PERILS
and
PROSPECTS
of a
UNITED
IRELAND

PERILS

and

PROSPECTS

of a

UNITED
IRELAND

PADRAIG O'MALLEY

THE LILLIPUT PRESS
DUBLIN

First published 2023 by
THE LILLIPUT PRESS
62–63 Sitric Road, Arbour Hill
Dublin 7, Ireland
www.lilliputpress.ie

ISBN 978 184351 8518

10 9 8 7 6 5 4 3 2 1

A CIP record for this title is available from The British Library.

The Lilliput Press gratefully acknowledges the financial
support of the Arts Council/An Chomhairle Ealaíon.

Set in 11pt on 15.3pt Minion by iota (www.iota-books.ie)
Printed by Walsh Colour Print in Kerry

For Peter and Mary

Contents

Acknowledgments

Perils & Prospects of a United Ireland was mostly researched during the worst days of the global COVID-19 pandemic throughout 2020 and well into 2021, when the world went into lockdown, commerce and travel came to a halt and Zoom replaced person-to-person contact. I would like to acknowledge the over six million that the World Health Organization (WHO) estimates died from the insidious virus, whose mutations time and again outwitted our best efforts to contain it. The pandemic leaves us with at least one disconcerting lesson: in a moment of great peril, the global community did not come together and act in unison to counteract the threat. Each country looked after its own interests.

In contrast, the people who helped me with *Perils & Prospects* came together to form a small, tight community, although separated by thousands of miles. Foremost among those is Allyson Bachta, a PhD student at the John W. McCormack Graduate School of Policy and Global Studies at the University of Massachusetts, Boston, whose tenacious research and comments, unstinting diligence and generosity with her time guided the passage of the book through many drafts. Without her, this book would never have seen the light of day. I also benefitted from the fact-checking assistance of Kate Butterworth and Kelsey Edmond. Allan Leonard in Belfast became close to indispensable overseeing the latter stages of preparing the manuscript for publication – from a detailed and meticulous reading of the manuscript, to creating maps, to finding appropriate photographs and visual art, often his own work.

Debby Smith near Valley Forge and then Djinn von Noorden at The Lilliput Press in Dublin both made sense of my mangled prose, offering a keen eye for identifying repetitive paragraphs. They both turned an unwieldy manuscript into a reader-friendly book. Ruth Hallinan oversaw the production process with patience and utmost professionalism. Josh Hall in Belfast scheduled interviews – a formidable task during the pandemic years, as he had to rely almost exclusively on potential interviewees' official email addresses that few appeared to check on a daily basis. In this task, and in transcribing many of the interviews, he was helped by visual artist Stephanie Heckman, also in Belfast. Andy Pollak in Dublin gave invaluable feedback on an earlier draft of the main chapters and assisted with his extensive Rolodex to identify potential interviewees with their contact information. Professor Brendan O'Leary, at University of Pennsylvania, responded immediately to my many queries about the report of the Working Group on Unification Referendums on the Island of Ireland. Likewise Professor Liam Kennedy in Belfast, who responded with alacrity and source details on punishment beatings in Northern Ireland. Marcy Murnaghan, a close friend of long standing, prepared a bibliography that reflects the extent of my readings on Northern Ireland; rather than being specific to *Perils & Prospects*, it acts as more a source of material for future researchers to draw on.

My decades-long partner, Patricia Keefer, Washington DC, is a continuing source of inspiration; daughter Ntombikayise Gladwin Gilman a continuing source of joy; and my brother Peter my biggest booster, who pushed me to work on when my energy flagged and from whom I took inspiration, learning to deal with challenges with grace.

Others in that small group I relied on for strength and sustenance were my sister Mary in Dublin, the poet Tracey McTague in Brooklyn, Rebecca Thornley in Minnesota, Edris Kelly and Rhett Nichols in Boston, Caroleen Feeney in San Francisco, Kirsten Thomsen in Portland, Maine, and Marcie Williams in Lansing, Michigan.

My thanks, too, to Rita 'Kiki' Edozie, Interim Dean of the John W. McCormack Graduate School of Policy and Global Studies at the University of Massachusetts, Boston, and my colleagues with whom I have enjoyed warm relationships spanning forty years.

To Antony Farrell, founder of The Lilliput Press, I extend my gratitude for his faith in this project, encouragement in bringing it to fruition and the privilege of publication in one of Ireland's most prestigious presses.

And finally, my thanks to the ninety-seven interviewees who gave unsparingly of their time. All conclusions reached are mine alone. And I take responsibility for their content.

Padraig O'Malley
September 2022

ABBREVIATIONS

B/GFA	Belfast Good Friday Agreement
Dáil Éireann	lower house of the Irish parliament
DUP	Democratic Unionist Party
ESRI	Economic and Social Research Institute, Dublin
IRA	Irish Republican Army
MLA	Member of the Legislative Assembly, Northern Ireland Assembly
MP	Member of Parliament, UK Parliament
NILT	Northern Ireland Irish Life and Times
NIP	Northern Ireland Protocol
Oireachtas	Irish parliament, consisting of Dáil Éireann, Seanad (Senate upper house) and the President
PIRA	Provisional IRA
PSNI	Police Service of Northern Ireland
PUP	Progressive Unionist Party
RHI	Renewable Heat Incentive
RUC	Royal Ulster Constabulary
SDLP	Social Democratic and Labour Party
TD	Teachta Dála, member of the Irish parliament
TUV	Traditional Unionist Voices
UDR	Ulster Defence Regiment
UDA	Ulster Defence Association
UL	University of Liverpool
UUP	Ulster Unionist Party
UVF	Ulster Volunteer Force
WGR	Working Group on Unification Referendums on the Island of Ireland

Introduction

Hundreds of others and I thronged Queen's University Belfast's Whitla Hall on 10 April 2018, the twentieth anniversary of the Belfast/Good Friday Agreement (B/GFA), where the principals who had negotiated it and its stepchild, the St Andrews Agreement (2006), looked back at their work, pronounced themselves well pleased and shared their hopes for the future. It was a celebratory occasion and we lapped it up. We had come to applaud, not to question.

The fact that key elements of the agreement and the institutions that it gave rise to were in abeyance since the collapse of the Stormont power-sharing government in January 2017, and with little sign that they would be resuscitated any time soon, chastened the proceedings but did little to dim the optimism about the future.

The former protagonists on stage were there – including David Trimble, Seamus Mallon, Gerry Adams and Peter Robinson – and also the luminaries from outside – Sen. George Mitchell, Bill Clinton and Bertie Ahern – and all were focused on the big picture. The present impasse was a hiccup, just the latest in a series dating back to the first stages of implementation in 1998, not an indicator that the agreement itself might need rethinking.

Former Irish Taoiseach (prime minister) Bertie Ahern, one of the architects of the agreement, captured the moment: the B/GFA negotiators, he
reminded the audience, had to confront issues of great complexity in order
to reach agreement, 'like the release of prisoners, decommissioning and the
reform of the police and ... the shape of new political institutions'. All that
it would now take to get things back on track was for 'the two governments
at top level to give it total commitment', and within a month a deal would be
hammered out.[1] The agreement was, after all, in the judgment of that political savant Bill Clinton, 'a work of surpassing genius'.[2] Sometimes, however,
even genius short-changes its most ardent cheerleaders. Brexit, the elephant
in the hall, was mentioned only in passing, in keeping with the benign spirit
of the occasion.

Part of the 'genius' of the agreement was its ambiguity. It allowed David
Trimble to sell it to the Protestant community as a destination reached and
assured – Northern Ireland would remain a part of the United Kingdom
(UK) with no qualifications to the permanency of its position, the ship of
state docked securely within the union. It allowed Gerry Adams and John
Hume to sell it to the Catholic community on the basis that it was a temporary stop at a waystation on the road to a united Ireland – demographics
alone assuring that outcome. At some point, the two interpretations would
clash – and Brexit has become that point.

Never quite enunciated above a whisper was that in the final analysis
both aspirations – to remain in the UK and to become part of a united
Ireland – cannot be simultaneously accommodated. No serial invocation
of 'parity of esteem', itself a phrase of ambiguity, can perform the political
jujitsu of having both sides come out the winner.

I grew up in Crumlin, Dublin, in the 1950s in a family so strictly Catholic it
made the puritanical and all-powerful Archbishop John Charles McQuaid
look like a rabid reprobate. The words 'Northern Ireland' were never mentioned, other than at election time when both Fianna Fáil and Fine Gael
accused England of being responsible for partition and demanded that
England put an end to it. Like magic, the wave of a political wand would
reunify the two parts of Ireland. I left a well-paying job at the Agriculture
Institute in 1965 to pursue graduate work in economics in the United States,

and, in a turn of events that would not have happened if I had stayed in Ireland, found myself in Northern Ireland for the first time in 1972 after Blóody Sunday.

From that point, over a fifty-year span, I have been immersed in the political life of the North. I arranged for a cross-section of political players, including senior republican and loyalist paramilitaries, to attend the Amherst Forum at the University of Massachusetts (1974);[3] organized the Airlie House Forum (1985),[4] which was attended by the most senior civil servants and ministers holding Northern Ireland portfolios from Ireland, Northern Ireland and Britain; worked on the Opsahl Commission (1993);[5] and arranged for the key political negotiators from across the political spectrum to travel to South Africa to meet with Nelson Mandela, Cyril Ramaphosa, later president of South Africa, and others who had been instrumental in negotiating the transition from apartheid to democracy (1997).[6] I interviewed the key political players for *The Uncivil Wars* (1983) and again for *Questions of Nuance* (1990) and the families of the hunger strikers for *The Irish Hunger Strikes* (1990).

In short, I've done an awful lot of listening over half a century.

Since Brexit (2016) – when the UK voted to leave the European Union (EU) by a 52 to 48 per cent margin, but Northern Ireland voted to remain by 56 to 44 per cent, and the subsequent border down the Irish Sea requiring checks on goods entering Northern Ireland from Britain was drawn to demarcate the trade borders of the EU with the UK – the word 'consent' has entered the political conversation with recurring vengeance.[7] Nationalists and republicans argued that Northern Ireland had not given its consent to leave the EU, yet were stuck with the outcome; unionists and loyalists argued that they had not given their consent to a border down the Irish Sea that diminished Northern Ireland's status as part of the UK. Increasingly, too, republicans called for a border referendum. The B/GFA stipulates that the Secretary of State shall call a referendum 'if at any time it appears likely to them [the Secretary of State] that a majority of those voting would express a wish that Northern Ireland should cease to be part of the United Kingdom and form part of a united Ireland'.[8]

Reams have been written about just precisely what an imprecise instruction this is, with interpretation running from the Secretary of State being able to do so at a whim or in concert with the Irish government or in the most literal sense of what constitutes 50 per cent + 1, devoid of context or in the context of which (if any) strands of the B/GFA agreement are working. The Republic of Ireland is under a legal obligation to hold a concurrent referendum should the North hold one. Here, too, there is a vagueness. If concurrent means simultaneous, then one could end up in a situation where the North votes to stay in the UK but the South votes to reunify Ireland. If there is a lag between the two polls, how long can it go on for? Long enough for minds to change should unrest in the North spread in the wake of a close pro-unity result? Would an Irish government call a referendum if support for reunification were to hover around the 50 per cent + 1 mark or would they wait to build a broader consensus?

In this book, I explore the factors that might lead to the Northern Ireland Secretary of State calling a border referendum and the challenges both Northern Ireland and the Republic of Ireland would face if and when such a poll took place. What does 'appears likely' mean? How might that majority for unity, a simple 50 per cent + 1, emerge? Has it got to be just 50 per cent + 1? What criteria might a Secretary of State draw on to make his or her judgment call? Must a referendum take place in conditions of relative normalcy in Northern Ireland, or simply when it seems the required threshold is crossed? Is there any obligation on the part of the Secretary of State to consult with the Irish government before making his or her decision? Who would provide the wording? What referendum scenarios are there to consider? How would prevailing political and socio-economic considerations in Northern Ireland be factored into decision-making? Or is the consent formula pristine, to be invoked as soon as the minimum threshold for holding it is met? Would institutions like the National Health Service (NHS) in the North and the Health Service Executive (HSE) and Sláintecare in the South have to be aligned beforehand? What of the two educational systems, especially at primary level? Would the Stormont Assembly have a role to play? What direct input would the Republic of Ireland have?

What kinds of costs might be involved in merging the two jurisdictions? What obligations does the guarantee in the Irish Constitution that unification will take place 'in harmony and friendship' entail? What kind of Northern Ireland would an Irish government want to see in place before sanctioning holding a referendum in the South? How would the South reach a consensus on what model of a united Ireland reflects the will of the Irish people? How would unionism be made part of that process? Would the recommendations of a Citizens' Assembly, the preferred route to consensus for nationalists, be debated and amended in the Dáil in order to reach cross-party consensus that whatever united Ireland arrangement is agreed is on behalf of the Irish people and not a particular government? What if a consensus cannot be reached?

Would political unionism be part of this process? And how? Can it stay above a rising tide of pro-unification sentiment in the wake of Brexit to meet the challenge of creating a more inclusive Northern Ireland? Should it make it more appealing to 'cultural Catholics' who might be quite content to stay in Northern Ireland rather than risk the disruptions that would accompany a bitter and polarizing border campaign, likely followed by even more intense disruptions in the event of a successful pro-unity outcome? Meanwhile, is it in Sinn Féin's interests to see Northern Ireland become a 'success' story? Under what circumstances might a referendum result in violence, either in the lead-up to it or immediately after a poll? How might that impact attitudes in the South? Why are unionists so impervious to the transformative socio-economic and cultural changes in the South since the early 1980s? In the event of reunification, how would the B/GFA's requirement of 'parity of esteem' for the British identity be accommodated?

These are among the key questions I address in this book. There are no hard and fast answers; sometimes there is the posing of more questions and an examination of uncertain outcomes, predicated on assumptions that may have relevance at the present but which, over time, may see that relevance evaporate. External shocks, like Brexit, Scotland voting for independence or the war in Ukraine may reverberate in unforeseen ways, requiring a recalculation of the calculus of analysis.

My overarching focus is on Sinn Féin and political unionism/loyalism as the principal tribunes of their respective constitutional dispositions, one with its relentless pursuit of Irish unity, sensing that the prize is within grasp, the other hunkered down, primed for trench warfare, in opposition but unable to grasp that the nature of constitutional warfare has changed and that staying in place in the trenches exposes it to being outmanoeuvred or simply overrun.

I interviewed ninety-seven political players, academics, political influencers, a cross-section of the political grandees who negotiated the B/GFA and faith leaders between February 2020 and June 2021, mostly from Northern Ireland but also with a sampling of opinions in the South.

From the political parties in the North, interviewees included party leaders Jeffrey Donaldson (Democratic Unionist Party, DUP), Doug Beattie (Ulster Unionist Party, UUP), Naomi Long (Alliance), Colum Eastwood (Social Democratic and Labour Party, SDLP) and Billy Hutchinson (Progressive Unionist Party, PUP). Jim Allister (Traditional Unionist Voice, TUV) declined to take part. Across these political parties I interviewed eight from the DUP, six from the UUP and SDLP, five from Alliance, two from the PUP and seven from the loyalist community. In addition, I interviewed four from the former Women's Coalition political party, eighteen prominent commentators/opinion influencers, seventeen academics, three from Fine Gael, nine from Fianna Fáil, seven faith leaders and three former senior Irish diplomats who held Northern Ireland briefs during their careers.

Only with Sinn Féin did I encounter a number of refusals: Declan Kearney, chairperson; Alex Maskey, Assembly speaker; Mitchell McLaughlin, former chair; Jim Gibney; and Tom Hartley never responded. I got in touch with the Sinn Féin office in Belfast to try and arrange an interview with Michelle O'Neill but received no responses. I also reached out repeatedly to Conor Murphy and Pearse Doherty but received no responses. Eoin Ó Broin did respond to say he was busy. However, Matt Carthy Teachta Dála (TD) and Chris Hazzard MP – both members of the Ard Comhairle – did respond, and, in all, I interviewed six Sinn Féin representatives: three from the North and three from the South.

The political landscape during this time was kaleidoscopic, ever-changing, strewn with the detritus of political upheavals and the impact of a global pandemic. It spanned the careers of four British prime ministers (Theresa May, Boris Johnson, Liz Truss and Rishi Sunak); three secretaries of state for Northern Ireland (Brandon Lewis, Shailesh Vara and Chris Heaton-Harris); two Taoisigh (Micheál Martin and Leo Varadkar); two leaders of the UUP (Steve Aiken and Doug Beattie); three leaders of the DUP (Arlene Foster, Edwin Poots and Jeffrey Donaldson); several waves of COVID-19; over a year of argumentation, agitation and negotiation over the Northern Ireland Protocol (NIP), the border down the Irish Sea; the toxic effects of Brexit on relations between Dublin and Stormont, and Dublin and London; Assembly elections in Northern Ireland; the meteoric rise of Sinn Féin in the republic and its emergence as the largest political party in the North; a collapsed Assembly; the deaths of Seamus Mallon, John Hume and David Trimble, three titans of the peace process that culminated in the B/GFA; the death, too, of Queen Elizabeth II, an incalculable loss for the unionist community; and finally the invasion of Ukraine by Russia with its far-reaching and ongoing repercussions, including an energy crunch across much of Europe that tested its resolve to stand united against Russian aggression, surging inflation and a cost-of-living crisis that has affected the economies of both Northern Ireland and the republic.

I conducted fifteen interviews in Belfast in February and March 2020 before the COVID-19 pandemic closed down much of the world, and then conducted eighty-two more by Zoom from Boston through late 2020 and 2021, roughly half during the transition year for the NIP and half in 2021, the first year of its implementation.

In-person interviews and Zoom interviews are very different. In-person interviews provide a degree of intimacy and allow you to establish relationships with the interviewees, make strategic interventions to move the conversation along without appearing to be intrusive and, most importantly, establish and maintain eye contact, the key to establishing an empathetic connection with the interviewee. You have a greater degree of control. The Zoom interviews lasted longer, responses tended to wander off point and the internet quality often varied considerably, posing problems for transcribers. That said, I am immensely grateful to all interviewees, who gave freely of the time asked for and, despite the handicaps I've mentioned, were exceedingly co-operative.

At one level, conversations about the issues I raised were surreal. Many of them were intense and passionate over an event (a border referendum) that might not take place for another ten years, perhaps longer. Some interviewees predicted a pro-unity outcome, looking forward with absolute certainty to a united Ireland that remains vague and vacuous; some presented 'facts' that will change multiple times in the coming years, evidence-based facts and alternative realities commingling, making assumptions about the future when we have learned – once again with the invasion of the Ukraine by Russia, which is redefining relations across Europe and bringing the skeletons of history out of the closet – that such peering into the unknown and making decisions based on hunches is a hazardous exercise.

The conclusions are stark. None of the metrics identified as potential markers of the emergence of a pro-unity majority among the electorate in Northern Ireland meet the test of a majority in the making. These markers fall short of being able to deliver a pro-unity majority in large measure because the binary nationalist/unionist framework that is the foundational bedrock of the B/GFA no longer reflects how large segments of the Northern Ireland electorate behave, how they identify themselves or their likely voting preferences.

Both the North and the South are ill-prepared for a referendum, and it may be a decade or more before the necessary basic political requirements are in place. Neither electorate is willing to pay higher taxes if that is what unity might entail. The South is shockingly ignorant about life north of the border. Unionists harbour ideas about the South that are decades out of date with the reality of the Irish state. Governance in the North doesn't work. When the Assembly and Executive are functioning – they have been collapsed for almost one-third of their lifespan – they function sporadically and badly, closer to an ongoing drunken brawl between the DUP and Sinn Féin than a progressive, functional legislative process. And few interviewees other than unionists believe that a border referendum would produce a result indicating that the will of the majority is to remain within the United Kingdom. The B/GFA needs a reboot.

Nationalists and unionists both cherry-pick data that support their side of the debate on what constitutes a majority and how it is measured. On one side, nationalists insist the conditions for a referendum are about to be met or are at least relatively imminent. On the other, unionists insist that the conditions for one might never be met or, if they are, that it will occur at least ten years from now, but more likely fifteen or more. One side says reunification of the island is inevitable, the other that there is nothing at all inevitable about it. One side says the other had better get into a conversation now regarding the future of the island. The other says there is nothing to talk about.

One community (nationalist/republican) is gung-ho to talk about the future, because if unionists join in that means they are open to discuss the terms and details of a united Ireland. The other (unionist/loyalist) refuses to engage in any conversation because nationalists are not open to one about Northern Ireland continuing as part of the UK. Worse still, entering into a conversation might be perceived as the unionists signalling their readiness to contemplate a future united Ireland, and they would thus, in effect, be negotiating their terms of surrender.

I was repeatedly reminded by unionist/loyalist interviewees that Leo Varadkar, then Taoiseach, raised the threat of dissident republican violence should there be a post-Brexit land border across Ireland between the EU and the UK. On the other hand, few unionists would rule out loyalist violence in the event of a close and polarizing border poll that results in a narrow margin in favour of unity. Responses were always framed in terms of 'Of course we would accept the democratic result, but there are others …' – precisely the same response I received forty years ago when I broached the question then. In April 2021, when young loyalists engaged in bouts of rioting that threatened to get out of hand and metastasize into something more serious, even the Biden administration warned of the necessity to safeguard and protect the B/GFA. There were hurried meetings between Brandon Lewis, the Secretary of State for Northern Ireland, and David Campbell, Chair of the Loyalist Communities Council (LCC), the umbrella group for loyalist paramilitaries. Loyalists got the message: violence gets attention.

In the run-up to the May 2022 Assembly elections, the Ulster Volunteer Force (UVF) – not some 'dissident' group of former paramilitaries but B Company – announced that it still had weapons, some dating back to a cache of arms that had arrived in Northern Ireland in 1987, and warned that it was going to target Irish government property, first in Northern Ireland and then in Dublin.[9] Not all arms had been decommissioned; it is hardly surprising that paramilitaries would hold on to some just in case a future scenario might call for their use. In a peculiar twist of logic, the UVF considered the Irish government responsible for the NIP because it had convinced the EU that the alternative – a land border across Ireland demarcating the border between the EU and the UK – would lead to dissident republican violence.

What the threat of loyalist violence is supposed to accomplish is unclear, unless its purpose is to force the Irish government to intercede on the behalf of unionism by having Article 16 triggered, essentially suspending the protocol.[10]

Logic, however, is not the purpose of the enterprise, just the endangering of the 'fragile' peace, with intimations of violence being enough to send shivers of apprehension down the spine of the country, threatening a downward spiral into renewed conflict. Indeed, a putative republican paramilitary group calling itself Oglaigh na hÉireann emerged out of the shadows to threaten retaliation if the UVF carried out their threat against the Irish government.[11]

Loyalist interviewees were in common agreement: the protocol had to go.[12] Billy Hutchinson of the PUP and part of the loyalist delegation during the B/GFA negotiations wrote on a unionist website in March 2022 that 'there was no chance loyalism would have supported the Belfast Agreement had they known in 1998 that the principle of consent was merely symbolic'.[13]

'It seems the loyalist mainstream has turned its back on the peace process,' the security analyst Allison Morris wrote in the *Belfast Telegraph*:

> There is no one within loyalism selling the benefits of the Good Friday Agreement. There is no influential figure within loyalism speaking out against the hardline, for they are all hardline now. Loyalism, once fractured with bloody feuds, has united around a common cause. Previous internal fractures are being set aside in opposition to the protocol, and increasingly the Good Friday Agreement itself.[14]

Should things unravel and the UVF/UDA (Ulster Defence Association) carry through with its threats of violence, we will say that in hindsight we should have seen it coming all along.

For as long as paramilitarism remains 'a clear and present danger', to quote successive reports of the Independent Reporting Commission (IRC), a monitoring organization created under the Fresh Start Agreement (2015), there will always be some set of circumstances that will breathe fire into the ashes of their violent pasts. Some paramilitaries justify their continued existence as having become key figures in the conflict transformation phase of the peace process, as they manage the tensions at the interfaces between their respective communities.

In short, we have the contradictory phenomenon of paramilitaries as peace-builders, but hardly a reason to condone their continued existence after twenty-five years. Unless the steps the IRC outlines in great detail

– especially massive measures to address the scale of deprivation in both communities – are implemented, and the paramilitary presence and their dissident counterparts in republican and loyalist communities permanently eradicated, the IRC will continue to wail 'a clear and present danger' in their reports, and tentacles of paramilitarism will continue to exert their vice-like grip on these communities. In March 2022, the 'terror threat level' was downgraded from 'severe' to substantial in the North for the first time in twelve years.[15] Days later, Irish Foreign Minister Simon Coveney was evacuated from the Houben Centre in Belfast, where he was attending a peace dialogue, due to a bomb scare. And almost immediately the UVF issued its own threat.[16]

The political scientist Adrian Guelke has written that 'in a deeply divided society conflict exists along a well-entrenched fault line that is recurrent and endemic and that contains the potential for violence between the segments'.[17] That fault line in Northern Ireland is still a yawning geopolitical gap between two sets of competing perspectives on the present and the future. In a divided society saturated with binary choices, every decision, from the trivial to the existential, receives the same zero-sum stamp. Going on a full generation after the conflict, on the way to a milestone where the B/GFA peace has more years behind it than the decades of conflict, that potential for violence still exists and is invoked very effectively by one side or another when it perceives a threat to its interests. 'Is a return to violence on the cards?' asked *The Financial Times* after reviewing what the political endgames might be following the May 2022 Assembly elections. And it answered its own question: 'No one expects a full-scale return to the Troubles, but there have been worrying flashbacks – a van hijacking/car hoax last month, and petrol bombs hurled at police this week.'[18] Small-scale stuff, but sufficient to push the alert button.[19]

In one breath we are told that unity is around the corner, that it is inevitable; in the next that the peace is fragile, that if reunification happens, it may take a generation or more. In one breath Sinn Féin emerging as the largest party in Northern Ireland is hailed as 'historic', an inflection point hastening reunification; in the next that objective evidence reconfirms that a majority wish to remain part of the UK. This tension between 'there ought to be a border poll' republicanism/nationalism, as if it were a moral imperative divined by a higher power, and 'we are the bulwark against Irish unity' unionism/loyalism, as though it were a contagious disease, infects the relationship between Sinn Féin and the DUP and has a corrosive if not calamitous impact on their working relationship in government.

The peace process is fragile, says Professor Graham Spencer, who has written extensively about unionism/loyalism and researched their communities, because:

> From the start, the peace process was never really embraced by unionism and so it was sold under duress from the beginning. Once that happened it became very difficult, if not impossible, to promote the peace process as something to be welcomed. If you don't sell it that way at the moment of birth it is unlikely you will be able to convincingly make the case thereafter. Communicating the agreement as something that would 'copper-fasten' the union was also a mistake since that obstructed any real receptiveness to the value of process and ongoing change.[20]

Most interviewees believe Sinn Féin is the biggest obstacle to unity (acknowledged in its own way by Sinn Féin) and that it should not be leading the charge for unity, despite being addicted to calling for a border poll.[21] Unionists made a sharp distinction between a united Ireland with Mary Lou McDonald as Taoiseach or Tánaiste and one with Leo Varadkar or Micheál Martin as either. The elusive 'lower-case' unionists, who might be open to being persuaded that they would be better off in a united Ireland, would shun a united Ireland with Sinn Féin in control. Pro-union non-voters, I was told, would emerge from the woodwork in droves to vote.

On one aspect of a border referendum there was unanimity: avoid a Brexit-like situation – no simple up-or-down vote on whether to stay in the UK or become part of a unified Ireland. What kind of united Ireland is envisaged should be worked out in considerable detail beforehand. Most interviewees believed that, while unity called for a change of sovereignty, it did not collapse other strands of the agreement. The existing institutions, including the Stormont Assembly, would continue in place with Westminster MPs becoming TDs in Dublin, and the transition period itself before the final phases of reunification were implemented should last ten to fifteen years.

Thus, at some point there is a Hamlet-like question for the republic's government: whether to launch serious preparations for a united Ireland

– even if unionists collapse the B/GFA in protest – on the grounds that a Secretary of State could call a referendum with little warning (though the probability of one doing so is perhaps close to zero, it would be highly imprudent for an Irish government to be caught off-guard with all the negative consequences that would follow). Or whether to take the foot off the reunification pedal, pursue a different route at a more tortoise-like pace, work the Shared Island initiative and give the North more breathing space to heal its wounds? If reconciliation is only possible when it isn't directly linked to the prospect of a referendum, time may provide unionism with the space to dig itself out of the constitutional silo it has hunkered down in since the conflict erupted in the late 1960s.

Sinn Féin wants to opt for the former route, Fine Gael and Fianna Fáil the latter, although if Fianna Fáil were to find itself in a coalition with Sinn Féin after the 2025 general elections, it might be tempted to veer more towards Sinn Féin's position – or require Sinn Féin to veer more towards its current position as the price of that coalition. This latter approach, of course, has its own set of assumptions – one being that unionism can adapt to change about the future – which are problematical at best.

Commentators, such as Alex Kane, close to unionist thinking say unionism is turning a corner. The fact that this can be seen as some kind of breakthrough speaks volumes about the paucity of unionism's continuing ability to articulate a 'vision' of a future Northern Ireland which is inclusive of its diverse identities. Perhaps it can never get to that spot. Every gesture that would signal inclusivity, making Northern Ireland a 'warmer house' for Catholics, is seen as a concession to Sinn Féin. Hence unionists' trenchant opposition to every move in that direction. Hence, too, their derisive dismissal of Sinn Féin's promise to fully protect the British identity in a united Ireland, even their being open to the idea that the British monarchy should play a role. In the unionist view, Sinn Féin instigated a thirty-year conflict to destroy Northern Ireland, continues post-conflict to disrespect Northern Ireland and all its appurtenances as illegitimate, is unable even to call Northern Ireland by its legal name and is relentless in the ongoing culture war to dilute the Britishness of Northern Ireland. Unionists find Sinn Féin's expressions of its willingness to protect, secure and accommodate the British identity in a united Ireland to be laughable and highly hypocritical, smacking of the chutzpah that characterizes its political wheeling and dealing.

Indeed, the unionist preoccupation with Sinn Féin borders on obsessive. Sinn Féin is 'winning'; therefore, in the binary arithmetic that frames everything, unionism must be losing. Hence, the political Rubik's cube: the more republicanism focuses on the future, calling for a border poll and talking up the inevitability of a united Ireland, the more unsettled unionism becomes, reinforcing its fierce determination not to engage in a conversation about the future, which it regards as being synonymous with negotiating terms of surrender.

Re-reading *The Uncivil Wars*, I am struck by how much some things have changed while others have resolutely stayed the same. The violence is over, but paramilitarism still exists. Indeed, no matter what the shortcomings of the B/GFA, the fact that it underpins a ceasefire by republican and loyalist forces is reason enough to treasure its existence. The rantings of Rev. Ian Paisley in our interview in the early 1980s – on the Irish Republican Army (IRA) as part of the Pope's army, the satanic rituals practised by the Vatican and what the nunneries got up to – would have made it difficult to imagine the DUP emerging as the dominant voice of unionism and impossible to believe that Paisley would form a warm partnership with his arch-nemesis, Sinn Féin's Martin McGuinness, and that the pair would be jocularly referred to as 'the Chuckle Brothers' during their tenure in office, such was the obvious delight they took in each other's company. Impossible, too, to imagine Sinn Féin as the largest political party in Northern Ireland and odds-on favourite to emerge as the largest political party in the South in 2025.

And hard to imagine that Alliance, then a small blip on most electoral maps, would become the third-largest party in Northern Ireland, with the surge in support for that party threatening some of the basic architecture of the B/GFA – anchored as it is on a two-traditions paradigm – and calling into question the relevance of this binary model for governance. Unimaginable, too, the collapse of the Catholic Church in the South, a fall from a degree of power and authority of epic proportions, the result (*inter alia*) of multiple child sexual abuse scandals and related cover-ups. But unchanged, the basic constitutional positions of the two main protagonists: one remains adamantly pro-reunification – the prize, Sinn Féin believes, within grasp – the other adamantly committed to staying in the UK, but apprehensive of fatal British government duplicity.

Nevertheless, with so many 'unimaginables' that wound their way into social and political fabric of everyday life since the B/GFA, it is not unimaginable to believe that other seismic changes North and South and within and across the UK and the EU will have a transformative impact. In the short run, the pivotal necessity is for a revamped B/GFA that allows the political middle ground to fully participate in governance and redefines power-sharing without the limitations of mutual vetoes, and for first and deputy first ministers to become joint first ministers. These simple concepts slip easily off the tongue but are time-consuming to negotiate and difficult to achieve where the minutiae of differences, often apparent only to the protagonists themselves, amplify the zero-sum calculus that informs every decision.

I hope this book helps to unpack the complex issues raised by a border referendum on the island's constitutional future and provides food for thought rather than argumentation. Were everyone to talk less about the imminence of a border poll, it would perhaps, paradoxically, hasten the day one is achieved, with Ireland's voters, North and South, going to the polls in relative harmony and friendship.

ONE

Brexit: 'taking back control'

By unleashing English nationalism, Brexit has made the future of the UK the central political issue of the coming decade. Northern Ireland is already heading for the exit door. By remaining in the EU single market, it is for all economic intents and purposes now slowly becoming part of a united Ireland.[1]

    – George Osborne, First Secretary of State (May 2015–July 2016)

The great political success of the Brexiteers is that they have convinced a narrow majority of the British people that most of their woes, even the weather, derive from Europe. In truth, scarcely any do, but foreigners make convenient scapegoats.[2]

    – Max Hastings, British journalist and historian,
    Bloomberg Opinion columnist

Brexit has spooked the moderate liberal Northern niceness, there's no question about that, because in their European identity there was a wideness, so you can designate yourself as British or Irish singly, British and Irish both, British and Irish and European, British and European, Irish and European ... That's all been snatched away from people. That

1

widening of national identity, in a strange way, Brexit has sharpened that distinctive of Britishness.[3]
– Rev. Gary Mason, Methodist minister, Director, 'Rethinking Conflict'

Unionists' and loyalists' support for the Good Friday Agreement is predicated on there being no diminution of Northern Ireland's place within the United Kingdom … That's the bedrock on which unionists and loyalists have supported the Good Friday Agreement. Anything that begins to undo or in any way detract or dilute Northern Ireland's place within the United Kingdom … presents the risk for serious disorder, which could very easily spill over into something much more looking like a conflict, and a militarized situation … In effect, it [Brexit] will see Northern Ireland become a rule taker … without a seat at the Brussels table … I think that has the potential for a serious breach in terms of the UK sovereignty, in relation to Northern Ireland. I think that could have serious consequences for the stability here that we enjoy.[4]
– Winston Irvine, former Progressive Unionist Party (PUP) Director of Communications, Loyalist Communities Council (LCC) member

The government of the republic need to be very careful about putting too much weight on Europe to help them and deal with the problems for them in the future … The South needs to be very, very careful, and it hasn't been careful. It has, instead of seeing itself as a bridge between Europe and Britain, it has seen itself as a bulwark for Europe against Britain. But Europe will not help bail the South out if it runs into a balance of payments deficit with Britain. And Britain will not be so prepared to help out as it was in the past, because they will feel that Ireland was not helpful to them in their Brexit debate. So, I think the Republic of Ireland is not in a good place at the moment.[5]
– John, Lord Alderdice, former Alliance Party leader and Northern Ireland Assembly speaker, Belfast/Good Friday Agreement (B/GFA) negotiator

Brexit is a game-changer. In *Breaking Peace: Brexit and Northern Ireland*, Feargal Cochrane expounds on a meteor metaphor to analyse the impact of Brexit on the Northern Ireland peace process in the context of conflict transformation, focusing on the need 'to provide peacebuilding shock absorbers that can withstand fundamental unforeseen circumstances – meteors – that hit peace processes with the potential to knock them off their conventional axes and change the local context'.[6]

The meteor analogy can be applied to the whole of the United Kingdom (UK). When the time frame to negotiate the terms of British withdrawal from the European Union (EU) and a trade agreement ended on 30 December 2020, four and a half years after the initial vote, there were signs that the future of the union itself was in jeopardy. A four-country poll in *The Times* in January 2021 revealed the extent of disaffection and disarray among citizens and the depth of the strains on the union: Scotland's seemingly unstoppable march to independence; Northern Ireland wanting a border poll; England's agnosticism with regard to the union; signs of a growing nationalism in Wales; and the overarching sense of Britishness fraying at the union's seams.[7] If one of the purposes of Brexit was to restore and aggrandize the UK's sense of Britishness, the irony was that it achieved the opposite result. Only in England did voters put Britishness ahead of Englishness, in contrast to the Scots and Welsh whose national identities took precedence. English voters expected Scotland to become independent within ten years. Northern Ireland voters expected Northern Ireland would be united with the rest of Ireland within ten years.

Brexit not only changed the trading relationship between the UK and the EU, it changed the political relationship between the constituent nations of the UK. Above all, Brexit was driven by English nationalism.[8] Unlike Scotland, Wales and Northern Ireland, each of which has its own devolved government, England is the only country in the UK not to have one. But England sends hefty subventions to the other three – 84 per cent of the population subsidizing a 16 per cent increasingly seen by the English as spongers on the British Treasury.[9]

After forty-three years (1973–2016) as a member of the EU, on 23 June 2016 the UK voted to leave by a vote of 52 to 48 per cent.[10] The referendum question was a simple Leave or Remain choice, with no consideration as to what the divorce would entail or what kind of relationship the UK would subsequently have with the EU, whether it would be a 'soft' Brexit, which would see the UK continue to be aligned with the EU in a number of regards, or a 'hard' one, which would see the UK severing most links with the EU. Northern Ireland voted to remain by a 56 per cent to 44 per cent margin. Eighty-five per cent of the Remain vote came from voters with a Catholic background, 60 per cent of Leave votes from voters with a Protestant background. For self-defined

nationalists, 88 per cent voted Remain, 66 per cent of self-defined unionists voted Leave and 70 per cent of those who chose to define themselves as
neither voted to stay in the EU.[11] Once identity labels are attached, the impact
of political leanings became more pronounced.

It was not supposed to happen. Prime Minister David Cameron held the referendum in the certainty, shared by most elites, that it would fail, allowing
him to see off the Eurosceptic wing of the Conservative Party. No one
had thought through the ramifications. The mantra 'Taking back control'
galvanized support in England's heartland, which had borne the brunt of
de-industrialization over decades and seen little economic recovery, leaving
communities with only the nostalgia for a past that no longer existed – a
once-upon-a-time Britannia.[12]

Both the Leave and Remain campaigns were either ignorant of or
oblivious to the B/GFA and the paramount importance of an open border
between Ireland and Northern Ireland being one of the planks underpinning the agreement. Both campaigns were oblivious, too, to the fact that
the agreement was embedded in EU law, to which Britain and Ireland were
parties, and that the EU played a significant and ongoing role in the peace
process. In terms of financial support, over €500 million had been pumped
into the region 'in structural funds for economic regeneration and cross-
border co-operation' under the EU's second Programme for Peace and
Reconciliation in Northern Ireland.[13] In addition, on an ongoing basis 'two
other EU programmes, INTEREG and PEACE IV, funnel approximately
£470 million per annum into Northern Ireland, 85 per cent of which is bank-
rolled by the EU'.[14] The European Convention on Human Rights is etched
into every stitch of the agreement.

Cameron immediately stepped down after the Brexit vote to leave the
EU, and Theresa May, the formidable Secretary of the Interior, took the
helm. Touted as a Margaret Thatcher in the making, she turned out to be
anything but. Just about every move she subsequently made was a mistake,
some the result of hubris, some of ignorance, but most of them because of
incompetence and miscalculations.

In a major speech at Lancaster House on 17 January 2017, May outlined a UK future outside of the EU that would see the UK leave both the

Single Market and the Customs Union but remain a close member of the European community. She committed the UK to maintaining the Common Travel Area (CTA)[15] and emphasized that 'nobody wants to return to the borders of the past' and that a 'stronger Britain demands that we do something else – strengthen the precious union between the four nations of the United Kingdom',[16] a statement that was met with incredulity in Scotland and Northern Ireland, which had both voted to remain (the former overwhelmingly and the latter less so, but still substantively). May's speech was long on the aspirational but short on clarity regarding how the objectives it enumerated might be achieved.

On 18 April 2017, in another catastrophic misjudgment, May announced plans for a snap general election.[17] Rather than increasing their majority in Parliament, the Tories fell short of one. To form a government and stay in power, May had to enter into a 'confidence and supply' arrangement with Northern Ireland's Democratic Unionist Party (DUP).[18] The 10 seats this arrangement provided gave May a cushion of 2 seats and returned the Tories to power, albeit in a party still torn almost equally between Leave and Remain factions.

Under the terms of the agreement between the DUP and the Conservative Party, the UK government poured an additional £1 billion into Northern Ireland, the Tories pledging 'never to be neutral on expressing support for the union' and 'never [to] countenance any constitutional arrangements that are incompatible with the consent principle'.[19] However, being locked into the parliamentary deal with the DUP undermined the government's ability to be impartial between the competing interests in Northern Ireland, making nonsense of the UK government's requirement under the B/GFA to act as an impartial guarantor and ensure parity of esteem for both aspirations. The new arrangement gave the DUP a veto over EU/UK negotiations on how to deal with the Irish border question. The party's agenda was straightforward: it would veto any UK/EU withdrawal agreement that would result in Northern Ireland being treated differently from the rest of the UK.

Implicit in the B/GFA is a frictionless border between the two parts of Ireland that ensures the free movements of people, goods and services. The island of Ireland is, for all intents and purposes, a single economic and geographic entity. Only after the Brexit referendum did the hitherto ignored fact that Brexit would mean a land border between Northern Ireland and

Ireland become glaringly obvious. Ireland would become the western perimeter of the EU, the only part of the EU to share a land border with the UK, and hence would necessitate the physical paraphernalia and security personnel a customs border requires.

The re-imposition of customs checks along the 300-mile-plus border, the Irish government strenuously argued, would violate provisions of the agreement referring to cross-border co-operation in listed areas; wreak havoc with economies, both North and South; and reinforce divisions between nationalists/republicans and unionists, spurring a widespread sense of betrayal and raising the prospect of renewed violence.[20] In these circumstances, according to some assessments – including that of the Police Service of Northern Ireland (PSNI) – the peace process, so carefully nurtured over two decades, could unravel at frightening speed.[21]

According to a 2018 UK in a Changing Europe survey, in Northern Ireland there were 'strong expectations that protests against either North-South (between Northern Ireland and the republic) or East-West (between Northern Ireland and Great Britain) border checks would quickly deteriorate into violence'.[22] In the South, meanwhile, 57 per cent of those polled feared that a hard border would result in violence.[23]

To ensure free movement of goods and people between the two parts of Ireland, the Withdrawal Agreement would have to include a mechanism keeping either the UK or Northern Ireland in the Single Market. One arrangement, the so-called 'Irish backstop', was agreed by May and Michel Barnier, the negotiator handling Britain's exit for the EU. It would have involved the UK continuing to align itself with the EU's Single Market and customs area. This was an anathema to hard-line Brexiteers and the DUP. In one of a number of humiliating climbdowns that came to define her tenure as prime minister, May had to abandon lunch with Barnier before unveiling their joint position on the backstop when she was informed that the DUP would not support the position.[24] The DUP insisted that there should be no divergence between Northern Ireland and the rest of the United Kingdom in any Brexit withdrawal agreement, tying May's hands – indeed, forcing her to back off from the first arrangement she had reached with the EU.[25]

In Belfast, after he resigned on 9 July 2018 as May's Secretary of State for Foreign Affairs because of her handling of the backstop,[26] Boris Johnson, to rapturous applause, told the annual convention of the DUP that under no circumstance should there be an agreement to any backstop, as it would tear the union apart.[27]

On three occasions May tried and failed to get Parliament to pass her withdrawal bill.[28] Battered by the incessant infighting between Leave and Remain Tory MPs, and having lost support in both factions, May stepped down in March 2019. Months later, the Tories chose Boris Johnson, who promised to 'get Brexit done' as their new party leader and the country's prime minister. Parliament, however, passed legislation ruling out a hard Brexit, or the UK simply crashing out with no deal on 31 October 2019.[29]

After much posturing and talk of preferring 'to die in a ditch' before asking for a further extension of the 31 October exit date,[30] Boris Johnson embraced his metaphorical death unscathed: he met with then Taoiseach Leo Varadkar at Thornton Manor Hotel, Liverpool, and reached an agreement: the Northern Ireland Protocol (NIP), or what amounted to a border in the Irish Sea between Northern Ireland and the rest of the UK.[31]

Having lost the support of the DUP, Johnson called a snap election on 12 December 2019 that returned the Conservative Party to a whopping majority, reducing the DUP to irrelevance in the Westminster Parliament.

The NIP calls for checks on goods entering Northern Ireland from Great Britain to ensure compliance with EU regulatory standards and customs requirements, especially with regard to foodstuffs. (Medicines are dealt with separately.)[32] There are no checks on goods originating in Northern Ireland going into the South. For the purpose of trading – for goods, but not services – Northern Ireland is in both the Single Market and the British internal market.

The Withdrawal Agreement, incorporating the NIP, was reached on 17 October 2019 and ratified by Parliament on 29 January 2020.[33] It became legally operational after a transition year on 1 January 2021.[34]

But uncertainty about the future lurked. A poll of Tory Party members – showing they were quite prepared to toss Northern Ireland out of the union if that was the price to be paid for a hard Brexit – added to the unionist sense of isolation.[35] The Conservative and Unionist Party had morphed into an English nationalist one. Says former Alliance leader David Ford:

> There's absolutely no doubt that the decision that the UK should leave
> the European Union, which was basically an English decision, has been
> very destabilizing for the prospect of the United Kingdom. There's

no doubt that support for independence in Scotland has increased. There's no doubt that support for a united Ireland has increased to some extent ... It's probably fair to say that those who would have been described as nationalists, who were basically quite content with the Good Friday arrangements, as long as they saw fairness within Northern Ireland, partnership and sharing here, and North-South links, they weren't particularly pushing [for a united Ireland]. Some of them are now significantly more Nationalist with a capital 'N'.[36]

Brexit disrupted the delicate peace process, which works only when the three interlinked strands it encompasses are working together. When Strand I (the Northern Ireland Assembly and Executive) collapses, Strand II (the North-South Ministerial Council) automatically collapses. In the absence of devolved government in the North, only Strand III – the British-Irish Intergovernmental Conference (BIIC) – remains functional. This is the only forum in which the two governments working together can act as mediators to try and resuscitate Stormont after it collapses.

Says Sam McBride, the highly respected political editor of the *Belfast Telegraph*:

> [Brexit] has both polarized and poisoned those relations ... There had been a thawing of the ice there that had existed [between unionism and the Irish government] after the Anglo-Irish Agreement ... Within Northern Ireland, I think what Brexit has done is forced people who were otherwise quite comfortable, maybe not enthusiastic about the status quo ... to question whether Northern Ireland is what they thought it was ... It is almost the precursor to what would happen in a border poll where people that otherwise don't spend their waking hours consumed by these issues suddenly think, 'What do I think about this? I have to pick a side here.'[37]

For Ireland, says Fianna Fáil's Jim O'Callaghan, Brexit has complicated both North-South and East-West relations. Besides being 'a divisive issue within unionism', it has had 'huge impacts' on political relationships between the North and the South.[38] The East-West relationship, says O'Callaghan, is under strain 'because there's a strong element of English nationalism in the UK government now', making politics in every part of the island more complicated.[39]

From its earliest days, close co-operation and a common sense of purpose between British and Irish governments were prerequisites for a successful peace process. In 1985, had it not been for the personal relations between Dermot Nally, secretary to the Irish government, and Sir Robert Armstrong, British cabinet secretary (and between his cabinet deputy Sir David Goodall and Michael Lillis, a senior Irish diplomat), it is unlikely that the Anglo-Irish Agreement would have passed muster with Margaret Thatcher.[40] In 1993, Albert Reynolds's and John Major's trust in each other opened the way to the Downing Street Declaration. In 1998, Tony Blair's and Bertie Ahern's ability to work in lockstep was key to getting the political parties in Northern Ireland to agree to the B/GFA. Frequent EU meetings provided a space at the margins for British and Irish officials, where either government could raise its concerns but, more importantly, both could foster personal relationships.

The importance of these meetings, says Seán Ó hUiginn, former head of the Anglo-Irish Division in the Irish Department of Foreign Affairs, cannot be overstressed: 'For the first time in history their [British-Irish] relationship was under a structure of wider laws and regulations, which mitigated somewhat the enormous imbalance between them in terms of power and influence. This enabled them to pursue common interests within the EU, free of the baggage of the past.'[41]

Throughout the Brexit years, the Irish government had punched above its diplomatic weight and cultivated relationships with EU countries, especially France and Germany, skilfully played the diplomatic circuit and brought all twenty-six EU countries onside to ensure a backstop.[42] 'This was not an Irish referendum,' Tony Connelly, RTÉ's reporter on Brexit wrote, 'but it might as well have been.'[43]

There was, however, one fundamental imperative: if Britain voted to leave the EU, the Irish state would have to show its citizens – and the world – that it could withstand the immediate impact and that, no matter what, Ireland would be remaining in the EU.[44]

For unionists, the DUP in particular, Brexit came with a contradiction that may yet come to haunt it on the constitutional issue. As the only political party in Northern Ireland that campaigned on a Leave platform, it had to argue, after the Northern Ireland vote to remain, that the democratic vote that counted was the sovereign vote – the 52 per cent who voted Leave represented the wishes of the majority in the UK, that the 56 per cent who voted Remain in Northern Ireland did not matter. But if a slight majority was a sufficient degree of consensus to leave the EU, why should Northern Ireland be any different? Why wouldn't 50 per cent + 1 be a sufficient barometer of support for Irish unity?

Brexit catapulted the question of a border poll into the public discourse. The conventional wisdom holds that Brexit makes Irish unity more likely; that some Catholics who were hitherto prepared to live in a UK where the B/GFA was working reasonably well and Northern Ireland was part of the EU were now more disposed to looking for a relationship with the rest of Ireland; and that 'soft' unionists[45] who had voted Remain would be looking South and seeing a cosmopolitan country with a roaring economy firmly embedded in the EU. In contrast, the North would increasingly appear as an economic backwater, the ugly appendage in a union on its way to being dismembered, with Scotland taking the road to independence and the English nationalism that had fuelled Brexit all too happy to unload the sponging North. An increasing number of Catholics support unification (the proportion of Catholics wanting to stay in the UK declined from 17.8 per cent in 2010 to 13.6 per cent in 2019),[46] and an increasing proportion of Alliance voters support unity.[47]

'Brexit,' says Naomi Long, Alliance leader, 'has contributed to a change in dynamic in Northern Ireland and one that has challenged some of those who traditionally were content with the status quo. Perhaps (but not necessarily) unionists … felt that Brexit and being removed from the EU is something that has changed … an important part of their identity.'[48]

The Northern Ireland Life and Times (NILT) 2021 survey reports 63 per cent of respondents saying Brexit makes a united Ireland more likely, up 5 percentage points from NILT 2020 and 27 points since NILT 2019.[49] Disaggregating the 63 per cent reveals that 83 per cent of nationalists, 45 per cent of unionists and 67 per cent of 'neithers' believe that Brexit makes a united Ireland more likely. To the question 'Has Brexit made you more in favour of a united Ireland?', 73 per cent of nationalists say it has, up 39 points since 2016, while 32 per cent of unionists say it had made them less in favour, up 20 points since 2016. These evolving attitudes are reflected in a hardening of identities. For the first time more respondents identified as 'Irish only' (26 per cent) than 'British only' (21 per cent).[50] Reviewing the results of the NILT data between 2016 and 2021, Sam McBride opined that:

What is beyond doubt is that the 2016 vote for Brexit undermined the Union. In 2016, 54% of people thought that the long-term policy for Northern Ireland should be to remain part of the UK; that has now fallen to 37% – a dramatic slide in just five years. In that same period support for Irish unity as a long-term solution has risen from 19% to 30% (and there is reason to believe that this underestimates the true figure).[51]

Dutch TV news has aired footage of customs officers confiscating ham sandwiches from drivers arriving by ferry from the UK under post-Brexit rules banning personal imports of meat and dairy products into the EU. Officials wearing high-visibility jackets are shown explaining to startled car and lorry drivers at the Hook of Holland ferry terminal that since Brexit, 'you are no longer allowed to bring certain foods to Europe, like meat, fruit, vegetables, fish, that kind of stuff'. To a bemused driver with several sandwiches wrapped in tin foil who asked if he could maybe surrender the meat and keep just the bread, one customs officer replied: 'No, everything will be confiscated. Welcome to the Brexit, sir, I'm sorry.'[52]
    – Jon Henley, *The Guardian*

The word fish appears 368 times in the new agreement compared with 90 for financial services.[53]
    – George Parker et al., *The Financial Times*

At 11 pm GMT on 31 January 2020, the UK formally exited the EU. Brexit is 'done', Prime Minister Boris Johnson boomed to the nation.[54] This was the new Britain, unshackled from the vassalage of the EU, poised to regain its rightful order on the world stage, a bridge between the EU and the United States, Singapore on the Thames, free to strike trade deals with whomever it wished, no longer constrained by the layers of bureaucracy and regulation to which it had been fettered for almost half a century.

Of course, Brexit was anything but done. As the Institute of Government said, '[Brexit] will continue to dominate government for years to come. The prime minister may hope to end Brexit's dominance in the public debate after 31 January but in Whitehall it will continue to be the biggest and most challenging task faced by government in decades.'[55]

On the front burner was the negotiation of a trade agreement delineating the future relationship between the EU and the UK in a comprehensive trade treaty. Negotiations were ugly and contentious, more like a brawl than two parties trying to reach an amicable divorce, permeated with accu-sations and counter-accusations. The UK, the EU maintained, wanted to cherry-pick. Sticking points included the extent to which the UK govern-ment intended to maintain regulatory alignment with the EU – whether it would, as it staked out its negotiating manifesto, seek to diverge from EU regulations and set its own standards.

These roadblocks to progress had become apparent before the COVID-19 pandemic changed the world in March 2020. It relegated the possible impact of Brexit to the sidelines – a puny consideration in the circumstances of the possibility of collapsing economies and signs of a global meltdown. As second and third waves of the pandemic smothered Europe and the UK, the clock ticked inexorably towards 31 December 2020, before which point a trade agreement between the EU and UK would have to be reached or else see the UK exit the EU without any relationship in place.

The Withdrawal Agreement should have been the easy part, delineating the future relationship between the UK and the EU in a comprehensive trade treaty the hard part. In September 2020, Johnson upended the negoti-ating process itself when he tabled the Internal Market Bill at Westminster.[56] The bill sought to ensure that regulations between England, Scotland, Wales and Northern Ireland were in harmony with each other because, once the UK left the EU, each would have the power to set their own rules on areas like food safety and air quality.

The bill overrode several provisions of the Withdrawal Agreement, including key portions of the NIP. If enacted into law, it would allow UK ministers to 'disapply' previously agreed rules relating to Northern Ireland, should there be no trade deal with the EU. Brandon Lewis, Secretary of State for Northern Ireland, admitted in Parliament that the bill violated international law, but only 'in a specific and limited way'.[57]

The pushback was furious. The EU gave the British government until the end of September to rescind the proposed legislation, otherwise it would invoke legal action. The EU parliament announced that 'under no circumstances would it ratify' a trade bill reached between the EU and the UK should the bill proceed in its initial reading.[58] US Speaker of the House Nancy Pelosi and President Elect Joe Biden weighed in with warnings: any semblance of a hard border across Ireland because of application of provisions in the Internal Market Bill relating to the NIP would slam the

door on a UK-USA trade agreement.[59] All living former UK prime ministers – Blair, Major, Brown, May and Cameron – were vocal in their opposition: Britain's international reputation as a keeper of the rule of law was at
stake.[60] What moral right did the UK have to condemn China for violating
the Sino-British Declaration guaranteeing Hong Kong's limited autonomy
until 2047? How could they expect to play a role as an international mediator? The government's most senior lawyer, Sir Jonathan Jones, resigned
in protest.[61]

The UK Parliament, Boris Johnson insisted, was sovereign and could
breach international treaties. He asserted that the future of the Union was
at stake; he wanted to 'stop a foreign power [the EU] from breaking up the
UK'.[62] Johnson, Micheál Martin said, 'knows well that is not the case'.[63] Irish
Foreign Minister Simon Coveney called it 'inflammatory language coming
from Number 10 which is spin and not the truth'.[64]

Both Scottish and Welsh leaders said the proposed bill '[undermined]
their powers', that it was 'an attack on democracy' and that, rather than safeguarding the Union, the bill was an 'abomination', a step toward dismantling
the Union.[65]

In Parliament, Johnson doubled down: the bill was 'a safety net'[66] to
ensure the EU did not exploit ambiguity in the Withdrawal Agreement to cast
Northern Ireland adrift from the rest of the UK; 'What we cannot tolerate now
is a situation,' he told the Commons, 'where our EU counterparts seriously
believe they have the power to break up our country.'[67] In short, Johnson was
saying that he did not fully understand the ramifications of the agreement he
struck with the EU in relation to the NIP and hence would simply abrogate it,
claiming the sovereignty of Parliament. In the end, the offending clauses were
removed from the final reading of the bill. As an intended negotiating ploy,
it had badly misfired, only making more manifest the widely held belief that
Johnson was unprincipled, untrustworthy and incompetent.

Johnson and Ursula von der Leyen, the European Commission's president, announced the Trade and Cooperation Agreement (TCA)[68] on
Christmas Eve 2020.[69] The bare-bones agreement covered just the manufacturing sector of the economy, with nothing on financial services and
other service sectors that accounted for 80 per cent of the economy.[70] The
agreement was a 'skinny' free-trade agreement – a 'no tariffs no quotas'
arrangement, one step removed from a hard Brexit.[71]

It did not bring much in the way of Christmas tidings. In a UK desperately trying to cope with the COVID-19 crisis, there was little of the celebratory festivities from the previous year, when it had formally exited the EU. The public had soured on Brexit. A YouGov poll in November 2020 found that 51 per cent of respondents thought it was 'wrong' to leave the EU, 38 per cent thought it was 'right' and 11 per cent 'don't know'. Excluding the 'don't knows', 57 per cent said it was wrong, compared with just 43 per cent who said it was right – the highest level of support for 'wrong' ever recorded by YouGov.[72] 'There will be no non-tariff barriers to trade,' Johnson declared.[73] But that too was a lie. In fact, the fraught, year-long negotiations centred on moving from a free-trade arrangement to one putting barriers in the way of free trade.

Rather than the comprehensive free-trade agreement that Johnson had promised, the 'skinny' agreement fell well short. It ensured 'zero-tariff', 'zero-quota' free trade, but a slew of paperwork and VAT made a mockery of any claim to 'frictionless' trade. Better than a no-deal, but only just.[74]

The bad faith that clouded and enveloped the negotiations would continue to contaminate future EU-UK relations. It also put Ireland in an invidious position. 'We are in for a period of continued flux,' says Professor Katy Hayward, who extensively researched the impacts of Brexit:

> The UK and the EU are on different trajectories; Northern Ireland is in the middle … It's not a place that's well able to cope with those tensions. The way [internal tensions] have been managed the past twenty-plus years have been through British-Irish co-operation … Now we have [the two governments] on very many issues themselves on different paths and trajectories. And this is why Brexit has been quite significant for Northern Ireland.[75]

As a member of the EU 'team', Ireland is presumed to be onside in disputes between the EU and the UK, which, in turn, damages London-Dublin relations. The more contentious the EU-UK relationship, with ongoing arguments about interpretations of parts of the Withdrawal and the TCAs – but especially the former over the NIP – the greater the chasm between Dublin and London. Rather than closer working arrangements to manage the daunting political challenges in an increasingly fractious Northern Ireland beset with governance difficulties and calls for a referendum on its constitutional status, the gulf between the two has made it more difficult for both to exercise their dual responsibilities as the impartial co-guarantors of the B/GFA. They reached a nadir in May 2022 after Johnson announced his government's intention to introduce legislation to give his ministers authority to override the NIP.[76] Condemning the move, Taoiseach Micheál Martin accused the British government – not the DUP – of being the main stumbling block to a settlement of the protocol issue.[77]

Whatever spirit of generosity and goodwill that had existed since 1998 has largely dissipated.

TWO

The Northern Ireland Protocol: breaching sea walls

There is no escaping the following: the Northern Ireland Protocol, described at the time by Boris Johnson as an 'excellent deal' that resolved all the issues around Northern Ireland, was a bad deal and didn't resolve those issues; that this was apparent at the time to anyone studying the detail; that the UK government is now effectively in disorderly retreat from the agreement it made; and that, if left unresolved, the issues at the heart of the protocol have the capability of causing an enlarged trade conflict between the UK and the EU, or undermining the Good Friday Agreement – and quite possibly both.[1]

– Tony Blair, former UK prime minister; architect, Belfast/Good Friday Agreement (B/GFA)

My 24-year-old daughter lives in West Sussex ... My dad's not that well, she wanted to go home and see her grandad a couple of weeks ago and she wanted to bring her dog with her in the car. She was going to have to go to her vet and get a veterinary certificate at £110 to bring her dog back to the farm. Now that's crazy. That's just wrong within the UK, within our own country.[2]

– Ian Marshall, Ulster Unionist Party (UUP), former Independent Ulster Unionist Senator, Seanad Éireann

This year marks Northern Ireland's centenary. But, given the effects of Brexit, few are betting on there being a 125th birthday. The Brexit terms keep Northern Ireland inside the EU customs union and single market for goods, weakening its legal and commercial ties to the UK. The first weeks of Brexit have amplified this. British retailers halted some supplies while they grappled with the new trade rules. Customs checks stymied hauliers with multiple loads, and there are fears over the looming expiry of a grace period on health certification for food products.

The arc of history may bend towards reunification but it can be very long. Polling does not suggest a majority in the province for a united Ireland. It also shows deeper ties, such as attachment to the UK's NHS. But nationalism has a secret weapon: the Democratic Unionist Party. The strategic judgements of the province's largest party have been among the most consistently witless in recent politics. One Tory MP fumes: 'The DUP have done more damage to the union than the IRA, Sinn Féin and all the nationalist forces combined' ...

As EU regulations on goods evolve, Brussels – and Dublin – will exert a greater pull.[3]

– Robert Shrimsley, *The Financial Times*,
UK chief political commentator

The political landscape for Northern Ireland has been completely trans-formed by Brexit ... mainly because the underpinning of the Good Friday/Belfast Agreement in terms of the relationship between the UK and Ireland has been transformed. ... Within Northern Ireland, we've seen not only growing pressures and differences between unionism and nationalism in relation to this matter, but also we've seen the intro-duction of a new, strong line of division ... Leave-Remain identities in Northern Ireland [are] very strongly held ... this is a very acute line of division, separation within Northern Ireland ... It's difficult to talk now about Brexit without also talking about the protocol on Ireland/ Northern Ireland because in essence, we do have harder borders all around Northern Ireland. Over time those borders will become more significant and more hard, which is a really uncomfortable position for Northern Ireland given that, as is recognized in the Good Friday Agreement, Northern Ireland is integrated closely with Britain and with Ireland in very meaningful and significant ways. In essence, [in] the process of Brexit ... we've had a great deal of uncertainty.[4]

– Professor Katy Hayward, Senator George J. Mitchell Institute for Global Peace, Security and Justice at Queen's University Belfast; Senior Fellow, UK in a Changing Europe

If the application of this protocol leads to serious economic, societal, or environmental difficulties that are liable to persist, or to diversion of trade, the union or the United Kingdom may unilaterally take appropriate safeguard measures. Such safeguard measures shall be restricted with regard to their scope and duration to what is strictly necessary in order to remedy the situation. Priority shall be given to such measures as will least disturb the functioning of this protocol.[5]

– Article 16(1), Northern Ireland Protocol (NIP)

The impact of the first year of Brexit on Ireland has been revealed after official data showed cross-border trade between Ireland and Northern Ireland jumped by €2.8bn (£2.3bn) in 2021. Full year figures from Ireland's Central Statistics Office show that imports to Ireland from Northern Ireland were up 65% to €3.9bn, a rise of €1.5bn compared with 2020. Exports from Ireland to Northern Ireland also rocketed, up 54% to €3.7bn, an increase of €1.3bn compared with 2020 – a total trade rise of €2.8bn.[6]

– Lisa O'Carroll, Brexit correspondent for *The Guardian*

The Withdrawal Agreement, incorporating the NIP, exposed the shortcomings of the B/GFA when it came to meeting an extraneous political upheaval never envisaged at the time of its signing. It exacerbated disagreements over conflicting interpretations of the core principle of consent, shook the peace process, soured relations between the British and Irish governments and stoked the antagonisms between the United Kingdom (UK) and European Union (EU) that had marked their Brexit negotiations. This antagonism would become low-level hostility when the British government insisted the protocol be substantively modified because it undermined the constitutional integrity of the UK. The protocol did not hammer a stake through the agreement, but it left a thousand stab wounds.

For unionists, the protocol was one more psychic shock to its political nervous system, threatening their sense of security as part of the UK, already on high alert. The demands from republicans for a border poll were relentless, the issue now very definitely in the public realm as some polls appeared to show a tightening of opinion on the constitutional issue. The protocol left unionism grasping at political straws over how to respond to demands that the protocol be replaced.[7]

Bellows of betrayal from loyalists greeted the announcement of the protocol – a betrayal, on all accounts, more devious than the hated and despised Anglo-Irish Agreement (1985)[8] – which added to the unionist catalogue of grievances and confirmed its worst fears, yet again, that it could not rely on a British government to safeguard its position in the union. 'We are in the final days of the union if this withdrawal act goes through,' Jamie Bryson, an influential loyalist blogger, warned a group of fellow loyalist protesters. 'When it comes to regulations that would affect Northern Ireland on goods, the Dublin government would have a greater say over Northern Ireland than the sovereign government in Westminster.'[9] According to Bryson, resistance from the unionist camp would be massive if the deal passed in Parliament; however, he 'wouldn't advocate violence, but there are people who feel that republicans have been rewarded because of their threat of violence over Brexit.'[10]

Even though a majority of Democratic Unionist Party (DUP) voters (70 per cent) and UUP voters (58 per cent, 63 per cent in support twelve months later) voted Leave,[11] the DUP bore the brunt of the criticism for what was now perceived as a strategic blunder. To stave off the criticism, it began to spin the protocol as something positive, as a mechanism whereby businesses could have 'unfettered access' to both the UK and EU markets, thus an attractive destination for inward investment.[12]

On 16 December 2020, two weeks before the protocol went into effect, senior DUP MP Jeffrey Donaldson, not yet the DUP leader, told me with regard to the protocol, 'I don't accept that Brexit has fundamentally changed the constitutional arrangements in the United Kingdom. What it has done is changed the way that we trade. What it has done is changed the way we do business …' Within months he would be eating his own words.

COVID-19 lockdowns ruled out mass protests giving full vent to the frustration and anger people were feeling. The seething under the surface was left to fester, with only graffiti in East Belfast and the Shankill conveying hints of defiance. Political unionism remained silent. With no ostensible change in trading arrangements during 2020 (the transition year) between the 'mainland' and Northern Ireland, there appeared to be a begrudging acceptance of the protocol. With the pandemic raging, potential impacts were downplayed, an attitude reinforced by repeated assurances from Boris Johnson that there would be unfettered trade between the North and Great

Britain and no border down the Irish Sea, even while his ministers were saying the opposite.[13]

The rancour between the UK and EU, and the uncertainty with regard to what the protocol might actually involve and what disruptions it might lead to in people's daily lives in Northern Ireland throughout 2020 – the transition year – set the stage for the political repercussions that exploded in 2021. Throughout 2020, when it was unclear until the very last moment whether the EU and UK could reach a trade deal, Johnson was unequivocal that, trade deal or no trade deal, the movement of such goods across the Irish Sea would be 'unfettered'. He declared in a press conference on 13 January 2020:

> we are the government of the United Kingdom. I cannot see any circumstances whatsoever in which there will be any need for checks on goods going from Northern Ireland into Great Britain. The only circumstances [for] the need for checks coming from [Great Britain to Northern Ireland], is if those goods were going on into Ireland and we had not secured, a zero-tariff, zero-quota agreement with our friends and partners in the EU.[14]

Which, of course, he secured. And which, of course, did nothing to mitigate the impact of the protocol. His pledge of frictionless trade between Britain and Northern Ireland was in outright contradiction of what his ministers were stressing would be unavoidable paperwork for Northern Ireland businesses. Months before the protocol went into effect, Johnson was telling Northern Ireland businessmen 'to bin' customs forms.[15] The EU was unimpressed: the protocol called for red tape, paperwork and physical checks at the Northern Ireland end.[16] Michel Barnier, the EU's lead negotiator, was unequivocal on the question, telling the European parliament that 'the implementation of this [deal] foresees checks and controls entering the island of Ireland'.[17] Mixed messages, for sure.

As the year wore on, Johnson's propensity for political gamesmanship compounded the uncertainty in Northern Ireland about the future along with the uncertainty permeating life during COVID-19. Having to choose between competing narratives regarding the possible impacts of the protocol, unionists chose, again, to take Johnson at his word: the protocol would do little to disturb their daily lives. Northern Ireland, if not quite as British as Finchley, was not significantly different either.[18] A Command Paper (May 2020) rubbished the protocol, proposed a 'trust and verify' system for traders from Britain selling into Northern Ireland and unfettered access to the whole UK market.[19] None of this came to pass. It amplified Johnson's mantra that there would be no border down the Irish Sea, as if by repeating it often enough he could convince unionists that it was true. A second Command Paper (July 2021) followed,[20] calling for wholesale revisions to the protocol and essentially neutering huge chunks of its key provisions. In their place it proposed, once again, a '"trust and verify" system for traders selling from Britain into the Northern Ireland market'.[21] Any role for EU institutions including the European Court of Justice would go.

A joint committee oversees implementation of the protocol. It screens goods entering Northern Ireland from the rest of the UK to ensure they meet EU regulatory standards. Widespread disruption to trade between Great Britain and the North accompanied the roll-out of the protocol in January 2021, in good measure because Northern Ireland was woefully ill-prepared to cope with the situation. In addition to commodities having to be vetted to ensure they met EU regulatory requirements, there were also prodigious amounts of procedural rules and volumes of paperwork to be filled out before goods could be transported across the Irish Sea.

'Absurdities on the border between Great Britain and Northern Ireland,' *The Economist* editorialized. Among the more egregious: plants grown on British soil could not be exported to the North, but plants grown in peat could be; fish food exported there needed a certificate completed by a vet, as well as a customs declaration; bringing a dog or cat into Northern Ireland required a rabies injection for the pet even though Britain is rabies free.[22] The chairperson of the giant food and clothing retailer Marks & Spencer told the BBC that 'Wagons have to carry 700 pages of documentation. It takes eight hours to prepare the documentation, some of the descriptors have to be written in Latin, has to be in a certain typeface, it takes 30 per cent more driver time. So it's highly bureaucratic, very onerous and pretty pointless.'[23] As a result, many British companies simply stopped selling into Northern Ireland because oceans of red tape – from customs declarations to phytosanitary certificates – swamped many transactions, making them too costly and time-consuming. This led to empty shelves after supermarket chains stopped sending hundreds of items to retail outlets.[24]

The anger among unionists was palpable once it became clear that costs and disruptions were not just teething problems but the new normal; among nationalists, there was silence. Even their common experiences – the half-empty shelves in some supermarkets, the obvious burdens on businesses owned or run by nationalists as they strove to comply with complex regulations – could not move either Sinn Féin or the Social Democratic and Labour Party (SDLP) to join the chorus of unionists' voices demanding remedies. The protocol was strictly a zero-sum issue. The prevailing nationalist/republican sentiment was that the DUP had campaigned for Brexit. They had brought the consequences on themselves. Besides, why complain about a trading arrangement that makes a united Ireland more likely? If not a border in the Irish Sea, then what? Once again, a land border could loom.

On 24 December 2020, when the Trade and Cooperation Agreement (TCA) was announced, DUP First Minister Arlene Foster said:

> We will, of course, examine the details both of the trade deal itself as well as other issues such as security where agreement will be particularly important from the Northern Ireland viewpoint. Given the government's Northern Ireland Protocol, a sensible trade deal between the United Kingdom and the European Union was always the most favourable outcome for Northern Ireland. Moving forward, we will continue to work to seize the opportunities and address the challenges which arise from the United Kingdom's exit from the European Union. This is the start of a new era in the relationship between the UK and the EU and in Northern Ireland we will want to maximise the opportunities the new arrangements provide for our local economy.[25]

A week later, on 3 January 2021, days after the protocol went into effect, Foster on the BBC pledged 'to mitigate the worst effects of the protocol'.[26] 'What we have is a gateway of opportunity for the whole of the UK, and for Northern Ireland,' she said, 'and it is important that in this centenary year that we look forward to that and step through that gateway and take all the opportunities that are available for our people.'[27] That said, she hoped that when the protocol came up for a vote in the Assembly, 'people will see that it is much better to move out of these regulations and into the global market'.[28] Her remarks preceded the tsunami of the protocol's regulatory provisions about to turn trade between Northern Ireland and Great Britain into a bureaucratic and administrative nightmare. Not a whisper, however, about Northern Ireland not having given its consent to a border down the Irish Sea.

That would change. Six weeks into the protocol taking effect, the EU – in a row with the UK over the supply of the AstraZeneca vaccine – unilaterally invoked Article 16 of the protocol, the 'nuclear option' open to both the UK and EU, only to be resorted to in extraordinary circumstances.[29] Neither Dublin nor London had been consulted; both were swift in their protestations and the decision, by an unnamed official, was reversed within twenty-four hours. But the damage was done. The EU had lost its moral high ground. Its commitment to the Irish peace process, so carefully burnished over four and a half years, was called into question. The UK used the incident to demand an extension of the grace period to implement the full range of checks at Northern Ireland ports for two years, in the hope of silencing increasingly agitated unionist voices, and it emboldened the DUP's efforts to get the UK government to invoke Article 16.[30]

The protocol row morphed from being about how to mitigate its deleterious repercussions on trade and commerce into a constitutional one. 'A part of the [United] Kingdom is governed by [EU] laws that it cannot amend ... ' DUP MP Ian Paisley Jr decried in our interview:[31]

> If those laws can be altered in [the European Court of Justice] of which [Northern Ireland] is no plea at the bar of, it's inherently undemocratic and it's also completely different from how the rest of the United Kingdom is managed and organized and it is not true to what the people voted for in 2016, which was to leave the European Union as a United Kingdom.[32]

> The protocol undermined the constitutional integrity of the UK. Article 16 must be invoked. It allows for one party to say that there are either societal or economic issues which unilaterally we need to change. If we do, these are our proposals for how we change them and what we would put in their place. I think we need that to come into play and the British government needs now to do what it didn't do over the last three years, and that's crack the whip in terms of saying we're negotiating on behalf of Northern Ireland.[33]

DUP MP Sammy Wilson goes further:

> The Belfast Agreement has been ripped up in pieces and deliber-
> ately so. The very first declaration, which was made in the Belfast
> Agreement, was that 'There cannot be any change' – those are the
> words – '... in the constitutional status of Northern Ireland, unless
> there's the consent of the people of Northern Ireland.' The Belfast
> Agreement is effectively dead.
>
> Quite clearly our position has been changed: laws are now made
> in another jurisdiction, courts in a foreign jurisdiction will adjudicate
> on those laws, and as a result of that, we have been cut off from our
> main market in GB. Article Six of the Act of Union has been removed
> and has been altered ...[34] Another part of the Belfast Agreement [says
> that where] there were controversial issues, they have to be dealt with
> on a cross-community basis in the Executive and in the Assembly.
> That part was deliberately removed in relation to the protocol so that
> there is no longer any need for cross-community consent.
>
> The two pillars of the Belfast Agreement, first of all, the consent
> principle and secondly, the Safeguards for Minorities Principle have
> been removed, so the Belfast Agreement is effectively dead. That's
> one of the reasons why we're refusing now to take part in some of the
> agreement's institutions.[35]

Contrary to what nationalists held, Wilson insists that although nationalists had not given their consent to leaving the EU – indeed, they had voted over-whelmingly to remain – the consent stipulation in the B/GFA only applies to Northern Ireland and the UK, not Northern Ireland and the EU. Trying to equate the two is a red herring.

David Frost, the pugnacious UK Brexit negotiator, bore down on British objections to the protocol Boris Johnson himself had negotiated and called 'fantastic', advancing a novel negotiating posture.[36] Johnson, he argued, had negotiated under duress. Had he not agreed to the protocol, the UK would either have crashed out of the EU or found itself stuck indefinitely in it. Hence the imperative to agree a protocol at any price to avoid either of these disasters.[37] The protocol, Frost maintained, threatened the constitutional integrity of the UK and was an infringement on British sovereignty. (Later, it emerged that Johnson had been fully briefed on the extent of the checks on goods coming from Britain to Northern Ireland but had hoped 'the EU would not apply them'.)[38]

Unionist objections became more focused – the sea border violated the Constitution of the UK as embedded in the Acts of Union 1800; it violated the Northern Ireland Act 1998; and, they maintained, it violated the consent formula of the B/GFA.[39] If a land border across Ireland violated the B/GFA because it disrupted a seamless border between the two parts of Ireland – although one could not point to any clause in the agreement with that explicit provision – then the same logic held with regard to Northern Ireland: the sea border violated the seamless border between one part of the UK and another. If a land border would trigger violence, surely it was equally valid to argue that a sea border would also result in violence? In political terms, the Irish government 'won' the argument; years of assiduously cultivating governments across the EU had paid off. Unionism had no advocate to make the case against an Irish Sea border by laying out how it might instigate loyalist violence. The protocol was a done deal before they could fully comprehend its consequences.

If one steps back from the arguments advanced by the Irish government on the one hand and unionists on the other, the justifications for their positions become a little more nuanced. There is no specific reference to a border in the B/GFA because both Ireland and the UK were members of the EU. Trade and travel between the three entities was seamless. The agreement is embedded in EU law. The absence of a border was a given. With respect to North-South relations and the implementation of projects agreed by the bodies under the remit of the North-South Ministerial Council, the B/GFA stipulates that implementation will be 'on an all-island and cross-border basis'.[40] A land border across Ireland would severely disrupt the work of these bodies, inconvenience travellers and reinforce the physical partition of Ireland, but it would not change the constitutional relationships between North and South, or the North and Britain. While nationalists would angrily object to a land border, saying they had not given their consent, the consent formulation in the B/GFA refers only to the relationship between Northern Ireland and the United Kingdom. No one doubted, however, that violence would follow the imposition of a land border.

Likewise, the B/GFA has no provision regarding Northern Ireland and the rest of the UK, other than the consent formulation requiring a majority voting to enact a change to its constitutional status. Nor was one necessary because seamless trade and movement of people between the two was explicit – they are, after all, two parts of the same country. Former First Minister Peter Robinson complained that:

> [it is] infuriating to hear people, some of whom should know better, recite the mantra that a land border on the island of Ireland would have been a breach of the Belfast Agreement. While they struggle to show where in the agreement such a stipulation exists, they, at most, rely on the scrawny defence that it is contrary to the spirit of the agreement. Naturally, they ignore the equally valid truth that a border in the Irish Sea is contrary to the spirit of the agreement.[41]

Much of unionist anger at Dublin is because of what they see as hypocrisy, the refusal of Dublin to acknowledge that unionism's case against the sea border is as legitimate as Dublin's case against a land border.

David Frost repeatedly threatened to invoke Article 16; the EU promised retaliation. For much of 2021, Northern Ireland was a useful pawn in openly hostile relations between the EU and UK over interpretations of the TCA. Once it appeared that a settlement to the protocol dispute was in sight when the EU offered to alter EU law so as to ensure the free flow of medical supplies into Northern Ireland,[42] Frost pulled another obstacle from his negotiating toolbox: under no circumstances would the UK agree to having the European Court of Justice as the arbiter in disputes over the protocol between the EU and UK.[43] Any suggestion that the UK should be bound by a ruling of a foreign court – a regulatory purgatory that the UK had exited – was unacceptable, an infringement of UK sovereignty that Brexit was designed to protect against. Ireland's Foreign Minister Simon Coveney slammed 'UK protocol demands as insatiable'[44] and became the target of unionist anger for his 'ignoring unionist concerns and hoping they'll just go away',[45] for 'gravity-defying levels of arrogance and hypocrisy',[46] for 'trashing East-West relationships … with barely disguised triumphalism and bombastic belligerence'.[47]

In a scathing *Irish Times* op-ed, an angry and at times sorrowful David Trimble – who could legitimately claim stature to address protocol issues because of his key role in formulating the consent language in the B/GFA – lashed out at both governments.[48] There were '70 pages of EU laws to which Northern Ireland must adhere'.[49] Northern Ireland now had to follow future EU laws without having had any say in how these laws were enacted. These changes represented 'a seismic and undemocratic change in the constitutional position of Northern Ireland and runs contrary to the most fundamental premise in the Belfast Agreement'.[50] Trimble continues:

> This false mantra of protecting the Belfast Agreement and keeping the peace in Northern Ireland has become the shield behind which the EU, the Irish government, nationalist parties in Northern Ireland, UK politicians, and even US president Joe Biden hide behind when challenged about the damage to democracy and the economy in Northern Ireland as a result of the protocol. They believe, by invoking the hard-won agreement that I helped negotiate 23 years ago, they can justify the indefensible attack on the rights and livelihood of all Northern Ireland citizens that the unprecedented and unreasonable protocol requirements impose on the part of the UK in which I live.[51]

He issued a warning: 'If the genuine grievances and resentments caused by the protocol are not addressed politically, then there is real potential for those who have engaged in past violence to take action again into their own hands.'[52] The protocol, he asserted, 'changes fundamentally the constitutional relationship between Northern Ireland and the rest of the UK'.[53] Laws across a range of activities 'no longer will be made at our parliament in Westminster or the local Assembly in Belfast. They will instead be determined by a foreign authority in Brussels'.[54]

He goes on:

> The very first clause of the Belfast/Good Friday Agreement states: 'It is hereby declared that Northern Ireland in its entirety remains part of the United Kingdom and shall not cease to be so without the consent of a majority of the people of Northern Ireland voting in a poll held for that purpose.' And the second clause is clear: 'it would be wrong to make any change in the status of Northern Ireland save with the consent of a majority of its people'.
>
> Thus, the Northern Ireland Protocol ignores the fundamental principle of consent. Northern Ireland is no longer fully part of the UK – it has been annexed by the EU, subject to EU laws and an EU court without any right of dissent.[55]

Furthermore, there was the implicit duplicity:

> Under the heading of 'Safeguards', the agreement stipulates that 'key decisions are to be taken on a cross-community basis'. Nothing

could be more 'key' than the demands made in the Northern Ireland Protocol. Yet, any vote on them is held back for four years and, when a vote eventually is taken, the cross-community safeguard will not be applied.[56]

Nationalists were unmoved.

Trimble's warning that the NIP 'risks a return to violence', 'that the protocol ripped the heart out of the agreement'[57] and undermined key principles of the B/GFA, were dismissed as the bitter whining of a hardline Brexiteer, as Trimble being Trimble – aloof, dour and rather graceless, his blind anger leading him to misinterpret the agreement he had been instrumental in designing. The fact that he had been one of the key architects of the B/GFA, had earned a Nobel Peace Prize for his contribution and hence should be listened to and his views given great attention, went ignored. But when he died in July 2022, the tributes poured in across the political divide – from Dublin, London, Belfast and Washington, DC. He was hailed as a transformational unionist leader, a visionary, a risk-taker willing to compromise on the most contentious issues, courageous and brave in the face of the animosity towards him from his own tribe after he led Ulster unionists – balking all the way – into a post-Agreement Northern Ireland. Even Sinn Féin paid a tribute. Trimble was praised for his moral rectitude, his equanimity in the face of the savage and endless personal attacks from the Rev. Ian Paisley and his DUP acolytes who branded him a traitor. Only he could have brought the UUP onside and secured a post-conflict future. 'His legacy will endure,' Bill Clinton intoned, although Trimble himself believed that the NIP eviscerated his legacy. 'Even if David Trimble opposed the Northern Ireland Protocol,' Sam McBride asked, 'How can the EU play the Good Friday card?'

In March 2021, in short order, Johnson unilaterally suspended until 1 October the requirements for the end to the grace period on 1 April for some businesses and/or products to comply with EU rules. The EU threatened legal action:[58] the Loyalist Communities Council (LCC) – the umbrella organization for loyalist paramilitary groups including the Ulster Defence Association (UDA), Ulster Volunteer Force (UVF) and Red Hand Commandos – wrote to Johnson on 4 March, saying it was withdrawing its support for the B/GFA until the NIP was replaced,[59] albeit stressing that it was not calling for a land border and not threatening violence. Donaldson said unionist support for the B/GFA 'was rapidly diminishing'.[60]

Over several days in early April 2021, including the twenty-third anniversary of the B/GFA, young Protestants took to the streets protesting the
protocol. At first the protests resulted in confrontations with the police and
the hijacking and burning of a bus. Then they threatened to spread into
Catholic areas with skirmishes across peace walls, coming to a climax on
8 April at the Lanark interface separating Catholics on Springfield Road
from Protestants on the Shankill Road in West Belfast. Loyalist rioters on
the Shankill Road side hurled rocks and petrol bombs across the interface;
Catholic youths on the other side responded.[61]

Older members of paramilitaries were on hand, some said, to contain
the youths and police the situation from getting out of hand; others said
they were behind the rioting (a subsequent police investigation cleared the
paramilitaries of any involvement).[62] These were social media-organized
protests, many using fake media accounts. Had the rioters breached the
interface and come into contact with the Catholics gathered on the other
side, the situation could easily have spiralled into a new phase of violence.
Father Tim Bartlett, the influential Catholic priest who was on the nationalist side of the Springfield Road interface, recalls:

> During the riots in Lanark Way, at a certain point on the loyalist side, I
> heard a car burning at the gate, but then the rioters still commandeered
> this BMW X5, a very powerful four-by-four vehicle. The assumption
> was that they were simply going to burn it as well, but they got into
> that vehicle, and they rammed the gate again and again. No one had
> any doubt that what they were trying to do. The gate, however, was
> strong enough to stop the car. Had the car come through and drove
> over people it would have flipped everything on its head.[63]
>
> What I saw with my own eyes, and I've been in a lot of riots and
> watched a lot of those kinds of situations over the years, it was the
> sheer viciousness of it and the determination and the anger behind
> it on the loyalist side.

Despite the small scale of the violence, in much of the West and the
United States, the media reported the rioting as threatening to spiral into
a more violent phase of conflict, a view which many governments shared.
Micheál Martin, Boris Johnson and even US President Joe Biden issued
statements: the 'fragile' peace had to be protected.[64] Only the B/GFA provided the necessary safeguards. Loyalists weren't listening to the bromides

about the agreement: the republic had shamelessly used the threat of violence to get its way over a land border; loyalists would use it to get rid of the
sea border.[65] Says Ian Marshall:

> What the loyalists said to me on when I met them was, 'Ian, for three
> years no one has listened to us. For three years our voice has been
> lost in the wilderness about our concerns about what was going on.'
> They said, 'Three weeks ago, violence erupted as a consequence of
> an Irish Sea border, and people came onto the streets. What's hap-
> pened in those three weeks is that the establishment, both British
> government, Irish government and Northern Ireland Executive,
> now want to talk to us.' I said, 'What does that say to you? That says
> that violence definitely pays' … The perception for the loyalists …
> is equally as important because it's the feeling that one border was
> more important than the other, and one border threatened a return
> to violence and the other border … they'll just have to suck it up and
> get on with it. That's the feeling that's there …

David Frost's threats to invoke Article 16 became more frequent. Meanwhile,
negotiations between Frost and Barnier's replacement EU vice president,
Maroš Šefčovič, became more contentious as the impacts of Brexit were felt
across the UK. The Biden administration warned the British government
on at least two occasions not to act in a way that threatened the B/GFA.[66]
Speaker of Congress Nancy Pelosi and Richard Neal, who chaired the powerful Ways and Means Committee and was a good friend of Sinn Féin, let it
be known that there would be no trade deal for the UK if the government
messed with the Agreement.[67]

Getting rid of the protocol became the new unionist mantra.[68] The DUP
had championed Brexit. During Theresa May's government, it had maintained unwavering inflexibility on every manifestation of Brexit that might
have seen Northern Ireland being treated differently from the rest of the UK,
eventually backing itself into a corner of its own making.[69] Once it opposed
even an outcome that might have seen the UK as a whole stay in the Single
Market and Customs Union until such time as a better solution to the Irish
border question was found, a border down the Irish Sea became inevitable
simply as a process of eliminating alternatives.

The DUP allied themselves with Johnson, who betrayed them. Thereafter,
seeking to put distance between itself and the protocol, it joined with

other Northern Ireland parties in voting against the TCA when it reached Westminster on 30 December 2020, again bellowing betrayal.[70]

It sought to justify its own actions while it held the balance of power at Westminster, arguing that even if it had backed Theresa May's backstop, eventually it would have led to 'Northern Ireland being locked into a separate arrangement from Britain'.[71]

Voters weren't buying the explanation. In a May 2021 LucidTalk Poll, Sinn Féin outpolled the DUP, 25 per cent to 16 per cent, with Alliance also at 16 per cent, the UUP at 14 per cent and the Traditional Unionist Voice (TUV) surging to 11 per cent.[72] By any measure, a drop of 40 per cent in support since Assembly elections in 2017 was precipitous, reflecting grass-roots concerns about how the party had handled Brexit and anger at how the NIP was disrupting trade and commercial life – and holding the party partly accountable for the outcome. The haemorrhaging of support continued throughout 2021.

David Frost resigned from the cabinet on 19 December 2021, ostensibly over restrictive measures curtailing a number of activities to halt the spread of the Omicron variant of COVID-19.[73] He was replaced by Liz Truss, foreign secretary and a former Remainer, now intent on out-Brexiteering the Brexiteers themselves[74] – and by all accounts a putative candidate for Johnson's job should his myriad troubles force him to resign.[75]

It appeared that Russia's invasion of Ukraine in February 2022 would put the EU-UK 'wars' on hold and their disputes into a broader perspective as Europe united in opposition to Vladimir Putin's invasion of Ukraine, which made other issues seem trivial in comparison. Premonitions of a wider war in the making that could quickly escalate to heretofore unimaginable levels preoccupied most of Europe, still conscious over a hundred years later of how the First World War had not been meant to happen, how a slow unfolding of events – none of which appeared particularly threatening – resulted in Europe almost accidently sleepwalking into a devastating war.

But Johnson needed his quarrel with the EU to distract from his multiple home-front problems, and from the fact that Brexit was not delivering the socio-economic benefits its advocates had promised, making his tenure as prime minister increasingly problematic.[76] He needed an enemy, someone or thing he could point his finger at as the source of Britain's misfortunes and use that as a continuing diversion. Hence, he ratcheted up his dispute with the EU to a point where it invited the EU to take retaliatory action, even when European solidarity as a counterweight to Russia's invasion of Ukraine and the threat of a wider war had never been more necessary. In early June 2022, Johnson barely survived a vote of no confidence in the House of Commons: 211 votes supporting him, 148 against. But the laws of political gravity are inexorable: he would be gone sooner rather than later.[77] 'The Conservative Party will not be able to move on,' *The Economist* editorialized, 'whatever the prime minister hopes.'[78]

In the end, nothing could save him from himself. Almost inevitably, he hoisted himself by his petard of lies. 'Enough is enough,' Sajid Javid, Secretary of State for Health, said in his resignation letter when it emerged that Johnson knew, but had denied having known, even though he had been given a 'first-hand account' of the misconduct allegations against Chris Pincher before appointing him deputy chief whip. After fifty cabinet members and senior staff resigned, Johnson bowed out.[79] 'Them's the breaks,' he shrugged, announcing his intention to step down as soon as his successor was chosen.[80]

Following a bruising and vicious campaign between former Chancellor Rishi Sunak, whose resignation from the Cabinet had triggered the tsunami of resignations that led to Johnson's downfall, and Elizabeth Truss, who had stayed loyal to Johnson, Truss emerged the winner, party leader and new prime minister after Conservative Party members voted in September.

Truss was, on all accounts, the prime minister unionists – especially the DUP – had hoped for. In June 2022, weeks before Johnson's tumble from power, she had tabled the Northern Ireland Protocol Bill in the Commons. This legislation would empower UK ministers to make unilateral changes to the protocol, essentially cannibalizing its content and ending most checks on goods entering Northern Ireland from Britain.[81] It went further than Article 16, giving UK ministers sweeping powers to override virtually all provisions of the protocol and eliminating any role for the European Court of Justice (ECJ).[82] The key component would set up a two-lane system for trucks entering Northern Ireland from Britain: a check-free green lane for trucks carrying goods that that would stay in Northern Ireland and a red lane for checking trucks on their way to the republic, and thus into the EU Single Market.[83]

The uproar was predictable. Relations between Dublin and London took a further turn for the worse. 'It would be a historic low if the British government proceeds with plans to unilaterally introduce legislation to override the Northern Ireland Protocol,' Micheál Martin said.[84] Johnson's actions were 'a fundamental breach of trust', 'profoundly dispiriting', 'had the potential to destabilize politics in Northern Ireland'.[85] Maroš Šefčovič, the EU commissioner for Brexit, promised legal action.[86] He warned of the irreparable damage to the UK-EU relationship that would follow either the UK triggering Article 16 or unilateral action scrapping the protocol.[87] A majority of the Members of Assembly (MLAs) wrote to Johnson condemning his 'reckless' action and rebutting his assertion that he was simply protecting the B/GFA.[88] Nancy Pelosi, Speaker of the US House of Representatives, warned that it put a UK-US trade deal in jeopardy.[89]

Undeterred, Truss pressed on, exhibiting a political tone-deafness that would ultimately be her undoing. The bill worked its way through the House of Commons, cleared all hurdles on 20 July and was subsequently sent to the House of Lords where it faced stiff opposition and numerous amendments, setting the stage for protracted 'ping pong' exchanges between the two chambers. 'The government will have to work hard to get it through the Upper House,' said Lord Alderdice, 'because it does not have an absolute government majority there, unlike in the Commons.' Moreover, 'There is a view amongst many in the Lords, including some on the Conservative side, that the bill is proposing a breach of international law, or at the very least a breach of trust, and there is talk of a long stand-off between the Commons and the Lords over passing the legislation.'[90]

Getting rid of the protocol spearheaded the DUP's campaign for the 5 May 2022 Assembly elections. It promised unionist voters that it would not become part of the Northern Ireland Executive until the protocol had been replaced and there were no impediments to the movement of goods and people between Britain and Northern Ireland. The Northern Ireland Protocol Bill satisfied these demands. But such an in-your-face disavowal of the Withdrawal Agreement by the UK was sure to result in the EU responding with 'all measures at its disposal'.[91]

To fend off that eventuality, the EU held out the olive branch with an offer to resolve the dispute with a proposal to hold checks on goods entering Northern Ireland from Great Britain to a near 'invisible manner' involving just 'a couple of lorries' a day. Physical checks would be made only 'when there is a reasonable suspicion of illegal trade smuggling, illegal drugs, dangerous toys or poisoned food'.[92]

The groundwork was laid for a compromise.

However, should the UK government's Northern Ireland Protocol Bill become law, it may fall to the Irish government to protect the Single Market. In short, it may have to impose limited checks on the border between Ireland and Northern Ireland and at Irish ports. Should that happen, one likely consequence will be a decisive swing among cultural Catholics in Northern Ireland presently content to stay in the UK, or who respond 'don't know' on the constitutional question in opinion polls, to supporting reunification.[93] The other consequence could be the dissident republican violence the Irish government had warned of in 2016 in the event of a hard border materializing.

The DUP should listen to the adage: 'Beware of what you wish for.'

— THREE —

The Northern Ireland Statelet: a place apart

It is clear from the structures that were fashioned at the birth of Northern Ireland that our forefathers did not envisage creating a permanent state. The apparatus of the Council of Ireland suggests our separateness from the South was to be short term and transitory.[1]
— Peter Robinson, First Minister of Northern Ireland, 2008–16; leader of the Democratic Unionist Party (DUP), 2008–15

What is normal is change, and not even change for the better, just change. The world of fifty years ago is gone; it was probably not even as we remember it. And the world we bequeath to another generation will not be as we have conceived it. Between a garbled past and an inconceivable future there is today, which would be enough if there was equality and universal neighbourliness ... Some people edged us closer to that while others were obsessed by narratives of sovereign destiny and trying to clear the way to a future we may not want or recognize anyway when it arrives – if it arrives.[2]

— Malachi O'Doherty, journalist

Facing possible home rule for Ireland twice in the late nineteenth century, Ulster unionists, overwhelmingly Protestant, turned to threats of violence, expressed by Randolph Churchill: 'Ulster will fight and Ulster will be right.'[3] Were home rule for Ireland to pass, unionists would go from being part of a Protestant majority in the United Kingdom (UK) of Great Britain and Ireland to being a Protestant minority in an all-Ireland Catholic state – hence the rallying cry, 'Home rule is Rome rule'.

On 28 September 1912, 471,000 Ulster men and women signed a solemn league and covenant pledging to use 'all means which may be found nec-essary to defeat the present conspiracy to set up a Home Rule Parliament in Ireland'.[4] They established the Ulster Unionist Council (UUC) as a pro-visional government and the Ulster Volunteer Force (UVF), a paramilitary force of 90,000 men. The UUC imported huge quantities of arms from Germany in a ship named *Mountjoy II*, after the ship that had broken the siege of Londonderry in 1689.[5] The UVF flaunted its strength with intimi-dating military-type parades across Ulster. It was the bedrock of militarism on which the Northern Ireland statelet was founded. 'Between July 1920 and July 1922,' historian Donnacha Ó Beacháin writes, '453 people were killed in Belfast alone. Catholics constituted the vast majority of deaths, despite the fact that they constituted only a quarter of the city's population. Of Belfast's 93,000 Catholics, nearly 11,000 had been ejected from their place of employ-ment and 23,000 had been driven from their homes. In addition, over 500 Catholic-owned shops and businesses had been destroyed.'[6]

Sectarian violence was rampant, casting in hatred and blood a pattern that would repeat itself in the following decades until the late 1960s, when the British government had to deploy the army to Northern Ireland to protect Catholics from what seemed an imminent pogrom.

No one wanted Northern Ireland to exist as a political entity within the UK. Pro-union Protestants wanted to preserve the union with Britain; Catholic nationalists wanted a unitary Irish state. Northern Ireland's first prime minister, James Craig, said in 1921: 'In this island we cannot live always separated from one another. We are too smart to be apart or for the border to be there for all time. The change will not be in my time, but it will come.'[7] Edward Carson, who led the unionist campaign against Home Rule, was no less hopeful: 'There is no one in the world who would be more pleased to see an absolute unity in Ireland than I would.'[8]

Actions spoke otherwise. Within two years, Craig's government had mobilized the Protestant community, which accounted for two-thirds of the statelet's population, to become members of its newly established security apparatuses: in 1922, for every two Catholic males, there was a member of the state security forces.[9] Northern Ireland was always a conditional part of the UK, composed of six of the nine counties of historic Ulster to ensure a Protestant majority in perpetuity. The Government of Ireland Act (1920) made provision for a Council of Ireland to lay the groundwork for eventual Irish unity.[10]

The 1921 Anglo-Irish Treaty gave Northern Ireland the right to opt out of the new Irish Free State. The Ireland Act (1949), passed after the Free State declared itself a republic, thus severing all ties with the Commonwealth, gave the Northern Ireland parliament the right to determine the constitutional status of Northern Ireland.[11]

In 1920, the unionist government established a special paramilitary police force, the B Specials, to protect the new state against the assaults of republicans, and introduced a Special Powers Act in 1922 that gave the government draconian powers to intern people without trial. The unwillingness of nationalists to recognize the new statelet and their abstention from the Stormont Parliament during its formative years – and periodically thereafter – meant they had no say in the crucial early years of the statelet when governance institutions were being shaped, further facilitating unionist hegemony.[12]

Michael Collins had, after all, told Dáil Éireann during debate on the treaty in January 1922 that it gave the 'freedom to achieve freedom'.[13] The Boundary Commission, established under the auspices of the 1921 treaty to rule on final borders between Northern Ireland and the rest of Ireland, would, nationalists believed, result in boundaries that would make the North an unviable socio-economic unit.[14] The activities of the Northern Ireland Irish Republican Army (IRA) tried to hasten the day.[15]

The perceptual lens that framed both communities' political behaviour was the same: that of the aggrieved minority. While Catholics saw themselves as the minority in a majority Northern Ireland Protestant state, Protestants saw themselves as the minority in a majority Catholic all-island Ireland. Articles 2 and 3 of the Irish Constitution, claiming the North as part of the national territory, exacerbated their sense of insecurity.

The unionists' great fear throughout most of the twentieth century, especially during the years of the conflict – and particularly when republicans targeted mainland Britain – was that the British government would somehow seek to coerce them into a united Ireland without their consent. Hardcore loyalist unionists were prepared to fight Britain to stave off any measures that came to be seen as undermining Protestant hegemony. The result was widespread electoral gerrymandering, discrimination against Catholics in every economic and social arena and a society that put the utmost premium on geographic divisions and used religion as a badge of allegiance.[16]

Protestant response to partition was reflexive: behind every Catholic was the intent to destroy the Northern Ireland state. Accordingly, when Catholics organized a civil rights movement in the late 1960s, demanding impartial police protection, an end to electoral abuses, equal employment opportunities, fair allocation of public housing and the disbanding of the B Specials, Protestants responded according to their prior perceptions. Since any organized Catholic effort was seen by many to be an act of subversion to bring about a united Ireland, their predictable response to thwart the threat was violence. In August 1969, when the police could no longer handle the situation, the British government had to deploy troops onto the streets of Northern Ireland to protect the Catholic community.

One of the first casualties of the conflict was the Northern Ireland parliament and government, prorogued by the British government in April 1971 when direct rule from Westminster was instituted. After Stormont fell in 1972, the principle was re-embodied in an amendment by Ian Paisley to the Northern Ireland Constitution Act (1973) that affirmed the status of Northern Ireland as part of the United Kingdom.[17]

By the early 1970s, the civil rights movement had achieved its major goals, but the British army's presence had become the symbol of old hatreds – a symbol that provided a nascent IRA, which sought to reunify Ireland through force of arms, with a situation to exploit. So began the long war, a near thirty years of violence, some 3,500 killings, 20,000 injuries, disruption, economic depression and social upheaval before the IRA renewed its ceasefire in July 1997, opening the way for Sinn Féin to join the talks process that culminated in the Belfast/Good Friday Agreement (B/GFA).[18]

History in Northern Ireland, like every slice of life you interrogate, is highly contested, and pro-union historians give a different emphasis to how events have unfolded there. From the onset, they maintain, Northern Ireland was under threat – both from the Catholic minority within and the Catholic majority on its border, exacerbating the historic sense of siege.[19] Nationalists never understood the nature of unionism – how differences in religion, ethnic background, culture and political aspirations set Ulster apart from the rest of Ireland. There was no acknowledgment of how the deep bonds of blood and sacrifice forged at the Somme on behalf of Great Britain and again during the Second World War copper-fastened their commitment to a British identity. Rather, Irish nationalists questioned the integrity of their commitment to the Union, insisting that the Irish nation was one indivisible territorial unit covering the entire island and unwilling to concede that, just as they had the right to secede from the Union, unionists had the right to stay in. Partition, according to nationalist political theology, was perfidious England's fault. Once it was abolished, the people of Ireland would be magically united; pro-union Protestants would discover that their British identity was due to false consciousness and become born again with an Irish identity.

The Irish Free State rejected the principle of consent – that Northern Ireland would remain part of the UK until a majority decided otherwise. Irish Taoiseach Éamon de Valera famously said that 'Ulster must be coerced if she stood in the way',[20] without saying who would do the coercing and with no thought given to the militant opposition such an effort would undoubtedly galvanize. The opportunities for co-operation – and possible unity the putative Council of Ireland might have offered – were not taken advantage of because the South regarded the North's government as illegitimate. It discouraged Northern nationalists from participating in the North's government and encouraged abstentionism, passive resistance and civil protest.

The Irish state evolved into a Gaelic Catholic one where Catholic moral values were pervasive and insular. The Protestant population was marginalized in the organs of the state where a knowledge of the Gaelic language was a prerequisite for success. Sectarianism in the North had its counterpoint in the South: working-class Protestants were only marginally better off than Catholics, and much of the difference could be explained by Protestant geographic proximity to the North's industrial heartland: the Harland & Wolff shipping yards and Shorts engineering in East Belfast.

Similarly, there were claims of large-scale discrimination against Catholics in the allocation of public housing.[21] Contrary to these claims, Catholics, the supremely pro-union economist Dr Graham Gudgin asserts, 'were over-represented, not under-represented, in social housing at the end of the unionist regime in 1971. The Housing Trust built almost 50,000 dwellings between 1945 and 1971 and was scrupulously impartial.'[22] Yet while nationalists were wont to draw attention to Lord Brookeborough's assertion that Northern Ireland was 'a Protestant state for a Protestant people', it was a case of the pot calling the kettle black, as the South was as much a Catholic state for a Catholic people.

The IRA's was a 'long war' against the Protestant people; refusing to recognize the depth and intensity of the Protestant British identity, they determined to bomb and shoot a cowed population into submitting to a united Ireland, achieving by terror what could not be achieved by persuasion. Now republicans promised a New Ireland where that identity would be accommodated and respected, after a hundred years of unrelentingly disparaging its constitutional context within the UK and the legitimacy of Northern Ireland's status. In the political propaganda realm nationalists have won hands down, their narrative of oppression and grievance bolstered by a hyper-nationalist diaspora in other countries and the United States in particular. But even allowing for some levels of discrimination, there was no moral justification for the IRA's campaign of terror.

FOUR

The Belfast/Good Friday Agreement: the perils of ambiguity

The big 'give' from Irish republicans in 1998 was that for the first time ever we all came to the acceptance of the so-called principle of consent. Prior to that, it would have been referred to as the unionist veto over the self-determination of the island of Ireland. What was the 'give' in the Good Friday Agreement on the part of republicans? We accepted that there won't be a united Ireland until the majority of people in the North vote in favour of such a prospect.[1]

– Matt Carthy, Sinn Féin Teachta Dála (TD)

We live in angry times. The political atmosphere has been soured by the debate over Brexit and its impact on Ireland, by the failure to restore devolved government at Stormont and the mooted end to Troubles-era prosecutions of British troops. The hopeful days that followed the Good Friday Agreement have long vanished and with them, I fear, the possibility of more nuanced responses … These are perilous times. Taking a step back to the spirit of conciliation that marked the end of the Troubles in the North seems impossible to imagine.[2]

– Fergal Keane, BBC correspondent

On 10 April 1998, the Belfast/Good Friday Agreement (B/GFA) was signed, bringing to an end the thirty-year-long Northern Ireland conflict. The centrepiece of the document was parity of esteem for Irish and British aspirations in Northern Ireland and the principle of consent on the issue of Irish unity.

The next week, at the penultimate session of the Northern Ireland Forum, Ulster Unionist Party (UUP) leader David Trimble expressed his satisfaction at securing Northern Ireland's place within the UK: 'The Act of Union – the fundamental legislation defining Northern Ireland's position within the United Kingdom – remains firmly in place.'[3]

A week later at a special Ard Fheis, Sinn Féin endorsed the agreement as transitional, providing a path to a united Ireland.[4] Such was the use of 'constructive ambiguity' in the agreement that it allowed diametrically opposed aspirations to co-exist within their respective cocoons.

For a conflict once called intractable, there has been no lack of peace talks. The Northern Ireland peace process stretched across four decades.[5] The cycles of violence and talks existed in parallel. The problem was that at any given time not all the actors would participate in the process: some parties would sanction the exclusion of others, and not all agreed on who should be among the parties to the talks. Unionists were more intent on ensuring that nationalists did not exercise power than they were on exercising power themselves. According to David Trimble: 'They were content at that, even if they could only participate vicariously in British politics. While a return to Stormont was desirable in theory, it was not considered worth the compromise entailed in an accommodation with nationalists.'[6]

The core issues protagonists had to settle remained stubbornly the same: internal governance arrangements for Northern Ireland in some form of power-sharing between the political representatives of the two communities; the nature of the relationship between Northern Ireland and the Republic of Ireland; and majority consent as the determinant of the constitutional status of Northern Ireland.

The B/GFA provides a framework for settling disputes among protagonists – Protestant/unionist/loyalist and Catholic/nationalist/republican – a template for governance and a formula for settling constitutional issues.

On the governance side, the agreement addressed three sets of relationships: Strand I, between the two communities in Northern Ireland (setting up a devolved power-sharing Executive and Assembly at Stormont); Strand II, between Northern Ireland and the republic (establishing the North-South Ministerial Council); and Strand III, between the government of the Republic of Ireland and the government of the United Kingdom (UK) (setting up two bodies, the British-Irish Intergovernmental Conference to liaise between the two sovereign governments and the British-Irish Council to forge links between those governments and the various devolved and island administrations). Strands I and II are interlocked: if Strand I collapses, Strand II also falls.

The agreement was not negotiated from scratch by parties in Northern Ireland that had been locked in the three-decades-long conflict. Nor had any level of trust evolved over the years among the protagonists. The foundations of the agreement were laid by the two governments. They drew up the template and presented it to the Northern Ireland parties who offered amendments and negotiated trade-offs. The process was iterative: the parties' evolving positions and the scaffolding of the political edifice under construction were conveyed to the parties' respective governments. The governments crunched the positions and came up with compromise language to reconcile demands, conveyed the reworded drafts back to the parties and repeated the exercise until compromises on all sides dovetailed. For each strand there were different sets of negotiators. 'Nothing was agreed until everything was agreed' set the ground rules.

The notes kept by John Holmes, Tony Blair's principal private secretary who accompanied him to Belfast and was at his side during the final five-day stretch, reflect seemingly irreconcilable negotiating concerns.[7] Holmes captures the mood and behaviours of the main protagonists at the time, the high levels of distrust among the main actors, the crucial role of the British and Irish governments and the reliance on constructive ambiguity to hammer out an agreement that allowed every party to read into it an interpretation that reflected its political predispositions.

The relationship between the North and the South was the main concern for Dublin and the Ulster Unionists. The latter would give little ground on Strand I until the planks of Strand II were in place. Holmes's account is peppered with telling observations. 'It gradually became clear,' he wrote, 'that the two [the Ulster Unionists and the Irish government] were not capable of solving their problems bilaterally – the [mutual] distrust and hostility was too great. From now until virtually the end of [the] talks, we negotiated with both by proxy and kept them apart.' And he warned:

> In the longer term the building of trust is essential. But the Ulster Unionists will prove difficult to deal with. The fact that we were only able to reach agreement on key issues by keeping them and the Irish apart because of their deep mutual suspicions is not a good sign for the future. All sides have the sword of Damocles of mutually assured destruction written into the text hanging over them. This, if not more positive thoughts, should keep their minds focused on the tasks in hand.[8]

Differences were exacerbated by what language means in both cultures and how it is used – the English language itself, though common to both traditions, often becomes a barrier to communication. This linguistic bifurcation complicated negotiations. Republicans, according to Jonathan Powell, Tony Blair's chief of staff, 'are very discursive, very florid'.[9] He continues:

> [Martin] McGuinness would get on a rant about fairness, but it really did not mean a lot. On the unionist side, they were extraordinarily literal … where you say this and you don't mean anything else. They would talk past each other because the florid stuff that was coming from republicans was seen by unionists as rude and offensive and [they] often did not understand what they were on about. The role of the two governments was important in interpreting between the two, where they would say to the unionists: 'Look, republicans really mean this and here's where you might be able to go.' They would say to the unionists that when republicans seem to be promising this, that does not mean that they are going to do it because they could mean this.[10]

In a telling anecdote, Powell reveals the depth of the zero-sum mentality most prevalent among unionists: the sight of nationalists smiling or laughing during the hectic final days in April at Stormont led unionists to re-scrutinize negotiating texts, looking for what they had missed that accounted for the good humour nationalists were in.[11]

After the deal appeared done, on Good Friday afternoon, with everyone waiting to sign, the Ulster Unionists baulked because the agreement called for a power-sharing government that would include Sinn Féin before decommissioning of their arms began. Unbeknownst to the other parties, Blair immediately wrote a letter to David Trimble saying the agreement called for the reverse, decommissioning before Sinn Féin could participate in government. And with that swipe of the pen, the Ulster Unionists were brought onside.[12]

Some parties were pulled across the finishing line, some pushed. 'We had managed to get an agreement,' Jonathan Powell wrote:

> because of the unstoppable momentum we had built. It was a case of an irresistible force meeting an immovable object and moving it … Both sides were surprised to end up with an agreement the other side could sign up to[13] … They met in plenary session on Good Friday, 10 April 1998 to approve the agreement; there was no applause, just stunned silence.[14]

Decades later, the parties are still at odds over what the agreement calls for on many contentious issues.

At the core of the agreement was the principle of consent on the constitutional issue: Northern Ireland remains part of the United Kingdom as long as that is the wish of a majority voting in a referendum. The Secretary of State for Northern Ireland, whose sole prerogative it is, shall call a border poll 'if at any time it appears likely to them that a majority of those voting would express a wish that Northern Ireland should cease to be part of the United Kingdom and form part of a united Ireland'.[15] Thereafter, a poll no sooner than seven years later must be called.

A reciprocal poll on the Irish side is also called for. The South repealed Articles 2 and 3 of the Irish Constitution that claimed the territory of the island of Ireland as the national territory and replaced them with an aspiration:

> It is the firm will of the Irish Nation, in harmony and friendship, to unite all the people who share the territory of the island of Ireland, in all the diversity of their identities and traditions, recognizing that a united Ireland shall be brought about only by peaceful means with the consent of a majority of people, democratically expressed in both jurisdictions in the island.[16]

Should polls in both jurisdictions give consent for unity, both sovereign governments will enact the legislation to give legal remit to the outcome.

The agreement was designed deliberately to allow for different interpretations: the Ulster Unionists had to reassure the Protestant community that the agreement strengthened the union; Sinn Féin had to be able to assert that it provided a pathway to a united Ireland. In the referendum to ratify it that followed, 71 per cent voted in favour and just 29 per cent against.[17]

But when this result is disaggregated, a different picture emerges: 99 per cent of Northern Catholics had voted for the agreement compared with 57 per cent of Protestants. Almost immediately, however, Protestant support began to shrink; it dropped to 53 per cent in 1999, 47 per cent in 2000 and 46 per cent in 2003: in the last of these years, the agreement still had 96 per cent support from Catholics.[18]

In the 2021 Northern Ireland Life and Times (NILT) survey, 77 per cent of Catholic respondents, 57 per cent of Protestants and 67 of Neithers expressed support for the agreement, with 37 per cent, 41 per cent and 44 per cent respectively supporting with the caveat that it needs revision to make it work better.[19]

This dichotomy between Catholic and Protestant support for the agreement reflects the ongoing Protestant belief that the peace process is pro-nationalist. Nevertheless, consistently up to two-thirds of respondents in NILT surveys say the B/GFA is the best basis for governing Northern Ireland and managing the relations between the North and South. Usually up to 25 per cent of respondents fully endorse the agreement, and up to 40 per cent endorse it but with the qualification that it needed reform.[20] Almost one in four Protestant respondents, however – compared to almost one in twenty Catholics – believe the agreement is no longer the best way to govern and either requires radical change or should be scrapped.[21] Still, if voters are ambivalent about the efficacy of the agreement, the disillusionment is tempered with the knowledge that there is no good alternative.

The 1998 Agreement calls for parity of esteem for the opposing aspirations: the Protestant/unionist aspiration to remain in the United Kingdom and the Catholic/nationalist aspiration to become part of a united Ireland. The worm at its core, however, is that these aspirations are not only irreconcilable but asymmetrical: should the Catholic aspiration be achieved, the Protestant aspiration will become defunct.

In short, there will be winners and losers, airbrushed out of public discourse for years, and while nationalist sentiment is wrapped around the phrase 'an agreed Ireland', republican sentiment is more blunt: once it becomes apparent that consent for a united Ireland meets a 50 per cent + 1 threshold, a border poll should be called to bring about that result.[22]

In the immediate aftermath of the B/GFA, attention was focused on elections for the new Northern Ireland Assembly and Executive and getting these institutions up and running. The structure of Strand I ensured that the political parties would compete for power within their communities, not across them, thus further embedding sectarian politics.

During the first decade after the 1998 Agreement, the slow and fractious rate of change, a political environment where the promise of change did not live up to the expectations the agreement had created, early unionist disillusionment and an Assembly as often suspended as governing caused a tectonic shift in electoral support from the Ulster Unionists and the Social Democratic and Labour Party (SDLP) – the two parties most closely associated with reaching an agreement on Strand 1 – to Sinn Féin and the Democratic Unionist Party (DUP), the more extreme parties in both communities. The DUP had walked out of negotiations in 1997 when Sinn Féin was admitted to the process, and it had campaigned against the agreement during the referendum and thereafter. But when realpolitik demanded, it held its nose and took up its ministerial posts in the power-sharing Executive, the alluring odour of power snuffing out the stench of compromise.

Across the board, interviewees agreed that the devolved power-sharing government at Stormont is dysfunctional, more like a combat forum where Sinn Féin and the DUP square off than a working Executive and Assembly. 'Neither the DUP nor Sinn Féin wants Northern Ireland to work particularly well', Katy Hayward says:

> As a result of that, we have the perpetuation of this sense of protest, repeated by the two largest parties and thus, ultimately, a lack of a sense of responsibility from either the DUP or Sinn Féin for the future of this place ... This is the tension in the B/GFA. It created the agreement generation, some of whom are very strong unionists, some are very strong nationalists and many of whom don't really

care either way. It created the conditions for having that generation of 'Neither' and yet the dominant forms of political representation and the dynamics for political debate are still about unionism versus nationalism. Unfortunately – and this is my worry about the protocol – this has reinforced the binary nature of politics in Northern Ireland.[23]

Everything, *Belfast Telegraph* journalist Sam McBride says, is a negotiation: not only on matters relating to the COVID-19 pandemic, but even on 'the most basic things, such as calling an Executive meeting, since such a meeting cannot be called without the First and deputy First Ministers jointly agreeing to it':

> There were points over recent weeks [interview held 11 December 2020] where there was an urgent need to take a decision on either easing or extending restrictions around the COVID pandemic. You had businesspeople crying out for a decision – any decision, even if they didn't like it – but the DUP and Sinn Féin couldn't agree even to hold the meeting, let alone as to what the decision could be. That is partly, I think, the fault of the personalities of the people leading the DUP and Sinn Féin. They have to take their share of the responsibility for that. It's also a structural problem that a system in which diametrically opposed parties, for reasons which we well understand, were shackled together and expected to produce good government.[24]

Yet, despite its myriad shortcomings, its starts and stops and periodic times of paralysis as Sinn Féin and the DUP stymie each other, the public believes that it is better to have Stormont up and running, even if the running is mostly in place, than the alternative: direct rule or another election after the two governments have cobbled together one more agreement to resuscitate the body.[25] The political cost of collapsed institutions with uncertain but probably deleterious knock-on effects is deemed greater than the cost of a fractious Executive operating in a semi-permanent state of crisis with every dispute raising questions about whether it will collapse the institutions. But with each crisis the doubts grow. 'The ugly scaffolding of the agreement,' the SDLP's Member of Assembly (MLA) Matthew O'Toole says, 'has become less useful as a way of ensuring good consociational buy-in to governance.'[26]

Devolved government has a chequered history. In the decade following the B/GFA (1998–2007), because of disagreements over arms decommissioning, the release of prisoners and policing, its functioning was sporadic.

Nineteen months elapsed before the Executive finally took office on 2 December 1999. Thereafter, it was suspended in February 2000 by Secretary of State Peter Mandelson (restored on 30 May), August 2001 by Secretary of State John Reid (twenty-four hours), September 2001 (twenty-four hours), 15 October 2002 to 8 May 2007 by Reid again and most recently from 9 January 2017 to 11 January 2020 in a series of protest resignations.[27]

The St Andrews Agreement (2006) resulted in an uneasy rapprochement between Sinn Féin and the DUP, the two mutually loathing parties that have dominated the political stage ever since. On 8 May 2007, the devolved political institutions were restored under the leadership of First Minister Ian Paisley and deputy First Minister Martin McGuinness for a ten-year run until Stormont collapsed in January 2017. That collapse raised a question: if ten years in government was not enough for the parties to develop trusting relationships, what would be?

Sometimes they have worked in tandem, sometimes they have collapsed the institutions. From January 2017 to January 2020, there was a three-year hiatus. From January 2020 they had a two-year run, collapsed again in February 2022, months before scheduled elections in May for a new Assembly,[28] and still in abeyance when this book went to print in December 2022.

Is the absence of trust simply endemic, a by-product of the deeply sectarian nature of Northern Irish politics and society? Or is it partly the fault of the B/GFA itself, because of the way in which the requirement to share first and deputy first minister positions between the largest unionist and largest nationalist parties embeds sectarian politics? Does the formulation of the consent provision for calling a border poll encourage unionists, as time passes and demographic shifts signal inexorable change, to pull up the drawbridge, perceiving more threats to their place in the Union? 'If people are genuinely unable to work together in the structures of the Good Friday Agreement,' Naomi Long says, 'it is hard to say how we could then as a society actually take a rational and logical look at our long-term future on this island.'[29]

The B/GFA is built on the principle of consociational governance, which accorded equality of status to the two competing national identities, whose aspirations are, for the most part, diametrically opposed. On taking their seats, members of the Legislative Assembly must register as 'Unionist', 'Nationalist' or 'Other'. Elections are conducted using the proportional representation through single transferable vote (PR-STV) system to encourage

cross-community voter transfers. Committee members, chairs and ministerial roles are assigned on the basis of party strength using the complex
d'Hondt system. Concurrent majorities of unionists and nationalists – 'parallel consent' – or a weighted majority of 60 per cent with at least 40 per cent
support from both sides is required for key legislation.

This form of consociational government was the preferred choice of
the SDLP and the UUP, who assumed that since they had consummated a
successful negotiation, which the DUP had boycotted, the electorate would
reward them at the ballot box. The result, however, was that it entrenched
sectarian politics, ensuring a coalition of opposites. Political competition
is intra-community rather than inter-community, with no party having an
incentive to reach across the religious/political divide.

It has been argued that had Assembly votes required weighted majorities of both traditions, it would have encouraged and perhaps fostered
cross-community outreach. But deciding where to set the bar, avoiding its
being either too high or too low, would have been beyond the abilities of
the already stressed-out negotiators in the final stretch to the April 1998
Agreement deadline.[30] If, however, the Neither (self-identifying as neither
nationalist or unionist) cohort continues to grow – and the younger generation of voters are more inclined not to identify with either of the two established traditions as the drift to the neutral-on-the-constitutional-question
Alliance Party continues – the present arrangement will become increasingly lacking as a reflection of democratic intent.

Approximately 40 per cent of the electorate now define themselves as
Neithers – neither orange (unionist/loyalist) nor green (nationalist/repub-
lican) – bringing into sharp focus the democratic deficit at the core of the
governing structures. The binary choices lock them into a dichotomy that
fails to reflect their representation. If support for the Neithers is reflected in
electoral support for parties other than the mainstream nationalist/repub-
lican and unionist parties, former Alliance leader David Ford says, 'it is
simply not tenable to continue to discriminate against that group. It will be
necessary to reform the system.'[31]

At a more fundamental level, Paul Nolan says, the architecture of the
agreement is in need of restructuring because one of the key premises on
which the foundations were laid – the majority/minority dichotomy – is
redundant:

> There are some predictors like the 2017 Labour Force Survey[32] or the school census that allow you to assemble a picture. And the most likely scenario is one where we're heading towards a 40:40:20 [voting] population – 40 per cent unionists, 40 per cent nationalists, and 20 per cent other. So, the old paradigm, which was majority/minority, is obsolete. Northern Ireland routinely would be described as a majority/minority problem in the political science literature of the 1970s. And, in fact, a lot of the provisions of the Good Friday Agreement were constructed on that model with protections for the minority community, but actually we're all minorities now.[33]

Thus, there is an inbuilt dysfunctionality in these government arrangements, which were premised on the assumption that they would work in partnership for the overall good of the populace, with each able to put a check on the other. Instead, they evolved into a mandatory coalition of the DUP and Sinn Féin, who each pursue their own partisan interests, working only on behalf of their own communities and feeding their respective bases enough political red meat to copper-fasten their support.

An analysis by *The Guardian* revealed that of 871 debated motions and amendments between 2000 and 2021, 442 (51 per cent) received zero cross-community support – either no nationalist Assembly member or no unionist member voted in favour.[34] 'Just 32 per cent passed with at least one or more votes from an Assembly member from the opposing designation,' as UUP leader Doug Beattie puts it:

> It's [Stormont] worked to a degree … But everything is a battle all day, everything is a compromise … Five political parties in a power-sharing Executive … It's hard enough doing it with two, but we're trying to do it with five … [But] it is also dysfunctional because it can't change. There's no development within it. There's no proper opposition, to be able to say: 'You're in government now, but here's a better vision for five years from now, let's change government' … Ultimately, it's so rigid, it's going to fail.[35]

The Petition of Concern allows the parties to veto each other's legislative proposals as long as they command 30 seats, a mechanism often deployed by the DUP until the 2017 Assembly elections when its vote dropped to 28 seats. From 2011 to 2016 it was used 115 times, 86 times by DUP and 29 times each by Sinn Féin and the SDLP.[36]

A change that will have a profound impact on both main tribal parties may be required in the foreseeable future. Under the 2006 St Andrews Agreement, the first minister's job goes to the largest unionist or nationalist party. Thus, even if Alliance emerged as the largest or second-largest party, the posts of first minister and deputy first minister would still go to the largest unionist and nationalist/republican parties. This inbuilt democratic deficit requires fundamental reform because it calls into question the efficacy of a system designed to accommodate two opposing traditions when the political land-scape has shifted. The new landscape no longer reflects these absolute binary divisions, but will have become more nuanced: two traditions, yes, but con-tracting, as a growing centre, itself a minority, becomes the choice of the 'neither orange nor green' cohort of voters.[37] These trends have accelerated since 1998 (see Table 4.1):

Table 4.1: Number of seats won (percentage of first-preference votes in parentheses) for Northern Ireland Assembly[38]

YEAR	NATIONALISTS	UNIONISTS	OTHER[39]	TOTAL SEATS
1998	42 (39.7)	58 (49.4)	8 (8.1)	108
2003	42 (40.5)	59 (50.5)	7 (6.6)	108
2007	44 (41.4)	55 (45.6)	9 (9.7)	108
2011	43 (41.18)	55 (45.71)	10 (10.95)	108
2016	40 (36)	55 (45.2)	13 (14.7)	108
2017	39 (39.8)	39 (43.6)	12 (15)	90
2022	35 (38.1)	35 (40.1)	20 (17.57)	90

Uncertainty about the future ensures that politics hew closely to the embrace of the more extreme parties. 'When you have any sense of uncer-tainty in flux ... particularly, when it's about borders or the border, or about UK-Irish relations,' Katy Hayward points out, 'then the tendency is to go to what you know, fundamental foundations, and of course, these will be in stark opposition, unionist and nationalist.'[40] More than twenty-four years on, these traditional identities no longer reflect the profusion of identities that have evolved since 1998 – yet, when it comes to existential political choices, like a border poll referendum, voters will be forced into these binary silos.

Over the twenty-four-year stretch between June 1998 and May 2022, seven elections were held for the Northern Ireland Assembly. Over the same period, the Assembly did not sit for a 'a third of its lifespan',[41] the institutions collapsed by either unionists or nationalists/republicans. The results reinforce trends that were decades in the making, some because of changing demographics and some because of seismic changes in voting behaviour: changing demographics as younger voters – especially Catholics – enter the voting pool and there are fewer Protestants in the older age cohorts, reflected in their declining proportion of the population; shifting voter preferences within nationalism and unionism; and a turn to politics that eschews these narrow tribal labels.

The May 2022 Assembly results reflect the extent to which these trends have translated into a redrawing of the electoral map (see Table 4.2).[42] Overall, they reflect the rise of Sinn Féin, primarily at the expense of the SDLP; a slowly declining unionism; and the confirmation of Alliance, the only cross-community party, as a political force to be reckoned with in its own right.

Sinn Féin becoming the largest political party was heralded as 'historic', 'a landmark', 'unprecedented', 'stunning', all appellations that apply in the context of a party which refuses to acknowledge the existence of Northern Ireland – refusing to call it by its name and for thirty years acting as the mouthpiece of the Irish Republican Army (IRA), itself dedicated to destroying what it derisively referred to as the 'six counties' – now having the right to nominate a first minister, a position hitherto exclusively held by a unionist party. It is hard not to overstate the huge symbolic importance of the party's success in a political environment where perceptions are everything and optics always take precedence over substance. Sinn Féin rammed a stake through the heart of unionism's dominance, which had lasted for 100 years, feeding perceptions that the momentum for Irish reunification was becoming unstoppable. A party whose sole raison d'être is the abolition of the statelet is at the governing helm. Post the election, spin doctors went into overdrive issuing hyperbolic pronouncements heralding the pending end of partition.[43] Simply by holding on to its 2017 total seats, Sinn Féin was able to emerge on top of the political league. Screeds were written about the imminence of a united Ireland without there being a shred of evidence of a significant shift in public opinion in that direction.[44]

Table 4.2: First-preference percentage of those parties winning seats (rounded figures) (seats won in parentheses) for the Northern Ireland Assembly[45]

PARTY/YEAR	1998	2003	2007	2011	2016	2017	2022
UUP	21.3% (28)	22.7% (27)	14.9% (18)	13.2% (16)	12.6% (16)	12.9% (10)	11.2% (9)
SDLP	22.0% (24)	17.0% (18)	15.2% (16)	14.2% (14)	12.0% (12)	11.9% (12)	9.1% (8)
DUP	18.1% (20)	25.7% (30)	30.1% (36)	30.0% (38)	29.2% (38)	28.1% (28)	21.3% (25)
Sinn Féin	17.6% (18)	23.5% (24)	26.2% (28)	26.9% (29)	24.0% (28)	27.9% (27)	29.0% (27)
Alliance Party	6.5% (6)	3.7% (6)	5.2% (7)	7.7% (8)	7.0% (8)	9.1% (8)	13.5% (17)
UK Unionist Party	4.5% (5)	0.9% (1)	No seats won	—	—	—	—
Progressive Unionist Party (PUP)	2.6% (2)	1.2% (1)	0.6% (1)	No seats won	No seats won	No seats won	No seats won
Northern Ireland Women's Coalition	1.6% (2)	No seats won	—	—	—	—	—
Independents	2.9% (3)	0.9% (1)	0.5% (1)	0.5% (1)	0.5% (1)	0.6% (1)	1.6% (2)
TUV	—	—	—	2.5% (1)	3.4% (1)	2.6% (1)	7.6 (1)
People Before Profit	—	—	—	No seats won	2.0% (2)	1.8% (1)	1.1% (1)
Green Party	No seats won	No seats won	1.7% (1)	0.9% (1)	2.7% (2)	2.3% (2)	No seats won

But the political terrain is more complex. Sinn Féin's share of first pref-erences increased by just 1.1 per cent. The party did not increase its rep-resentation in the Assembly, holding still at 27 seats. Parties supporting reunification lost 4 seats. In terms of first preferences, nationalism secured 38.1 per cent overall compared with 39.8 per cent in 2017. Sinn Féin became the largest party not because of a groundswell surge in support, but thanks to the fragmentation, disarray and discombobulation of unionism.

The DUP's first-preference share fell by 6.7 per cent, the UUP's by 1.7 per cent, while that of the more extreme Traditional Unionist Voice (TUV) increased by 5.1 per cent (an almost 200 per cent increase in first preferences), signalling a decisive move of unionism to the right. The DUP, a party that since its inception in 1971 had always ensured it was never outflanked on the right, finds itself in the invidious position of being out-flanked. Liberal unionism fared no better: the more inclusive brand UUP Doug Beattie campaigned on found few takers, and Beattie barely scraped into the Assembly on the eighth count.[46]

In the Assembly, unionism also lost 4 seats. The contest between unionism and nationalism resulted in a stand-off, each standing at aggre-gate totals of 35, no swing in either direction, both contracting compared with their 2017 positions. In terms of first preferences, unionism secured an aggregate of 40.1 per cent compared with 43.6 in 2017, continuing its down-ward trajectory which began in 1998. Hence, both unionism and nation-alism are slowly shrinking, nationalism moving to the left and unionism to the right. The gap between aggregate unionism and aggregate nationalism is also shrinking, from a peak of ten percentage points in 2003 to two points in 2022.[47]

The Alliance Party emerged as the real 'winner', increasing its first-preference votes by 4.5 per cent but more than doubling its Assembly representation because of voter transfers. The Assembly now cements three major blocks – nationalism, unionism and a growing centre – with both ideologies hovering around the 40 per cent mark, an outcome the framers of the B/GFA never could have foreseen.[48]

No clearer message could be conveyed: the two-traditions paradigm is obsolete. In the absence of a fundamental overhaul of the governance pro-visions of the B/GFA, the large swathe of voters who had voted for 'no more of the same' has to settle for 'more of the same'.

Within nationalism, Sinn Féin – the more radical voice of nationalism – has emasculated the moderate SDLP; within unionism, there was a similar drift of votes from the moderate UUP to the more radical DUP, and more recently from the DUP to the still more radical TUV. Support for the broad centre has fallen precipitously since 1998. If the UUP, the Alliance and SDLP represent the moderate centre, support for these parties has declined from 'about 50 per cent of the overall vote and 58 seats of 108 members' for the first Assembly election in June 1998 to '34 per cent with 34 seats [in a chamber] of 90' for the seventh assembly election in May 2022.[49] Underlying these trends are demographic upheavals that will impact Northern Ireland for decades to come.

More ominously for unionism, the 2022 elections signalled the end of whatever pretences were left of unionism's ascendency and hold on the coveted position of first minister, as much a psychological punch to the gut as an electoral one. Unionism's hope that enough unionists would return to form a majority and vote to rescind the Northern Ireland Protocol (NIP) in 2024 was cruelly dashed.

Even though the first and deputy first minister posts are co-equal in every regard, and one cannot as much sneeze without asking for a handkerchief from the other, both Siamese twins tied at the political waist, such is the perception that 'first' conveys some infinitesimal advantage over 'deputy first' that more than 60 per cent of voters said 'it was important' to have a party from their community emerge as the largest and take over the first minister portfolio.[50] Throughout its campaign, the DUP warned ad nauseum that Sinn Féin as the largest party would pave the way to a border poll and that unionist voters, therefore, had better fall in behind the DUP. Nor would it commit to nominating a deputy first minister should it finish second.

The strategy backfired, galvanizing nationalists – all too happy to make the DUP's apocalyptic visions of the future come true – to vote Sinn Féin. (Such, too, is unionism's antipathy for Sinn Féin that even the hint of being perceived as somehow subordinate – deputy first minister to Sinn Féin's first minister – was enough to split its vote, with 45 per cent of its voters saying they shouldn't share and 44 per cent that they should.)[51]

True to his campaign rhetoric that the NIP had to go before the DUP would return to government, Jeffrey Donaldson refused to nominate a deputy first minister, arguing that DUP voters expected no less, thus pre-empting Michelle O'Neill's nomination as first minister and the forma-tion of an Executive.[52] He also blocked the appointment of a Speaker, closing down the Assembly.[53] A return to government is predicated on the protocol meeting 'the seven tests against which we will judge any outcome so that it meets these requirements,'[54] says Donaldson. 'Any legislation and subse-quent measures introduced by the UK Government must protect Northern Ireland's place within the UK Internal Market and uphold our rights under Article 6 of the Acts of Union. This should mean that goods travelling from Great Britain to Northern Ireland and remaining within the UK should not be subject to unnecessary customs paperwork or checks, the so-called green lane.' On this demand Donaldson had cross-community support. Almost 75 per cent of unionists, 60 per cent of nationalists and 60 per cent of people identifying themselves as 'Neither' believe there should be no checks on imported goods that remain within Northern Ireland. With a modicum of good will between the government and the UK, this component of the dispute should not prove to be insuperable to resolve.[55] An air of déjà vu pervaded. For old-timers, it was the political merry-go-round one more time. Practice did not mean perfect.

In August 2022, a LucidTalk tracker poll supported Donaldson's reading of sentiment in the unionist community. Unionist voters endorsed the DUP's hard-line stance on the protocol. The party polled 24 per cent, up three points since the May elections, and 82 per cent of unionist voters said the DUP should not return to Stormont unless it is scrapped or significantly changed – six points higher than when the question was posed in the pre-vious LucidTalk poll in May 2022.[56]

But for sure, Michelle O'Neill being denied her tenure as first minister is reflected in increasing support for the party, up another point in three months to 30 per cent, six points clear of the DUP over the same period.[57]

Do both Sinn Féin and the DUP believe they have more to gain by holding out for another election, Sinn Féin increasingly confident it can consolidate its place as the largest party in Northern Ireland with a 30+ per cent performance? Can the DUP recoup most of the votes it lost to the TUV? On all fronts, uncertainty. Not that an election producing the same result would do much to alleviate the uncertainty if the DUP were to run on the same platform.

According to the 2017 Labour Force Survey, the percentage of respondents who did not self-identify as either Catholic or Protestant has been growing. Between 1990 and 2017 it more than doubled, from 6 per cent to 17 per cent. In the 16–24 age cohort it more than trebled, from 7 per cent to 22 per cent. During the period of 1990 to 2017, the percentage self-identifying as Protestants aged 16 and over dropped from 56 per cent to 42 per cent, while the proportion of Catholics in the same age group increased points from 38 per cent to 41 per cent.[58] These trends are beginning to be reflected in the electoral sphere, with Others or Neithers emerging as a significant political force for the first time.

In the medium term, the demographic direction of the two communities' population share will continue to reset the parameters of electoral outcomes. The outlook is for more polarizing elections as both Sinn Féin and the DUP work to maximize their voter shares, Sinn Féin continuing their periodic calls for a border poll and the DUP selling itself – now sensing the future electoral threat of a lurking TUV – as the bulwark against the republican threat. No longer being the largest party may make the DUP more amenable to reform, exploring the possibilities of cobbling together a coalition with the Ulster Unionists and the TUV, all of whom would find a Sinn Féin first minister an anathema. But Doug Beattie poured cold water on the suggestion months before the Assembly elections.[59] Following the elections, he vowed to continue orienting the UUP in the liberal and inclusive direction he promised when he was elected leader.

Beattie sees the need for reform: 'Everything is identity politics,' he says. 'We need to be able to move away from that but the structures aren't there for us to move away in any meaningful way. They would have to be fundamentally overhauled if we made those huge changes that we think are likely to come down the road.'[60] Nor is the DUP wed to mandatory coalitions. But 'Reform,' Donaldson says, 'should be about more than just looking at the possession of the middle ground. The Alliance Party is pushing for reform. It is an area that will be looked at in due course. Reform, however, should look at when are we going to move from the concept of a mandatory coalition to a voluntary coalition style of government.'[61] With the Assembly elections done with and Alliance winning 17 seats, 'in due course' has arrived. But no one is holding their breath that the reforms needed to make the government reflect what the public voted for will come to pass.[62]

If perchance the DUP does eventually step up and accept the deputy first minister post and an Executive is formed, the stage is set for more of the same in the absence of some fundamental reform: dysfunctionality, stalemates, paralysis. Indeed, on the eve of the elections, Sam McBride ruefully wrote that:

> [In] the desperate clamour to restore the Executive, there is the danger that an irretrievably broken system is reassembled, that something broken which cannot deliver good government and involves inevitable incoherence is preferred to the more painful business of reform which can start to restore public confidence in our political and civil service machine.[63]

At some point, he said, 'putting off what needs to be done will lead to a day of reckoning'.

The period between 2007 and 2012 – when first Rev. Ian Paisley and Martin McGuinness, and then Peter Robinson and McGuinness, served as first minister and deputy first minister respectively – is remembered as the most stable period of devolution. Devolved government was working, if not always smoothly at least with a degree of commitment on the part of both the DUP and Sinn Féin, and in particular because of Martin McGuinness's determination to make this unlikely partnership of old enemies work.[64]

That changed in December 2012 after loyalists took to the streets for days across the North to protest about the restrictions the Belfast City Council had placed on flying the Union Jack outside City Hall.[65] Thereafter, relations fell apart piecemeal, especially after Arlene Foster became First Minister. In January 2017, Martin McGuinness resigned in protest over Foster's refusal to step aside as first minister pending the outcome of an investigation into the Renewable Heat Incentive (RHI), a green energy scheme devised by the DUP in 2012 to encourage firms, businesses and farmers to switch from fossil fuel heating to biomass systems such as wood-burning boilers. For every £1 that users spent on green heating systems, they got back £1.60 in subsidies. There was no cap to the level of subsidies a business might receive, hence the appellation 'cash for ash' – the more a business burned, the more it earned.[66] With McGuinness's resignation, the Stormont institutions were collapsed.

The RHI scandal was the final proof that Stormont is broken, says Sam McBride, author of the definitive book on the subject, *Burned: The Inside Story of the 'Cash-for-Ash' Scandal and Northern Ireland's Secretive New Elite*.[67] 'It was broken to the point that it imploded on itself.'[68] The official inquiry into the scandal found extraordinary levels of incompetence among the Executive's ministers and their civil servants. Records of ministerial meetings routinely went undocumented, due diligence was non-existent and expert advice frequently went unread or was dismissed. It also illuminated the implicit collusion between the DUP and Sinn Féin, each accommodating the other on sharing the spoils of the public purse, to the detriment of the community at large. What the report also revealed was the shocking degree to which the special advisers had usurped many ministerial prerogatives, and a level of overall incompetence of the civil service to an extent that raised questions about its administrative efficacy as the arm of a broadly dysfunctional government.[69]

There were also deeper divisions simmering under the surface: what Sinn Féin regarded as the DUP's failure to treat it with respect and that party's disdain for 'parity of esteem', one of the building blocks of the B/GFA. But, says the SDLP's Alex Atwood, there was a more fundamental cause of the collapse – in government, the DUP were humiliating Sinn Féin at every opportunity:

> That government – and I was a member of it for over three years – was government on DUP terms. They wiped Sinn Féin's eye, left, right and centre. It was only when the republican grassroots began to react against their own leadership ... that Sinn Féin decided it was time to jump ship. You could see the DUP trying to recreate the past ... [to] manage government to serve their own constituency and sectoral interests. That went on for ten years. At that point nationalism and republicanism said, 'That's it.' ... The collapse had been coming for a long time because nationalism and republicanism were saying, 'This is not a government on equal terms between the two main traditions.'[70]

Ironically, the political writer Robin Wilson observed in the foreword to the 2016 Northern Ireland Peace Monitoring Report,[71] 'Devolution appears more secure than at any time in most people's living memory. And it is a

power-sharing devolution – a genuine partnership between the largest political parties representing opinion across the community.' Within months
it had come crashing down amid recriminations and invective, not to be
restarted for another three years.[72]

The murder of Lyra McKee in Derry in April 2019[73] shamed the parties
back to the negotiating table, but no amount of shaming could push them to
resolve their differences, especially with regard to the Irish language. After
Boris Johnson's big win in the December 2019 general election, the British
government was no longer dependent on the DUP to keep it in office, and
both the DUP and Sinn Féin feared that they would be punished by the
Northern Ireland electorate for their intransigence. Thus, they were forced
to comply with a government ultimatum that, in the event of accommodation not being reached by mid-January 2020, they would face new elections.

The resulting New Decade, New Approach agreement, which was
mostly the work of the two governments, laid out the basis of an accommodation largely based on an agreement to bring in Irish language legislation
and extra money from London.[74] In January 2020, the parties reconvened
in the Stormont Assembly and a new Executive was formed, with the DUP's
Arlene Foster as first minister and Sinn Féin's Michelle O'Neill as deputy
first minister, replacing Martin McGuinness[75] who had died in March 2017.

The DUP and Sinn Féin, Sam McBride wrote in the unionist *Belfast
News Letter*, had come together 'in the knowledge that this is a loveless
political arrangement, a shotgun marriage enforced by the circumstances
of an electoral backlash and the absence of alternatives'.[76] In fact, after
more than twenty years of on-off power-sharing, the distrust between Sinn
Féin and the DUP remains unalloyed. The suspicions are only likely to be
heightened as Sinn Féin ups the ante for a border poll and unionists react
in their timeworn ways, trying to tie themselves more closely to the union,
even as the union itself begins to fragment and their constitutional status in
the UK, as they perceive it, is undermined by the NIP.

The new agreement added layers of bureaucracy, commissioners for
the Irish language and Ulster Scots, a preventative committee to anticipate
problems in governance before they once again led to collapse. The Petition
of Concern was tweaked. Sinn Féin and the DUP signed up because the
political cost of not doing so had become greater than the political benefits.

'Sustaining a revived Stormont,' *The Irish Times* editorialized, may be as testing as the protracted negotiations. One poor omen was that the cross-community Alliance, the SDLP, the Ulster Unionists and the Greens were sidelined to the end, yet Alliance and the SDLP have been far more vocal throughout about the need for real cooperation. That is in sharp contrast with the excited welcome for an emergent centre vote in last month's Westminster election.[77]

The hope, as always, was that, as imperfect as the agreement was, it would provide a starting point once again for sufficient cross-party co-operation to germinate, enabling the parties to plan for a shared future. Given the seismic impact of Brexit, such hope seemed greatly misplaced. The overwhelming impact of the COVID-19 pandemic, however, constrained the room for difference. The Executive grappled with having to agree to a lockdown strategy and chart a path to reopening the economy and social activities that was appropriate to Northern Ireland.[78] There were the usual breaks along a right-left continuum. Inevitably, there were also tensions between the two on policy alignment: the DUP was inclined to advocate policies closer to England, Sinn Féin closer to the South, preferring to co-operate as much as possible with the Dublin government. To their credit, they hewed a line somewhere in between. Initially, dealing with the pandemic had shown that First Minister Arlene Foster and deputy First Minister Michelle O'Neill and their parties could work together.[79] A hopeful sign, Peter Robinson said in early March 2020:

> I think that the parties need to prove themselves yet. One thing I always argued was that they needed to have some issues that they were on the same side … Strangely, coronavirus gives them something that there isn't a unionist and nationalist perspective on … they can work together on something and build up a relationship on something that isn't controversial from a political standpoint, but has a major impact on Northern Ireland.[80]

The pandemic created a brief solidarity. The wall murals in unionist East Belfast were decorated with images of the masked faces of NHS workers. Unusually, similar murals appeared in republican areas saying, 'Supporting our front-line workers.' Every Thursday evening, residents from both communities came to their front doors, stood on balconies and porches, clapping hands and banging saucepans to show their appreciation for front-line health workers. 'There [were] no orange and green versions of the rainbows the children [posted] in their windows,' Paul Nolan, Research Director of the Northern Ireland Peace Monitoring Survey, wrote. 'No Protestant or Catholic way to wrap coloured wool around a tree, no sectarian way to hand paint a message of hope on a pebble. It's a strange thing to say, but Northern Ireland is experiencing an outbreak of kindness.'[81] The Orange Order cancelled the 12 July processions, while its members raised funds to supply hospitals with PPE kits. In Larne, the Craigy Hill Bonfire Committee scrapped its bonfire plans and used the money saved to send food and toiletries to those in need.[82] Amnesty International reported that two-thirds of people across Northern Ireland had taken part in the 'Clap for Carers' movement.[83]

In November 2020, a second wave of infections stretched the NHS to breaking point. The Executive debated extending the duration of existing health restrictions. When the DUP could not get its way, it resorted to invoking the Petition of Concern, the cross-community veto mechanism, effectively bringing matters to a standstill. This begged the recurrent question: if the COVID crisis could not engender collective co-operation without bringing the Executive to the verge of collapse, what could? According to Alex Kane, 'It took almost a week … two DUP vetoes and a series of on-again, off-again meetings for the Executive to reach agreement on restrictions last week, and even then, the SDLP abstained and Sinn Féin voted against them.'[84]

No sooner was that agreement placed in the public domain than the briefings against each other began again, with rumour and counter-rumour flying about what was likely to happen next. It had been a bad week for the Executive, Arlene Foster ruefully admitted; more accurately, it was another bad week.[85] 'Even in terms of COVID,' says the psychiatrist Philip McGarry:

> there have been huge splits in the Executive [on how to address the COVID-19 pandemic], after two or three months of initially getting it together fairly well. So often things are being seen through a sectarian lens. Our politics aren't about values, it's about tribes: you vote Super Prod or Super Taig. The Good Friday Agreement undermined the centre and brought the extremes. Then we're surprised that twenty-three years on we've still got peace walls and a bitterly divided society.[86]

The shenanigans in the Assembly took a toll on public perceptions of how the Assembly was dealing with the pandemic: 55 per cent of people faulted the actions of the Executive as impeding the response to the pandemic; just 35 per cent approved.[87]

When the Executive was collapsed again in February 2022, this time by the DUP, no one was surprised. No compromise can endlessly square circles of political incompatibility. Says loyalist community leader and DUP MLA Sammy Douglas:

> If you don't trust these people, but you want to work to keep the peace … you build up a sense of trust with them. And that's exactly what happened up in Stormont with Ian Paisley and Martin McGuinness, and then Peter Robinson and Martin McGuinness. They worked together to try and make this place better. That doesn't seem to be the case at the moment.[88]

'Over the last five to ten years,' Brandon Hamber says:

> there has been an erosion of trust between the political parties … you talk to each other via press releases rather than in a more relational, compassionate type of way, which is the way that got people to the 1998 Agreement. Yes, there was hard, pragmatic political stuff too, but there was a lot of relationship-building … Then once we got everybody over the line, what do we do? We say, 'Oh, the institutions will figure it all out. It'll be fine.' Then we abandoned all the trust-building work that was needed and cut right back to an adversarial political system.[89]

Even the pandemic, which affected both communities in equal measure, could not forge a sense of common purpose among the parties in the Assembly, in contrast to the cross-the-divide 'clappers'. The DUP and Sinn Féin, in particular, often remained at loggerheads, engaging in bitter public feuding rather than trying to forge a consensus on best ways to make their partnership work in the face of the grim toll of the coronavirus. The common experience of their respective communities counted for little in their political behaviour. Every disagreement raised the question of whether it might collapse the government. 'It's like a bad marriage,' former SDLP politician Alban Maginness wrote in the *Belfast Telegraph*, 'where there are endless rows and petty disagreement, which could be resolved, but for the depth of marital bitterness and irreconcilable differences.'[90]

Stormont is dysfunctional in part because the society it governs is dysfunctional, and even if Stormont had the budget resources to chip away at some of the structural obstructions standing in the way of avenues to reconciliation, it would not address the core problem, the sectarian DNA of Northern Ireland itself.

Some of the provisions within the B/GFA, particularly the Petition of Concern, have made it unworkable as a system of governance, says Paul Nolan. However, the Irish government successfully convinced the European Union (EU) that a land border across Ireland as the western border of the EU would violate the 1998 Agreement. With the B/GFA having been 'sold' as a sacred treaty that could not be violated under any circumstance, the sole bulwark against a return to violence, reforming parts of it now would amount to refuting the arguments so ardently promulgated in the corridors of power in Brussels. As Nolan explains:

> The Good Friday Agreement was presented as the shield against Brexit. This was the thing that you can't touch: the Good Friday Agreement ... But when you've got two political groups of equal size, and they're blocking each other with a mutual veto, then government can't work ... In contrast to the Assembly, Belfast City Council doesn't have the complex constitutional engineering. It works in a much simpler way ... votes are taken and it's a simple majority parties will determine something ...
>
> With hindsight, the Assembly would have been much better to have used [the simple voluntary coalition] mechanism, rather than ... the majority/minority paradigm, which no longer held, and so twenty years on from it you could see this didn't work. But the point where it was so obvious it wasn't working, that became the point when it couldn't be touched, and it remains that way.[91]

Attitudes toward devolved government differ to a considerable degree between the two communities. The NILT Survey (2021) found that 44 per cent of respondents believed Stormont should have more power and that 'the devolved powers of the NI assembly should be increased', a view enjoying 51 per cent among those from a Catholic background but only 40 per cent among those with a Protestant background. Overall, just 18 per cent supported maintaining the current power balance with Westminster, with London retaining decision-making powers on issues like trade and immigration policy.[92]

The 'culture wars' that spiked in June 2020 after the murder of George Floyd in Minneapolis resulted in international Black Lives Matter protests that spread to British and Irish cities, including London, Belfast and Dublin.[93] Protesters in England called for Britain to come to a reckoning with its colonial past and demanded the removal of statues of colonial masters and slave traders from earlier centuries. In Belfast, a republican-affiliated group, Lasair Dhearg, briefly renamed streets after IRA members who had died on hunger strike or in clashes with British security forces. Thus, street signs were erected in the names of Bobby Sands, Joe McDonnell and Kieran Doherty, and Queen's University was renamed the Máiréad Farrell University. Belfast's streets, Lasair Dhearg said, are:

> littered with the poverty of its people ... with the names of those whose attitude to Ireland was one of subjugation, and who, by force of arms, forced a political and economic system upon our people, which became the foundation for partition and for the current economic struggles faced by the Irish people. It is our inheritance as republicans to end the oppression immortalised in these street names and statues. It is our duty to end colonialism, to end the normalisation of imperialism and, consequently, the political and economic system that maintains it.[94]

Not to be outshone in this non-violent variant of guerrilla warfare, the DUP proposed to rename the Castlereagh Leisure Centre the Centenary Leisure Centre, to commemorate the founding of the Northern Ireland statelet in 1921. 'This proposal by the DUP is nothing more than a political stunt,' the SDLP objected. 'They want to call it after something that I would describe as the worst thing to happen to Ireland since partition ... The DUP continues to try to drag us back to the Ballygobackwards days of Craigavon council.'[95]

The Northern Ireland Office used the image of Seamus Heaney – without permission from the Heaney family – to promote Northern Ireland's centenary celebrations. Nationalists decried the usage as 'cultural appropriation'.[96] Although he wrote, 'Be advised, my passport's green/ No glass of ours was ever raised/ To toast the Queen' following his inclusion in 1983 in an anthology of British poets, during his life Heaney had assiduously sidestepped the minefield of the sectarian politics of Northern Ireland. Now his memory was reduced to being part of an ugly verbal brawl.

The DUP and the UUP refused to engage with the Irish government's Shared Island initiative, although this was specifically designed to be about mutually beneficial cross-border projects so as to avoid being tagged as a united Ireland initiative in disguise. The two unionist parties refused to become involved because they said it was precisely that.[97] Nationalists refused to have anything to do with the celebration of Northern Ireland's centenary.[98] President Michael D. Higgins declined an invitation to attend an ecumenical service in a Church of Ireland cathedral in Armagh organized by the four major church leaders (including the Catholic primate), which Queen Elizabeth was also scheduled to attend, because he objected that the title of the service ('a service of reflection and hope to mark the centenary of the partition of Ireland and the formation of Northern Ireland') was not 'a neutral statement politically'. Unionists expressed disappointment that he would refuse such an opportunity to make a significant gesture of reconciliation.[99] Sinn Féin vetoed erecting a modest stone at Stormont to mark the occasion despite the four other main parties, including the SDLP, agreeing to the proposal.[100] And Sinn Féin opposed illuminating Belfast City Hall to mark the centenary of the founding of the statelet.[101]

Each of these is a small thing in its own right, among many small things, all of some symbolic significance. But they are overlaid on the scabs of the past, still raw from the constant rubbing of the small divisive gestures each side compulsively engages in, ensuring they cannot heal, making agreement on how to deal with legacy issues more problematic. Mindsets over how to reach an accommodation on equality issues in the present overlap with mindsets on how to deal with the past.

— FIVE —

Referendum Metrics:
the numbers game

I have always been of the view that we need all of the parts of the Good Friday Agreement to be functioning and we need stable government in place, and that is part of the conditions set for a poll on a united Ireland. If we can do that for a sustained period of time successfully, then we are much more likely to be resilient enough to be able to sustain in a peaceful and lawful manner the run-up to any kind of border poll, which will in itself be divisive and contentious. If you layered that on an already volatile political situation, it could be very dangerous.[1]

– Naomi Long, Minister of Justice, Alliance Party leader

There's a good chance of a border poll within the next ten years and possibly quite a lot sooner than ten years, and there's a good possibility of a united Ireland, which raises all sorts of horrific problems. A Tory Secretary of State in a Johnson government would be inclined to refuse to hold one, but he has to be careful because he will be subject to judicial review on this. But if he was faced with a series of opinion polls that show on a sustained basis a majority for a united Ireland and a reasonably sized majority, not 2 per cent but 5 per cent or more, and if those were respectable polls, not those held by Sinn Féin, he'd find himself in a difficult situation.[2]

– Jonathan Powell, Downing Street Chief of Staff
under Prime Minister Tony Blair

Certainly this side of a Scottish independence poll, the British government is unlikely to want to call a poll in Northern Ireland. The Secretary of State has to be convinced that there is a clear wish for unity. You would need to have support for Irish unity in the high fifties. Fifty per cent + 1 doesn't represent a wish for unity. That's opinion being evenly divided. I think Sinn Féin is a bit like the dog chasing the car and not sure it necessarily wants to catch it. Chasing the car probably helps to maximize their support and that's why they do it.[3]

– Martin Mansergh, adviser to Taoisigh Charles Haughey
and Bertie Ahern

The Irish government has said it will not support a call for a border poll, and it is inconceivable that you would have one without the Irish government saying so ... The Tories [are] not going to accept this critique of Brexit. They're active persuaders for the union in a way that they were not in the '80s and '90s. That is the great asset from the unionist point of view. They are determined to show that all this talk about English nationalism is crap.[4]

– Paul, Lord Bew, Professor of Irish Politics at
Queen's University Belfast

Regarding a border poll, there are two mechanisms that might apply that do not involve either opinion polls or surveys. One would be a resolution of the Northern Ireland Assembly passed by a majority that the Secretary of State should hold the referendum in such-and-such a time. If a majority of the Assembly does that, I think a border poll would be very difficult to avoid.

Secondly, this hasn't happened yet, but it might happen. If you add up the votes cast in Westminster elections for the SDLP [Social Democratic and Labour Party] and Sinn Féin and pro-referendum Alliance and those were in a majority, that would be a clear signal ... that the change of opinion is present.[5]

– Brendan O'Leary, visiting professor of Political Science and Mitchell
Institute International Fellow at Queen's University Belfast

> *On the process of handover, pension liabilities, the acceptance of other liabilities, debt liabilities, the British government is going to play hard-ball before a first referendum. You need to have that out of the way before you can get involved in the more detailed negotiations. It needs to be a process of several years.*[6]
>
>   – Paul Gosling, freelance journalist specializing in the economy, accountancy, co-operatives and government and the public sector

> *Identifying the best path for the people who are in the Neither category [self-identifying as neither orange nor green, Catholic nor Protestant] is almost impossible to predict ... The nationalist groups who want the referendum need to win over the centre – the Greens, Alliance, Neithers, the Don't Know voters who have to be convinced that this is a necessary and rational next step.*[7]
>
>   – Duncan Morrow, Professor, University of Ulster; former Chief Executive of the Northern Ireland Community Relations Council

The requirement in the Belfast/Good Friday Agreement (B/GFA) that the Secretary of State for Northern Ireland shall call a border poll 'if at any time it appears likely to him that a majority of those voting would express a wish that Northern Ireland should cease to be part of the United Kingdom and form part of a united Ireland' bristles with equivocations.[8]

What does 'appears likely' mean? A gut feeling on the part of the Secretary of State? What verifiable, empirical evidence would be required to back it up? With whom should he consult beforehand? What kind of notice will be given to parties that a poll is under consideration? 'One thing that is clear,' Katy Hayward points out,

> is that it's the Secretary of State for Northern Ireland who calls the poll. There's no requirement on [the Secretary of State] to consult with the Irish government in advance to allow the Irish government and Irish state to prepare. It's a peculiar situation in which the British government minister has that responsibility. He could completely upend the Irish Constitution by triggering that process.[9]

The phrase in the B/GFA is that 'if at any time it appears likely to him that a majority of those voting would express a wish that Northern Ireland ...' suggests that a putative majority should exist at the time the Secretary of State announces a border poll but may dissipate over the course of the referendum campaigns conducted on both sides and no longer exist on polling day. In Scotland's referendum on independence in 2014, the pro-independence vote had a secure lead until close to voting day; the Remain vote had a comfortable lead in all Brexit pre-referendum-day polls, raising questions about the utility of opinion polls as a metric that might inform the Secretary of State's decision. For sure, a binary referendum, with all the psychological baggage that would accompany one, is more than likely to rekindle and exacerbate the visceral sectarianism, always poised to take advantage of any opportunity to spread its toxic poison. In the run-up to the Brexit referendum, identities hardened – more voters identified as either British or Irish. A border poll would be far more polarizing, as voters hunkered down in their ethno-national silos. Such is the nature of binary choices.

The 50 per cent + 1 formulation has gained traction among republicans and some nationalists, dominating much of the political conversation in the wake of the Brexit poll. If the 52 per cent of the British public voting to leave the European Union (EU) was deemed sufficient to be stamped as the will of a democratic majority,[10] then a similarly small margin in favour of Irish reunification had an equal legitimacy.

A perceived small margin for unification in any poll to justify calling a referendum would likely see unionists challenge the Secretary of State in court, demanding that he show that his decision to call a poll was evidence-based. There is both a legal and a political problem here. If there appears to be a small but solid majority for unity, it is the Secretary of State's duty to call a poll, though the agreement does not say that such a poll has to be held immediately. If the Secretary of State holds back, however, hoping that a more pronounced majority will emerge, republicans will cry foul, perhaps emboldening dissident republicans to renewed violence. If Sinn Féin leads the government in Dublin – an increasing likelihood after the 2025 elections – matters become more complicated, ensuring a more hardline response, unless it is tempered by its coalition partners.[11] Once the prize – so ferociously fought over for so long – is within the republican party's sights, the impulse to try to fast-track it may be impossible to check.

On the question of consent, unionists are at sixes and sevens: 82 per cent grudgingly say they would accept an outcome of 51 per cent favouring unity, but with a caveat that, while they are after all democrats, one could not be sure whether a razor-thin margin might result in an eruption of violence

– much the same response as they gave forty years ago.[12] Back in 1982, James Molyneaux, leader of the then dominant Ulster Unionist Party (UUP), told me that:

> if 51 per cent of the people of Northern Ireland in a free and open election opted for some form of unification, my party would have to accept it democratically. But then you'd be leaving out of account people who wouldn't be under the influence of politicians – and there would be a growing number of them under these circumstances. If they felt they were being pushed into a united Ireland against their will, then I think you'd find the strength of the paramilitaries vastly increased. You'd have a reverse terrorist situation.[13]

The threat of violence cuts two ways, says Peter Shirlow:[14]

> There will be loyalist violence. It might not be very sustained, but it will happen, and one would assume the target would be Dublin … On the other hand, say we have a border poll and it's 65–35 – to stay in the union, dissidents will turn around and say that Sinn Féin's strategy is failing. Everybody keeps thinking about violence from loyalism. If you have a lot of expectation built up that there's going to be a united Ireland and it doesn't happen, the probability of dissident republican violence is high.[15]

Polls suggest that voters have a more realistic response to the 50 per cent + 1 formulation. An *Independent*/Kantar poll (April 2021) on the centenary of the founding of Northern Ireland reported that 74 per cent in the North and 81 per cent in the South favoured a threshold of either two-thirds or 70 per cent for a border referendum outcome to be acceptable to both sides of the community.[16]

Would loyalists accept the legitimacy of a 50 per cent +1 referendum outcome, having so stridently endorsed the legitimacy of the United Kingdom (UK) Brexit vote, despite the narrowness of the Leave victory and the fact that a majority in Northern Ireland voted to remain? Apples and oranges, some say. Why should loyalists accept the legitimacy of a border poll that would transfer them into an all-Ireland state when the republican minority in the North never accepted the legitimacy of being part of the UK and are violently opposed to it? Unitarian Church Minister Rev. Chris Hudson, who maintains close ties with loyalists, says:

There are pockets within loyalism that are making angry noises, saying things like, 'Well, if there is a border poll and 51 per cent of the people vote for a united Ireland and 49 per cent vote against, we're not just going to accept it. They [republicans] never accepted Northern Ireland as part of the United Kingdom, so why should we accept a united Ireland? And we will make it unworkable.' These voices are not widespread, but you'd still be left with a rump of people who are going to make sure that it [a united Ireland] doesn't work.[17]

If one wants to game a scenario where a border poll results in a small majority emerging for unity, one should also game the opposite result – a small majority emerging to stay in the UK after a bitter and highly divisive campaign that saw what appeared to be a small majority in favour of unity dissipate in the course of such a campaign. Would dissident republicans cry foul? Or would they use the outcome to vindicate their belief that Ireland can be unified only by violence, since all the peaceful alternatives are shown not to work? Billy Hutchinson, leader of the small Progressive Unionist Party (PUP), says:

Do you think that [people in the Republic of Ireland] want a million Protestants being dragged into a united Ireland against their will? Through a border-poll vote? I don't think they would. No matter what happens, a large minority will be disaffected. It will be the same with disaffected republicans. They're fighting for the same thing as the Provisional IRA were fighting for before the ceasefires. But if there was a border poll and we decided to stay within the United Kingdom, does that not actually give those dissident republicans some sort of mandate to say, 'We're going back to war?' No matter what way it goes, there will be a large minority that will be angry and disaffected. I don't think the Irish or British government will want that.[18]

Complex factors must be taken into account when holding a border poll: the metrics a Secretary of State should use to determine whether there is enough evidence of a majority for unity to call it; when it should be called and how it should be worded; whether the decision would be made in concert with the Irish government; when and how the type of the new all-Ireland state on offer should be drawn up (after a border poll in negotiations with Northern Ireland's political parties or before, in some form of Citizens' Assembly or other all-Ireland forum, so that voters would know what type of Irish state they were voting themselves into); and for how long such a forum should sit before reaching their recommendations. If such a deliberative forum met before a referendum, how could it ensure the participation of a political unionism that was unwilling to engage, because to participate would in effect mean they were conceding the outcome? Is this an argument for a negotiating forum after a pro-unity referendum when unionism would be compelled, if only to protect its interests, to come to the table? What kind of majority in the poll itself would produce a stable result? And what kind of transitional arrangements would be needed – and for how long – to con-summate the new all-Ireland state?

Unionist interviewees are vague about the metrics: some because they believe that a referendum is not in the offing, or because they are con-vinced that if one were called they would win, or because they think that the metrics for calling a referendum should be overwhelming, or because they believe a border poll is so far into the future that it is not a 'clear and present danger'. Former UUP leader Steve Aiken says: 'There would have to be overwhelming evidence that showed there would be a considerable majority of people who'd be willing to vote for Irish unity in a border poll. I can't envisage the circumstances where that's going to happen anytime within ten, twenty years or maybe longer.'[19]

In contrast, the Social Democratic and Labour Party's (SDLP) Colum Eastwood says whatever the metrics for a poll, post-Brexit there is an 'an unstoppable momentum' for reunification. 'People see what's happening in Scotland. It is pretty clear that there will be a referendum of one type or another there. I'm pretty sure … that there will be a positive outcome for Scottish nationalism then.'[20]

Either way, he says:

> if there's a border poll tomorrow, I will vote one way, Arlene Foster [at the time of the interview first minister] will vote another. But in the middle [are] those who are young, liberal, outward-looking, interna-tionalist, not defined necessarily by the old two blocks [nationalist and unionist]. To have the EU taken away from them, particularly when they didn't vote for it, changes the dynamic … plus the fact that because of Brexit and the resulting protocol, economically we're reorganizing ourselves in terms of where we get many of our goods from … The union is coming to an end. It's now a case of how you manage that in such a way that that is not damaging, not divisive.[21]

While 50 per cent + 1 is a democratic majority, Alliance Party leader Naomi Long says that in real terms there should be a decisive majority in favour of unity, the three strands of the B/GFA should have been working harmoniously for a period and voters should know what a united Ireland entails. Otherwise, any united Ireland would be unstable. Election results, however, she is quick to add, do not necessarily reflect constitutional preferences. The Secretary of State,' she elaborates:

> needs to look much more broadly than simply at the likelihood of a 50 per cent +1 vote for unity based on election results. He needs to look at the *conditions* in which elections are fought. We will have to weigh [election results] against other polling evidence. A Secretary of State would need to be reasonably confident that the polling would show us a majority in favour of change before he would go down that route. It would need fairly robust evidence. Some evidence of that would have to come from direct polling, as opposed to simply taking the results of a general or an Assembly election.[22]

In many of the polls taken to gauge support for a border poll, assumptions are made about the nationalist vote. One is that a vote for Sinn Féin is a vote for Irish unity. That assumption is false. A University of Liverpool Northern Ireland Survey poll conducted in December 2019 found that 10 per cent of Sinn Féin supporters and 20 per cent of SDLP supporters said they would vote against a united Ireland in a border poll.[23] In other words, support for a nationalist or a republican party does not necessarily translate into support for a united Ireland.

Social researcher Paul Nolan, who tracks social and demographic trends in Northern Ireland, says should a border poll be called the lessons of Brexit tell us that it should be preceded by years of preparatory work.[24] The phrase 'uniting the people on the island of Ireland' in 'harmony and friendship' in Article 3 of the Irish Constitution surely precludes any notion that opinion polls indicating a small margin for unity would meet that constitutional requirement:

> What seems to be evolving within Sinn Féin is the view that we need to have the discussion first and the vote afterwards. That process would take a period of years in itself. It may well be, for example, that people decide they want an Ireland with a fully comprehensive

healthcare system. At some point, the Irish government has got to say, 'Well, if we take on all of that, how much is it going to cost? And what about the North's share of the UK national debt – are we expected to take that on too?' All of those things will have to be costed in. The people have to decide what they want. The Irish government has to decide whether or not they can pay for it. The question then could still be framed in simple terms, 'Do you want a united Ireland?' but with a clear understanding of what it would involve.[25]

Jane Morrice, a founder of the now defunct Northern Ireland Women's Coalition, says the B/GFA itself provides the mechanism for starting a conversation about Northern Ireland's future. The agreement called for a civic forum – drawn from employers, trade-union and voluntary-sector organizations – which was established in 2000 but mothballed in 2002. 'The Civic Forum should be reinstated to mirror the Citizens' Assembly, which has operated down South before referendums on abortion and gay marriage,' she says, adding:

> The forum should sit for five years, followed by a referendum on whatever proposal emerges from its deliberations – and, in the event of a border poll favouring unity, another five-year transition period. Whatever proposals emerge would have to be fed to both governments: the Irish government, because it will be the responsible party for working out the details of a united Ireland, and the British government, because it and the Irish government will have to negotiate the future of the Treasury subvention and the National Health Service. Both would be matters of hard bargaining.[26]

Alex Attwood, part of the SDLP's Good Friday Agreement negotiating team, outlines several variables in play in the path to a possible border poll. Some are external: the impact of the UK leaving the EU with a bare-bones free-trade agreement; the changing character of the union because of devolved government in Wales and Scotland; a possible Scottish referendum on independence; and generational shifts, with an incoming generation in both the North and South for whom the conflict is 'ancient history'. An overriding consideration will be making Northern Ireland work, a sustained period during which the Stormont government is not collapsed, and there is the substance of a genuine partnership between Sinn Féin and the Democratic Unionist Party (DUP).[27] He believes what is needed is a new, sustained dialogue between unionists, nationalists and others, which is what happened in the years leading up to the B/GFA. 'You have to grow the process organically. The danger is that if it is too aggressive, elements of unionism will run into the hills. This is a conversation that has to be properly paced.'[28]

However, Sinn Féin, Attwood believes, is unlikely to adopt this approach: 'I have a fear that there are people within Sinn Féin whose strategy is to again overwhelm unionism, demoralize them, and thus get Irish unity over the line. And then you're going to have this hostile conversation, and God knows where hostile conversations go in this part of the world.'[29]

In the wake of Brexit, with Northern Ireland voting to remain in the EU despite the DUP campaign to leave, a few DUP voters, more 'liberal' unionist voters and younger people deciding that climate change and sexuality issues were more important to them than the 'national question' gravitated to Alliance for the 2019 European and Westminster elections, significantly increasing its electoral share from 7–8 per cent to 15–20 per cent.[30] Professor Duncan Morrow, former Alliance Party chair, cautions that the increase in support for a border poll among some Alliance voters signified a comfort level with an Ireland led by moderate leaders such as Leo Varadkar and Simon Coveney.[31] An Ireland led by Sinn Féin would be another matter. 'They're not convinced that a united Ireland, and certainly not a Sinn Féin-led united Ireland, is the answer to their problem,' Morrow says:

> They're not responding to the union flag in the way they used to but they're also not convinced by Sinn Féin … If the Shinners [Sinn Féin] decide that a hard-line Sinn Féin-fronted united Ireland is the way they want to go, they would lose a referendum. If nationalism genuinely wants a united Ireland, then the question is, how do you appeal to that central group who absolutely doesn't want a hard-line policy?[32]

According to Sam McBride, the key measure of readiness for a border poll lies with the Alliance Party – when and if that party signals it is prepared to bring the issue to a debate and vote in the Assembly. Other measures are flawed:

> My sense is just how remarkably complex and ambiguous even the calling of a border poll would be, and the modalities and methodologies for how it would be held on both sides of the border. The fact that we're only now starting to seriously consider this shows that [Sinn Féin are] not really serious about it.

They have never really addressed the issues surrounding a poll, let alone the far more substantive issue of what Irish unity would look like. There are various criteria. There could be a vote in the Assembly chamber. That's one of the most convincing mechanisms because … you would not just need nationalist parties to vote for it, you would need to persuade the Alliance Party to vote for it, possibly also the Greens, so it would be much more representative of where Northern Ireland is than simply saying nationalist parties want this.

Traditionally, the Alliance Party has been very hostile to the idea of a border poll. They see it as divisive, as tribal, as something that should only be called if it is going to be won. Therefore, if they were to move in that direction, I think that would be quite significant. It would show that they believed that this was at least winnable by nationalism.[33]

However, Alliance deputy leader Stephen Farry MP does not foresee the party initiating a conversation in the Assembly on holding a referendum any time soon:

We [the Alliance Party] take a very deliberate decision not to define ourselves around the constitutional question. Some members will be pro-union, some pro-united Ireland. Many people will be open-minded on the issue. Our focus is on reconciliation, integration, making Northern Ireland work. Before 2016, if a border poll had been called, I would say that most supporters of the Alliance Party would have defaulted to the status quo, which often happens at referendums … Since Brexit, it's a much more fluid situation. There is much more open-mindedness to consider the various options for the future.[34]

And what would convince Alliance that the time had arrived for a border referendum?

You would need to see a very consistent pattern [for unity] over a sustained period of time. Measuring possible support for unity through election results is also a possibility, but then you have the problem of how you count and interpret the votes for the Alliance Party and other non-aligned parties. Do you count them as people who don't want a border poll, or who do want a border poll, or who are not particularly keen on a border poll either way but may be open-minded if they were asked their opinion regardless? We would be very wary of

voting for a border poll in a vacuum. Certainly, the bar for us doing
so will be very high.[35]

In short, Alliance would have to know what kind of united Ireland is on
offer before joining in a vote in the Assembly requesting the Secretary of
State to call a referendum.

Alex Kane, the commentator who is regarded as having his finger on the
pulse of unionist thinking, says:

> If unionists were to take another massive hit in the 2022 Assembly
> election, and if Sinn Féin were to eclipse the DUP; if nationalism were
> to increase its vote again in the Assembly; if the Alliance Party were
> to increase on its base; if unionism were to go down from 40 seats to,
> say, 32 or 33, and a couple of years down the line, you have Sinn Féin
> not simply a junior partner in government in the South but the senior
> partner, then there would be a number of metrics in play that could
> result in unionism suddenly being confronted with a border poll.
> A referendum is not inevitable, but it's more likely than not.[36]

On these criteria, the 2022 Assembly elections were indecisive. A mixed bag
at best for unionism. But unmistakably the trends are in the wrong direction.
Since 1969, unionism has lost more than 40 per cent of its share of the vote.[37]

A border poll will be a major chicken-and-egg dilemma for the politicians. Which comes first: a straight question on unity *before* any details
have been worked out, or having sufficient details in advance of such a
poll? There is consensus among interviewees that under no circumstances
should there be a simple Brexit-type up-or-down poll. In which case, is the
onus on the Irish government to jump-start that process? And if so, when?
Especially since, as things stand, none of the metrics invoked as barometers
of pro-unity dispositions point to a likely majority for unity, not now, and
perhaps not for at least a decade to come.

Across the interviews there was no consensus about the route to a
border poll. Nationalists retreated to the comfort zone of the 50 per cent + 1
mantra. Unionists treated the question dismissively, mostly pointing to the
potential for violence such a small margin for unification would unleash,
but were caught on the horns of a dilemma of their own making: if the UK
Brexit vote (52 per cent to leave, 48 per cent to remain across the UK) constituted 'the will of the people' – legitimately imposed on Northern Ireland,

which had voted to remain – why should a similar slender margin not legit-imize a vote for unity in a border poll?

Age and immigration will also be issues. Would voting be extended to the 16–18 age cohort in a border poll, as happened in the Scottish independence referendum – a proposal that would be opposed vehemently by unionists because of younger people's larger presence in the Catholic community, hence creating a perceived pro-unity propensity? Another quandary will be whether 'a majority of the people of Northern Ireland voting in a poll' includes domi-ciled EU citizens and immigrants.[38] Would the thousands of immigrants who have become British or Irish citizens, and who have made Northern Ireland their home, have a say in what jurisdiction they will live under?[39]

The B/GFA lays down that consent to unity should be 'freely and con-currently given', which is interpreted by some analysts as meaning a poll at the same time, North and South, as happened with the referendums on the 1998 Agreement. But such an interpretation means, on the face of it, that the British government would be dictating the time of the Irish referendum, regardless of whether the republic felt itself ready for one. Such a situation is hard to imagine, underscoring yet again why the process for holding a border poll will have to be agreed by the two governments working together.

Concurrent does not mean simultaneous. Simply as a matter of logic, a lag between the two polls is called for: before the South voted on the ques-tion it would want to see how the referendum turned out in the North, since the option of staying in the union would also be on the ballot. The lag could affect the outcome in the South. A divisive, highly polarized campaign in the North, with perhaps some instances of violence, might cause some emo-tionally pro-unity voters in the South to have second thoughts. Indeed, the 2021 *Independent*/Kantar poll found that over two-thirds of people in the republic feared a return to violence 'at the prospect of a united Ireland'.[40]

Interviewees were inclined to think the consent provision in the B/GFA is a necessary but not a sufficient condition for a border poll. Unless the Irish government indicates that it is prepared to call a poll, no Secretary of State is going to call one in the North. The wording of the poll has to be worked out by both sovereign governments because it will fall to both to oversee the transition to unity if there is a vote in favour of unification, and to negotiate a plethora of complicated issues associated with the transfer of sovereignty.

The Irish government is highly unlikely to call a referendum in the South if it appears that the metrics used for gauging support for unity in the North may result in a tiny margin for unity, with the Catholic community overwhelmingly in favour and the Protestant community even more overwhelmingly against. In these circumstances, while both governments wait for a more substantial majority for unity to emerge, loyalist paramilitaries would, no doubt, do their utmost to reverse that sentiment, which would erode support for unity because of the perceived mayhem that might accompany it, aside from economic and other costs.

It can be argued that this scenario makes the case for pressing ahead even if the apparent majority emerging is small, because proponents of unity would cry foul. In the end, the call for a referendum will be a political decision, arrived at after careful examination and risk assessment of different scenarios, with the Secretary of State weighing the pros and cons of each and ultimately making a judgment call.

The DUP's Peter Robinson says:

> There is a deliberate vagueness about the terms used within the Belfast Agreement that gave the Secretary of State the role to call a border poll ... But I think the [consent provision] was deliberately left vague. Every sensible person recognizes that to have a border poll with a 50 or 51 or 52 per cent result, on a constitutional issue like the future of Northern Ireland, is certain to be violent. There is no other likely outcome in those circumstances, if the result is tight. By the time a Secretary of State might feel that they could just edge it, you're going to have a situation where Northern Ireland is on a knife edge, and one section of the community or the other will be aggrieved at the result. I suspect that you will not see a Secretary of State calling a border poll until there is overwhelming evidence that there would be a united Ireland as an outcome.[41]

The East Belfast loyalist community leader Sammy Douglas echoes Robinson's sentiments:

> It certainly has to be more than 51 per cent. I know that's been agreed as part of the Good Friday Agreement. But it will be a disaster for us all. People here say you'll end up with violence. It's inevitable that will happen. It's clear if you look at the recent violence up around the north-west, in Portrush and Ballymoney; we had eighteen-gun

attacks there by loyalists on their own people, feuding.[42] It wouldn't take much for those people to turn their guns on the nationalist community – and that's only one area. In parts of East Belfast, you see the paramilitaries still very much ruling those communities. Sinn Féin is the worst party to be pushing for an agreed Ireland. People here would listen more to the likes of the Taoiseach, or Leo [Varadkar] or some of those people. Certainly not Mary Lou [McDonald]. There's a mistrust there that I can't see it ever evaporating.[43]

On the Shankill Road, community leader Jackie Redpath takes a similar view:

> There's only one other option and that is to die in the ditch when faced with the inevitability of this truck of a border referendum leading to unity coming down the road. What happens then is you either get out, suck it up or fight … It would be a recipe for disaster because such a fight, of course, will be bloody but it will be short. It would not be successful, and it would put a desperate shadow over the future in Ireland for another one hundred years.[44]

Harping on about 50 per cent + 1 as the defining metric for a Secretary of State's calling a border poll, no matter what the political circumstances prevailing in the two Irish jurisdictions at the time, is a policy of madness. SDLP leader Colum Eastwood says:

> The two governments need to come together and create a high-level panel to advise them on this because otherwise it will become party political. There was a mistake made in the agreement: just leaving it up to the Secretary of State and a fairly flimsy set of criteria there to make the decision. However, if the polls are consistent in terms of people wanting change, then it would be fairly divisive if the Secretary of State refused to act at that point.[45]

The Working Group of British and Irish academics, led by University College London's Constitution Unit, examined how a referendum might be worded and conducted. Titled 'Unification Referendums on the Island of Ireland', it looked at five possible configurations of a referendum, some including the details of the united Ireland on offer in the referendum question, and some including the process that would be followed to negotiate a future all-Ireland state in the event of a pro-unity vote.[46] The group also outlined the criteria that would ensure a referendum result all parties would accept as valid.

These include 'procedural legitimacy, stability, clarity, informed choice and inclusivity'.[47] It emphasizes that '*all these criteria point towards the importance of advance planning of the referendum processes; and about the shape of a united Ireland, or a continued union* [my italics]'.[48]

A referendum presaging a 50 per cent + 1 outcome taking place in circumstances of social turbulence, rampant sectarianism and sporadic bouts of low-level violence would undoubtedly not meet the conditions the working group enunciates. Nor would it be a precursor of the unification promised in the Irish Constitution that the people on the island will be unified 'in harmony and friendship'. In fairness, the group stresses that it is 'focused on technical and procedural questions'.[49] 'As a group,' the report states, 'we take no view on whether holding such referendums would be desirable or not, or on what the outcomes should be if referendums were to be held.'[50]

But the group's members were open to questions on a range of matters relating to the process that will lead up to a referendum. In this regard, I asked Brendan O'Leary, a co-author of the Working Group report, whether there is any requirement that the two governments should work together to safeguard against a Secretary of State from calling a Brexit-type binary poll. 'There's nothing in the Good Friday Agreement,' he says, that 'obligates' the two sovereign governments to work in that way:

> It would, of course, be entirely sensible and rational for the two governments to co-operate both with regard to the timing of the referendum and on its implementation if it were to be in favour of unification; and then to ratify the result in their respective parliaments and give institutional effect to the result.
>
> However, there is a worrisome set of scenarios that need to be considered. It is possible for the Secretary of State to trigger a referendum in the hope that it might be lost in the sense that it would be a vote for the union, but it could turn out to be a vote with a narrow majority in favour of Irish unification, with the South caught completely unprepared, and indeed the UK government also caught unprepared. That's one possibility.
>
> The other possibility is for the South to signal that it doesn't want the Northern referendum to happen, but legally and politically the Secretary of State in Northern Ireland might reasonably feel obliged and perhaps required by a court to hold a referendum if sustained objective evidence had indicated a shift in Northern opinion on the

union. It's precisely because of those scenarios that I think it's vital
that the government of Ireland spend much of the next decade – after
the recovery from the pandemic, of course – in preparing for these
eventualities.[51]

Under the referendum scenarios the Working Group considers, voters
will not know how the present UK subvention to Northern Ireland will be
dealt with; how it will be apportioned into the part still owed by the British
Treasury, such as pensions; and the part a united Ireland would have to pick
up. To this extent, a yardstick the group stipulates for the conduct of a border
poll is not met. 'One of the criteria that we have for evaluating different referendum configurations,' Alan Renwick, Chair of the Working Group, says,
'is that people are able to make an informed choice … We heard lots of different views as to how big a part of the issue that [the subvention] really is.'[52]

The Working Group appears to believe that matters such as the subvention would be settled after a unification poll and before the transfer of
sovereignty. 'The British government,' Renwick continues, 'might calculate
that by sowing uncertainty on this point [the subvention], they would discourage votes in favour of unification. It clearly diminishes the degree to
which there's informed choice. But people we spoke with … were very clear
that the subvention was not a major issue.'[53]

The Working Group's finding that the subvention is not a matter of
major concern is contrary to what unionist and loyalist interviewees told
me. Many of these people simply dismissed the prospects of unification on
the grounds that the South couldn't afford it. Time and again the subvention
is mentioned, a mantra for the superiority of the North's economic well-
being. It is sown into the fabric of the North's economy, underpinning its
standard of living.[54] Undoubtedly, the campaign to remain in the UK will
invoke it. Uncertainty over who will pay will exacerbate one of the most
contentious issues in a border poll and influence that segment of voters who
haven't made up their minds about Northern Ireland's constitutional future
to opt for the status quo. In opinion polls a large majority of people, North
and South, say they would not support unification if they had to pay higher
taxes to subsidize it.[55]

'The core subvention is now £15 billion,' says Lord Bew, formerly one of
David Trimble's closest advisers:

The funding of it is very hard work and there's the argument that it would require a very high level of taxation to support it. How do we get by without the British Treasury paying for it is a huge problem. If there is a border poll, they'll be saying on every street corner, 'You're getting 15 billion a year[56] from us [the UK]. It's keeping you in the first world. You're not getting a penny after.' They'll be saying it in Scotland too. So, it is very heavily subsidized … On every street corner, it'll be a message.[57]

In highly contentious referendums, the winning side is frequently the one most successful at reducing complex issues to simple messages and then saturating the media with short, snappy sound bites. Certainly, this was the case with Brexit. The Vote Leave campaign collapsed a host of extraordinarily hard-to-understand issues into the simple message: the UK was sending £350 million to the EU every week, which once the UK was out of the EU would be available to upgrade the National Health Service (NHS). Of course, the £350 million was a fabrication, but no matter to the spin masters. So successful was the messaging that more than 40 percent of the British public who had heard about the claim still believed it to be true two years after Brexit.[58] Dominic Cummings, the mastermind behind the Vote Leave campaign, admitted after the referendum that 'all our research and the close result strongly suggests that Remain would have won without the advert. It was clearly the most effective argument, not only with the crucial swing [vote] but with almost every demographic.'[59] My point: Northern Ireland voters know what the subvention is. What will happen to it if a united Ireland is tailor-made for a similar kind of messaging as what the Vote Leave campaign deployed?

Could the B/GFA be amended to reflect a different consent formulation? Unlikely. It would require levels of trust, goodwill and reconciliation between republicans and unionists that would obviate the need for it. Article 7 of the Review Procedures for the Good Friday Agreement states:

If difficulties arise which require remedial action across the range of institutions, *or otherwise* [my italics] require amendment of the British-Irish Agreement or relevant legislation, the process of review will fall to the two Governments in consultation with the parties in the Assembly. Each Government will be responsible for action in its own jurisdiction.[60]

The agreement is not sacrosanct; it has been amended several times, most notably by the St Andrews Agreement with regard to governance.

It is argued that the constitutional provision regarding consent is immutable, the heart of the agreement, that only this provision allowed the Irish Republican Army (IRA) Council to signal its assent and for Sinn Féin to buy into the process, that any tampering with it will have violent consequences. Nevertheless, if the two governments and Northern Ireland's two nationalist parties listen to their respective publics, who have indicated in opinion polls that they want a threshold higher than 50 per cent + 1, they can move forward in lockstep to determine whether a sufficient margin for a referendum is reached to ensure minimum disruption in the North.[61] However, nationalists argue that requiring a super-majority in a referendum would mean that their votes were worth less than unionist votes. Moreover, such a scenario, the Working Group on Referendums concludes, is highly unlikely. 'It seems to us,' Alan Renwick says, 'that absent some extraordinary circumstances, it would not be possible to get the consensus on changing the agreement that was achieved in order to reach the agreement in the first place in 1998.'[62]

Undoubtedly, Sinn Féin in government in the South would reject out of hand any move in this direction. Indeed, if a UK government were persuaded by unionists, when a majority for unity appeared imminent, to toy with the idea of amending the consent formula, the pushback from an Irish government, most likely one with Sinn Féin in charge, would be fierce. It would consolidate support among nationalists/republicans for a 50 per cent + 1 threshold, rather than opening the possibility of raising it.

More likely, it would galvanize dissident republications righteously claiming, 'We told you so! Perfidious Albion tricked us in 1921 and again in 1998 – only armed struggle can finish the job of Irish unity.' As long as the gun lurks across the penumbra of Northern Ireland's political landscape, the threat of violence in response to what is perceived to be existential danger will hang like a dark cloud over Northern Ireland.

Interviewees across the political spectrum acknowledge that a sufficient number of unionists should be on board; opinion poll respondents North and South endorse a higher threshold in a border poll vote by significant margins.[63] Of course, for nationalists and republicans the 50 per cent + 1 formulation is now sacred dogma: if 50 per cent + 1 keeps Northern Ireland in the UK, 50 per cent + 1 is sufficient to take it out. This is what Sinn Féin signed up for. This is its default position. That said, the inherent drawback of relying on 50 per cent + 1 in favour of unity at the starting gate, when the poll is called, is that over the course of the race it can quickly be overtaken and 50 per cent + 1 against unity prevail in the home stretch as unionists who are traditionally non-voters flock to the polls. In 2019, non-voters numbered around 500,000.[64] Unionism in particular has a problem getting its supporters to vote compared with nationalism and republicanism. The 2019 University of Liverpool general election survey revealed that the preferred choice of Northern Ireland's non-voters is to stay in the union by a three to one margin.[65] How successful unionists are in galvanizing their voter turnout will have a significant impact on a future referendum.

The 1998 Northern Ireland Act (incorporating the B/GFA into British law) allows for a referendum on the question of Irish unification to be called by ministerial order, subject to parliamentary approval. But the B/GFA has nothing to say on how a referendum poll should be worded. In a literal sense, it requires no more than a simple yes/no vote on whether voters want to remain part of the UK or become part of a united Ireland. The 2016 Brexit referendum exposed the folly of such simplistic formulations, and there is unanimous agreement among interviewees – and the wider publics North and South – that the electorates in both jurisdictions should know before the referendum in the North what kind of united Ireland is on offer.

This poses a dilemma: the calling of the referendum is the sole prerogative of the Secretary of State, but the delineation of what kind of new Ireland is on offer is the sole prerogative of the Irish government. How then is the kind of united Ireland on offer conveyed to the Northern electorate? Either it is embedded in the referendum question the Secretary of State proposes or it is widely promulgated by the Irish government before and during a referendum campaign.

The Secretary of State must consult the UK's Electoral Commission on the question's wording before laying the draft order before the Westminster

Parliament. Parliament may amend the wording. Court action could follow if proponents of unity think it is in violation of the B/GFA. Court action, too, could also be pursued by pro-union advocates arguing that the Secretary of State has not met the threshold of a likely majority being in favour of unity. The Irish government has no veto over when the referendum might be called or how it might be worded. In both cases it is 'reliant on the good behaviour by HMG [His Majesty's Government]'.[66]

The Irish government has to decide whether it will follow the model route to unification or the process route. Under the model route, the shape and form of a united Ireland is worked out in some detail before the referendum in the North. Under the process route, the consultative steps the government will follow to lay the groundwork for a negotiated united Ireland are laid out.

Whichever course a government follows, its choice will have to be brought before Dáil Éireann, debated, subjected to amendments and consensus reached across all parties on the final package. The united Ireland on offer will not be on behalf of an Irish government; it will be on behalf of the Irish people.

All this must be known *before* a referendum. It is imperative, says Professor Brendan O'Leary, 'for the South to do long-run preparation for the possibility of unity after a border referendum. If we can see that this is an above-zero probability, then there is absolutely no harm and all good in preparing for such an eventuality'.[67] In the event that unionism refuses to engage prior to a referendum and the Irish state chooses the model route, 'the most difficult thing for any Irish government will be to try to estimate and evaluate unionist and loyalist opinion and their political and institutional preferences in the event that they might lose the vote'.[68] Under the most benevolent scenarios, the Working Group on Unification Referendums on the Island of Ireland, envisages 'discussion between the UK and Irish governments, consulting with the Northern Ireland Executive, political parties and civil society and with the UK Electoral Commission'.[69] It believes the latter body 'ought to be able to prevent differences in question wording that could lead to confusion for voters or difficulty for campaigners'.[70] This, however, presupposes that unionism is on board, which O'Leary himself believes will not be the case until after a referendum, when it will have to engage, even if reluctantly, to safeguard its interests in a future all-Ireland state. Now, he argues, is the time for planning, a ministry and multiple Citizens' Assemblies, and building a cross-party consensus in the South:

> I see no reason why over the next decade there couldn't be a series of fully funded Citizens' Assemblies in the South – and with the consent of the North perhaps also in the North – looking at either modes of improved co-operation or at the institutional and policy design of a united Ireland. Citizens' Assemblies do not have to be government-sponsored. Researchers, funded properly, could organize such assemblies in the North and the South. And if unionists refuse to participate? So be it![71]

The absence of precedents illustrates the perils of missteps in this process. Unless the Irish government has completed its preparations for a poll, no matter how far distant on the horizon it might appear, it could be wrong-footed by a Secretary of State calling a poll. Or, worse still, a border poll could take place with no clear understanding of what it entailed while the Republic of Ireland's political parties squabbled over the timing, form and shape of a future Ireland.

But for an Irish government to start the process of developing models of a united Ireland now would undoubtedly draw the ire of unionism and feed its paranoia that the British and Irish governments are secretly working in cahoots, preparing to offload Northern Ireland into an all-Ireland state. Most of mainstream unionism has refused to engage with the Irish government's low-key Shared Island Unit, dismissing it as a Trojan horse for Irish unity.[72]

Francis Campbell, the former private secretary to Tony Blair who understands how the inner sanctums of Whitehall work, says the UK will be preoccupied with the fallout from Brexit, and thus no Irish government should instigate any consultation of the options regarding some new constitutional dispensation in Northern Ireland. 'Such an effort,' he points out, 'would come across as predatory, irresponsibly immature and dash any hope of mending fences and the trauma of Brexit.' He adds:

> If the Irish government were to begin to come up with proposals now, that would further inflame unionism. It's not that such proposals don't need to exist. The proposals and the talking and the ideas need to come from another space. Their absence creates a vacuum. The

question is, who puts these proposals forward? My fear would be that
if it is the Irish government that puts forward ideas and proposals on
what this [united Ireland] might look like, it would backfire. It would
not help politics on the ground, or community cohesion or relations
in Northern Ireland. You're trying to think what the reaction would
be within Northern Ireland's unionist community that feels the link
with London is weakening.[73]

With no timetable as to when a Northern Ireland Secretary of State might
call a poll, the Irish government needs to be prepared for any eventuality.
Unless unionism comes on board at some point in this process, it is hard
to envisage a scenario that would not elicit an angry and hostile unionist
reaction once an Irish government takes up the cudgels of unification. There
would certainly be very serious repercussions, very definitely damaging
North-South relations. A border poll called because the Secretary of State
believes a narrow majority for unity appears to have materialized would
only add to the disruption. All roads to the future are strewn with highly
combustible, unknown obstacles.

Ideally, the two governments would be working together through the
British-Irish Intergovernmental Conference and advancing slowly towards
a border poll in close collaboration, working on proposals that are put into
storage for use some time in the future. However, as co-guarantor of the
B/GFA, the British government cannot be seen to overtly encourage the
Irish government on any path to unity.

No matter how you envisage the different scenarios, their paths are lit-
tered with pitfalls. A Northern Ireland Secretary of State agreeing to insert
an Irish government wording on unity into the referendum question would
require the deftest of political finessing. But still there would still be nothing
to preclude either the UK Electoral Commission or the UK Parliament from
passing amendments that distorted the intent of the wording, another scenario that would invite court action.

> There are no criteria anyone can point to that suggests the Secretary
> of State should act upon the wording in the Good Friday Agreement
> that he or she should consider a border poll when a clear majority was
> in favour of unity, because that majority is not in sight. Whether you
> do it by election results, whether you do it by demography, or whether

you do it by opinion poll, there is no sign of that majority taking shape. Which isn't to say it won't happen, because extraordinary things happen in politics.[74]

– Dr Paul Nolan, Research Director, Northern Ireland
Peace Monitoring Survey

The Working Group identifies six possible sources of evidence a Secretary of State might draw on to assess the state of public opinion in Northern Ireland: 'votes cast in elections; the results of surveys and opinion polls; qualitative evidence; a vote within the Assembly; the seats won at elections; or demographic data'.[75] It states that the Secretary of State '*must* [my italics] *take all relevant evidence into account*'.[76] (There is no requirement in the B/GFA stipulating this. The Secretary of State can call a referendum at any time and is not obliged to provide any justification other than saying that it 'appears likely' a majority for unity exists.)

All of the suggested metrics the group identifies are wanting: opinion polls contradict each other; they are only snapshots at a point in time, and only a few since the B/GFA show a majority for unity. In Assembly elections, both nationalist/republican and unionist parties' shares of votes have levelled off, pegged at around 40 per cent each, and those of centrist parties at 20 per cent.

After the 2022 Assembly election, both an aggregate of nationalist parties and unionist parties fell well short of having a majority of seats. 'Assembly elections are hard to read because you have a wide spread of candidates,' says Naomi Long:

> not all of whom will have strong views when it comes to the constitutional position. It doesn't follow that if someone votes for Sinn Féin in a local or Assembly election, they automatically will vote for a united Ireland in a border poll. Local and Assembly elections are often driven by a member's constituency work and reputation, rather than by party political brand. There would have to be some independent polling measure to get a sense that we were at the point of a majority in favour of unity.[77]

In the December 2019 election for Westminster, parties representing the Catholic community won more seats than those representing the Protestant community for the first time in history, but not a majority of votes because the Alliance Party picked up a seat. 'The danger of using a Westminster election,' Long continues, 'is that in a general election people's votes are skewed by the fact that it's a first-past-the-post contest. It doesn't necessarily reflect the breadth of people's opinions, and voters will often look for someone as the least-worst option rather than because they support them or their policies.'[78]

Most elections in Northern Ireland have relatively low turnouts. In 1998, the referendum on the B/GFA attracted an unprecedented turnout of 80.2 per cent, which fell dramatically to 64 per cent in the subsequent first election for the Northern Ireland Assembly.[79] Average voter turnout in five Assembly elections has not surpassed 64 per cent since.[80] The Assembly 2022 elections turnout was 63.52 per cent, down 0.48 per cent from the 2017 turnout.[81] The 2019 University of Liverpool survey concludes: 'If a similar turnout was achieved [more than 80 per cent], and non-voters engaged, then the poll would be to remain within the union.'[82]

Other than a vote in the Assembly – supported by Sinn Féin, the SDLP, Alliance and the Greens – on instigating a conversation on constitutional futures, thus opening the way for a broader discussion on a referendum, the other metrics that have been cited fall short of indicating majority support for one. 'At the moment,' Alan Renwick says, 'it's very clear that there is not a majority in favour of unification on any criteria. We don't take a view on what might happen in the future. All we can say is, there is not a majority at present, there might be in the future. Who knows how opinion might change?'[83]

According to the 2021 census, '46 per cent of Northern Ireland's population were Catholic or brought up Catholic, 44 per cent were Protestant or brought up Protestant'.[84] For the first time since the founding of the statelet, those from a Catholic background outnumbered those from a Protestant background. The result was not unexpected, but for unionists it was another psychological blow, having to absorb the loss of both political and numerical ascendency in one year, what had once been intended to be a permanent Protestant majority, hewn from the nine counties of Ulster 100 years back to ensure the link with the UK in perpetuity, now simply a footnote for the history books.

Of the eleven local government areas, only Mid and East Antrim, and Ards and North Down, represent a majority Protestant population. Four areas represent clear Catholic populations, with the rest having no religious majority population (see Table 5.1).[85]

Table 5.1. Three highest rates for combined religion identity, by local government district (2021)

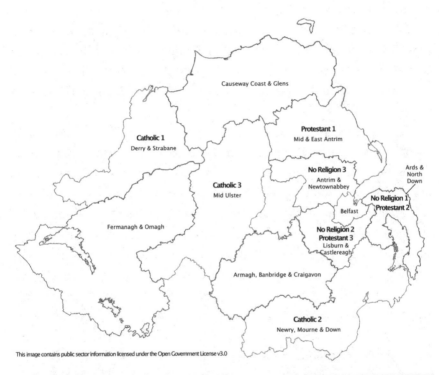

CATHOLIC		PROTESTANT		NO RELIGION	
1. Derry City and Strabane	68%	1. Mid and East Antrim	58%	1. Ards and North Down	31%
2. Newry, Mourne and Down	68%	2. Ards and North Down	56%	2. Lisburn and Castlereagh	24%
3. Mid Ulster	62%	3. Lisburn and Castlereagh	49%	3. Antrim and Newtownabbey	23%

For the local government district council areas, Derry City and Strabane had the highest prevalence rate of those with a Catholic religious identity (68 per cent), followed by Newry, Mourne and Down (68 per cent) and Mid Ulster (62 per cent). The areas with the highest rates for a Protestant religious identity were Mid and East Antrim (58 per cent), followed by Ards and North Down (56 per cent) and Lisburn and Castlereagh (49 per cent). Those with the highest rates for no religious identity were Ards and North Down (31 per cent), Lisburn and Castlereagh (24 per cent) and Antrim and Newtownabbey (23 per cent).

In age cohorts over sixty-five, Protestants are in an increasing majority. In the 2020 Life and Times Survey, of those identifying as Protestant, 40 per cent are under thirty-five; of those identifying as Catholic, 51 per cent are under thirty-five, and 54 per cent of those having no religious affiliation are under thirty-five.[86]

School attendance figures replicate these trends. There were 177,843 Catholics and 109,475 Protestants in Northern Ireland's schools in 2021/22; in addition, there were 66,500 children who classified as 'other Christian, non-Christian, or no religion' who will eventually make their way into the electorate and lean one way or the other on the union.[87] The numbers at Northern Irish universities are equally telling. In 2015, the student populations at Queen's University Belfast, the University of Ulster, Stranmillis, St Mary's Colleges and the Open University were 45.3 per cent Catholic and 29.5 per cent Protestant.[88] In 2021, these figures were 52.8 per cent and 32.0 per cent respectively.[89]

Although the Catholic community emerged as the largest of the three main population groups in the 2021 census, it still fell well short of a majority.[90] Close to one-fifth of the population said they had no religion, almost doubling since the 2011 census. A more nuanced contextual framework has to take account of an emerging Catholic plurality as the largest religious designation and a growing propensity among Catholics, and Protestants in particular, to self-identify as 'other/no determination'.[91] Northern Ireland is increasingly becoming a secular society. Moreover, religious background and political identity are no longer automatic predicators of voting intentions. But the long-run forecast is that the increasing numbers of Catholics as the 16–24 cohort comes of voting age may produce an overall segment for unity. However, this process may not be as seamless as it appears.

Between 1998 and 2014, Northern Ireland Life and Times (NILT) surveys reported that on average 41 per cent of Catholics defined themselves as neither unionist nor nationalist; in 2020, this number was 37 per cent.[92] This cohort appears to decrease in number when Northern Ireland is perceived not to be working. These opposing trends – an increasing proportion of the population from cultural Catholic backgrounds and an increasing number of Catholics self-designating as neither orange nor green – can pull in opposite directions, making predictions of future voting behaviour speculative at best.

> *The question is, what about those who are undecided? What would make them change their mind on these things? Depending on the different polls, around 10 to 25 per cent of people say that they would vote, but they don't know yet which way they would vote. That is quite a considerable proportion of the population.*[93]
> – Professor Katy Hayward, Senator George J. Mitchell Institute for Global Peace, Security and Justice at Queen's University Belfast; Senior Fellow, UK in a Changing Europe

The defining characteristic of voting patterns in Northern Ireland since the founding of the state in 1920 is that Catholics invariably vote for nationalist or republican parties, Protestants for unionist parties.[94] This remains true, but with smaller majorities for nationalist and unionist parties, and more Protestants and Catholics voting for non-sectarian parties like Alliance and the Green Party.[95] Moreover, there has always been a significant minority of Catholics opting to stay in the UK, if they had to make a choice between staying or joining a united Ireland. Professor Richard Rose's 1968 Loyalty Survey, which predated the outbreak of the conflict, asked Catholics several questions about partition.[96] In response to whether they approved or disapproved of the controversy at the time about the constitutional position of Northern Ireland, just 33 per cent approved, 34 per cent disapproved and 32 per cent didn't know. In a further question, Catholics were asked how they would react if nationalists agreed to stop debating partition and accept the present borders as final: 46 per cent disapproved, 30 per cent approved and 24 per cent didn't know.[97] Hardly a bandwagon for a united Ireland.

In 1989, after another decade of horrific warfare, 32 per cent of Catholics wanted to stay in the UK.[98] This fell to 19 per cent at the time of the B/GFA in 1998 and thereafter began to rise, first to 39 per cent after restoration of the Stormont Assembly and Executive in 2007, to 52 per cent in 2013, declining in subsequent years (particularly after Brexit) to 35 per cent in 2019, dramatically to 25 per cent in 2020 and continuing its descent to 21 per cent in 2021.[99]

There is a proliferation of polls in Northern Ireland competing for relevance and legitimacy. On the one hand, there are rigorous academic surveys: the NILT survey, conducted by Queen's University Belfast and the University of Ulster, the University of Liverpool Tracker surveys and the *Irish Times*/Ipsos. There are also the online polls – Red C, LucidTalk, Lord Ashcroft, BBC *Spotlight*/LucidTalk, *Belfast Telegraph*/Kantar, *Irish Times*/Ipsos and *Irish News*/University of Liverpool both in person and online.[100]

The university polls adhere to strict statistical sampling in both in-person and online interviews. The latter group use online sampling that lacks this rigour. Each has a built-in bias. The NILT survey is considered to be the gold standard for the depth and breadth of its questions and its time-series analysis. It is used by policy practitioners to help them analyse a wide range of socio-economic issues and is especially helpful in detecting trends in public opinion. But the gold is tarnished somewhat because the survey underestimates support for Sinn Féin – residents in republican areas are more suspicious of strangers knocking at their doors wanting to quiz them on a wide range of matters, including their constitutional preferences.

LucidTalk relies on computer-generated interviews and is more likely to attract interviewees who are more familiar with online interactions and how to manipulate responses – thus, its bias. Unlike the NILT surveys that are conducted in October with results posted the following June, LucidTalk polls are tracker polls that occur at regular intervals throughout the year and cover a much narrower range of questions. While the NILT and University of Liverpool polls put support for unity in the low thirties, LucidTalk puts it at the mid- to high forties. Across thirty-four polls conducted between 2013 and 2022, online polls averaged between 10 to 15 per cent more support for a united Ireland than in-person polls. The former averaged 30 to 45 per cent in favour of one, the latter 20 to 30 per cent.[101] For the six years prior to Brexit, unionism support for staying in the UK averaged 61 per cent; post-Brexit between 2016 and 2020, it averaged 53 per cent.[102]

Because of differences in methodology and how the question is framed, there are huge disparities among polls. On occasion they contradict each other, in part because of how questions are framed and the sample drawn. For example, a University of Liverpool/*Irish News* poll (February 2022) placed the protocol as a major concern of just 10 per cent of unionists; a LucidTalk opinion poll (March 2022) in the run-up to the Assembly elections reported that constitutional issues and opposing the protocol were their top priority. But on the question of Irish reunification or staying in the UK, the trend is towards a 50-50 pro-unity/pro-union convergence (see Table 5.2), or more accurately under 50 per cent opting to stay in the UK.

Table 5.2: Aggregated results for a variety of polls (2019–22, rounded figures)

POLL	METHOD	POLL DATE	FOR UNITY (%)	AGAINST UNITY (%)	UNDECIDED OR WOULDN'T VOTE (%)
Ipsos MRBI (*Irish Times*)[103]	Face-to-face	March 2019	32	45	23
Lord Ashcroft[104]	Online	September 2019	46	45	9
University of Liverpool[105]	Face-to-face	December 2019	28	54	15
LucidTalk (The Detail)[106]	Online	February 2020	45	47	8
NILT[107]	Multi-mode[108]	October–December 2020	30	53	16
LucidTalk (*Sunday Times*)[109]	Online	January 2021	42	47	11
LucidTalk (BBC Spotlight)[110]	Online	April 2021	43	49	8
Kantar (*Belfast Telegraph*)[111]	Online	April 2021	35	44	21
LucidTalk (*Observer/Belfast Telegraph*)[112]	Online	August 2021	42	49	9
University of Liverpool[113]	Online	October 2021	30	58	12

NILT[114]	Multi-mode	October–December 2021	34	48	18
Lord Ashcroft[115]	Online	December 2021	41	49	10
University of Liverpool (*Irish News*)[116]	Online	March 2022	30	45	25
University of Liverpool (*Irish News*)[117]	Online	July 2022	43	40	13
LucidTalk (*Sunday Life*)[118]	Online	August 2022	41	48	11

Of the twenty-four-plus opinion surveys in Northern Ireland taken between 2017 and May 2022, only four have shown more respondents in favour of a united Ireland than against.[119] Averaging these poll results shows support for a united Ireland at 38 per cent, backing for the union at 48 per cent and undecideds at 14 per cent. For the cross-section of polls presented in Table 5.2 (2019/22), the online polls averaged 9 per cent more support for a united Ireland (40 per cent) than in-person polls (31 per cent). In short, on the twenty-fifth anniversary of the B/GFA, support for a united Ireland – no matter how you manipulate data – falls short of 50 per cent.

Table 5.3: Results of youngest-age cohorts surveyed in a variety of polls (rounded figures; all respondents' results in parentheses)

POLL	AGE	FOR UNITY	AGAINST UNITY	UNDECIDED OR WOULDN'T VOTE
Lord Ashcroft (Sept. 2019)[120]	18–24	60 (46)	40 (45)	—
	25–44	55 (46)	45 (45)	—
LucidTalk (The Detail) (Feb. 2020)[121]	18–24	41 (45)	55 (47)	4 (8)
	25–44	58 (45)	37 (47)	5 (8)
NILT (Dec. 2020)[122]	18–24	38 (30)	40 (53)	16 (16)
	25–34	34 (30)	50 (53)	13 (16)
LucidTalk (*Sunday Times*) (Jan. 2021)[123]	18–24	40 (42)	55 (47)	5 (11)
	25–44	50 (42)	40 (47)	10 (11)

LucidTalk (BBC *Spotlight*) (Apr. 2021)[124]	18–24 25–44	50 (43) 50 (43)	44 (49) 43 (49)	6 (8) 7 (8)
Kantar (*Belfast Telegraph*) (Apr. 2021)[125]	18–24 25–34	50 (35) 42 (35)	26 (44) 34 (44)	25 (21) 24 (21)
University of Liverpool (Oct. 2021)[126]	'Under 35'	54 (30)	35 (58)	11 (12)
NILT (Dec. 2021)[127]	18–24 25–34	35 (34) 36 (34)	37 (48) 43 (48)	28 (18) 20 (18)
Lord Ashcroft (Dec. 2021)[128]	18–24 25–44	71 (41) 46 (41)	24 (49) 45 (49)	5 (10) 9 (10)
LucidTalk (*Sunday Life*) (Aug. 2022)[129]	18–24 25–44	57 (41) 48 (41)	35 (48) 42 (48)	8 (11) 10 (11)

For some polls for which disaggregation by age is available (see Table 5.3), results suggest that the support for reunification among 18–24 and 25–34 age cohorts is above average, some by significant margins, reflecting the increasing proportion of Catholics making their way into the voting pool. Although here, too, the survey data varies significantly, and bearing in mind that being Catholic is not synonymous with being pro-unity, if these trends hold over time – and if younger voters don't change their minds as they age – a majority for unification will emerge as the trends in different age cohorts converge. It's a matter of when, not if.

The volatility of polling (see Table 5.2), the hugely differing outcomes and the incompatibility of their various methodologies makes relying on the results of polls to gauge support for unity or staying in the UK in a future border poll highly problematical.[130] This is especially true of the NILT surveys, which underestimate support for a united Ireland. SDLP leader Colum Eastwood says he is 'fairly unconvinced' by NILT, 'not just because it doesn't say what I want it to say, but because I've looked at some of their previous predictions on party percentages in terms of party strength; they've put Sinn Féin in the low teens and stuff like that. I'm not convinced that their weighting is right'.[131] Brendan O'Leary also cautions:

> I wouldn't want to rely on either polls or surveys on their own, partly because there appear to be specific problems with both of them [the Life and Times surveys and the LucidTalk polls] for reasons that may

not have anything to do with bias, it may be some kind of meth-
odological problem. They underestimate the support for hardliners,
and they appear to indicate a very significant section of the electorate
that doesn't care at all about anything, but might actually turn out at
a referendum. For a Secretary of State to work out how things are
going to go on the basis of polls and surveys, to my mind is not easy.[132]

Volatility in polling results is not specific to Northern Ireland. A YouGov
voter survey after polls closed in the Brexit referendum on 23 June 2016
showed 52 per cent for Remain and 48 per cent for Leave.[133] In the United
States, polls taken before election day on 3 November 2020 consistently
showed Joe Biden with comfortable leads over Donald Trump in key swing
states that turned out to be extremely tight. The polling industry has yet
to find ways to reach the less politically engaged in a mostly post-landline
telephone era. In Northern Ireland, a lot of non-voters are not apathetic
(although in some unionist areas they are); these people are Neithers – they
repudiate orange/green political categorizations.[134]

Opinion polls on a border referendum are largely devoid of context. They
ask vacuous questions. Are you in favour of staying in the UK – an option
that is tangible, concrete, something voters experience living there every
day – or are you in favour of a united Ireland, an option that is intangible,
illusory, whatever the voter wants to believe? Respondents can fill in the
blanks for themselves, meaning that no two respondents will have the same
understanding of what a united Ireland might look like. Party spin doctors
weave their interpretations into the results, driving the conversation in
one direction or the other, with no acknowledgment of biases or margins
of error, sometimes acknowledging a poll's shortcomings before blithely
ignoring the caveats they themselves have cautioned against.

Polls are weaponized. Proponents and opponents choose survey results
that buttress their positions. Sinn Féin looks at one set, declares itself well
satisfied and calls for a unity poll; unionists look at another set and declare
the union is safe, though with a trepidation that comes from what they see
as decades of betrayal by UK governments.

The commentaries are repetitive, raising expectations in the nationalist/
republican community and eliciting demands for a border poll from Sinn

Féin, while reinforcing among the unionist community the sense of denial that there is a need to engage with nationalists about the future. They give the impression that the two communities are preoccupied with the constitutional question when in fact what the ordinary people in those communities prioritize, according to most polls, are bread-and-butter issues such as the NHS, recovery from COVID and the economy.[135]

Multiple series of polls show that support for unity is increasing, albeit more slowly than what many commentators believe, while support for staying in the union is slowly declining.[136] However, the 2019 University of Liverpool poll reported that 63 per cent of those who did not know what the long constitutional future should be (15.2 per cent of the sample) were Catholic.[137] How they shift would have a significant impact on the border poll.

The Working Group also surveyed polling data. Brendan O'Leary noticed 'an upward tick in support for Irish reunification. That level of support I think will vary between now and 2030 depending on how well the protocol works or doesn't, and how well the Assembly does its business, or it doesn't'. He adds:

> It is [not] something … which will simply change at a steady rate per annum. Before 2001–2 the growth in the Northern nationalist vote amounted approximately to three-quarters of a percentage point a year since 1969. Of course, there's lots of complexities behind that. In the early part of the twenty-first century through 2016 the Northern nationalist vote stabilized. That reflects partly a considerable degree of satisfaction with the institutional arrangements of the Good Friday Agreement. That is what has been put in jeopardy by all things Brexit.
>
> We saw no further growth in the Northern nationalist vote, and we saw an overall decline in turnout, reflecting partly the trends that have occurred throughout European democracies: lower participation rates in elections. There was a certain degree of calm in both communities that votes for the Assembly were not existential votes. The unionist share of the vote has stabilized at about 40 per cent. It still continues on a very slight falling trajectory overall. That of course has magnified since 2016 with the growth of the Alliance Party, which is largely, in my view, a by-product of liberal Protestants who were pro-European and unhappy with the performance of both the major unionist parties. [138]

According to the University of Liverpool General Election Survey (December 2019), a majority in the 18–29 age cohort did not vote in the 2019 general election, yet they are the ones who are more socially progressive – more in favour of abortion, mixed relationships, same-sex marriages. Importantly, pro-union non-voters outnumbered pro-united Ireland non-voters by more than three to one.[139]

As Marcus Leroux, a London-based investigative journalist, points out in an opinion piece in the pro-union *News Letter*, 'it is not hard to see' why a swathe of younger Protestant non-voters, who were 'the cohort least keen on sending their children to an "own-religion school"; the least bothered by the suggestion a close relative married someone of a different religion; and most in favour of gay marriage equality', are 'politically homeless'.[140] Young Catholics and Protestants share the same attitudes on social media. Leroux continues:

> Taken in the round, a clear-eyed look at the numbers suggests that our template for understanding Northern Ireland is a generation out of date … The saviours of unionism are no longer found in the garden centre – they are more likely to be found on Instagram and TikTok and they are increasingly unlikely to call themselves unionists. On the other side, nationalism, too, needs new recruits to achieve a breakthrough: Northern Ireland's fate will not be determined by demography.[141]

According to his analysis: 'The better the pollsters were at seeking out the views of those who did not vote, the lower the support the poll showed for a united Ireland. The scale of the effect is dramatic: of polls that had at least half the proportion of non-voters as the wider electorate, none reported support for a united Ireland above 30 per cent.'[142] Unionist interviewees insisted that these pro-union non-voters would surface for a border referendum, which for unionism will be an existential election.

In the two decades since the B/GFA, there has been a significant realignment of identities in Northern Ireland. The proportion of the population self-identifying as neither unionist/Protestant nor nationalist/Catholic, especially the latter, has given rise to the 'Neithers'.[143] Consistently being reported at over 40 per cent since 2006, Neither was the designation of choice for 49 per cent of the 18–45 age cohort in 2019, rising to 55.9 per cent among 18–29-year-olds.[144] If this sizeable section of the electorate is one key to how a border poll could turn out, it is also germane to a referendum being called by the Secretary of State in the first place.[145]

The Neithers are 'persuadables',[146] open to changing their minds on the question of the union. They are now one of the key demographics. In terms of voting patterns, the most significant movement has been to the Alliance Party, officially neutral on the constitutional question, whose voting share rose to 16 per cent across three elections in 2019.[147]

'In the December 2019 general election,' says Katy Hayward:

> we saw Alliance take votes from both the DUP and Sinn Féin for the first time in a surge of the middle ground. That was connected to Brexit and the hope of many Remainers that there might be a second referendum. We need to put it in that context, but generally speaking, it's all too easy to imagine Neithers deciding just to opt out of the formal democratic process.[148]

It is not clear at this point whether this is a trend or a once-off occurrence. So, who are the Neithers?

- They are much more likely to be female (62 per cent), to have 'no religion' (63 per cent), to be of both British and Irish identity (63 per cent), but are also most likely to identify as 'Northern Irish' (50 per cent).[149] They are also more concentrated in the 25–44 age cohort, although Neithers are spread fairly evenly across the generations, and it is not just a trend among the young.[150]

- They have gone to a religiously mixed school, are more likely to be highly qualified and have well-paying jobs and are more likely to have lived outside Northern Ireland.[151]

- By 2021, two-thirds of those with no religious affiliation described themselves as Neither.[152]

- According to the 2019 UL survey, only one in three of the Neithers voted in the 2019 UK general election that year. Two-thirds of those aged 18–44 who did not vote in that election self-identified as neither nationalist nor unionist.[153]

- 55.9 per cent of 18–29-year-olds identify as neither unionist nor nationalist. According to the UL 2019 survey, approximately 23 per cent of this 18–29-year-old cohort who do not state an identity preference are 'Don't Know' on the constitutional question.[154]

- Neithers are more likely to support Northern Ireland staying in the UK – almost twice more likely to favour devolution than Irish unification.[155]

- After 2012, Neithers began to swing towards supporting Alliance, at first slowly and then as a surge: in 2021, Alliance secured 34 per cent support of the Neither vote, doubling what it had in 1998.[156]

The Neithers are a malleable cohort, with a signifyingly higher proportion of Don't Knows on Northern Ireland's constitutional status than the overall electorate; the Neithers are susceptible to moving in either direction, but predominantly into Don't Know, depending on the prevailing political winds. Support for a devolved power-sharing government within the UK has been the constitutional preference of this group over a twenty-year stretch. Support for unity peaks among both Catholics and Neithers when the Executive and Assembly are not working, and it reverts to support for a devolved power-sharing government within the UK when these institutions are functioning. When their support for the union falls, they tend to become Don't Knows, which was one in four Neither voters in 2017.[157]

Malleability cuts in both directions. The better the Stormont Executive functions, the more open people in the republic will be to a marriage of the two jurisdictions.[158] But the more the Neithers – and this includes a sizeable proportion of the Catholic community – are satisfied with the certainty and stability a smooth-functioning Stormont brings, the more reluctant they will be to trade their position in the UK for a new constitutional dispensation with all the uncertainty and disruptions that will entail. They will also be conscious that the transition to Irish unity will bring its own set of disruptions and uncertainties to their communities, with possibly a return to sectarian violence. Should the Stormont government continue to malfunction – which has been the pattern over the past decade and more – perhaps more Neithers will be open to moving towards some form of unity. Conversely, the existence of a badly malfunctioning Northern system will make Southerners less disposed to unifying with it.[159]

The argument that if Northern Ireland cannot work ('a failed political entity', to use Charles Haughey's phrase) the alternative is a united Ireland brings false equivalence to a new level. It is a form of magical thinking to believe that an entity, which fails in one political dispensation partly because one community (the nationalists) wants it to fail, can successfully be transferred into a new dispensation where another community (the unionists) works just as diligently to ensure it fails. 'You need to remember that most of those people who say "Neither" or "Don't know" are middle class. They're not going to be like turkeys and vote for Christmas,' says Billy Hutchinson, the former Ulster Volunteer Force (UVF) member who heads the PUP:

> They see that they have a very good living in Northern Ireland, within the United Kingdom, and that they have a good level of salaries and public services and all the rest of it, and those people will always vote to stay. They're not going to go into the republic and not have free education or free healthcare.
>
> People like me will vote because it's a political decision – I want to remain British. There's no economics to it. But there will be others who are dithering in the middle, who are neither unionist or nation-alist, and they will make an economic decision. And that economic decision will always drive them towards the UK, because they're better off there. But we don't know what's going to happen in two generations' time. People won't remember the Troubles then. I hope, in another two generations, people will have their own brand of pol-itics and they'll move forward.[160]

In a border poll campaign, both nationalists/republicans and unionists will target voters self-defined as Neither who are perceived as malleable on the constitutional issue. Their votes will be swayed by the prevailing political circumstances and the traffic on social media the opposing cam-paigns generate, one relentlessly and vociferously pro-unity, the other just as relentlessly and vociferously pro-remaining in the UK. Just as social media contributed to the bitter polarization of the Brexit referendum cam-paign, consider what social media would do with an impending border poll, spewing torrents of disinformation into an internet void with a capa-cious appetite for divisive content, feeding on itself and ultimately getting reflected in public opinion.

In this era, social media has emerged as a vehicle for hate, virulence, dis-information, conspiracy theories, spurious argumentation, turbulent alter-native realities, the trashing of expert opinion and evidence-based facts. In a divisive border referendum campaign, what Hannah Arendt called 'the fabric of factuality'[161] will be largely absent. Social media will create a toxic campaign atmosphere that will probably exacerbate the propensity for low levels of loyalist and republican violence, sufficient to drive Neither voters into their ethno-national silos.

The social infrastructure in Northern Ireland is delicate. Both com-munities easily succumb to the sectarian social biases that define them, retreating to the refuge of their respective narratives.[162] The dynamics of group behaviour, especially in situations of great insecurity and uncertainty which a contentious border poll would foment, will invariably result in a retreat to particularistic identities, as was the case, for example, in the former Yugoslavia.[163] 'Group identity may become increasingly important,' political scientists J. Snyder and R. Jervis write, 'not only intrinsically but because the security of individuals becomes implicated with the fates of the contending groups. Group identity can then be a consequence of conflict as much as a cause of it and can be fuelled by security concerns.'[164] Perceptions of threat solidify in-group solidarity and out-group hostility. After the 2016 Brexit ref-erendum, when uncertainty regarding the impact on Northern Ireland was high, there was significant retreat to their respective communal in-groups by Catholics and Protestants. A far more polarizing border poll campaign would almost certainly see a stampede to opposing ethno-nationalist silos.

'One of the most interesting aspects of the work of the Working Group on Referendums,' Katy Hayward, one of its members, says:

> was to begin to think about the regulations regarding referendum campaigns. I found that really fascinating, not least because I had just read Peter Geoghegan's book *Democracy for Sale*,[165] which is about the huge challenges to the democratic processes that we see particu-larly through the use of dark money, online campaigning, use of social media and manipulation of public opinion through this. Both the UK and Ireland are completely unprepared in terms of regulating that area [referendum campaigns] in a way that will assure people about the outcomes of a referendum. The report is pretty good on this.[166]

Among the Working Group's recommendations were that:

- Public authorities should 'provide a certain amount of necessary information in order to enable voters [in a referendum] to arrive at an informed opinion ...'

- 'Voters should be able to know so far as possible what each option entails before choosing ...'

- 'There are *adequate measures to constrain misinformation and manipulation* [my italics].'

- 'People should be able to find information on how each of the options would affect their lives.'

- The 'processes [that will be followed to unify the island] are mapped out in advance'.

- The question in Northern Ireland is worded so as to maximize clarity, allow campaigners to project their messages effectively and avoid any bias.

- The issue of the languages on the ballot paper is taken into account. All of these considerations matter for the public legitimacy of the vote and voters' ability to make an informed choice.

The Irish border poll campaigns will be highly polarizing, particularly in a society like Northern Ireland, which is already deeply divided along ethnic and religious lines. (Over two-thirds of voters North and South believe a border poll will be accompanied by violence.)[167] Binary choice referendums are inherently divisive.[168] Differences of opinion morph into contagious, polarized groups; expose existing cleavages in society; allow latent grievances to reappear; and often bring to the forefront contentious issues once thought to have been settled. It is highly likely that the promulgation of falsehoods, distortion of positions, pillorying of one's opponents and smearing of reputations one step short of libel will characterize a referendum campaign. Such behaviours are not uncommon during referendums on divisive issues in societies far less divided than Northern Ireland.

To expect that somehow there is a set of codes of conduct that both protagonists will be required to abide by, as though they were boxers in the ring being instructed by the referee on the Marquess of Queensbury rules, is utopian. The British government trying to enforce standards, especially if the rules are set by that government, would be perceived by nationalists and republicans as being an intervention in favour of the pro-union side.

The Working Group on Referendums also suggested that there should be a period of three years at most between the Secretary of State announcing a border poll and the poll itself. This – and a substantial lag is absolutely necessary – sets the stage for its own mischief. One cannot even begin to fathom how matters might play out in the interregnum if the Secretary of State is proceeding on the basis of a stated belief that the likely majority for unity is 50 per cent + 1 or some similarly narrow margin. How would the tenuous power-sharing administration stay functioning during that period? How would loyalist paramilitaries respond? And dissident republicans?

The problem is that opinion polls can only give a measurement of how respondents are likely to make decisions at a point in time. Desired outcomes are of course rarely achieved, assumptions about the future course of events are invariably faulty, disinformation is rampant. A border poll that fails but will be repeated not sooner than seven years afterwards until one succeeds is a prescription for instability, and the Secretary of State would be better off now making it clear that opinion polls on unity will not be a criterion unless it emerges that they provide unequivocal support for unity, including a significant element in the unionist community over a sustained period.

The key variables that will decide how a referendum will turn out are: how successful unionists are in motivating their traditionally non-voting pro-union voters to vote; how successful nationalist republicans are in shifting the approximately 9–10 per cent of Catholics who are Don't Knows on the constitutional question into the pro-unity column; how successful the pro-unity and pro-union campaigns are at targeting the 31 per cent of non-voters who have no position on the constitutional issue; and how successful both campaigns are in targeting the Don't Know cohort on the issue among those who do not identify as either nationalist or unionists voters.

The great majority of interviewees for this book are emphatic that there should not be a Brexit-type referendum, with a simple, binary choice between Irish unity and staying in the United Kingdom. Voters should know what kind of united Ireland is on offer. There is no easy route to determining what criteria a Secretary of State should draw on to merit a referendum.

While interviewees across the board mention opinion polls, they recognize their shortcomings. Nevertheless, they turned to a series of consistent opinion poll results showing support for unity within a certain amount of time as the best barometer of public opinion. Peter Robinson, for example, would not accept LucidTalk polls as a fair indicator; Colum Eastwood would not accept NILT.

There are other takeaways. There is a huge disparity between when nationalists and republicans think a border referendum should be held.[169]

Across the board, political party interviewees accept 50 per cent + 1 as a democratic outcome in a referendum. But whereas nationalists and republicans believe the same metric should be used to convince the Secretary of State to call a poll, unionists argue for a much higher threshold. Voters, North and South, would also like to see a higher threshold. They fear that violence would accompany a referendum poll that passes with a narrow margin.[170] If a referendum resulted in a very slender pro-unity outcome, there would be loyalist violence; if a very slender pro-staying in the union, there would be dissident republican violence. Loyalists are most concerned about republican violence but suggest there might be an uptick in loyalist violence too.

The most cogent case for a super-majority in a unity referendum was put by the late Seamus Mallon of the SDLP. 'I do not believe in the kind of "democracy" that leads to conflict,' he wrote in 2019, shortly before his death:

> If we have a 50 per cent + 1 vote for unity, that is when the real problems for the whole island will begin. I believe there is a real risk, based on the precedents of Irish history, that it could lead to a major resumption of violence, this time led by the loyalists. I believe Dublin and other Southern cities and towns would not escape that loyalist-led violence, which would be aimed at making the new all-Ireland solution unworkable, in the way loyalist bombings of Dublin and Monaghan in May 1974 were aimed at making the Sunningdale Agreement unworkable. Will a narrow vote for unity lead to harmony and friendship, as laid down by the new Article Three of the Irish Constitution, between unionists and nationalists? I very much doubt it.[171]

Most interviewees agree that 50 per cent + 1 pro-unity is a necessary but *not* a sufficient condition for a border referendum. At present and for the foreseeable future – unless there is an external seismic shock to the Northern Ireland body politic like a successful Scottish independence referendum – none of the criteria a Secretary of State might draw on to signal a majority of voters in favour of unity are evident. The key requirement, as Naomi Long points out, before a peaceful border poll can even be contemplated, should be a B/GFA that is functioning through its three strands.

In short, all paths to a referendum run through Alliance.

— SIX —

The North: Jekyll and Hyde

Sinn Féin and even some Social Democratic and Labour Party people can't even say the words 'Northern Ireland'. This really angers a lot of unionists. However, the fact is that some unionists won't say 'Republic of Ireland' – 'they'll say 'the South' or 'that place down there'. We can't even agree on what we call the country we're trying to govern together. Unionists will talk quite often about 'the Northern Ireland Executive'. But Sinn Féin only talk about 'the Executive'. On the key issues like the name of the state, the name of the government, the name of the building you're using, we can't even agree on things as commonplace and basic as that.[1] How the hell do you even begin to start the conversation about legacy? Whose fault is it that we ended up in thirty years of terrorism, and we have ended up still poles apart twenty-two years after we signed the Good Friday Agreement?[2]

– Alex Kane, journalist, former Press Officer for the
Ulster Unionist Party (UUP)

Nationalism in Northern Ireland, even the more moderate kind, is not friendly towards unionism, and they should stop pretending that they are. Unionists don't pretend that they're particularly concerned about or interested in nationalism. Nationalists won't, of course, recognize

111

Northern Ireland. They didn't recognize the state, they didn't recognize
the police. They got a reward, it took a long time, the better part of a
century before they got a reward for not recognizing it.[3]

– Ben Lowry, *Belfast News Letter* editor

The physical and economic transformation of Northern Ireland is
obvious, but after a few days back in the province I began to realize that
this new veneer of normality is misleading. Beneath the surface, several
elements of peace – closure, justice, reconciliation, healing and strong
leadership – are still sorely lacking. The failure to address the legacies
of the Troubles matters. It nourishes hatred. It hampers reconciliation.[4]

– Martin Fletcher, former NBC News Middle East correspondent
and Tel Aviv Bureau chief

Since the 1998 Agreement we have had divided politics, but increasingly
blended lives. Our political structures moved us forward. But we have
outgrown them. The Covid-19 pandemic might be seen as a trial run for
future politics. For climate emergencies. For events that we cannot even
imagine yet, which will blow orange and green politics out of the water.[5]

– Claire Mitchell, freelance journalist

From one perspective, things are very different. There's almost no killing.
Having said that, when you scratch below the surface, it's not a 'normal'
society. The political debate is probably more bitter than it's been for
a long time. It's not actually over current violence, it's about past vio-
lence ... The main issue is that Sinn Féin believes that killing people was
justified. There are no Protestants nor any free-thinking people from a
Catholic background who will accept that scenario.[6]

– Philip McGarry, psychiatrist and former chair of the Alliance Party

This new Northern Ireland which we've all been trying to live in since
1998 hasn't really had a vision attached to it ... One side will feel they're
gaining, one side will inevitably feel they're losing. Unless we develop a
vision of something better for us all, I think we will have failed at that
vision part. Then that's where the narrative – particularly in loyalist
communities – comes from, where they say 'there was no peace divi-
dend for me' ... the sense of loss rather than the sense of gain.[7]

– Rev. Lesley Carroll, Presbyterian minister and prisoner ombudsman

We don't have a mature, reflective approach to dealing with what
happened over the course of the conflict here. We still have fault lines,
which are run through green and orange sectarian lines. However, on a
positive note, I have a nine-year-old daughter, Saorlaith, so the life that
she is living now is markedly different from the life I have had in this
society. That progress should never be discounted.[8]

– Máiría Cahill, former Sinn Féin activist, former Seanad Éireann
senator, former Social Democratic and Labour Party (SDLP)
Councillor, Sunday Independent columnist

Northern Ireland is beset with paradox: at once normal and abnormal,[9] robust and fragile, forward-looking and trapped in the past, stable and unstable, vibrant and stagnant, where the detritus of the conflict, mined by elites for partisan polarizing purposes, can cause the political axis to tilt in one direction or the other. In 2001, political scientist Jennifer Todd and sociologist Joseph Ruane wrote: 'Powerful structurally based tendencies towards conflict remain, while the uncertainty about the future produces new divisions within as well as between the political parties. This makes for a crisis-prone political environment. It follows that current political crises are not simply transitory but endemic within the new situation.'[10] More than twenty years on, it is striking how apposite their analysis is. A sense of pre-cariousness overhangs a Northern Ireland still unsure of itself and where it is heading. The North oscillates uneasily between haunting memories of a low-level war and the vagaries of an uncertain peace; everything is scrutinized for whether it might tip the balance in one direction or another.

Since the Belfast/Good Friday Agreement (B/GFA), life in Northern Ireland has changed immeasurably for the better: the violence that was pervasive for three decades is over. Belfast has been transformed beyond recognition. 'Ordinary' crime is the lowest in the United Kingdom (UK).[11] Tourists flock to see the Titanic centre in Belfast, named the world's leading tourist attraction in 2016.[12] The Giant's Causeway, the Dark Hedges, the Cushendun Caves and the twenty-three other locations where *Game of Thrones* was shot in its beautiful landscapes, sea-to-sky horizons and undu-lating hills put Northern Ireland on a global tourist map.

Belfast joins the ranks of only nine cities in the United Kingdom that employ more than one-fifth of its workforce in the technology sector.[13] Northern Ireland is the best place to live in the UK and start a business, according to a 2021 PWC study.[14] The Organisation for Economic Co-operation and Development (OECD) ranks Northern Ireland as among the top-performing regions internationally according to several socio-economic indicators which measure well-being, and on a par with the best-performing regions in the republic.[15]

In the political arena, young people in particular find common cause across many issues.[16] They are less interested in the incessant talk regarding a border poll or Irish unity and want a government that attends to the problems that are priorities for them, such as finding good, well-paying jobs and access to higher education. They are progressive on issues like abortion and LGBT+ rights. They tend to identify as Northern Irish or 'equally British and Irish', not as either 'Irish only' or 'British only'.[17] For many, the past is 'ancient history'.

The SDLP leader Colum Eastwood says:

> If we make the conversation about the past, it's done before we get started. It has to be about a promise of a vision for the future and a perspective for a different kind of country. If you look at the electorate that will decide the future – the Alliance and Neither-type voter – they're not going to buy into some sort of statement that is about righting old wrongs. It's not going to be built on the rubble of our past.[18]

Parallel with this young, outward-looking Northern Ireland[19] there exists – a full generation after the B/GFA – a Northern Ireland that is still deeply divided, unable to unshackle itself from the chains of its past, still haltingly stepping into an uncertain future, still sharpening oppositional narratives of what the conflict was about and who to blame for the bloodshed and death. This Northern Ireland experiences ongoing levels of paramilitary activity, albeit mostly criminal in nature; chronic unemployment in the most deprived areas;[20] and community coercion and 'gatekeeping'. Here the past is still prologue to the present, and the remnants of collective trauma can trigger spirals of regression, fragmentation and implosion. A flag flown on the wrong day or not at all can provoke a riot. 'It's a deeply scarred community', says conflict resolution specialist Rev. Gary Mason.

> One in five ex-prisoners drink themselves to death. We have the highest prescribed antidepressant prescription rates in Western

Europe, and one of the highest in the world. We are a very traumatized society, particularly in the inner cities. There is an uncertainty
about where things are actually going to go.[21]

This division between the Catholic nationalist/republican community and
the Protestant unionist community has become sharper since Brexit and
the resulting increased noise around a border poll.[22] Nationalists for the
most part embrace the Northern Ireland Protocol (NIP), perhaps a little too
warmly because it is so opposed by unionists. The Protestant community,
once ascendant, is on the decline; the Catholic community, once under its
thumb, is now ascendant. For the first time in 2020, Catholics were more
likely to be employed in the public sector workforce than Protestants, with
the gap closing in the private sector as well.[23] One community is anxious
and uncertain about the future, the other is confident and forward-looking.

The influential Belfast priest Father Tim Bartlett points out that in the
aftermath of the B/GFA:

one of the critical changes we are observing that proves that we
didn't really deal with the deeper fissures is that there's a new generation of nationalist republicans that is incredibly self-confident,
[that] has grown up with no memory of the awfulness of violence
and its consequences. The conflict has been very romanticised into
a narrative about the older Irish Republican liberation cause, back
to the 1916 Rising.[24]

This generation is 'unaware of the Troubles and how terrible they were in
terms of human tragedy, other than in a very vague sense that this was just
a simple struggle, a continuation of the old struggle and a continuation of
its valiant ideal'.[25] In contrast, he adds, 'the young people of that generation
on the loyalist side have grown up with a narrative, not of religious hatred,
which would have been a stronger part of the narrative in my day within
the Protestant/unionist/loyalist tradition, [but] of betrayal, risk, threat
and insecurity'.[26]

While the post-B/GFA period has led to significant gains to society in
the North, the expected economic bounce has been insignificant in the
communities most in need. Northern Ireland remains reliant on the UK for
welfare and public-sector spending, making it the most highly subsidized
of the UK regions. A 2019 paper by Ireland's Economic and Social Research

Institute (ESRI) finds 'no evidence to suggest that Northern Ireland has benefited from any peace dividend [and] it remains one of the poorest UK regions'.[27]

Sinn Féin in government, according to Bartlett, has done little to alleviate the most pernicious social and economic needs of the communities it represents. 'West Belfast, parts of Derry, North Belfast still have the highest levels of childhood poverty, food poverty, working-family poverty, of any part of these islands. Where the hell was the "we're in this to raise everybody's boat" revolution from Sinn Féin and the republican movement?'[28]

This continuation of poverty and deprivation has provided the oxygen for paramilitary groups to squeeze their communities into staying in lockstep. Areas of East and West Belfast and Derry/Londonderry are among the most deprived in the UK, with little prospect of a more prosperous future, fuelling alienation that in turn feeds sectarianism.[29] Sectarianism and the hatred it spawns remain largely unaddressed, not because of insufficient effort by multiple public-sector agencies, NGOs, ample resources and the heroic work of individual community leaders and workers, but because the gestalt of sectarianism is so encompassing and the serial socio-economic structural deficits so impervious to change.

There is little in the Northern Ireland Executive's pipeline that could bring in the massive investments these communities need to crack the hundred-year toxic core of poverty and sectarianism, to eradicate the structural barriers that maintain and reinforce them. Huge sums of money would be required beyond the fiscal limits of Stormont, let alone a British government with more pressing concerns and priorities. Between December 2019 and December 2021, the average Northern Ireland household income increased by a meagre £90 a year, while the top 5 per cent richest across the UK have increased theirs by £3,300.[30]

What has been established is that across a wide political landscape, seemingly random events can trigger eruptions at any time, hindering reconciliation. 'The absence of stable government and the implication that socio-economic factors are treated as politically secondary,' concludes Duncan Morrow in his book *Sectarianism in Northern Ireland*, 'means that these factors, and the way in which they interact with issues of peace and conflict, continue to be dealt with in a disjointed fashion.'[31]

Sectarian divisions complicate efforts to apply equality-based criteria to social policy. Furthermore, the ways in which actions designed to address poverty and interventions aimed at reducing conflict interact are poorly developed, often setting policies at odds. Although it receives relatively little attention, economic inequality across society – especially in the area of employment – is now clearly more significant than the differential between communities.[32]

A 2016 study by Ulster University's Economic Policy Centre found that the gap 'between the lowest skilled and highest skilled' is greater in Northern Ireland than in any other OECD country.[33] Despite improvements, the centre's 2020 study showed that Northern Ireland 'has a significantly lower proportion of its population educated to at least secondary-level education (often regarded as an overall base level of skills) compared to other EU countries'.[34] In parts of Belfast's Shankill Road and Falls Road areas, containing key interfaces between Protestant and Catholic working-class communities, more than two-thirds of school leavers fail to achieve the General Certificate of Secondary Education (GCSE) or an equivalent qualification, providing fertile ground for recruitment by the paramilitaries.[35] However, Catholic boys have higher levels of educational attainment than Protestant boys.[36] Graham Spencer and Chris Hudson write that 'many loyalists feel ostracized from the socio-economic benefits of peace and look upon the idea not with interest but disdain, removed from its appeal and excluded from participating in the brighter future it suggests has arrived'.[37] Instead, loyalist youth may look for opportunities in other ways. Says Naomi Long:

> Most of the young people who get involved in the paramilitary these days are vulnerable young people, often from very deprived backgrounds … who are lured into … organized crime gangs, whether it's through drug dealing or other kinds of racketeering. They see these people in their communities. They have good cars, they have cash in their pocket, they get to go away for holidays to nice places. We need to identify those vulnerable young people … We need to go in and start tackling the underlying problems in those communities, so they become more resilient.[38]

What has not changed stands starkly in contrast to what has. Segregated housing and education seem impervious to change. Primary and secondary education remains as segregated as ever,[39] with only about 7 per cent of students attending Northern Ireland's 68 integrated schools out of Northern Ireland's total of 1,091 schools.[40] In general, children born after the B/GFA are educated in the same schools as previous generations.[41] For the most part, history is taught along communal lines. The curriculum offers two units: Catholic schools overwhelmingly choose to teach the 1968–98 unit, covering the civil rights movement and the Troubles; 40 per cent of state schools teach the unit covering the period 1920–49, including the Second World War, compared with one in ten Catholic schools.[42]

A 2021 LucidTalk poll reported that 71 per cent of voters were in favour of having children educated together, including 72 per cent of Sinn Féin and 59 per cent of Democratic Unionist Party (DUP) voters.[43] The 2020 New Decade, New Approach agreement between the parties declared that the present three-sector system – the Catholic, state (i.e., majority Protestant) and integrated education system – was 'unsustainable', and it pledged to examine the prospects of moving towards a single system.[44] Any effort to implement a single system would face formidable obstacles. The Catholic Church has a huge economic interest in maintaining the status quo and will not easily give up its role in shaping young minds. 'If you start to dismantle that system,' Brandon Hamber of the International Conflict Research Institute at the University of Ulster points out:

> you're not only dealing with the deep, psychological, moral reason as to why people think it's a good system. There is the financial imperative. Now you also have an institution [the Catholic Church] which is slowly falling apart internationally. Here, in Northern Ireland, it still can get to young minds and educate them with the belief system that it's slowly losing across the world.[45]

There are other obstacles to integration, with parents' choice of schools for their children also constrained by geography, wealth, the availability of integrated schools and car ownership.[46] While housing segregation has been declining slightly in Belfast since 2001, 90 per cent of houses are still either in entirely Catholic or entirely Protestant areas.[47] 'Peace walls' have proliferated – approximately a hundred are still in place.[48] But the peace walls are only the most visible and blatant manifestation of the bulwarks in place to reinforce segregation between the two communities, ensuring that social divisions remain. Hamber, who is part of a group called 'Hidden Barriers' that tracks and documents the less visible and more subtle markers of segregation, says:

> We look for streets which are closed, streets where there are bollards, where shopping centres have been built or a business park has been built to divide the two communities. If you take the big, emblematic things like peace walls as your marker of social change, you could say, 'Well, some peace walls have come down, but society is still divided.' If you take those actually more hidden barriers like tree lines, roads that separate communities, those that don't even register in the public discussion, you'll see they're much more insidious in terms of the divisions that exist between communities.[49]

According to the highly regarded economic analyst Paul Gosling,

> In March 2019 there were nearly 39,000 applicants on the social housing waiting list, of which almost 28,000 were recognized as being in 'housing stress', while 11,323 households were accepted as statutorily [sic] homeless. With less than a thousand new social homes built in 2018–19, at that rate it would take more than a decade to house just those who are accepted as homeless. Instead of the construction of large numbers of new social houses, there has been a growth in the private housing sector.[50]

Moreover, 'Northern Ireland has become the only part of the UK where the private housing rental sector is larger than the social housing sector.'[51] Two and a half years later, the situation had gotten worse. Over 44,000 households were on a waiting list for social housing, just 834 units had been built in 2021/2022. It would take up to fifty years to clear up the existing backlog.[52]

Higher education is another fault line. Northern Ireland has a net outflow of thousands of students (17,425 undergraduate and postgraduate students studying in Great Britain in 2018–19), most of whom do not return.[53] On average, just 36 per cent have returned to Northern Ireland six months after graduation.[54] Add the 15 per cent of graduates of Northern universities who migrate for employment after graduation, and the picture that emerges is of a significant brain drain – a cohort of well-educated young adults who for one reason or another do not want to live in Northern Ireland – which affects innovation and productivity, significant drivers of economic growth, as well as the vibrancy of wider society.[55] A significant proportion of these students who go to study in English and Scottish universities and do not return are from unionist backgrounds.[56]

> *We can't pretend there isn't a deep trauma in the society.*[57]
>   – Matthew O'Toole, SDLP Member of Assembly (MLA)

> *Northern Ireland represents what you would call a negative peace: where political violence has certainly decreased dramatically, but the underlying issues like social division, housing division, educational division, although changing slightly, are the same as what they were before. Then there are other factors, which actually have not dropped dramatically: the so-called political punishment beatings, or the physical and violent assault of adolescents and children by paramilitaries, have continued. The statistics over the last ten years have not changed dramatically.*
>
>   *It's not a particularly good diagnosis for a peace process. In terms of decrease in violence and general physical security, you would have to say it was successful, but in terms of those other issues, you couldn't really make the argument that it was a success.*[58]
>   – Brandon Hamber, Professor, International Conflict Research
>   Institute (INCORE) Ulster University

The lingering psychological impacts of the conflict, especially the continued existence of deeply traumatized communities, pose a different kind of threat to social cohesion. Despite several commissions of inquiry and agreements among the political elites to address them, issues concerning the past – including flags and emblems, parades and sectarian flashpoints – keep the drivers of division humming. In 2002, only three years into the B/GFA, Duncan Morrow, shortly to become head of the Northern Ireland Community Relations Council, observed:

> After all the effort spent on resolving the constitutional dispute through the Agreement, the conflict turns out to be driven as much by a need to protect against and avenge the legacy of conflict itself than by the future of the Irish border. In other words, the conflict continues even after the 'reasons' for the conflict have been resolved: conflict ends up being about the conflict. For Northern Ireland, this holds out the prospect that a constitutional settlement, no matter how far-reaching, will be threatened by the internal 'common sense'

that makes trusting a mortal enemy absurd and makes into a potentially fatal mistake any acknowledgement that 'our team' inflicted
injury rather than merely suffering it.[59]

More than two decades on, these observations have not lost their salience.

Areas of Northern Ireland that bore the brunt of the conflict continue to
experience trauma from three decades of sectarian violence, undermining
social cohesion and precluding the emergence of empathy – a necessary
ingredient for developing intercommunal trust and a willingness to forgive.
There is little ground for a shared understanding of the past and a commitment to a shared future, both prerequisites for reconciliation. 'It's still a war,'
says the Rev. Lesley Carroll, Presbyterian minister and prisoner ombudsman,
'We haven't moved to that new place of building something together':

> We're still in that space of trying to work out who was responsible
> for the conflict. Even when we get into a better place on that issue, as
> sure as anything, somebody will say something that annoys some-
> body else and we'll go back into the old blame game. A large part of
> that can be connected to the experience of trauma, where resisting
> blame, blaming others, looking for somebody to pin it on, are all
> trauma behaviours.
>
> We have learned how to react, overreact and react again to prac-
> tically everything that we hear. Trauma is a large part of it. The fact
> the war is not over is a large part of it; so too is the fact that nobody
> appears willing to step up and say, 'this was my bit' without asking
> what your bit was. If people would come at it that way, it would be
> better, but we haven't yet found that capacity to step up and say 'this
> was my part' and then to stop. There's always a 'but' or 'you did' or
> 'you provoked'.[60]

The two communities, especially in working-class areas – those bastions of
republican and loyalist support – are sealed in their respective physical and
mental enclaves. 'An isolated community that disengages from the broader
community,' Dr Eugen Koh, who has been studying trauma in Northern
Ireland for several years, writes:

> will only redefine their existing culture; they are self-referential and
> self-reinforcing. They will not be enriched by new elements from the
> outside. Some communities in Northern Ireland are so isolated that

they are more like potted plants that require constant feeding and are easily manipulated; unlike those that are grown in the ground with deep roots [and] are more resilient.[61]

The Commission for Victims and Survivors estimated that about 500,000 people – almost one-third of Northern Ireland's population – exhibited either physical or mental problems attributable to the conflict, the latter alone for 200,000 people.[62] Brendan O'Leary and John McGarry point that 'nearly two per cent of the population of Northern Ireland have been killed or injured though political violence', a figure close to one in fifty of the population. On an equivalent ratio of victims to population, this would have amounted to 100,000 killed in the UK or 500,000 in the United States, about 10 times the number of Americans killed in the Vietnam War.[63]

Post-Traumatic Stress Disorder (PTSD) is pervasive.[64] One estimate puts 39 per cent of Northern Ireland's population as having experienced at least one traumatic event related to conflict.[65] According to the World Mental Health Survey Initiative's Northern Ireland study of Health and Stress, the rates of mental illness in Northern Ireland were among the top three highest out of the countries surveyed, and 8.8 per cent of the Northern Ireland adult population met the criteria for PTSD at some point in their life, while 5.1 per cent had met the criteria in the previous twelve months.[66] The rates of PTSD were the highest of the countries in the initiative, including Lebanon, Israel and Iraq.[67] Accounts of the conflict are handed down from one generation to the next through deeply ingrained tribal lenses. Collective memories reinforce starkly contrasting narratives of the conflict: one tribe's victim is another's terrorist, with binary thinking obviating more nuanced versions of incidents of violence that might lead to empathy with the 'other side'.

At the individual level, trauma associated with the conflict can be transmitted inter-generationally, in addition to toxic stress of household trauma. At the societal level, historical trauma across generations is embedded in cultural trauma, culture as the 'social consciousness that holds the collective experience together'.[68] 'That inter-generational trauma and animosity, that sense of fear and injustice has been carried down through the generations,' says loyalist community leader Winston Irvine. 'The main fault line is the allegiance, or the identity divide between those who affiliate with Irish nationalism and those who affiliate to British Unionism (or Irish Unionism), which lies the very heart of the underlying conflict.'[69]

Between 1965 and 1997, 3,983 deaths by suicide were recorded in Northern Ireland; from the 1998 peace agreement to the end of 2014, 3,709 people died by suicide – almost the same number in half the amount of time.[70] In contrast, 3,636 deaths due to the conflict took place over the period 1966–99.[71] In their comprehensive review of suicides in Northern Ireland, academics Siobhan O'Neill and Rory O'Connor report that 'Northern Ireland has the highest rate of suicide in the UK, [rising from] 143 registered in 1996 to 305 in 2017'.[72]

Lower rates of suicide during the conflict have been attributed to 'increased social integration as a result of the perceived need to protect families and neighbourhoods from threat'.[73] Suicides in the most deprived areas were almost three times higher than in the most affluent.[74] The higher suicide rates are related to the conflict.[75] 'Most of the main violence ended twenty-five years ago,' says Philip McGarry, 'but an Irish ceasefire means you keep on shooting people for a long time after that.[76] When you have violence being accepted, then violence in the home and suicide become more acceptable.'[77]

The suicide rate in Northern Ireland almost doubled from 1998 to 2008, following the previous decade during which the rate declined from a low level of 10 per 100,000 of the population to 8.6. Queen's University sociologist Michael Tomlinson suggests the once quotidian violence – which saw external expression during the conflict – has been turned inward.[78] In the decade after 1998, the age group most susceptible to suicide was adults who had been children during the 1970s, the most violent decade of the conflict. Recent studies have shown that through epigenetic molecular changes to DNA, trauma can be biologically transmitted, and that PTSD may be as much biological as psychological.[79]

There were also 35,000 shooting incidents and 15,000 bomb explosions over the course of the conflict.[80] Over 42,000 people were injured as a direct result of the conflict.[81] One in every five eighteen-year-olds suffers from a significant mental health problem.[82] Surveying the literature for her study, 'Suicide: Northern Ireland,' the research analyst Dr Lesley-Ann Black reported that Northern Ireland 'experiences 20–25 per cent higher levels of mental health illness than the rest of the UK', and that 'one in 10 ten children experience anxiety or depression, which is around 25 percent per cent higher than in other UK jurisdictions'.[83]

Domestic abuse is at epidemic levels, Police Service of Northern Ireland (PSNI) figures show.[84] In 2020–1, there were 19,036 domestic abuse crimes and 31,196 domestic abuse incidents, the highest figures since recording began in 2004–5 – this equates to 85 incidents and 52 crimes every day.[85] More women are murdered per capita in Northern Ireland than in any other part of Western Europe, other than Finland, at three times the rates in England and Wales.[86]

'It's not just enough to say it's just about the conflict,' Brandon Hamber explains, 'it's about the fact that the conflict also intersects with social divisions. Issues like high use of prescription drugs or alcoholism, these things are going to intersect in those poorer communities, added to the legacy of the conflict. That is of course, a recipe for more mental health challenges.'[87]

In 2011, the United Nations Office of Drugs and Crime found that Northern Ireland reported the highest annual prevalence of prescription opioids (8.4 per cent), antidepressants (9.1 per cent) and sedatives (9.2 per cent) in the world.[88] In Northern Ireland health surveys, between 18 and 20 per cent of the adult population consistently report signs of a mental health problem.[89] In neighbourhoods controlled by paramilitaries, people learned to keep whatever resentments they might have to themselves. Seamus Heaney's famous line 'Whatever you say, say nothing' is the most succinct and telling expression of the ethos in these ghettos. 'The level of undealt-with anger,' says Máiría Cahill, daughter of a prominent republican family who went public with her claim that she had been raped by a member of the Irish Republican Army (IRA), 'that hardness about people, the complete inability to process or manage emotion, and high-anxiety stress levels, moves on to your children if you haven't dealt with it yourself.'[90]

> *Women in some communities, most pronounced in loyalist communities, feel the pressure of unreconstructed paramilitaries and their continuing imposition on communities. There are women acting as gatekeepers in those communities. There are women who were threatened in those communities when they tried to stand up and do something different. They were very concerned about the young boys being groomed and the young girls being used as trophy girlfriends. Women articulate this in different areas of Northern Ireland.[91]*
>
> – Bronagh Hinds, co-founder of the Women's Coalition party

All of the eulogizing and mythologizing of the Troubles is really dangerous, because it weakens the resolve of young people and particularly vulnerable young people who may not feel that they will ever amount to much in this life, whose aspirations are low, who expect that they will live and die in the same community, in the same streets, and have no real impact on anybody. How do you talk to those young people if somebody hands them a gun and says, 'Take this, son, and shoot somebody and then you'll be a hero. You'll end up with your mural on a wall. You'll end up with people writing books about you and singing songs about you'? How do you break that cycle?[92]

– Naomi Long, Minister of Justice, Alliance Party leader

You know what it's like when you're in Belfast? You can't walk in inner-city areas more than twenty metres before you're looking at some mural memorializing violence. Hubert [Butler, the Irish historian], he says, 'The sores of Irish history are present every single day.' You have kids at five, six, seven years of age meandering to school, and they're seeing a picture of a man on a wall and they're saying: 'He's dead. Who killed him? He's being commemorated. Why?' Edna Longley said, 'I think we should build a monument to amnesia in Ireland, and then forget where we put it.' Because these murals are everywhere.[93]

– Rev. Gary Mason, Methodist minister, Director, 'Rethinking Conflict'

Paramilitary organizations have not gone away, nor have all their stockpiles of weapons. While not engaged in overt military activity, they are not out of the business of violence either. In the poorer urban Protestant and Catholic neighbourhoods, their tentacles reach into most socio-economic activities. These dissident republican and loyalist groups still administer punishment beatings and kneecapping to maintain a control over their working-class estates; they deal in drugs and other criminal activities, known to the authorities but tolerated as a price worth paying for deflecting them from re-engaging in sectarian killings and targeting members of each other's community. As psychiatrist Philip McGarry says, 'We are a society where violence is normalized. Of course, the IRA haven't stopped. There has not been a single year in the last fifty years when the IRA haven't stopped shooting people ...'[94]

There were 1,460 paramilitary shootings and 3,691 paramilitary-style attacks between 1994 and 2014. Between 1990 and 2014, 519 young people under the age of 18 were victimized by paramilitaries in so-called 'punishment shootings' or beatings.[95] 'When you have this kind of violence being accepted, then it is no surprise that violence becomes less unacceptable,' says McGarry,

> but in effect the violence was licensed by the government. 'Internal housekeeping' is the cynical term that is used to describe IRA punishment beatings of young people. Sadly, the governments have allowed the IRA to keep on doing that. To be seen to be dealing with 'petty criminals', if quietly, was approved by many people. As long as our politics remain separate, segregated and poisoned, and we honour the myths of the past, there will always be organizations which seek to use non-democratic methods. Nothing will change if our politics remain sectarianized and in thrall to Irish and British nationalism.[96]

In October 2015, according to a report by the PSNI and MI5, 'paramilitary groups remain a feature of life in Northern Ireland … all maintain a relatively high public profile in spite of being illegal organisations'.[97] Their leaderships were committed to 'peaceful means to achieve political objectives',[98] and paramilitary groups had played 'an important role in enabling the transition from political violence to political progress'.[99] However, despite these positives, it concluded:

> [We] judge that individual members of paramilitary groups with a legacy of violent activity still represent a serious threat to national security, are engaged in organised crime and undermine Northern Ireland's post-conflict transformation. They cause serious harm to the communities within which they are embedded and undermine support for policing.[100]

With the continual glorification of the past, a post-conflict generation is attracted to paramilitaries. Says loyalist community leader Colin Halliday:

> There is an element coming through, a younger element here, who were not involved in the conflict, who somehow believe they've missed out; you can see it amongst the young ones now, we hear it being said: 'We are not going to be the generation that lets Ulster down.' As if by some reason, the 15,000-odd people who ended up in prison for fighting republicans and the hundreds of our members who died somehow let the people down.[101]

One threat to the peace process comes from dissident republican groups – the Continuity IRA/the Real IRA/the New IRA – who rejected the B/GFA. Dissident republicans are still mounting terrorist attacks, primarily directed at the PSNI and other security forces. Although the number of such attacks has fallen in recent years, they are still in double digits. Between April 2019 and March 2020, there were 21 bombings, or attempted bombings; 40 shootings; 30 firearms seized; and 774 rounds of ammunition found.[102] The IRA remains an illegal organization in the South, unlike in the North, where ignoring the IRA's public presence is a matter of political pragmatism. As long as the constitutional status of Northern Ireland remains conditional, republican paramilitaries will continue to portray themselves as custodians of the national cause, sentinels guarding their communities in the event of a resurrection of violent loyalist sectarianism.

The British government does not treat dissident republicans and loyalists as criminals: they have a special status. Republican and loyalist prisoners are segregated from other prisoners and each other at Maghaberry Prison.[103] Republicans wear their own clothes and have access to special amenities. In September 2020, dissident republicans staged a thirteen-day hunger strike to get their demands met and the government acceded.[104] A special committee liaises between the prisoners and the government. Says one official:

> If it means bigger sausage rolls, or a bigger television screen in their cell, if the choice is that they're going to chuck bombs into prison officers' houses and perhaps kill their children, we will give them the bigger screen. That's the moral of this. You could say there are limits, but it's down to that ridiculous level.[105]

And the two prison officers who were killed by dissident republicans, David Black in 2012[106] and Adrian Ismay in 2016,[107] 'were killed over things that for one reason or another we couldn't get movement on, which weren't significant'.[108] However, the flip side of this treatment is that, in the eyes of the dissidents, it confirms the legitimacy of their cause. Acquiescence to these demands is a corollary of the larger imperative to keep the peace at any price.

In 2016, an influential investigative report for the period 2005–6 to 2014–15 attributed '22 killings, more than 1,000 shootings and bombings, 787 punishment attacks, and nearly 4,000 reports of people forced from their homes' due to paramilitaries.[109] Security alerts halted more than 4,000 train services.[110] Paramilitary activity is not sectarian. For the most part it takes place within each community in areas that are almost exclusively loyalist or republican – attacks are against members of their own community, for criminal control in their own communities, and against the police.

The Fresh Start Paramilitary Panel Report (2016) concluded that a 'culture of unlawfulness' in many parts of Northern Ireland related to paramilitarism.[111] The committee conceded that the state cannot, of itself, disband paramilitary organizations:

> Continuing punishment attacks, evidence of economic crime, symbolic challenges such as flags, emblems and bonfires continue to create the impression that the rule of law is limited. This has a continuing impact on the long-term stability of Northern Ireland and on the ability to decisively tackle issues such as peace walls and segregation in residential areas.[112]

In November 2019, two years after the collapse of Stormont, the Independent Reporting Commission (IRC) provided a sobering analysis of ongoing paramilitarism: 'Continued paramilitarism is a profoundly de-stabilising factor and as long as it persists, peace and reconciliation will be much more difficult to achieve … Wishing it gone has not made it happen … so there needs to be a wider, deeper and more realistic understanding around what is required for a definitive end to paramilitarism.'[113] The report did not prescribe policy proposals, observing only that 'the task is a complex one that will require a sustained, long-term and holistic effort that combines a policing and justice response, side by side with a major and energetic tackling of the deep socio-economic issues facing the communities where the paramilitaries operate.'[114] The problem, of course, is that the Provisional IRA (PIRA), Ulster Defence Association (UDA), Ulster Volunteer Force (UVF) and their dissident spin-offs are deeply embedded in republican and loyalist communities, in which calling on the PSNI is synonymous with being an informer and thus a 'punishable' offence.

While this may be true, a complicated and symbiotic relationship is also present between paramilitaries, politicians and police. In efforts to maintain the status quo, police and politicians find themselves in an ironic predicament that requires them to groom relationships with paramilitaries to keep them engaged in peace-making while trying to eliminate their presence in communities in which they continue to be enmeshed. 'The response of government, politics and the public sector to paramilitarism is widely believed to be "two-faced" … rhetoric in favour of tackling paramilitarism is seldom matched by action on the ground,' says Duncan Morrow.[115] 'Over a long period of time the press has regularly carried allegations that former paramilitaries and alleged current paramilitaries hold visible positions of formal and informal authority and influence. Where these allegations are both denied and repeated but not investigated, many in the wider community are left unsettled and ambivalent.'[116]

Both governments are at fault. They make payments indirectly – through intermediary organizations – to paramilitaries, explained by a Northern Ireland youth worker as: 'You get the money because of the trouble. But if you stop the money, then they go back to the trouble.'[117]

The nationalist commentator Brian Feeney elaborates:

> They [the British and Irish governments] pay them. It's effectively bribery, and guys like Jim Wilson, Winky Irvine, Jackie McDonald, operating through the Loyalist Communities Council [LCC] purporting to represent the Red Hand Commando, UVF, UDA, are all salaried as 'community leaders' by the British and Irish governments. The Irish government operates through Cooperation North.[118] Wittingly or otherwise, they channel tens of thousands of pounds through men linked to unionist paramilitary organizations using the front of community groups. If violence broke out, these guys would be out of business. They wouldn't be able to employ any of their supporters in loyalist districts, which is what they do. They control the money that flows into loyalist districts.'[119]

Both Sinn Féin and the DUP pay supporters through the Social Investment Fund (SIF),[120] which disburses a lot more money than Cooperation North. The SIF, which the UUP and SDLP have called 'a slush fund', is in excess of £100 million a year.[121] It's controlled by Sinn Féin and the DUP. Both look after their own people through this. Loyalist front organizations are the recipients of tens of thousands of pounds from the British and Irish governments as an incentive to behave themselves. For example, in 2018 Dee Stitt, a North Down UDA commander and convicted robber, was forced to resign as CEO of Charter NI, which received £1.7 million from the SIF, because of his paramilitary background.[122]

Framing the narrative of the conflict, competitive victimhood and para-militarism are interconnected, says the Rev. Gary Mason, who leads work-shops on legacy-related issues:[123]

> Legacy is the biggest issue. It's not just about victims, it's about memo-rialization. It's also about commemorations. In his book *In Praise of Forgetting*, David Rieff tells a graphic story where he's in a room with a group of Serbs. He leaves the room, and some guy comes out and shoves a piece of paper into his hand. He opens it and sees some obscure date – 1389 – is on it. He looks at it, he goes back in the room with the Serbs, and he says, 'What is this?'
>
> They say, 'You don't know?' It was the battle of Kosovo, which the Serbs lost to the Ottoman Turks, which led to the disintegration of the medieval Serbian empire. One Serb said: 'You take away the battle of Kosovo, you take away the soul of the Serbian nation.' Over 600 years later, they used the loss in that battle [as justification] for the murder of 8,000 Bosnian Muslims at Srebrenica.[124] That's how powerful the past is. Unless we deal with the legacy, unless there's some architecture put around it, these stories are passed from gener-ation to generation to generation.[125]

In 2020, the Independent Reporting Commission called the presence of republican and loyalist paramilitaries a 'clear and present danger'.[126] In some areas, paramilitary groups are viewed as the go-to people to deal with anti-social problems. There were thousands of 'signed up' paramilitary members. Although 'only a relatively small number' were directly involved in illegal activity, issues around Brexit and dealing with the past had the potential to 'further and greatly complicate' the ending of paramilitarism, says Monica McWilliams, a member of the IRC and the former leader of the Northern Ireland Women's Coalition. 'The armed groups, paramilitaries that haven't disbanded, say "we're not going anywhere because we're needed", either to defend the union or an eventual united Ireland.'[127] The IRC's fourth report (December 2021) reiterated the warnings: 'We remain deeply worried about the risks posed to society by the continuing existence of paramilitary struc-tures which can be harnessed for the purposes of violence or the threat of violence … paramilitarism remains a clear and present danger.'[128]

Naomi Long, Alliance Party leader and Minister of Justice, says that getting a grip on paramilitarism and successfully implementing the programmes and policies that address its underlying causes in communities in West Belfast, East Belfast and Creggan in Derry and North Down 'will take us five to ten years at least of intensive work'. This will require 'asset-stripping the godfathers … making sure that there is no incentive whatsoever for young people [to want to join a paramilitary group]' and for 'politicians to stop giving the paramilitaries cover':

> It will also require from other parties the need to confront some of the issues in our community around coercive control, whether that's flags, emblems, memorialization and all of the other things that go with paramilitary activity … Until we can have those serious conversations we are trying to start in the Department of Justice with the political advisory group, then our options for being able to do anything meaningful will be limited.[129] As long as politicians give paramilitaries cover, it will be exceedingly difficult to root out the paramilitaries.[130]

> *There's no shortage of approaches that have been put forward for dealing with legacy issues. The real question is why. One of the reasons is that because this is a small and divided place, political power is balanced in a 50-50 way. Everybody has something to lose by delving into the past.*[131]
> – Brandon Hamber, Professor, International Conflict Research Institute (INCORE) at Ulster University

> *Legacy issues are not going to go away when our generation leave the stage. If we don't deal with it we will continue to have these competing narratives about the Troubles, these competing understandings of what is truth, and about what happened. I think that those will continue to poison the well in terms of good relationships on this island until it's resolved.*[132]
> – Naomi Long, Minister of Justice, Alliance Party leader

> *Some people in the British and Irish governments have honourably tried to deal with legacy in order to bring about reconciliation, but it has just not happened. There's no sign that spending another million or £500 million would do it.*[133]
> – Paul, Lord Bew, Professor of Irish Politics at Queen's University Belfast

In January 2020, when the Stormont government was relaunched after three years of suspension, the British government, as part of the New Decade,

New Approach Agreement, committed to introducing legislation to implement the legacy aspects of the Stormont House Agreement (2014) within
100 days. It also committed to engaging with Northern Ireland's political
parties and the Irish government in 'an intensive process' to 'maintain a
broad-based consensus' on these issues.[134]

The Stormont House Agreement, hammered out by the political parties
themselves, represented a major step towards dealing comprehensively
with the past.[135] It established several bodies: a Historical Investigations
Unit (HIU), an Independent Commission on Information Retrieval (ICIR),
an Implementation and Reconciliation Group (IRG) and an Oral History
Archive (OHA), the last of these including a research project led by academics schooled in conflict resolution and related fields who would plot a
factual timeline and perform a statistical analysis of the thirty years of the
conflict.[136]

Among the areas falling under the agreement's broad investigative
umbrella, according to Brian Rowan, author of *Unfinished Peace: Thoughts
on Northern Ireland's Unanswered Past*, are:

> alleged collusion, British and Irish; alleged ethnic cleansing in border
> regions and in interface neighbourhoods; the alleged UK 'shoot to kill'
> policy; the targeting of off-duty UDR [Ulster Defence Regiment] sol-
> diers, prison officers and reservist RUC [Royal Ulster Constabulary]
> officers; the degree to which, if at all, the Republic of Ireland provided
> a 'safe haven' to republican paramilitaries; intra-community violence
> by paramilitaries; the use of lethal force in public order situations;
> detention without trial; mistreatment of detainees and prisoners; the
> policy behind the 'disappeared'; and the sources of financing and
> arms for paramilitary groups.[137]

In short, 'the recommendations included setting up structures to collect the
stories of the conflict in and about Northern Ireland, investigating unresolved
cases, seeking information for victims from responsible groups, ensuring
statements of acknowledgement for past hurts and identifying steps to build
reconciliation'.[138]

In 2016, the Stormont House Agreement was tabled at Westminster. A
public consultation followed during which over 17,000 responses were
received. The UN Special Rapporteur for transitional justice came to Belfast
twice with his own set of recommendations. The British government

responded that 'the recommendations can be best achieved through the full implementation of the Stormont House Agreement'. A summary of the consultation on the agreement was published in 2019. There was, the British government said, 'an obligation to seek to address the legacy of the past, reiterating its commitment to the Stormont House Agreement'.[139]

On the Northern Ireland front the proposals were stillborn, enabling legislation in the UK stalled, while a few prosecutions of British soldiers proceeded. Each community had its own priorities: for republicans and nationalists, the focus was on wrongdoing by the security forces and collusion with loyalists who had murdered 'known' republicans or random Catholics; for unionists, it was the murder of RUC and UDR personnel, who were often off duty or had retired from the security forces.

Like other issues of consequence, legacy fell into the maelstrom of zero-sum politics: the parties squabbled belligerently, accused the 'other side' of being responsible for the worst atrocities, tried to entrench their own narratives of the conflict as the overarching architectural framework for the Stormont House Agreement and fought over who should be called a victim and who should be prosecuted and on whether amnesty should be offered in return for truth.

'Trying to find a consensus on legacy is even more difficult than Brexit and the protocol,' says Alliance deputy leader Stephen Farry. 'We're now in a situation where the UK government has given up on the Stormont House Agreement and are promising to bring forward their own proposals, which aren't going to work at all. We're probably back to square one on legacy if we have that particular scenario played out.'[140]

'You're talking about things that happened thirty years ago,' Rev. Gary Mason says. 'Yet every day they're part of someone's story. That is why unless we deal with this legacy – I'm not saying we will go back to war – we're going to be in a very damaged, trans-generational trauma space forever.'[141]

In 2020, matters came to a head over who should qualify for a Troubles pension.[142] The scheme was repeatedly delayed by political wrangling over who should pay for it, and whether those injured by their own hand should be eligible. Individuals who had sustained severe or permanent injury caused by 'no fault of [their] own' qualified for a pension. This included physical injury, such as a loss of limbs, or psychological, such as being in the vicinity of a bomb explosion.

Sinn Féin refused to nominate a Stormont department to administer the scheme after objecting to the eligibility criteria in the Westminster legislation, which excluded former paramilitaries convicted of causing serious harm. Michelle O'Neill only agreed to sign off on implementing the scheme in August 2020 after being at the receiving end of an extremely critical court judgment accusing the Executive Office of acting 'unlawfully' in its delays.[143]

Asked in the 2019 University of Liverpool poll whether only innocent people should be called victims, the responses varied as widely as 80 per cent and 72 per cent among UUP and DUP voters respectively, to 41 per cent among Sinn Féin voters in agreement – a two-to-one ratio differential.[144]

Rev. Harold Good, the Methodist minister who helped oversee IRA arms decommissioning, adds:

> There are those who still demand retribution, for the want of another word. There's a lot we could learn from South Africa's Truth and Reconciliation Commission, which we are not willing to consider because, for many people, you cannot put the past where it belongs until you have full retribution … The whole legacy thing is what also makes it very difficult to think in terms of moving towards a new dispensation on the island of Ireland, because until that is resolved, and until we can be a happier, more contented, more united Northern Ireland, what part could we have within a new Ireland, either for the sake of the total island or for any of us [here in Northern Ireland]?[145]

The British government changed its commitment to the Stormont House Agreement on the back of concerns about possible prosecutions of British army veterans. Legislation proposed in March 2020 called for the creation of a single body primarily focused on information recovery and reconciliation rather than investigating killings. The legislation would have set a presumptive five-year time limit on prosecutions for members of the British army who had served overseas as well.[146]

The DUP applauded the proposed legislation;[147] Sinn Féin rejected it out of hand.[148] The Catholic Church also felt compelled to enter the dispute.[149] It rejected Lewis's assertion that his proposals were 'consistent with the principles' of the 2014 Stormont House Agreement. In a letter to Lewis, Archbishop Eamon Martin (the Catholic primate) and his fellow bishops emphasized that victims must be 'given priority' and 'justice would be pursued, where possible, regardless of the identity of the perpetrator'. The UK government, they asserted, had moved the goalposts from the position of 'equal access to justice for all', and 'state and non-state actors must be equally accountable before the law. Otherwise, no authentic reconciliation can be achieved'.[150] Lewis's proposals, they argued, were a 'departure from the understanding inherent in the Stormont House Agreement to which all parties signed up to with goodwill'. They warned that legislation on the proposals 'could destabilise the Executive and other institutions', which were fragile, having only resumed operations 'after three years of political sclerosis'.[151]

Once again, the past became a contentious issue as the parties lined up on either side of the proposals. The primate's intervention simply reinforced the Protestant perception that for all the blather about the Catholic Church eschewing politics, that Church was a republican arm in clerical clothing. Whenever the North has an opportunity to bury a stereotype, it goes out of its way to reanimate and even strengthen it.

Unable to deal with the past, despite the innumerable models from other countries, Northern Ireland turns inward, as its emotionally crippled communities compel their political leaders to lash out at each other with accusations that the other is at fault for the interminable delays in righting legacy's wrongs. It is almost a cliché to recall William Faulkner's apt line that 'the past is never dead. It's not even past'.

Soldier F epitomized the depth of the seemingly unbridgeable divide. In 2019, he was charged with two counts of murder for the deaths of William McKinney and James Wray during the Bloody Sunday massacre by British paratroopers of fourteen civil rights demonstrators in Derry/Londonderry in January 1972.[152] Unionists decried his prosecution. Banners and other symbols supporting Soldier F were on display throughout loyalist communities. Nationalist communities demanded their pound of flesh and called for the prosecution of more soldiers. In July 2021, prosecutors decided not to proceed with the case and moved to have the charges against Soldier F dismissed. William McKinney's brother Michael was granted leave to seek a judicial review of the determination that Soldier F should not stand trial.[153] (In March 2022, a high court judge quashed a decision by the Public Prosecution Service [PPS] to drop murder charges.)[154]

Other prosecutions also fell through: Soldier B for the murder of fifteen-year-old David Hegarty in 1972 and Soldiers A and C for the murder of Official IRA leader Joe McCann, also in 1972.[155] In July 2021, the UK government announced it would be proposing legislation to ban all Troubles-related prosecutions of paramilitaries as well as state forces from before 1998.[156] Scholars have argued that doing so would be in violation of human rights laws,[157] and Northern Ireland's political parties across the spectrum have condemned the plan. (COVID-19 may have been more influential in ending these prosecutions than legislation. In October 2021, Dennis Hutchings – a former member of the Life Guards regiment on trial for the 1974 murder of John Pat Cunningham, a young man with special educational needs[158] – died of COVID-19 while his trial was still in session; instead of a conviction or acquittal, his file was simply closed.)

Going on half a century after such killings, the families of the men murdered – many now next generations – fill the court rooms, intent on seeing justice done. There is no forgiving.[159]

In the book *In Praise of Forgetting*, David Rieff employs the therapeutic perspective via psychiatrist Janet Baird, who has argued that:

> both individuals' traumatic memories and the collective historical memories of groups, for all the obvious differences in the way that they are formed, retained and transmitted, retain the quality of 'now' rather than receding into the subjective past.[160] Baird says: 'Social stress seems to waken and activate the historical memory in such a way that the protagonists of the past become resurrected into the "now".'[161]

This alleviates social stress. Individuals self-medicate on their historical narratives. Perhaps also ameliorating a condition akin to continuous traumatic stress disorder, grievance – tightly held in affected communities – is a social glue that binds them.[162]

Under mounting pressure from Tory MPs to protect British army veterans from what Boris Johnson called 'vexatious prosecutions in their seventies and eighties', in July 2021 the British government unilaterally slammed the door on further prosecutions.[163] Brandon Lewis tabled new legislation at Westminster that included a statute of limitations on prosecutions of possible crimes committed before 1998 by paramilitaries and the security forces. Instead, Lewis proposed an independent body that would focus on truth recovery and reconciliation.[164] Legislation was supposed to follow that fall.[165] However, Lewis put the brakes on further legislation and continued to engage with victims' groups.

For once there was unanimity of agreement across all political parties and victims' groups in the North and from the Irish government that the proposals were unacceptable, although for starkly different reasons. DUP leader Jeffrey Donaldson said: 'There can be no equivalence between the soldier and police officer who served their country and those cowardly terrorists who hid behind masks and terrorized under the cover of darkness. We find any such attempted equivalence offensive.' (The DUP, both publicly and privately, continues to oppose any form of amnesty.)[166] In contrast, Sinn Féin deputy First Minister Michelle O'Neill said: 'The British government amnesty proposals are clearly an attempt to put state forces beyond the reach of the law and to continue to deny truth to families.'[167] In a rare moment of cross-community solidarity, the proposals were rejected by the Assembly.

Lewis's proposals provide a shield for British army veterans. The notion that the British government would ever agree to members of its armed services, especially soldiers of advancing age, confessing to some tribunal, is far-fetched. As recent failed prosecutions have shown, getting evidence-based facts that meet the threshold for criminal prosecutions is difficult after such a long number of years. Nor is the government about to reveal the Byzantine clandestine operations of M15, M16 and other intelligence agencies that colluded with loyalist paramilitaries and infiltrated republican paramilitaries.[168]

But the proposals also provide a shield for paramilitaries. As part of the peace negotiations, Sinn Féin insisted to Tony Blair that it might have trouble bringing the IRA on board the B/GFA – its arms-decommissioning element in particular – unless it secured guarantees of immunity from prosecution for over 200 IRA operatives who were 'on the run' (i.e., wanted for offences they could be prosecuted for) and who then received 'letters of comfort' from the prime minister given without the knowledge of other parties to the 1998 Agreement.[169] The fact that Sinn Féin objected to amnesty for others when it had demanded one, albeit in secret, for IRA members over twenty years ago, is one reason why non-republicans think of it as utterly duplicitous and snake-tongued.

Still, some fundamental questions need to be addressed. Are victims seeking truth or justice? And what comparative weight do they attribute to each? Most truth and reconciliation processes emphasize truth recovery over justice.[170] But perpetrators do not get off scot-free. Amnesty is held out in exchange for perpetrators giving a full accounting of possible crimes they may have been party to. In exchange, there is full amnesty for some and punishment for others in proportion to the offences committed.

A radical variant of this model has been proposed by the Committee for the Administration of Justice.[171] Prosecutions called for by the Stormont House Agreement would proceed, and cases would be brought to court. In the event of conviction, a prison term would be commuted once the Independent Commission on Information Retrieval was satisfied that the prisoner had fully co-operated and had made a full disclosure regarding the offence in question.[172]

A crucial test looms with respect to prosecutions. Superintendent Jon Boutcher,[173] head of Operation Kenova, handed over thirty-three 'charging decisions awaiting' files to the Director of Public Prosecutions 'containing evidence regarding serious criminal offences that include murder, kidnap, torture, misconduct in public office, perverting the course of justice and perjury'.[174] The evidence referred to relates to the activities of paramilitaries and the security forces. A full report on his investigations has yet to be published.[175] Meanwhile, more evidence of 'collusive behaviour' between loyalist paramilitaries emerged.[176] The past, as noted, is always present.

Then Secretary of State Brandon Lewis further antagonized parties across the political spectrum – some feat, given his standing in both communities – when he announced his 'compromise', which would supposedly deal comprehensively with the sheaves of protest crossing his desk. He promised legislation in 2022–3 incorporating 'a new approach … to immunity for those involved in Troubles-related incidents'. Now, 'an independent body will only grant immunity from prosecution on a case-by-case basis, based on an individual's co-operation with the body's inquiries'. In short, immunity is tied to a 'truth-recovery' process: amnesty is granted to those who agree to provide information on the nature of their actions in the past.[177]

Again, his unilateral legislative proposals – the Northern Ireland Troubles (Legacy and Reconciliation) Bill (2022) – were denounced by victims' groups, Northern Ireland's political parties and across the spectrum in Dublin as a back-door attempt to secure amnesty for British war veterans.[178] In a rare display of bipartisanship, Taoiseach Micheál Martin and opposition leader Sinn Féin president Mary Lou McDonald said the UK move demonstrated 'the same contempt for the kind of joint London-Dublin diplomacy that had made the Good Friday peace agreement possible twenty-four years earlier'.[179]

Meanwhile, the Northern Ireland Troubles (Legacy and Reconciliation) Bill made its way through the Commons. In the House of Lords, however, it encountered scathing criticism and a slew of amendments.[180] The incoming Secretary of State, Chris Heaton-Harris, in one of his first press conferences after his appointment in September 2022, admitted that the Bill could be improved. He would, he said, await the recommendations of the Lords.[181] Meanwhile, the trial of Soldier F resumed in October 2022.[182]

SEVEN

The South: 'The old order changeth, yielding place to new'

The Republic is not that Catholic 'green' edifice that it was back in the 1980s.[1]
– Will Glendinning, Alliance Party and former chief executive of the Community Relations Council

There are people who previously would have described themselves as unionist, have now preferred to describe themselves as coming from a unionist background.

They then look at the Republic of Ireland, and they see phenomenal change within their lifetimes. These are people who previously might have said, 'You know when you're going across the border because you're in a country where the roads are better, no little thanks to the European Union, and where the Catholic Church is no longer in charge.' They look at what the people of the republic have done in terms of same-sex marriage, in terms of reproductive rights.[2]
– Mike Nesbitt, Ulster Unionist Party (UUP) Member of Assembly (MLA)

What it [Sinn Féin in government in the South] would do would be to destabilize things, given their current stance on Northern Ireland. Their policy is that we need a border poll, and we need it now. I don't believe they will care if they only won that poll by 1 per cent. They will declare victory. They would have won their war and I'm not sure if they care much after that.[3]

– Niall Blaney, Fianna Fáil, Seanad Éireann senator

The rise of Sinn Féin in the republic had nothing to do with nationalism. It had to do with a poor government in the South and poor social issues. When Sinn Féin gets elected in the South it starts talking about having in the South the kind of social services we have here in the North. But the republic couldn't pay for it, so who is going to pay for it?[4]

– Billy Hutchinson, Progressive Unionist Party (PUP) leader

The Irish economy was most like Humpty Dumpty – bloated, fragile, sitting smugly at a great height and headed for a fall.[5]

– Fintan O'Toole, journalist, *The Irish Times*

During the long conflict, while Northern Ireland imploded, and in the decades following the Belfast/Good Friday Agreement (B/GFA), the South underwent an unprecedented social and economic transformation, shedding its image – assiduously cultivated after independence in 1921 – as holy Catholic Ireland, becoming an economic powerhouse and socially liberal society. The metamorphosis transformed a country, once the poorest in Europe, into one of the most prosperous. The impact of these political and societal upheavals is still being felt, signalling another round of transformational change in the works. Some of these potential changes, on the religious and economic side – cited by unionists in an earlier era as obstacles to a united Ireland – should mitigate that opposition among that coveted cohort, lower-case unionists. Other changes on the political front, most significantly the meteoric rise of Sinn Féin, are sure to harden opposition across all strands of unionism.

On the religious front, those decades witnessed the collapse of the moral authority of the Catholic Church and the marginalization of its influence on Irish public life and private behaviour.

The authority of the Roman Catholic Church was terminally undermined by the paedophilia scandals that rocked the country at the beginning of the twenty-first century, sounding the death knell for an institution that had been the bedrock of Irish society for hundreds of years. A series of scathing reports revealed the depth of collusion between paedophiles and their superiors. A government commission reported widespread rape and molestation as 'endemic' in Irish Catholic Church-run industrial schools, orphanages and 'any other place where children are cared for other than as members of their families'.[6]

The Church hangs on, performing baptisms, holy communions (now a social outing, signalling the coming of age of young children, rather than a religious event), marriages and death rituals, more transactional than faith driven. Its slow decline accelerated after the extent of the paedophilia scandals became public knowledge and it fumbled its response, displaying more defensiveness than absolute contrition. Yet, even as a decaying institution, it has tried to assert its relevance, fighting rear-guard actions opposing – though to no avail – amendments to the Constitution legalizing divorce, abortion, gay marriage and LGBTQ+ rights. Even in primary education, where it had iron-fisted control throughout most of the state's existence, the Church lost its grip. The parish priest, once the sole school manager with absolute authority, now has to share management with boards that include the laity. Attendance at Catholic schools no longer requires proof of baptism.

After a disastrous recession in the mid-1980s, the Irish economy began to recover in 1987. The historian Roy Foster succinctly documents the extent of the economic transformation that followed: 'Output in the decade from 1995 increased by 350 per cent a year,' he writes, 'personal disposable income doubled, exports increased five-fold and trade surpluses accumulated into the billions, employment boomed, migrants poured into the country.' Between 1987 and 2001, the annual rates of growth of gross national product (GNP) grew on average by 7 per cent a year, often reaching double digits.[7] The 1990s and early 2000s ushered in an era of spectacular and unprecedented prosperity during which Ireland had some of the highest economic growth rates in the European Union (EU).

The Celtic Tiger had arrived, and it swung its tail with gusto and abandon across the moribund corners of Irish society. Real gross domestic product (GDP) grew by an average of 9.4 per cent a year between 1995 and 2000, the year after the South became part of the eurozone, and by 229 per cent between 1989 and 2007.[8] Multinational companies accounted for 45 per cent of Ireland's growth in the first half of the 1990s and for 85 percent in the second half.[9] By 2000, with fourteen years of uninterrupted growth behind it, Ireland was on its way to becoming one of the richest countries in the world in terms of GDP per capita.[10] The growth engine was primed by several factors: low taxation; pro-business regulatory policies; a young, educated and tech-proficient workforce; and sterling performance in attracting foreign direct investment (FDI), especially from tech companies.[11]

Over the following decades as new technologies emerged, Ireland with its low tax laws – the 'leprechaun tax' of 12.5 per cent on corporations was well below the EU average – attracted a disproportionate share of their businesses in the EU.[12] The new multinationals – including Facebook, Google, Microsoft and Apple – established their EU headquarters in Ireland. Twenty-four of the world's leading pharmaceutical and biotech companies also have headquarters there.[13] The EU built the country's infrastructure, a transportation network criss-crossing the country; what once was a three-hour-plus drive between Dublin and Belfast now takes less than two hours. EU membership was also the gateway to lucrative markets in Europe, which diversified the economy and weaned exports away from Britain, though Britain remained the country's main trading partner. Between 1970 and 2000, imports grew eight-fold and exports twenty-fold.[14]

With modernization came secularization and consumerism. For a population that had once been taught that it is more difficult for a rich man to get to heaven than for a camel to go through the eye of a needle, the abundance of material undercut the old shibboleths. The days of 'Rome Rule' are over, a crucial obstacle to a united Ireland done with, according to Irish nationalists. 'At the time of partition,' Matt Carthy of Sinn Féin says:

> the most vociferous argument against Irish unity and Irish independence on an all-Ireland basis was the proposition that home rule would mean Rome Rule. The influence of the Catholic Church would be such that people of other denominations would be isolated and maligned in an Irish state. Certainly, the Irish state has moved a long way from Rome Rule. I don't think that any argument against unity would be based on religious reasons. The twenty-six counties now are arguably more pluralist and less dominated by religious tendencies than probably even the North.[15]

All this good luck, the vertiginous ascent to one of the world's top economic performers from one of the poorest within such a short time frame, was bound to become undone: Irish fatalism – nurtured on centuries of poverty, famine and emigration – demanded as much. In 2008, when the economy imploded, that implosion was accompanied by a certain perverse collective sense of its being inevitable. Many saw the previous decades of phenomenal success not as the product of a careful stewardship of the economy but as a stroke of good fortune – like winning the lottery – and good fortune eventually runs out. While it lasted, the craic had been great.

The worldwide recession, triggered by the collapse of Lehman Brothers, devastated the Irish economy. The banking system tanked. To prevent total collapse, the government underwrote its liabilities, requiring it to go cap in hand to the EU to borrow the €64.5 billion it needed – a liability Irish taxpayers had to meet.[16] The repayment schedule imposed by the EU was draconian and accompanied by prohibitive interest rates. The government responded by making huge cuts in public services and imposing extreme austerity measures. At the peak of the recession, the unemployment rate was 14 per cent. The economy contracted by 10 per cent and emigration surged to levels not seen since the 1950s and as bad as those during the recession of the mid-eighties, though a large percentage were migrants from other EU countries.[17] It took the economy several years to recover, regaining its 2008 per-capita income level only in 2015, but subsequently going on, again, to have the highest GDP growth rates among EU countries. And, again, the country consolidated its position as the beneficiary of huge inflows of FDI and as a global hub for tech companies.[18]

In 2022, one in every three workers in Dublin is a foreigner; overall, 18 per cent of the workforce is foreign born.[19] Nearly half of all adults (25- through 64-year-olds) in Ireland (47 per cent) have earned a tertiary qualification, one of the largest shares among member countries of the Organisation for Economic Co-operation and Development (OECD). The tertiary attainment rate is even higher among women (51 per cent compared with 43 per cent among men). Among the younger generation (25- through 34-year-olds), the share of tertiary-educated adults reaches 52 per cent of men and 60 per cent of women.[20]

Diversity is no longer an abstraction but a defining characteristic of Irish society. The country has one of the youngest populations in Europe with one-third of the population under twenty-nine years of age.[21] It has one of the most educated workforces in the world.[22] The share of 25–34-year-olds in Ireland with a third-level qualification in 2020 was 58 per cent compared with an EU average of 41 per cent.[23] Ireland's education system is among the best in the world. It ranks among the top ten globally for the quality of its secondary and university education.[24] According to the 2020 UN Human Development Index, Ireland ranks second in the world for quality of life in terms of income, education and health and mortality rates, outscored only by Norway. Gross national income per capita in 2020 stood at $68,371, fifth highest in the world.[25] Another study put Ireland among the five to survive global societal collapse.[26] The 2019 World Economic Forum (WEF) Global Competitiveness Report ranked Ireland as the twenty-third most competitive economy globally; the Institute of Management Development (IMD) placed Ireland seventh in its competitiveness ranking of 190 countries.[27]

Because of societal changes in the South, Colum Eastwood, leader of the Social Democratic and Labour Party (SDLP), says, the old arguments unionists raised against unity no longer hold water: 'Opportunities exist in terms of access to the global economy as a result of all of the new major companies being headquartered there. The South decided, as a society, to turn on the old institutions, and basically to run them out of town, and to decide what kind of progressive liberal society they wanted for themselves. And they've done that.'[28] Many unionist interviewees were not impressed. What they see is an economy that is subject to wild swings, boom or bust. Good times are fleeting, the arc of the economy dips too often, unlike their own economy, which, while underachieving, is primed by the United Kingdom (UK) treasury to withstand economic shocks. They choose stability over the uncertainty of a more dynamic economy, preferring one that is public-sector driven, more risk averse.

Much of this phenomenal growth is illusory, however, because it consists of the huge profits of the high-tech sector – including companies like Apple and Microsoft – that are exported to the United States.[29] Patrick Honohan, governor of the Central Bank of Ireland, calls GDP growth of 26 per cent 'a farce' and 'meaningless' as a measure of Ireland's economic performance.[30] (Perversely, Ireland has a higher GDP than GNP. The former includes all the profits of the multinationals, which are repatriated to the United States; the latter is what is left over after these transfers are made.)

As well as GDP per capita being a very skewed measure of well-being, Ireland is the most unequal society among the richer countries.[31] The top 10 per cent hold between 42 and 58 per cent of the country's wealth, the bottom 50 per cent a mere 12 per cent.[32] The high-tech/big pharma bubble in the Dublin region obscures multiple levels of poverty, a scarcity of affordable housing, poor access to healthcare, a severe shortage of social housing, a dysfunctional mental health system, one of the highest costs of living in the EU and huge levels of debt scheduled for repayment in a post-COVID-19 era.

The country is increasingly reliant on corporate tax receipts as a source of revenue.[33] Corporate tax revenue almost doubled between 2015 and 2021, with €68.4 billion in tax revenue in 2021, more than one in four tax euros collected.[34] Add in the income tax multinationals pay, and overall these companies account for about one in three tax euros.[35] What is troubling is Ireland's overreliance on a small number of foreign-owned multinationals for tax revenue. Ten foreign-owned multinationals, Fintan O'Toole notes, 'accounted in 2019 for 49 per cent of all income tax, USC and PRSI paid by companies amounting to €10.4 billion. They also contributed 42 per cent of VAT paid by companies that year – another €4 billion'.[36] Stripped of these sources of revenue, he concludes, 'the republic as a functioning fiscal entity would shrink so drastically that it would not be viable'.[37] But this reliance on the multinational golden goose means Ireland is increasingly beholden to decisions made in boardrooms in New York and elsewhere, revenue decisions the Irish government has no say in. Typically, when recessions threaten, multinationals first rein in their foreign operations.

On the horizon is the huge cost of meeting Ireland's pledge at COP26 in Glasgow to cut greenhouse gas emissions by 51 per cent by 2030.[38] This elephant in the room no government will be able to ignore. If Sinn Féin is in government, it will be called on to make unpopular decisions – as is the case with the present government – that impact its base and bring home to it the difference between hollering from the sidelines about the shortcomings of the players on the field and being a player themselves.[39]

While the agricultural sector will bear much of the brunt of Ireland's pledge to cut greenhouse gas emissions, the impact will be felt across all sectors of the economy.[40] The cost of transforming the economy to fall in line with the plan's goals, estimated at €125 billion, is sure to be a contentious issue.[41] The inevitable process of changing to a carbon-free society will be both transformative and painful.[42] However, in her address to the Sinn Féin Ard Fheis in October 2021, weeks before COP26, Sinn Féin president Mary Lou McDonald called on the government to 'scrap these carbon tax hikes', insisting that they 'push more families into poverty … will make life harder … [they] won't change behaviour or reduce emissions'.[43] This position is contrary to what the collective science says on the matter.[44]

On the surface, the economy seems extraordinarily resilient, posting a 3.4 per cent growth in 2020, the highest among OECD countries, despite the prolonged lockdowns and stringent sanitary measures implemented during the pandemic.[45] In October 2021, the Central Bank and Economic Social and Research Institute (ESRI) reported that Ireland's economy and GDP would grow by 7 per cent and 12.6 per cent respectively.[46] Unemployment, at 6.9 per cent, reached a pandemic low in December 2021.[47] FDI in Ireland rose by €71 billion in 2021 despite the COVID-19 crisis, mostly reflecting increase flows from the United States.[48]

The Central Bank of Ireland estimated that for 2020 and 2021 the total estimated expenditure on pandemic-related measures was €37 billion: 'A key challenge for government in the post pandemic period will be ensuring that measures designed to be temporary do not become a permanent part of the expenditure base.'[49]

The country will shoulder a total government debt of approximately €237 billion for 2021, up by almost €33 billion since the start of the pandemic.[50] Per capita this is a debt burden of €48,291, the highest across the EU and the UK.[51] If interest rates had stayed low – that is, close to zero – this would be a sustainable repayable amount. But any significant rise in rates due to the inflationary pressures the global economy began to experience in the latter part of 2021 will leave the country exposed. Ireland needs to be lucky. Concluding his study of change in Ireland between 1970 and 2000, Roy Foster writes that 'it is hard … not to recognize that in several spheres, not just the economic, a certain amount of good luck was maximized by good management'.[52]

In the decade ahead, the country is going to need another dose of the proverbial 'luck of the Irish' to cope with a deglobalizing world intent on shortening supply chains in an uncertain post-pandemic era, as mutations of the virus continue to outwit best efforts to contain it. The omens are not reassuring. Annual inflation soared to an almost forty-year high of 6.7 per cent by March 2022, the result of supply-chain bottlenecks, tight labour markets and, most significantly, the economic and political repercussions of Russia's invasion of Ukraine, especially skyrocketing energy and commodity prices.[53] 'A recession,' said Irish Taoiseach Micheál Martin, 'cannot be ruled out.'[54] Irish households, the ESRI warned in June, were facing the biggest fall in living standards since the 2008 financial crisis.[55] In August 2022, residential electricity bills increased by 10.9 per cent, which equated to €13.71 per month on the average electricity bill, and residential gas increase of 29.2 per cent, which equated to €25.96 per month on the average gas bill.[56] Almost 30 per cent of households were in energy poverty – where more than 10 per cent of a household's net income is spent on energy bills – the highest on record.[57] Fuel across Europe was in short supply. The government warned of rolling blackouts during the winter months,[58] and further increases in the price of electricity loomed.[59]

All is not going well in this new Ireland, which has thrown off the shackles of Catholicism and evolved from a poor, rural-based economy to a mega-high-tech, vigorous, vital and progressive society that prides itself on being a meritocracy, with the usual riders that a rising tide lifts all boats. According to a Behaviour and Attitudes Survey, 'Sentiment is pessimistic across all demographics. Whether young or old, male or female, "white collar" or "blue collar", a parent or not, whether living in Rathmines in Dublin, Rathmullan in Co. Donegal or Rathcormac in Co. Cork, almost half of people living in Ireland have indicated they see no end in sight to current hardships.'[60] In September 2022, one-third of the population was economizing on food.[61]

A report by SDG Watch Europe notes:

> Gross income inequality is higher in Ireland than [in] any other EU country. However, the impact of low taxation and social transfers is significant, bringing Ireland's net income inequality close to the EU average. Economic policies since the 2008 financial crash have exacerbated wealth inequalities, with a shift in income towards the top 10%. Between 2015 and 2017 the bottom 50% of people experienced a 2% fall in their share of gross income, while the top 1 per cent saw their share increase by 27%.[62]

The study concludes:

> Stark wealth inequalities exist alongside persistent social discrimination and low wages. This in particular affects members of the Traveller community, women, persons with disabilities, older persons

and people who identified as 'black' in the study. One in eight people experience some form of discrimination. Members of the Traveller community are ten times more likely to suffer discrimination while seeking work, and twenty-two times more likely to face difficulties in accessing private services, than people who identify as 'white Irish'. Women are twice as likely as men to face discrimination at work, while persons with disabilities are twice as likely to experience discrimination at work or while accessing private and public services. People who identify as 'black' are three times more likely than 'white Irish' people to experience discrimination at work and in accessing private services, and four times more likely in public services.[63]

However, research also indicates that real disposable incomes are higher for many in Ireland than in the UK. Using disaggregated Eurostat survey statistics, the economist David McWilliams shows:

> The people right in the middle in Ireland have 20 per cent more income, after tax, than the people in the middle in the UK, while the people in the middle in Norway, Switzerland and the US are richer. If you are in the middle in Ireland, your standard of living is about the same as the middle in most developed countries. The poorest 10 per cent in Ireland rank well above the developed-world average and some 45 per cent above their counterparts in the UK, while the bottom 5 per cent of Irish earners have a standard of living which is 63 per cent higher than that of the poorest people in the UK. [64]

'Socially,' McWilliams concludes, 'Ireland left the UK behind a long time ago.' Yet, for all the good fortune these statistics would portend, the Behaviour and Attitudes study referred to concludes that a million people – 20 per cent of the population – struggle to make ends meet.[65] Thus, the paradox: Ireland is well off by any measure with its EU neighbours, but anxiety about the future is pervasive.

On the positive side of the economic status equation, in 2021 the ESRI reported that income distribution disparities had narrowed significantly, and it estimated that real disposable income – after taxes, inflation, pensions and transfers – grew at 3 per cent a year between 1989 and 2019. Disposable income inequality had shrunk to its lowest level in the thirty years prior to the pandemic, a finding that contrasted with what was happening in other OECD countries where inequality increased over the same period.[66]

The impact of Brexit on the economy has been less severe than projected.[67] A study by Copenhagen Economics seems wildly off the mark, as Ireland has adapted to the new patterns of trade with remarkable alacrity.[68] Brexit disrupted historic trade patterns between the South and Britain, and between the South and Northern Ireland, setting in motion a reorientation of trade away from the UK to internal trade between the two parts of Ireland, thus changing the dynamics of the multiple relationship between the three entities in ways that have yet to fully play themselves out.

Before the Brexit vote, Britain accounted for almost 25 per cent of the value of all imports to the South. One year into implementation of the Trade and Cooperation Agreement (TCA), the value of imports had dropped to 7 per cent.[69] Or, to use a different metric, over the time period 2016–21, Britain's share of imports to Ireland dropped by two-thirds.[70] Irish exports to Britain, however, remain robust, rising 17 per cent to €14.4 billion in 2021.[71] In April 2022, the British government announced that it was rolling over the imposition of import controls on goods coming from the EU, this time until late 2023.[72] When it does, a further redirection of exports to the EU is likely.

In contrast, trade (in both directions between the South and Northern Ireland) is surging, as businesses find it less costly and cumbersome to buy from each other than from Britain. The value of Irish exports to Northern Ireland increased by 54 per cent in 2021 to €3.7 billion, a historic high. The acceleration of trade from North to South was even more pronounced – exports to the South jumped 65 per cent to €3.9 billion. This included '€1 billion in food and animals, a 43 per cent gain from 2020, and a tripling of chemicals and pharmaceuticals to €850 million'.[73]

Trade routes are undergoing adaptation. To avoid customs and regulatory checks, Irish hauliers are increasingly dropping the British land bridge – the route via Holyhead that connects Ireland to the rest of the EU via mainland Britain and across the Channel – to reach their markets in the EU. The number of trucks using the land bridge dropped by 30 per cent between 2019 and the first six months of 2021.[74] In its place, hauliers are using direct ferry services.[75] Thirty-two new ferry services ship goods directly from Rosslare to Le Havre, Cherbourg and Dunkirk in France and Zeebrugge in Belgium. The volumes of goods shipped directly from the South to the EU using these routes rocketed by 50 per cent in the first six months of 2021.[76] Traffic between Dublin Port and the UK fell by 21 per cent in the first nine months of 2021.[77]

All these trends signal a pattern – a weakening of the economic link in both jurisdictions with Britain – that is likely to deepen and broaden after the implementation of further regulatory and customs checks. 'By unleashing English nationalism, Brexit has made the future of the UK the central political issue of the coming decade,' former Chancellor of the Exchequer George Osborne wrote. 'Northern Ireland is already heading for the exit door. By remaining in the EU single market, it is for all economic intents and purposes now slowly becoming part of a united Ireland.'[78]

Irish voters went to the polls on 8 February 2020 and produced an historic result. For the first time in more than a hundred years since the founding of the state in 1921, neither Fianna Fáil nor Fine Gael emerged as the largest party. Sinn Féin won the most first-preference votes (24.5 per cent), which translated into 37 seats, one seat less than Fianna Fáil – which won 38 seats (22.2 per cent) with fewer first-preference votes, an anomaly of the single transferable proportional representation voting system – and the governing party, Fine Gael, at 35 seats (20.9 per cent). The combined vote of Fianna Fáil and Fine Gael also fell to a historic low.[79]

The results represented a huge generational shift in voter preference.[80] On a breakdown by age, Sinn Féin won pluralities of voters in every age group – in the 18–24 and 25–35 cohorts – a share greater than the combined share for Fianna Fáil and Fine Gael; only in the 65+ cohort did its support fall significantly to 12 per cent.[81] This is the age group that had witnessed the conflict in Northern Ireland since the late 1970s and are therefore most likely to identify Sinn Féin with the Irish Republican Army (IRA). For younger voters, especially in the pre-35 age cohorts, the conflict in Northern Ireland is something from times gone by, frozen in history, war stories their parents might talk about. It was peripheral to their concerns, and they couldn't associate Sinn Féin candidates (a lot of whom were in the same age range as themselves) with any of the gruesome details they sometimes heard. Sinn Féin was overwhelmingly the choice of a young population for whom Ireland, despite having an economy with the highest growth rate in Europe, did not address their concerns.[82]

The trajectory of Sinn Féin's rise underscores a fundamental politics in the South, anchored in parties that emerged in the 1920s after the founding of the state and that took a more right/left tilt after the civil war, though not to the extent prevalent in some European countries. 'Their strength is growing,' former Fianna Fáil Taoiseach Bertie Ahern, a past master of voting arithmetic, told me in November 2020. Soon, he predicts,

> Sinn Féin will be sitting on 30 per cent of the electorate, Fianna Fáil will be on, probably, 20 per cent or less at the moment … Fine Gael are probably sitting on about 30 per cent and then there's 20 per cent between Labour and other left-wing parties. That has totally changed. It's not that long ago that Fianna Fáil and Fine Gael between them held three-quarters of the votes. I'm afraid those days have moved on.[83]

Irish unification was not an issue in this election. In fact, exit polls revealed it didn't figure among voter priorities, not even receiving a recorded mention.[84] The lack of affordable housing (median housing prices doubled between 2013 and 2017), a broken healthcare system and the high cost of living were foremost in voters' minds.

Sinn Féin capitalized on the anger, especially among young people, at the prohibitively high cost of housing and the inability over the years of long-established governments of Fianna Fáil, which led the country into recession in 2008, and of Fine Gael, in government since 2011, which failed to redress the crisis. Young people flocked to Sinn Féin, whose election manifesto made a pledge to build 100,000 social housing units over 5 years[85] and to revolutionize healthcare along the lines of the British health service, without of course, mentioning the National Health Service (NHS) by name.

A second historic breakthrough from the 2020 election broke the mould of Irish politics. Fine Gael and Fianna Fáil had emerged out of the blood-soaked civil war of the early 1920s. One or the other (usually Fianna Fáil alone or Fine Gael in coalition with other parties) had governed the South for a hundred years. On policy issues it would be hard to find much difference, but the cleavages of that war had become entrenched in the body politic. After the election they faced a Hobson's choice: form a coalition, either with Sinn Féin or with each other.

They chose the latter, a variation on the theme that 'the enemy of my enemy is my friend'. They cited their concerns about Sinn Féin's close association with the IRA during the conflict and about who was pulling the decision-making strings, mentioning how decisions had to be cleared with the party's central structures, which included former members of the IRA, not elected officials – a throwback to how Cumann na nGaedheal (later Fine Gael) sought to define Fianna Fáil in the 1932 general election (the first one Fianna Fáil contested) as a party with a legacy of violence. A campaign poster had warned of 'the shadow of a gunman, keep it from your home'.[86] Now, under pressure from Sinn Féin, they set aside their residual differences and went into government together, with the Greens as a junior partner, in June 2021.[87]

Under the coalition's governing arrangements, Micheál Martin, leader of Fianna Fáil, serves as Taoiseach until the end of 2022, Leo Varadkar for the following two years. They are also to rotate the office of Tánaiste (deputy prime minister).

The new government got off to a rocky start: a dinner in Clifden, Connemara, attended by senior politicians and public figures, that violated mask-wearing and social distancing guidelines, sparking a rare bout of concerted public anger; the badly handled resignation of Phil Hogan, the EU trade commissioner, in its aftermath;[88] dissent among Fianna Fáil back-benchers; gnawing questions about Martin's leadership; perceived lack of discipline in the cabinet; and trouble trying to cobble together a coherent post-lockdown COVID strategy. Political mishaps diverted attention from the consequential issues the government had to address.[89]

Perceptions once formed are difficult to dislodge. In post-lockdown Ireland they continued to linger. When things were going well, members of the government tended to shoot themselves in the foot.[90] And with two major parties in a coalition where the head of government would rotate after two years, it was impossible to maintain absolute cross-party discipline.

In the end, Ireland had one of the most severe lockdowns in the EU, according to Oxford University.[91] Too often it found itself in the invidious position of alternating between having the highest infection rates in Europe or the lowest. In October 2021, Ireland was ranked best country in the world in Bloomberg's COVID Resilience Ranking, which measures where the pandemic is being most effectively managed with the least economic and social upheaval.[92] A study in the *Lancet*, a premier medical journal, cited Ireland as having one of the lowest rates of excess deaths in the world during the pandemic.[93] November 2021, just before the Omicron variant of the virus

swept across Europe and the United States, Ireland had the highest vaccination and lowest death rates from COVID-19 in the EU, according to the
European Centre for Disease Prevention and Control.[94]

None of this impressed the public, who were tired of shutdowns, re-
imposed restrictions, quotas established for gatherings, travel plans
aborted. It needed a scapegoat, and the government became the target of
its frustrations – all to the benefit of Sinn Féin, who gleefully attacked the
government from the sidelines, promising no such underperformance on a
Sinn Féin watch. Nevertheless, as Omicron began to crest in December 2021,
the public approved of the government's performance by a large margin.[95]
But nothing, it seems, could halt the inexorable rise of Sinn Féin. A Red C
tracking poll (January 2022) reported Sinn Féin at 33 per cent of first-
preference votes for the third poll in a row. At the beginning of December
2022, it had almost tripled its potential vote share in less than two and a half
years, a feat unprecedented in the annals of Irish electoral politics.[96]

Much of Sinn Féin's electoral success came from its relentless concentration on the housing crisis during the campaign. Exit polling showed that the
lack of affordable housing and healthcare had been the priority issues for 58
per cent of voters; among Sinn Féin they had been higher still at 66 per cent,
with housing taking precedence over healthcare.[97] Sinn Féin, in the course
of the election campaign, rarely went off message on these two issues and
were amply rewarded on election day.

Owning a house in Ireland is out of the income range of all but those in
higher-income occupations. Ownership rates collapsed from '60 per cent at
age thirty for those born in the 1960s to less than 20 per cent for those born
in the late 1980s'.[98] Renting eats into disposable income, absorbing greater
amounts than in any other country in the EU. Most economic activity is
centred in the Dublin metropolis, which accounts for 40 per cent of the
population and 55 per cent of GDP. It has a highly diverse and educated
workforce and draws workers into its economic web from eleven adjacent
counties. Its growth, according to the ESRI, is 'unsustainable'.[99] Dublin is
ranked fifth in the EU for financial services.[100] According to the price comparison website Numbeo, Ireland is the thirteenth most expensive country
in the world to live in, the tenth most when rent is included, and the fourth
most expensive in Europe, behind Jersey, Luxembourg and Switzerland.[101]
The EU's statistical agency, Eurostat, estimates that prices for goods and

services in Ireland are 40 percent above the EU average. Along with Denmark, it is the most expensive country in the EU to live in.[102]

Young people are caught in a no-win vice – because of the chronic shortage of housing combined with an ever-increasing demand, rents and the price of new housing are also among the highest in Europe. In 2019, just 8,000 houses built that year were for sale on the open market,[103] and just over 20,000 new dwellings were built in 2020 and 2021. During Q1 2022, 5,669 new dwellings were built, representing a 14.5 per cent increase in production over Q1 2021.[104] The price of a house in Dublin soared to €405,999 in 2021, resulting in long commutes and high rents.[105] According to a report from the Banking and Payments Federation Ireland (BPFI), the median total household income of new first-time buyer borrowers increased from €71,000 to €77,000 between 2019 and 2021. The median household income in 2021 was €56,659, according to the Central Statistics Office, a shortfall that makes buying a house out of reach for most of the population.[106] Market rents increased by 38 per cent between 2017 and 2022 and more than doubled over a decade. In May 2022, just 851 homes were available nationally for rent.[107] One result is that the number of homeless families increased 350 per cent between 2014 and 2019.[108]

Sinn Féin promised that Sinn Féin in government would deliver the largest public housing-building programme in the history of the state and a three-year lid on rents and reduction.[109] Its plan calls for building 100,000 houses in 5 years, including council housing and affordable homes for renters and first-time buyers, at a cost of €6.5 billion – possible, it says, because 50,000 social homes are already budgeted for under the National Development Plan.[110] Of the 50,000 remaining, 30,000 are budgeted at a cost of €50,000 per unit; the additional 20,000 include 10,000 rental units and 10,000 affordable homes.

Entering the second half of the coalition arrangement where Leo Varadkar and Micheál Martin switched roles, with Varadkar becoming Taoiseach and Martin Tánaiste in December 2022, there was little light at the end of the political tunnel this luckless government had blindly navigated during the first half of its tenure. It had been handed COVID, post-COVID supply shortages, soaring inflation, a surging cost of living, initial steps to meet carbon emission reduction pledges, disruptions caused by the war in Ukraine, including devastating increases in energy prices, and a housing crisis it just couldn't get a handle on. It watched a frazzled electorate take out its frustrations by turning in huge numbers to Sinn Féin, which sat in gleeful opposition calling out the government for crises very often beyond the government's control (though on occasion of its own making). But in one stroke of good fortune the government amassed almost €44 billion in tax receipts for the 7 months ending in July 2022, mostly big increases in corporations, leaving the exchequer with €5 billion to cushion residential energy costs or splurge on the October 2022 budget. This is the highest tax-take for the first seven months of any year. [111] The weary old Tiger still had a little wag left in its tail.

The coalition knows that its future in the next general election will be determined in good measure by its success in matching Sinn Féin's housing programme and getting it off the ground before the next election. Micheál Martin hailed what he described as 'the most ambitious programme of social and affordable housing delivery in the history of the state' as he unveiled the plan that aimed to increase the supply of housing to an average of 33,000 homes per year by 2025.[112] The government pledged €4 billion per year in 'guaranteed state funding', which it says is the 'highest-ever level of government investment in building social and affordable housing'.[113] That was before post-pandemic labour shortages, inflation, rising interest rates and soaring energy prices as a result of sanctions on Russian oil underwrote many of the plan's assumptions regarding cost into question.[114]

The influential economist David McWilliams writes: 'Politically, this coalition is in the last-chance saloon – and they know it. The future of the coalition parties at the next election is tied to housing. This is the government's Stalingrad, a last gasp effort to stop Sinn Féin. They'll live and die on housing.'[115]

— EIGHT —

The Two Economies: a study in contrasts

Because of the economic, single-island economy, increasing numbers of people who come from Northern Ireland are working in the republic and people from the republic are working in Northern Ireland … [Before the South would want to embrace the North in unity], we'd have to have the potential of a growing economy in Northern Ireland, instead of one that is completely held up by the public sector. The difficulty with that is … you're not going to get that vibrant economy until you have the all-Ireland structures and until the economy actually fully functions on an all-Ireland basis. That is the only way that our economy will grow.[1]
– Will Glendinning, Alliance Party and former chief executive of the
Community Relations Council

None of the Northern parties on the unionist side are prepared to use the autonomy Northern Ireland has to develop a distinctive Northern Ireland economy in collaboration with the South. They're terrified that the moment they appear to be able to stand on their own two feet and they become integrated economically with the South, the British will wash their hands of them. They don't want that. It's a paradoxical situation …[2]
– Dr John Bradley, international consultant on analysis and
modelling of economic development and industrial strategy

Remember, a hundred years ago, when partition happened, the twenty-six counties were leaving the biggest economic bloc in the world. You flip that on its head a hundred years later. The South is part of the biggest economic bloc in the world, we just left it.[3]

  – Colum Eastwood, MP, Social Democratic and
  Labour Party (SDLP) leader

I would be uncomfortable with a united Ireland because the South is a more neoliberal society. Fifteen per cent of the people in Ireland are living in poverty. That's never mentioned. GDP [gross domestic product] figures are skewed by transfer pricing … The Southern economy and its neoliberalism and the cost of living and no health service … none of that is in a blueprint, because if Sinn Féin are telling us in a united Ireland there'll be a public health sector, that's not what the Irish state is saying. There's no unity of purpose within those who supposedly want the united Ireland.[4]

  – Professor Peter Shirlow, Professor, Director, Institute of
  Irish Studies, University of Liverpool

People in Northern Ireland get better housing but at a much lower cost and are left with a lot more money to spend on things like holidays or whatever. Living standards are good in Northern Ireland, whether you're comparing with Great Britain or with the republic.[5]

  – Dr Graham Gudgin, Policy Exchange's Chief Economic Adviser

If we go down the route of trying to compare both economies and trying to assess is this economically going to succeed, or which way will we be economically better off, my assessment is it's going down a completely partitionist attitude as well. If you want to do this, you do it on the basis it's a political decision, it's not an economic decision …

What people don't talk about is the opportunity that will arise as a result of this new country that will get significant support from the country you're living in … from the European Union. I don't think we should just do this on the basis of totting up two ledgers … The debt at present in this country is enormous … it's enormous in the United Kingdom now as well. At some stage, we're going to have to, not pay it back, but we're going to have to stop borrowing at the same level.

There obviously will be economic consequences, but I don't think economic issues should dictate whether or not this happens … We'll

have nearly two million people in Northern Ireland joining five million people here. It would be an exciting prospect if it's handled properly.[6]

– Jim O'Callaghan, Fianna Fáil Teachta Dála (TD)

My fear is that at that point [Scotland voting for independence], if not before, English nationalists start looking at Northern Ireland. They say, 'We are paying you £11 billion a year to be a part of our club. That's a lot more than we were not prepared to pay for our continued membership of the European single market of 500 million customers.'

£11 billion to an English nationalist is a lot of money for acute hospitals, for policemen on the beat, for classroom assistants. My fear is once Scotland goes they look at us and they say, 'That's a lot of money. Half of you don't even want to be in our club. I tell you what, we'll just wind down the block grant over a number of years, as you prepare to get into bed with your colleagues across the border.'[7]

– Mike Nesbitt, Member of Assembly (MLA),
former Ulster Unionist Party (UUP) leader

At the time of partition, they controlled 80 per cent of the manufacturing in all of Ireland, was based in and around Belfast – 80 per cent. At the time of the 1916 rising, Belfast was bigger than Dublin. Now it's a shadow of that. The North used to be an economic powerhouse; now it's a basket case, and what we want to do is to see it reach its potential once again but within the context of an all-Ireland economy.[8]

– Séanna Walsh, Sinn Féin, member of Belfast City Council

You're looking at subvention that's more like 2–3 billion than 10 billion and that is even without looking at the opportunity benefits of a united Ireland and what that is likely to produce. That's some of the work that we'd be doing, but everything that we do and every portfolio in Leinster House is done on an all-island basis.[9]

– Rose Conway-Walsh, Sinn Féin TD

At one level, the questions are very basic: which economy, Northern Ireland or the Republic of Ireland, offers the better standard of living to its citizens? Which has the potential to offer a better life and job opportunities? Which is the more equitable? Which has the better health service? The best social safety net? What are the real costs of integrating the two economies? Would reunification cause severe economic disruption to the North's economy? Could the South afford to absorb the North and the subvention from the United Kingdom (UK) Exchequer that underpins its economy without significant cost to its own citizens?

On all of these matters, Sinn Féin answers in the affirmative: the dynamic Irish economy is up to the task. Others are less sure. Some say the South can't afford the North or that unification will involve significant costs to the South's citizens or that its problematic roller-coaster economy, swinging between ups and downs, from prosperity to austerity, does not provide the stability Northern Ireland enjoys as part of a trading block of sixty-seven million, where falls are cushioned by the largesse of the UK Exchequer.[10]

A considerable number of interviewees say that unionists and the cohort of voters who self-identify as Neithers might consider Irish unity if they are convinced that they would be better off (provided the health service is on a par with the National Health Service [NHS]) and that the opportunities the South promises for their children far outweigh anything Northern Ireland can offer. The economy, Peter Robinson says, is the 'centre ground which will determine whether we have a united Ireland or whether we remain within the United Kingdom, because you're not going to change the mind of the passionate unionist or nationalist on economic issues'.[11]

Comparing the two economies is a fraught endeavour, full of technical issues, methods of measurement and interpretation, and the assumptions that support them: cyclical dynamics, the intricacies of currency fluctuations, competitiveness, tax structures, differences in economic structure, interconnected variables, differences in terminology itself and whether per-capita gross national product (GNP), gross domestic product (GDP), gross national income (GNI), actual individual consumption (AIC) or gross value added (GVA) is the best measure of economic well-being. Each measures something different, and a case can be made for each that it is the best basis for a comparison of the performance of the two economies.

No matter how sophisticated, no analysis is likely to change many minds on these questions. Pro-union and pro-unity advocates are armed with their respective metrics and experts that argue for the superiority of their economic scenarios.

Rather, the subvention – the difference between what Northern Ireland taxpayers contribute to the Treasury and what it receives, amounting to between 20 and 25 per cent of Northern Ireland's national income – is fated to become the pivot for argumentation about the affordability of union.[12] Not because it is the most critical element on the cost side of unification but because it is the most tangible, and voters can relate to it as something that will be met, in full or in part, by a united Ireland, either easily absorbed by a single-island economy or requiring a tax hike to cover or prorated by the United Kingdom over a decade or so to ease the burden of transition.

Several studies address the question of who is better off – that is, whether citizens of Northern Ireland have a higher standard of living than citizens of the South – and what portion of the subvention the South might have to bear.[13]

John Fitzgerald and Edgar Morgenroth characterize the North's economy as low investment, low productivity, low levels of human capital and low incomes.[14] The North was the slowest among regions in the United Kingdom to recover from the 2008 financial recession.[15] It has a relatively small private sector compared with other regions in the United Kingdom.[16] The shipbuilding company Harland & Wolff and the aviation company Bombardier, once-fabled global giants of industry, were the engines of growth in Northern Ireland: now the only vestiges that remain are the huge yellow cranes that stand like lonely sentinels overlooking East Belfast. Northern Ireland has the lowest productivity level region among UK regions, accounting for about 85 per cent of the average when measured by GVA.[17] It is low skilled and lacks qualified labour to fill a significant tranche of well-paying, skilled jobs; consumption is overly dependent on the Northern Ireland subvention.[18] Average household incomes have stagnated, and its productivity gap relative to the rest of the United Kingdom continues to persist.[19]

Since the signing of the Belfast/Good Friday Agreement (B/GFA), the economy of Northern Ireland has been the slowest growing of any region of the United Kingdom, averaging an anaemic 1.2 per cent a year.[20] 'In its current form,' Fitzgerald writes, 'the Northern Ireland economy would be exceptionally challenging to merge into any united Ireland.'[21]

In 2020, Ireland's GDP per capita was $85,475; Northern Ireland's $32,810.[22] At 121.0 per cent of the European Union (EU) average, that figure suggests Ireland is the second-richest country in the EU, second only to Luxemburg, which also has economic distortion issues due to being a tax haven.[23] But, as a measure of any economic outcome, the South's figure is deceptive. Ireland's GDP data is distorted by multinational accounting practices that vastly overstate the size of the economy. Former Central Bank of Ireland governor Patrick Honohan calls Ireland's GDP data 'worse than useless'.[24]

GNI discounts the impact of profits of multinationals going to foreign shareholders and is a better measure of relative income, but distortions remain.

In 2019, Ireland's Central Statistics Office (CSO) devised a special measure, GNI*, to eliminate all the distortions to GNI caused by multinational factors. GNI* per capita was about 40 per cent below the level of GDP, whereas GDP and GNI are about equal in most countries.[25] Using yet another measure, AIC, Ireland drops to 97 per cent of the EU average, on a level with Italy.[26]

Writing in the Central Bank newsletter in February 2021, Honohan says:

> Ireland's AIC ranks in the EU28, having jumped from 11th in the late 1990s to 6th in 2007, fell precipitously to 14th in 2009, after which it recovered, but only to 12th place by 2019. On this measure, then, Ireland falls behind not only the United Kingdom but all six of the original founder members of the EEC [European Economic Community], along with Austria and the three Nordic member states. Indeed, Ireland's AIC per capita is only about 95 per cent of the EU average, down from 115 per cent in 2006–7.

He concludes:

> Ireland is a prosperous country, but not as prosperous as is often thought because of the inappropriate use of misleading, albeit conventional statistics. There is less consumption per capita than in the United Kingdom, and on this metric, we are closer to New Zealand, Israel and Italy, than to the United States, Switzerland or Norway (which is where the GDP comparison would put Ireland). The same conclusion is drawn if GDP is replaced with the Ireland-specific GNI* indicator. Using GDP as a measure can mislead analysis of such matters as debt, carbon-intensity and inequality.[27]

For unionists, what appears to be sleight of hand with regard to statistics and indices of well-being, especially those conjured up with asterisks, are all signs of an economy that can swing dangerously between booms and busts.

If AIC is restricted to private goods, the South has the edge.[28] If the basket of goods in AIC includes government spending on public services – health, education and the public service, mostly free goods in Northern Ireland – then the North has the edge.[29] If disposable household income controlled for prices is used then, according to Adele Bergin and Seamus McGuinness, the South has a considerable edge. If GNI per capita is used, the South again has the edge.[30] If GNI* in the South is pitched against GNI in the North, the results become more problematic. Per-capita public consumption in Northern Ireland is higher than in the South; per-capita investment is lower.[31]

In 'Modelling productivity levels in Ireland and Northern Ireland', Bergin and McGuinness strip out the sectors of the Irish economy with a high concentration of multinationals, such as pharmaceuticals and technology. They found that productivity per head in the South is about 40 per cent higher than in Northern Ireland and 'noticeably higher' in 14 of the 17 sectors they examined, accounting for about 90 per cent of employment in both jurisdictions. They attribute the divergence in sectoral productivity to lower levels of investment and skilled workers in the North, especially at upper secondary and post-secondary levels.[32]

The pro-union economist Graham Gudgin is scathing in putting down studies suggesting the South has a higher standard of living. He argues that they do not take account of price differentials; if they do, they use the wrong one. The cost of housing is so much lower in Northern Ireland, the value of a pound so much greater than a euro. He dismisses Bergin and McGuinness's conclusion that GNI* per capita is higher than GDP per capita in Northern Ireland, because 'they wrongly compare current price GNI* in the republic with constant price GDP for Northern Ireland'. When he concludes his analysis, the North emerges comfortably as having a higher standard of living. He goes further:

> The fact that the Republic of Ireland has not managed to overtake living standards in one of the United Kingdom's poorer regions, even after 60 years as a tax haven, is likely to be at least one reason why half of Northern Ireland's Catholics regularly tell the Life and Time survey they would prefer to remain in the United Kingdom rather than join a united Ireland.[33]

(This statement requires a correction: on two occasions only – 2010 and 2013 – did a majority of Catholics [52 per cent on both] tell a Northern Ireland Life and Times [NILT] survey that they would prefer to stay in the United Kingdom. The figure for 2021 was 21 per cent, the lowest since the question was asked in 2007.)[34]

The North is a consumption-oriented economy with underinvestment for long-term growth; the South an investment-oriented economy with the emphasis on long-term growth. If unification required Irish taxpayers to subsidize the North so that the people there could continue to enjoy a higher level of consumption and government spending than those in the South, it would be without precedent and sure to meet with vociferous resistance. Though since 2012 public consumption in the South has been catching up with public consumption in the United Kingdom, Fitzgerald and Morgenroth say, 'Personal consumption per head in Northern Ireland in 2016 was around 92% of that in Ireland.'

However, the gap in living standards was much greater for public consumption – expenditure on health, education and public service. Funded by a transfer from central government, public consumption per head in Northern Ireland was 45 per cent higher than in Ireland. As a result, when public and private consumption are taken together – an appropriate measure of current living standards – people in Northern Ireland were approximately 4 per cent better off than people in Ireland.[35]

According to these calculations, the gap in living standards had narrowed from Northern Ireland being 14 per cent better off in 2012.

Should there be border polls North and South giving the imprimatur to unity, the subvention will be disaggregated, with some costs apportioned to the new Ireland state and others continuing to be costs on the UK Treasury. Which costs are allocated to either would be a matter of intense negotiations, often with no sure-fire methodology to give guidance other than ideological biases. This transfer from London increased from under 18 per cent of GDP a year between 1980 and 1999 to 20 per cent of GDP since then, amounting to a £5,000 per-capita subsidization of the region.[36] While the size of the subvention can vary from one year to the next, the base amount is in the region of £10 billion.[37]

In an article published in the *The Irish Times* in June 2019, Fitzgerald says:

If the North came without an albatross of UK debt, then the Northern
Ireland deficit to be shouldered by a united Ireland would be €8.4
billion, not €11.4 billion … However, even with this lower sum, if
Ireland had to take over funding services in the North, it would
reduce GNI in Ireland by more than 3 per cent and would reduce
Irish consumption by about 8 per cent. This reduction in the Irish
standard of living could leave the standard of living in the North
around 20 per cent higher than in the South, sustained by transfers
from poorer Southern households, possibly giving rise to resistance
to the idea of unification.[38]

If, on the other hand, Northern Ireland as part of a united Ireland had to
get by without the subsidy, a cut of the necessary magnitude would see a
collapse in the Northern economy, with unemployment rising well above
20 per cent.[39]

The Sinn Féin analysis outlined in 'The Economic Benefits of United
Ireland' writes off military and defence, servicing British debt and overseas
spending – bringing the subvention down to £6 billion – and adds a further
reduction of £3.5 billion for accrued pension rights. Thus, it argues, 'the ultimate subvention figure will be determined by the outcome of negotiations.
The figure will range from £2.5 billion to £6 billion'.[40] But, given the dyna-
mism of the Irish economy, economies of scale and inward investment flows,
the Irish economy, Sinn Féin asserts, will easily be able to absorb the lump
sum, perhaps with some borrowing, but without an increase in taxation.[41]
The analysis by Professor John Doyle reduces the subvention to approximately £3 billion of a subvention of between £9 billion and £10 billion.[42]
That would 'require once-off economic growth and tax revenue growth in
a future united Ireland of about 5 per cent to absorb this deficit without
disruption'.[43]

The Fitzgerald and Morgenroth study calls into question the Sinn Féin
projections:

If Northern Ireland were to leave the United Kingdom, for example
to join a united Ireland, this could trigger an ending of transfers from
the UK central government and Northern Ireland could also have to
share responsibility for its share of the net liabilities of the UK … An
alternative option, which might be considered most favourable terms
for Northern Ireland leaving the UK, might involve an agreement to

waive Northern Ireland's liability for the UK net debt and to phase out the transfers from London over a period of five to ten years.

Even if Northern Ireland joined a united Ireland debt free, so that there was no contribution towards national debt interest payments, the 2016 deficit of £9.3 billion [€11.4 billion] would be reduced to £6.9 billion [€8.4 billion]. However, if the usual approach to be the break-up of a Union is taken, and Northern Ireland took its share of UK net liabilities, the deficit would be £8 billion [€9.8 billion].[44]

This scenario would cost the funding of existing welfare rates and rates of public at their present UK rates. But, as Fitzgerald told me:

> It is likely that Northern Ireland would come [into an Irish state] with a share of the UK national debt. In return, the accrued pension rights of people in Northern Ireland having paid into the social insurance fund in Britain would be a continuing charge on the United Kingdom after a united Ireland …
>
> Then there's the fact that public servants are paid 25 per cent more in the republic than in Northern Ireland, and welfare payments are about a third per head more. If you had Irish unity, but the North stays separate with Stormont [still functioning] and you don't rerate pensions and wages, then there isn't a liability. But there's a very big cost to rerating to Irish rates.[45]

Under the first scenario, the South would absorb subvention and harmonization costs; effectively, a country with a slightly lower standard of living would subsidize one with a higher one so that the latter could maintain that standing. Funding this transfer, Fitzgerald and Morgenroth write, 'would require a fiscal adjustment in Ireland amounting to cuts or tax increases of €20 billion to €30 billion'. This would 'reduce GNI by around 4% and also reduce consumption per head by around 9% and employment in Ireland by around 4%'.[46] A prospect that would be 'economically disastrous'.[47] Furthermore, if the republic 'took over responsibility for the transfer currently coming from the UK central government … those living in Northern Ireland would be between 10% and 20% better off than those living in Ireland, purely due to a huge continuing transfer from Ireland'.[48]

The second scenario, rerating civil service salaries and welfare payment to reflect funding levels in the South, would put considerable strain on the Irish economy. 'That would be a problem,' Fitzgerald says:

especially if the higher standard of living comes from public services, and that the republic would have to pay the £6.7 billion to Northern Ireland, in spite of the fact that when you took account of public service, people were slightly worse off in the republic, and you'd also have to pay Northern Ireland to keep their public service better off than the republic.[49]

Should these steps require a tax on all citizens, North and South, the political calculus changes, becoming more precarious if the perception lingers that the North continues to have a higher standard of living that is being underwritten by the South.[50]

With regard to Irish government policy for Northern Ireland, Fitzgerald maintains that 'successive Irish governments have recognized that Irish unity can only follow the establishment of a workable political and economic system in Northern Ireland, where the sectarian divide no longer determines all outcomes and where co-operation between North and South develops organically'. That, he says, may take another generation, hardly on a timeline that advances the nationalist/republican agenda. Sinn Féin, he advises, should pause their hyperbolic fixation on unity to take cognizance of the immense structural costs involved.[51]

Professor Peter Shirlow says:

> If you get an articulate unionism that points out how much a united Ireland will cost, that you're looking at economic decline in the South, and if you actually get in beyond the fantasy economics of a united Ireland and look at this the way John Fitzgerald does and if that is articulated and if you've got the pandemic and, say, you have a collapse of the Irish economy, why would Southerners vote for a headache? There hasn't actually been any serious debate about a united Ireland.[52]

In agreement with Shirlow, Fitzgerald says:

> [Sinn Féin would] have to spell out what the economic implications were, how rapidly they were going to rerate wages and salaries in the North, pensions and so on … If you did it today, you'd be telling the people of the republic, 'Vote for Irish unity and it's going to cost you an awful lot and you're going to have a million people or half a million, whatever it is, who don't want to be part of us, part of you, and don't

want to play ball.' The Sinn Féin paper [*Economic Benefits of a United Ireland*] makes this point, there would be economies of scale.

Basically, [Sinn Féin] point out you'd have to fire a lot of Irish public servants in order to make space in a united Ireland [for civil servants] from Northern Ireland. You lay this out and ask the people of Ireland to vote for it. Now, I think that some of Sinn Féin of the republic know that the Irish people would quite likely vote against it and you then have a complete disaster ... So as Seamus Mallon suggested, this is not a 51/49 [per cent case]; you need to be very certain that it's going to work on both sides of the border before you go ahead, or else, you'll have a complete disaster.[53]

High on the list of issues to address to mitigate 'disaster' is the extent of the divergence between the two economies and how to bring the two into closer alignment. The North, according to Fitzgerald and Morgenroth, has 'the worst educational system of any region in the UK', and 'upgrading it to deliver comparable economic performance with the republic would take 30 years'.[54]

Stormont's Department for the Economy cites 'a lack of basic employ-ability skills among graduates' and shortages of qualified workers at all levels in most fields.[55] As a result, sectoral productivity is considerably higher in the South. Bringing Northern productivity to a par with the South would require a restructuring of the educational system.[56]

The education system in the North is unequal and discriminatory in three distinct, though overlapping, ways: the Protestant/Catholic divide, the grammar-school/secondary-school divide and the divide between secondary schools themselves. These divides reinforce each other. At age eleven, the top 40 per cent of children based on ability are selected to go to high-quality grammar schools; the others attend secondary schools. The former group of students go on to university; relatively few of the latter do. In addition, Northern Ireland has the highest share of early school leavers in the UK. It also has the lowest share of graduates in the UK, in part because a significant cohort of young people from unionist backgrounds choose to study abroad and the number of university slots available for them is capped every year.[57]

'Northern Ireland's post-primary secondary schools fail to meet the minimum acceptable standard for post-primary schools in England of 40% of Year 12 pupils,' Vani Borooah and Colin Knox write after dissecting the North's education system:[58]

This collective failure masks an even deeper failure at the level of individual schools. Of Northern Ireland's 142 secondary schools, 82 (or 58 per cent) performed below the '40 per cent standard' and, in these underperforming schools, the average proportion of Year 12 pupils obtaining the requisite GCSE [General Certificate of Secondary Education] passes was just 28 per cent while, in the secondary schools that were not underperforming, it was 51 per cent.

As a result, Fitzgerald and Morgenroth observe, there

is a high proportion of children not completing high school and a reduced level of progression to third level. In addition ... a substantial share of those who progress to third-level emigrate. [For the 30–35-year-old cohort] the share ... with a third-level education (35%) is well below that in the UK as a whole (50%) and even further below that in Ireland (55%). Also, the share of the 30–35-year-olds in Northern Ireland who had not completed high school education, at over 20%, is more than twice the figure for Ireland.[59]

Yet, despite these dismal results, per-capita expenditure on education in Northern Ireland is 110 per cent of the UK average.[60]

There is little political pushback to change the system, and it suits the elites, Fitzgerald says:

Middle-class parents get their kids into grammar schools and 90 per cent go on to university, so they do well. They don't want to give up a system which discriminates massively against working-class kids, because their kids do better. Both Catholics and Protestants, unionists, the DUP [Democratic Unionist Party] and Sinn Féin don't want to change the system because it benefits middle-class kids. Now, Sinn Féin did get rid of the 11-plus exam but they didn't get rid of selection so it's actually worse after getting rid of the 11-plus. [In the North] grammar schools work very well and [are] very good for the kids there but the secondary schools, even if they are a good school, the research shows that integrated education – where you can have bright kids and kids of mixed ability taught together, the brighter kids aren't disadvantaged but the weaker kids have a major benefit.[61]

Pro-unity advocates often point to the German experience of unification as one Ireland could emulate. Besides the fact that Germany is one of the wealthiest countries in the world and an economic powerhouse, the Germans wanted unification of East and West. The fall of the Berlin Wall was a global event, signalling the collapse of Soviet communism; Germans on both sides of the divide greeted each other tearfully and joyfully; they embraced each other as kith and kin too long separated from each other. West Germans were willing to make whatever financial sacrifices were necessary to bring the East's moribund economy into something approaching parity with the West's. Every taxpayer paid a solidarity surcharge called *Solidaritätstzuschlag*, up to 5.5 per cent of income, which is still being phased out.[62] Nevertheless, huge economic and social upheaval accompanied the sharp transition from a centrally planned economy to a market one. It is estimated that West Germany splurged almost €2 trillion on helping integrate the two countries.[63]

Thirty years on, huge disparities remain in Germany.[64] By every social indicator, the East lags significantly behind the West, fostering a sense of isolation, grievance, disillusionment and political radicalization. In the East, voters are more than twice as likely to support the right-wing Alternative for Germany (AfD) party, and while over 70 per cent of West Germans simply feel 'German', a recent survey by the Allensbach Institute found that in the East this was true of only 44 per cent, with there being a growing propensity to identify as East German.[65] Convergence, despite huge capital inflows (additional transfers of €50 billion were also received by the East from the EU), the process has been slow and has come at a high social cost. Around three-quarters of people in the former East Germany (74 per cent) and around two-thirds of those in the former West (66 per cent) say the East still has not achieved the same living standards as the West.[66]

A West German economy with a GDP more than six times larger absorbed the East's; a West German state with a population almost four times as large absorbed the population of the East German state.[67] In contrast, Irish unity would involve the South with a population two and a half times as large integrating the North. The absorptive capacity of Ireland is far more limited.[68] Rather than being a beacon of how a successful convergence of two diametrically opposing economies might proceed, the German experience underscores the enormous social and economic disruptions involved, even when there seemed to be no limit to the money available to mitigate its worst upheavals and lay the groundwork for a more equitable distribution of income across the two regions. In fact, the German case shows how entrenched structural deficits are, how wrenchingly difficult the barriers to increasing productivity and economic growth are to surmount and how bureaucratic sclerosis can stymie the best policy prescriptions. Few of the social engineers of German unification would have believed that the drag on the German economy would enter a fourth decade and still not have achieved equality across the two regions.[69]

Brexit is causing North-South trade to grow, and unless there are other unforeseeable circumstances this trend will accelerate, signalling a more robust all-island economy in the making – much to the chagrin of unionists who see the growth of an all-island economy as expediting unification. In his review of the two societies in *A New Ireland: A Ten-Year Plan*, Paul Gosling observes that 'Northern Ireland is a dysfunctional society, kept segregated, with a duplicated and wasteful structure of public service delivery; a failing health service, weak economy, low productivity, absence of regional policy and in places under the grip of paramilitaries … This set of deeply institutional problems will take years to resolve.'[70]

Meanwhile, the North remains a low-wage economy, perhaps more attractive for foreign direct investment because it has access to both the UK and the EU markets, yet hampered as a place for foreign direct investment because of a low-skilled labour force. The educational system is dysfunctional, duplicative and inordinately expensive. The NHS in the North is the worst in the UK, with over 50 per cent of patients waiting for more than a year to see a consultant.[71] The economy is dependent on public consumption for its well-being and is excessively subsidized. All of these factors may pose near-insuperable political problems for the South. In successive polls over decades, Irish respondents have made it clear that their support for unity does not extend to having to pay more taxes to support it, even without the caveat that they might be supporting one at a higher standard of living than themselves. An all-Ireland state pivoting to a single-island economy will mean acute economic dislocation for some Northerners as the province is weaned off public consumption, the school system is rationalized and brought more into line with the South's and stringent steps are taken to unlock human capital and close the productivity gap – all of which might have to be accomplished without the co-operation of hundreds of thousands of unionists bitterly opposed to unification. As was the case with Germany, it might take decades to achieve.

A study by Kurt Hübner and LKC Consulting – frequently quoted by advocates of Irish unity, in particular Sinn Féin – uses econometric modelling applied in Germany following unification after 1989 to forecast that incomes would rise across Ireland, especially in Northern Ireland, between five to ten years following unification.[72] Pre-Brexit, the study forecast a €36 billion boost in GNP within the first decade of unification; post-Brexit, a €23.5 billion surge in output. 'With this increase in overall economic output and higher-skilled employment,' Sinn Féin asserts, 'comes a direct boon in tax revenues available to the unified state.'[73]

The results are questioned on several grounds, mostly with regard to its underlying assumptions, summarized in *TheJournal.ie*:

> That taxes in Northern Ireland become fully aligned leading to more foreign direct investment; the costs of cross-border trade are lower if there is no border, coming down by five per cent a year; that there are no political frictions to unification and an all-island government is cheaper to run, coming down by two per cent year compared with government spending in Northern Ireland would have been; that Northern Ireland joins the euro, devaluing the currency; that the subvention is paid in full by the republic instead of the UK.[74]

Fitzgerald faults the study on three other grounds:

> It's said if you get rid of the border between the republic and Northern Ireland, you'd get a big increase in trade. That took no account of the fact that the Northern Ireland economy is totally integrated into the Great British economy. There'd be a huge loss to Northern Ireland from leaving the United Kingdom. The loss of trade and particularly in services would be massive. With Brexit, the loss would be even greater than when they did the study.[75]

According to Fitzgerald, the Hübner report also says that 'there'll be lots of foreign direct investment, which will raise productivity in Northern Ireland'. He continues:

> A study done for the Northern Ireland Department of the Economy in 2019 by Iulia Siedschlag of the ESRI … shows that the Northern

Ireland foreign direct investment … is strictly limited because of the very poor educational attainment to the population.[76]

The productivity is low because of the low education attainment. There is no way that the productivity of Northern Ireland would converge in the republic any time soon. If [the North] reformed their education system today, it would take twenty to thirty years before the effects of that increased productivity would come through in Northern Ireland. That's what Ireland did in the 1980s and 1990s. We invested massively in education and thirty years on you see the benefits. First, keep kids in to complete their high school, which is not happening in Northern Ireland. Then they go on to university and then they replace people gradually as they get older in the labour force … In one paragraph they [the Hübner study] said the republic would pick up the tab for Northern Ireland without taking account of the fact that the cost of that would have a significant negative effect on the standards of living in the republic.[77]

After reviewing the literature on the economics of unification and the importance of factoring in different assumptions about the size of the UK's fiscal transfer to Northern Ireland and which government might meet it, J. Esmond Birnie, a senior economist at the University of Ulster, concludes:

In economic terms the argument for the union remains but the real strength of that argument has declined … [In] the absence of a very large degree of fiscal forbearance from the rest of the UK either in terms of refusing to transfer any debt obligations to a united Ireland or in terms of continuing to subsidise Northern Ireland, it remains unlikely that the Republic of Ireland could afford Northern Ireland.[78]

There are studies, however, that come up with the opposite results: for example, the analysis for Sen. Mark Daly's Oireachtas Committees on the Good Friday Agreement and Professor John Doyle's analysis.[79] Reviewing different scenarios positing what deductions would be made to the subvention, *Irish Times* columnist Eoin Burke-Kennedy writes:

In many ways, the North's subvention is a red herring in the debate about Irish unity. All economies are centralised around richer, more industrialised parts and the United Kingdom is no different. Dublin is wealthier than Connemara or Leitrim, but we don't view the republic's economy through the prism of Dublin's surplus versus Connemara's or Leitrim's deficit.[80]

Perhaps, but the subvention will become the focal point of unionist declarations that the South cannot afford to pick up the costs involved. The uncertainty of the outcome on the question will increase the likelihood that some undecided voters will vote for the status quo.

Former First Minister Peter Robinson is dismissive of these varying estimates. For him, it's an open and shut case: the South can't afford to absorb the North on terms that would allow it to continue to enjoy the advantages of being in the United Kingdom: 'The argument for a united Ireland can only economically stack up if the president [Joe Biden] leaves his chequebook behind.'[81]

Billy Hutchinson espouses a perspective prevalent in the loyalist community:

> There is no way that I would want to go into a united Ireland … it's a failed state. We know [Ireland] collapsed in 2010. We know that the World Bank had to pull them out. And we know that Europe had to pull them out. And we know that they had to borrow money from the British to actually survive, because they made a mistake. They went into the eurozone; they had no control over their currency; the same as Greece: their economies collapsed. And if it hadn't been for people coming in and helping them out, it would still be collapsed … It's a bad economy. And it will collapse again.[82]

Arguments that are fact-based won't change minds. During the Brexit campaign in the UK, both the Leave and the Remain sides produced studies purporting to show the economic benefits or costs of their positions. As was referred to in Chapter 5, the most infamous promise of the Leave campaign, the propaganda splattered across every campaign bus, was that leaving the EU would return £350 million every week from Brussels to the UK. It was pure nonsense, but it pointed to a more insidious problem. In the era of 'fake' news, there is a strident propensity for parties on different sides of an issue to create arguments that have no basis in fact, and hope that a sufficient number of voters will buy into the lie if it is repeated often enough. Any campaign on a border poll will result in a slew of studies. Nationalists will come up with studies showing that the South can easily absorb the North, that the North will be better off, that the costs to the South will be minimal; unionists will produce studies showing what a disaster unification would be, not just for Northern Ireland but for the South because of its inability to absorb the cost of doing so. Caught in the detritus of these competing narratives, studies by the academy and research institutes will likely sink in the swamp of disinformation. When numerous studies were published after the Brexit vote warning of dire economic impacts should there be a hard Brexit, they did little to sway Leave voters to consider a second vote, hardening Leave positions among those most likely to be affected.

For both unionists/orange and nationalists/green, given the intensity with which they hold their respective positions on the constitutional issue, forecasts of adverse economic consequences are unlikely to sway their propensities to vote either to leave or stay in the UK. But as to the 40+ per cent of Neithers, we are told (the evidence is largely anecdotal) that the future performance of the South's economy may be the key to convincing a sizeable number of this cohort that their future lies in an all-Ireland state, with the island secure within the EU and the Single Market economy. Certainly, the future of healthcare in both jurisdictions would loom large.

In 'The Political Economy of a Northern Ireland Border Poll', Seamus McGuinness and Adele Bergin, after reviewing the 'known unknowns' that will have to be taken into account in any consideration of the costs of unification, conclude:

> It is difficult to be specific about [the costs of unification] as it is determined by a number of unknowns including (a) the length and nature of any adjustment or transition period (b) the relative role of both governments during any transition period in addressing some of the key issues ... in reforming educational, industrial and regional policy (c) the relative success of such policies in raising Northern Ireland productivity levels (d) the role and significance of both the EU and USA in potentially reintegrating a post-Brexit Northern Ireland into the EU and assisting in promoting FDI (Foreign Direct Investment) to the region, and (e) the outcome of discussion on the issue of debt obligations.[83]

There is no clear-cut way to ascertain which of the two economies is the better off: every measure has a drawback and is open to question; none can capture a people's own beliefs. Large population segments of the North believe they are better off there economically when things such as, for example, the NHS are factored in (even though the North has the poorest health service among the regions of the United Kingdom) and account is taken of property prices and rentals, currency differentials and other extra-neous intangibles. The public and private costs of unity, much of it unquan-tifiable, cross every spectrum of individual and collective activity. On one hand, the disruptions due to the continuing external costs of Brexit as more of the Withdrawal Agreement provisions are implemented may cause some cultural Catholics who feel comfortable and at home in a Northern Ireland that is working to have second thoughts about a border poll. On the other hand, voters may feel daunted facing what would almost certainly be polarizing border referendum campaigns and the economic upheavals and uncertainty that may accompany a united Ireland – even one that is phased in over a number of years and incorporating what appears to be a more dynamic Irish economy. This cohort, especially that considerable segment working in the public sector where concerns about job and pension take precedence over constitutional status, may dictate that the more prudent decision is to stay in the UK.

A similar situation arises regarding attempts to compare and contrast the respective healthcare systems, North and South – the NHS and the Health Service Executive (HSE), respectively.[84]

The main issue by a large margin among voters North and South is healthcare. The *Irish Times*/Ipsos MRBI poll in the South before the February 2020 general election found that healthcare had been the leading priority for 42 per cent of voters.[85] In the North, the University of Liverpool/ *Irish News* poll (February 2022) found among voters preparing to vote in the May 2022 Assembly elections that healthcare was the priority of 30 per cent. Concern cut across nationalist and unionist communities.[86] There is across-the-board agreement among interviewees that one of the decisive factors in a border poll will be healthcare and that nationalists/republicans will have to persuade unionists that there is a healthcare system in the South, free of charge at the point of delivery and with all the benefits they associate with the NHS. The importance of the issue is grasped by Sinn Féin. It is proposing, says Chris Hazzard, MP, 'the idea of a "National Health Service in Ireland", free at the point of delivery. Similar to the British model of the National Health Service but perhaps looking to Western Europe and some of those very successful models from Scandinavia'.

In an NILT (2019) survey, respondents were asked whether a Northern Ireland healthcare system free at the point of use and paid for by National Insurance contributions or the HSE in the South paid for by private insurance would make them more likely or less likely to favour unification. Fifty-two per cent said it would make them less likely to vote for unification: a spread across 45 per cent of Catholics and 59 per cent of Protestants, and 46 per cent among self-identifying as 'no religion'.[87] In a University of Liverpool/*Irish News* (March 2022) poll, just 25 per cent said they would vote for reunification if they had to pay higher taxes or a fee for health.[88]

The NHS in Northern Ireland is the worst in the UK.[89] During the quarter April/June 2021, over 349,000 people were waiting for a first appointment, 53 per cent for over a year, an increase of 39,000 for the same period in 2020.[90] Adjusted for population size, waiting lists in Northern Ireland are 100 times greater than those in England, a country 50 times its size.[91]

'One of the things that is interesting is the difference in perception of the National Health Service and the reality of it,' says Paul Gosling, author of *A New Ireland, A New Union: A New Society*:[92]

> Anyone who says that we have a National Health Service that has to be saved in Northern Ireland is ignoring the reality that it is a system that was not performing well before Covid. It was a system that needed major reform, but because of the fragmented political system, it could not be reformed, and it is not being reformed. That is an example of why the current structures of politics in Northern Ireland do not work because we've got a health service that is completely failing people. You can't get an appointment; you can't get treatment. The fact that it's free is irrelevant if you can't get the treatment. Meanwhile, in the South, you've got a system that is based around insurance. So, what we need to do is have a unified system, free on the point of delivery based around the principles of Sláintecare and the NHS, but a system that works.[93]

In the South, the situation is as bad. In August 2021, more than 900,000 people were on a hospital waiting list, waiting be treated or assessed by a consultant, an increase of 66,167 people or 8 per cent over a year.[94]

In their study 'Who Is Better Off? Measuring Cross-border Differences in Living Standards, Opportunities and Quality of Life on the Island of Ireland', Adele Bergin and Seamus McGuinness examined a series of metrics

and concluded that health-service levels across the two regions were con-
verging mainly 'as a result of higher spending and the extension of universal
access in the South and the impacts of austerity and the poor relative performance of the NHS in NI [Northern Ireland]'.[95]

Both health systems fare poorly among OECD (Organisation for
Economic Co-operation and Development) countries in terms of having
acute-care bed occupancy rates exceeding 90 per cent. General practitioner
(GP) and hospital appointments and prescription costs in Northern Ireland
are free at the point of use, paid for by the UK-wide National Insurance
contributions. In contrast, in Ireland a GP appointment costs around €60, a
visit to the emergency department costs €100 and prescription costs are out
of pocket for the patient.

The South has a two-tier healthcare system. Almost one-third of the
population has a means-tested medical card. This provides access to healthcare for free, while about 46 per cent of the population has private health
insurance. Unlike most countries in the EU, where GP visits are free or
heavily subsidized, in Ireland a large proportion of the population pay in
full for visits.[96]

The most recent data indicate that there were 3.3 active physicians per
1,000 population in the South compared to 2.1 in Northern Ireland; conversely,
the number of hospital beds was marginally higher in Northern Ireland at
3.1 per 1,000 population compared to 3.0 in the South. In 2018, children born
in Northern Ireland had a life expectancy 1.4 years lower than those born in
the republic. Life expectancy trends for those aged sixty-five and over was
0.5 years higher among persons living in the South by 2018.[97] Whereas in 2018
healthcare spending per person in Northern Ireland was ahead of the South's,
by 2021 the South had caught up, with Ireland spending €4,204 per person in
2021 and Northern Ireland spending the equivalent of €4,182.[98]

A complete overhaul of the healthcare system is underway. Sláintecare
is an initiative that will abolish the country's two-tier health system and
replace it with a universal healthcare model, as is in place across much of
Europe, along the lines of the UK's NHS. Legislated for in 2018, the initiative has run into several roadblocks. Implementation has been piecemeal
and not fully budgeted for. Huge costs are involved. There are turf wars
with the existing HSE, and several resignations of key personnel have called
into question the government's commitment to fully fund the initiative.[99]

Reform has stalled. Halfway through the Sláintecare plan, waiting lists had grown by 54 per cent. In June 2022, over one-quarter of the population were on health services' hospital waiting lists. Estimates to get rid of the backlog ran to eleven years.[100]

'The current Irish policy when it comes to healthcare [is] the Sláintecare document,' Fianna Fáil TD Jim O'Callaghan told the audience during his talk at Sydney Sussex College Cambridge on 23 March 2021, 'as agreed by all parties in the Oireachtas. It's referenced and recognized in the current Programme for Government of the Irish government, which is entitled "universal healthcare" ... a clear statement of where we are going.'

> The path that we are on ... is going to lead to the convergence of standards between the two parts of the island. We've short term commitments that include extending free GP care to more children and older people. Although [not] free at the point of delivery as yet, it is, I would have thought, a very clear point of direction to where Ireland is heading. There would be a convergence between the two jurisdictions when it came to healthcare if the endpoint would be free at the point of delivery.[101]

Despite their innumerable flaws, the two healthcare systems working together have had some successes – cancer treatment and child heart health services are on an all-island basis, and there is widespread agreement that these North-South initiatives are a huge success and a harbinger perhaps of what might yet be accomplished on a co-operative basis.[102]

One key difference between the two healthcare systems is respective attitudes to each. The emotional attachment of both Catholics and Protestants to the NHS transcends their standing on the constitutional issue. The NILT (2020) records 92 per cent of respondents as valuing the NHS 'a lot'.[103] For unionist interviewees, it was intertwined with their sense of Britishness. 'Since its introduction in 1948,' says the Alliance Party member Will Glendinning, '[the NHS] has become part of our psyche ... There is something built into our psyche about the fact that [the UK] is one of the few countries where you have, technically, that ability to get that care.'[104]

The NHS is not something unionists believe can be replicated in the South, which they associate with a system that requires patients to pay on points of use. There is a form of psychological fusion between Northern

Protestants and the NHS, no matter the frustrations of long waiting times, the constant complaints, airing of horror stories and other shortcomings. The NHS is 'theirs' in a personal sense. In fact, fusion studies show frequently that the less well-performing the object of psychological attachment, the greater the loyalty.[105]

Unionists will take some convincing that an all-Ireland Sláintecare, or even some integration of Sláintecare and the NHS, will result in a system that provides them with all the benefits the NHS currently provides. Who pays and how will also be a matter of intense debate. The cost of the NHS in Northern Ireland is spread across the 68 million people of the UK; an all-Ireland health system will be borne by fewer than 7 million people.

— NINE —

A Shared Island: a Trojan horse?

My view is that [a united Ireland is] a constitutional inevitability because of demographics, because of economics, because of Brexit. Whereas it might not come around for some years, it will come around this decade and now is the time to commission detailed economic projective models.[1]

– Niall Murphy, Belfast solicitor, Secretary of Ireland's Future

There's a lot of work going on behind the scenes with the Shared Island Unit. There's a lot of engagement with communities and community groups. There's a lot of research going on by universities and the likes of the Economic and Social Research Institute in Ireland. I think an awful lot could be achieved if we knuckle down and get on with it.[2]

– Niall Blaney, Fianna Fáil, Seanad Éireann

We're nowhere near to saying what that would look like, having the conversation as to what people want, what they would like to see, who's going to pay for it, how we're going to align, how our traditions will be having a shared future together with respect and neutrality. The Taoiseach's new Shared Island Unit is an attempt to start having that

conversation, but … I fear we're talking to ourselves in little groups of
interested people, as opposed to talking to the seven million people on
the island.[3]

– Regina Doherty, Fine Gael, member Seanad Éireann

Micheál Martin's whole Shared Island nonsense is designed to avoid
the issue and to sideline Sinn Féin and to distract from their policy.
The Shared Ireland Unit is going to die with him when he ceases to be
Taoiseach, which might be sooner than he thinks.[4]

– Brian Feeney, Political columnist, *The Irish News*

For a hundred years, Southern politicians have been able to pay lip service
to the idea of a united Ireland, safe in the knowledge that it was unlikely
to become a reality, certainly for the last quarter of a century. Now that
they have to confront the possibility … and they are ill-equipped, they're
clearly ill-equipped. Even we have Micheál Martin's Shared Island Unit.
This in itself is not a bad idea … but more needs to be done. All the ques-
tions you're asking need to be answered by greater minds than mine and
certainly considered about how we move this process forward.[5]

– John Manley, Political correspondent, *The Irish News*

I don't believe the Irish government or the people of the twenty-six
counties get a share in the six counties. We share separate parts, and I
think that's the distinction. We don't have commonalities economically
with the Republic of Ireland … Seventy per cent of our trade is with GB
[Great Britain], so our look is not south in that trading relationship. In
terms of goods shared, infrastructure projects, no problem with that.
We have a shared electricity market. We could have a shared hydrogen
market. We could work on those things and be constructive in those
things. Our linkage is over to the UK mainland, it is not a Southern
look. Nice as that might be and cozy as it would be, the hard stats are
that it accounts for less than 10 per cent of the things we do.[6]

– Ian Paisley Jr, Democratic Unionist Party (DUP) MP

The creation of the Shared Island Unit earlier last year has indicated
that even the Irish government are aware that this conversation [about
unity] is taking place.[7]

– Chris Hazzard, Sinn Féin MP, Ard Chomhairle

I can easily see the situation that a border poll passes by 1 per cent in Northern Ireland but fails in the South at this stage because it hasn't been thought through. It can't be enough to simply be a slogan. It has to be a practical, economic and social movement, and unfortunately that can't happen within ten years.[8]

– Neale Richmond, Fine Gael Teachta Dála (TD)

In the South, attitudes towards Irish reunification are ambivalent: the aspiration is strong, but the commitment is weak; sentiment is frequently contradictory, the result of Southerners not having to give much thought to the matter. For many, the North remains an enigma, a strange and foreboding place, rife with sectarianism, endless squabbling between Catholics and Protestants and teetering on occasion towards violence again. Old grievances appear to reassert themselves under new guises with a disquieting frequency.[9] The peace is called 'fragile', which suggests that it could break. Few in the South have visited the North, other than Belfast, and fewer still rank it as among the issues that concern their daily lives.[10] A majority believe violence could accompany a united Ireland.[11] Food for pause. But not enough to dampen enthusiasm. Almost half believe they will see a united Ireland in their lifetime; a whopping 70 per cent are in favour of a poll within five years, with no caveats attached.[12] But when one is added – that the Irish public might be called on to pay higher taxes to pay for the merger of North and South – support for unification dissipates.[13] In short, the public supports unification if it involves no cost, is risk-free, entails no sacrifice. It is a much-honoured element of the national grail, historically preordained, the only question being when it will happen – not if.[14]

Support for unification is straddled along age, class and party affiliation lines.[15] The younger generations (a generation that has no memories of the Troubles) are overwhelmingly in favour, as are Sinn Féin voters; among older voters (a generation still with vivid memories of the Troubles) and supporters of Fine Gael and Fianna Fáil, support drops off significantly.[16] Salaried and managerial/professional cohorts and those earning above-average incomes are less in favour, with the more blue-collar voters, the more in favour.[17] Besides differentials in support from different ideological bents and demographic cohorts, support varies between strongly supporting and moderately supporting in equal measure. There is no national consensus on the question, and if the differentials according to these metrics persist, calling a border poll in the South after a referendum in the North – a decision of Dáil Éireann – could be highly divisive.

Southerners for the most part display an almost blissful ignorance regarding Northern Ireland, paying scant attention to its politics other than when a derailment of the Executive threatens, and even then the attention is only cursory. Most would be familiar with names such as the late John Hume, Ian Paisley and Gerry Adams, but few would recognize Colum Eastwood or Doug Beattie.

In addition, few could say what the North-South Ministerial Council is or how it works or what it has achieved. Few could reel off areas of co-operation between North and South, though everyone is gung-ho about further co-operation between the two parts of the island. Everyone is in favour of 'generosity' in accommodating the British identity, but few can articulate what it entails. When details are added, the generosity quickly evaporates.[18]

'Nobody has ever asked the question,' former Alliance Party leader David Ford says, 'are you in favour of a united Ireland, and by the way it happens next week, your taxes go up 20 per cent and you get 800–900 thousand extra citizens who want no part of you. [If they had] I think the numbers favouring a united Ireland would go down significantly.'[19] The *Independent/*Kantor poll (April/May 2021) answers the question – just 22 per cent of respondents in the South who were in favour of a united Ireland were prepared to pay extra taxes to bring it about.[20]

'In the nearly 50 years I have lived mainly in Dublin,' Andy Pollak, who co-wrote *A Shared Home Place* with Seamus Mallon and writes the influential blog *2Irelands2gether*, told the Hewitt Summer School in July 2022, 'I can't recall a single well-informed conversation with the journalists, academics, teachers, civil servants and voluntary sector workers who make up my friendship group about what unity might entail for the politics, economics and culture of the Southern jurisdiction.'[21]

A sampling of eleven surveys in the South (see Table 9.1) on the question of reunification since the Belfast/Good Friday Agreement (B/GFA) show clear majorities, usually in the range of two-thirds of respondents, in favour of the idea of a united Ireland, leaving it to individual voters to decide for themselves what it might look like and what it might cost.

Table 9.1: Aggregated results for a variety of polls (1979–2021, rounded figures)[22]

DATE	POLL	UNITED IRELAND	UNITED IRELAND, DESPITE HIGHER TAXES	AGAINST A UNITED IRELAND	AGAINST IF HAD TO PAY HIGHER TAXES/ WOULD REFUSE IF HIGHER TAXES	DON'T KNOW (IF HAD TO PAY HIGHER TAXES)	WANT A BORDER POLL IN THE NEXT FIVE YEARS	THINK IT WILL HAPPEN IN NEXT TEN YEARS	THINK IT WILL HAPPEN IN MORE THAN TEN YEARS
1979	ESRI	68[23]	46	9[24]	51[25]	—	—	—	—
1999/2000	European Values Study[26]	54	—	10[27]	—	—	—	—	—
Oct. 2010	RED C/Sunday Times[28]	57	—	22	—	21	—	—	—
Oct. 2015	RTÉ/BBC[29]	36[30]	31	44[31]	31[32]	17[33] (25)	—	—	—
Dec. 2016	RTÉ's Claire Byrne Live/ Amárach[34]	46	—	32	—	22	—	—	—
Mar. 2017	Ireland Thinks[35]	—	33[36]	—	33	(34)	—	—	—
Dec. 2017	Ireland Thinks[37]	—	47[38]	—	32	(22)	—	—	—
May 2019	RTÉ/RED C exit poll[39]	65[40]	—	19	—	15	—	—	—
Jan. 2020	The Times[41]	80[42]	—	20	—	—	—	40	39
Feb. 2020	RTÉ/Ipsos MRBI[43]	57	—	40	—	—	57 [44]	—	—
Apr. 2021	Independent/ Kantar poll[45]	67	22	16	54	17	69[46]	21	6[47]
Nov. 2021	RED C[48]	62	41	25	43	15 (16)	—	62	—
Dec. 2021	Irish Times/Ipsos MRBI[49]	62	15	16	79	13	15	42	16

A comprehensive benchmark survey of attitudes in the South towards Northern Ireland, carried out by the Economic Social and Research Institute (ESRI) in 1978, reported that, overall, 68 per cent of respondents were in favour of a united Ireland: 41 per cent for a unitary state and 27 per cent for a federal solution.[50] There was widespread opposition to partition (72 per cent); only 46 per cent said they felt either strongly or moderately about it. And although 69 per cent agreed that unification was essential for any solution to the problem, only 52 per cent felt strongly about it. Only 46 per cent of respondents were willing to pay higher taxes in order to achieve it, 51 per cent were not.[51]

Fast-forward forty years and the results are not much different (see Table 9.1).[52] In addition to the *Independent*/Kantar poll, the *Irish Times*/ Ipsos MRBI poll (December 2021) also showed a large majority in favour of a united Ireland. But when voters were told they'd have to pay higher taxes to support one, support collapsed to 15 per cent in the former survey and 15 per cent in the latter. Across the decades, the attitude towards reunification is the same: an ambivalence – widespread support for, but no urgency to do so.

There could not be a starker difference between the Sinn Féin position on a border poll and the position adopted by the new coalition government. The government's Programme for Action does not mention either a border poll or a united Ireland, nor even the nationalist mantra of an 'agreed Ireland'.[53] A unit was established in the Taoiseach's department 'to work towards a consensus on a shared island'.[54] This unit, the Shared Island Unit (SIU), would 'examine the political, social, economic and cultural considerations underpinning a future in which all traditions are mutually respected'.[55]

The government pledged to work with the Northern Ireland Executive and the British government to 'deepen multi-agency cross-border co-operation on crime, including information sharing between the Police Service of Northern Ireland [PSNI] and An Garda Síochána'.[56] It would 'seek to develop an all-island strategy to tackle climate breakdown and the biodiversity crisis'.[57]

A particular focus is on cross-border infrastructure initiatives. The government 'will work with the Northern Ireland Executive to deliver key cross-border infrastructure initiatives, including the A5, the Ulster Canal connection from Clones to Upper Lough Erne, the Narrow Water Bridge, and cross-border greenways, in particular the Sligo-Enniskillen greenway'.[58] The government committed €500 million out to 2025 for cross-border capital projects.[59]

On Brexit, the key priority was having the Northern Ireland Protocol (NIP) work smoothly to forestall a land border and in doing so 'actively participating' with the Joint Committee, the committee overseeing its implementation.

Hardly a week into the new coalition government, on 7 July 2020, in response to a question from Sinn Féin's Mary Lou McDonald (now the leader of the opposition) on calling a border poll, Taoiseach Micheál Martin outlined the government's position. Martin responded that the focus on a border poll 'was too divisive, too partisan and would only run counter to what you [Sinn Féin] wanted to achieve'.[60] He emphasized the need for 'a stronger North-South relationship' and argued that 'the agenda for the future of this island is how we engineer and develop an accommodation where we can all live in peace and harmony … and to not try to dictate to one tradition about what the solution is going to be, which seems to be the agenda you're [Sinn Féin] pursuing'. The focus of the SIU 'is to see how the Government can develop a shared future [but] irrespective of what may emerge' – these three sets of relationships (in the B/GFA) will have to underpin any future arrangements.[61]

Three weeks later, on 31 July, Martin met with First Minister Arlene Foster and deputy First Minister Michelle O'Neill – the first meeting of the North-South Ministerial Council since November 2016. The meeting took place in Dublin Castle.[62] Martin did not bring up the SIU and its ramifications for North-South collaboration, leading Foster to say: 'It does not threaten our constitutional position, or what we believe in, so I don't feel threatened at all by the unit.'[63] But within weeks she had changed her mind, sensitive to how negatively the SIU was being received in other unionist quarters. The Catch-22 is that every gesture by nationalists, no matter how benign, is microscopically examined by unionists for the hidden intent they suspect it conceals.

Foster sharply rebuked Martin for remarks he had made in an interview with the *Irish Independent* when he said he planned to 'beef up' the SIU.[64] He had drawn attention to the paramount role English nationalism played in the Brexit vote and suggested that Scotland could maybe opt for independence. 'What happens,' he asked, 'if England gets turned off Northern Ireland? We've got to be thinking all this through.'[65]

Unionist reaction was swift and condemnatory. Did this 'beefing up' mean that he was beginning to prepare for Irish unity? Trying to blindside Sinn Féin for domestic political consumption? Was he suggesting that if it appeared that England, in the aftermath of Scotland voting for independence, 'turned off' Northern Ireland, the British government might be more amenable to a border poll? Was he making a calculation that fallout from Brexit, the Scottish vote, English antipathy towards Northern Ireland and a prime minister with no particular attachment to it would all be enough to swing a border poll in favour of nationalists?[66]

'Although the conflict was never a religious war, extreme brands of Protestant fundamentalism sociologically have shaped the Protestant mindset,' says Gary Mason:

> Micheál Martin sets up the Shared Island Unit. Unionism says, 'We're not talking to that.' That sort of fundamentalist, religious, separatist mentality spills into a political identity. It's the Paisley scenario: if we disagree with you, we withdraw, we become a separatist people. In many ways, that sometimes describes our politics. Whereas the late David Ervine's logic was, 'Unionism needs to get into the ring, and actually lay out its stall instead of withdrawing continually from conversation.'[67]

What most upset unionists was Martin insinuating what many of them ruminated about among themselves, their own darkest fears about one more possible betrayal by a British government. Every suggestion that Northern Ireland is a place apart is met with fervid protestations, exaggerated to compensate for the insecurity unionists have about their status. Martin says that the SIU would commission studies not on attitudes to a united Ireland, but on how the two jurisdictions work and where there may be fruitful collaboration: the health services, school curriculums and non-constitutional issues like joint infrastructure projects – roads, bridges, high-speed railways, greenways.[68]

Interviewed by *The Irish Times* in September 2020, Martin was asked whether the endgame for the unit was paving the way for Irish unity. He prevaricated, making a Jesuitical distinction between setting a process in

motion without a defined end in mind, the process itself creating the circumstances that make a desired outcome more likely: neither a means to an
end nor an end in itself. The work under its remit 'will be very substantial
and will help to deliver the new norm, whatever the new norm is', but 'not
actually a stalking horse to a certain political objective'.[69]

Won't he have to persuade unionists that engaging on the array of North-
South issues he cites is worth doing in itself and not a slipway towards a
united Ireland? 'It can be an end in itself,' Martin responded.[70]

But is it also a means to an end for him? 'Not necessarily. I'm not as
obsessional about the end result, provided where we end up is that we genuinely share the island.' Was he a persuader for Irish unity? He shared Seamus
Mallon's view that 'we have to learn to share this island'. For Martin, 'the
genius of the Good Friday Agreement is that we don't always have to end up
talking about the constitutional status of the island. We just have to get on
with the agreement'.[71]

For Martin, 'getting on with the agreement' required the government
to perform a number of balancing acts: on the one hand, threading its way
delicately between what might be perceived as constituting preparation for
unification and what were just old-fashioned construction and engineering
projects that benefited both parts of Ireland; on the other hand, presiding
over a proactive SIU perceived as robust enough to placate nationalists
that the government is serious about unification, yet not threatening to
unionists.

The SIU, if implemented in full, facilitates a more integrated all-Ireland
economy. Insofar as this will both precede and succeed a border poll and
Irish unity, the SIU is laying the groundwork for the future. For nationalists,
the 'new norm' is the inevitability of Irish unification. 'This idea of saying
the SIU will look at everything except the question of a united Ireland is
wrong,' the Social Democratic and Labour Party's (SDLP) former leader,
B/GFA negotiator and former deputy First Minister Mark Durkan cautions:

> Micheál Martin is saying that the Shared Island Unit isn't a stalking
> horse for a united Ireland and giving unionists that assurance, but he
> also needs to assure people it's not a stalling vehicle around a united
> Ireland. They also need to assure people ... that it's only when there's
> a Sinn Féin mandate for government that you will get a move towards

a united Ireland. It's somewhat derelict to be suggesting that you can afford to leave this question for five years, because in five years' time Sinn Féin is going to be very strong in electoral politics in the South and that will make it easier for people.[72]

A steady stream of polls on both sides of the border asking questions about a border poll and Irish unity muddy the political waters. The results are regurgitated in endless commentary and hostile exchanges on social media. Martin's 'getting on with the agreement' posture is frequently drowned in a torrent of words suggesting a border poll is just around the corner, though the evidence for one is lacking, or tenuous at best. Proponents of a referendum believe that by sheer repetition of calling for a referendum they will end up willing it into actuality. Since Brexit, the ingredients of a tipping point for a referendum are coalescing.

Certainly, with Sinn Féin holding the office of first minister in the North and potentially also in government in the South after the 2025 elections, the bullhorns for a border poll will blast a 'unity now' message, and the SIU will most likely be replaced by a dedicated unit advancing preparations for Irish unity or a 'department of reunification'. The SIU will have done some of the necessary spadework, though none of the deep digging into the national psyche that will be required when Ireland eventually puts a unity project on the topsoil.

The quandary for the present Irish government is whether to set the agenda for Irish unity, for which it has no electoral mandate other than in a benign way, or else leave it to a Sinn Féin government. Nationalist pressure networks, including those in the United States, call for the Irish government to begin the work of setting out how a united Ireland might be achieved. 'Although they're extremely careful not to put it in this way,' Katy Hayward says:

> the Shared Island Unit and initiatives around it are not around preparation for unification per se. But they are, in part, a mapping of what do we need to think about. It's extraordinary how little thinking has happened on this matter to date. Not least because of the border poll issue [in the North] even though nobody was expecting it and it hadn't seemed imminent. But that was pre-Brexit. It's always a live issue in politics in the North. It's not in the South.[73]

But should the present government pre-empt Sinn Féin and start putting in place the template for detailed preparation for a united Ireland? What is the role of Fianna Fáil? A party to one policy now, will it simply morph to a more republican stance if it is part of a future coalition with Sinn Féin? 'I would accept that they could and probably will be in government in the republic after the next election,' says Fianna Fáil TD Éamon Ó Cuív. 'I don't accept they will be necessarily the lead part of the government, but that's a question that Fianna Fáil have to decide. At the end of the day a lot of Irish people would like to have a republican [Fianna Fáil] government because of our experience and because we don't have the legacy issues.'[74]

Sinn Féin's call for a border poll, Micheál Martin says, would only have added 'a further level of divisiveness to an already difficult situation' Sinn Féin hadn't thought through.[75] There is a difference between electioneering slogans and governing: 'We're trying to unite people here, in a common purpose. I don't think it should be a majoritarian, territorial approach. That will not suffice.'

In response to Sinn Féin's arguments that there is no clarity related to calling a border poll and preparation should be prioritized, Martin disagrees: 'That's not only what the Good Friday Agreement was about. Most people in the North felt that the Good Friday Agreement was giving people a respite from this endless pursuit of a constitutional target.'[76]

'The spirit behind what Seamus Mallon was arguing (parallel consent in both communities),' Martin told *The Irish Times*, is the 'key point'. 'He [Mallon] said his neighbours "have been here for 400 years [and] it's about time we learned to live together". This idea, that we must have it in five years' time or 10 years' time – it doesn't work. The sloganeering doesn't work. Anyone can do the rhetoric. I could do it.'[77]

Whatever the intent, what most unionists saw was a cleverly crafted document with a series of proposed projects whose implementation will put the economic and social infrastructure of an all-Island economy in place, a precursor for a united Ireland, if only by default. Steve Aiken, leader at the time of the Ulster Union Party (UUP), refused to bite, foreswearing any interaction with the SIU and describing it as 'political expediency' designed to counter 'the scourge of Sinn Féin'. 'If the structures put in place by the Belfast Agreement were working effectively and appropriately,' he said, 'there wouldn't be any need for a SIU and what is an extra unnecessary layer of bureaucracy ... No unionist sees any merit in the SIU and we've told the Taoiseach that directly.'[78]

No one disputes the breadth of the co-operation in the seven areas in Schedule 2 of the B/GFA that provides the work remit of the North/South Ministerial Council (NSMC).[79] John Bradley, however, a former economist at the ESRI who specialized in North-South economic issues, scoffs at the notion of in-depth co-operation:

> In all the many projects that I ran on North-South issues, I was often horrified when you actually got in a room with somebody and they trusted you and they told you the truth. You realized how skin-deep this co-operation was ... On the unionist side, they are constrained by what they can do other than cleave to Britain for sustenance ... Pragmatic policymaking, the kind of things that Germans did with the French ... the kind of pragmatic policymaking that doesn't in any way threaten your sovereignty ... that's never succeeded in Northern Ireland.[80]

On the COVID-19 pandemic, the issue that cried out for cross-border co-operation, it was egregiously limited.[81] 'Civil servants and politicians can create machinery at the high level to try and get people to co-operate, but unless people want to, they won't,' says Sean Donlon, the former secretary general of the Irish Department of Foreign Affairs. 'There's very little co-operation between North and South. Frankly, none at all, in dealing with the pandemic. It's a crazy situation where you have two different administrations, two different approaches to the same virus.'[82]

Some interviewees mentioned institutional rigidities, set-ups designed to prioritize twenty-six counties, without the flexibility to factor in an additional six counties: 'It doesn't come naturally after a hundred years to think through the wider all-island dimensions ... There's an inbuilt institutional bias to work on a twenty-six-county basis for large aspects of governance.'[83] Others mentioned the countervailing impacts of opposing political ideologies: 'One is very opposed to being seen to be working with Dublin if that means they're working in a different way to London.'[84] Still others point to competition, bias and arguments over which health system was better at handing the virus. 'On one hand,' Ian Marshall says:

> Arlene Foster was guided by Michael McBride, chief medical officer, who took all his direction from Westminster ... on the other

hand was the Sinn Féin deputy First Minister Michelle O'Neill, who wanted to take her direction from Dublin, not to be steered by Westminster ... We got into a situation where there was a lack of communication between Belfast and Dublin because each was trying to be one better than the other. For all the language around working together and sharing things, it was very much a competition between who could deal with this pandemic better. That was a huge failure.[85]

Some interviewees argue that Northern Ireland has more economic links with the UK than with the Republic of Ireland. In fact, the Northern Ireland economy and British economy are highly integrated.[86] But the Trade and Cooperation Agreement (TCA) between the EU and the UK is having foreseen and unforeseen impacts on the three economies; Brexit is changing the trading relationship between Britain and the republic, and the NIP is changing the trading relationship between Northern Ireland and Britain, and between Northern Ireland and the republic. The net result is a dramatic fall in Britain's share of imports to the republic and an even more dramatic surge in trade between both parts of Ireland, germinating another fear: the economic stranglehold the South might have on the North's economy in future years.

The quandary for the present Irish government is this: pressure, albeit republican alone, is mounting to prepare for a border poll, which will require that the public, North and South, have some detailed idea about how it is to be brought about and what it will entail. But objective evidence does not suggest there is majority support for unity in the North for a poll, and there may not be for some years to come.

This poses the question: should the present government pre-empt Sinn Féin and start putting in place the template for how the process should unfold, or should it cede the political ground to Sinn Féin?

Sinn Féin and its republican acolytes are well on their way to becoming the new establishment. The clash between the two will be one of the defining characteristics of the emerging Ireland: on one hand, the advocates of a more reasoned approach for unity in the Seamus Mallon model, emphasizing the necessity for a sufficient body of unionist buy-in for unity; on the other, a Sinn Féin-driven campaign for unity that acknowledges such a buy-in would facilitate unity, but is not about to wait for it to emerge once it appears the 50 per cent + 1 threshold has been crossed. The debate about a future united Ireland may prove as divisive as the debate in Northern Ireland.

TEN

Sinn Féin: 'whatever works'

Sometimes Sinn Féin's call for a border poll is misunderstood or misrepresented in the sense that people suggest that we are calling for a border poll immediately. What we're actually calling for is the preparations for a border poll ... to agree what a united Ireland will look like in terms of the constitutional, the economic and the political framework ... and then agree a template as to how we can persuade the majority to support that proposition.[1]

— Matt Carthy, Sinn Féin Teachta Dála (TD)

The biggest obstacle to a united Ireland is Sinn Féin. A lot of people would find Sinn Féin's approach off-putting, the kind of 'ourselves alone' approach – the Bobby Storey funeral, ignoring the rules as though they're above the law and some of their behaviour on social media – they're not a normal political party. It's not a reflection on their electorate because many of their electorate are post-ceasefire voters. These people are not interested in the history of the organization. They're interested in what they do on the ground in local communities. One of the mistakes that unionists make is to equate all Sinn Féin voters with people who support paramilitary activity. However, they're not a

*regular political party in the way they do business, in the way they're
organized, and that's fairly clear when you look at how they behave.*[2]
   – Naomi Long, Minister of Justice, Alliance Party leader

*A Northern Ireland Assembly whose members still represent a majority
of people who want to remain part of the union, led by a Sinn Féin first
minister with their version of a united Ireland which has no respect
for unionism and eulogizes murderers and terrorists – that's such an
appalling vista that it's not conceivable Northern Ireland could end up
in such a position.*[3]
   – Nigel Dodds, deputy leader of the Democratic Unionist Party
(DUP) 2008–21, leader of the DUP in the British House of Lords

*Sinn Féin will use their role in a future Irish government as a platform
to push for a border poll, and I think that will have a destabilizing
effect. The overall result of that will be to make the relationship between
Northern Ireland and the Republic of Ireland more difficult because
Sinn Féin will use their position in government in both the North and
South to push a particular agenda. In the end, the Sinn Féin party is
not a majority in Northern Ireland and it won't be a majority for the
foreseeable future in the Republic of Ireland, so the rest of us have to
have a say as well … I think we would have to look at whether we
require additional safeguards to be put in place to protect the other
political parties in Northern Ireland from Sinn Féin abusing its position
as being both a judge and jury.*[4]
   – Jeffrey Donaldson, Member of the Legislative Assembly (MLA),
leader of the DUP, MP

*My view [of the Sinn Féin in government in the South], in terms of
the cost of unity and creating a new Ireland, is that it's actually quite
damaging because we in the SDLP are engaged in an extensive process
of discussion with unionism, not with unionist parties but with people
from a unionist background. There is a door ajar there for us to have
a conversation about the future. People can see the sands, the constitutional sands are shifting. But they are worried, to a man and woman,
about a Sinn Féin-led government. I think this is a problem Sinn Féin
always have: are they more interested in themselves or the country?
They usually come back in favour of themselves.*[5]
   – Colum Eastwood, Social Democratic and Labour Party
(SDLP) leader, MP

Sinn Féin's narrative is that it was appropriate to bomb and kill to get a united Ireland. While that odour is in the air, you can understand people being uncomfortable about moving towards such a united Ireland. Unfortunately, the IRA have made a lot of people associate Irish unity and the Irish Republic with death.[6]

– Claire Hanna, SDLP MP

Interviewees across Northern Ireland agree: Sinn Féin is the biggest obstacle to a united Ireland. It is an irony that the party whose raison d'être is a united Ireland is perceived as making that goal more difficult to achieve. Yet the fact remains that Sinn Féin is likely to be part of a governing coalition in the South after the next election in 2025, perhaps as the lead partner, with Mary Lou McDonald as Taoiseach. Undoubtedly, the call for a border poll and the creation of either a dedicated reunification unit within the Taoiseach's department or a department of reunification will top its demands of its coalition partners.[7]

Founded in 1905 as a 'dual monarchy' party, Sinn Féin, chameleon-like, has reimagined itself in many iterations throughout its long and tumultuous history, but has never deviated from its razor-sharp focus on the promise of a thirty-two-county unitary Irish Republic. The party, elected to the first Dáil in the last all-Ireland elections in 1918, spearheaded the War of Independence (1919–21). In 1922 it split into pro- and anti-Anglo-Irish Treaty factions. A savage civil war followed (1922–3), pitting neighbour against neighbour, often dividing families against each other.[8] The pro-Treaty faction became the Cumann na nGaedheal and subsequently Fine Gael.[9] The anti-Treaty faction split in 1926 into Fianna Fáil and a rump Sinn Féin. For all of the twentieth century, the bitter residuals of the Civil War defined Irish politics. And for much of the century, the Fianna Fáil side – the losing side in the Civil War – ruled alone or in coalition with smaller parties. But, ironically, it was Fine Gael that declared Ireland a republic and took it out of the Commonwealth in 1949.

The rump Sinn Féin continued to deny the legitimacy of both the independent Irish state and Northern Ireland, referring to the Irish state as 'the twenty-six counties' – or derisively as 'the Free State' – and Northern Ireland as 'the six counties', a practice that continues to this day. On the margins of Irish politics, it contested general elections on the platform that if elected it would abstain, a promise the electorate rewarded with a vote commensurate with no representation. But no matter which iteration it found itself in, Sinn Féin clung tenaciously to one overriding goal: to reclaim the republic mandated in the 1916 Proclamation of the Irish Republic.

Throughout the decades of the Northern Ireland conflict, the party was the spokesperson for the Provisional Irish Republican Army (PIRA), a semantic difference deployed to either tie itself more closely to the Irish Republican Army (IRA) or create a little distance from it, depending on circumstances. As Danny Morrison, editor of *An Phoblacht* and a Sinn Féin spokesperson at the time, told me in 1982:

> The aim of the republican movement, going back sixty years, has been to establish a socialist republic based on the 1916 Proclamation. What we want to see is a fair and equal distribution of wealth throughout the country, an end to poverty, proper schools and hospitals, an end to exploitation, everyone having the right to a home.[10]

In 1997, with the party branding itself as a left-of-centre social democratic party, the first non-abstentionist Sinn Féin TD was elected to Dáil Éireann.[11] In 2002, it won an additional 4 seats.[12] In 2011, in the first election to be held after the 2008 economic recession that required a European Union (EU) bailout of Ireland's banking system and led to a period of austerity, the party secured 14 seats.[13] It added another 9 seats in 2016 and a further 15 in 2020, for a total of 37 seats.[14]

'It's a very different Sinn Féin,' says Bertie Ahern, former Taoiseach:

> Sinn Féin come across now as quite centrist. They don't come across as left-wing anymore. They're no longer anti-Europe, they're no longer against Ireland keeping its low tax rates for business. They support modern innovation. They support investing in infrastructure and education. It's a very different Sinn Féin than the one that I had to contend with in the early years of my political life, which was only about the North, extradition, prisoners.[15]

In a move to show that it had come in from the cold, and showing its readiness to assume the reins of government, the 2021 Ard Comhairle passed a resolution dropping its opposition to the republic's Special Criminal Court, established in 1974 primarily to try IRA members, and for decades an anathema to Sinn Féin.[16]

Over the years, Sinn Féin has built a powerful all-Ireland political machine. Its electoral bandwidth extends across four political jurisdictions. With MPs at Westminster (absent but using the perks and allowances of the United Kingdom [UK] Parliament, the European parliament, the Northern Ireland Assembly and Dáil Éireann), the party dwarfs all others, somehow maintaining its mystique as an outsider. Yet, this self-proclaimed anti-elitist and anti-establishment party is well on the way to becoming the new establishment. It is by far the richest party in Ireland, with more than 50 properties and a staff of more than 200.[17]

Alex Attwood, a former SDLP minister and a member of the SDLP's team that negotiated the Belfast/Good Friday Agreement (B/GFA), calls Sinn Féin's open boasting about the fifty properties it owns and its flaunting of its wealth, while simultaneously selling itself as the little guy fighting for the public good against the Southern establishment, 'brazen'. It was 'an astounding, ultra-confident move … And how do they fund all these properties? That, I've always said, is one of the biggest legacies of the conflict – IRA money. It's what Des Mackin [Sinn Féin's long-time director of finance] was publicly, arrogantly announcing'.[18]

One avenue of inquiry leads to the Northern Bank robbery in Belfast in December 2004, widely believed to have been carried out by the IRA, when £26.5 million disappeared and was never traced. This was the IRA's swan-song, according to most accounts.[19] (That, and money from other bank robberies in both parts of Ireland during the conflict, subsequently laundered into legitimate enterprises, also comes to mind.) But with the emphasis in the early 2000s on pressurizing or cajoling the IRA into decommissioning its arms, governments turning a blind eye to the robbery was in the spirit of realpolitik. Blind eyes have been turned to many paramilitary activities because, as the MI5 report conceded, the IRA was helping to implement the B/GFA.[20]

If present electoral trends continue, however, Sinn Féin will probably head governments both North and South. Were such a situation to emerge, the pressure on the British government to announce a border poll might become difficult to ignore. The consequences would be unpredictable, possibly provoking a violent backlash from elements of loyalism, which in turn could galvanize residual pockets of dissident republicans into action. Sinn Féin denies the likelihood of such a scenario, but veteran observers express caution.[21]

The Police Service of Northern Ireland (PSNI) and the Garda Síochána report that, according to intelligence reports in both jurisdictions, the Army Council oversees both the IRA and Sinn Féin, although stressing that the IRA is now committed to achieving its goals through peaceful means.[22] Mary Lou McDonald, Sinn Féin president, rebuffs the claim that Sinn Féin still answers to the IRA: 'The war is over, the IRA has gone away and democracy is the order of the day and there's no dispute around that.'[23] Five former Irish ministers of justice, however, have confirmed the relationship between the Army Council and Sinn Féin.[24]

Not quite nonsense, says Naomi Long, Minister of Justice in the Northern Ireland Executive:

> Until they [Sinn Féin] manage to find a way of commemorating and marking the dead that doesn't extend to glorifying the IRA's actions, they will continue to be a barrier to unity on this island. There are a lot of unionists who could picture themselves living peacefully in a united Ireland even if it wasn't their first choice, but who would struggle to do so if the Taoiseach were a member of Sinn Féin. That's not about sectarianism, that's about the concerns about Sinn Féin and how it operates.[25]

Sinn Féin in government in both Irish jurisdictions would raise questions about the relationship between the party and the institutions of the Irish state, especially policing and justice, where in the North its minister is determined by a cross-community vote – effectively ruling out any prospect of a Sinn Féin Minister of Justice.[26] There are also questions about how Sinn Féin in government in both jurisdictions would impact the working of the B/GFA. The British and Irish governments are guarantors of that agreement, meant to be neutral and impartial arbiters. They bang heads when the Stormont parties have disagreements and especially when the institutions are collapsed. How would this process work when one party is a mediator in a dispute and another one of the disputants? It doesn't. As Professor Duncan Morrow of the University of Ulster points out:

> The DUP's participation in a kind of coalition with the Tories at Westminster under Theresa May exposed a significant weakness of the agreement's structure in that it depends on the ability of the British and Irish governments to mediate disputes … If either Sinn

Féin or the DUP takes control of one of the referees, the whole system starts to wobble. The DUP providing the Tories with their majority for three years effectively disabled the British government in Northern Ireland, and so we had no government here. The situation was only addressed after the Conservative party won the December 2019 election with a majority large enough to ditch the DUP. Only then did they force the DUP and Sinn Féin back together.[27]

There are also lingering doubts about whether Sinn Féin recognizes the legitimacy of the Irish state's institutions. The IRA always claimed that it was the rightful heir to the tradition of 1916, and that the states in both North and South were illegitimate, contrary to the Proclamation of Independence and Dáil elections in 1918. When pushed to say whether it accepts the full legitimacy of the Irish state, Sinn Féin dances around the question, touching on but never quite giving an unequivocal response.[28] In this regard, some of the most scathing criticism of the party comes from the SDLP, and while some of that may be attributed to lingering resentment over Sinn Féin's success in eclipsing the SDLP as the party of preference for most Northern nationalists, suspicions about the party's real intentions run deeper. Sean Farren, a member of the SDLP's B/GFA negotiating team, says:

> Do they give allegiance to the police? They say so but … I have very strong questions that need to be answered by Sinn Féin as to their position on the Irish Constitution and the key institutions of the state for which they've shown a lot of disregard over the years … I don't want to see Sinn Féin in government. I would be very worried about them having control of the police in the South, and I would be very worried about them having control over Anglo-Irish affairs and North-South affairs.[29]

When I asked Pádraig Mac Lochlainn TD, Sinn Féin's Dáil whip – who refers to himself as an 'activist', not a politician – about the matter, he was unapologetic:

> I refer to the state that I live in as the twenty-six counties and I refer to the state that is just over the road from me [in Buncrana, County Donegal] as the six counties. That's our way of acknowledging and openly stating our objective that we want to live in a thirty-two-county Irish Republic, and we accept that it's our responsibility to win the hearts and minds over to that objective. I refer to my nearest

city as Derry City, not Londonderry … I regard the state that I live in
as a transitionary state. As I say, we've come a long way.[30]

If Sinn Féin limits its acceptance of the legitimacy of the Republic of Ireland
to seeing it as a transitional political arrangement and not a functioning democratic constitutional state (regarded as such by the overwhelming number
of its citizens), it begs the question: 'what other parts of the Constitution
does Sinn Féin not subscribe to?'

Now that Sinn Féin is in position to head a future Irish government, will
it uphold the Constitution and acknowledge the present republic unequivocally as the state it governs? Or will it continue to see it as a state that will
only become legitimate when the two parts of Ireland are united? Will a
future coalition partner demand its unequivocal embrace of all the institutions of the state and the state itself? Or will Sinn Féin take a leaf out of
an old Fianna Fáil playbook? On joining Dáil Éireann in 1927, even though
the country's dominion status required an oath of allegiance to the king, its
newly elected TDs 'pretended' to do so, 'fingers crossed'. It was, after all, at
that point a 'slightly constitutional party', an appellation some would ascribe
to present-day Sinn Féin.[31]

What does Sinn Féin stand for? Among the six Sinn Féin interviewees,
only Rose Conway-Walsh used the phrase 'socialist republic'.[32] Pádraig Mac
Lochlainn said:

> I've always felt that being an Irish republican is a more active way of
> achieving a united Ireland. Somebody who is an Irish nationalist, in
> my opinion, is somebody who would like to see a united Ireland but
> isn't terribly motivated about making it happen. An Irish republican
> is somebody who is more energized to campaign, to work, to win
> hearts and minds, for a united Ireland …
>
> I have to convince a section of unionism that their best interests lie
> in a united Ireland. My problem right now is that too many people, both
> in the Irish political establishment and in the North, are reticent. Even
> though we are twenty-three years after the Good Friday Agreement
> … people are still saying that we shouldn't even make the case.[33]

The best summary of Sinn Féin's modus operandi came from Brian Feeney,
author of *Sinn Féin: A Hundred Turbulent Years*.[34] Sinn Féin, he says, stands
for 'what will work', what 'gets them into power'.[35] 'The South is where the

power is now. It used to be the power of the party was in the North. That's why Mary Lou McDonald is the president and Michelle O'Neill is vice president':

> Five years ago, it was the other way around. [Gerry] Adams was the president and Mary Lou McDonald was vice president. The balance has swung to Dublin. The A-team is in Dublin. They switch people from Belfast to Dublin, if they're any good. The hope is, from Mary Lou's point of view, that she's going to make this a squeaky-clean party of people who have no IRA associations.
>
> What's working now and has been working for the last ten years is that they've been moving to the centre as much as they can to attract voters in the South. They've been developing expertise in finance and housing in a big way. Eoin Ó Broin is the expert on housing in the republic now. He's written a book on it. Pearse Doherty is really a dominant figure in finance. They're trying to present a sensible economic position, but they're also staying radical because they believe that's what gets them votes. They will do what they think needs to be done to get the votes. If it means changing economic policy, changing financial policy, they'll do it. [36]

Feeney's words are echoed in the sentiments of others. Sinn Féin, a wide cross-section of interviewees said, is not a normal political party. Sinn Féin itself is quite open about this characterization. Indeed, they wear it like a badge of honour, as a symbol of not being like the entrenched parties and sclerotic elites that have ruled Ireland and divvied up the spoils of political office for a hundred years.

In March 2020, *The Irish Times* published a report on the inner working of the party.[37] Sinn Féin does not want its elected representatives controlling the party, Des Mackin, the long-time director of finance, told the paper: 'We don't want a parliamentary party running the organisation. We want to stay a party of activists. It's a totally different model. There's nothing mysterious about it.'[38]

TDs Pádraig Mac Lochlainn and Rose Conway-Walsh describe themselves as activists who are in politics only to bring about Irish unity, not to have a career. Conway-Walsh says:

> Sinn Féin has evolved, and it continues to evolve … It doesn't mean that you lose your core values. It moves in a direction of a united thirty-two-county socialist republic … For me, as a member of Sinn Féin,

> I want Irish unity before I die. Now Irish unity can mean different
> things to different people. I appreciate that.[39]

According to *The Irish Times*, the party's standing committee, the Coiste
Seasta, is a key body in the running of the party.[40] There were eight people
on the committee, only one of whom was an elected representative; in
March 2020, three of these people had IRA convictions. Five of the eight
were from Belfast. Sinn Féin's forty-eight-member Ard Comhairle is the
ultimate ruling body. It meets every six weeks or so, has eleven MLAs and
two MPs against six TDs. The Coiste Seasta, which meets every fortnight,
has the power of the Ard Comhairle when the latter is not sitting, and runs
the party on a day-to-day basis. All the party's national departments report
to the Ard Comhairle through the Coiste Seasta. This committee approves
all payments out of party funds that are above €250. Once a decision is taken
by the Ard Comhairle, it becomes the agreed position of the party.

All members are expected to speak from the same playbook in public,
a top-down decision-making and discipline model akin to a form of 'democratic centralism'. Among the other major parties in the South, the parliamentary party meeting, where a party's elected representatives meet in
private to thrash out party positions, is a key structure. Not so with Sinn
Féin. Political staffers who work for TDs meet at Sinn Féin HQ on Monday
mornings, without TDs present, and work out the agenda for the week.[41]

Sinn Féin made its case to the Irish electorate in its 2020 general election
manifesto, 'Giving Workers and Families a Break',[42] and in its discussion
document, 'Economic Benefits of a United Ireland'.[43] In the manifesto, Sinn
Féin finds government badly wanting after a hundred years of independence,
describing Irish society as a place where one finds 'homeless children eating
their dinner off the pavement outside the GPO', 'elderly people left to suffer
for days on hospital trolleys', 'working couples unable to afford a home', 'families unable to provide meals for their children or to meet domestic bills' and
'citizens who have worked all their adult lives being forced to draw the dole
because they are refused the right to a pension'. 'A political establishment
shamelessly sticks its head in the sand in the face of growing support for
Irish reunification and refuses to prepare responsibly for that eventuality.'[44]

At all levels, the manifesto argues, government has failed the people
and only Sinn Féin can remedy the dysfunctionality and corruption of the

Fianna Fáil/Fine Gael cabal that has sided at every stage 'with landlords, developers, insurance companies and vulture funds'.[45] Successive governments, it asserts, 'have delivered for their friends and cronies. They have delivered for big business, for vested interests and for golden circles'.[46]

The case the manifesto makes for the economic benefits of reunification rests on different grounds, some of it in terms of the adverse effects of partition, some the obvious appeal of an economy that is among the fastest growing in Europe. Northern Ireland is one of the poorest regions of the United Kingdom.[47] Sinn Féin cites 2018 figures showing that per-capita output in the South of Ireland is the highest in these islands: £40,637 in the South, £32,857 in England, £29,660 in Scotland, £25,981 in Northern Ireland and £23,866 in Wales.[48] The labour market in the North, it asserts, is characterized by jobs that are lower-paid and less secure than anywhere else in the UK.[49]

The manifesto says that the subvention to Northern Ireland, once it is disaggregated and such things as UK pension contributions factored out, is manageable. The EU will step in if necessary to stabilize the financial system, just as it poured huge amounts into East Germany to harmonize living standards in East and West Germany in the early 1990s. 'It is not a matter whether we can afford Irish unity,' Sinn Féin argues:

> the fact is that we cannot afford partition. A united Ireland economy would enjoy significant benefits by way of infrastructure, investment, taxation and employment. Brexit, the economic consequences of the Covid-19 pandemic and the climate and biodiversity crisis are best faced with a united Ireland economy operating to its full potential.[50]

The doomsayers who proselytize that the South cannot afford the North, cannot afford to take on the British Exchequer's subvention, are ignoring evidence to the contrary. 'There is no evidence,' Matt Carthy says, 'to suggest the people in the South would have to pay more taxes in the event of the united Ireland. In fact, there's every argument to suggest that they will be economically better off in that scenario, or certainly that the overall financial situation of our country will be better.'[51]

Twenty-four years after Sinn Féin committed itself to the B/GFA, what it stands for, other than a thirty-two-county republic, is still opaque. 'They didn't get where they are today by staying exactly the same, staying loyal to some immovable, ideological, theological position about republicanism,' Brian Feeney says. 'Privately, some of them would laugh at you if you said that the IRA was fighting for a thirty-two-county socialist Ireland. That was then, this is now.'[52]

Sinn Féin appears to be seeking to create the largest possible tent for ideas of what a united Ireland might look like and the processes required for its implementation following a pro-unity border poll. It claims to be prepared to subjugate its own core beliefs to the ideas of others in a forum yet to be established – but without disclosing its own ideas at this point. Its republican base is still committed to a thirty-two-county republic, no matter how narrow the margin of approval: 50 per cent + 1 is sufficient to rectify one of the most enduring wrongs of Irish history.[53] The unionist electoral majority in the North is gone. 'There is no need to second-guess the position of the people; instead, let us measure it in a referendum.'[54] The British government 'in line with the agreement should set a date for a referendum. A discussion on the future and of unity without a conclusion is a worthy yet ultimately pointless exercise.'[55]

In the 2016 Sinn Féin discussion document *Towards a United Ireland*, we are told that the party is open to considering

> constitutional recognition of the unique identity of Northern unionists and the British cultural identity of a significant number of people in the North; expression being given to the relationships between unionists and the British monarchy; and recognition of the place of the loyal institutions (including the Orange Order) in the cultural life of the nation.[56]

Also, 'transitional arrangements' might include 'devolution to Stormont and a power-sharing Executive in the North within an all-Ireland structure', or 'federal or confederal arrangements'.[57] One is left to surmise that all transitions lead to a unitary, all-Ireland state.

'Sinn Féin have two options,' Carthy says:

> We can actually set out what we expect a united Ireland to look like, or we can work with others to agree a collaborative formula as to what we think a united Ireland will entail, what mechanisms will need to be put in place – I'm talking about things like how long a transition

period would follow a referendum, and what would happen during
that transition period.[58]

The path to unity as laid out in *Towards a United Ireland* is perceived as a
series of processes – of discussion, persuasion, change, transition, transformation and reconciliation. In addition, 'the agreement of a significant
section of people who are now described as unionists is required for the
building of a new Ireland'.[59] A united Ireland is not simply 'new', it is 'agreed'.
There is 'a real need for all those who wish to see a united Ireland to engage
with unionist neighbours. We must listen to and engage with their hopes
and fears regarding unity'.[60]

For a party that is itself in a process of continual adaptation to the political environment it finds itself in, the emphasis on process is part of Sinn
Féin's DNA. But Sinn Féin has to find a route to squaring the political circle,
on the one hand avowing that if 50 per cent + 1 is sufficient to keep Northern
Ireland inside the United Kingdom, then 50 per cent + 1 is sufficient for
leaving – what's good for the unionist goose is equally valid for the republican gander. On the other hand, it must engage in the painstaking steps
involved in the healing and reconciliation it so eloquently expounds but
does little to put into practice.

In *Towards a United Ireland*, Sinn Féin pledges that the kind of 'truly
united Ireland' it seeks is 'one that means the unity of people ... one that
is agreed, inclusive, pluralist and which is constructed by all our citizens,
from all backgrounds and traditions'.[61] Nor should a referendum 'be seen or
portrayed as a threat to any section of our community'.[62] Which community
being referred to here is unclear, whether it is the Protestant/unionist community or those cultural Catholics (especially the significant number in the
public sector) who are content to stay in the union as long as it gives sufficient space for their Irish and European identities and who might fear losing
jobs or pensions in a reconfigured all-Ireland public sector. 'We've never had
a poll on the maintenance of partition,' says Chris Hazzard MP, a member
of Sinn Féin's Ard Comhairle. 'The Good Friday Agreement sets out that
it's going to be a straightforward vote like it was in Scottish independence
... We certainly want to be making the case that it should be much bigger
than that.'[63] (The Scottish independence vote in 2014 was lost by a margin of
ten points [55/45].) To facilitate getting a significant section of the unionist
community on board, he emphasizes engagement:

For many years now, we have had a department of engagement within the party that has reached out and that has been facilitated by our national chairperson, Declan Kearney. He has run several engagements around tackling sectarianism and racism and any forms of discrimination.

[That effort] has reached out to those people who have suffered loss as a result of the conflict in recent decades, people who have come from traditionally the other side of the community than ourselves, and that's been a process … Life and times are changing on the island, [and] these conversations are taking place much more readily now. In fact, even Brexit, I think, has pushed some of that stuff on …

We also need conversations to take place on an East-West basis because most people probably have a cavalier attitude and [are] saying, 'Oh the British government will want to leave this place [the North] in the morning.' To a large extent there's some truth to that, but there's also a connection between our islands. There's a connection deep in the DNA of people in the North with the people in Scotland.[64]

What does Sinn Féin point to as evidence that the metric for a poll has already been met and that such a poll would be successful? Says Séanna Walsh, the former senior IRA volunteer who announced the IRA ceasefire in 1994:

In December 2019 there was a Westminster election. There are eighteen seats in the North of Ireland. Sinn Féin took seven and the SDLP took two. The Alliance Party took one and the unionists took the other eight. You have nine nationalists, eight unionists and the Alliance Party. It's a majority nationalist outcome in regard to unionism versus nationalism.

In the most recent Assembly election in 2017, unionism lost their majority for the first time. If you look at the two major cities – Belfast and Derry – again it's a majority of nationalists in both. The unionist majority is gone. The strong unionist areas are only parts of County Down and County Antrim.

The [reason] for the union, which was the economy of the empire and the way that big business wanted to maintain the link with the empire for their own economic interest – all of that is now in the past. There are no good economic reasons to maintain the union. Brexit has done real damage to the cause of unionism in that there were a lot of people from a unionist persuasion who felt quite comfortable being members of the European Union, as well as being part of the United Kingdom.

Where it has come to a choice between membership of the union with Britain or membership with the union of the rest of Europe, that has taken its toll in regard to some unionists as well. On top of that, you have the whole demographic shift where the big majority of schoolchildren are from a Catholic background. Whenever I say Catholic, I'm not talking about religious Catholic. I mean more about cultural Catholics.[65]

How will the process itself unfold? 'The British government,' Hazzard says:

may say something like, 'after consultation with the Irish government we believe that there should be a border poll in such-and-such a year'. If the Scottish process is anything to go by, it's likely to be a two- or three-year process. The British and Irish governments are not yet at that point. But we know as [then Taoiseach] Leo Varadkar said almost three years ago, 'Tectonic plates are moving, and the British and Irish governments understand that they're in the ready-for-a-border-poll terrain …'[66]

The mechanism for having the referendum is the British government. We are actively asking them what criteria are you using to jumpstart that process. It appears that it is the issue of which parties have the electoral strength. We obviously must wait and see … If and when an Irish government says it's time, the British government will probably move. If the current Irish government was to say to the current British government, 'It's time now to have this referendum,' I would be confident that they would set down a date.[67]

Once a date is set, Walsh says, 'the real discussion begins'. It will force unionists to engage:

Unionists have adopted a strategy of burying their heads in the sand. They say, 'I don't want to talk about that. A referendum is never going to happen.' Therefore, it's very difficult to have a conversation with them. But once the date is set … that will force them to engage. However, whenever Sinn Féin talks about a referendum within five years, they're not looking at five years plus a week and that's the end of the union.

Look at what happened in Hong Kong – the British and the Chinese reached agreement that the British mandate would finish in Hong Kong in 1984. [Yet] it wasn't until 1997, thirteen years later, that the British furled their flag and departed the shores [of Hong Kong]. The border referendum would be a starting point, a 'well, that's it' point. We have to now start looking at building a new society together.[68]

Hazzard agrees:

If Brexit has taught us anything, if German reunification has taught us anything, it's that this will be a process. It won't be a big bang, it'll be done over a five-, ten-, fifteen-year period. Baby steps and doing it sensitively – I'm all for that because it brings more people along on the journey.[69]

These steps – consultation with the British government, setting a date in the future for a poll, making public the metrics the Secretary of State will use, thus opening the public space for political unionism to come to the negotiating table and articulate what measures would best accommodate their British identity in a new agreed Ireland – are the ones Sinn Féin in government will follow. Hazzard says:

If and when we enter government in the South, we can work with whoever we're in power with ... That's not to suggest that we wouldn't tread carefully. We understand the sensitivities nationally to all of this – it can't be seen as a pincer movement. It needs to be seen as a genuine process of national reconciliation ... We would want to see a department established underneath the Taoiseach's office that would be following this very carefully. There will be a white paper laying out the steps in the process, beginning the conversation in order to create the forum for people to come in and talk about the future. That's the process that a [Sinn Féin] government will follow.[70]

Things, however, are not that straightforward. There would be constraints on what Sinn Féin in government in the South could accomplish, especially if it is also heading up government in the North. It is highly unlikely, given the complicated proportional representation system by means of the Single Transferable Vote (PR-STV) Ireland uses, that Sinn Féin could govern alone. In July 2020, former Taoiseach Bertie Ahern – still a very astute observer of the Irish political landscape – pointed out:

Sinn Féin are picking up a lot of quality candidates who were not involved in the Troubles. A lot of their new members are third-level, educated people, and although they want a united Ireland (as Fianna Fáil does), their agenda is more focused on social issues. Health and education and agriculture and industry are the issues … It's a very different Sinn Féin.[71]

After the Assembly 2022 elections, Sinn Féin emerged as the largest party in the North. Michelle O'Neill is poised to become Northern Ireland's first minister whenever the DUP signals it is prepared to nominate a deputy first minister, something it refuses to do until the Northern Ireland Protocol (NIP) is 'sorted out'.[72]

Down South, every poll since the 2020 general election has the party going from strength to strength, easily outperforming its political rivals. In May 2022, after the Assembly elections in Northern Ireland where Sinn Féin emerged as the largest party, it benefited from a knock-on bounce of support in the South, receiving 36 per cent of the vote in a Red C/*Business Post* poll, greater than Fine Gael and Fianna Fáil combined (35 per cent).[73]

Mary Lou McDonald, meanwhile, has pronounced herself ready to become Taoiseach.[74]

However, even support in the mid-thirties percentage-wise would translate into 50–60 seats in the Dáil, well short of a majority in a chamber with 160 members.[75] If that level of popular support is reflected in the general election scheduled for 2025, Sinn Féin will undoubtedly emerge as the largest party, poised to form a government. And while forming a coalition with Fianna Fáil in tow would appear to be the most likely outcome, other parties might have to come on board: Labour, the Social Democrats, the Greens or groups of independents. But no matter which parties might be open to coalition with Sinn Féin, each will have its own set of demands; Irish unification will *not* rank among their key priorities. Moreover, in negotiations on forming a coalition, the parties being wooed will have disproportionate bargaining power because Sinn Féin wants above all else to be in government. And if this should call for some dilution of its core agenda of prioritizing, above all else, the drive for unity, so be it.

Forming a coalition might prove more difficult than conventional wisdom holds. A January 2022 poll showed Sinn Féin at 33 per cent, well ahead of Fianna Fáil and Fine Gael, but voters preferred the Fianna Fáil/ Fine Gael/Greens coalition (38 per cent) to a Sinn Féin-led government (34 per cent) with smaller parties, identified as the Greens, Labour, Social

Democrats and others on the left. Just 10 per cent of voters responded that they would like to see a Sinn Féin/Fianna Fáil coalition, and a meagre 3 per cent a Sinn Féin/Fine Gael coalition.[76]

Among 'the unknowns' that stalk the future, however – one that might derail Sinn Féin's advance to government – is the Russian invasion of Ukraine. An ongoing war that grinds on inconclusively, unsettling whole populations[77] and with growing uncertainty as to where it is ultimately heading might lead voters to opt for steady hands rather than a novice at the helm – especially since the novice was 'soft' on Russia prior to the invasion. Sinn Féin dealt with this embarrassing problem with a volte-face, scrubbing all references to its past 'soft' statements on Vladimir Putin and Russia from its social media following the invasion of Ukraine. When evidence of Russian atrocities came to light, McDonald led the charge calling for the expulsion of the Russian ambassador from Ireland.[78]

Even with Fianna Fáil there would be problems to be sorted out. Fianna Fáil TD Jim O'Callaghan, who has ambitions to lead the party, says the 50 per cent + 1 threshold is unrealistic. 'When there's a referendum in Northern Ireland,' he says:

> there will be a significant group of people arguing coherently for a pro-union position, and the status quo is always hard to defeat … People advocating reunification need to recognize the strength of the pro-union position and also that it will never be possible to get consensus amongst everyone. The objective in a debate on reunification should be to try to get over 60 per cent of the Northern Ireland population saying, 'Yes, we'll go along with this.' That would be a remarkable achievement.[79]

Sinn Féin will also face other realities, underscoring the difference between being in government and being in opposition. Sinn Féin points to polls in the South that consistently say that at least two-thirds of voters are in favour of unity.[80] But they fail to provide any caveats, not the least of which is that when asked what size majority would be sufficient for a border poll result to be accepted by both sides of the community in Northern Ireland, 81 per cent of respondents in the South say they believe either a two-thirds or 70 per cent majority would be needed.[81]

'Sinn Féin government in the republic would be part of a coalition so they won't be calling all the shots,' says John FitzGerald:

They will need two referenda, North and South, and they'll have to
sell that in the republic. Pearse Doherty [Sinn Féin spokesperson on
finance], I'm convinced, knows that it will be an exceptionally difficult sell.

This issue is not high on the agenda of the people of the republic
… People may say, 'Oh, we want Irish unity,' but when they're asked
what the priority issues are, they are health and housing and so on.
Sinn Féin is unlikely to get a referendum in the North, and if they got
one in the South, they could well lose it.

Sinn Féin in the driving seat in both jurisdictions might force
them to face reality on this. Because they can't deliver on it, it will
pose problems with some of their electorate, especially in the North.
If they focus too much on delivering it, it will cause them significant
problems with their electorate in the South.[82]

Sinn Féin may be on the way to becoming the leading party in governments
North and South, but neither of these scenarios, Brendan O'Leary believes,
'enables a very fast move to Irish unification'.[83] There's no point calling for a
poll in the North without evidence in favour of unification, and in power
Sinn Féin will realize the merits of being careful what it wishes for. The key
question, he says, 'is whether Sinn Féin will behave like Fianna Fáil in the
1930s or arguably Cumann na nGaedheal in the early twenties, that they will
see that their party's success is best accomplished through stabilizing both
entities on the island. Their ideological goal of unification is best accomplished through not having any impatient push'.[84]

How, then, would dissident republicanism respond to unification
without that 'impatient push'? After the British vote to leave the EU, the
Irish government successfully used the threat of dissident republicanism to
convince the EU that a land border across Ireland would result in violence.[85]
Would Sinn Féin find itself behaving like Fianna Fáil in the 1930s and 1940s?
Would it, irony of ironies, haul reactivated dissident republicans before the
Special Criminal Court – which it had so despised and condemned during
the Troubles, and only recognized as a legitimate arm of law enforcement in
October 2021 – as part of the party's makeover of its image as a respectable,
electable party? Far-fetched, says Andy Pollak: 'Sinn Féin will drive on to
unity in a way Fianna Fáil never could.'[86]

As Matt Carthy says:

> One of the more disappointing aspects of the unity debate is that the argument has actually been articulated by Irish government representatives to move the goal posts to suggest that 50 per cent + 1 wouldn't be sufficient because it could lead to turmoil … If 52 per cent across Britain was enough to drive the North out of the European Union against its wishes, then 50 per cent +1 or 52 per cent in favour of Irish unity would be enough to do that in a democratic process.[87]

The message that the desired majority in the North for unity is nowhere near materializing is not one Sinn Féin is open to hearing, despite fewer than 40 per cent of Northerners voting for nationalist parties and over 80 per cent of Southerners telling pollsters that unity would require at least a two-thirds majority in Northern Ireland.[88]

The Sinn Féin newspaper *An Phoblacht* is a platform for 'uncomfortable conversations'. In recent years, there have been few such conversations, and too often they occur within a wider republican bubble – unionists hardly flock to the paper, which they see as the IRA's propaganda rag, to share their thoughts on constitutional futures.

The paper says all the right things. Reconciliation between the two traditions, if not quite a prerequisite for unification – that would be a bridge too far – implies at least having enough (lower-case) unionists on board, a slice of 'civic unionism'. Increased dialogue and engagement are essential. Sinn Féin, according to party chairperson Declan Kearney, has to be 'prepared to take the lead in helping to shape an authentic reconciliation process and embrace the discomfort of moving outside [its] political and historic comfort zones'.[89] Kearney calls on Sinn Féin 'to be courageous [and] … recognise the healing influence of being able to say sorry for the human effects of all actions caused during the armed struggle'.[90] But there would be no apology for the IRA's armed struggle, he said, no suggestion that it might have been wrong.[91] It did not start the war; the war came to it.[92]

These sentiments were expressed in 2012. Now, Sinn Féin's 'reaching out to unionism' reconciliation project is moribund: the mellifluous words still flow, the exhortations are still as appealing, the response still as muted. Relations between Sinn Féin and unionists are at an all-time low, exacerbated by the fact that Sinn Féin has emerged as the largest party in Northern

Ireland and claims the prize of first minister, putting unionism in a subordinate position for the first time in 100 years.

In the Sinn Féin documents *Towards an Agreed and Reconciled Future*[93] and *Inclusion and Reconciliation in a New Ireland*,[94] the party spells out the route to healing, reconciliation, ending sectarianism and dealing with the legacy of the past – much of which, it implies, has to be accomplished before a border poll, because 'creating the positive conditions in which a unity referendum is held will be as important as the outcome of the referendum'.[95] This means 'facilitating an open, including and informed societal dialogue that engages the broadest section of stakeholders'.[96] The huge steps Sinn Féin envisages itself taking as part of its reconciliation project will be impossible to accomplish in the near future, as it requires the kind of engagement unionists eschew, not least because the Sinn Féin narrative of the conflict is such an anathema to the Protestant community.[97]

Matters were further complicated by the Bobby Storey funeral controversy. Michelle O'Neill's attendance at Bobby Storey's funeral on 1 July 2020 in the middle of the COVID-19 pandemic, along with twenty-four Sinn Féin members of the Assembly, took a sledgehammer to the relationship between herself and then First Minister Arlene Foster, as well as with the broader nationalist and unionist communities. Yet again, it was revealed how fragile the Stormont institutions were, just months into their resuscitation.[98]

Storey, a former director of intelligence for the IRA and among its most senior members, was a staunch Gerry Adams ally and chairperson of Sinn Féin in Northern Ireland for a period. He had also been the IRA's enforcer. His support of the peace process was critical in republican circles. He died during an operation for a lung transplant in England.

His funeral in West Belfast had all the trappings of an IRA funeral: pipers leading the funeral cortege from St Agnes' Church to Milltown Cemetery; an honour guard, paramilitary style, along the length of the route; men in white shirts, black trousers and matching black ties; streets lined with up to 1,800 mourners; graveside eulogies – in short, perfect choreography for the myth-making grandiosity that is the hallmark of how republicans bury their dead. In pre-pandemic times, it was an event that on its own would have had the potential to derail the Executive.

The event, however, was also in violation of the COVID-19 regulations that O'Neill herself had helped draw up and regularly called on the Northern

Ireland public to adhere to during the weekly press conferences she and First Minister Arlene Foster jointly convened to keep the public informed of the virus's progress. These regulations restricted attendance at funerals to a maximum of ten, and to only relatives of the deceased. Public gatherings of more than thirty were forbidden, with rules of two-metre social distancing and mask-wearing in place. When the Nobel Prize-winner John Hume, widely regarded as the godfather of the B/GFA, died, his family adhered strictly to the guidelines. So did the family of the DUP's Edwin Poots at his father's funeral.

The sense of hurt and anger across Northern Ireland outside the republican base was palpable. Families who had lost loved ones and restricted funeral attendance to ten close family members – keeping in line with the Assembly-approved rules – were outraged, and they demanded accountability. The airwaves and social media crackled with people calling out Sinn Féin for being hypocritical: the party that prided itself on its principled advocacy of equal treatment across all aspects of life in Northern Ireland had gone and placed itself above the rules everyone else was following. For others, it confirmed what they already believed: Sinn Féin couldn't be trusted to act within the bounds of moral inclusion, or to take responsibility for its actions. On the positive side, some pointed out that in the past an act like the Bobby Storey funeral would have collapsed Stormont.

O'Neill's presence in the church in violation of several regulations led the DUP, Alliance, the SDLP and the Ulster Unionist Party (UUP) – the four other parties in the Executive – to call for O'Neill to step aside while the PSNI investigated to ascertain what rules had been breached. Unless O'Neill apologized, Foster said, she could no longer share a platform with her for their weekly briefings. Sinn Féin itself also came under fire: it had had a week to plan the funeral and could have asked its supporters to stay at home and follow the COVID-19 guidelines, but it chose instead to stage a grand public spectacle, as if to assert Sinn Féin's exceptionalism and entitlement to transcend the regulations it called on others to obey.

The contrast was striking: O'Neill at the podium with Foster for the weekly COVID-19 media briefing exhorting the public to stick with the guidelines – especially the ten-person, family-only limit for funeral services – and O'Neill defiantly saying, 'I will never apologise for attending the funeral of my friend.'[99] Fears that the imbroglio could lead to the collapse of the Executive less than six months after it being restored for the fifth time as the parties struggled to find an acceptable fudge was a reminder of just how fractious relations between the DUP and Sinn Féin were.

They are locked into cycles of self-reinforcing abuse: a disagreement, a crisis, a meltdown, two governments scrambling to find some formula to avert the collapse of the Executive one more time. Unionists took note of the Storey funeral arrangements: a set piece of republican theatre, with the implicit message that the IRA had not gone away, and Sinn Féin President Mary Lou McDonald's attendance in violation of Dublin's lockdown. In the Dáil, McDonald defended her attendance, adding that if she were Taoiseach and had been invited to attend she would have done so. The reaction in the South to the brouhaha surrounding the funeral reflected the divide between an older generation – for whom the IRA was still a lingering presence, evoking memories of violence and horror – and a younger generation for whom such considerations are what it would expect an older generation to obsess about: point-scoring about matters of no import to anyone.

Ten months on, in April 2021, the Northern Ireland Public Prosecution Service (PPS) issued a detailed report making the case for its decision not to pursue prosecution of the twenty-four Sinn Féin members of the Assembly who had attended the funeral. It cited too many technical loopholes, provisions of the law that might be construed in different ways and the fact that there were Sinn Féin members who had attended saying they did not fully understand the law (despite having been co-authors of the legislation).

Then came the revelation that the PSNI and Sinn Féin had met prior to the funeral.

The uproar was furious: unionists accused the PSNI of being Sinn Féin's lapdog; they said the police force was two-tiered – one for Sinn Féin and one for everybody else. Lord Bew, one of the key advisers in David Trimble's inner circle during the B/GFA negotiations, said:

> The Bobby Storey funeral is going to be around for years ... You just play back those scenes, with Gerry Adams, Michelle O'Neill, Mary Lou McDonald, all the Sinn Féin MLAs and TDs. Everybody else who lost a father or mother to COVID was restricted to four people at the funeral. It's emblematic, a dramatic moment. It's a real assertion of entitlement ... Indeed, the police have been very, very reluctant to pursue them for obvious reasons.[100]

Immediately the Parades Commission was inundated with applications from loyalist bands to take part in parades to mark the beginning of the Orange marching season. Loyalists were demanding their pound of flesh: if Sinn Féin could so flagrantly disregard COVID restrictions, loyalists were asserting their right to parity of esteem. Upwards of 250 applications were received, swamping the commission with notifications from bands outlining their intention to parade within their communities, adhering to the thirty-person public gathering guideline.[101]

Gable walls and the peace walls in West Belfast and the Ardoyne are shrines to republicans who were killed by security forces or otherwise gave their lives for the cause. Sinn Féin holds its dead close. The mantra 'the war came to us' is at the core of Sinn Féin's push to define the narrative of the conflict. The IRA's war was a heroic war to end the British presence in Northern Ireland and achieve a united Ireland. The 1916 uprising and the first Dáil in 1918 are continually invoked to provide legitimacy to the war. Memorialization is essential to the narrative. Every volunteer killed by the British security forces is commemorated.

In his book, *Who Was Responsible for the Troubles?*, historian Liam Kennedy provides a clinical dissection of the deaths and injuries over the thirty-year period of the conflict. His conclusion is stark and unequivocal: the IRA was the most responsible agent. Of the 3,636 deaths, 49 per cent were attributable to the PIRA; loyalist paramilitaries were responsible for 29 per cent and the security forces for 10 per cent. Deaths suffered by IRA volunteers came to 293 (8 per cent) compared to 1,032 (28 per cent) for the security forces – a ratio greater than 3:1. Of these 293 IRA volunteers, just 40 per cent met their deaths at the hands of the security forces, 60 per cent by forces other than the security forces – vendettas and internecine quarrels between rival republican paramilitaries. The number of civilian deaths due to the IRA amounted to 636 – just over 17 per cent of all deaths. Kennedy writes:

> Contrary to populist accounts, only a small minority of civilians' casualties were due to the security forces. The RUC [Royal Ulster Constabulary], despite being the object of much ideological and communal hatred, was responsible for less than 2 per cent of *civilian* deaths.

Security-force deaths were two and half times more frequent than those of republican paramilitaries and seven times more frequent than those of loyalist paramilitaries. This sets Northern Ireland apart from many [other] insurgencies in the twentieth-century world where state forces typically inflicted disproportionate casualties on other armed groups.[102]

According to the [republican] script, the 'war' was not against the Protestant and unionist people of Northern Ireland … The 'war' was against the British army of occupation … One might imagine that the soldiers of the British army would be the principal targets and would be heavily represented among the casualties. Was this the case? The fact is that of the 3,600 or so Troubles-related deaths, less than 15 per cent of the total – 13.8 per cent, to be precise – were soldiers of the regular British army. The equally startling, or perhaps more startling, fact is that more than *four-fifths* of the fatal casualties of the Troubles were *Irish* (in the sense of being born on the island of Ireland). In practice it would seem that the Troubles was a form of communal and civil war, man against man, fought out largely within the confines of Northern society.[103]

Kennedy's meticulous analysis, using data drawn from *Lost Lives*,[104] hardly fits Sinn Féin's narrative of a heroic war fought against an imperial oppressor who was responsible for the partition of Ireland. Yet, such is the power of republican myth and propaganda that the evidence-based facts seem counter-intuitive.[105] In speeches and in his blog articles in *An Phoblacht*, Sinn Féin chairman Declan Kearney (who refused to be interviewed for this book) frequently and elegantly calls for 'reconciliation', emphasizes the need for 'difficult' conversations and expresses willingness to acknowledge 'the hurt' the IRA's campaign of violence caused others. What Sinn Féin can never do is abandon its narrative of the conflict. Anyone who wore the uniform of the Crown – or had in the past – was a legitimate target. This group includes the RUC, the locally recruited and mainly part-time Ulster Defence Regiment (UDR) and former UDR members, almost all Protestants with deep roots in that community.

The IRA's campaign was in large measure a war against Northern Protestants. Until Sinn Féin can acknowledge this, without innumerable qualifiers and whataboutery, it will continue to be oblivious to Protestant anger and hurt regarding the past. In fact, there is little likelihood of it doing so. In the 'war' of the narratives, Sinn Féin has emerged the clear winner. A LucidTalk poll (August 2022) found that 69 per cent of nationalists/republicans believe there was no alternative to violent resistance to British rule. The figure among 18- to 44-year-olds is higher, at 74 per cent.[106] So successful has Sinn Féin been at selling its narrative of the conflict that a generation that saw little of it retrospectively condones it, whereas in 1998 a generation of nationalists/republications that had experienced it were over-whelmingly condemnatory.[107] The more the conflict recedes in time, the greater the support expressed by the nationalist/republican community for the narrative promulgated by Sinn Féin.[108]

Northern Protestants see Sinn Féin as attempting to establish a hierarchy of victims, with its own dead in the most deserving positions and the secu-rity forces – especially the British army, whom they see as the enforcers of the remnants of colonial oppression – painted as heinous perpetrators who must be brought to justice, even if fifty years have elapsed since the incident in question. The case of Soldier F personifies this double standard.[109]

What unionists fear is that in an all-Ireland state under a Sinn Féin government, the dominant and celebrated national narrative will be that of Sinn Féin and the IRA. In the public space, they ask, would that party sanc-tion commemorations for members of the RUC and UDR murdered by the IRA? Public space for eulogies for their heroes who fought a decades-long war against IRA terrorism? Parity of esteem for their fallen, sometimes shot dead because at one time they happened to be members or former members of the RUC and the UDR?

The South has little understanding of or interest in the loathing that most unionists harbour towards Sinn Féin, a visceral hatred that shows no abating a generation since the B/GFA. The South is a country of young people: more than 62 per cent of the population are younger than forty-five years old, and the median age is thirty-seven.[110] 'A new generation of young people are emerging, who do not remember the IRA campaign,' says Lord Alderdice, former Alliance leader and Speaker of the Northern Ireland Assembly. 'For them, it is ancient history. And therefore, when you talk about … [accusa-tions of] Mary Lou McDonald, leader of Sinn Féin and connections with the IRA … a young generation says, "What are you talking about? We don't remember any of that stuff, that's all ancient history."'[111]

The current generation of young people in the republic is focused in particular on trying to make ends meet in a country where housing costs are among the highest in the world, and the current coalition government seems incapable of doing anything to change this. Sinn Féin, led by its impressive housing spokesman Eoin Ó Broin, has outlined detailed plans to deal with the housing crisis, and this, more than any other issue, is what is likely to see them cruise into first place in the 2025 general election.

Sinn Féin has a two-track strategy: on one hand, hammering home to its base the republican narrative, reinforced with serial memorializations; on the other, holding out an olive branch of sorts to unionists, calling for national reconciliation and mutual acknowledgment of the hurt each may have inflicted on the other. Reconciliation, however, is seen not as an end in itself, but instrumental in facilitating the route to a border poll and to unity. At every turn, unionists see all roads leading to Dublin; this 'process' stuff is antithetical to the way they think, a far cry from the biblical incantation Northern evangelicals frequently quote: Matthew 5:37: 'But let your communication be Yea, Yea; Nay, Nay: for whatsoever is more than these cometh of evil.'

I asked Pádraig Mac Lochlainn about this: on the fortieth anniversary of the hunger strikes, would Bobby Sands and the nine other young men who died for a united Ireland recognize Sinn Féin today, a party that is open – on paper, at least – to constitutional expression of British culture, the monarchy and the Orange Order in a new Ireland? 'Well, there's no doubt that they were motivated first and foremost by gaining dignity and equality for their communities in the North of Ireland, and to that end they would have wanted a united Ireland,' he said. 'So, I like to believe that they would see that the path we're on, our positive republicanism in a space that's peaceful, as the same path they were on back then.'[112]

When I tell Mac Lochlainn that I have some difficulty in understanding what Sinn Féin stands for these days, as compared to 1981, he replies:

> I'm very clear. I've told you about the background where I came
> from: my father was imprisoned. He was motivated by the same
> issues that motivated the men who died in the 1981 hunger strike.
> He would have been on a hunger strike himself at that time only

for [the fact that] it was not agreed to by the republican leadership. I certainly would regard myself as being on the same path as my father. What is that? It's the path towards a united Ireland. I see the Stormont Executive as transitionary. That is not my endpoint as an Irish republican, but I've accepted that I have to achieve my goals by peaceful means only, and I agreed to the process of dismantling the Irish Republican Army and to putting arms aside and to focus solely on political means. My primary objective as a political activist today is … to achieve a united Ireland.[113]

I put the same question to Chris Hazzard, who is of the opinion that

it's for the people to decide. A large section of the people [in the North] do have that allegiance to a British monarch and come from a cultural identity with the Orange Order. Their links to Scotland are very dear to them. It's in their very DNA. I'm not the sort of person, and my party probably aren't the sort of party, to be able to dictate what [the expression of these links] will look like. That's the space for unionism to come forward with the types of protections they would like to see …

Political unionism, of course, is opposed to a border poll. That's understandable. [Unionists have] seen themselves lose the majority in the North. They're having an identity crisis at the moment through Brexit. They championed Brexit even though we were told time and again that this was like constitutional roulette, no one knew where the chips would land. It created the uncertainty and instability that we are seeing.

I get the feeling that there are those within political unionism who understand the current lay of the land, who would be up for a process of negotiation now about protecting their rights and their identity going forward … There are those in the North who are opposed to any ideas of Irish unity. They will always be opposed. Economic arguments won't matter to them. They want to maintain the union until the day they die.[114]

On the question of a united Ireland re-joining the Commonwealth, Hazzard responds:

As a republican I am opposed to that. I believe most Irish people are opposed to that type of idea as well. I want to see a genuine thirty-two-county republic established. However, I'm aware that a large proportion of people might want to do something different ... I'm up for the conversation. As I say, I think there is an onus upon those particular people to bring forward those ideas.[115]

Peter Shirlow asks: 'Where are Sinn Féin's own proposals on these issues? They produce papers saying Northern Ireland is a basket case, and you'd be better off in a united Ireland, but there is nothing about structures, how you link policy ... I say this to Shinners and nationalists all the time: where's the blueprint? Where can I go and find out about this united Ireland? There's nothing there.'[116]

'Everything,' Des Mackin, Sinn Féin's long-time director of finance, says, 'should be thought of in terms of a united Ireland. It is important to ensure and promote the united Ireland vision, to make sure that it goes right through and that all our policies are thought of in these terms.'[117]

In the 1970s, Sinn Féin had a vision of Ireland's future. The *Éire Nua* (New Ireland) document was a radical governance proposition: a federal Ireland, with regional governance in each of the four historical provinces and an overseeing all-Ireland national government. 'There is no document comparable to *Éire Nua*,' Walsh says:

> It's about addressing the whole problem around homelessness. It's about addressing an all-Ireland health service. It's about tackling the cancer of sectarianism, which still eats away at the heart of politics here in this part of Ireland.
>
> The overall model has to include input from unionism ... If there is to be a continuation of some sort of a Stormont administration, well then let's talk about that. If there is to be a new relationship between all of Ireland and Britain, well then, let's talk about that. There's no sense in us saying, 'This is how it going to be, folks.'[118]

Sinn Féin's position is that it doesn't have a position; it prefers to wait for a Citizens' Assembly (CA), which – confident that it will be in government in the South in the near future – Sinn Féin would be in a position to convene. Sinn Féin would, at that point, try to persuade the Assembly of the merits of its proposals. In government it would be in a better position to direct the proceedings and impose its ideas than in opposition.

That said, Sinn Féin is more open to there being a devolved government at Stormont as part of a unification outcome. Carthy points out:

> Most people who have analysed the Good Friday Agreement have come to a view that there would be a role for a Stormont Assembly in a united Ireland scenario; whether it would be in line with the Good Friday Agreement is possibly a point for the discussion. Many people would say … following reunification, that there would absolutely be a need for an Assembly to be in place.
>
> Rather than operating under a Westminster Parliament, which clearly has little consideration or concern for any part of Ireland, it will be operating under a Dublin parliament with a vested interest in seeing the North succeed because our relationship is so intertwined (arguably even more so than the East-West link in terms of the economic fortunes). Many people whom we've had dialogue with have been of the view that is certainly something that would be a persuader to many people who fit into that category.[119]

Note the Jesuital distinctions: these are the opinions of others, not necessarily Sinn Féin's, and while Sinn Féin will give them consideration, it may not endorse them. Whether such a devolved government would be a holding arrangement or part of the final unification package is open for others to pursue. It may not fly with the republican base, which might see it as partition by another name. The option may be more palatable, however, if Sinn Féin emerges as the largest party in the North and at the helm of government in the South – heading both a regional government and a national one might maximize its overall electoral potential as the only all-Ireland party with the political infrastructure in both jurisdictions to match its political ambitions.

Sinn Féin is open to hearing unionists expound on their vision for the future within a continuing UK constitutional framework: not to be persuaded regarding its merits, but the better to understand it. 'In order to counter an argument, you have to understand what the argument is,' Carthy says:

> We need to understand what [attachment to the status quo] is across all varieties. There's the issue of identity and there's issue of the cultural attachment. Arguably, they will not be undone in advance of a unity referendum to convince them to vote otherwise just on that basis. There are also many who have arguments with respect to the

economics … they will want assurances with regard to the protection
of and the advancement of that in a united Ireland scenario.[120]

Fianna Fáil and Fine Gael are not serious about unification; only a Sinn Féin
government can deliver both a border poll and Irish unity. Sinn Féin TD
Rose Conway-Walsh says:

> I would like those who call themselves republican parties to [actively
> pursue unification], but, in all honesty, I can't see that happening
> until we have a Sinn Féin Taoiseach. In the North, if you have a Sinn
> Féin first minister … you have an opportunity for real leadership that
> could deliver a referendum on Irish unity. There's a big job of work
> to be done, to persuade people that we are better off making our own
> decisions, that we are better off as an independent nation, and that
> we are better off as a free and united Ireland.[121]

Most of my interviewees, I tell Pádraig Mac Lochlainn, say that Sinn Féin
itself is the biggest obstacle to unity; that unionists will never trust the party;
that the IRA destroyed their way of life, and that Sinn Féin was the political
arm of the IRA. How to deal with that distrust? 'This is an important question,' Mac Lochlainn replies:

> I'm very clear that I understand that on the pathway to Irish unity
> Sinn Féin will be just one voice on that journey. Obviously, for the
> unionist community, I absolutely accept that it's not a terribly long
> time ago that we were inflicting terrible hurt and pain on each other.
> There's a long way to go in peace and reconciliation. I will do all I can
> in my political lifetime to heal the wounds and build relationships,
> but that's why I say on our own, Sinn Féin cannot achieve this.
>
> I share the same belief system as those who died [in the 1981
> hunger strikes]; I want to live in a united Ireland based on the prin-
> ciples and the promise of the 1916 Proclamation … those words are
> powerful, and bringing them to life in the modern era, that's my
> life's objective.[122]

What Mac Lochlainn intimates is that whether or not unionists trust Sinn
Féin is irrelevant. In a CA on the design of the future all-Ireland state,
republican-leaning participants will be only one voice among many, not
even necessarily the dominant one. Sinn Féin will then feed the CA with its
proposals. Others will feed theirs. The CA can summon experts, interrogate

them and invite the wider public to make submissions. Out of the mix of proposals, oral testimonies and summonses, all interrogated at length, the CA finally votes on a series of recommendations on what the form and shape of a united Ireland should look like, which are submitted to the government. But there are caveats.

Sinn Féin wants an all-island national CA. Whatever the political propriety of selecting citizens of the UK to participate in a CA convened by an Irish government for the purpose of severing the union, this, one can assume, would not pose a problem for Sinn Féin because it does not regard Northern Ireland as a legitimate political entity. Getting representatives of the estimated one million unionists who voraciously object to the entire proceedings would be highly problematical – the Assembly might at best be pan-nationalism flexing its muscles. And if some lower-case unionists agreed to participate, how representative would they be of the broader recalcitrant unionist community? To what extent could they articulate a British identity that would resonate with unionism's fears and anxieties? Given unionism's propensity for constitutional paranoia, would it not regard the Assembly as a trap, a false flag to lure them into the kind of conversation they are adamantly against having? Moreover, while a CA can table recommendations with the government, the government is under no obligation to legislate its findings. Any proposal in this scenario would have to be put to Dáil Éireann and debated, opening the way to amendments, and, if passed, the final form would have to be agreed by all the major parties.

Sinn Féin recognizes the problem of bringing political unionism, or at least a sufficient section of it, on board, but sees this as a task for others, not itself – a tacit admission of the abhorrence with which it is held. 'I understand completely that [Sinn Féin] will not win the hearts and minds of some people,' Hazzard says. 'That doesn't mean that we have to win all the hearts and minds ... We want to be part of a national coalition of voices making the case. There will be others who will reach out to unionists just as equally as we do and might be able to go even further in being able to make those connections.'[123] Sinn Féin's game plan is to try to bring sufficient numbers of civic unionists on board, those elusive lower-case unionists more likely to be swayed by the case made for the economic benefits of unification and more ecumenical on identity questions, most likely those who vote Alliance or self-designate as Neither.

'Increasingly,' Hazzard adds:

> we are starting to see more civic figures entering the conversation. People from civic unionism beginning to speak about how they might be interested in having a conversation about the future. What we're saying is, 'Look, we shouldn't be afraid of this.' In fact, there's a duty on the Irish government to step forward into that space and ensure the planning takes place.[124]

The roles of the two governments are asymmetrical: the British government's is restricted to setting a date for a poll and ensuring that it is safely and expeditiously carried out. The role of the Irish government is to be an active persuader.

Understanding unionism's arguments for the benefits of the union puts Sinn Féin in a better position to refute them. It is not a matter of unionists being able to persuade republicans otherwise. Unionism must make its case on two fronts. 'There are two levels in which they need to engage,' Carthy says. 'The first is to set out what they consider to be the benefits of the status quo. That's legitimate and that's absolutely to be expected. The second is to engage on the basis of, if things don't go the way we would like in a united Ireland poll, this is what we would like to see happen.'[125]

And if unionism refuses to engage? According to Walsh, unionists must put their endemic mistrust aside:

> Unionists have to tell us how they wish to ensure that their identity will be secured. It's up to them. They have to do it on their own legs. We can't do it for them … That's why it's all a negotiation. You know how these things work. It's not up to us to set out the plan for them, they have to draw up their own plan.
>
> Unionism is constantly looking over its shoulder. [Unionists] don't trust the English government, and rightly so as the whole Brexit thing has proved. They don't trust Sinn Féin. They don't trust the Dublin government. They have to trust themselves. They have to be the people who define their own requirements within the new Ireland. Nobody else can do that for them.[126]

The Irish government has to step up and jumpstart the process. 'Otherwise,' Carthy says, 'big moments of change happen in an unplanned way. It's quite possible that support for unity would actually overtake the political preparations, which would be a scenario that wouldn't be optimum.'[127] In government, Sinn Féin 'will make no apology for advancing Irish unity. We will conduct that mandate with vigour and transparency'. The present coalition government's Shared Island initiative 'misses the really important opportunity' to plan for unity. 'We need to move beyond co-operation and towards integration … We think the Irish government should commission the Economic and Social Research Institute [ESRI] or a body like it to carry out a comprehensive analysis of what the cost of reunification will be.'[128]

Post-referendum, Hazzard says, a period of joint authority may be warranted:

> I certainly foresee a process where the British and Irish governments would have to work through. It could be something similar to joint authority. There would be financial handovers and transactions that would take many years to rebalance … I would foresee a period of time where the British government, the Irish government and the European Union – and, indeed, the US administration – would be playing a role at different levels. That may involve a piece of joint authority between Britain and Ireland.[129]

To give effect to the new constitutional arrangements, either the existing 1937 Constitution will have to be amended or a constitutional convention convened to draw up a new Constitution. Sinn Féin is open to either, Carthy says:

> The first is that the current Bunreacht na hÉireann that covers the twenty-six counties would be amended in the immediacy of a united Ireland, but then amended point-by-point following reflective discussions on each of the points, and as amendments need to be made to remove provisions or to insert provisions.
>
> The second is a brand-new Constitution. Bunreacht na hÉireann has served us well and has a large buy-in. It would be easily amended to address some of the issues … What we need to try to do is broaden and have the largest cohort possible of pro-united Ireland voices. We need to get consensus within that cohort [on what a new Ireland would look like] … One of the questions will be the Constitution. It's probably in that scenario, most likely, that the broadest consensus would be found for amendments to the current Constitution of the twenty-six counties.[130]

How would Sinn Féin bring the South on board?

News coverage of the North in the South is sporadic at best. It comes to the public's attention only when there is a crisis. The public looks north and sees a dysfunctional government; bilious relations between Sinn Féin and the DUP; every crisis a question of whether it will collapse the devolved institutions; frenetic attention to the constitutional question, more pronounced now with the NIP becoming an existential issue for unionists. The spate of loyalist rioting in the Shankill, the Protestant enclave in West Belfast, in April 2021 overlapped with a LucidTalk poll in the South on the question of unity – just 51 per cent of respondents were in favour of unity, with a substantial majority fearing that a united Ireland would be accompanied by violence.[131] Why should the South be open to embracing this mess? What would it want to see in place before giving its imprimatur to unity?

Hazzard's view is that:

> not everybody will be convinced. There's a proportion of the population I have no doubt who will think 'we just simply don't need this'. However, I think as the conversation grows, as the Irish government become champions for [unification], I think the upcoming referendum on extending presidential voting rights to the North and the diaspora will be a good marker for this.[132]

In the South the mindset is partitionist, so reunification must be a process, accomplished over a ten- or fifteen-year period, not a simple once-off transfer of sovereignty. Hazzard continues:

> I have seen first-hand how partition-ism [thinking] is ingrained in the Southern system and ingrained in the political establishment … Whenever TDs maybe talk about building on the opportunities that exist, there is that reluctance, there's that fear very often … All too often in recent years I would argue that the political establishment and especially Fianna Fáil and Fine Gael have used the North at times as a political football to score points against ourselves in the Dáil.[133]

Brexit, he says, 'has changed an awful lot … it has just thrown all the chips in the air. You're dealing now with a serious identity crisis within the unionist community on the back of Brexit'.[134] In this political miasma, to expect that Irish unification should await a working Stormont is imposing a condition that cannot be met: the North will always be unstable:

> Sectarianism will always be a feature of political life in the North. The
> state itself was of a sectarian design … Everything is cast in an orange
> and green light, how could it not be? Our political structures have
> been designed around that division … Everything is viewed through
> that lens. Until we break out of that into genuine national parameters
> … only then can the divisions ever be overcome.[135]

In short, end partition and you'll go a long way to ending sectarianism.
'Genuine national parameters' is Sinn Féin parlance for conversations about
a united Ireland.

The implicit message for the South is: do not expect any change in sectarian behaviours or the confrontations and constitutional hiccups they
inevitably spawn. See them as a product of partition. Once you remove the
source of the infection, things will normalize, perhaps not immediately, but
over succeeding years as different stages of the new Ireland governance and
constitutional arrangements are implemented.

But it's not that straightforward. This kind of simple arithmetic logic
typifies much of Sinn Féin's thinking: it summons a linearity of cause and
effect, states an outcome (Irish unity) and works backwards to show how
it is possible. Complications are the fault of partition. Sectarianism and
inter-communal violence, an endemic malignancy, have been entrenched
in the societal fabric of the Ulster counties since the plantations of the seventeenth century.

Sinn Féin is a movement, not a political party in the normal sense of the
term: it does not follow protocols the way mainstream parliamentary parties
in Dáil Éireann do. At this point, it chooses not to go public with details of
what it might want an all-Ireland state to look like, preferring to wait until
the process of preparing for unification is formally underway. (One understands that behind the scenes Gerry Adams leads a Sinn Féin team busily
working on these issues.)[136] Its preferred vehicle for conducting a conversation about the future is an all-Ireland CA, though it is open to a constitutional convention.

Sinn Féin appears to be open to almost every suggestion on the constitutional question on the assumption that such suggestions are in the context
of unity, including continuing devolved government in the North, ties to

the British monarchy – even returning to the fold of the Commonwealth.[137] The metrics for a border referendum have already been met; the economics alone would justify it. The Northern Ireland Secretary of State should say what metrics he will use to justify calling a poll. The British and Irish governments together will agree on a date for the referendum 'once the Irish government says it's time'.[138] Other than facilitating a smooth and safe referendum, the British government's role is limited. The Irish government, however, should have a proactive role: providing a forceful voice for unification, orchestrating the proceedings of a CA and preparing the marriage offer to the Northern bride.

The party wants to engage with unionism to facilitate reconciliation. It points to several documents it has published addressing the issue, knowing this may involve 'uncomfortable conversations'. And though it does not expect to have much success with political unionism, it claims that increasing numbers of civic unionists are participating in dialogues about the future. These will provide the basis for a border poll that ensures a greater margin for unity than the legal requirement of 50 per cent + 1. Unification will be implemented in stages, Hong Kong-style, over ten or fifteen years, or more. Meanwhile, the narrative of the Northern conflict as a war of national liberation conducted by the IRA, the unfinished business of the first Irish Dáil (1918), is memorialized on every occasion the death of one of its volunteers is remembered.

Among interviewees, there is an unbridgeable dissonance between how Sinn Féin sees itself and how others see it. What comes across in my interviews with members of Sinn Féin is the reasonableness of their arguments, their willingness to engage with unionism, their openness to making far-reaching concessions to unionism to accommodate its British identity, some of which are antithetical to core republican ideology. There is none of the stridency and belligerence others associate with it, whatever about the across-the-board perception of its relentless drive towards unity regardless of the hurdles that stand in its way.

It's all too simple – no mention of potholes on the road to unity; no off-ramps that might derail the process; no acknowledgment of the extraordinarily complex arrangements that will have to be put in place; no suggestion of costs the people of the North and South might have to meet. Indeed, it claims the opposite when economies of scale across an all-Ireland economy and public institutions kick in. It promises to produce a white paper once in government that will address what the various stages of implementing reunification might look like. It blandly dismisses the possibility of loyalist violence with 'there is no appetite for it', stating that much of the loyalist violence during the 1968–98 conflict was in collusion with British state security agencies. 'All I have to do as an Irish republican is convince somebody who today isn't a united Irelander to become one,'[139] Carthy says. Would that it were it so uncomplicated! (I should add that Carthy stood out among Sinn Féin interviewees as the most direct and least ambiguous in his responses.)

But there is also an absence of substantive content. Words roll off tongues; flourishes of language often fail to address directly the question asked while sounding as if they have; mellifluous soundbites are strung together. Were any of the interviewees making their case for unity in a public platform or on television, it would sound compelling, hard to disagree with. The responses to questions are in sync, hardly a deviation from one interview to the next. All march to the beat of the same drummer, with occasional solo flourishes, but none deviating too far from the singular focus of a thirty-two-county united republic.

The same proclivity for soundbites that lack any substance, but create the illusion of great things to come, marked Mary Lou McDonald's address to the party's Ard Fheis in October 2021. In her bullet-point address, the message was the drive for change to a new Ireland, a refrain rhythmically and repetitiously hammered home:

> The people of Ireland are ready for change … ordinary people creating extraordinary change … driving home change … people define change … change is about people … [Fianna Fáil and Fine Gael] can delay change but they cannot stop it … there are attempts to block change … those of us who desire change have to work harder, to be more determined and more united than ever.[140]

In short measure, change would deliver the promise of the 1916 Proclamation, affordable housing for all, free healthcare, the end of poverty and inequality, higher wages, lower greenhouse gas emissions, lower taxes, increased public expenditure at the end of the republican rainbow – all gift-wrapped for the people of Ireland from the party of the people.

Sinn Féin in government in the North and South will signal seismic shifts in politics in both jurisdictions, setting politics on an uncharted course.[141] To prepare the way for the CA it will launch once in government in the South, Sinn Féin established a Commission on the Future of Ireland in July 2022, chaired by Sinn Féin Chairperson Declan Kearney (who refused to be interviewed for this book).[142]

Launching the initiative, which will last eighteen months, Mary Lou McDonald said, 'The Commission will seek to engage with the protestant, loyalist, and unionist section of our people.' The Commission 'is also an opportunity for alternative proposals to be presented by those with different visions of Ireland. This can be done privately as well as through a series of People's Assemblies. These will be moderated by an independent chairperson'. People's Assemblies will be held across the island of Ireland. Assemblies will include 'Women's assemblies, youth assemblies and assemblies in Gaeltacht areas'. Among its goals, this initiative is intended to silence the party's critics who watch with dismay its seemingly inexorable march to political power in both parts of Ireland and accuse it of being full of hot air on the constitutional question.

Sinn Féin in the North will continue to keep the matter of a border poll upfront, but less abrasively, while Sinn Féin in the South will act as a responsible opposition, the better to prepare it for entering government after the next election. Its remarkable inroads into all sections of the Southern electorate continues. In the February 2020 general election, there was a clear bifurcation of voters' preferences – a majority of voters under forty-five chose Sinn Féin, a majority of those over forty-five went for either Fianna Fáil or Fine Gael. Those with little or no memory of the Troubles voted one way; those with memories of the violence another. Since the *Irish Times*/MRBI poll in December 2021, Sinn Féin has made significant inroads into the over-45-year-old and wealthier vote and is no longer the choice only of the working class.[143] The party has moved into the mainstream as the transformation of Irish politics gains momentum.

In each case, North and South, it has a different base, not necessarily holding similar views on the urgency of a border poll. But, like a trapeze artist, Sinn Féin navigates both. Francie Molloy, a Sinn Féin MP for the Westminster Parliament, called the B/GFA a 'bluff', adding that nationalists had been 'sold a pup', that the two governments were doing nothing 'to implement the agreement on a border poll'.[144] His comments fit snugly into Sinn Féin's strategy: repeatedly call for a border poll, with no expectation that there will be a positive response from the British government but that the drumbeat of the constant barrage of demands and the predictable knee-jerk responses they elicit will normalize the idea in the public domain. Implicit, too, in this is that no matter how strongly unionists 'make the case for the union', or make Northern Ireland a 'warm house' for all its citizens and accommodate all things Irish, their efforts will be insufficient to move Sinn Féin from its relentless focus on achieving unity. Mary Lou McDonald called COVID-19 'an accelerant in terms of the unity debate',[145] adding that the necessity for a single health system across the island of Ireland dwarfed Brexit 'in terms of reflecting the danger of partition, the fact that it's not sustainable, and the necessity of having us work as one island'.[146]

In 2000, when Seamus Mallon complained of the attention Blair was paying to Sinn Féin, Tony Blair told him: 'The trouble with you fellows is you have no guns.'[147] The guns now are strictly political, but one must ask – what happens if the trend towards unity levels off and a majority in Northern Ireland, even a small one, is content to stay in the UK?

This is the conundrum at the core of the agreement: it cannot reconcile irreconcilables; diametrically opposing aspirations cannot both be accommodated in the long run. One aspiration will be fulfilled, one will not. Unionists are told that the best way to secure their future in the United Kingdom is to build a 'warm house' for Catholics: that is, full equality and respect for their traditions, and the legitimacy of the nationalist aspiration for unity. But the purpose of that warm house is to ensure that this nationalist aspiration can never be achieved. Under these circumstances, why should Sinn Féin connive for any significant period of time in a functioning government of Northern Ireland?[148] Fortunately for them, the DUP seems genetically incapable of understanding the crucial importance to the survival of Ulster unionism of the warm-house policy on key issues like recognition of the Irish language.

Sinn Féin is not interested in sharing a warm house, just a short-term rental. But there are factors beyond its control that may determine the length of its tenancy. If, for example, the South's economy is hit with recession, reconjuring impressions of it being 'a basket case' among sections of unionism, the 'soft' unionists – predisposed to being persuaded of the merits of unification on economic grounds – may no longer be up for a grand marriage once the dowry disappears.

Sinn Féin signed up to the B/GFA only because it was convinced it would lead to the unification of the island. If it holds the reins of government, North and South, and fails to deliver reunification within a relatively short period of time, would dissident republicans reinvent the mantra that unity can be only achieved through violence, and if that takes resumption of the armed struggle, so be it? Again, many may say 'far-fetched', but one of the lessons of the conflict is that in a divided society with criss-crossing political fault lines, political earthquakes can shake its foundations at any time. Nothing is far-fetched: remember Martin McGuinness and Rev. Ian Paisley as 'the Chuckle Brothers'?[149]

ELEVEN

Unionism: running into culs-de-sac

I can't remember a moment when unionism has been so unsettled. The fall of the Stormont Parliament (1972), the Sunningdale Agreement (1974) and the Anglo-Irish Agreement (1985) all meant challenges and anger, but all were offset by the fact unionism remained electorally strong. And, crucially, none of those moments required Northern Ireland to be in one political/economic entity (the EU in this case) while the rest of the United Kingdom was in another. That's why this is now a full-blown constitutional crisis: it's not just the economy, stupid.[1]
   – Alex Kane, journalist and commentator, former Press Officer
for the Ulster Unionist Party (UUP)

Unionists always had two options to secure the Union. What you needed to do was get a section of Northern nationalists to support unity with Britain. The Good Friday Agreement did that. You could be a citizen of the United Kingdom while feeling yourself to be Irish and experiencing your Irish identity through all sorts of cultural expressions. That was the deal the middle-class nationalists bought into. Unionists would have been wise to have embraced them and shown a little generosity …

Instead, they went the other way, to insult that sense of national identity by pointless, childish insults about the Irish language, in particular. While most middle-class Catholics don't speak Irish, it has totemic importance for them, and they don't like to see it insulted. But the DUP [Democratic Unionist Party], in the way of which they have treated Irish national identity and their understanding of government as a form of state capture ... exposed all of that. Basically, unionism did a very bad job of safeguarding the Union.[2]

In fact, had the DUP gone with an Irish language act, that would have been the most British thing to do, because both Scotland and Wales have their own language acts – it's a very UK thing to safeguard cultural identity. But the DUP did diametrically the opposite. Having alienated Northern nationalists, they've now got a situation [with] a resurgence of Irish nationalism and so they've got an alternative strategy – to make themselves so unattractive, so belligerent, so warlike, so bellicose, so threatening that nobody would want them.[3]

– Paul Nolan, Research Director, Northern Ireland
Peace Monitoring Survey

Unionists would be dead set against any suggestion that there could ever be a united Ireland in [our] lifetime ... Protestants, the unionist community, are living in denial – the denial of the demographic reality that they are heading towards being a minority within Northern Ireland ... the demography is such that it will only be a matter of time. I can't understand why they don't realize this ...

If you really are serious about wanting to sell Northern Ireland within the United Kingdom ... you need to do an awful lot more to try and give good reason to nationalists and republicans to stay within the United Kingdom.[4]

– Rev. Harold Good, Methodist Church minister, one of the two
independent witnesses who oversaw the decommissioning
of paramilitary arms

The biggest thing that unionism needs to do, in the immediate term, is to talk to itself ... It needs to develop a strategy ... to convince enough people within Northern Ireland who are not naturally – if I could put it – unionist, that staying in the United Kingdom is a much better way forward than any notion of joining a united Ireland.

There's only one other option: to die in the ditch in the inevitability of this truck coming down the road of referenda and potentially alienating so many people within Northern Ireland that they would go the other direction in terms of that referendum. What happens then is you either get out, suck it up or fight. Sadly, the history is that there will be enough people willing to fight.[5]

– Jackie Redpath, Shankill community leader in Belfast

If you're a unionist yourself, why would you want change if what you've got is what you want? If you want the union, why would you even be thinking about other things? It's not about intransigence. It's about being satisfied with what you've got and not seeing any value to change. That's where I think the message has fallen down.[6]

– Rev. Lesley Carroll, Presbyterian minister and
Prisoner Ombudsman

Northern Ireland unionists feel that there is no one really prepared to fight in their corner or to support their position. Both Margaret Thatcher and Boris Johnson have been unreliable partners. In the world's media they are portrayed as the problem. The North American diaspora have overwhelmingly supported Ireland and Irish republicanism, I think sometimes naively so. The Northern Ireland unionists feel that they've been on their own.[7]

– John Kyle, former Interim Leader, loyalist Progressivist Unionist
Party (PUP), switched to UUP in 2022

Unionists know that they have to change the way they operate. They know they have to keep the Catholic minority who are pro-union on board. They know they have to generate a positive message about Northern Ireland to a younger generation … An activism within political unionism is starting to influence people, to promote the merits of the union …

Boris Johnson wants to keep Scotland within the union. You can't throw Northern Ireland under the bus and then keep Scotland within the union. Johnson is surrounding himself with people who are pro-union. He's bringing in advisers from Northern Ireland who are pro-union. There's a space, post-Brexit, when Boris Johnson will be starting campaigns that are pro-union campaigns … Anybody who knows what's going on in Downing Street knows that it is now preparing pro-union strategies. Northern Ireland is a thirtieth of the population of the UK. It supplies 10 per cent of the armed forces. You can't get people to join the army in Britain, but you can get people in Northern Ireland to join …

> *Look at the data: 65 per cent will state they're pro-union. Pro-*
> *unionism is the only perspective which gets both Catholics and*
> *Protestants. You can get a significant Catholic share of support as well*
> *as a very high share of Protestant support. Virtually everybody who's*
> *pro-unification is Catholic. The DUP have realized that they have to*
> *change their way of being.*[8]
>
> –Peter Shirlow, Professor, Director, Institute of Irish Studies,
> University of Liverpool

In October 1981, a group of 'professional and businesspeople of the Unionist tradition', led by the liberal unionist Robert McCartney, came to Dublin in the aftermath of Garret FitzGerald's Constitutional Crusade.[9] FitzGerald described their manifesto, 'The Case for the Unionists',[10] as 'the authentic voice of Unionism', while Dublin's *Irish Independent* editorialized that the document should become 'required reading on this side of the Border'.[11]

According to the manifesto, the unionist case rested on one reality: 'Over one million Northern unionists are totally opposed to the concept of a united Ireland and the activities of the Provisional IRA [Irish Republican Army] have done nothing but entrench them in such opposition.'[12]

Opposition came from two sources. First, the nature of the Southern state itself: 'The Northern unionist believes it inevitable in a country where 95 per cent of the population subscribes to the Roman Catholic faith, that the teaching of that Church as reflecting the view of the overwhelming majority will be mirrored in the laws of the state.'[13] And second, the claims of the Southern state: 'The national aspiration of the republic, its people and its parties are claimed to be the absorption of the North into a united Ireland. This objective is given legal validity by articles 2 and 3 of the Constitution.'[14] This claim is a fundamental source of offence to the Northern unionist because it 'belies his most basic political belief and heritage'.[15] Such claims also give a 'spurious legitimacy to the worst excesses of the Provisional IRA'.[16] And 'since the objective of the IRA is also favoured by the Catholic hierarchy, it is hardly surprising', the manifesto continued, 'that the great mass of Roman Catholics find that the legitimacy of the Provisional IRA campaign can be couched in terms they find difficult to reject'.[17]

The territorial claim, it argued, was fundamental to the Provisional IRA (PIRA) campaign for the withdrawal of the British army from Northern Ireland, since 'the whole concept of the British Army as one of occupation is founded on the premise that Northern Ireland is not a legitimate part of the United Kingdom'.[18] Hence, 'the most significant blow that can be struck by the republic against the pseudo-legitimacy of the Provisional IRA is the abandonment of the territorial claim in the Constitution of the republic'.[19]

Northern unionists, it goes on, 'hold the view that the Roman Catholic Church is in such a position of entrenched power because of the control it exercises indirectly through the minds and attitudes of the faithful, as to be able to dictate policy to the state which the Church considers essential to the maintenance of its position'.[20] Such is the extent of this power that 'conflict between Church and state barely arises and the power is so effective in real things that the badges of it such as the special position of the Church in the Constitution are no longer necessary and can be dispensed with'.[21]

Accordingly, 'the Northern unionists considered that the amendment of the Constitution to remove the special significance clause was of no significance'.[22]

Northern unionists also believed that the Roman Catholic Church has 'a grip on education unique in strength',[23] and that while there are other countries in the world with 'educational systems which are denominationally controlled, only in the Republic of Ireland is it clerically controlled'.[24] In addition, they were also convinced that the Catholic Church's insistence on 'separateness of education for its members' in the North has been 'a significant factor in the polarisation of the (two) communities'.[25]

The machinery for perpetuating a Roman Catholic theocracy is built into the Irish Constitution. Article 41, the manifesto notes, enshrines the Catholic moral code. They noted that legalizing divorce would not just require the passage of a statute but the passing of an amendment to the Constitution. Article 42 stresses the rights of the Church in the area of education, 'thereby placing the education of 95 per cent of the population effectively in the hands of the Roman Catholic Church'.[26]

A statement by Éamon de Valera during the Dáil debates on the Constitution in 1937 that is quoted in the manifesto provides the raison d'être for resistance:

> There are 93% of the people on this part of Ireland who belong to the Catholic Church and 75% of the people of the people of Ireland as a whole who belong to the Catholic Church who believe in its

teachings and whose whole philosophy of life is the philosophy that comes from those teachings. If we are going to have a democratic state, if we are going to be ruled by the representatives of the people, it is clear that their whole philosophy of life is going to reflect that and has to be borne in mind and the recognition of it is important.[27]

This was grist for the mills of unionist opposition. 'One million Protestants', the manifesto declares,

would find the above expression of opinion close to anathema. It expresses exactly what they fear, that in a united Ireland the will of the majority would be a Roman Catholic will in circumstances where the Constitution not only did not recognize their right to divorce, contraception, state schools, uncensored reading and other matters involving the exercise of individual conscience but might require constitutional amendments to secure them.[28]

Hence, 'the aspect of the republic's present arrangements which reinforces Northern unionist opposition to any form of unification is the absence of any real possibility of change'.[29] If there is any hope that the two traditions in Ireland might ultimately meet upon the same road, then 'the process of transforming the republic from something bordering theocracy to a pluralistic society' has to be undertaken.[30]

Accordingly, the challenges before the people of the republic were first 'to decide whether they are willing to abandon their claim to the territory of Northern Ireland which is used by [the Provisional IRA] as a license to murder', and second 'to decide whether the current relationship between Church and state and the power the Church exercises in education and health are to be drastically modified so that the state becomes a pluralistic and non-sectarian state'.[31]

But even if these changes were made, it would be wrong to assume that Northern unionists would 'consent to any unification of Ireland' because 'the position of Northern unionists is dependent on neither the guarantees of the British government ... nor on the posturing of loyalist extremists but on identification of interests with Britain in peace and war'. The unionists are 'psychologically bound to her [Britain] with bonds of blood, history and common adversity, which cannot be bartered away in some political package no matter how attractive that might seem'.[32]

Even more important, the Northern unionist embodies:

> theological, philosophical, cultural and political principles and ideas
> that materially affect his attitude to government, clerical authority
> and morality so that his views in these matters are profoundly dif-
> ferent than his Roman Catholic neighbour. The real partition is not
> a line across the map of Ireland but in the minds and hearts of men
> ... The failure to remove the territorial claim almost totally precludes
> the necessary preconditions for any settlement of the minority's
> claim within Northern Ireland and the United Kingdom.[33]

In short, on one hand, the manifesto argues that unionists cannot join a
united Ireland because it is a Catholic state; on the other hand, even if the
South 'cleaned up its act' and weaned itself off the influence of the Catholic
Church, unionists could not join a united Ireland because they are British.

In the forty intervening years, the South did 'clean up its act'. The Catholic
Church's influence is now marginal in terms of the influence it exerts over
both social legislation and the minds and hearts of the laity; its teaching is
more often honoured in the breach; offending articles of the Constitution
have been removed or amended; legislation on minority rights, divorce, marriage and abortion are now among the most liberal in the European Union
(EU); the economy, disparaged forty years ago for its backwardness, is among
the most vibrant in the EU, while that of the North underperforms. Sinn
Féin, the political party associated with the Provisional Irish Republican
Army (PIRA), became the largest party in the North and appears well on its
way to emerging as the largest political party in the South after elections are
held there in 2025. For a younger generation, the conflict that has convulsed
Northern Ireland for thirty years is something for the history books.

But in the North, the detritus of that conflict, especially unresolved
legacy issues and the incessant tug of wills between Sinn Féin and the DUP,
keeps memories of the conflict front and centre, permeating and spoiling
political discourse. One result is that Northern Protestants cling to their
union more tenaciously, even as others would argue that the bond has
become more tenuous: between 2010 and 2019, the share of Protestants who
support remaining in the United Kingdom (UK) grew from 90.3 per cent to

94.5 per cent; 97.6 per cent of DUP voters and 94.9 per cent of UUP voters reported being Protestant.[34]

The Protestant psyche is convulsed with episodic bouts of betrayal by British governments. On all socio-political and economic sides, unionists see potential threats that feed into the paranoia that they are being either pushed or pulled into a united Ireland. The detested Northern Ireland Protocol (NIP) is reorienting trade patterns, loosening ties with Great Britain, increasing trade flows between North and South and beginning to imperceptibly cop-per-fasten a single-island economy, widely seen as a harbinger of a unified political entity. 'The difficulty with unionism,' Alex Kane says, is that

> it was almost bred and fermented and weaned in paranoia. Because it never wanted the six counties … it never wanted what it ended up with. Getting what you don't want, usually in political terms, does make you paranoid. Unionists assumed that everyone was an enemy. Edward Carson saying about the way we were just puppets. It's still quoted …[35] They assumed the new Southern state is going to be the enemy, they assumed British governments are going to be the enemy. They assumed anyone that spoke out of turn or criticized unionism or asked questions of unionism [to be an enemy].[36]

Unionists have a shrinking Protestant demographic presence in the province as their majority number contracts to just two of the eleven local govern-ment districts: Mid and East Antrim; and Ards and North Down (see Table 5.1). The Protestant population had slipped beneath the magic 50 per cent mark on the occasion of Northern Ireland's centenary founding. 'Within a decade,' says Professor Duncan Morrow, 'Belfast will almost certainly have a Catholic majority.'[37] In effect, 'a majority Protestant Northern Ireland is now restricted to the suburban area surrounding Belfast.'[38] Gone, too, when the DUP agrees to form an Executive, will be the first minister post to Sinn Féin – the adversary they loathe and hold responsible for destroying their way of life. Henceforth, unionists will have to stomach the humiliation of playing second fiddle in an orchestra of republicans.

Political unionism is warned repeatedly by an array of pundits, indepen-dent political commentators and civic unionism that, though a referendum on a united Ireland is not inevitable, it is extremely likely at some point, and they had better make their case for the union if they are to convince a cohort of cultural Catholics that they will be better off in the new, improved union than taking their chances in a united Ireland with all the disruptions and unrest that might result in. They are told they should talk about the future, among themselves first and then with their Irish neighbours about the future of the island.

The Protestant population sees little purpose in such conversations because they might mistakenly signal acquiescence to the prospect of a united Ireland as hoisting a white flag of surrender to the political onslaught of the republican agenda and the inevitability of a united Ireland. Says Steve Aiken, former UUP leader:

> Is a border poll inevitable? No. Show me when the conditions are likely to be set when there's going to be a border poll in the next twenty, thirty, forty years ... I'm not saying it won't happen, but I don't anticipate it happening ... You will have to have very clear indications from either elections or from opinion polls or other areas for the Secretary of State to make that call.[39]

The current UUP leader Doug Beattie says, 'I am a unionist who identifies as Irish, but I want to remain part of the United Kingdom.' He goes on to explain:

> A poll on a united Ireland is not on the horizon and may not be for years. It won't happen because the people won't want it to happen. There is a middle demographic of people who view themselves as being Northern Irish [so] the constitutional question isn't one they feel they have to answer anymore. What they're saying is, 'Northern Ireland as it stands now is my home and can do the best for me.'[40]

Unionism sees the republican narrative gain an increasing foothold in history's first draft, the expression of triumphalism in small but humiliating ways. Sinn Féin, as the largest party in the North and poised to be in government in the South after 2025, poses almost insuperable political challenges for unionism to grapple with, such is its antipathy for the party it equates with the IRA, testing the political scaffolding that has held the Belfast/Good Friday Agreement (B/GFA) in place for a generation.

'People need to understand something,' Beattie says:

> There's a psyche within unionism – and maybe wider than unionism, maybe in some degree of nationalism as well – that when we talk

about Sinn Féin, we are talking about the IRA because Sinn Féin are the political arm of the IRA. It's not the other way around, it's not the IRA are the military wing of Sinn Féin. It's Sinn Féin are the political wing of the IRA.

They still excuse and condone and celebrate the murder of the IRA over many years, some of the most heinous crimes imaginable. Burning people to death, strapping people to bombs, blowing people up as they attend charity events. There's a psyche in unionists who will just not give ground to the likes of Sinn Féin. If Sinn Féin become the largest government in the Irish Republic, and they are the government, they will be viewed as a hostile government ... We have a real problem here. That problem is that we cannot move forward as a society while you have a political organization, linked into a terrorist organization. It wouldn't happen anywhere else.[41]

Moreover, Sinn Féin in government North and South, as a party to a dispute in Northern Ireland on one side of the table and on the other side part of a government whose responsibility is to mediate that dispute, unbalances the delicate mechanisms of the agreement. 'The whole balance of the Good Friday Agreement will become unstuck.'[42]

Unionists watch Scotland's campaign for independence, not convinced it will succeed but anxious and apprehensive about the knock-on effects for the rest of the union should it be successful. They hope the extraordinarily complex negotiations it would take to unravel a union of almost 400 years and create a hard land border between England and Scotland would give pause to those seeking to undertake a similar uncoupling for Northern Ireland.

For northern Presbyterians, the ties of kith and kin are strong and Scotland is much more Northern Ireland's natural hinterland than the English mainland. 'The majority of Northern Protestants don't actually have any allegiance to England,' Lord Alderdice says:

They have an allegiance to Britain, to the Crown. If Scotland were to leave the United Kingdom, there would be many Northern Protestants who wouldn't know where they were. A great part of the Northern Irish Protestant identity is tied up with the relationship with Scotland ... If Scotland decided to leave, the consequences are absolutely huge for Northern Protestants. I don't think we're as close to Scottish independence at the moment as some people would say, but it could happen.[43]

Northern Protestants watch, too, the rise of English nationalism and the pos-sible repercussions because Northern Ireland must compete for resources from the UK Treasury with the new Tory voting base in what were once impregnable Labour strongholds in de-industrialized Northern England. At some point the financial spigot may get turned off, or at least turned down. Overarching these concerns is the impact of the protocol that requires customs checks and paperwork for goods travelling from Great Britain into Northern Ireland – a clear violation of the B/GFA, say unionists, because it represents a change in the status of Northern Ireland with respect to the rest of the United Kingdom. On this matter, all unionist/loyalist interviewees are aligned.[44]

Jackie Redpath, the Shankill community leader, says:

> Unionism's problem is essentially within itself, as opposed to exter-nally with the threat of a united Ireland or a problem with what British governments do or not do. The problem for unionism is for it to have a positive view of itself and of its future, and also a recog-nition that things change, and that the United Kingdom, of which we're a part, is undergoing change. Therefore, I think part of the problem of unionism is implicit in a famous hymn it identifies with, *Abide With Me*, when it says, 'Change and decay in all around I see,' where change is associated immediately with something negative, as in decay. In fact, change is inevitable and we need to grapple with it as a positive, because the United Kingdom that we belong to is a changing United Kingdom and a very diverse United Kingdom.
>
> The threat to the United Kingdom is not coming from the Republic of Ireland. It is not coming primarily any longer from the IRA. It is coming from the United Kingdom itself, from Scottish nationalism, and more recently from emerging English nationalism.[45]

To accommodate the demographic changes that are occurring, that is, an increasing plurality of Catholics,

> Unionism has to promote a very positive image of the future of Northern Ireland. What unionism needs to do is to ensure that those that are unionist with a small 'u' and nationalist with a small 'n' are made comfortable within Northern Ireland and the UK. That's more and more complex as days go on and Brexit has made that process much more difficult. Nevertheless, it's a prize to be sought after.[46]

Indeed, Protestant, unionist, and loyalist interviewees (the PUL community) say the right things: they want a Northern Ireland for all of its people that shares common values with respect to inclusivity and mutual reciprocity, much like the Northern Ireland promised by the B/GFA with the emphasis on mutual respect and parity of esteem for the multiple identities that have evolved and blossomed in the past twenty-five years.

But they see no urgency in having conversations about the island's future and their place within it. Much like a bucket list, these are things that they hope to get around to, but not immediately. 'I don't really see why unionists would engage in a debate about how you would create a more palatable, united Ireland,' says one of the DUP's influential special advisers, Richard Bullick:

> I don't see the logic of it before there is any evidence that a united Ireland is likely to happen ... I don't really see why you'd be nego-tiating on something which, in honesty, would make it more likely. There's no doubt, because once you start that discussion, you would be very much engaged with the debate and are almost opening the way up for a united Ireland to be the outcome. You're almost negoti-ating surrender at that point.[47]

But unionists insist that, if and when there are conversations about the future, there must be equal time and engagement given to making the case for maintaining the union. Just as a united Ireland remains a vacuous concept, a 'new, warmer house' Northern Ireland is equally vacuous. The skirmishing around the margins of both provoke passions and challenge intensely held convictions, but few if any can actually articulate what's in the political vessels on offer.

As Sammy Douglas says:

> Sinn Féin and some of the groups who are pushing for an agreed Ireland are saying, 'Great, a united Ireland ... come and talk to us and tell us what your role could be in the new dispensation,' which is a bad place for negotiating. But you've got Mary Lou McDonald, Michelle O'Neill, Gerry Kelly and other republicans who continue to eulogize people who have committed heinous crimes ... This just keeps on fanning the flames of division and creates a lack of trust. It also creates problems for unionists when they hear An Garda Síochána and the PSNI [Police Service of Northern Ireland] Chief

Constable stating that the IRA Army Council are still directing Sinn Féin. Although it's inferred that they don't pose a threat but the fact that they are still in existence spooks many in that community.[48]

The leaders of political unionism take their cues from two highly respected surveys: the annual Northern Ireland Life and Times (NILT) surveys and the periodic University of Liverpool polls, both of which show that support for Irish unity is still relatively low, despite Brexit. What comes across from the cross-section of unionist interviewees is a world-weary defensiveness, a low-burn irritation at being either lectured to or cajoled by well-meaning nationalists that they had better get engaged in conversations about the future or find themselves sidelined when inevitable change comes knocking. Especially post-Brexit, one finds a benign resignation in their responses. And why raise questions about the outcome of constitutional issues that are unlikely to arise for at least a decade and perhaps never? Raising them affords credence to their likelihood. Says Richard Bullick:

> Just as unionism sometimes can be dispirited, political nationalists in recent years have an entirely misplaced analysis on where sentiment is in Northern Ireland in terms of a border poll being held on the likelihood that it would be won, which makes them less effective in campaigning for one. Unless unionists make a big hash up of things, I don't see a border poll in the next decade.[49]

'I get a little bit frustrated about people who say that unionists should join a conversation about a united Ireland,' Doug Beattie says:

> That's like me co-designing a united Ireland for people who want a united Ireland when I don't want it. It doesn't make sense to me. I understand that people want a united Ireland. They can work on it and then they need to come up with an offer ...[50] I'm quite liberal, but for people like me there is no economic box to tick. I'm a constitutional unionist, not an economic unionist. It doesn't matter to me if I would be better off in a united Ireland or staying with the United Kingdom because I know that economic circumstances rise and fall ... You could have a united Ireland and be well off for five years. Then there could be an economic crash and you're going to be in a worse state than what you were.[51]

Because unionism does not see a border referendum happening at any point soon, the issue is moot, though the short answer, where one is forthcoming, is that a united Ireland can't happen. When pollsters ask voters whether there should be a border poll in the next ten years, a majority say yes, but unionists say that this is a speculative answer into the unknown future on a question on the unknown contours of an abstract choice, interpreted by nationalists/republicans as implicitly supporting an outcome for unity.

This, the DUP MP Gregory Campbell argues, is a misreading of the data. A Secretary of State, he points out, 'would have to see a whole series of opinion polls and a whole series of elections where the will of the people is reasonably demonstrably clear that they want constitutional change. There's no sign of that whatsoever'. As he points out:

> When I look at the percentage in my constituency [East Londonderry] who voted for united Ireland parties in the year I got elected, 2001, and compare it to the percentage of votes given to united Ireland parties in 2019, it has declined.[52] The question was: will there be a united Ireland within the next ten years? Forty-three per cent said no, 32 per cent said yes, and 25 per cent said [they were] neutral.[53]
>
> Now, that's a two-to-one majority thinking there won't be a united Ireland, and that's before we spell out any costings. This was not a question like, would you vote for united Ireland in the next ten years if it meant A, B and C? If it meant more violence? If it meant your taxes going up? If it meant increasing tensions in Northern Ireland? My guess is when you put those things into the mix, the 43 [per cent] and 32 [per cent] would probably change, but it wouldn't change in a way that Sinn Féin would be pleased with.
>
> That's a country that is 95 per cent nationalist electorate saying, 'No, there's not going to be a united Ireland.'[54] They appear to realize, even if Sinn Féin don't, that there's no way Northern Ireland is going to be incorporated within an all-Ireland state, whether it's agreed island, shared island, united Ireland. We are British, we're not giving up our identity ... But when you flip that over and say, 'Can an Irish identity be incorporated within the UK?' The answer is emphatically yes because it already is.[55]

Both unionism and nationalism/republicanism have a propensity to selectively cite polling data that support either maintaining the link with the UK or suggest that a united Ireland is on the way. The two tribes may as well exist on different planets, not within the small and narrow geographical confines of Northern Ireland. The new mantra is, 'We're all minorities now.' Ensconced within their respective silos, they plan for world views that are antithetical to each other.

In 'Same but different? The Democratic Unionist Party and Ulster Unionist Party Compared', Jonathan Tonge and colleagues conclude that differences between the two parties have diminished, and that 'as the DUP came to eclipse its rival and then accepted the B/GFA, some distinguishing features of the two parties became less marked'.[56] In the DUP, they point out, the pre-eminence of the Free Presbyterian Church is much reduced, Orange Order membership is at the same levels in the DUP and the UUP, both parties have failed to attract any Catholic members and both overwhelmingly embrace a British identity. Although they were on different sides of Brexit – the DUP campaigned for Leave, the UUP for Remain – a majority of both their respective electorates voted to leave. Following the pro-Leave result in the UK referendum, the UUP changed its stance and became a pro-Brexit party.[57] 'If the main differences are historical rather than contemporary,' the authors write, 'the obvious question begged is the purpose of maintaining two unionist parties, particularly if intra-unionist rivalry assists nationalism.' The authors point to 'the narcissism of small modern differences [that] cannot erase the proudly held fierce party memberships who would fight fusion. Their unionism might be similar but the organisations representing the ideology will always be different in the view of those most committed to either party'.[58]

Beattie and Donaldson – the leaders, respectively, of the UUP and DUP – allude to the 'narcissism of small differences', though Beattie believes there are more pronounced differences.[59] 'From education to social issues to environmental issues to animal welfare,' he says:

> we have a whole range of different policies from the DUP … One of our biggest failings was that we supported not leaving the European Union. We were against Brexit. We alienated people who would be unionist voters who wanted Brexit. Then after the Brexit vote came in with the decision to leave, as a democratic party we accepted that decision. That, of course, alienated the unionists who wanted to stay. Having a nuanced message over Brexit has not helped us at all. That

has seen our decline. Brexit has been one of the biggest thorns in our side because we haven't managed to tackle the message properly.[60]

That's something we're going to have to address so that people understand better what the Ulster Unionist Party stands for, what our vision is, and how we see Northern Ireland in the future … If we all want to live in Northern Ireland, then we have to make it a place for everybody. It's a union of people within a geographical United Kingdom.[61]

During the campaign for the 2022 Assembly, Beattie steered the UUP closer to the political centre, articulating a more liberal message. The party manifesto emphasized progressivity and inclusivity.[62] He refused to take part in rallies protesting the protocol and calling for its abolition, saying they were divisive and raised communal tensions.[63] He proposed instead 'common sense alternatives', such as labelling goods coming from Britain to Northern Ireland and not onto the EU single market in the Irish Republic as being for 'UK sale only'.[64] He was open about his position as pro-abortion[65] and defended the party's proposal for an anthem specifically for sports.[66] He refused to enter a pan-unionist election plan, intent on differentiating the party from its rivals.[67] In the end, the message and the messenger found little voter traction. The party took a battering, which would have been a lot worse had it not been for transfers from both the DUP and the Traditional Unionist Voice (TUV); Beattie himself almost missed the cut.

Jeffrey Donaldson is more critical of the political rather than the policy differences between the two parties. 'The Ulster Unionist Party', he maintains:

has positioned itself on the middle ground, but has hopelessly failed to hold it in the face of the advance of the Alliance Party … I fear that the UUP is drifting towards a more extreme position [and] is at times reflective of the politics of Jim Allister, itself reflective of the politics of people like Jim Molyneaux. If [the UUP] wants to truly battle for votes on the middle ground, then this hard-line, extreme position it continues to take is simply haemorrhaging votes on the middle ground for unionism to the Alliance Party.[68]

Donaldson's interview took place in late December 2020, before the potentially catastrophic collapse of support for the DUP, as reported in a series of LucidTalk polls for much of 2021. Its voters were punishing it for the deleterious effects the NIP was having and flocking to Jim Allister's party, the TUV, further to the right than the DUP. The one-man party has been unrelentingly anti-protocol, calling unequivocally for its termination and no checks on goods coming from Great Britain to Northern Ireland, positions Donaldson adopted once he became party leader.

None of the mainstream unionist parties, however, can advance themselves as the authentic voice of unionism. According to a 2021 University of Liverpool survey, just 52.3 per cent of those who wish to remain in the United Kingdom intended to vote DUP, UUP or TUV in the 2022 Assembly elections.[69] 'It is evident,' the survey report concludes, 'that constitutional preference for those wishing to remain in the UK does not equate strongly with regard to voting for unionist parties.'[70] (In comparison, 92.9 per cent of voters wanting a united Ireland intended to vote Sinn Féin or SDLP.)[71]

In his seminal review of unionist ideology, *Unionist Politics* (2001), Feargal Cochrane argues that unionism 'contains diverse interest groups with little in common other than a commitment to the link with Britain', but that the coherence of the ideology begins to disintegrate when unionists are forced to establish a consensus for political progress.[72] Conflicting perceptions of identity between those who saw themselves 'in isolationist terms as the guarantor of Protestant religio-cultural hegemony' and those who saw themselves 'as simply another region of Britain that should be governed in the same way as the rest of Britain'[73] created two political poles, the former group advocating restoration of legislative devolution with majority rule, the latter full integration with the UK: the UUP only very reluctantly signed up for the B/GFA; the DUP vociferously opposed it. Eventually, internal arguments in the UUP post-1998 toppled David Trimble and the party imploded. 'Is unionism a finished product or a work in progress?' asks Professor Graham Spencer and Reverend Chris Hudson:

> [and if] it's a finished product, what did it end up creating? If it's a work in progress, what does it aspire to create? … If you ask those two questions, that's where the absence of a response indicates a problem. Nobody really now is clear what the union means anymore. One hears that unionists are becoming increasingly detached from London and Scotland. This again feeds into the siege mentality.[74]

But who speaks for the union? The prominent group of Northern unionists who trekked to Dublin in 1981 to make their case for the union were at best speaking for themselves, despite Garret FitzGerald's endorsement of their views as the authentic voice of unionism. Other than this attachment to the union, Protestants speak many tongues.

The Protestant community in Northern Ireland is fragmented. Unable to advance a collective political vision that will accommodate their interests as they face adverse demographic trends in rapidly changing internal and external political environments, Protestants find common purpose only in their determination to maintain the link with Britain – even as there is ambivalence in Britain about whether it is worth preserving. What is unionism, absent the Union?[75]

There is a diversity of religious underpinnings. The Shankill alone, a community of 27,000 people, supports twenty-four different congregations, each competing for community support: Scots Presbyterian, evangelical Protestant and Episcopal Protestant coexisting under the broad umbrella of Protestant, and an ancillary umbrella, unionist.[76]

Some academics stress the importance of the Presbyterian tradition, a Calvinist mindset reflecting moral superiority that makes it resistant to change. Marianne Elliot writes, 'Presbyterians tend to believe their faith to have preserved the original purity of the Reformation from the dangers of prelacy and popery and have used this perception to inform their conceptualization of Ulster.'[77] For Elliot, 'the notion of a church as a covenant between God and man' has also been used to challenge 'excessive executive influence and unrepresentative government' and helped shape 'a nonconformist tradition of contract between Presbyterians and centres of power, which has created a problematic relationship with the forces of state and state control.'[78] Hence, 'the intellectual superiority felt by Protestants in general, but more particularly etched in Presbyterian consciousness by their conviction of their own purity of principle' and thus the 'resistance to political reform.'[79]

John Dunlop stresses the value put on 'an ongoing suspicion of power and authority.'[80] Anthony Stewart concludes that among Protestants 'there is "a natural instinct to distrust the outward forms of civil government unless they are consonant with his religious principles"'.[81] This defensive position took place in a predominantly Catholic Ireland, which, by its theological unity, is seen as contradictory to the contested space of Presbyterian/ Protestant identity and so an influence on the '"defensive, intolerant and uncritically loyal to traditions and institutions" which have sustained the radicalism of the Protestant tradition.'[82] For Steve Bruce, 'an incapacity to agree on the foundations of religious belief and an encouragement to rein- terpret how that belief intersects with identity offers an explanation as to why unionists find it so difficult to agree about anything, and, accordingly, why they find it so difficult to articulate a reassuring or consistent message about what they stand for.'[83]

'There are so many Protestant denominations,' Dermot Nesbitt, the former UUP Member of the Legislative Assembly (MLA) and at one time private secretary to Brian Faulkner at the time of the Sunningdale Agreement, observed,

> that if they don't agree, they fall out and form their own grouping. Whereas Catholicism has traditionally been more hierarchical … the [nationalist] party structure was somewhat reflective of that disci- pline. On the other hand, the unionist party structure was reflective more of the Protestant discipline, where if we don't like it, we form our own. And that's why unionism has been all over the place.[84]

Words such as 'intransigent', 'distrustful', 'moral certainty', 'cantankerous', 'suspicious', 'paranoid' and 'lack of tolerance' pepper the different analyses of unionism and its theological undercurrents. Hardly behaviour characteris- tics that fit the criteria for nimble-minded negotiators, if there are at some point negotiations about the future constitutional shape of the island. Rev. Harold Good echoes these sentiments: 'We need to remember that, largely, the Protestant population within Northern Ireland are the descendants of the settler people and settler people are the most unsettled of people.'[85] In Northern Ireland, to a large extent, 'the Protestant population are the descendants of the Scottish settlers, of English and Scottish planters':

> They're always seeing enemies and always wary of change or chal- lenge. Calvinistic theology plays its part in our political ideology, which is a chosen-people theology, where this is the land that God gave us. That's why we're here and we must defend it … I believe it's very influential in our political or theological thinking. Take the Free Presbyterian Church, which was built on this theology then trans- lated into the politics of the DUP. Paisleyism was there before Paisley was born.[86]

Perceived threat is a defining attribute of how a divided society frames its response to every issue, seeing them as binary choices, reducing complexity to a matter of us versus them.

One hundred years since the foundation of the state, the inbuilt two-to-one majority – to assure an enduring Protestant ascendency – has come to an end. It can't be legislated back. 'That,' Paul Nolan says, 'makes the Protestants feel insecure':

> They had Boris Johnson, a British prime minister [who they trusted] until he threw them under the bus with the deal that he agreed with the EU, a line down the Irish Sea. On the question of the border between the UK and EU that Brexit called for, the EU took the view that Ireland was a natural *political* entity, that it wished to maintain Ireland North and South as a natural political entity, which wasn't of course the unionist view and wasn't the British view … So now you've an arrangement [that] has edged Northern Ireland a bit closer to the republic and further away from what unionists consider 'the mainland'. That is psychologically very upsetting for unionism. Add to it the fact that you've got a situation where at the time of those negotiations over Brexit, the opinion polls show that it would not have been an issue for the British public to see Northern Ireland go in return for the Brexit they wanted.[87]

Alex Kane asks:

> Who would represent unionism in any conversation with the Irish government? Unionism is not united like nationalism. Whatever the differences may be between Sinn Féin and the SDLP [Social Democratic and Labour Party], it's clear what the end goal is. They've done the work; they've opened up a number of areas. Even [Ireland Senator] Mark Daly's report,[88] which is a bit heavy and flaky in places, is evidence that there is work being done. The trouble is [that] there's no collective unionist voice to go to any meeting.
>
> I remember Micheál Martin telling me once that even up to a few years ago they'd gone to see the various unionist parties, and he said, 'Alex, I feel like I have been in different countries sometimes. They don't have the same priorities.' He said that unionist parties are more concerned about the treachery of their fellow unionists than they are about what we're doing, about what Sinn Féin is doing.[89]

Nor do unionists talk to their own base, Kane says:

> They don't talk to themselves about what it is they value and what
> it is they stand against, what it is they fear. They don't do that with
> each other ... I just get this feeling that they'll just have a completely
> petulant breakdown, some new fatuous argument or disagreement
> between them. Then they'll continue fighting each other and then
> one day they'll wake up and be told, 'Well actually the British and
> Irish governments have agreed to a border poll' ... They will lose not
> necessarily because [it's a] united Ireland versus United Kingdom ...
> they will lose as they haven't a clue how to make the argument, let
> alone what argument they're making.[90]

The predominant unionist view of the peace process is that it has been primarily a nationalist project, that unionists have done all the giving and
nationalists all the taking.[91] Such was unionist antipathy towards sharing
government with nationalists that, after Stormont was prorogued in 1972,
they were prepared to forego exercising power themselves rather than
sharing government with nationalists if that was the price to restore a
Stormont parliament.

The 1985 Anglo-Irish Agreement (AIA) had a profound impact on the
Protestant psyche.[92] Not only was the agreement negotiated behind their
backs without consultation, but it specifically gave the Irish government a
consultative role in how Northern Ireland was governed and a physical presence in Northern Ireland – a republican Trojan horse in Northern Ireland's
territory. To show their anger, unionists boycotted meetings with British
government officials for several years, essentially shooting themselves in the
foot as the agreement took a greater institutional hold and the two governments grew closer. In 1991, unionists participated in the Peter Brooke
talks. As a gesture of encouragement, the British and Irish governments
suspended meetings of the AIA for their duration. The implicit message to
unionists: if you want to get rid of the AIA, you will have to negotiate a
settlement with nationalists that would include power-sharing and an Irish
dimension. Mainstream unionists reluctantly accepted the B/GFA, aware
that their failure to agree to a compromise with nationalists would result
in the two governments working with the hated AIA more broadly, likely

morphing into a form of joint authority. Even then, the B/GFA tore the UUP apart.

The DUP sat out the B/GFA negotiations and campaigned vociferously against the agreement during the referendum campaign to ratify it, turning only to embrace the St Andrews Agreement when it had electorally emasculated the UUP and eliminated all electoral threats. In the decades since, it has struggled to reconcile believing that the B/GFA is primarily a nationalist document and using it as a tool to advance a unionist vision of the future, a project it has been singularly inept at pursuing. However, in 2021 unionism – and the DUP in particular – wrapped itself in every provision of the B/GFA to make its case against the NIP, having belatedly discovered that it threatened its constitutional status in the United Kingdom. Hence, the weaponization by both sides of the agreement: for nationalism/republicanism it was invoked to argue that a land border would constitute a violation of the agreement; for unionism/loyalism it was invoked to argue that a border down the Irish Sea constituted a violation. Dublin sides with the former, London with the latter. The years of relationship-building with the South were abruptly cut, meetings of the North-South Ministerial Council curtailed, then ceasing altogether.[93] But, true to form, while unionism railed mightily against the protocol and demanded that it be rejected in toto, it had little to offer with regard to what should replace it, except that whatever arrangement was agreed would ensure the free movement of goods between Northern Ireland and Great Britain.

Unionists, Peter Robinson advises his erstwhile colleagues, must 'sell' the union to nationalists, showing that it will provide them with a better future and will act as insurance in case of a border referendum: 'I don't expect my own house to burn down but I still insure it because it could happen,' he advised in July 2018.[94] That requires a vision.

Unionists, however, are poor at the vision stuff. They have, Robinson adds, been almost complacent about their position within the UK:

> They don't feel that they have to sell it. They don't feel that they have to prepare for a border poll. We have reached a stage where the unionist community now finds that there's a challenge to their position within the union [as a result of Brexit], and they've made no preparations for selling membership in the United Kingdom as being the best alternative [to a united Ireland].[95]

Unionists should be working the Stormont institutions: 'The stronger Stormont becomes, the more stable it becomes, the more likely people will be to retain the status quo. Why fix it when it's not broken?'[96]

That interview took place in March 2020, four months after the Brexit Withdrawal Agreement incorporating the NIP was signed.[97] Nary a word was spoken at that point about the protocol's violation of the consent formulation in the B/GFA, which stipulates that no change will be made in the constitutional status of Northern Ireland without the consent of a majority. One year on, only months after the first phase of the protocol had been implemented in January 2021, Robinson called for dramatic measures to protest the protocol unless it was abolished in its entirety.[98] The protocol, he said, 'was a devilish ploy that will, unless it is removed, spread like a cancer through the blood and into the bones and organs of the Union'.[99]

Unionism may as well have been Rip van Winkle, sleepwalking through the transition year, giving no thought to what the protocol would eventuality entail. As Mervyn Gibson, the Orange Order Grand Secretary says: 'Unionists realized things were going wrong when there wasn't unfettered access for goods coming to Northern Ireland. They were not able to buy British goods,' and thus were 'being forced to buy from the Republic of Ireland'.[100] That, Gibson adds:

> leads to an all-island economy, which is a precursor to a united Ireland. That unfettered access needs to be immediately reinstated, so if I order something from England, it comes from England, there's no customs label on it, there's nothing else, it's an internal trade within the United Kingdom. I understand that if they want goods to go to Europe, you need special checks, that's grand. Deal with that. You don't need a whole Irish Sea border infrastructure to do that. There's always been smuggling on the island of Ireland … There should be no restrictions on any goods coming to Northern Ireland from mainland UK.[101]

'For unionists it is the impact of the Northern Ireland Protocol on our constitutional position that cries out for change,' Robinson writes:

> It's quite simple really, either suck it up in its present or minimally changed form or resist it … You cannot try to ditch the protocol and administer it at the same time … Is the scrapping of the protocol

more important than the continued operation of the Assembly? A choice may have to be made ... Can those opposed to the Northern Ireland Protocol gain a majority in the Assembly and withhold the democratic consent required under Article 18?[102]

He warned of the potential of violence 'lurking in the background', 'stirred up by opposition to the protocol ... What is needed is a pan-unionist response that all unionist parties can support. The inclination to outdo or criticize others who have the same objective must be overcome'.[103]

Eventually unionism coalesced around the issue, issuing a joint statement calling for replacement of the NIP.[104] Unless action was forthcoming, the DUP threatened to collapse Stormont.

Dermot Nesbitt says:

> I want unionism to be embracing of the broader community. They should have said more clearly 'yes' to an Irish language act, but of course then Sinn Féin has to reciprocate and recognize Westminster ... I do not presume that all Catholics are nationalists, neither would I presume all Protestants are unionists. We [the UUP] as a unionist party must articulate a broadly based Northern Ireland within the United Kingdom fundamentally subscribing to international law with all rights and equality ... We should be pragmatic, progressive, out-reaching. Of course, a lot of unionists are not doing that.
>
> If or when there may be a [border] poll and if there was a decision to secede from the United Kingdom, then we could discuss how cessation could take place but I'm not going to discuss that now because it would hypothetical. Equally, I would not ask Sinn Féin 'come and discuss about how you should remain in the United Kingdom'. They wouldn't do it. They argue for a united Ireland; I argue for a United Kingdom.[105]

Yet while Sinn Féin says the party is 'committed to the full implementation of the Good Friday Agreement in all its aspects',[106] it will not acknowledge the fact, stated in the opening pages of the agreement, referring to 'the legitimacy of Northern Ireland as part of the United Kingdom'. Nor can it call Northern Ireland by its proper name: it calls it the North of Ireland, not Northern Ireland. 'They neither recognize nor abide by the integrity of the

United Kingdom, yet in international law Northern Ireland is part of the United Kingdom, so I have no doubt in my mind the hypocrisy of Sinn Féin, but I'm prepared to work with them. I've been in government with them.'[107]

Similar sentiments are echoed by Peter Robinson:

> Nobody is going to get into a process of saying, here's the kind of united Ireland we're going to have, even though nobody has voted for it. It's just not gonna happen. No unionist is going to sit down and say, 'Well, we'll have a united Ireland on this basis, if the referendum decides that there's going to be united Ireland.' That's to concede the case. Unionists are not going to concede the case that it is inevitable. I don't think it is inevitable either.[108]

Among unionist interviewees this view was widespread: when nothing is on the table to discuss, why open a conversation on something as vague as a united Ireland? Moreover, before it could even contemplate a conversation with nationalists on the future, it had to engage with itself, all its fractious and disparate pieces coming together to try to forge a future that would go beyond simply restating ad infinitum that unionism stands for the union. 'There's a recognition at last,' Alex Kane says, 'that they are no longer the kingmakers, they're no longer the unassailable leaders of Northern Ireland, that things have changed. It's a slow recognition that they need to adapt but it is happening.'[109]

The DUP seems fixated on preserving the status quo, a longing for the remnants of ascendency that is not in their own interests to cling to. 'We don't want a conversation because we don't want a united Ireland,' former DUP MLA Jim Wells says.[110] 'Are the Alaskans having a conversation about becoming Canadians? No, because they still wish to be American. It seems quite illogical that we, given the fact that we are absolutely resolute as a community wanting to remain British, that we facilitate negotiations about changing that? We don't want anything to do with it.'[111]

Voters may be inclined to go for Alliance, but Alliance, he asserts, remains staunchly pro-union. 'We are confident,' Wells continues,

> that 99 per cent of the Protestant community wish to remain British and a significant number of the Roman Catholic community, any-thing from a quarter to a third, don't want to change their status either … Nationalists are very good at upping the ante, trying to convince us

that we've changed our minds. But despite all of the scaremongering, no unionists are changing their minds. But what has happened is that a lot of unionists are now voting for the middle-ground parties … [but] they haven't changed their view on constitutional change.[112]

Many interviewees said that political unionism is 'dead', in the sense of being unable to adapt to changing circumstances. By holding firm to the belief that there is no potential referendum in the offing until some date in the distant future, they are in denial of the possibly tidal impacts as the union reinvents itself post-Brexit. 'There's absolutely no question that political unionism is in a state of flux at the moment,' the loyalist community activist Winston Irvine says,

> but we need to be careful not to be drawing simplistic conclusions from what are complex political points. For example, most people in Northern Ireland voted Remain in the Brexit referendum. However, some people try and conflate the fact that quite a number of unionists, myself included, voted to remain in the EU in that referendum with some kind of benign support for constitutional change for Northern Ireland.[113]

Unionism, Richard Bullick says, may be losing ground, but so, too, is nationalism, as more identity configurations have emerged:

> The number of people … who would vote for Northern Ireland to remain in the United Kingdom is far in excess of the number of people who'd vote for political parties that have a capital U in their names … It would be useful for unionist parties to have a fuller understanding that they can't simply rely on the approach that has been taken down the years. A hundred years gives them an opportunity to rethink about how best to create a situation where 60 or 70 per cent of people support the constitutional status quo.[114]

And why isn't unionism up to the challenge of laying out a vision for the future? The problem, Bullick says, is one of bandwidth:

> Most of the people who are involved in unionism are tied up in being government ministers or party leaders or doing other things … the difficulty is that what you would need to do in order to win a border poll big is not necessarily the same as what you would need to do to

make sure you win at the next Assembly election. While the short-term electoral advantage outweighs the long-term strategic advantage, you're more likely to take up an approach which is popular in the short term and plays to your base, because the DUP have been enormously successful winning a greater and greater percentage of a smaller and smaller pie.[115]

The UUP, Bullick adds, is partly to blame:

The Ulster unionists, rather than trying to be broadening unionism by moving to the left into the centre ground, have sort of shadowed the DUP at most opportunities, so they're fighting on the same turf as the DUP, and in a way in which they can never outflank the DUP … That's why the Alliance Party have now been able to take over in the centre, because people became disillusioned with the DUP in the last election. Most of them didn't jump to the Ulster unionists, they jumped to the Alliance.[116]

'Political unionism has been badly led by the DUP,' the UUP leader Doug Beattie says:

They never give ground. This no, no, no approach that they had has left us in the position that we are now. Everything that they do has a short-termism to it which leaves unionism losing out. The Assembly had 106 members and a unionist majority. The DUP pushed for it to be reduced from 106 down to 90. Fourteen of the seats that were lost were unionist seats. They just are not bright in what they're trying to achieve. There's no sense of strategic thinking.

Unionism is in a decline in regard to open support. The people are not coming out to vote as much as they used to, the demographic is older. If you alter the message for people, then that can change quite easily. That needs to happen. There's this ebb and flow, which you just need to deal with in politics. Unionism is on the decline from a very big high, but it's not on a decline where it's irrelevant anymore. Half the population in some shape or form are unionist even if they don't own up to it, or even if they don't vote for it. They are willing to say, 'I want to stay in the United Kingdom because I'm happy with Northern Ireland as it is now.' Unionism as a brand might be on the decline, but not unionism as a movement.[117]

Not so, says the DUP leader Jeffrey Donaldson:

> I think that there is a future for unionism, but it needs to recognize
> the changes that have occurred in politics in Northern Ireland and to
> adjust to those changes. The 'New Decade, New Approach' document
> sets out the mechanisms that we intend to use to do this. The UK
> government is going to fund a new foundation that will undertake
> academic research on the benefits of the union, provide us with the
> up-to-date information that we need to enable people to fully appre-
> ciate the benefits of being in the United Kingdom. New Ulster British
> commissioners [need] to be appointed to ensure that the British
> identity of unionists is protected, something we feel is important
> because it has been eroded, in our opinion, in recent years.[118]

Political unionism, according to Donaldson, must also reposition itself in
a way that broadens the appeal of unionism. 'That is not something that is
unique to the DUP.'[119]

The interview with Donaldson took place in December 2020, several
months before the DUP imploded. The leaked minutes of a meeting of the
South Antrim Constituency Association on 25 February 2021 provides a
snapshot of the turmoil brewing in the party.[120] Fears were expressed that
the DUP might not be the largest party after the next Stormont election:
'DUP on back foot, lose seats, drastic change is needed,'[121] one note reads.
Another, with respect to Brexit, says, 'bringing down the Assembly is not an
option. The protocol [had to be] removed totally'.[122]

In the space of a month (May 2021), the party, wracked by internal divisions – partly driven by what many of its MLAs regarded as First Minister
Arlene Foster's tepid reaction to the protocol, too inclined to stress the
possible benefits of Northern Ireland's unique access to both UK and EU
markets – unceremoniously dumped Foster as party leader after an MLA
coup led by agriculture minister Edwin Poots.[123] Poots replaced Foster after
a leadership contest that saw him defeat Donaldson by a single vote. After
twenty-one days at the helm, he resigned after losing support of the party's
MLAs and MPs.

As required by the B/GFA, the first minister and the deputy first minister have a veto over each other's appointments to the posts, effectively collapsing the Executive and Assembly. In the case of Poots's choice as first
minister, Paul Gavin, Sinn Féin demanded that he initiate legislation on an

Irish language act during the rest of the Assembly legislative session. Poots balked; a compromise was reached. If the Assembly failed to act, Secretary of State Brandon Lewis promised to introduce Irish-language legislation at Westminster in October 2021. The DUP parliamentarians, who had not been consulted, furiously opposed such a compromise and effectively gave Poots the heave. Donaldson stepped into the breach, unopposed for the leadership. For the duration of the Assembly's sitting, Gavin continued as first minister. Replacing him would have required repeating the process all over again, with Sinn Féin no doubt having one more political card up its sleeve.[124]

It was a precarious time for the DUP. The haemorrhaging of support had accelerated since the January 2021 LucidTalk poll. A LucidTalk poll in May 2021 showed Sinn Féin at 25 per cent and the DUP and Alliance at 16 per cent.[125] The UUP stood at 14 per cent, SDLP at 12 per cent and the TUV at 10 per cent.[126] The unionist vote was fracturing, the DUP losing voters to Alliance and the more moderate UUP at its left, and to the TUV at its right.[127] Months later, the political landscape had worsened. An August 2021 LucidTalk Tracker poll had Sinn Féin holding still at 25 per cent, the UUP at 16 per cent, the TUV at 14 per cent and Alliance and the DUP at 13 per cent.[128] DUP support had more than halved from 31 per cent at the Westminster elections three years earlier.[129] Electoral catastrophe loomed.

Donaldson moved to reverse the DUP's plummeting support, putting a premium on fending off further defections from the party's base to the TUV. He laid out seven 'tests' that a renegotiated trading arrangement between the EU and Northern Ireland would have to meet.[130] If met, these tests would essentially emasculate the protocol. In what many political pundits saw as a gamble, he repeatedly threatened to collapse the Executive unless he saw progress towards sweeping revision to the protocol. He pulled the DUP ministers out of meetings of the North-South Ministerial Council.[131] He worked in lockstep with David Frost, the UK's chief negotiator, calling for the British government to trigger Article 16.[132]

Donaldson positioned the DUP to take credit for whatever concessions the British government won from the EU and wrap them in a package the party could sell to unionist voters. If no concessions were forthcoming, then he would resort to the nuclear option – collapsing the Assembly. After repeated threats to do so, and being accused of bluffing, Donaldson pulled the plug. Paul Given resigned as first minister on 4 February 2022, which automatically removed Michelle O'Neill from her position of deputy first minister.[133] But – unlike in 2017, when McGuinness's resignation as deputy first minister collapsed the Stormont institutions in their entirety – ministers stayed in their posts in a caretaker capacity through the Assembly elections in May, although the Executive could not meet and key decisions could not be made, especially in regard to the three-year budget the Executive had hoped to agree on before the Assembly elections.[134]

Donaldson's decision left the party in a vulnerable position, open to UUP accusations of putting DUP interests before Northern Ireland's.[135] Nevertheless, the DUP upped the ante: unless the protocol was resolved to its satisfaction, it would not go back into government after the Assembly elections.[136]

At one level, it was delusional and hubristic for the DUP to believe that a small party representing a few hundred thousand voters from the smallest region of the United Kingdom could force the EU to bend to its wishes and renegotiate an international treaty between two economic powerhouses – one representing more than 60 million people, the other more than 400 million – or it would collapse the B/GFA's institutions with unforeseeable consequences for the peace processes. However, in the narrow parochial context of Northern Ireland, and a looming election where the DUP was hard-pressed to recover the votes it had lost to its more extreme right-wing rival, it made perfect sense. As the election campaign progressed, the DUP's relentless assaults on the protocol, and its warnings of a constitutional catastrophe should the protocol stay in place, began to pay dividends. A March 2022 LucidTalk poll vindicated Donaldson's hard line. It reported that, contrary to the earlier University of Liverpool surveys, the most important concern for unionists was Northern Ireland's constitutional position in the UK, which 61 per cent of those surveyed cited.[137] Opposing the protocol was the next priority for unionists at 54 per cent, followed by the Northern Ireland economy and jobs at 52 per cent.[138]

If Sinn Féin's credo is 'whatever works', the DUP's was 'whatever it takes'. There were few lengths to which it would not stoop as it clawed back support from the TUV, and if that meant cuddling up to the fringe loyalist Orange Volunteers to protest the protocol, the party held its collective nose to curtail the stench.[139] Knowing Sinn Féin had a virtually insurmountable lead, it doubled down on its messaging that only the DUP stood in the way of Sinn Féin becoming the largest party and calling for a border referendum.[140]

Moreover, the DUP reiterating that it would not serve on the Executive unless its uncompromising demands on the protocol were met also flew in the face of public opinion, which was against Stormont being collapsed in the first place and overwhelmingly in favour of it being restored.[141] Were it not to finish second – and, worse, were it no longer the largest unionist party – the DUP would effectively be out of business. The DUP's nightmare was not Sinn Féin finishing first, but itself not finishing as the largest unionist party.

The public wants the institutions to work. The huge vote for the Alliance Party in the Assembly 2022 elections is a bellwether of change – of a voting public, no longer hostage to timeworn catchwords, that wants a government that functions, that does not lurch from crisis to crisis but addresses the everyday issues that affect the way people live. Just 6.5 per cent of unionists and 4 per cent of nationalists want constitutional issues to be the Executive's number one priority when the Northern Ireland Assembly is restored.[142]

> *Unionism is in an absolute mess at the moment, political unionism and the DUP in particular ... The identity politics that enabled unionism to rule for a hundred years is dying out. These elements are all converging and threatening unionism.*[143]
> – John Manley, political correspondent, *The Irish News*

Among unionists, Lord Ashcroft concludes in his comprehensive survey, 'Ulster and the Union: the view from the North', there is 'gloom ... the feeling that, in the political arena, they have simply been outclassed ... many believe that through a combination of patience, strategic discipline, reinvention, presentational genius and sheer persistence, the nationalists have put themselves on course to achieve their aim, maybe not in this decade, but within their lifetime or that of their children'.[144]

The psychological impact of Michelle O'Neill preening as first minister added to the angst. Slowly, almost imperceptibly, the Northern Ireland carved out of Ulster to ensure a lasting Protestant majority has disappeared, unionism fighting a rearguard action for a Northern Ireland that no longer exists.

In unionists' own words, unionism is 'unsettled', 'has done a poor job at safeguarding the union', 'is in decline', 'is living in denial', 'cannot speak with a collective voice', 'needs to talk with itself' and 'is always seeing enemies'; 'its problem is with itself', 'its back is against the wall', it is unsure of its place in the United Kingdom and it is watching Scotland's pursuit of independence and the rise of English nationalism. It continues to conflate Sinn Féin with the IRA, which it considers still active and a threat, and it sees no reason to begin conversations about the future, which it would regard as tantamount to surrendering to the idea of a united Ireland. A Sinn Féin government in the South would be perceived as 'a hostile government': unionism may have lost its dominance, but neither has nationalism superseded it. Unionism 'has to be about more than flags and parades', has to declare its intent to create a 'broad church', yet for both the DUP and UUP, for all of Jeffrey Donaldson's and Doug Beattie's talk of the need for inclusivity – 'an island of its peoples' – passing an Irish language act is a red line that cannot be crossed.

'They're trapped,' says Bronagh Hinds, a Women's Coalition co-founder. 'They can't see any way forward. They're told on the one hand that they should start setting out for what a new Northern Ireland would look like or why conditional Catholics should vote for it in the future. On the other hand, they're told that they should get into negotiations for a united Ireland.'[145] However, 'The pro-union community is very robust,' Peter Shirlow says. 'It's been thrown under the bus many times, but it doesn't give up on its faith of articles. It doesn't give up on its desire to stay within the union.'[146] Although adrift in churning political seas, buffeted on one side by English nationalism and on the other by Irish nationalism, they cling to a constitutional life raft: the choppier the seas, the more vice-like their grip. They intensely oppose a united Ireland, more intensely than nationalists crave a united Ireland, but stall at making Northern Ireland a warmer house for Catholics.

Once the ramifications of the protocol seeped in, all talk of warmer houses and broadening the electoral base came to an abrupt stop. In less than a year, Peter Robinson went from urging unionists 'to work the institutions' of the B/GFA to calling on unionists to smash them:

> Unionists dwell under a cloud of injustice ... pilloried for not meeting each of the ongoing, incessant, and unending demands from republicans to erase everything British and indulge everything Irish. ... There is a feeling of deflation and disappointment ... [unionists] speculate that the laws which will apply here will, in the greater part, be made not in Stormont nor at Westminster but in a Dublin-influenced European Union, without a single elected representative from Northern Ireland having a vote.[147]

Furthermore, Robinson adds, 'there have been many occasions when unionists were under fire or faced overwhelming adversity and have been more
angry than today, but I can think of no period over my fifty years in politics
where unionists have felt more alienated than they are now'.[148]

'Betrayal', 'alienation', 'anger': three words encapsulate unionism's state of
mind since the proroguing of Stormont in 1972. The AIA was met with the
DUP's 'Ulster Says No' campaign, which came to naught; the Orange Order
marches from Drumcree Church down the Catholic Garvaghy Road were
curtailed despite vehement opposition; the Parades Commission is still in
place; the B/GFA, denounced by the DUP during the referendum campaign
to ratify it as another act of betrayal, is now embraced; the flags protest that
turned ugly and menacing eventually petered out; the Brexit Withdrawal
Act incorporating the NIP was demonized as an act of betrayal. At every
turn unionists see their cultural markers weakened, vilified or erased.

Hence the predicament of unionism, succinctly enunciated by Graham
Spencer and Rev. Chris Hudson:

> Objections to the Northern Ireland Protocol provide unionism with
> a meaning that it is used to: the politics of rejection and resistance.
> And the inability of unionism to provide a compelling and inclusive
> political alternative to the enduring picture of loss and decay con-
> tinues to provide solace only for those who value protesting against
> something. However, this reactive mentality reveals not just an
> absence of imagination but an absence of hope.[149]

This mindset can galvanize support against a perceived threat but cannot
articulate an alternative because of 'an inability to grasp the importance of
proactive thinking'. It provides psychological relief at the time of a crisis, but
only until the next crisis when the cycle of protest galvanizes support again.
Thus, 'the long-term condition of anxiety continues'. Even more worrying
[they write] 'is how there appears to be such little attention given to the
inadequacies of this reasoning or how the reactive approach hinders the possibility of building social stability, forward-thinking and confidence'. How,
then, 'given this tendency, can unionism be anything other than fearful of
the future?' Hard-line reactions to the protocol, the authors postulate, 'draw
from a deep well of anger that, over time, has taken energy from having no
positive way of thinking about change itself'.[150]

The refrains of protest echo across the decades. In 1989, five years after the AIA was implemented, I interviewed Peter Robinson when I was writing *Northern Ireland: Questions of Nuance.* He told me then that the union is 'already broken'. The question unionists have to ask themselves, he said, is, 'Are we wanted in the UK? Is our future in the United Kingdom?'[151]

Three and a half decades on, unionism is still asking itself the same question but without any further insight into what futures might lie ahead. They are, perhaps, too painful to contemplate.

— TWELVE —

Protestant Fears: ghosts of the past

It's not so much a fear, it is an attachment to what they have ... Now, the relationship with the Catholic Church actually is a very interesting development. It would be fair to say that, in his early career, Ian Paisley feared Rome, Rome rule, the Catholic Church. I think in later years, you'll find strange bedfellows and lots of issues between the Catholic Church and the very religious Presbyterians who don't particularly like liberalism ... They share a lot of the social values of church-going Catholics. They might have an issue with the mass and so on, but I don't think they have the same fear any more at all in terms of the shared values, in terms of social values.[1]

– Éamon Ó Cuív, Fianna Fáil Teachta Dála (TD)

In terms of fears, what do they think? They think they're going to be moved against their will into Leprechaun Land, for some of them. Some of them are much more nuanced and feel they're going to be moved into a system of government that they never identified with ... that they're going to be forgotten about, that their children are going to be starving, that they're not going to have access to proper educational support, that, God forbid, they're going to be completely discriminated against, because they will essentially be living in a land that they don't identify

270

*with, and, therefore, will be treated as second-class citizens. That they
may end up having to defend their section of the community against
things which they haven't given consent to. I don't know what that looks
like for them, I presume some of them would very much welcome the
fact that they want to get a bit of aggro in, largely younger members of
the loyalist community, who don't remember how bad the conflict was.
I think that they feel that they're going to be sneered at, that their right
to practise their culture isn't going to be protected, whatever that is ...
These are just random things that you hear. Their kids are going to be ...
forced to play GAA matches, for example.*

*All of that is ridiculous, but that is a genuine and real fear for
them. That they're not going to be able to identify with the Royal
Family, for example ... that they won't be able to have an allegiance
to a Tory Party government or whatever [British] government is in
position at that time, that they don't recognize the Dáil, will never
recognize the Dáil, and certainly don't want it imposed upon them.
I think a lot of it, actually, is probably a reverse position in terms of
where society went when Northern Ireland came into existence in the
first place. You had these sections of community in the North which
didn't really buy into the political process, and felt completely alienated for it. That's why I'm saying when those conversations take place,
and if they are at a micro level, not at a macro level, on the ground
amongst your ordinary Joe and Mary or Nigel Bloggs, that those fears
need to be articulated in a proper way, and they shouldn't be treated
as nonsense ... [You have to] say, 'Well, okay, that's a real fear for you.
Let's put this on the list and see how we can mitigate the risk of that
ever happening to you ...'[2]*

– Máiría Cahill, Sinn Féin activist, Former Seanad Éireann senator,
former Social Democratic and Labour Party (SDLP) Councillor,
Sunday Independent columnist

*My wife, she didn't learn Irish [so] she couldn't get a job that was paid
for by the public purse. She went to England for her first job ... there
are still the images and the stories that people have in their minds of a
hostile environment. There was [the] Ne Temere decree. There were all
sorts of ways in which Protestants felt isolated and alienated from the
state, and they just kept their head down. I think that's why my family
in business did well. They didn't take any part in local affairs. They just
carried on their business. That's all changed dramatically.*

The Northern Protestants who've had no understanding of what it's really like to live within the republic would still have these images, and would not want to be a part of that. Now, I think the republic has to work hard to try and show and demonstrate that other than through very liberal things – same-sex marriage and divorce and all that – because a lot of the conservative Protestants in Northern Ireland, that doesn't appeal to them because [chuckles] they're against those things. The DUP [Democratic Unionist Party] and the Free Presbyterian Church would be much more conservative. To say to them, 'Well, all of those things have changed.' There's still that image. The psyche is it's not a welcoming place for Protestants … They're fearful of being further diminished.[3]

– Rev. Harold Good, Methodist Church minister, one of the two independent witnesses who oversaw the decommissioning of paramilitary arms

[Protestant fear] goes back to partition in 1921 and the civil war in 1922. The expulsion and the murders that took place of Protestants, the businesses that were destroyed or the homes that were burnt. People still remember that because we have still got people from that generation living up here. I hear them saying, don't repeat the past, don't repeat the past.

That is a big fear that will be carried out again if we were to go into a united Ireland, that somehow that would re-emerge. Look at what went on, especially along the border during the conflict. That can only be described as genocide, ethnic cleansing by fascists. To shoot somebody sitting on the tractor because they owned that land and then go back and say, we were told he was security force, when they knew rightly he was the only son of two elderly people – but that was a policy that they pushed, and people have a fear of that … I think it's a valid fear.

Nobody else would have been allowed to buy the land because they wouldn't have got in, and that's what they'd done … Newry used to be known as a border town, but it's not really now because it has pushed out so far. It's basically if you go out to the other side of Banbridge, there's people that will tell you, 'Oh, we're at the border now, so it is. Because you see the Irish-language signs, you see the tricolours. It's in your face, so it is. Once they've gained power in the council the first thing they do is change the street and road signs. I could drive from here, six, seven miles, and you would swear you were in the Republic of Ireland, so you would. That's with every county along the border.[4]

– Colin Halliday, Former Ulster Defence Association (UDA)

I'm involved in a number of initiatives bringing loyalists and unionists to engage with the Irish government, really just to clear channels of communication as well as chairing across the island dialogue group. They are in a very edgy place at the moment, particularly loyalism, I think, wondering where things are going to go. There is a deep concern. I've heard extremes like, 'Will people want their land back that was taken from them [in the seventeenth century]?' ... I've even heard, 'Do you think they'll end up putting us in concentration camps?' Those are genuine fears within a number of communities ...

We all know the future is not going to be decided on this island. It's going to be decided in Westminster, in London ... People do not trust the current [Westminster] administration ... It's a very precarious position. You have 900,000 people [in this] north-eastern part of this island, who are wondering where are we going to go, what is going to happen. The whole border poll debate has been ratcheting things up continually. I would say part of it is ... [Republicans are] not expecting a united Ireland in the next couple of years any more than they were expecting it in 2016. I think if [a united Ireland] does evolve, I see it over a ten- to fifteen-year block.[5]

– Rev. Gary Mason, Methodist minister, Director, 'Rethinking Conflict'

It seemed like a good idea and would set an example to unionists and nationalists in Northern Ireland endlessly grappling, often bitterly, with legacy issues. And so, in January 2020, 'in the new spirit of inclusivity and reconciliation on the island', the Fine Gael Minister of Justice Charlie Flanagan proposed an event to include the historic Royal Irish Constabulary (RIC) in one of the events commemorating Ireland's Decade of Centenaries.[6]

Prior to the War of Independence, the RIC and the Dublin Metropolitan Police were the local police in their communities, back to their founding nearly 100 years earlier.[7] Some 90,000 policemen served in both. Because they wore the uniform of the Crown and were on the British side during the War of Independence, they were regarded as legitimate targets by the Irish Republican Army (IRA). There were killings on both sides, and on occasion in the wake of IRA attacks the RIC carried out reprisals against locals. In post-independence Ireland, the RIC was disbanded and replaced by An Garda Síochána. Former RIC members were ostracized and stigmatized for having fought on the British side during the war. Their unpatriotic act relegated them to the wrong side of history.[8]

The backlash against Flanagan's proposal, including from some senior Fianna Fáil former ministers and councillors across the country, was immediate and vitriolic, and the event was cancelled. Taoiseach Leo Varadkar decried the backlash, saying it set back the cause of Irish unity. A united Ireland, he said, 'must be one that recognizes a shared history and that there are "one million people on the island who identify as British and as being from a unionist background".[9] The incident, however, was revealing, a microscopic example of the unaddressed baggage in the subconscious of the collective memory, dormant until some event jars it to the surface.

In drawing up its 'imagining' of a united Ireland, one of the factors the South will have to offer unionists will be how to accommodate the British identity. But, say unionists, the South cannot accommodate something it does not understand, platitudes about 'a shared Ireland', 'an agreed Ireland', which Protestants see as code words for a border poll within a time frame that suits the South.

Unionists' response to the RIC imbroglio was immediate and condemning, a kind of 'gotcha' moment. 'Those leading the vehement opposition to this event,' Jeffrey Donaldson of the DUP said, 'are the same people who tell those of us in Northern Ireland that British identity would be respected and accommodated within some mythical "new Ireland".'[10] He added: 'When agreement cannot be found to commemorate those who died 100 years ago it is a clear demonstration of how far we still have to travel in terms of respect and reconciliation, particularly in relation to the British identity in Northern Ireland by republicans.'[11] Those who served in the RIC and the Dublin Metropolitan Police, he added,

> were Irish men and women from all religious backgrounds who lived and worked in an Ireland that was politically united. Many of them suffered or were murdered for no reason other than the fact they wore a crown on their uniform, and it is difficult to escape the conclusion that opposition to this commemoration is based again on that.[12]

The then Ulster Unionist Party (UUP) leader Steve Aiken called the decision to defer the commemoration 'disappointing, but not surprising given the tone of the debate and the language used by some of the leaders and elected representatives of political parties in the Republic of Ireland. It exposed a direct and underlying contradiction to their previous public statements about reconciliation.'[13] Furthermore, he said, 'the comments from Fianna Fáil and Sinn Féin … will further affirm the view among many unionists in Northern Ireland that there are many within the Republic of Ireland who continue to hold a deep animosity against anyone or any organization linked to "the Brits"'.[14] Describing members of the RIC as 'colonialists' and 'oppressors', he says,

> is an insult to their memory and their descendants. These types of comments do nothing to build reconciliation and demonstrate that some elements of society with the Republic of Ireland remain openly hostile to the British identity or those perceived to be associated with it. This hostility will not be lost on unionists who are the subject of repeated entreaties to consider embracing Irish unity and who are constantly assured that all would be well. Actions really do speak louder than words.[15]

If the South finds it difficult to forgive members of the RIC for being on the wrong side during the War of Independence, or if it sees them as insufficiently Irish to be counted among the casualties of that war, how, unionists asked, might it treat former members of the Royal Ulster Constabulary (RUC) or the Ulster Defence Regiment (UDR) in a united Ireland? The RIC fiasco does not inspire confidence.

But the episode raises a larger question. Why is unionist opposition to a united Ireland so unrelentingly steadfast now that two of the bogeymen most cited as obstacles – the influence of the Catholic Church and a backward economy – were disposed of at the end of the first decade of the twentieth century?

In *The Uncivil Wars* (1983), I wrote: 'Protestant fears are endemic. They encapsulate the entire Protestant experience in Ulster. They are so deeply rooted, so pervasive, so impervious to the passage of time that it is almost possible to think of them as being genetically encoded – a mechanism, like anxiety, necessary for the survival of the species.'[16] Little has changed to alter that observation. While some of the fundamental aspects of Protestant fears of a united Ireland have undergone a metamorphosis, evolved to take account of changing circumstances, and some have intensified because Brexit catapulted the Northern Ireland Protocol (NIP) into the political mix, the psychological core remains impervious to change.

Focus groups conducted by the scholar Jennifer Todd as part of her study for 'Unionism, identity and Irish unity: Paradigms, problems and paradoxes', found that the overarching fears of a united Ireland in the unionist community are:

> extreme fears of sovereignty change that would make unionists a minority in a strange land … intense fear of assimilation and of being treated as 'second class Planter citizens' and 'alien planters who don't belong here'. There was concern that close connections with 'kith and kin' in Great Britain would be lost forever, that the primacy given to the Irish language would marginalise them and that they could not be truly British in a united Ireland, under rule by triumphalist republicans, with their British heritage removed: 'effectively our home would become a foreign state'. There were continuing fears of violence among all groups … that loyalists would provoke violence, and, like some of the everyday nationalists we interviewed, worries that the transition period would bring instability and economic and security dangers. For participants in the focus groups, the fear was of republican triumphalism and unionist defeat and humiliation; nationalists would expropriate unionists' farms and take their land; there would be show trials of ex-members of the British security forces; there would be a return to murder and violence.[17]

The exegesis of these fears reflects a modern variant of Protestants' historical belief that the Catholic majority is surreptitiously poised to rise up and drive Protestants from the lands they settled. From the early seventeenth century, plantations in Ireland were settled by Episcopalians from lowland England and Presbyterians from Scotland. These settlers lived in fear that Catholic natives would rise up to reclaim their lands. According to the Protestant narrative, the foundational starting point is 1641, when the remnants of the Old Gaelic Catholic aristocracy rose up to reclaim their confiscated lands. This uprising confirmed the worst fears of the Protestant minority. It gave birth to the myth of massacre and reinforced the myth of siege. These two myths have replicated themselves in different circumstances across centuries to ward off every perceived threat to either physical or spiritual dispossession, including Protestant fears of being catapulted into the cauldron of an Irish Catholic state where they would be a minority and vulnerable to dispossession and marginalization.

'Most Catholic gentry lost their lands after the 1641 Rebellion and Williamite wars,' Professor James Wilson told the Oireachtas Committee in his submission:

> There was a sectarian competition for tenure which fostered the rise of agrarian solidarity groups: Defenders, Oak Boys, Hearts of Steel, Peep of Day Boys, Orange Boys, Ribbonmen, Fenians. It is a matter of record that – particularly in the nineteenth century – many Catholics lost their tenancy to Protestants, as landlords perceived Protestants as loyal to the Crown. In 1870 Gladstone's Liberal government passed the Land Act that gave tenants the right to purchase, and many Catholics saw their ancient rich tribal lands now 'legally owned' by Protestants, while they had to settle for less favoured areas. This resentment has festered for over one hundred years and resurfaced during the Troubles.[18]

The Protestant narrative thread of the thirty-year conflict includes the IRA murdering the sole sons of Protestant farm owners in border areas who were members or former members of the UDR or of the UDR Reserve, often forcing the parents to sell the land they were now unable to farm due to their age or lack of manpower. Invariably, the sale was made to Catholics, bidding below market price. This was perceived by Protestants as territorial gain for republicans as they pushed the border deeper into Northern Ireland. They fear that in a united Ireland some farms, especially in border areas where memories are long and unforgiving, will revert to the descendants of the original owners. 'Many unionist landowners,' the Oireachtas study reports, 'believe that there is an expectation among some Catholics west of the River Bann that, as a result of Irish unity, the lands of unionist farmers will be confiscated and redistributed to Catholics.'[19]

Protestants fear, too, that they will be submerged in an all-Ireland state that suffocates their cultural identities. These beliefs have retained their potency since the Belfast/Good Friday Agreement (B/GFA). They are expressions of the lingering chosen trauma – the inner fear of extinction that lies deep within the Protestant psyche.[20]

The past is recalled every year with commemorations of the Williamite Wars, the Battle of the Boyne and the Apprentice Boys; Orange Order parades, castigated as triumphalist and smacking of ascendency by republicans, are reminders for Protestants to stay vigilant in the face of known and unknown threats. People feel that the past is now and what happened in the past can happen again.[21] Some unionists believe that in the post-B/GFA political environment, 'implementation of measures designed to redress historic discrimination against Catholics have, in fact, created a discriminatory environment for Protestants'.[22]

No understanding of the Northern Ireland question is complete without an understanding of the basis and intensity of Protestant fears. And while no constitutional future is possible without addressing them, it may also well be that those fears are so integral to the Protestant psyche that no number of accommodations may suffice to ameliorate their impact. The propensity in the South to dismiss these fears as superficial fails to grasp how collective insecurity with tentacles reaching back in the early seventeenth century can continue to exhibit itself.

Says Jennifer Todd:

> To dismiss the claims is also to mistake their status. They speak as much to ontological fears as physical insecurity. The respondents are so concerned about their identity, their past, their sense of belonging and the meaning of their lives that they may be prepared to unleash the security problems they fear … Their fears will not abate until their ontological insecurity is addressed, and this, notoriously, cannot be reassured by reasoned argument, pragmatic appeals or appeasement.[23]

The report on submissions on 'Unionist concerns and fears of a united Ireland' to the Oireachtas Committee on the Implementation of the B/GFA cautions:

> Many of the submissions referenced a fear of a united Ireland being that of triumphant nationalism. This fear is not without foundation and that is why we in the South must change not only our vision of a united Ireland but also how we speak about it. Language was a key component of negotiating the Good Friday Agreement and it remains a key component of the peace process. With hard work, we must move from the language of the past such as a 'united Ireland' and all the dread and fear which it creates in the minds of our unionist friends and neighbours. We must instead change to the language of the need to protect the peace process, build a vision for a shared island and a united people in a New Agreed Ireland.[24]

Rather than reassuring unionists, such reasoning is itself part of the problem. For them, it smacks of the duplicitous use of language to conceal what is at its core: a united Ireland.

In *A Troubled Sleep: Risk and Resilience in Northern Ireland*, James Waller draws on the work of Walter Stephan and Lausanne Renfro to elucidate how the sectarian divide in Northern Ireland finds expression in perceived threat, a metric 'by which we can understand how a particular out-group becomes a target of hostility'.[25] What matters, Waller points out, 'is not only the actual threat posed by the "other" … it is also the degree to which threats posed by the "other" are perceived to exist'.[26] In Stephan and Renfro's intergroup threat theory, he adds, 'perceived threats come when members of one group perceive that another group is in a position to cause them harm'.[27] Perceived threats, whether realistic or symbolic, do not have to be accurate, nor do they have to be fulfilled, to have intergroup behaviour. The perception of threat becomes its own reality.[28]

In Northern Ireland, one such perceived threat comes from the Irish language, an insidious forerunner of Irish unity. Fears involving the Irish language are based in part on a clause in the B/GFA that places a statutory duty on authorities to encourage Irish education, though that obligation remains largely unfilled. The 2006 St Andrews Agreement calls for the Irish government to introduce legislation 'to enhance and protect the Irish language'; the 2020 'New Decade, New Approach' document calls for legislation to create a commission 'to recognise, support, protect and enhance the development of the Irish language in Northern Ireland and to provide official recognition of the status of the Irish language in Northern Ireland'.[29] Unionists will point to the less than 12 per cent of Northern Irelanders who have some fluency in the language and the less than 1 per cent who use it as their primary language.[30] They see the hidden agenda in agreements involving the Irish language: roads, bridges, schools, public records and court proceedings will be named or published in Gaelic. They fear the diminution of Northern Ireland's Britishness and see the Gaelicization of the North as a step to Irish unification. Such is the grip of this threat that it cost Edwin Poots his job as leader of the DUP.

In the event of a border campaign where the prospect of a united Ireland looms large, confirmation bias will lead unionists to embrace aspects of reality that reinforce their belief system and affirm their perceived threats.[31]

The fact that the South is one of Europe's more socially liberal countries with respect to such cultural wedge issues as LGBTQ+ rights and abortion cuts little cloth with unionists. They point to the primary education system still, they say, firmly in the domain of the Catholic Church, with little appetite among political elites to secularize schooling, or they will hold that the Irish economy, no matter how booming, is one step away from the next recession.

With Northern Ireland having free access to EU and UK markets, it could as easily be marketed as a dynamic driver of growth, pulling those more open to being persuaded regarding the economic virtues of unity back into the pro-union fold. The Irish government is seen as working *sub rosa*, conniving with the European Union (EU) to ensure that it will not renegotiate the NIP because it has led to a significant increase in cross-border trade and hence the backbone of an all-Ireland economy, a harbinger, as unionists see it, of unity.

Boris Johnson was highly distrusted for his heinous betrayal. Having promised that never, under any circumstances, would he countenance a border down the Irish Sea, he acceded to the EU to do just that. Unionists nonetheless clung to his coattails, believing he would protect their interests, even as he showed disinterest in doing so. Belief polarization is rampant: Catholics and Protestants look at the same data and it strengthens them in their prior opposing beliefs.[32] What Catholics see as facts, Protestants see as fabrications. A LucidTalk poll in January 2021 reported that 72 per cent of unionist party voters believed Northern Ireland would still be part of the United Kingdom in 2050.[33] In contrast, a stunning 97 per cent of SDLP and Sinn Féin and 68 per cent of Alliance thought Northern Ireland would have left by that date.[34] Catholics may see the Catholic Church's implosion in the South as signifying the final erosion of the Church's authoritarian hold on Irish society; Protestants see a sufficiency of its continuing influence. Catholics see a turbo-charged Irish economy achieving new heights; Protestants see one highly leveraged on a small number of multinationals who could pull the plug on their presence, an economy on a roller coaster where the only sure thing is that it will collapse again, as it did in 2008. And besides, they say, the North has a higher standard of living.

The former Alliance Party leader David Ford alludes to the treatment of Protestants in the Irish Free State but also to how they assimilated. 'The precedent of 1921 [regarding how Protestants were treated in the new Irish state] is not good on accommodating Britishness for those who were, as some people term it, "left behind" in Donegal and Monaghan and Dublin/Wicklow areas ... The precedent is that those people did not retain any feelings of being British at all.'[35]

Though Protestants retained control of their hospitals and schools and other institutions after 1921, the South made little attempt to accommodate their British identity in post-independence Ireland. A low-intensity anti-Englishness was fostered by the de Valera government, in power for most of the 1930s through to the 1960s. Partition was England's fault and England alone had the power to remove it, which, quite miraculously, would result in a united Ireland as Protestants awoke from the false consciousness that they were Brits and discovered they were Irish.

Even their souls were victims of the false consciousness. The souls of Protestants, Catholics were educated to believe, could not ascend to heaven – not even the most virtuous. Instead, they got stuck in limbo, denied the rapture of God but not suffering from the loss since they lacked knowledge of His infinite presence. Catholics knew something Protestants didn't, and that knowledge compensated for a sense of inferiority in the face of things perceived as English.

Anti-Englishness was inculcated and fostered. 'English' games – rugby, soccer and cricket – were not allowed at Christian Brothers schools. The 50,000 Irish men and women killed during the First World War on the battlefronts in France fighting on behalf of Britain were marginalized, as if their deaths had somehow been unpatriotic. There was no acknowledgment that, for thousands, joining the British army was done in the hope of bringing the war to a quick end and seeing home rule – postponed at the beginning of the war – become a reality. Even wearing a poppy on Remembrance Day was stigmatized – the best the South can do on Poppy Day is mostly to wear a green shamrock poppy commemorating the Irish men and women who were part of the slaughter of the First World War.[36]

The Protestant population of the South declined by approximately one-third between the pre-independence census of 1911 and the first post-independence census in 1926 – most precipitously between 1920–2. From a near peak of 10 per cent in 1911, the Protestant population in Ireland declined to 4 per cent in 1971 and to between 4 and 3 per cent since (see Table 12.1).

Table 12.1: Protestant population in Ireland, by census year (%)[37]

CENSUS YEAR	POPULATION	PROTESTANTS	PROTESTANTS % OF POPULATION
1891	3,468,694	356,786	10.3%
1901	3,221,823	328,850	10.2%
1911	3,139,688	311,461	9.9%
1926	2,971,992	207,307	7.0%
1936	2,968,420	182,746	6.2%
1946	2,955,107	157,054	5.3%
1961	2,818,341	129,645	4.6%
1971	2,978,248	119,437	4.0%
1981	3,443,405	115,411	3.4%
1991	3,525,719	107,423	3.0%
2002	3,917,203	146,226	3.7%
2006	4,239,848	161,291	3.8%
2011	4,588,252	165,897	3.6%
2016	5,123,536	162,505	3.2%

Many socio-economic and political factors were at work: migration to Northern Ireland or Britain; political changes that were not supported by most Protestants; the disproportionate targeting of Protestant landowners during the War of Independence and the civil war that followed; land-grabbing under the veneer of political emancipation.[38]

John Kyle, a former member of the Progressive Unionist Party (PUP), who switched to the UUP, compares the fortunes of the two minorities:

> The unionists – or the Protestant minority – in the South have almost disappeared. The nationalists and Catholic minority in the North have prospered and grown. Unionists would say, 'Well, that says

something about the two states at their institution a hundred years ago.' ... We recognize that the times have changed, that the Catholic Church's position is far different than what it was a hundred years ago. We do recognize our identity, that it comes with an emotional dimension. Our identity is a British identity. Primarily, we look towards the east, not towards the South. Therefore, emotionally, we are tied to that and that is who we are.[39]

In *Buried Lives: The Protestants of Southern Ireland*, Robin Bury documents 'the widespread intimidation and attacks on Southern Protestants from 1920 to 1923, the enforced migration of up to 48,000, the burning of 276 of their so-called "big houses", further widespread sectarian attacks in 1935, the Church of Ireland's futile opposition to compulsory Irish in primary and secondary schools'. [40] Included are details of 'the mini pogrom in the Bandon Valley in April 1922 when thirteen Protestants were murdered and a further sixteen targeted'.[41]

The enforcement of the Catholic Church's Ne Temere decree that required the Protestant partner in a 'mixed' marriage to raise the children as Catholic meant that as the smaller Protestant population married into the larger Catholic one, the population did not reproduce itself. In 1911, there were 311,461 Protestants in the South; in 1991, there were 107,423, a precipitous decline of 66 per cent. Representation in the Irish parliament remains marginal: of the 144 TDs elected to Dáil Éireann in 1969, four were Protestants; in 1973, three; in 1977, one; and, between 1981 and 1989, between one and two.[42] Discrimination was not official, but the overwhelming Catholicity of the state coupled with the association of Protestants with Britishness sufficed to sustain a narrative that Protestants were insufficiently Irish. Absent from public life was 'the energy, intransigence, and the fierce radicalism which marked the Protestant tradition'.[43]

Proficiency in Gaelic as a requirement for the civil service and public institutions led to the absence of representation in the public sector and cultural bodies. The Irish language, Tom Garvin writes, was 'an ideological weapon for nationalists and fundamentalist Catholics, feared by Protestants and used for moral supremacy. The extremists confiscated the language much as they had confiscated Gaelic games for a particular political ideology'.[44] The efforts to Gaelicize the state came to naught – in 1922, 17 per cent of the population spoke the language; in 2016 it was 1.7 per cent.[45]

A Gaelic, Catholic Ireland was promulgated in the 1937 Constitution, which opens:

> In the Name of the Most Holy Trinity, from Whom is all authority and to Whom, as our final end, all actions both of men and States must be referred, We, the people of Éire, Humbly acknowledging all our obligations to our Divine Lord, Jesus Christ, Who sustained our fathers through centuries of trial …[46]

Of course, the historical contexts are different a hundred years on, and the legal protections in the South prohibit seizures of property.[47] The Catholic Church's influence was eviscerated by the paedophilia scandals that engulfed it in the 2000s. From the embers of economic depression in the 1980s rose the Celtic Tiger revolution of the 1990s, propelling Ireland into a top-tier economy among the most prosperous in Europe.[48] Regardless, unionists continue to claim to have a superior economy and that the South cannot afford to absorb it. The territorial claim in Articles 2 and 3 of the Constitution, claiming the whole of the island of Ireland as the national territory – so abhorrent to unionists – has been removed. But in the post-Brexit political reconfigurations, calls for a border poll have intensified.

A conservative society morphed into a socially liberal one: it is the first country in Europe to legalize marriage equality by popular vote; to have a gay prime minister; and to hold a referendum abolishing the constitutional provision prohibiting abortion by an almost two-thirds majority. In contrast, in the 1980s, unionists proclaimed their heritage of religious liberty in contrast to the South's suffocating Catholicism; in 2019, the DUP refused to legislate in the Assembly to bring Northern Ireland into line with UK law on abortion, and it fell to the UK parliament to legislate for Northern Ireland over DUP objections.[49] Indeed, for some unionists, the South is not sufficiently religious. Fr Tim Bartlett warns:

> Ironically, there's an element within unionism that still has a strong religious ethos. One of the things that the South hasn't really grappled with in its transition to an aggressively secular and antireligious culture is [that] they need to be ready to deal with a very sophisticated evangelical Christian tradition in the North that is able and willing to claim its religious rights freedoms.[50]

> Whereas in the 1980s Protestants could take issue with the domi-
> nant, socially conservative ethos of the South, the situation forty years
> on is the obverse: a liberal South and significantly conservative North.[51]

Has anything happened in more than twenty years since the B/GFA that would persuade a unionist that the South is open to the 'generosity and harmony' it promises in accommodating Britishness? Is there something tangible that would signify that openness? That one could point to as indicative of a warmer house? Sinn Féin TD Matt Carthy says:

> It's not really for me to say to a unionist or to somebody who is
> British living in the North, 'This is what we will do for you in the
> event of the united Ireland.' Part of the conversation must and even-
> tually will come to the point where unionists are saying to us, 'This
> is what would need to happen in order for us to feel confident and
> ownership of Irish unity.' Then the test will be whether we have the
> generosity and the ability to respond in kind.[52]

Among interviewees, this question largely drew a blank. Other than referring to the erosion of the authority of the Catholic Church and the emergence of a liberal social polity, few could point to much that might be interpreted as a concerted effort to accommodate a British identity. 'We have an electorate in the Republic that doesn't want to make any significant changes in its political and societal arrangements to accommodate unionists,' Andy Pollak said in his address to the John Hewitt summer school in July 2022:

> And a unionist community in the North who feel zero identification or
> fellow feeling with the 26-county Irish state; in fact the great majority
> probably feel hostile to it, not least because what they see as Southern
> support for the Provisional IRA's 30-year campaign of murder and
> mayhem in the North. As that most liberal of men, former Ulster
> Unionist Party leader Mike Nesbitt, after defining himself as a 'Brit',
> puts it: 'What I haven't heard from nationalists is that "We want you
> in this new dispensation and here's why" … Somebody has to explain
> to me why we've gone from "Brits Out" to "Brits In".'[53]

On the contrary, Brexit stirred a dormant Anglophobia, disquieting enough to draw a rebuke from President Michael D. Higgins.[54] His decision to not attend an interfaith service at Armagh Cathedral to commemorate the 100th year since the founding of Northern Ireland drew rebuke from unionists.[55] 'The Anglophobia that was unleashed in all the mainstream media during Brexit was huge,' Lord Bew says. 'Irish tribalism is alive and well. It was on full display during the Brexit years. It just turns out that Irish Catholicism is an optional part of it.'[56]

The Angelus bell still introduces RTÉ's 6 pm evening newscast.

— THIRTEEN —

Loyalism: loss and change

*Unionism will never admit that loyalism has anything to do with it.
It will never take ownership of it in the way that Sinn Féin has done
and has to do with the IRA; admit that they were two parts of the
same organization. They want to have plausible deniability, but they
will always invoke the threat of loyalism if something is not going their
way, and they will do it in a 'Well, of course, we wouldn't be violent, we
wouldn't do the wrong thing, but some people out there might.'*[1]

– Naomi Long, Minister of Justice, Alliance Party leader

*I detect a growing sense of anger and frustration among loyalist para-
militaries … There is a sense that Northern Ireland is outside of the
rest of the United Kingdom. The rest of the United Kingdom [UK] left
the EU [European Union]. We're half in and we're half out. The whole
push for a referendum from Sinn Féin is causing major problems. I'm
not quite sure what's going to happen after the latest polls that show
clearly that it doesn't meet the requirements for the Secretary of State
and that's who, at the end of the day, makes the call.*[2]

– Sammy Douglas, Democratic Ulster Party (DUP); Member of
Legislative Assembly (MLA) 2011–17

All we can do is protest. We can't ever go back to the days of violence ... There is no appetite for loyalism to return to violence.

Where that might change is if you look down the line and there's a bigger threat to a united Ireland. A columnist was down in Dublin a few years ago. He would have come from a unionist background, but he's a journalist, and he was asked a question, where would loyalism fit in a united Ireland? He says, 'Listen, two or three well-placed bombs in the Republic of Ireland will put an end to a talk of a united Ireland' ...

We have engaged with the republicans about what a united Ireland would look like [and] ... as part of that engagement, you have to have a bit about staying within the United Kingdom, and republicans flatly refused to do that.

It's the centenary here and Sinn Féin and nationalists all have said, 'We're having nothing to do with that.' That's having a hardened stance within loyalism, because in 2016 loyalists engaged with republicans, done training with republicans, went down to Dublin and showed respect to their hundredth anniversary. I don't want republicans to show respect or anything. See, if they don't want part of 2021, I have no problem with that, but they have to show a level of tolerance.

[How] republicans show tolerance to their unionist neighbours in the celebrations of our centenary ... will have a big knock-on effect on to what engagement we'll take after this here ... If they don't, the biggest problem will come after this year where people will say, 'Well, they're talking about a united Ireland, and that's the way they treated us when we were celebrating our centenary, not a chance.' Republicans, I think, are starting to think a wee bit differently here.[3]

– Colin Halliday, Former Ulster Defence Association (UDA)

There has been a massive revolution in loyalist identity over the last twenty years. Lots of anti-racism projects, anti-misogyny projects, job-creation projects, social-economy projects. The band culture is very much tied to anti-sectarianism, running Orange bands, playing with Somalians, North Africans, Chinese, challenging racism, challenging educational disadvantage, setting up restorative justice. There's been a massive shift. One of the biggest social-economy projects in Northern Ireland is Resurgam in Lisburn.[4] *There's a largely unknown shift within those who were the peacemakers within loyalism who are [now] using every effort to build social justice, inclusion and anti-racism, anti-sectarian projects.*

Both unionists and loyalists are pro-union – I don't even know what a unionist identity or a loyalist identity is … the difference now is probably just class. Both have traditionalists and progressives. Clearly loyalism has a structure which is linked to bands or former paramilitarism. The whole idea that these are monoliths is wrong: pro-union and loyalist groups are made up of all types of people and with different perspectives. The one thing that holds them together is their desire to stay in the UK.[5]

–Peter Shirlow, Professor, Director, Institute of Irish Studies,
University of Liverpool

Loyalists are beginning to rattle their sabres. They will say, on one hand, we're not going to go back to violence, but on the other hand, 'Well, we'll use whatever means are necessary to resist.' It's a bit like going back to 1912. We fight the British to stay British.

The loyalists are saying it [violence] worked for the others, so we'll have to resort to that as well. We'll have to give the threat of violence even though we don't particularly want to. There are those within the loyalist community who say there's no way we're going back to that. At the same time, they're making it known that they will hold that in abeyance as a resource if necessary.

In spite of having been influential in supporting the Good Friday Agreement, they are now saying we withdraw support for the Good Friday Agreement. What that actually means in practice nobody's quite sure.[6]

– Rev. Harold Good, Methodist Church minister, one of the two
independent witnesses who oversaw the decommissioning
of paramilitary arms

One side will feel they're gaining, one side will inevitably feel they're losing. Unless we develop a vision of something better for us all, I think we failed at that vision part. That's where the narrative, particularly in loyalist communities, comes from … the sense of loss rather than the sense of gain.[7]

– Rev. Lesley Carroll, Presbyterian minister and
Prisoner Ombudsman

There is a group of people who have the flexibility educationally to have choices, but [for] many folk within working-class loyalism, that choice is not open to them. Identity becomes the all-prevailing concept, because there's no education to give you those options. If you analyse that, you can see how British identity, battles of the past, who we are as a people, becomes the all-prevailing mechanism of why we don't want a united Ireland. Because we don't have any other options. This is our space.

We're not going anywhere, and if we're forced into something, the uncertainty of what may evolve with republicans … we just don't want to be there. You think of people on the border, I've heard them say, 'Look, from our perspective, there was an ethnic cleansing of Protestant families in the border. We had at that stage the RUC [Royal Ulster Constabulary] and the British army to protect us.

What's it going to be [in the united Ireland] when they're no longer there? What happens if the republican movement or elements within that [say], 'You know what? That land was never yours in the first place. We're taking it back.' It's probably not dissimilar to the South African Afrikaner mentality. That when you go into this allegedly rainbow nation, will the Blacks take our land back?[8]

– Rev. Gary Mason, Methodist minister, Director,
'Rethinking Conflict'

There is a pervasive belief in Protestant working-class areas that they have lost the peace-agreement game – and, as they witness their community's decline through immigration and a high mortality rate due to having an older population, their expectations for the future mirror their experiences of the present. Says Professor Graham Spencer, who works closely with the loyalist community:

> There has been a frustration building amongst some sections, not all, some sections of loyalism since the B/GFA [Belfast/Good Friday Agreement]. This perceived notion that loyalism has been left behind in the peace process. The reason that many bring to the table as to why they think that is not so much because of social circumstances but because of the gains of Sinn Féin … [these] are interpreted as evidence of loss and detachment.[9]

There is a palpable sense of loss, an anxiety for a retrieval of a past they fought to perpetuate, that is as much now of mythology as of fact, forever rubbished. The Protestant working classes were a little better off than Catholic working classes, but the knowledge that they belonged to the ruling class was an expression of their supremacy – they took satisfaction in the narcissism of small differences.

When the symbols of the cultural manifestations of unionist dominance are dismantled, loyalists cling fiercely to them. Hence the violence after the decision of the Belfast City Council – where the Alliance Party holds the balance of power – to restrict flying the Union Jack over Belfast City Hall to eighteen days.[10] Although barred since the mid-1990s from making the march from Drumcree Church to Portadown centre on 12 July through the Catholic estates on Garvaghy Road, every Sunday four Orangemen march from Drumcree Church to Portadown with a petition for a license to hold the parade.[11] The death of Queen Elizabeth in September 2022 was an almost unbearable loss. The losses are held fast, nurtured, the resentments they feed accumulating until they reach a breaking point. The border down the Irish Sea is such a point.

The losses accumulate: the 1998 agreement is referred to as the Good Friday Agreement, not the Belfast Agreement. On a comparative basis, fewer Protestant youngsters complete high school.[12] Catholics get higher grades.[13] Queen's University, once synonymous with Ulster's Protestant elites, now graduates a higher proportion of Catholic students.[14] There is little that generates hope for Protestants as they look across the political horizon. In contrast, Catholics – convinced for the most part that eventually there will be a united Ireland if that is their wish – have emerged as a self-confident, forward-looking community, poised to embrace the challenges of the future.[15] From Protestants being the majority population in Northern Ireland since its founding, they are no longer even the largest plurality.[16] Having once ruled everything, they now look ahead and imagine a future where they may rule nothing. Not that they see a united Ireland around the corner, but it hangs, like the Sword of Damocles. And, as they wait for it to fall, their best way to deal with it is with denial – it is not to be spoken of – lest engaging in the hypothetical might put scaffolding on it.

'I grew up in a city where wall murals were all of King Billy,' says Paul Nolan:

> And as somebody from the Catholic community, I resented that triumphalism. That sense of 'we were the victors; you were the losers' that you've got all the time. If I drive around Belfast now, I don't see King Billy, I see the Somme. And it's all about sacrifice and loss and

this sense that Ulster unionism has always had to become the sacrifi-
cial lamb, and that sense of fatalism that goes with that. You know, all
these silhouettes at sunset and all the rest of it and this, you know, it's
a rebuke to the English, who have forgotten how much Ulster gave to
protect the United Kingdom.[17]

In his submission to the Committee on the Implementation of the Good
Friday Agreement, Professor James Wilson reported on focus groups he
had conducted among a cross-section of loyalist communities.[18] Among
his findings: the period of 'direct rule' had been 'elevated in the Protestant
collective memory to what historians call "a heroic period"', on a par with
the Siege of Derry, the Battle of the Boyne and the Battle of the Somme; it
was recalled as a 'time of heroism, unionist unity and valour'.[19] He found,
too, that many 'plebeian Protestants' had a strong nostalgia for the Troubles,
'when, financially and psychologically they were much better off', and that,
'retrospectively, Protestants now voice a carefully couched nostalgia about
the Troubles'.[20] A younger generation is denied – and envious of – the well-
paying careers in the security forces during the conflict that an older generation of Protestants enjoyed, the high status of respect their communities
lavished on members for the risks they took on their behalf and the job
satisfaction that came from tracking 'terrorists' and making their communities safer. But the reality check is that there is no going back to the past
under any circumstances; no matter the future, direct rule will never again
be part of it.[21]

The ethos of conflict provides both meaning and a sense of belonging
and social cohesion that manifests itself in a strong sense of community.
Protracted conflict becomes part of the identity of its protagonists. Peace
erodes these interconnected communal bonds, the acute sense of belonging
to a cause greater than oneself. It signifies a loss.

The social psychologist Peter Marris, a pioneer in this field, wrote that
the ideology of conflict has a very powerful appeal for those who have lost
their sense of belonging:

> it relieves the threat of personal disintegration because the structure
> of conflict offers a side to take, a reference for behaviour, a meaning
> to the experience of loss: and with this reassurance life becomes
> manageable again.[22]

Unionist/Loyalist opposition message to Northern Ireland protocol post-Brexit on placard in Lurgan, County Armagh. 5 March 2021. Photo: CAZIMB/Alamy.

Anti-Brexit billboard on the northern side of the border between Newry in Northern Ireland and Dundalk in the Republic of Ireland. 18 July 2018. Photo: Niall Carson/Alamy.

Taoiseach Leo Varadkar and British Prime Minister Boris Johnson meet in Thornton Manor, Cheshire, England, after which they said that they 'could see a pathway to a possible deal' on Brexit negotiations. 10 October 2019. Photo: Irish Eye/Alamy.

Fianna Fáil leader Micheál Martin shakes hands with Fine Gael leader Leo Varadkar as Sinn Féin President Mary Lou McDonald looks on at the final TV leaders' debate at the RTÉ studios in Donnybrook, Dublin. 4 February 2020. Photo: Niall Carson/Alamy.

Sinn Féin President Mary Lou McDonald (right) and Vice President Michelle O'Neill speaking to the media at City Hall in Belfast. 10 February 2022.
Photo: Brian Lawless/Alamy.

DUP leader Jeffrey Donaldson (right) announcing that Edwin Poots (left), previous DUP leader, will fill Belfast South constituency seat of Christopher Stalford, who died suddenly. Belfast. 7 March 2022.
Photo: Liam McBurney/Alamy.

Nick Mathison with arm held up by Alliance Party colleague Kellie Armstrong after being declared elected in Strangford constituency to the Northern Ireland Assembly. Titanic Exhibition Centre, Belfast. 7 May 2022. Photo: Allan Leonard.

Sinn Féin leader Mary Lou McDonald (centre right) and Michelle O'Neill (centre left) arrive at the Northern Ireland Assembly Election count centre at Meadowbank Sports arena in Magherafelt, County Derry/Londonderry. 7 May 2022. Photo: Liam McBurney/Alamy.

Campaigners for an Irish Language act protest outside Parliament Buildings, Belfast. 16 December 2019. Photo: Niall Carson/Alamy.

Irish Republican mourners line the route in Andersonstown, west Belfast, for the funeral of veteran republican Bobby Storey. 30 June 2020. Photo: Irish Eye/Alamy.

Rioters are seen at the 'peace wall' gate into Lanark Way, Belfast, as part of anti-Protocol protests. 7 April 2021. Photo: Jason Cairnduff/Alamy.

'The People's Monarch.' Her Sovereign Majesty Queen Elizabeth II: 1926–2022.
Mural erected and adorned with memorial flowers and tributes.
Crimea Street, Belfast. 17 September 2022. Photo: Allan Leonard.

God bless our NHS. Banner affixed to gate at St Paul's Church. Falls Road, Belfast. 1 February 2022. Photo: Allan Leonard.

House with steel caging at Cupar Way 'peace wall' interface. Bombay Street, Belfast. 6 June 2022. Photo: Allan Leonard.

Newtownards stands with Soldier 'F', referring to a former soldier charged with two counts of murder and five counts of attempted murder on Bloody Sunday. Banner affixed to housing, Bangor Road, Newtownards. 25 April 2020. Photo: Allan Leonard.

Table used by Edward Carson to sign Solemn League and Covenant on 28 September 1912. City Hall, Belfast. 31 January 2018.
Photo: Allan Leonard.

*The 25th Anniversary of the Good Friday/Belfast Agreement takes place on
10 April 2023. Taoiseach Bertie Ahern, US Senator George Mitchell and
UK Prime Minister Tony Blair pictured. Castle Buildings, Belfast. 10 April 1998.
Photo: RollingNews.ie/Alamy.*

McArt's Fort, where United Irishmen met atop the summit in 1795.

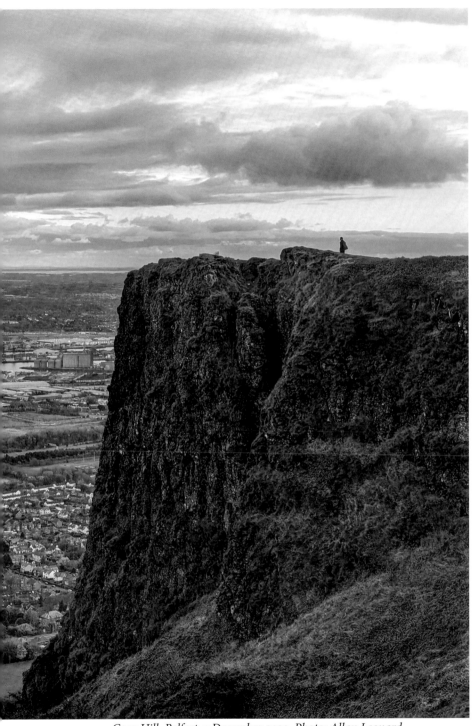

Cave Hill, Belfast. 3 December 2022. Photo: Allan Leonard.

Derry Girls mural by UV Arts, depicting five main characters of popular TV show. Orchard Street, Derry/Londonderry. 11 March 2019. Photo: Allan Leonard.

Lamppost placards for 'yes' and 'no' votes on referendum on the Eighth Amendment, addressing rights to abortion. Dublin, Ireland. 8 May 2018. Photo: Allan Leonard.

Protest for equal marriage rights for gay and lesbian people.
City Hall, Belfast. 28 March 2014. Photo: Allan Leonard.

'It Won't Always Be Like This.' Mural of journalist Lyra McKee after her murder
by dissident republicans. Kent Street, Belfast. 25 May 2019.
Photo: Allan Leonard.

Protestants are at risk of losing their sense of belonging. The community lacks the cultural cushion the Gaelic language, the Gaelic Athletic Association (GAA) and its accoutrements provide for nationalists and the richly developed historical narrative anchored in the belief of the inevitability of a united Ireland. Without a similar cultural crutch, it is in freefall.

In 'The Battle of the Somme in Ulster Memory and Identity', academics B. Graham and P. Shirlow write that 'conflict in Northern Ireland is not between ideologies of equal strength, unionism having failed to create an identity myth and sense of place, which might compete with the cultural coherence of republican nationalism'.[23] The quandary for unionists is that any kind of cultural identity that places them in Ireland 'challenges their Britishness by requiring some acknowledgement of an element of Irishness to their identity'.[24]

On how loyalism differs from unionism, they say:

> Loyalism is not a coherent ideology, [rather] embracing diverse discourses as Ian Paisley's right-wing populist and fundamentalist Christianity, the left-wing Progressive Unionist Party [PUP], which is relatively pro-British and the various and often murderous paramilitary factions ... This fragmentation of unionism reflects a real sense of a fragile identity undermined by the British government; the Ulster Protestant people seen as no more than pawns in a bigger game. Even worse, that betrayal is seen as being internal to unionism itself. Class conflict is fundamental to understanding the fragmentation of unionism ... After decades of abuse and misuse by their own politicians, working-class Protestants see themselves as 'puppets no more'. They are far less interested in notions and symbols of reconciliation than in establishing a place for themselves, a place that demands its own past and claim to that past.[25]

Nor are loyalists particularly pro-English. In fact, many have a strong anti-English streak ('I don't think anybody hates the English more than the loyalists,' says one prominent interviewee, understandably not wanting to be quoted by name); they regard themselves as 'British only' in the most generalized cultural sense; what they most represent is determined opposition to becoming part of a united Ireland. Allegiance to Britain is therefore conditional, their side of the ledger writ in blood and sacrifice on behalf of the Crown and hence the 'the obligations of the imperial government to uphold the interests of its kith and kin over those of non-British peoples'.[26]

For loyalists, the Somme embodies Ulster's blood sacrifice for the Crown, a counterpoint to republicans' blood sacrifice in 1916. On the morning of 1 July 1916, the 36th (Ulster) Division, composed for the most part of members of the Ulster Volunteer Force (UVF), which had been formed in 1912 to fight home rule, advanced from the trenches in front of Thiepval Woods towards the German lines and were cut down. On the first day of the offensive, some 2,000 members of the Ulster Division were killed.[27]

The Somme is central to loyalist identity. 'Linda Colley's book, *Britons: Forging the Nation 1707–1837*,[28] explains how the British identity was forged on war,' says Graham Spencer:

> and if you look at Northern Ireland it is clear that for some union-
> ists and loyalists the expression of that central component of British
> identity is vital in relation to the imagined community. Many rituals
> and commemorations prioritize the centrality of war, and so as a
> representation of Britishness it reinforces a sense of patriotism that
> keeps the narratives of conflict and sacrifice current.[29]
>
> Although commemorations of Remembrance Sunday and
> remembrance of the war are still looked upon with tremendous pride
> and passion throughout the union, the fact that Northern Ireland is
> always seen as under siege amongst swathes of the unionist and loy-
> alist population provides rituals with even greater meaning around
> themes of resistance and defence. One senses that for many young
> people the significance of moments like the Somme does not hold
> the emotional attachment it does for older generations; it is also
> apparent that as unionists and loyalists feel more under threat so the
> images that symbolize the importance of such events become more
> important. The past becomes a key referent for the present.[30]

After it became apparent that the Northern Ireland Protocol (NIP) involved significant physical checks on commodities coming from Britain to Northern Ireland, loyalists took to the streets in 2020 and 2021, despite COVID-19 regulations, decrying what they called the 'betrayal act'.[31] They held rallies at Belfast City Hall and town halls across the province, lashing out at an enemy they could not easily identify. Was it Boris Johnson, for negotiating the deal after his repeated assurances he would never countenance a deal that saw Northern Ireland treated differently from the rest of the UK? Or was it the

DUP for mishandling its brief at Westminster during Theresa May's tenure
as prime minister? But if the DUP was to blame, what were Nigel Dodds and
other senior DUP figures doing on protest platforms? 'It fizzled out,' says
Paul Nolan, 'because they had no political project at this stage to express it,
but the emotional thing underneath it, that sense of insecurity, that sense of
incipient betrayal, that need for it to be vigilant. That's very definitely there
in Ulster loyalism at the moment.'[32]

'Some of the main loyalist paramilitaries were saying recently,' says
Sammy Douglas:

> that the anger wasn't directed at the DUP or Boris Johnson or even
> the European Union, but it was the Irish government's attitude
> towards unionists, particularly through Leo Varadkar and Simon
> Coveney who are perceived as the real enemy. During early discus-
> sions around the Brexit Withdrawal Agreement, nationalist politi-
> cians had said that if there is a border between Northern Ireland and
> the republic the dissidents would come in and there'd be violence.
> Then when the protocol was being implemented between Northern
> Ireland and the rest of the UK, they supported an Irish Sea border.[33]

It became an article of faith among unionists and loyalists that the Irish
government – personified by Simon Coveney and Leo Varadkar – had, like
snake-oil salesmen, sold a bill of goods to the European Union (EU), successfully arguing that a land border across Ireland would result in violence
that might easily get out of hand. It poisoned the relations between Dublin
and the loyalist community, many of whom had visited Dublin on a number
of occasions to meet with Department of Foreign Affairs officials who would
assuage any insecurities they might have been expressing regarding Anglo/
Irish relations. Says the Ulster Unionist Party's (UUP)'s John Kyle:

> The border down the Irish Sea has annoyed loyalists who would not
> support violence. It has annoyed loyalists that Leo Varadkar implied
> that there would be violence if there was a border on the land, yet the
> fact that there's a border now at the ports is seen as something that is
> acceptable. Loyalists say, 'Well, the republicans threatened violence,
> we didn't, and look what's happened, we have lost.' I think that's part
> of the narrative in certain loyalist quarters. There are more extreme
> views within loyalism that feel that this is unacceptable and that we
> will never accept this. I think that broader unionism does not go

down that road, but there are sections within loyalism who would
be very outspoken and angry about what has taken place. I think that
the threat of violence should not be dismissed. Much as I abhor it and
condemn it, I think we would be foolish to think that there could not
be loyalist violence as a result of the situation.[34]

For many young loyalists, it was also about 'getting skin in the game', taking
up their cudgels to continue the struggle their parents and cousins had
been part of, now memorialized on gable walls across the province. Colin
Halliday states:

> Young people have no memory of the past. When you speak to young
> people as we do, and you've got sixteen and seventeen year olds, and
> you ask them, 'What do you aspire to be?', you're hoping [they will
> say], 'I want to be an MLA,' 'I want to be a councillor,' 'I want to be
> this, I want to be that.' But they're all coming, 'I want to be a para-
> military, I want to kill republicans.' … I always say to them … 'Before
> anybody asks you to go out and do anything, you ask them to do it
> first, see when they have done it first, then I can understand.' Because
> people using these young ones, it's like the flag protests.
>
> We kept thousands of young people out of jail by going in, and
> saying, 'This is not right.' I disagreed with the flag coming down.
> If people had taken ten minutes to vote, the flag would never have
> come down. Here we are nine years after the flag came down still in
> the same scenario where people are going out on a weekly basis to
> protest, it's madness. I would like to ask how many of those people
> vote or voted.[35]

A survey of loyalist attitudes (August 2021) to the protocol and attitudes
to Stormont and the Police Service of Northern Ireland (PSNI) reveal
a pattern of responses that mirror the observations of loyalist interviewees.[36] The survey elicited 1,000 responses and was circulated through social
media platforms and directed towards individuals and groups within the
loyalist community. It lacks the scientific rubric, as it was not conducted
according to strict statistical methodology that called for random sampling.
Nevertheless, it provides a glimpse of what mainly middle-aged male loyalists were thinking in August 2021.

Almost all loyalists view the NIP as a threat to Northern Ireland's position within the United Kingdom, while 90 per cent want the NIP abolished.[37]

Only 8 per cent would prefer it was amended to 'make it tolerable'.[38] Over 90 per cent think the NIP creates the risk of a return to violence in Northern Ireland; 80 per cent think that political unionism should withdraw from all North-South ministerial meetings 'due to the Irish government playing an integral role in creating the Northern Ireland Protocol'.[39] Ninety per cent of respondents supported collapsing the Northern Ireland Assembly in protest against the NIP.[40]

The seven days of violence in April 2021 protesting the protocol either petered out, due to the leadership of former paramilitaries and the concerted efforts of community leaders, or have been put on hold, awaiting the outcome of negotiations between the UK and the EU.

'There are a small number of [loyalists] who called the border down the Irish Sea a betrayal act,' says Professor Peter Shirlow, who has researched and written extensively about the loyalist community:

> Other loyalists said that you had to accept Brexit and the consequences. Loyalism's not a homogenous group. Loyalism's made up of people who are right wing, who are rabble-rousers, who are traditionalists, and it also has people who are the complete opposite of that. Think about that betrayal act. What happened? A couple of hundred people sat in town halls, Orange halls. It went nowhere. Nothing happened, the same as the flag protest. Nothing happened. The majority of people who have leadership positions in loyalism are working to stop violence. They're working to build a better society.[41]

Yet the questions regarding potential for violence will linger as long as paramilitarism maintains a presence in working-class Protestant and Catholic communities. 'The recent riots in West Belfast on the peace line [in April 2021] could have led to much more serious violence,' says Sammy Douglas:

> My fear is that some violent republicans could bring the guns back on to the streets during street confrontation. That will bring violent confrontation with loyalist paramilitaries. I'm not saying we'll go back to the level of violence we experienced during the Troubles, but there's no doubt about it that lives will undoubtedly be lost if we can't get a resolution to our present difficulties.[42]

The lesson of the April violence – some petrol bombs, burning a few buses, trying to breach an interface between a Catholic and Protestant community

– is that in a deeply divided society a minority of a minority can attract inordinate attention, threaten the 'fragile' peace. The smallest spark can ignite a conflagration.

FOURTEEN

Accommodating the British identity: conundrums and contradictions

*In both communities there are psychological forces at work that inten-
sify the strength of feeling beyond what the real conflict of interests
would appear to justify. These psychological forces display themselves
in terms of an intense concern about identity. These concerns appear
to be even stronger among Protestants, perhaps because their identity
is less certain.*[1]

*The problem with proposing unity by agreement ... lies in the fact
that agreement manifestly does not exist ... The unionist community
is passionately opposed to unification with the Republic. Its opposition
has if anything grown in intensity over the last twenty years and does
not seem likely to lessen for years to come.*[2]

*The persuasion ... will have to come from Britain, as Irish national-
ists have been unable over 100 years to find any argument to convince
unionists that their interests would be better served in a united Ireland.*[3]
— John Whyte, Irish historian

*The type of united Ireland that we put forward must be one that is
agreed, inclusive, pluralist and which is constructed by all our citizens,*

from all backgrounds and traditions … In any referendum campaign, those advocating a united Ireland must demonstrate an understanding that we have different traditions on this island. That there are people on this island who consider themselves British. We must emphasize that the British identity can and will be accommodated in an agreed, united Ireland. This may involve constitutional and political safeguards and we must be open, flexible and imaginative in that discussion.[4]

– Matt Carthy, Árd Comhairle, Sinn Féin Teachta Dála (TD)

[In] 1969–70 there was a housing committee [in Sandy Row] and they basically demolished all the houses and moved [the residents] up to lower Malone Road … They put them into [an estate] which they called Taughmonagh and gave them trees and a few lawns. Within I think ten years, almost every family that moved in had gone back, wandered the way back to East Belfast. My mum lived up near there and I remember asking someone she'd got to know working in the shop [why]. He said, 'I know it's only like two miles away, Mr Kane, but it wasn't my home.' I remember telling that to an audience: 'That's the problem, guys. If these people didn't feel comfortable a couple of miles from where they've been brought up, imagine if you said to them, "The country you were born in doesn't exist anymore. It's no longer, Northern Ireland has gone completely. You are no longer citizens of the United Kingdom [UK], but hey, we can accommodate your identity."[5]

– Alex Kane, journalist, former Press Officer for the
Ulster Unionist Party (UUP)

I said [to some republicans attending Féile an Phobail in West Belfast], 'For years the Union Jack was reprehensible to you [Irish republicans]. It's symbolic of imperialism, colonialism, occupation, all of those things.'

The flip side of that is for most unionists in Northern Ireland here from my generation and older, the Irish flag was something I would have burnt at school because for me it was an IRA [Irish Republican Army] symbol. It was draped over the coffins of all the terrorists or volunteers, whatever you want to address those people as. For all the combatants who were buried at a paramilitary funeral, it was the Irish flag that was draped over the coffin … For most Northern unionists, the Irish flag is still something that is anti-Brit, anti-union, anti-Protestant. That comes from when we were at school, when we were schoolboys at school, the flag and the Irish language were actually weaponized. The

Tiocfaidh ár lá [Our day will come] was daubed on the walls around Armagh where I went to Protestant grammar school. Effectively it was a symbolic gesture of Irishness that, for want of a better term, we Prods couldn't understand. The flag was waved at – it was flown all around as an anti-British statement.

I said to the two republicans that night, 'Look, guys, if you're serious with this, then if I went and bought a house in Cork and I wanted to put a flagpole up in the rebel county and I wanted to fly a British flag because I have still British identity, would you be comfortable with that?' They said, 'That can never happen, Ian.' These are all really uncomfortable parts of the conversation. For me, it's dangerous to have an oversimplified view of what this would be like.[6]

– Ian Marshall, UUP, former Independent Ulster Unionist Senator,
Seanad Éireann

The diversity and richness of the United Kingdom is something that we value. The fact that we are a mixture of Scottish, Welsh, English – not to mention the newcomers and the ethnic and cultural richness that is developed within the United Kingdom over the past fifty years – is something that we admire and want to be a part of. We feel that our history rests with the United Kingdom ... that the British history is our history. I think that institutions like the BBC are ones that we admire and trust and consider to be our own. Those would all be unionist reasons for wanting to remain in the United Kingdom.[7]

– Dr John Kyle, former Interim Leader, loyalist Progressive Unionist
Party (PUP); switched to Ulster UUP in 2022

This might sound trite, but [people] simply feel British. That's been a way of life, it's been the Royal Family, but it's also Coronation Street, British football teams, The Proms and so on.[8]

– Sammy Douglas, Democratic Unionist Party (DUP); Member of
the Legislative Assembly (MLA)

I'm British. I don't wake up in the mornings wondering, 'Am I British?' It's what I am, any more than anybody that says they're Irish wakens up in the morning saying that they're Irish or worrying about it. They don't. The only reason that this becomes an issue is when your identity, or nationality, or whatever you want to call it, gets called into question or attacked ... it then becomes an issue. I'm very, very comfortable with

*my Britishness and don't feel the need to question it or in any other way,
except that the notion of Britishness is undergoing change as is many
other things in the world.*[9]

     – Jackie Redpath, Shankill community leader in Belfast

*People have tried to bomb us and bribe us into a united Ireland. We
simply do not want to go because we're British. I don't care what way
they change the state, I don't care if they have the Twelfth every day, I
am a citizen of the United Kingdom and I wish to remain a citizen of
the United Kingdom.*[10]

    – Mervyn Gibson, Grand Secretary to the Orange Lodge of Ireland

                                  since 2016

*The Catholic Church ... need to be ready to deal with a sophisticated
evangelical Christian tradition in the North that is very able and willing
to claim its religious rights and its religious freedoms and all of that kind
of thing. They would actually find ... they wished they had built up a
better relationship with the Catholic Church, sir, rather than demon-
izing the religious side of it. Anyway, that's a slightly more obtuse point.*[11]

    – Fr Tim Bartlett, Secretary to the Catholic Bishops of
                                 Northern Ireland

In 1987, the scholar Jennifer Todd in her article 'Two traditions in unionist
political culture' described unionist ideology as essentially an umbrella organization with two distinct groupings: one, Ulster loyalism, 'firmly rooted
in [its] Presbyterian ancestry, defining itself by its primary imagined community of Northern Protestants and its secondary conditional loyalty to the
British state'. It treats religion and politics as inextricably interrelated. This
ideology is reproduced in 'potentially dominatory marches'. The other, the
Ulster British tradition, defines itself as being 'an integral part of Great Britain
with a secondary regional patriotism for Northern Ireland'. 'This ideology is
reproduced by the extensive linkages between Northern Ireland and Great
Britain which create typical life paths for Ulster British individuals.'[12]

    In 1988, Todd refined her analysis in 'The limits of Britishness'. In this
article she identified three specific features of Ulster Britishness: 1) 'a cultural
commonality and distinctive regional identity with the rest of the people of
Northern Ireland'; 2) civic unionism, or 'a celebration of and commitment
to state structures, such as Westminster and the monarchy ... the health and

education system'; and 3) an element defined as 'glorification of the history of Empire and British military adventures' – a propensity 'to want to be more British than the British themselves'; in short, 'a primary cultural identification with Great Britain and a secondary regional loyalty to Northern Ireland'.[13]

Accommodating a British identity in a united Ireland would require somehow weaving these various strands of Britishness into a broad, multi-layered mosaic that would stand the test of parity of esteem with the Irish state's pervasive Irishness. Looking at the South through the lens of the present, it is highly doubtful whether it will be up to the task or even wishes to be.

Parties in the North and in the South that favour a united Ireland pledge to secure and protect the British identity of Northern Protestants in a united Ireland. But, like a united Ireland itself, whatever that might entail remains an empty vessel. The Belfast/Good Friday Agreement (B/GFA), in Article 1(v) of 'Constitutional Issues', states:

> the two governments ... affirm that whatever choice is freely exer-
> cised by a majority of the people of Northern Ireland, the power of
> the sovereign government with jurisdiction there shall be exercised
> with rigorous impartiality on behalf of all the people in the diversity
> of their identities and traditions and shall be founded on the prin-
> ciples of full respect for, and equality of, civil, political, social and
> cultural rights, of freedom from discrimination for all citizens, and
> of parity of esteem and of just and equal treatment for the identity,
> ethos and aspirations of both communities.[14]

In the event of a united Ireland, this statement raises several interrelated questions: how pervasive is a British identity among Northern Protestants? Does it differ from England's Britishness? How strongly do Protestants feel about their Britishness? Do they share other identities? Are there identities other than the 'British only' that must be accommodated? Is British identity flexible? To what extent does Britishness in Northern Ireland define itself in opposition to Irishness? And, if the core of identity is an intense attachment to a particular ethnic group, how can that sense of belonging be replicated when its adherents are removed from a dispensation in which it is fully expressed to one in which it is bitterly opposed?

Despite endless chatter about cherishing all traditions and identities across the island in a future unified dispensation, when it comes to tangibles that might reflect these sentiments, the South comes up breathtakingly short of magnanimity. Respondents to opinion surveys seem impervious to the unity-in-harmony-and-friendship clause of the Constitution, unwilling to compromise on existing cultural norms, suggesting that, in the event of unity, the unionists would have to adjust to an Ireland as it is.

Illustrating this, the *Independent*/Kantar poll (May 2021) found that just 37 per cent were in favour of a new flag to reflect both traditions, and 36 per cent supported flying the tricolour North and South.[15] A comprehensive *Business Post*/Red C poll (November 2021) presented a series of questions to the Irish electorate about concessions it might be willing to make to accommodate the British identity.[16] The responses were far from reassuring.

Only 41 per cent would support a united Ireland if it meant paying higher taxes. There was strong resistance to discarding 'Amhrán na bhFiann', the national anthem; just 35 per cent were willing to do so. There was even less support to changing the tricolour, with just 27 per cent agreeing. Re-joining the Commonwealth received just 23 per cent support; 39 per cent say they would be willing to give unionists a guaranteed number of seats in the cabinet; 45 per cent would favour keeping the Northern Ireland Assembly.[17]

These findings were replicated in an *Irish Times*/Ipsos MRBI poll a month later.[18] A large percentage of voters favoured a united Ireland in the long term, with only 15 per cent saying they would want a referendum now and 20 per cent describing it as 'very important' and a 'priority' for them. By contrast, 52 per cent of people said it is 'not very important' to them, but they 'would like to see it someday'. This view was also the one Sinn Féin voters favoured the most, with just under half (47 per cent) agreeing with it. Thirty-six per cent of Sinn Féin supporters describe a united Ireland as 'very important'. Majorities were opposed to a new national flag and a new national anthem and to paying higher taxes, curtailing public spending or re-joining the Commonwealth to help make a united Ireland happen. Forty-two per cent of respondents thought a referendum should be held 'in the next 10 years' at the earliest.

An *Irish Sun* survey of a cross-section of members of the Oireachtas found that six in every ten members 'ruled out re-joining the Commonwealth to help secure reunification'.[19] Research conducted on behalf of Sen. Mark Daly for the Oireachtas Agreement on the B/GFA found 84 per cent of Irish people wanted to 'retain "Amhrán na bhFiann", the national anthem, as it is'.[20]

And, of course, few are willing to pay for unification. Ultimately, it would appear the South is reluctant to concede on the flag or national anthem or other symbols of Irish statehood to accommodate British identity in a united Ireland.[21]

At best, support for a united Ireland is lukewarm, something Irish voters support but not now; these polls suggest that few are willing to make the kind of overtures that might convince unionists that they are serious about exploring ways in which a British identity might be accommodated.

The South, says Duncan Morrow, is in 'for a shock' if reunification should happen. Post-independence in 1921, it never had to deal with its Britishness. That, Morrow says, is 'unfinished business'. In the North there have been difficult, contentious and often inconclusive reconciliation conversations on symbolic issues:

> But if the Unionists become part of a united Ireland, they will want to celebrate things, or publicly mark things, which Nationalist Ireland doesn't want to, doesn't see why it should, and hasn't had to for the last hundred years. We in the North haven't got this right, but we do know that there's an issue. And we constantly know we have to find ways to manage it. For example, 'Amhrán na bhFiann' is not just a song. Unionists have spent years walking out every time they hear it. There is a mythology around the tricolour that it is a flag about peace. The problem for Unionists is not the orange stripe or the green stripe, it's the white stripe! They do not believe that that flag was a peaceful gesture to them. It's the white stripe that's the problem. They think it's a black stripe or a red stripe. That's something which Northerners know, instinctively, even Northern Nationalists know it, but I'm not sure if Southern Nationalists know.
>
> In my view the South isn't prepared for what Northern Ireland being reunited with the rest of Ireland is going to mean. Conversations around symbolic issues will be brutal, difficult, endless, and emotive, as they have been for twenty years in Northern Ireland.[22]

Under the Irish Constitution, the right to vote, hold office, or sit in the Oireachtas is reserved for Irish citizens only, whereas the B/GFA confers the right – and equality under that right – for Protestants from Northern Ireland to be either British or Irish or both. Under existing constitutional provisions, British citizens in the republic would not have the right to vote on a referendum on Irish unity.[23] The B/GFA calls on the Irish government to 'continue to take further active steps to demonstrate its respect for the different traditions in the island of Ireland'. In this regard, successive Irish governments have been derelict, with nothing substantial to show in the twenty-five years since the agreement that specific measures have been taken to empower British citizens of Ireland. During that time, a slew of measures has been enacted at Stormont to give parity of esteem to the Irish identity.

Over fifty years, encompassing thirty of conflict and twenty of post-conflict transformation, trends in national identity have changed in terms of the prevalence of the identity and the meaning it holds.

On the Protestant side, any identification with Irish identity has been eradicated (5 per cent), with 49 per cent of Protestants self-identifying as 'British only' (down from 69 per cent in 2019), while the percentage identifying as 'Northern Irish' only has been increasing (36 per cent up from 23 per cent), according to the Northern Ireland Life and Times (NILT) 2021 survey.[24] Both the NILT and University of Liverpool surveys show significant numbers on both sides not identifying as Catholic or Protestant, or as orange or green. What emerges is a mosaic of interrelationships, ranging from 'British only' or 'Irish only' to 'more British than Irish', 'more Irish than British', 'equally British and Irish' or 'Northern Irish', and a small but growing cohort not identifying with any of these labels.[25]

Some identities are more rigid than others; some have varying degrees of elasticity. In the event of a border referendum, should there be a slim 51 per cent in favour of Irish unity, these complex identities will be forced into a binary choice: either British sovereignty or Irish sovereignty, regardless of whether a new dispensation can protect and secure some, especially the British identity.

In 1968, just before the outbreak of the conflict, the Rose Loyalty Survey on national identity in Northern Ireland[26] found that 39 per cent of Protestants saw themselves as British, 32 per cent as Ulster, 20 per cent as Irish, 6 per cent as sometimes British and sometimes Irish and 2 per cent as Anglo-Irish. The survey found that more than 66 per cent of Northern Protestants felt that generally people in England were very different to themselves.[27]

Over the decades of the conflict, the proportion of Protestants seeing themselves as British grew, hovering between 60 and 70 per cent and staying within these margins in the post-conflict-generation era. Self-identification as Ulster disappeared, replaced by self-identification as 'Northern Irish only' or mixed identities. In the 2011 census, 67 per cent of Protestants identified as 'British only', 15 per cent as 'Northern Irish only' and 11 per cent as 'British and Northern Irish only'.[28]

Another cohort in Northern Ireland to consider represents those who have no religious affiliation. The size of this 'no religion' cohort has increased from 17 per cent in the 2011 census to 28 per cent in the latest 2021 NILT survey.[29] Also, this cohort is more pronounced among younger people.[30] So, what national identities do these cohorts express? In the 2011 census, among those with no religious affiliation, 45 per cent identified as 'British only', 22 per cent as 'Northern Irish only', 7 per cent as 'British and Northern Irish' and 9 per cent as 'Irish only'.[31]

Colin Coulter et al. made further observations based on data drawn from the NILT and University of Liverpool General Election surveys since 2010:[32]

- The age cohort identifying as having no religion, especially among young voters, has grown steadily, from 9 per cent in 1998 to 13 per cent in 2013 and 20 per cent in 2018.[33]

- The no-religion cohort is less likely than Protestants and Catholics to identify as British or Irish only and more likely to have mixed identities, including equally British and Irish identities.[34]

- A quarter of those under the age of twenty-four describe themselves as having no religion and are less likely to describe themselves as British only or Irish only.[35]

A 'Northern Irish only' identity is increasingly the choice of younger Protestants. The NILT (2021) survey reported that 42 per cent of those under the age of 35 self-identified as Northern Irish (43 per cent of 18–24-year-olds and 42 per cent of 25–34-year-olds; see Table 14.1 on next page).[36] If these and younger cohorts over another generation continue to identify as Northern Irish in such numbers, there will be a profound effect on what it means to be British and what will have to be accommodated.

Table 14.1: NILT 2021, Ethno-national identity chosen by Protestants,
by age cohort (%)[37]

AGE	BRITISH	IRISH	ULSTER	NORTHERN IRISH	OTHER
18–24	28.6	7.1	7.1	42.9	14.3
25–34	43.6	7.3	1.8	41.8	5.5
35–44	49.4	1.2	2.4	41.0	6.0
45–54	45.8	5.0	4.2	40.0	5.0
55–64	50.4	2.4	2.4	42.3	2.4
65+	61.1	5.4	4.7	23.5	5.4

What will be the differences between accommodating a 'British only' identity
and a 'Northern Irish only' identity or mixed identities? Will the prevalence
of 'Northern Irish only' among younger Protestants morph into soft/hard
'British only' when they get older? Or will the 'Northern Irish only' achieve
a critical mass, diluting what accommodating a British identity means?

If there were a border poll within the next ten to fifteen years and the
trends in NILT and University of Liverpool surveys continue to project
greater swathes of younger Protestant voters professing no religion, with
approximately 40 per cent of the electorate expressing 'neither unionist nor
nationalist' as their preferred identity and a significant cohort identifying
as 'Northern Irish only', how might what constitutes expression of a British
identity have evolved?

Question: over the next ten to fifteen years, will the cohort of Protestants
who do not self-identify as 'British only' continue to self-identify as such?
If so, what would that mean for the imperative to accommodate the British
identity in a united Ireland? A similar question arises regarding younger
Protestants who have become eligible to vote. Or is it more likely that these
Protestants will retreat to their ethno-cultural silo, that the binary choices of
a border referendum will harden primary identities, in their case, elevating
their sense of Britishness?

What appears paramount in terms of Britishness to the current Protestant demographic may be of little consequence in ten years. Many of

the aspects of Britishness that are important to them now may be more amenable to being accommodated, certainly with regard to the Crown.

Attachment to the Crown is germane to the Britishness of unionists. Queen Elizabeth II was a constant presence, conveying calmness and reassurance in the face of conflict and crisis in Northern Ireland. Even the Royal Family's shambolic affairs and scandals left her untouched. 'The British connection is more than loyalty to the government,' Sammy Douglas said, 'It's loyalty to the Royal Family, and even bringing that down, it's loyalty to Her Majesty the Queen. I'm not so sure what would happen when she eventually dies.' Douglas added:

> I remember I met her one time; it was at [a lunch in] Hillsborough Castle. My mother – who lived in, do you remember, Sandy Row? – said to me, 'Do me a favour, Sammy. When you're talking to the queen, tell her that I've been thinking about her and praying for her because she's been having terrible problems with her sons and her family, and I know how she feels because I have two daughters and I've had problems with my two sons.' She wanted me to tell the queen, 'I can identify with you ...'[38]

Even though the queen was ninety-six years of age in 2022, her death on 6 September still came as a surprise. One day she was appointing Liz Truss her prime minister, frail and back bent but on the job, the next dying peacefully in her bed surrounded by family – it was somehow befitting that a life lived without fuss should end without fuss. A huge mural of a young Queen Elizabeth, radiant and ageless, dominates the Shankill, with the legend 'Sovereign of the People' symbolizing an unbreakable connection for loyalists between the Crown, their Britishness and their fealty to the queen.

Queen Elizabeth II personified the intrinsic essence of that relationship. The Shankill, East Belfast and Sandy Row teem with houses whose small sitting rooms display photos of the newly coronated Elizabeth – fresh and young, wearing pearls and a ball gown along with her crown, her smile calming and beatific – an omnipresent reminder of the immutable connection been between them and the monarch they had known from the cradle. Her death was like a death in the family, far more than just a political event put a profoundly personal one.

Over five decades of my conversations with loyalists, there has been a recurring constant: loyalists are not loyal to a British government – on the contrary, they were highly distrustful of them and their serial betrayals. They are loyal to the Crown, to the only monarch they had ever known. Elizabeth II was 'a final direct link to Empire, World War Two, central to their identity' and sense of mythmaking.[39] Like all deaths, hers elicited deep grieving and anxiety about the future. Loyalists have already formed their opinion about Charles, too long a prince: he is prone to be a little cantankerous, impatient and opinionated on occasion; he lacks the aura of serenity his mother exuded so effortlessly. Not quite the same safe pair of hands. 'Change does not sit easily with continuity for many in unionist and loyalist communities,' says Graham Spencer. 'No doubt a new king will be generally seen as yet another potential danger for the Union and so Northern Ireland itself. And, in response to that there will be a further unrest that will be used to resist rather than develop.'

'I grew up as a loyalist. I feel loyal,' Sammy Douglas, DUP MLA who has his finger on the pulse of loyalist sentiment, told the writer Susan McKay, 'But I'm not quite sure what I am loyal to. The thing that keeps us together to some degree is the queen. She's a wonderful woman. Absolutely wonderful. She's held Britain together and she's a global figure. But then the problem is when she dies, I can't see the same loyalty or attraction to the royalty as it is now.'[40]

There was anxiety, too, because unionism in 2022 seemed more under threat than at any time since its founding a hundred years earlier: unionists were no longer the largest party in the Assembly; they will have surrendered the coveted first minister post to the hated Sinn Féin (assuming the NIP dispute is resolved); an emergent demographic plurality, majority Catholics, of younger voters are more in favour of a united Ireland. Says Doug Beattie, UUP leader, 'there is anxiety of the unknown, but that is normal. The queen seemed to be the glue to the whole of the union, the four nations. With a new king we could have continuity. We'll just and wait and see.'[41] Says Jeffrey Donaldson, DUP leader, 'Whatever changes may occur in the monarchy, it remains the case that the future of the Union relies on the strength of the pro-Union vote and not on who is the head of state of our nation.'

Attachment to the monarchy, however, is waning. 'Among my own family and their contemporaries,' Rev. Harold Good says, 'the monarchy is an outdated frill that we could well do without. The new generation are saying, "We have no vested interest in the monarchy at all ... emotional or otherwise." I've grown up with great respect for the monarchy. I have things hanging in my wall here that the queen gave me. She's invited me to have lunch with her.'[42]

'Young people,' says Graham Spencer,

> are now engaging with expressions of popular culture, debates about the environment ... Although there would be a doffing of the cap still by many to the Royal Family, it is not as powerful as it used to be ... The conflict made that attachment to the monarchy much more important. It's a very strong marker of identity and I don't want to suggest it's still not powerful for a number of people. A lot of young people in Northern Ireland are ... not as tied to those convictions as perhaps their parents or grandparents.[43]

The 2011 UK census manifested the tenuousness of the British association in the union's countries. It reported an increase in 'national consciousness'; national identity in the United Kingdom had become 'multi-dimensional', a trend it suggested would gain more traction in future years.[44] Wales and Scotland have had their own devolved governments since 1996, which has encouraged the evolution of their own distinct ethno-nationalism. A successful Scottish referendum on independence – that could potentially lead to the fragmentation of the United Kingdom – would also have a profound impact on unionism, redefining Scotland's relation to the monarchy, the writ of the monarchy and the concept of Britishness.[45]

Just 8.4 per cent of Scotland identified as 'British only'; in Wales, 17 per cent identified as 'British only', with most others settling for Scottish or Welsh identities and variations.[46] Only in England did the proportion identifying as British exceed the proportion identifying as English – 80 per cent of the population felt strongly English, 82 per cent strongly British, the two inextricably intertwined.[47] In contrast, in Northern Ireland, 40 per cent identified as 'British only', 21 per cent as 'Northern Irish only' and 25 per cent as 'Irish only'.[48]

Among Northern Ireland's Protestants, identification as 'British only' is even stronger at 69 per cent: a superordinate identity for other countries in the United Kingdom is the dominant identity for Northern Ireland's Protestants.[49]

In terms of the total population of Northern Ireland (1.9 million in the 2021 Census), 606,300 people identified as 'British only', with a further 208,300 identifying as a mixture of British and another national identity – British-Irish, British-Northern Irish – meaning there are 814,600 people for whom some dimension of their British identity will need to be accommodated in a united Ireland.[50]

'British only' as the largest cohort of the population in Northern Ireland continues to fall, at 32 per cent barely the largest compared to 29 per cent 'Irish only' and 20 per cent 'Northern Irish only'.[51]

Table 14.2: Three highest rates for national identity, local government district areas (2021 Census)[52]

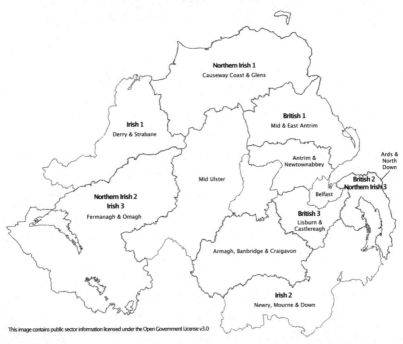

This image contains public sector information licensed under the Open Government License v3.0

BRITISH ONLY		IRISH ONLY		NORTHERN IRISH ONLY	
1. Mid and East Antrim	49%	1. Derry City and Strabane	54%	1. Causeway Coast and Glens	23%
2. Ards and North Down	48%	2. Newry, Mourne and Down	47%	2. Fermanagh and Omagh	22%
3. Lisburn and Castlereagh	41%	3. Fermanagh and Omagh	41%	3. Ards and North Down	22%

For the local government district council areas, Mid and East Antrim had the highest prevalence rate of those with a 'British only' identity (49 per cent, down from 59 per cent in 2011), followed by Ards and North Down (48 per cent, down from 58 per cent) and Lisburn and Castlereagh (41 per cent, down from 53 per cent). The areas with the highest rates for 'Irish only' were Derry City and Strabane (54 per cent, up from 48 per cent in 2011); Newry, Mourne and Down (47 per cent, up from 41 per cent); and Fermanagh and Omagh (41 per cent, up from 35 per cent). Those with the highest rates for 'Northern Irish only' were Causeway Coast and Glens (23 per cent, unchanged), Fermanagh and Omagh (22 per cent, down from 26 per cent) and Ards and North Down (21 per cent, up from 19 per cent).

However, when you add another identity choice – not only British or Irish, but also British-Irish, British-Northern Irish, Irish-British, Irish-Northern Irish – a more complex picture emerges: 43 per cent say British, 33 per cent Irish, and 32 per cent Northern Irish.[53] Nothing yet to conclude that the results call for a border poll. But the trends are unmistakeable: the 2031 census should show fewer 'British only' and more 'Irish only'. What will have to be accommodated is both shrinking and becoming more multi-layered. The census results were succinctly summarized by Sam McBride: 'If unionists insist on Northern Ireland being British and British only, it can't and won't survive.'[54]

Moreover, being British is not an ethno-national identity per se. It supplements national identification but cannot take the place of one. It is at best an umbrella identity subsuming English, Scottish and Welsh national identities. The upshot is that a lot of Northern Ireland's Protestant population are sure about what they are *not*. And because they are unsure of what they are, they compensate by feeling more strongly about it. The Rose Survey found that Protestants felt more strongly about their identity no matter what identification they chose, and those who identified most strongly with a particular national label had the most extreme political views.[55]

There is no concrete entity called Britishness. Its content and meaning varies among the constituent countries of the United Kingdom, and it has become a label from which they increasingly distance themselves. Brexit has accelerated the ethno-national trends, especially English nationalism, a disruptive and radical force that is reshaping British politics and which poses, in the view of many unionist interviewees, a greater threat to the union than the pro-Irish unity lobby. A YouGov poll found that a quarter of English respondents believed that English interests should be prioritized even if meeting them threatens the union.[56] A majority of Conservative Party members were prepared to jettison Northern Ireland in order to secure a hard Brexit.[57]

What is Britishness without the union? Flags, emblems, national holidays and a wide range of cultural accoutrements will, ostensibly, be on the negotiating table. But there is a deeper psychic dimension to identity. 'To simply reduce unionism down to a tradition or to a sense of identity that needs to be cherished, and needs to have a place found for it,' Winston Irvine, the loyalist community leader says, 'entirely misses the point as to what actually unionism is. It is predicated on the constitutional monarchy ... which is something rather different from a sense of tradition ... or some kind of expression of identity.'[58]

No amount of tinkering with the like of symbols can obviate the fact that once the Union is severed as the result of a border poll, unionism – predicated absolutely on maintaining the Union and with no social glue that can otherwise hold it together – becomes redundant, reduced to obsolescence by a triumphant nationalism. If a border poll does not succeed first time around, the B/GFA provides for further referendums. This is unionism's future: a nationalist battering ram methodically pounding the constitutional underpinnings of their position until it breaks through – shades of the trauma of siege revisited.

Accommodating the two communities/traditions/identities and ensuring parity of esteem for both is the cornerstone of the B/GFA. But in the generation since it was signed, it has not brought the two communities closer. Instead, they compete for cultural superiority, each trying to negate whatever marginal gains the other might make. Unionists, in particular, see parity of esteem for Irishness as somehow diminishing their sense of Britishness, believing not just that Sinn Féin is pursuing the assertion of Irishness as the dominant culture but that it runs a parallel campaign to undermine British identity. The loyalist leader Tom Roberts, who describes himself as 'British Irish', says that Sinn Féin's behaviour makes it difficult for him to acknowledge his Irishness:

I look at issues like the flag protests. I would probably argue that most unionists or nationalists, for that matter, weren't even aware that the Union Jack ... flew on the [Belfast] City Hall for 365 days a year. Sinn Féin in their wisdom decided it would be a good idea to take that down ... and then it became an issue. They've done that consistently with a lot of issues such as parades.

They created residents' groups to be opposed to parades. Then eventually, when they wanted the things to settle down, they couldn't get the genie back into the bottle ... I feel they've done that around victims as well, the Republican-created victims groups who would follow an agenda of 'It was all Britain's fault' ... It makes it very difficult for unionists to be magnanimous when they have this consistent onslaught, as they see it, against their culture and identity ... It will make unionists more resistant to ever even considering a constitutional change on the island.[59]

This sentiment – that the British identity in Northern Ireland has been systematically undermined since the B/GFA under the rubric of parity of esteem – is pervasive among unionists, reflecting the belief that every concession to Irishness has diminished Britishness, that it has diluted the British content of the province, as it were, like adding a dash of water to good whiskey. When history is contested, every cultural trope that spins the narrative in one direction or the other becomes weaponized. The UUP's John Kyle says:

Can a leopard [Sinn Féin] change its spots? We have seen almost no evidence to suggest that that would be the case. In fact, if anything, what we see points in the opposite direction ... There is a despising of all things British. For example, take the wearing of poppies. Republicans ... demanded the removal of the Union Jack from public buildings. They oppose the flying of the national flag and playing the national anthem. They objected to the city welcoming home the troops from Afghanistan. These patriotic practices, normal in other jurisdictions, were consistently opposed by Sinn Féin in Belfast.

Even the proposal to use the British Armed Forces to help in the health emergency caused by COVID-19 was opposed by Sinn Féin and by Sinn Féin supporters ... It leads many unionists to believe that we would be a despised minority and that our Britishness would not be respected but would be gradually undermined, just as some feel it has been over the past twenty years since the Good Friday Agreement.[60]

These questions are just the outer layer of identity fears. The deeper, emotional essence at the core of these layers of identity is something ethereal – that profound sense of belonging, of connection to something larger than the self.

After an in-depth review of the academic literature on the multifaced strands of unionist identity, Feargal Cochrane comments:

> Unionism is not based solely on rationalism or on political, social or economic self-interest. At its most fundamental it is based on *a sense of belonging* [my italics]. In addition to seeing the union as a protector of civil liberties, religious expression and economic well-being, there is a complex web of historical, emotional and psychological bonds [with Britain], although these go largely unreciprocated, which underlie the dynamics of unionist behaviour.[61]

If identity and a sense of belonging are inextricably aligned, how can a united Ireland accommodate this fusion? It can't, as Paul Nolan explains:

> National identity is something that's experienced in ways that people find hard to describe when you ask them, 'Why are you British? Why are you Irish?' I saw Gerry Adams being interviewed one time when he was asked this question, 'Why does it matter so much to you to be Irish and have a united Ireland?' He happily took on this question, which he found an interesting one, and he said, 'When it comes down to it, I can't explain it.' He said, 'It's like a mystical thing. I feel myself to be Irish.'
>
> And you [can flip that over to how] unionists feel themselves to be British. You can point out to them that there are certain disadvantages to being British or you can flip it over and say there are more advantages to being Irish ... It doesn't matter to them. They feel themselves to be British. That is it. It's like if I went to your house and noticed that the house next door looked a little bit better. And I said to you, 'Why would you not want to live in the house next door? You know, their paint works much better, their garden's slightly bigger?' You might say, 'I don't care' ... [So] it doesn't matter whether other people might regard it as a poor home or a good home or whatever, it's where you feel at home.[62]

That sense of 'home' cannot be replicated in a united Ireland. Better not to pretend otherwise. Sinn Féin tells unionists that in a future all-Ireland dispensation their cultural accoutrements, including the Orange Order and the loyal institutions, will be recognized and accommodated in a united Ireland, that the once unthinkable – some relationship with the monarchy – is not off the negotiating table.[63] The reaction is not disbelief but outrage at the hypocrisy. The UUP's Steve Aiken is scathing:

> There is absolutely no sense that there's going to be any accommodation for Britishness or unionism within Ireland. It's not happening … I find it amusing that people think that there's any form of dialogue about bringing in a sense of British inclusivity into Ireland, it's not. Matter of fact, it seems to be going the opposite direction … Bearing in mind that a lot of the vitriol that was coming was not coming from Sinn Féin; it was coming from people who identify themselves as Fianna Fáil or Fine Gael, and, indeed, a lot of younger people in Ireland who have never really managed to contextualize the whole situation.[64]

Unionists dismiss avowals that their identity will be secured in a united Ireland. Having gone to great lengths between 1921 and 1998 to ensure that Catholics lived in a cold house – and a further two decades post-B/GFA during which they fulminated against expressions of Irish culture as the gateway to Irish unity – unionists cannot imagine other than a cold house in a unified Ireland. They are unable to imagine an alternative outcome.[65]

How could unionism express itself in the absence of there being a union? 'The question,' Jennifer Todd writes:

> should not be how to protect unionist group identity in all possible constitutional circumstances. The question is rather how a future united Ireland might recognise and foster the values, experiences and everyday practices that allowed unionism past and present to express a valued way of life – not simply to organise contentious politics – so as to facilitate continuity and an evolution of traditions rather than a sense of identity under siege.[66]

The two traditions paradigm (British and Irish) that the B/GFA was designed to accommodate, Todd argues, is no longer up to the task. That

a shared island is a prerequisite of a united Ireland is a problematic claim.
'In conflicts where identity has been asymmetrically constructed and oppo-
sitionally defined, respect for one identity means disrespect for another.'[67]
Equality between the two traditions has been largely achieved, but the identity divisions are as intense as ever:

> The assumption that peoples will grow together in a stable equal
> environment assumes that the problem lies in lack of knowledge,
> contact and mutual understanding. But if antagonism is also gener-
> ated by asymmetric and oppositional constructions of identity, then
> there will not be gradual incremental improvement through equal
> interaction. The lesson of the last century of partition and the last
> half century of reform is that better relations do not evolve gradu-
> ally. Respect for the two traditions gave a path to equality, but it has
> become increasingly difficult to maintain those traditions in equality
> and harmony.[68]

She argues for a new Ireland paradigm:

> (i) Move the discussion away from given national identities. Reject
> the assumption that these are to be protected just as they are ... (ii)
> Focus discussion on the principles and values that will be relevant to
> all constitutional futures ... (iii) Critically assess the practices and
> principles of the British and Irish states ... (iv) Encourage a diver-
> sity of voices and a multiplicity of perspectives. The South has to be
> brought into the dialogue with the emphasis on its own divisions.[69]

If these steps become 'the cultural backdrop of public discussions of policy',
she asserts, 'then unionist and loyalist identity narratives are likely to change,
not to embrace nationalism but rather to contemplate and negotiate multiple possible alternative futures, and, should a united Ireland be democrat-
ically decided upon, to negotiate its optimal form'.[70]

In a scathing assessment of the state of the UK, journalist Tom McTague
wrote in *The Atlantic*, one of America's most prestigious magazines, 'The
grim reality for Britain as it faces up to 2022 is that no other major power on
Earth stands quite as close to its own dissolution':

> Given its recent record, perhaps this should not be a surprise. In the
> opening two decades of the twenty-first century, Britain has effec-
> tively lost two wars and seen its grand strategy collapse, first with

the 2008 financial crisis, which blew up its social and economic
settlement, and, then, in 2016, when the country chose to rip up its
long-term foreign policy by leaving the European Union, achieving
the rare feat of erecting an economic border with its largest trading
partner and with a part of itself, Northern Ireland, while adding
fuel to the fire of Scottish independence for good measure. And if
this wasn't enough, it then spectacularly failed in its response to the
coronavirus pandemic, combining one of the worst death rates in the
developed world with one of the worst economic recessions.[71]

What is Britishness? It's a question Joseph Ruane and David Butler pose in
their study 'Southern Irish Protestants: An example of de-ethnicization?'[72]
'British' is, they write, 'an ambiguous and slippery' concept:

> including in Britain itself. It has a host of national, state, and public
> institutional references and associated symbols as well as a patina of
> centuries. It once described an empire, then a commonwealth and
> still describes a state. It can describe a set of values and even a way of
> life. But there is no agreement as to whether or in what sense there is
> a British nation. It is a political allegiance and can generate a wider
> sense of belonging.[73]

Britishness is predicated primarily on there being a Great Britain, an entity
of the three nation–states: England, Scotland and Wales. Scotland wants
out of the union; Welsh nationalism is on the rise and English nationalism
gave birth to Brexit. According to an Ipsos MORI poll (2019), 50 per cent of
respondents thought the United Kingdom would not exist in ten years. Just
29 per cent said it would exist in its current form in a decade; '42 per cent
said the UK would exist in five years' time and 44 per cent said it would not.'[74]

Trying to project how a British identity might be accommodated in a
united Ireland may be a fool's errand. It presupposes that there is a British
identity to accommodate. That is increasingly problematical. Recent surveys
(2022) confirm the deep fractures in the UK polity that Brexit exposed and
sharpened. Almost half of Scots believe the UK will not exist in its current
form by 2027, a large majority that it will not by 2032.[75] Among Scots,
support for independence hovers at the 50 per cent mark.[76] Across the UK,
the proportion predicting the demise of the union also hovers at the 50 per
cent mark.[77] Just over half of people in England and Wales say they would
prefer Scotland to stay part of the union; for Northern Ireland, the figure

drops to 42 per cent.[78] In Wales, 25 per cent say the country should look for independence.[79]

There is no social glue binding the disparate parts of the UK tightly, just adhesive tape doing patchwork political maintenance. If the UK were to break up, no longer a hypothetical, what happens to Britishness? If Great Britain is no longer a Great Britain, or even a little Britain, what is Britishness? And if the UK were to break up following a successful referendum for independence in Scotland, what would we mean when we say that in a united Ireland the British identity will be protected in all its dimensions and afforded parity of esteem with the Irish identity?

— FIFTEEN —

Reunification: problems and prospects

A massive loss of nerve by the political leadership of the twenty-six counties is probably the greatest threat to the achievement of Irish Unity.[1]
— Richard Humphreys, author

We're drifting further away from a real interest in a coming together of the Irish people. I think the focus now has to become the narrow focus of bringing the people of Northern Ireland together. Let that sit for a generation before we even look again at the possibility of a North-South coming together.[2]
— Seán Donlon, Chair, Press Council of Ireland; former Irish ambassador to the United States

The bald reality is that this small island has not managed a coherent North-South unity in relation to dealing with a devastating pandemic over the last year. That, surely, is an indication of the unity mountain to climb, as is the underuse or neglect of structures already provided for or envisaged in 1998 in relation to dialogue and co-operation, such as an independent North-South consultative forum comprising social partners'[3]
— Diarmaid Ferriter, Irish historian, *Irish Times* columnist

What are the implications for the nation of Ireland to have a very significant section of its population NOT having allegiance to the new state – and not wanting to? Does the history of republican violence not warn us against this being even contemplated (to say nothing of tit-for-tat violence and the associated and deepening criminality)?[4]

– Rev. Norman Hamilton, former Moderator of the
Presbyterian Church

If there is a referendum, that was to say there was a united Ireland – well, there'd be a phase before there would be a united Ireland. So, what happens in that period? What kind of pressures will come to the surface when negotiations would be taking place? If you look at the period between the Brexit referendum and the Brexit result, the upheaval there was in a stable society in GB [Great Britain]. Can you imagine while negotiations are taking place, what's happening in Northern Ireland during that period?[5]

– Peter Robinson, first minister of Northern Ireland, 2008–16; leader
of the Democratic Unionist Party (DUP), 2008–15

After the Brexit vote, some people from the unionist tradition began to apply to get Irish passports ... For some, their minds were opening up to what the future might look like [in an all-Ireland state], but people I've talked to said the aggression of Sinn Féin has driven them back into their own silo – while they might carry the Irish passport, they have a mind closed to the island because of what they see as [Sinn Féin's] aggression.[6]

– Alex Attwood, member of Social Democratic and Labour Party
(SDLP) Good Friday negotiating team¬

Can a united Ireland work? Even if you get a simple one-vote majority and you're hauling a million people out of the United Kingdom [UK] into a totally new arrangement, can that work? Is that stable? ... It would only work if both communities actually agreed this is the best way forward. It's going to cost €2,300 for every man, woman and child in the Irish Republic to subsidize Northern Ireland in a united Ireland. It's costing the UK taxpayer £156 for every man, woman and child. Who do you think is more happy to pay? The Irish Republic has done well economically since the recession ... but they're still a very indebted country.[7]

– Jim Wells, DUP; Member of the Legislative
Assembly (MLA) 1998–2022

My argument is, 'Look, spend the next thirty years and promote genuine conciliation. Start really dealing with conciliation between the parties.' If young people at that stage decide to bring about constitutional change, then let them do it, but let them do it as friends. Let them do it in an economy that's succeeding and a society where they have a far better relationship.[8]

– Trevor Ringland, UK Government Special Envoy to the United
States on Northern Ireland

Maybe three or four generations from me a united Ireland will be different, but I don't worry about a united Ireland, because I just think it's not going to happen in my lifetime.[9]

– Colin Halliday, former Ulster Defence Association (UDA)

Any decision on a united Ireland will not be taken by dyed-in-the-wool unionists or dyed-in-the-wool republicans. The group that will form the majority will come from people in the centre ground who will have to be convinced one way or the other. At the moment nobody's really doing any significant convincing.[10]

– David Ford, Alliance Party leader 2001–16; first Northern Ireland
Justice Minister 2010–16

What I find hard to understand is why the Irish government and the Irish state is unprepared to do this, and there is enormous resistance there to this discussion ... People always want to defer this, which seems to me remarkable as we're heading up to the century of partition [is] that people still don't want to have the conversation ...

I think, by the time we get to 2030, we will have had these referendums and there's at least a reasonable possibility, given what is happening post-Brexit, what's happening to Boris and Britain and the Brexiteers, that a majority of the people here might say they've had enough, and want something different. But there is resistance. Obviously, partition has created two silos on this island to some extent, so you're working against that ... You have one bit of the island doing one thing and one bit of the island doing another thing, which seems, you know, remarkable to me.[11]

– Colin Harvey, Professor of Human Rights Law in the School of
Law, Queen's University Belfast; Fellow, Senator George J. Mitchell
Institute for Global Peace, Security and Justice

It is an incredible opportunity to realize an island of equality, the kind
of Ireland that is set out so poetically in the 1916 Proclamation.[12]
     – Mary Lou McDonald Teachta Dála (TD); President, Sinn Féin,

For Sinn Féin, the course of history is inexorably linear.

What is lacking in the discussions about the future of the island of
Ireland, especially the prospect for a united Ireland, is some political and
intellectual honesty. A border referendum is not likely to happen until 2032
at the earliest. The acknowledgment of this reality, especially by Sinn Féin,
would help immeasurably to bring political stability to Northern Ireland
and open the way for unionist/loyalist and nationalist/republican parties to
co-operate more efficaciously in the Assembly on the matters their constitu-
ents care about, without one eye always on the constitutional clock. Among
the major political parties, South and North, only Sinn Féin is calling for a
border referendum.

The phrase itself – 'a united or reunited Ireland' – is tossed around with a
staggering lack of clarity about what it would entail. The polls on the subject
that are routinely undertaken say little about what is involved. Social media
and mainstream media serving slices of society that thrive in parallel universes
amplify the results, adding commentary to buttress one position or another.
It often appears that whoever has the loudest bullhorn, the best propaganda
machine, the most sophisticated social media platform will carry the day.

In one universe, that of the nationalist/republican community, the pervasive belief is that a united Ireland is around the corner, waiting to happen,
perhaps within five years but definitely within ten. Staid, intransigent
unionism can be sidelined and unionists brought on board for a new constitutional future. In the other universe, that of the unionist/loyalist community, the pervasive belief is that Northern Ireland is nowhere near that point
yet; it may be generations down the road, or it may never be realized at all.

The pundits and commentators opine in an opaque political space, each
reflecting a received vacuous wisdom, acknowledging in a sentence or two
that a united Ireland would disrupt the status quo and then pressing on to
make their respective cases. Few bother to spell out the range of effects –
institutions either abolished or rethought; cultures accommodated; symbols
of statehood reconfigured; and routine aspects of daily life, such as healthcare, drivers' licences and ATMs, upended – that seem too inconsequential

to consider but that will have a profound effect on the way citizens live and interact with one another.

The dishonesty extends to how the consent formula of 50 per cent + 1 is treated. It is invoked without a context as if it is alone, divested from other provisions of the Belfast/Good Friday Agreement (B/GFA), a pristine pinnacle heralding unity, and without reference to the paramount importance of all strands of the agreement functioning or the caveat in the Irish Constitution that reunification must take place 'in harmony and friendship'. There is no acknowledgment that that phrase is as much a constitutional imperative as the consent formulation itself. 'Many nationalists and republicans probably imagine – if they think about it at all,' Andy Pollak warns,

> that when demographics and the consequent rise in the nationalist vote in Northern Ireland eventually bring about a narrow majority for unity in a border poll, unionism as a philosophy on this island will just disappear.
>
> I have to disabuse them of this foolish and self-serving notion. Large numbers of unionists, if they are voted against their will into a united Ireland which they have struggled fanatically against for the past 140 years, will continue to withhold their allegiance from that Irish state and will continue to feel, behave, and declare themselves as British. They will wave the Union flag; pledge their allegiance to the British monarchy; and reject Irish language and culture as nothing to do with them. They will be a sullen, alienated and potentially violent minority, just as the nationalists were in Northern Ireland. This is not a recipe for social peace and harmony.[13]

In 2017, Leo Varadkar, then a contender for the Fine Gael leadership, called the demand for a border poll 'alarming':

> It is a return to a mindset in which a simple sectarian majority of 50 per cent + 1 is enough to cause a change in the constitutional status of the North ... It represents a mindset of, 'There's one more of us than you, so now we're in charge. It's our turn to dominate ...' Bouncing Ulster Protestants into a unitary Irish state against their will would be as grievous a wrong as was abandoning a large Catholic minority in the North on partition. It could lead to alienation and even a return to violence. A unitary state formed on this basis would not be a good one.[14]

A former Taoiseach and one of the architects of the B/GFA, Bertie Ahern, cautions that the institutions in the North would have to be consistently operational for a long time. 'We still haven't ever achieved that since 1998,' he points out. 'The institutions would need to be stable, and they'd need to be functioning. The second thing is that the preparatory work would need to be done ... You need another ten years because the preparatory work has only commenced.'[15]

The disconnect between nationalists and unionists is immutable.

Most nationalist interviewees in the North echo Sinn Féin's call for a referendum within five years or at the most by the thirtieth anniversary of the B/GFA in 2028. They express both impatience and ebullience. Post-Brexit they feel the storied prize is within grasp. They can taste the future. They refer to an 800-year wait to throw off the yoke of English oppression. Some ground their remarks in the context of the first Dáil or 1916; most express commitment to giving full protection to a British identity, which includes considering re-joining the Commonwealth or some connection to the monarchy. How to accommodate the British identity, however, they insist, is not for them to say but for unionists to negotiate. All agree that a Brexit-style choice – an up-and-down vote followed by negotiations – should be avoided. When asked whether a united Ireland should take the form of a unitary state or a federal one, these interviewees said that the choice of what kind of state and the constitutional implications would be a matter of negotiations in which unionists would be involved.

Among unionists, too, there is a consensus. At this point, unionists do not feel any urgent need to engage with nationalists to begin a conversation about the future – that's what the same set of metrics tells them. They feel they are being upbraided, hectored and harangued for their reluctance to engage. The semantic problem precluding unionist engagement is the phrase 'a united Ireland'. It has toxic connotations; to cushion the intent, nationalists/republicans prefer to use the phrase 'an agreed' Ireland or 'a new' Ireland or a 'shared' Ireland. Unionists are not fooled; these phrases are just examples of nationalist prevarication.

Unionists are resentful: they are encouraged, on one hand, to make Northern Ireland a 'warm house' for Catholics and, on the other, to get engaged in 'uncomfortable conversations' about the future when these conversations will not include Northern Ireland remaining in the United

Kingdom. Why, they ask, should they engage about the future when nation-alists/republicans have yet to engage with themselves? They categorically dismiss republicans' promises to protect and secure the British identity in a unified Ireland, pointing to their failure to acknowledge the British identity in Northern Ireland.

Ultimately, unionists are their own worst enemies, seeing on all fronts threats to their constitutional position: a Tory government that humiliates them at every turn, a Dublin government that used the threat of republican violence to avoid a hard-border post-Brexit yet chastises them if they raise the threat of loyalist violence if the Northern Ireland Protocol (NIP) is not replaced; a European Union (EU) and a United States that are friends and allies of Dublin. Every gesture of co-operation between North and South is scrutinized for implications of its constitutional intent – mostly apparent only to unionists themselves – leading to political paralysis in which they are trapped between a London that cannot be trusted and a Dublin that will never be trusted. Such is unionists' paranoia that they raised a late-coming objection to the NIP when trade patterns post-Brexit showed a significant increase in North-South trade at the expense of East-West trade – the dreaded all-Ireland economy as leading ineluctably to political integration.[16]

The SDLP established a New Ireland Commission and joined Sinn Féin in calling for the Irish government to appoint a minister of unifica-tion.[17] Sinn Féin launched the Commission on the Future of Ireland and began to organize People's Assemblies across the island. Reports from the Working Group on Unification Referendums on the Island of Ireland lay out border referendum options in great detail.[18] The work of think tanks such as Ireland's Economic and Social Research Institute (ESRI) and the UK's National Institute of Economic and Social Research map the all-Ire-land economy. The Institute for British-Irish Studies at University College Dublin (UCD); Analysing and Researching Ireland, North and South (ARINS), an alliance of the Royal Irish Academy and the Keough-Naughton Institute for Irish Studies at the University of Notre Dame; and a slew of academics at UCD, Queen's, University College Cork and Trinity College Dublin are all beehive-busy conducting research into a wide range of ques-tions about the implications and possible consequences of different types of a united Ireland. The agglomeration of these activities, sure to accelerate in the coming years, would appear to be establishing a critical mass.

In a February 2022 University of Liverpool/*Irish News* survey, less than 5 per cent of respondents listed 'constitutional issues' as an issue of priority in the May Assembly elections.[19] Yet the chatter is constant. Hardly a week goes by without the Northern Ireland dailies running an opinion piece about a border referendum, Irish unification, the B/GFA or threats to the union. Down South, the North gets meagre coverage, and then most likely only when Stormont is about to collapse or an act of violence threatens the always 'fragile' peace. 'I don't think the establishment and the elite in Ireland want a border poll,' Peter Shirlow says. 'They want to find some fixes such as the Shared Island Unit or growing connectivity or working the protocol or working the institutions of the Good Friday Agreement. I think that many of the people who run Ireland have no interest in unification. I think they see it as damaging to their consensus.'[20]

These sentiments are echoed by others, including Rev. Harold Good, who for decades has been involved with other members of the clergy in reconciliation projects. 'My contacts in the South would suggest that people would be very, very nervous about wanting to take responsibility for these Northern, dysfunctional, as they would see it, six counties,' he says. '"We have enough problems of our own," they say. "Why should we take on responsibility for those dysfunctional counties in the Northern part of this island? We're okay as we are." That's what I'm hearing from people across a denominational board in the republic.'[21] Or former pro-union member of the Oireachtas Senate Ian Marshall, who says,

> I told Steve Aiken [then leader of the Ulster Unionist Party] that … the threat of Irish unity as he saw it wouldn't come from Dublin because, in my experience, the people in Leinster House didn't wake up every morning thinking about the Irish unity … The constitutional question and unity were a question, but one best described to me by a TD sitting in the members' bar in Leinster House. He said, 'You know, Ian, Irish unity is a bit like heaven. Sounds like a really good place, but we're just not ready for it yet.'[22]

Niall Murphy, the director of Ireland's Future, a highly organized uber-republican/nationalist lobby, says:

> There are vested interests in the South, establishmentarians who aren't reflective of Southern society. The concept of the Southern

partitionist is as great a threat to Irish reunification as Northern unionism. In that context is the academic integrity or robustness of the economic appraisals, which wrongly advise people that there would be an economic burden to the Southern electorate. That's not right and has proven to be wrong in successive economic reports. The most recent one is clear that there would be enhanced economic opportunities for everybody in the island. There will be a greater boom in the North as result of the legacy of the failed economic viability of the Northern jurisdiction.[23]

In the event of a pro-unity referendum result, Fianna Fáil senator Niall Blaney says, the 'transition [to a united Ireland] needs to happen possibly over a ten, maybe fifteen-year period. It'll have to involve the Irish government and the UK government and that needs to be not a full withdrawal the next day of the UK government, but a gradual withdrawal over that ten- or fifteen-year period'.[24]

Partition, according to the Fine Gael TD Neale Richmond, one of the few Protestant TDs in the Dáil, is as much a mental block as a physical one. Southerners have little interest in the North. 'The vast majority of people, unless they live in the border counties, never even consider going up to Northern Ireland,' he says, 'but they will consider regularly going up to Dublin or Galway, or across to Cork ... That's why we fundamentally need to get people understanding that this isn't two different countries on one island.'[25] Brendan O'Leary, who has researched Irish public opinion about the North in depth, summarizes: 'I'd want to emphasize that Southern opinion is radically out of date with developments in the North ... What gets highlighted in the South is any episode of violence. That's for normal media reasons, and it fits into standard narratives of what the North is like.'[26]

These views are prevalent among the present elites. But a new elite is knocking. 'A Sinn Féin Taoiseach would be the first left-wing government in Irish history,' says Niall Murphy. 'Having experienced the catastrophe of the failure of the banking system in 2008, and the scavenging of the vultures since then through NAMA [National Asset Management Agency] and the collapse in our housing system ... there would be wholesale seismic changes to the administration of our society.'[27]

As a younger generation comes to dominate the electoral vote, it may sweep to power a party whose relentless focus is reunification. In opposition,

Sinn Féin could do no wrong. Even as the government received high marks for its handling of the pandemic, support for Sinn Féin soared. In July 2022, the *Irish Times*/MRBI poll placed Sinn Féin at 36 per cent, Fianna Fáil at 20 per cent and Fine Gael at 18 per cent. Forty per cent of voters under thirty-five supported the party.[28] Sinn Féin has broken through to all age groups and income classes. It is also the beneficiary of the cost-of-living crisis and shortage of energy that gripped most countries in the EU as the war in the Ukraine dragged on and sanctions on Russia continued to bite. For large segments of the Irish public, Mary Lou McDonald is the Taoiseach-in-waiting.

The public's strong desire for change comes through in opinion surveys. The *Irish Times*/Ipsos poll (July 2022) reported 38 per cent were in favour of 'radical change' to the way in which the country is run, while 47 per cent said they were in favour of 'moderate change'. Just 11 per cent said they were 'wary of change'.[29] None of this is good news for Fianna Fáil or Fine Gael, especially the latter, which will have been in government for fourteen years when the next election is called.

But Matt Carthy's admonition that 'sometimes big moments of change happen in an unplanned way'[30] should be taken seriously. In *The Tipping Point*,[31] Malcolm Gladwell describes how things move from the fringe into the mainstream not according to linear extrapolations, but by geometric progression. Incremental change 'infects' the society that is experiencing it; it is contagious, doubling at every turn until it achieves a critical mass – the tipping point where it has infected the whole population. So it has been with the rise of Sinn Féin in the South. It has risen from the fringe of Irish politics, from 1 seat in Dáil Éireann in 1997, more than quadrupling to 5 in 2002, almost tripling to 14 in 2011, and again to 37 seats in 2020, now the official opposition and the largest party in Ireland according to a succession of polls.[32] Gladwell writes, 'We need to prepare ourselves for the possibility that sometimes big changes follow from small events, and that sometimes these changes happen very quickly.'[33] What appears as sudden change, however, is often a long time in the making.

For decades, Sinn Féin was the voice of the Irish Republican Army (IRA) (which a mere thirty-five years earlier had vowed to take power in Ireland 'with a ballot box in one hand and an Armalite in the other').[34] Now, primarily on the strength of their policies on the issues foremost in the minds of the electorate, it was on the cusp of taking power in both parts of Ireland through the ballot box.

Sinn Féin's ascendency will usher in a new breed of elite who are very definitely wanting a united Ireland and intent on seeing it happen on its watch. But, as it recognizes, if it is the most visible and vocal party leading the charge for a border referendum on a united Ireland, unionism's opposition will become more trenchant, a tacit acknowledgment of the loathing with which the party is held among the North's Protestant community. Nor is a British government likely to meet its two demands: setting a date for a referendum and going public with the metrics the Secretary of State will use to gauge support for unity. If they were to draw on the metrics analysed in Chapter 5, they can only conclude that there is no indicator yet of a majority supporting a change in the status quo. While the argument is made that Sinn Féin as the largest party in Northern Ireland and in government in the republic would create an inexorable momentum for unification and a hard-to-resist demand for a referendum, it should be borne in mind that in neither jurisdiction – Northern Ireland nor the republic – would Sinn Féin represent a majority of voters; at best, it would only be between 30 and 35 per cent. Indeed, such a demand could misfire as those unionists – once open to being persuaded of the benefits of a united Ireland – return to the pro-union fold, either because they find the prospect of Sinn Féin in government an anathema or they see Sinn Féin as a socialist party in disguise.

A united Ireland with Leo Varadkar or Micheál Martin as Taoiseach is a very different proposition to one with Mary Lou McDonald at the helm. 'There's all the difference in the world between a liberal Protestant in south Belfast,' Richard Bullick says:

> who likes Leo Varadkar and thinks the South's a jolly progressive pluralist place now and a liberal Protestant in south Belfast who looks at Mary Lou or some of the others who are on the scene and says, 'My goodness! These are the people who supported the murder of our kith and kin for forty years. Now they want us to go into a country with them and we know full well what that would look like.' You know you could look at any number of examples over the last few years of where the Sinn Féin mask slips slightly … Sinn Féin leading a unity campaign in the South would be disastrous for a pro-unity

message in the North, for people who are in the middle ground, and there ultimately will be people in the middle ground who decide the outcome of any border poll.[35]

Peter Shirlow adds:

[If] Sinn Féin are the government in the South, I bet you a penny to a pound, virtually everybody who's pro-union will come out to vote in a border poll. You will mass-mobilize the pro-union community because it will be a different world. It'll not be Micheál Martin … or Leo [Varadkar], [who are] soft on the constitutional question. It'll be a hardening of that and that will drive the pro-union community to vote in a border poll. It will mobilize them. I think that will be a very, very strong outcome.[36]

As spelled out in Chapter 10, there is near unanimity among interviewees that Sinn Féin in government in the South would be a major obstacle to a united Ireland. Jim O'Callaghan, whose party, Fianna Fáil, may find itself in coalition with Sinn Féin after Ireland's 2025 general election, says:

[If it is left] exclusively to Sinn Féin to do the running on the reunifica- tion of this island, then I'm fearful it will not succeed … I don't make political points, but … one of the biggest obstacles to reunification is the campaign of violence that was carried out by the Provisional Irish Republican Army [PIRA]. We would be at a much better position in trying to achieve reunification if we didn't have that.

It's a deciding factor for a lot of unionist people in Northern Ireland who will not engage rationally with the topic [because of what] happened in the past … If you look at the successes in diplo- macy in Ireland in the past thirty years, the B/GFA was the best one. It was steered by the centre-ground, non-violent republicanism of Fianna Fáil, the SDLP, and we brought people along with us. That's why Fianna Fáil is necessary.[37]

All interviewees agree that no matter when a border poll happens, its shape and form and as much detail as possible should be worked out beforehand, so that voters know exactly what they will be voting for to replace the status quo. That is the extent to which most unionist interviewees would volun- teer an answer. From others, questions about when this process should be initiated, whom it should involve and how it should be conducted elicited a range of responses. Some want the draft model of a united Ireland worked out beforehand; some the processes for designing a united Ireland agreed upon first.

A more depressing finding is that Northern Ireland, despite the passage of a quarter of a century since the IRA and loyalist ceasefires, remains a society on edge. Graham Spencer refers to the peace as fragile – a term repeated so often that it has become a cliché – because of the contradictory and ultimately incompatible ways in which it was sold to both communities:[38]

> The Good Friday Agreement was seen by many unionists as copper-fastening the union. In that sense, the agreement was presented as a door to close out any further unwanted change. At the same time, republicans and nationalists viewed the agreement as a stepping-stone, so one narrative was coming from unionism and a completely different narrative was coming from republicans and nationalists. If unionist politicians had presented the agreement as a stepping-stone towards a stronger union rather than the realization of that aim, they would have built some latitude into their approach and given themselves space to represent peace as a work in progress rather than a moment of revelation.[39]

A little dishonesty in how the B/GFA was sold to both communities was praised at the time, part of the 'genius' of the agreement's strategic ambiguity, of the intricate socio-political engineering at its heart. Dual messaging allowing the agreement to be read in two ways, each contradictory to the other, was seen as germane to achieving majority support in both communities. At some point in time, however, if a border referendum beckons, the two interpretations will clash, a collision which the B/GFA, for all its ingenuity, cannot indefinitely avoid.

Though there is a post-B/GFA society in Northern Ireland with all the accoutrements of normalcy and the glitter of modernity, it sits uneasily on unstable foundations. A distinctly abnormal Northern Ireland continues to exist, in some respects not much different after a generation of what Brendan O'Leary calls 'a dirty peace'.[40] The riots by young Protestants over the NIP at the interface between Protestant Shankill and Catholic West Belfast in April 2021 received wide media coverage. For young loyalists, a lesson: violence or the threat of violence attracts attention. Loyalist leaders say the violence was limited and reined in because of the work they did with young people; republicans say nonsense, the old guard were in the background controlling events. A more serious threat came from the Ulster Volunteer Force (UVF). First, it orchestrated a bomb scare at the Houben community centre in north Belfast that caused Irish Foreign Minister Simon Coveney to flee the scene.[41] And then came a warning that it would attack Irish government property to protest Ireland's support for the NIP, that it had the weapons to wage such a campaign. This received far less attention,[42] as the war in Ukraine had sucked the oxygen out of the news cycle.

Structural poverty remains as prevalent in republican and loyalist strongholds. Paramilitaries are still embedded – on call, so to speak, for the day yet to come when, they believe, their services on behalf of their respective causes are required. Violence, once directed at the other, is now inwardly directed at members of their own communities who are mostly the victims of the gangsterism paramilitaries engage in. According to many interviewees, unless paramilitarism and its appurtenances are permanently eradicated, a border poll producing a small margin for unity following campaigns fuelled by hatred and fearmongering will result in loyalist violence, either in the run-up to referendum day or afterwards, and will cause voters in the South to have second thoughts about what unification might entail. Another body says paramilitaries are so infiltrated by state security agents that such violence is unlikely. 'If you had a situation where there was a possibility of a united Ireland,' says Paul Nolan:

> you would see rallies on the streets of Belfast, Ulster Hall full, petitions and people marching. In a worst possible scenario, if you really wanted to block a border poll you would have a few car bombs in Dublin, and the Dublin electorate, which is so cheerfully voting for Sinn Féin, would think, wait a minute, do we really want to import this? I regret almost bringing in that illustration, but it's not beyond the bounds of possibility. My general argument isn't to predict violence, it's to say that when you get into the situation, that whole debate will be shaped not just by words, but by the movements of people, political mobilizations of people will shape how the issue will present itself.[43]

Despite dates set to dismantle peace walls, they remain as immutable reminders of the depth of the divisions between the two communities. Legacy issues and commemoration of the dead ensure that the past is always present. Reconciliation is still largely the province of academic literature. Claiming the narrative of the conflict is fiercely contested; Sinn Féin's attempt to define it in terms of a war against oppression where the valiant IRA volunteers fought the last remnants of British imperialism to set Ireland on course to achieve the independence promised in the Proclamation of 1916 is abhorrent to Protestants. Unionists fear a united Ireland with Sinn Féin at the helm of government. They are convinced that Sinn Féin would impose its narrative of the conflict as the national one, marginalizing theirs and trivializing their history and traditions. Stormont does not work. The institutions no longer reflect the political reality of the population it purports to serve. The B/GFA was designed to accommodate two identities – British and Irish. Today, almost 40 per cent of the people of Northern Ireland define themselves as Neither.[44] When the Assembly is operating, Sinn Féin and the DUP wage a war of political attrition. Every crisis becomes a matter of whether one or the other will collapse the institution, with both sides threatening to do so to squeeze out some marginal political advantage.

The rationale for keeping it going, dysfunctional as it may be, is because it is better than the alternative – direct rule from Westminster, which London is loath to invoke and which is anathema to republicans. The belief, promulgated by some nationalists, that Northern Ireland is a failed political entity – and, if not failed, on life support and the solution to its divisions therefore being to incorporate it into a unitary Ireland – is magical thinking. What came across strongly in these interviews is that an Irish government would want to see a working Northern Ireland before asking its electorate to partake in a referendum unification. Sinn Féin is an exception. But the party faces a conundrum. It is not in its interest to see Northern Ireland working too well, because if too many cultural Catholics are comfortable living there they might vote for the status quo in a referendum; at the same time, Sinn Féin has to show the electorate in the South that it can govern. Some of the support – outside its traditional base, lured from Fine Gael and Fianna Fáil since the 2020 general election – is soft and can be won back in the run-up to the 2025 general election.[45] A Northern Ireland that stumbles on with Sinn Féin and the DUP still at each other's political throats, still regurgitating the same timeworn clichés, immersed in tit-for-tat culture wars but with Sinn Féin now the largest party at the symbolic helm of government, will cause that cohort of voters to pause and ask whether Sinn Féin is a safe bet to govern well in the South.

The B/GFA's consent requirement of a likely 50 per cent + 1 can be deconstructed in two ways. One way would call for 50 per cent + 1 emerging for a united Ireland from an electorate that would have no idea of what that entails, other than that it's the opposite of staying in the United Kingdom.

'What seems to be evolving from within Sinn Féin,' Paul Nolan says:

> is the view that we need to have the discussion first and the vote afterwards ... They want either a Citizens Assembly or something like the New Ireland Forum of the 1980s, a constitutional convention that would hear presentations and sift evidence from the experts and come down in favour of one or possibly more, a number of different options.[46] And so that process would take a period of years in itself ... So, there may be some sequence like that, but it would be pretty unimaginable that there could be a border poll with just a simple question, 'Do you want a united Ireland?' Which of course is how it's framed in the Good Friday Agreement, but without ... the Irish government having decided whether they can foot the bill for the Ireland that emerges from those discussions.[47]

Thus, the second way. The shape and form of the united Ireland on offer has been worked out beforehand following robust public debate that takes account of what form would most appeal to unionist voters; which is best understood by electorates North and South; which provides the easiest path to institutional, legislative and constitutional alignments and integration; which would be the least costly to implement; which would entail the least social and political disruption; and which could be phased in over a number of years.

One model meets all these requirements, and rather than having to be negotiated from first principles such as a unitary state or a federal would have to be, it is already in place. In *Beyond the Border: The Good Friday Agreement and Irish Unity After Brexit*, Richard Humphreys argues that the 1998 agreement is an international agreement that provides for a change in sovereignty but does not specify that in the event of such a change the other strands and institutions of the agreement would be collapsed.[48] Which means that the institutions of the agreement, including the three strands (see Chapter 4), would still have legal force following a referendum in favour of Irish unity; that the agreement only specifies the conditions for a change in sovereignty; and that there is no provision that implies a collapse of the institutions of the agreement following a successful referendum. It refers throughout to 'sovereign governments'. The sovereign government, no matter which dispensation it presides over, must treat both communities with parity of esteem and rigorous impartiality. Interviewees from the nationalist/republican community are dismissive: both the Theresa May and Boris Johnson governments, they were quick to point out, were anything but impartial.

Thus, a devolved power-sharing government would continue to exist: MPs that went to Westminster become MP/TDs going to Dublin. The Working Group notes that in drawing up a blueprint for the talks that led to the B/GFA,[49] both the British and Irish governments 'seem to have envisaged continued power-sharing government in the North in the event of unification … evidence that the governments at least saw the agreement principles about *"equitable and effective political participation"* [my italics] holding sway indefinitely'.[50] Certainly, this is how Bertie Ahern, one of the primary architects of the agreement, sees things:

> That's how I envision this, that Stormont would remain a regional institution for the six counties and for Northern Ireland as we know it today, and they would still elect people to that region, but their national representatives then would be coming to Dublin to serve the people of Northern Ireland rather than to Westminster. In lots of ways, I think that's the best. I wish Northern Ireland's institutions were held in high regard by the people in Northern Ireland. Unfortunately, that isn't the case, and particularly after recent events and the pandemic, but let's hope that that improves. I think the idea of keeping Stormont there is certainly far better … and a better chance of us being able to frame a new Ireland in the future.[51]

That is also how Jeffrey Donaldson sees it:

> My understanding is that the concept of the three sets of relationships [or strands] continues at whatever any future political decisions,

any determination to change Northern Ireland's constitutional status. It doesn't remove the concept of the relationships and the need for [these] to continue and to be reflected in institutional arrangements. We're not planning for a constitutional change, but my view is that the three sets of relationships endure whatever the outcome of any future border poll and therefore, giving institutional expression to those relationships is necessary, whatever the future constitutional arrangements for Northern Ireland.[52]

In an interview by the *The Irish Sun* in December 2017, Fianna Fáil leader Micheál Martin said:

In our view, a future agreed Ireland will hold fast to the principles enshrined in the Good Friday Agreement: being the East-West relationship, the North-South strand and the strand within Northern Ireland between the two communities. That could mean in a future united Ireland you would still have a Northern Executive and Northern Assembly.[53]

Sinn Féin, too, can entertain this idea. Says Matt Carthy: 'Certainly, talking to people who might be described as coming from soft unionist positions in that, at the moment, they favour the status quo, but it's simply because they haven't been convinced otherwise yet. I think many of them are open to a conversation ... that the political structures in the North would remain in place.'[54]

Across the board, where interviewees ventured an opinion, including from Sinn Féin, Fianna Fáil and Fine Gael, they held to the view that in any future constitutional dispensation Stormont should stay, as either an interim stop on the road to unification or the final destination. In 1959, then Fianna Fáil Taoiseach Seán Lemass told the Oxford Union that Stormont would continue to exist if there was reunification.[55] Whether the republic would have its own parliament as a counterweight to the North's would be on the table. Otherwise, it would find itself in the invidious position that unionists in the North sitting in the Dublin parliament would have a say in legislation in matters affecting only the South – for example, healthcare and education – without Dublin having a corresponding say in matters affecting only the North – the 'West Lothian' question.[56]

This route to unification after a successful border poll would involve minimum legal changes in Northern Ireland. There would, of course, be amendments to the British-Irish Agreement to reflect the transfer of sovereignty.[57] Humphries argues:

> On such an approach, any ultimate realignment of sovereignty within an all-island framework would happen slowly, naturally and almost imperceptibly over a period of time within a stable constitutional context through a communitarian approach where the rights and identities of all were protected. There would be no jagged or unnatural discontinuities. There would be no sudden, triumphalist hoisting at Parliament Building in Stormont at 12 noon on some wet Tuesday following a border poll.[58]

But even minimal disruption would involve upheavals. The new dispensation would call for alignment of currencies – or would Northern Ireland retain sterling, to be phased to the euro over time (because a united Ireland would become part of the EU)? Would Northern Ireland still have 'unfettered access' to the British market for exports?[59] Proposals for dealing with structural inequities and legislative passage in both Westminster and Dublin parliaments suggests a transitional period of several years during which various phases of the unification protocol would be staged with benchmark stipulations met along the way.

Not that this is something that unionists yet see as a solution they could live with. But, in the longer run, if consent for unity did emerge it might be the optimal outcome, as it would address many of their fears. Francis Campbell, Tony Blair's former private secretary, says:

> If you have a situation where what's on offer in a referendum choice is the continuation of Stormont, all the checks and balances of the Belfast Agreement and very limited reserved powers at a federal all-Ireland basis, then in my view that is a lot less intimidating to some people than perhaps their worst fears about being absorbed into a system where there's no checks and balances.[60]

But 'If we're having a border poll,' Peter Robinson says:

> I would have thought the very least that would be necessary would be some kind of agreement as to what the process is ...
>
> If you look at Brexit there was no feeling at all during the Brexit referendum period of the centrality of the Northern Ireland issue, of the impact of the border issue in Northern Ireland. [It] didn't feature

at all, even within Northern Ireland … [Yet] it became the major issue with Brexit. … and I suspect the closer you get to the point where a Secretary of State might have to have a referendum, there will be issues that are not perceived at that time. Which if the result was to go in the direction of a united Ireland, you will have a long period [between the result and the implementation of the outcome], because if the disruption from Brexit was as polarizing as it was, you can imagine how much more polarized in Northern Ireland, and the consequences of that polarization … The issue of Brexit was just to unravel our relationship, which was about basically trade, although it went into some other areas, education and so forth … But the tentacles didn't go down as much as they would in terms of a constitutional change. Going from one nation to another nation. That'd be absolutely massive. The amount of negotiation that would have to take place to transfer education, health, all of the work of departments. Absolutely massive.[61]

In short, what happens the day after there is a successful pro-unity referendum? Do triumphalist republicans/nationalists parade in motorcades through Northern Ireland's cities and towns, waving the tricolour, tearing down the Union Jack and whatever symbols of Britishness they can lay their hands on? Do some, emboldened by their sudden empowerment, start painting letterboxes green? And what kind of backlash might such triumphalism provoke?

On *Claire Byrne Live*, former Taoiseach John Bruton (Fine Gael) shared his 'nightmare':

If we had a border poll and it was carried in either direction, like Brexit was carried with 51 per cent to 49 per cent, if it was in the direction of a united Ireland, do you think that would be acceptable and accepted in East Belfast? In County Antrim? In north Armagh? And places like that? Would the Guards be able to deal with the issues that would arise there? Also, if it went the other direction, you'd have a deep sense of disappointment and an agitation for another poll within seven years.[62]

With regard to the form a united Ireland might take, Brendan O'Leary believes that, after considering federal and confederal models:

the options on the united Ireland institutionally come down to two: an integrated Ireland in which Northern Ireland would disappear institutionally, and a united Ireland with a devolved Northern Ireland that is legally possible because of the way [Éamon] de Valera set up Bunreacht na hÉireann. There is a provision in there which allows for support in the legislatures to be recognized by the Oireachtas. There would be no constitutional barrier to recognizing a subordinate legislature in Northern Ireland. There would, however, be need for constitutional change in recognizing the Northern Executive because the Constitution doesn't recognize any subordinate executives.[63]

O'Leary, John Garry and their academic colleagues held two one-day mini Citizens' Assemblies (CAs): one in Belfast on 30 March 2019, and one in Dublin on 24 April 2021. Participants interrogated two constitutional alternatives.[64]

The Northern Ireland participants were asked to choose between the Stormont/devolution model, with most of the provisions of the B/GFA still in place but under Irish sovereignty, and an integrated Ireland state where Northern Ireland ceased to exist, absorbed into all-Ireland structures and an all-Ireland parliament with Dublin the governing entity. Over the course of the day, participants in the Belfast forum changed their minds from higher support for the devolved model to at least equal support for an integrated Ireland at the close of their deliberations.

'This change in support was most pronounced among Protestant participants,' the organizers concluded:

> [Some] thought that the transferred Good Friday model was unlikely to work politically because the power-sharing arrangements were not functioning, and in their view showed little promise of reliable functioning; the different policy powers in the different parts of the island were judged likely to cause confusion; and, indeed, some thought that because this model is neither the status quo nor a fully fledged united Ireland, it is unlikely to satisfy either nationalists or unionists and would hence prompt further acrimony and conflict. Relatedly, other participants saw such an arrangement as transitional – a 'semi-skimmed' united Ireland, one that would not last.[65]

There were qualifiers: participants could assume 'that in the short run a reunited Ireland would make only a small difference economically. Within the North some would be better off, some would be worse off, but in general there would not be a massive transformation.'[66] Deliberations took place almost two years into the Stormont institutions being in abeyance. One can ask: if Stormont had been up and working, which many interviewees see as a prerequisite for calling a referendum, would Protestant participants have continued to favour the devolved model?

The Dublin mini-Assembly considered the same constitutional alternatives.[67] Before presentation and discussion, they preferred an integrated Ireland to a united Ireland with a devolved Northern Ireland. After information about what a devolved Northern Ireland and an integrated Ireland would look like, they are even more strongly in favour of an integrated united Ireland. They wanted to know in advance what they are voting for.[68]

The participants shifted from wanting a referendum within two years to considering five to ten years. They wanted to know more about the costs. For the purpose of the exercise, they were told that there would be 'winners and losers from unification, but [to assume that] they and their families would experience no net loss'.[69] At best, 'some felt that recognising a devolved Northern Ireland could be a useful compromise, a transitional step towards an integrated Ireland'. Delivery of a single consistent and comprehensive economic, health and education policy was a prime consideration. And while participants thought 'it would be better if they [unionists] engaged', they 'thought that the South should nevertheless define a specific model of unification before the future referendums rather than having a simple vote on the principle – leaving everything to be decided by a future constitutional convention'.[70]

The academics who conducted the study concluded: 'If Irish policymakers eventually decide that retaining a devolved Northern Ireland is a wise pathway into unification, even perhaps as a transitional arrangement, then they will need to prepare the Irish public for what many of them would regard as an unwelcome surprise.'[71]

There are, however, other possible takeaways. The results also suggest there is a point of convergence between the two sets of findings. Both see maintaining a devolved government in Northern Ireland as at least an interim compromise, a starting point on a several-year path towards integration or, perhaps, the final point in the process.

Participants in Dublin were surprised to learn that there was more than one model of a united Ireland, which, if taken as representative of how unification is perceived in the republic, is indicative of the scale of ignorance regarding the dimensions of the myriad issues involved and the state of

Northern Ireland. But in the space of a day they were brought up to speed – itself a feat of singular pedagogical excellence on the part of the academics administering the exercise. Whereas most Irish CAs can take place over a year or more, these were compressed into a single day.[72] Nor can the influence of confirmation bias be dismissed – participants began with one set of ideas, and the information presented to them mostly reinforced them in their beliefs.

The mini CA in Dublin also took place within a few weeks of the disturbances in Northern Ireland over the NIP that catapulted Northern Ireland into news cycles in the republic. The fact that under these circumstances participants could begin their deliberations on whether to see a referendum within two years is breathtaking. Either they were unaware of the rioting or simply dismissed it as being of no consequence. If the former, probably more a reflection of the South's general blinders to what happens in Northern Ireland; if the latter, seeming indifference to how the B/GFA could unravel.

The assumption of a 'winners and losers but no net cost to themselves or their families' – with whatever costs reunification might involve being outsourced to others – avoided participants having to address *who* should bear the cost of reunification. One consistent finding from surveys since the 1970s is that substantial majority support for unity in the South slips to under 50 per cent when respondents are told they would have to pay higher taxes. Peter Shirlow says:

> I would say the commitment would be very weak post-pandemic if there was a decline in the Irish economy, if you pointed out that this was going to cost £3,000, £4,000, £5,000 per head, if you point out what happened when East Germany joined West Germany, that there was a tax that had to be raised, etc. One of the things that's really interesting about this debate is [that] it's not a debate. Nationalism or Republicanism are telling us: we're around the corner from a united Ireland.[73]

Issues thought to be highly contentious – such as flags, anthems, accommodating the British identity and policing – were parked, with the simple notation that they would require 'time to negotiate'.

Both CAs suggest that because Northern Ireland is not working in its devolved state, the best solution is to incorporate it within an all-Ireland state. Like polls, CAs are reflections of opinion at a point in time. If Northern

Ireland had been a better-working political entity – as the Alliance leader Naomi Long insists it must be before Alliance might consider becoming pro-unification – would participants have been more disposed towards a devolved Ireland state? My Southern interviewees in particular see a functioning Northern Ireland as necessary for the South's willingness to make a marriage offer. Moreover, having a unitary integrated model as the new Ireland of choice that is on offer, with details the subject of negotiation following a referendum, would narrow the range of constitutional choices open to unionists. One can only surmise how the results of both mini-Assemblies would have turned out if the probable costs involved – including some part of the subvention, possibly higher taxes, changes to political symbols such as flags and anthems and policing – had to be factored into the deliberations. And, in the case of the Northern Ireland CA, how a functioning Assembly might have influenced its work.

The appeal of the integrated model, the Working Group on Unification Referendums on the Island of Ireland reports, is that it is conceptually straightforward.[74] But, it cautions, it 'would involve significant adaptation of Northern institutions and practices to Southern ones, which might involve substantial delays, and potentially great friction'.[75] This observation alone might be grounds for ruling out the model. The WGR adds, 'it might be widely seen by opponents as the takeover of Northern Ireland, reducing their sense of belonging in the new state'.[76]

In the event of an integrated state, all structures of the North would be dismantled and replaced with all-Ireland structures.[77] Among the changes: application of EU law; the euro as the national currency; integrated health, welfare services and the public sector; harmonization of tax policies; agreement on who would be Head of State; integration of all-island sports bodies; provision for Catholic and Protestant schooling and equalization of funding; changes to third-level education; alignment of pension and redundancy arrangements; absorption of the Northern Ireland subvention; synchronization of infrastructure and environmental policies; formulation of policies to address representation in the all-Ireland parliament; integration of banking practices and postal services, including stamps; agreement on national flags and anthem; a possible all-Ireland party system, as parties in the North begin to organize in the South and parties there organize in the North; equalization of laws pertaining to abortion and gender rights determined by the Irish courts; legal systems aligned to Irish law. This list is not exclusive.

The point is that the degree of disruption and the uncertainty that could accompany an integrated Ireland would be wholesale, a disproportionate amount borne by Northern Protestants, but also a significant amount borne by Northern Catholics – many who are 'soft' on unity and work in the public sector, and who would look for job protection.[78]

Unitary state models could also lock in Sinn Féin's political dominance. As the only all-island political party, it would have an electoral bandwidth dwarfing other parties. Even if the established Southern parties began to organize in the North, it might take a decade or more before they gained significant political traction. In 2019, Fianna Fáil and the SDLP entered talks regarding a possible merger. 'We haven't done enough there,' Jim O'Callaghan says. 'It was announced in January 2019, then there was an election blah, blah, blah … If you're going to do it, there's only so long that you can be engaged to somebody, if you're going to get married or not, do it. I think we should engage with the SDLP.'[79] Looking ahead, Fianna Fáil must weigh up whether – should Sinn Féin emerge as the largest party in Ireland after the 2025 election – it would consider a coalition with Sinn Féin to form a government. Whether the combined strength of Sinn Féin and Fianna Fáil, the party nearest to it ideologically, could be offset by a coalition among Fine Gael, the unionist parties and the Greens is problematic. But under some electoral arrangement the best brake on a Sinn Féin ascendency might be a unionist block of votes in an all-Ireland parliament.

There are variations on the unitary state model. One proposed by Fianna Fáil TD Jim O'Callaghan is spelled out in his paper 'The political, economic and legal consequences of Irish reunification.'[80] He calls for a unitary state embedded in a new constitution, a new state with a new anthem, a new flag and a senate sitting in Stormont, a bicameral parliamentary system with the Irish parliament sitting in Dublin and the retention of a certain number of cabinet positions for representatives of unionist parties:[81]

> It's not about the South trying to buy another field ['Four Green Fields'] and saying, 'You can come in, and join our farm.' The purpose is for both jurisdictions to try to come up with something new and different … I think we'd have to get rid of the Irish constitution. We'll get rid of the Irish state … Northern Ireland, as part of the United

Kingdom, would go. We'd develop a new country; we'd probably call it Ireland. We'd get a new country, and we'd have a new constitution for it, but I think we need to get academics working on it in the first instance. If we can come up with a document, which is a constitution for a new Ireland that has something like an Irish senate up in Stormont … that sets out how we're going to protect minority rights in the Constitution … That sets out what an Irish flag would be, what an Irish anthem would be. We'd have two national languages.

This all needs to be done, and I think that can only be agreed if, after a border poll, people vote to go into a united Ireland. Then, obviously, unionism would engage with … this draft constitution. They may say, 'We want changes to that.' Hopefully, we should facilitate that.[82]

O'Callaghan argues that unionist parties could exercise considerable influence as coalitions. 'The reality here [in the republic],' he says, 'is that unionism and other centrist parties – there may be parties on the right down in the South – would probably dominate governance for quite a while here. They [unionists] need to move out to see the opportunities of this.' Academics, he says:

would draw up the draft Constitution. So that in the event of a border poll, [we can say], 'this is the draft that we think would be useful' … Obviously, we can't dictate it. It will be subject to what other people think, but that [it] is our best efforts of trying to put forward the architecture for a new country. This all needs to be done, and I think that can only be agreed if, after a border poll, people vote to go into a united Ireland. Then, obviously, unionism would engage with these draft documents and this draft constitution. They may say, 'We want changes to that.' Hopefully, we should facilitate that. Everyone votes on approving a new constitution. It's not easy; and it's complicated.[83]

Fine Gael – in government since 2011, in coalition with the Labour Party between 2011 and 2016, in a minority government along with Independent TDs from 2016 to 2020 and part of a coalition with Fianna Fáil and the Greens after the 2020 general election – allowed Northern Ireland to slip under the political radar, TD Neale Richmond says. Despite the agreement's undertaking that 'there will be regular and frequent meetings of the Conference', there were no meetings of the British-Irish Intergovernmental

Conference between 26 February 2007 and 25 July 2018, and only four meetings between July 2018 and December 2021.[84] 'We need to define our policy
a bit stronger; we haven't,'[85] says Richmond.

In his paper 'Towards a New Ireland',[86] like O'Callaghan's delivered at
Sydney Sussex College Cambridge, Richmond also supports a unitary state,
with the devolved Assembly structure, however, continuing in place for a
decade 'cognisant of the desire to achieve as great a buy-in as possible from
all communities'.[87] Richmond comes from a unionist background but says,
'I fundamentally consider myself a republican and a constitutional nationalist,'[88] and he does not foresee a border poll within the next ten years at
least. He emphasizes the pivotal role of the Shared Island Initiative as the
vehicle for establishing relationships across a spectrum of areas. He supports Ireland's re-joining the Commonwealth and calls for a lower and
upper house that would elect a speaker and deputy speaker, but for the first
decade of its existence 'at least one of these positions is always held by a
member from what would have been Northern Ireland'.[89] The same practice
would apply to chairs of parliamentary committees. Before a border referendum in the North, however,

> you need to see the nationalists considerably ahead of the unionists
> even if it's 40 per cent, 30 per cent and you have that 30 per cent
> middle ground, before you can start. It can't be just one election
> either. You need to see a shift. Have we seen that? We've seen a move
> towards nationalism for sure but it's still not in the big numbers. It's
> very hard to ask a perspective question.
>
> A lot of people, particularly republicans and nationalists in
> Northern Ireland, are not happy with this. That's why they call
> people like me partitionists … They say … 'No, no, nationalists are a
> majority. It's our time to have our say, we've never had our say.' That's
> understandable … but I think when it comes to responsibility … at
> the end of the day, it will also depend on who is the Secretary of State.
> Is it a Conservative, a unionist, or is it someone in the Labour Party?
> I think they may take distinctly different opinions.[90]

Richmond's path to unification schema would include having the Secretary
of State setting out what factors they will take into consideration in determining whether to call a poll, a date in a suitable timeframe – perhaps
within two years of agreeing to a border poll – and a CA across the island

that will shape what a united Ireland would look like, its deliberations debated and amended by a dedicated Committee of the British-Irish Parliamentary Assembly and subsequently referred to the executive committee of the Northern Ireland Assembly, the House of Commons Northern Ireland Affairs Committee and the Oireachtas Committee on the Good Friday Agreement. The reports of each committee would then once again be debated by the CA that will produce a vision for a united Ireland; referendums North and South are held on the same day.

The Irish government would be required to exercise its sovereign power with the same rigorous impartiality with which the B/GFA calls on the British government to act with respect to ensuring 'parity of esteem and of just and equal treatment for the identity, ethos and aspirations of both communities', as stated in Article (1)(v) of the British-Irish Agreement, annexed to the B/GFA.[91]

Before the B/GFA, the Anglo-Irish Agreement (AIA), much to the chagrin of the unionist community, provided for a consultative role for the Irish government in matters relating to the nationalist community in Northern Ireland and a physical presence in the North giving expression to that purpose. Why wouldn't unionists demand a reciprocal type of arrangement, in the name of parity of esteem and precedent, for the British community in a newly minted united Ireland? Seán Donlon, one of the architects of the AIA, says:

> My favourite option would be to have London basically begin to withdraw from Northern Ireland but to stay on in the same capacity as the Irish government did under the 1985 Anglo-Irish Agreement, where basically the Irish government became the guarantor of the position of the minority in Northern Ireland. I could foresee a situation where, increasingly, the British would withdraw … but stay on as the protector of unionists in exactly the same way.[92]

Indeed, the B/GFA infers such a British-Irish relationship for a united Ireland, especially if it takes the form of a unitary state, where British unionists are a minority of 15 per cent. The arrangement would simply replicate the British-Irish relationship in the AIA for Northern Ireland where Irish nationalists were a minority of 40 per cent. It fulfils the requirement of parity of esteem for both identities no matter which jurisdiction – Britain or Ireland – is the sovereign power. This, Andy Pollak says, will be

perhaps the most difficult discussion of all, the requirement – in a
republic that cast off British rule after a war of independence a century
ago – to talk about what kind of continuing British involvement in
Ireland we can live with for the sake of the peace and harmony of
the whole island. That, for many unionists, will be a *sine qua non*.
For many republicans and nationalists, it will be a huge step too far.
And of course, this vital dimension will not work if the British, as
they move out of the EU into their own strange post-imperial, post-
European orbit, want nothing more to do with us.[93]

Britishness in a united Ireland is not simply something that would have to be
accommodated. It is an entitlement; its various components would have to be
given legal expression and all its cultural dimensions given parity of esteem.
The two governments will be obliged to fulfil their respective separate and
collective functions to ensure the new arrangements work and continue to
step in to mediate differences, as they have throughout the past twenty-five
years, when the institutions in the North become dysfunctional.[94] A united
Ireland will not end the British presence in Ireland. It will recalibrate it. For
any model of unity, the fact of a united Ireland becoming the outer perimeter
of the EU will require a border between a united Ireland and Britain (which
itself would be a matter of intense negotiations), redefining or ending many
of the close socio-economic relationships between the two countries that
have existed for over 100 years. There is an odd paradox here: even as the B/
GFA calls for some role in a united Ireland for a British government, a united
Ireland will be gravitating away from Britain and towards the EU.

TheJournal.ie posed questions on unification to the parties before the general
election in 2020.[95] It is an understatement to call the responses embarrass-
ingly rich in their vagueness.

Answers to questions about the circumstances respondents would deem
appropriate for calling a poll in the South included:

- 'Should only be put to the people when we believe the poll would
  pass both North and South' (Fine Gael);

- A unit should be created within the Department of the Taoiseach 'to
  lead a formal study and cross-community consultation on a Green

Paper to outline how the Irish government should approach the handling of any unity referendum should circumstances arise where it can be called' (Fianna Fáil);

- '[We] want to see a referendum on Irish unity within the next five years' (Sinn Féin);

- 'Any referendum in Ireland should be a vote to agree to the reunification of Ireland if the majority in Northern Ireland had already voted in favour of this' (Labour);

- 'A border poll in the republic should come at the same time as a poll is conducted north of the border; it should only be carried out when there is a likelihood of it passing' (Greens).

As to the timing of the poll:

- 'Any holding of a border poll … would be inappropriate at this time … As such, any determination as to whether the polls should be held simultaneously or otherwise is, similarly, inappropriate as it would only exacerbate division and uncertainty' (Fine Gael);

- 'This sequencing should be considered as part of overall preparations for a united Ireland' (Fianna Fáil);

- 'That should be discussed by a Citizens' Assembly' (Sinn Féin);

- 'Any referendum in Ireland should follow the [Northern Ireland referendum], unless a wide range of political parties in Northern Ireland ask the Irish government to hold a simultaneous poll' (Labour).

And what type of Ireland?

- 'It is far too early to start making pronouncements and decisions on political structure. It would be divisive and counterproductive' (Fine Gael);

- 'This should be considered as part of overall discussions and considerations' (Fianna Fáil);

- 'That should be discussed by a Citizens' Assembly' (Sinn Féin);

- 'It is too soon for any party to set down a fixed vision of appropriate institutions for political unity across Ireland' (Labour);

- 'The continuation of the Stormont Assembly is likely to be retained in any united Ireland' (Greens).

A year later, the parties had another opportunity to share their views and visions for the future when they appeared on *Claire Byrne Live* on RTÉ to discuss what a united Ireland might mean.[96] There was little in the way of illumination for the large audience that tuned in. There were a lot of exchanges on the need for conversations, inclusiveness and recognizing and accommodating identities (although no one seemed ready to concede on the Irish flag): from Mary Lou McDonald – 'The truth is we need to begin preparation now for constitutional change, and that means all of us have to be involved in the conversation. This is not a Sinn Féin project ... this is a national project' – to Leo Varadkar warning that setting a date for a poll before the necessary preparatory work had been done, as he pithily put it, was akin to 'setting a marriage date before courtship began', to Micheál Martin's reverent invocation of the genius of the B/GFA. The banality of the responses stood out as the most public takeaway from the programme. Throughout, the B/GFA was frequently invoked by the Irish side as an antidote for all foreseeable contingencies.

But the B/GFA had begun unspooling. A month later, the Loyalist Communities Council withdrew loyalism's support for the agreement, followed by the April rioting climaxing at the Lanark interface and the DUP withdrawing ministers from the North-South Ministerial Council, collapsing the Executive with little immediate prospect of reconvening. All weapons, it turns out, were not decommissioned – hardly a surprise. Meanwhile, the calls for a border poll intensify, even as the agreement implodes, coming apart at the seams.

In short, the political parties in the South have not given any consideration to basic questions twenty-five years after the B/GFA, almost certainly reflecting the facts that before Brexit the question of a border poll was mostly a hypothetical, and a border poll on unity has never been an issue in Irish elections. Nevertheless, when asked whether they'd like to see a referendum within five years, 57 per cent were in favour and 40 per cent were not – no concern here about flying blind into the future. The collective 'positions' of the South's political class suggest a paucity of thinking. Bertie Ahern says:

> [A referendum at] the end of the decade ... it might be longer, but it shouldn't be sooner. If the financial model isn't clear, if the legal model isn't clear, if the institutional models aren't clear, and if there were a sizable minority, which I think there would be in the North, that would be opposed, it would have a big influence on the Republic of Ireland electorate. That's why whatever question and analysis is put to the people North and South must be comprehensive in nature and must be detailed in the papers that are prepared and must be under-standable to the electorate.
>
> If it's a half-baked, fuzzy kind of a referendum with too many unknowns, not enough clarity, then I think it would be rejected. I equally think that the *concept of a united Ireland* [my italics], the large minority that would be against it in the unionist community would turn into a majority of the unionist community against it. That's why it has to be in the *concept of a new Ireland* ...
>
> In the old days, the main problem with the unionists was that while we call them one time a failed state, they call those a Church-ridden state, and a state that was incapable of financially sustaining the South and being financially viable. Those arguments are gone now. When the ESRI analysis ... is finished, and we really see the real grant aid that the British government gives to Northern Ireland distinct from an arbitrary figure that's given now, then I think things would be far clearer.
>
> To make this referendum winnable – and there's no point in having a referendum that isn't winnable – it has to be comprehensive. It must be detailed, it must have clarity for the people, otherwise, it's a lost cause.[97]

Most nationalist/republican-aligned interviewees thought that Brexit made a border poll more likely, within ten years the target date for many; unionist-aligned interviewees refused to concede the inevitability of unifi-cation. A circular logic is at play, which says that because a majority are in favour of holding a referendum five to ten years hence, one ought to take place within that time frame, that somehow the metrics justifying one will have materialized, even if the objective evidence supporting the supposition is at best tentative, an extrapolation of trends of choice, or just speculative.

The data surveyed and analysed in the preceding chapters and an analysis of the ninety-seven interviews I conducted from February 2020 through 2021 strongly suggest that the most frequently cited metrics a Secretary of State might use to gauge whether there is a likely majority in favour of unification come up short. They are unable to deliver a definitive answer as to whether a likely 50 per cent + 1 at least would vote for unity in a border referendum. Rather than evolving in strict nationalist/unionist, Catholic/Protestant trajectories as the B/GFA envisioned, a robust centre, neutral on the constitutional question, has emerged.

The one metric that can produce a majority request for a referendum is the Alliance Party, now the third-largest party in Northern Ireland and growing.[98] Most interviewees agreed that if a majority of the Assembly's MLAs took a non-binding vote to ask a Secretary of State to set a date some two to three years hence for a referendum, the secretary should respond positively to that request. That majority in the Assembly would most likely emerge as a result of the Alliance Party's moving from its neutral stance on the union to a pro-unification one. 'We would be wary of voting for a border poll in a vacuum,' the Alliance Party deputy leader Stephen Farry says. 'Certainly, the bar for us doing so will be very high. You would need to have a fairly clear idea as to what a border poll was going to be on.'[99] Naomi Long is more explicit: 'The context in which the border poll is set in a functioning Assembly with a functioning North-South Ministerial Council, with a functioning British-Irish governmental organization and everything else.'[100] A LucidTalk poll (August 2022) recorded 31 per cent of Alliance voters would vote 'now' for a border referendum, 26 per cent said 'no' and 43 per cent said they would vote but were not sure how, the tilt being in the direction of a referendum.[101] But again, the conundrum: if, as Farry suggests, Alliance is to know what the united Ireland is on offer, then Dublin has to have its homework done. Niall Murphy, too, emphasizes that the middle ground will determine where the future lies:

> The referendum will be defined by the centre ground … They are
> the constituency that will be swayed by empirical evidence, facts,
> actual data, economic modelling and projections. Because we know
> that that constituency will define a yes or no, that's where the evi-
> dence and the argument will be targeted, I would expect, by both
> pro-united Ireland and pro-United Kingdom camps … I've looked

at some statistics, [which suggest that that constituency] could be
as little as 51,000 human beings who have the vote that will tip the
balance one way or the other.[102]

The challenges Sinn Féin will face if it becomes part of an Irish government
in 2025 – having to grasp the reins of government for the first time, famil-
iarize itself with its ministerial posts, pass and fund legislation to implement
its hallmark policies on housing and health, meet Ireland's COP26 climate
pledges by 2030 (sure to be contentious and demand unpopular decisions,
some of which will directly impact its voter base) as well as adjust to the
ongoing economic ramifications of the Russian invasion of Ukraine – will
stretch its political reach, put huge strains on the Exchequer and leave little
rope for addressing unification, which is not an issue the Irish public is seriously attuned to.[103] At the same time its Northern constituency, conditioned
by years of Sinn Féin's insistence that a border poll should be called, will
expect instantaneous action. Hence the outsourcing of questions relating to
a united Ireland to a Citizens' Assembly.

The differences between a position that calls for a referendum 'within
five years' and 'within five to ten years' are not just semantic, they are significant. Within five can mean by 2027, or ten can mean between 2027 and 2032.
Within five years would mean a border poll in years immediately following
general elections in the UK in January 2025 (where the governing party will
change), Ireland in March 2027 (where the governing parties will almost
certainly change) and Northern Ireland in May 2027, where the same parties
will be returned to govern. A border poll within this timeframe and in this
set of circumstances is so improbable we can write it off. In government in
the South after the 2025 elections would Sinn Féin immediately call for a referendum 'within two to seven years', or would its demands for one be reset
to the 'within five to ten years' position? If the latter, then the timeframe
becomes somewhere between 2030 and 2035.

A University of Liverpool/*Irish News* poll (April 2022) showed Sinn Féin
sitting on a comfortable lead of 7 percentage points over the DUP (27 per
cent to 20 per cent) as the parties headed into the May elections. But the poll
also reported that only 30 per cent would vote for a united Ireland 'tomor-
row'.[104] This would rise to just 33 per cent in '10 to 15 years'. Support dropped
to 25 per cent when higher taxes were raised. Sinn Féin found itself in the
awkward position of embracing the 27 per cent as an accurate reflection of

where the electorate stood – the actual result of Sinn Féin receiving 29 per cent of first preferences fell within the poll's margin of error – but questioning the accuracy of the 30 per cent pro-unity result. Moreover, two-thirds of nationalists agreed with the statement that 'if devolved politics worked better people would focus less on the constitutional question'.

Sinn Féin's Assembly 2022 election manifesto 'Make Politics Work' dropped the party's relentless prioritizing of a border poll. It scrubbed all mention of one from its campaign messaging, but once the election results were announced and pole position in the Assembly secured, old habits kicked in again. The party was back at the constitutional stuff. Within twenty-four hours, Mary Lou McDonald demanded a border poll 'within a five-year time frame'. 'Certainly, within this decade of opportunity,' she said, 'we are going to see constitutional change on the island of Ireland.'[105] Hence the elasticity of the Sinn Féin time band, between five and ten years, but also between five and eight years, a year or two chopped here and there depending on the intended audience.

If 'making politics work' means 'making Northern Ireland work', then we may witness a shift in strategy, away from the Northern Ireland as a failed political entity rhetoric and towards a realization that the best route to a united Ireland is through a Northern Ireland that is working. Its task is to woo the Alliance Party. As the largest party in the Assembly, Sinn Féin will be held responsible as the main governing party for how the Assembly and Executive work. Voters in the South will surely rank its performance in the North when they head to the polls in 2025. Certainly, the party's response to the death of Queen Elizabeth hit all the right notes. Alex Maskey, Sinn Féin Speaker of the Northern Ireland Assembly, welcomed King Charles to Stormont. He was gracious and respectful, eloquently expressing condolence on the Queen's passing, acknowledging her contribution to the peace process, with a deft nod to the transformation in the political landscape that allowed him, a former republican prisoner, to become Speaker. The new monarch did his part, conversing warmly with Michelle O'Neill, remarking that her party was the largest in Northern Ireland. For her part, O'Neill told him that his mother had 'played a great role in peacebuilding and reconciliation, it is the end of an era'. The small gestures conveyed a meaning entirely disproportionate to the acts themselves, yet will be recalled in time for their historical resonance, much like the queen shaking hands with Martin

McGuinness, then deputy first minister and former IRA mastermind, when she visited Dublin in 2011.

Thus: if the multiple pieces of the political jigsaws in London, Dublin, Brussels and Belfast fall into place, we are probably looking at a border poll in 2032 at the earliest. This scenario is based on the assumption that Sinn Féin is in government in the South after 2025; that on taking office it immediately calls a CA and the preparatory work takes a minimum of five years; that the Executive and Assembly remain operative for two election cycles; that the Alliance Party is brought on board following Assembly elections in 2027; that the new Assembly a few years into its term requests the Secretary of State to call a referendum and he or she responds. If all goes as predicted, this will set a referendum date sometime in 2032 – two to three years after the request for one – and, in the event of a vote for reunification, an elaborate and intricate process would thereafter begin, potentially lasting ten to fifteen years, phasing in the transfer of sovereignty and the final pieces of a united Ireland in 2042–7.

Of course, this scenario is too seamless – even optimistic – and there are numerous caveats. It would need Alliance to abandon its neutrality on the constitutional question (the party could split over the issue, hence a significant majority would need to be on board); Dáil Éireann to rubberstamp recommendations of a CA on the details of a united Ireland that would be part of a referendum question; the British and Irish governments to be in sync on the issue and working together; no external shocks such as Scotland leaving the union or a widening war in Europe as the Russian invasion of Ukraine worsens; no economic recession of consequence occurring in the republic; a full alignment of Sláintecare with the NHS and educational systems in the North aligned with those in the South; Sinn Féin to be returned to government in 2030; the NIP dispute to be resolved and not festering through 2024 when the Assembly will vote on whether to retain it; and security forces, including the Gardaí and the Police Service of Northern Ireland (PSNI), to be interlinked. It is extremely hard to envisage the Conservative Party – which went to such lengths to ditch the NIP, engaging in a protracted and bitter dispute (perhaps even a trade war) with the EU over the issue – now ditching Northern Ireland itself. But its full title is the Conservative and Unionist Party; if the union is to be torn asunder, it would seem to be the birthright prerogative of a Conservative Party government, rather than a task a Labour Party government would undertake in the face of fierce opposition from the Conservatives.

If Labour wins the 2025 general elections, Sir Keir Starmer will become prime minister. His immediate challenges will be getting a party that has been out of government for fourteen years to reacquaint itself with how government works, ascertaining what the levers of ministerial powers are and establishing a cabinet office that ensures the smooth running of the engines of government.

The focus of a Labour administration will necessarily be the economy and mending relations with the EU. The UK economy is in tatters, the worst performing in the G20 (apart from Russia), according to the Organisation for Economic Co-operation and Development (OECD).[106] On all fronts – whether trade, travel or financial services – Brexit has aggravated the situation.[107]

The UK is in the throes of a prolonged recession, experiencing the worst economic turndown since the mid-1950s.[108] Inflation is expected to reach 13 per cent, or even an astronomical 17 per cent, according to the National Institute of Economic and Social Research.[109] Living standards will fall close to 5 per cent over 2022/23.[110] On most economic indicators, Britain is in trouble.[111] Reversing these deleterious trends and halting the slide towards even worse depths will preoccupy whichever party forms a government post the January 2025 elections.

As regards Northern Ireland, Starmer is staunchly pro-union. On a two-day visit to Northern Ireland in July 2021, he reiterated his belief in 'the United Kingdom' and promised that he would campaign for Northern Ireland to remain in the UK in the event of a border poll.[112] Starmer also rules out sanctioning a referendum on Scottish independence.[113]

Were Scotland to pursue independence more vigorously, it might actually slow a border referendum on Irish unification, if only because a British government would find itself extremely stretched if it were to negotiate Scotland's departure from the Union – likely to make Brexit negotiations look rudimentary in comparison – simultaneously with Northern Ireland's. A more likely time frame would supplement the scenario with a question in the 2031 census form on whether respondents are in favour of a united Ireland and a referendum, and, if so, when.

Ultimately, no matter how the future unfolds, there will be the unknowns. Tipping points exist. Sinn Féin in government North and South – the largest party in both jurisdictions – would be a catalyst for its own set of dynamics. But Sinn Féin could find itself hostage to the vagaries of its ambition, unable to map out its course. It might get its referendum, but not the result it thinks is theirs for the taking.

In the Introduction to *Perils & Prospects*, I referred to the ubiquitous use of the word 'fragile' to describe the peace process, that is, it is easily shattered or broken. I invoke it on several occasions, a soft-sounding mantra to juxtapose the contradiction between the reality of Northern Ireland and the unreality of the incessant bugle calls for Irish unification. A quarter of a century on from the B/GFA, Northern Ireland, although a more tolerant society in many respects, remains a deeply divided one.[114] Despite huge investment of resources into 'good relations' projects and the best efforts of government and civic organizations, structural sectarianism is still deeply embedded; its malignant offshoots still flow through Northern Ireland's bloodstream, contaminating the social fabric.[115] We are reminded time and again that any random event can trigger political eruptions with adverse consequences.[116]

If perchance the Northern Ireland Bill – which is designed to effectively gut the protocol – survives House of Lords scrutiny and becomes law, consequences will follow, not just for Northern Ireland and the republic but for the UK, too. Erstwhile British Prime Minister Liz Truss promised US President Joe Biden that the UK and EU would resolve the matter by April 2023, the twenty-fifth anniversary of the B/GFA.[117] Should her successor Rishi Sunak not deliver on Truss's promise, there will be no US presidential visit to the UK to mark the occasion, no trade deal under Biden's watch. And in the unlikely event that the stand-off between the EU and UK remains unresolved, at some point the EU, as a remedy of last resort for the overriding imperative to protect the Single Market, might have to turn to a land border across Ireland, reluctant though it might be to do so.[118]

That, too, would have adverse consequences. If the Northern Ireland Bill gets bogged down in acrimonious exchanges between the Commons and the Lords, Northern Ireland is looking at a period with government institutions in limbo, the North-South Ministerial Council in abeyance and relations between the British and Irish governments continuing to deteriorate. If, in addition, the British government pushes through its legacy legislation, the deteriorating relations between the two will be further exacerbated. Moreover, the protocol has been operating in a 'grace period' phase – its harshest impacts are yet to be felt. The shrinking 'British only' demographic has consequences. There are lots of 'ifs', some more probable than others: some will have been resolved by the time *Perils & Prospects* is published; others will have morphed into a different kind of issue or become redundant.

On all fronts, however, uncertainties will remain.

Fragility loves uncertainty.

Epilogue

Liz Truss lasted forty-five days as the United Kingdon (UK) prime minister – from 5 September to 20 October 2022, the shortest time span in parliamentary history – before she was peremptorily dumped from office for reckless performance and pure ineptitude.

Just weeks into her tenure her mini budget called for unfunded tax cuts – mostly for the well-off[1] – but with no corresponding cuts in public services. This roiled the financial markets and triggered an immediate spike in interest rates, sent mortgage rates soaring, pension funds plummeting and the pound tumbling to its lowest exchange rate with the dollar in nearly half a century. To stem the rout, the Bank of England stepped in, citing 'potential risks to the stability of the financial system' and pledged to purchase £65 billion of UK long-term bonds.[2]

Forced to fire her chancellor, Kwasi Kwarteng, and replace him with Jeremy Hunt, a former Health and Foreign Affairs Secretary from the left wing of the party who immediately reversed all of Kwarteng's measures, Truss's humiliation was complete. She was finished. The markets had taken back control.

Also finished were fantasies promulgated by Brexit – that a country could sever its relationship with its biggest trading partner and get richer;

that the UK, unshackled from the regulatory constraints of the European Union (EU), was a global power; that making Great Britain 'great again' was a viable project. The economy was shrinking, not growing, with the country in the grip of the worst recession and cost-of-living crisis in decades.[3] After the years of bingeing on post-Brexit delusions, the painful hangover had set in. Support for re-joining the EU surged to 57 per cent compared to the 43 per cent who wanted to keep Brexit.[4]

Ironically, Truss had appeared ready to reset relations with Brussels and Dublin. She had adopted a more conciliatory tone towards both and expressed an openness to resolving the Northern Ireland Protocol (NIP) stand-off through negotiations rather than unilateral UK legislation.[5] In an extraordinary moment at the Tory Party conference in Birmingham in early October 2022, Steve Baker, the newly appointed minister of State for Northern Ireland and among the most hard-line of Brexiteers, apologized 'with humility' to Ireland and Brussels for how he and other hard-liners had behaved since 2016. They had not, he said, respected the 'legitimate interests' of Ireland or the EU during the Leave campaign.[6] Relations with Ireland 'are not where they should be and we will need to work extremely hard to improve them and I know that we are doing so'. After meeting with Truss, Martin reported that the mood music had changed. He 'detected a genuine wish to resolve the impasse over the Northern Ireland Protocol'.[7] Irish Foreign Minister Simon Coveney met Secretary of State for Northern Ireland Chris Heaton-Harris several times. The thaw was underway.

On 24 October 2022 the ultra-wealthy Rishi Sunak, son of Indian immigrants, a graduate of Lincoln College Oxford and Stanford University Graduate School of Business, became the UK's third prime minister in four months – the fifth prime minister since Brexit in 2016. He immediately turned his attention to recovering the public's trust, unifying the party, addressing the economy and repairing relations with the EU. Although he supported Brexit, he was free of hard-line Brexit baggage, a pragmatist with no ideological pre-dispositions to drag him into an ongoing protracted dispute with the EU over the NIP that could end up in a trade war, further damaging a British economy already experiencing its worst recession in decades. In early November 2022, Coveney said that he believed there was a 'real intent in London' that a negotiated settlement was 'doable by the end of the year'.[8] The EU's chief negotiator Maroš Šefčovič was even more ebullient and opined that the protocol dispute could be resolved 'in a couple of weeks'.[9] Sunak and Ursula von der Leyen, President of the European Commission, met on the margins of the COP27 summit at Sharm El Sheikh and between them committed to reaching a negotiated settlement on the protocol.[10] There were reports of 'major breakthroughs'.[11] Martin met Sunak ahead of a British-Irish Council summit and promised to 'deepen UK/Irish ties'.[12] The political elites in their three jurisdictions were aligned in their determination to find a compromise.

In Northern Ireland, the waiting game continued. Would a compromise reached by Sunak, Šefčovič and von der Leyen be sufficiently palatable for Jeffrey Donaldson and the DUP to return to Stormont government? Or would Heaton-Harris, in the absence of agreement being reached, call elections before 19 January or extend the grace period once again, even perhaps to coincide with local elections scheduled to take place on 4 May 2023?[13] Or what if the DUP refused to accept a protocol arrangement reached by the EU and the UK – would the following extended absence of a functioning government and animosity towards the DUP move 'soft' nationalists (or those content to stay in the UK while the Belfast/Good Friday Agreement [B/GFA] is working) from 'don't know' on the constitutional question (or content to stay in the UK while the B/GFA is working) into the pro-reunification column? Would this move 'soft' unionists to become more open to consider some form of Irish unification?

According to the LucidTalk November 2022 poll, in the absence of Stormont functioning, joint Dublin-London rule (undefined what that would actually involve) is the preferred option of 41 per cent of respondents and direct rule from Westminster the option of 40 per cent. Nationalists overwhelmingly prefer the former (85 per cent), unionists the latter (75 per cent), while 21 per cent choose direct role with a consultative role for Dublin. Just 3 per cent of unionists would prefer joint authority. Alliance voters are split on options: 37 per cent would opt for joint rule and 47 per cent for direct rule from Westminster with a role for Dublin.[14]

The November poll showed further polarization of the electorate, as the Democratic Unionist Party (DUP) and Sinn Féin squeezed support from their more centrist rivals.[15] The DUP continued to have overwhelming support (80 per cent) from the unionist community for its boycott of Stormont until the protocol is settled to its satisfaction. The party had clawed support from both the Ulster Unionist Party (UUP) and Traditional Unionist Voice (TUV): — at

27 per cent, up six points since the May elections, doubling where it had stood in August 2021. Although excoriated by nationalists and Alliance for his recalcitrance, Donaldson still had the backing of his electorate. Donaldson's dilemma: if the DUP accepts an UK/EU agreement on the protocol that falls significantly short of meeting its seven tests, it stands to lose the support it has won back from Jim Allister's TUV, perhaps even slipping to third place behind the Alliance Party in an Assembly election. Staying competitive with Sinn Féin and still harbouring hopes that it might beat it again requires that the DUP is not outflanked on its right.

Sinn Féin has consolidated its position as the largest party, at 32 per cent, gobbling up the SDLP and confounding the pundits who thought the party had hit its ceiling in the May elections. The Alliance Party, at 15 per cent, convincingly confirmed its status as Northern Ireland's third-largest party. For the first time, a Sinn Féin leader, Michelle O'Neill, emerged as the most popular leader (46 per cent), a reflection of Sinn Féin's empathetic response to the death of Queen Elizabeth II and King Charles's visit to Stormont. A significant majority of nationalists and Alliance respondents are convinced that the DUP will never return to a government where it plays a symbolic second fiddle as deputy first minister to Sinn Féin's first minister.

Among unionists, the waiting was fraught with fear – fear of the British government selling them out yet again or of making a deal with the Irish government that might amount to joint authority. Indeed, loose noise about possible joint authority brought immediate responses from unionists, more seriously with the Loyalist Communities Council (LCC) – speaking on behalf of the Ulster Defence Association (UDA) and the Ulster Volunteer Force (UVF) – warning of 'dire consequences' if joint rule was imposed.[16] Billy Hutchinson, leader of the Progressive Unionist Party (PUP), reported that tension within loyalist communities was 'greater than at any point since the ceasefires of 1994'.[17] Among nationalists, the waiting was tinged with antic-ipation of Michelle O'Neill becoming first minister and of a drift towards reunification now that Catholics were the largest plurality. Unionists see a future that is problematic, nationalists a future bright with the prospect of reunification no longer on a distant horizon. The political sands are shifting. Unionism is finding a firm footing increasingly difficult.

In the South, there is waiting too – waiting to see whether the slow dribble of job losses in the tech sector was the harbinger of more extensive lay-offs across the economy and whether a recession was in the making as the global economy slowly tanked.[18] Waiting to see whether the government, now led by Leo Varadkar (who had switched offices with Micheál Martin, honouring the Taoiseach 'swapping' arrangement the coalition agreement called for), would make good on its promise to go 'all out' to address the housing crisis.[19]

An *Irish Times*/Ipsos MRBI/ARINS December 2022 poll, North and South, complemented by a series of focus groups, threw a bucket of ice over calls for a border referendum – the drift towards unification is far from being a powerful tailwind.[20] In Northern Ireland, 50 per cent of respondents opted to stay in the UK, including 21 per cent of Catholics; 27 per cent voted for unity, 18 per cent were 'don't knows' and 5 per cent would not vote. A majority (55 per cent) opted for a border poll within ten years. Among those who self-designated as not being from either a Catholic or Protestant background, 35 per cent voted to stay in the UK, 20 per cent would choose unity, 31 per cent were 'don't knows' and 14 per cent would not vote. Among Catholics, just 55 per cent were in favour of unity, 21 per cent against, 21 per cent 'don't knows' and 3 per cent said they would not vote.

Hence, the most malleable pool of 'persuadables': the cohorts comprising 'don't knows' among Catholics and 'others' (neither Catholic nor Protestant). Considering that this poll was conducted after seven/eight months of political paralysis in Northern Ireland, the absence of a functioning Stormont government there and spiralling support for Sinn Féin, the survey results underpin the need for a distinction between 'Catholic' (or 'from a Catholic background') and nationalist/republican – the two are far from synonymous.[21]

The poll's results in the South reaffirmed the results of other surveys on the question. A large majority were in favour of unification (66 per cent) and a referendum within five years (76 per cent). But, as a similar *Irish Times*/Ipsos poll a year earlier reported, just 20 per cent see unity as a priority, while 52 per cent say that 'it is not important to them but that they would like to see it someday'. Moreover, respondents were not prepared to pay for it, change the national flag or national anthem, rejoin the Commonwealth or take any measure that would accommodate the British identity.[22] Hence, a question that will arise should Sinn Féin find itself in government: how would Sinn Féin square its key priority – a united Ireland – with an electorate for whom it isn't?

With their eye on 10 April 2023, the twenty-fifth anniversary of the B/GFA, the British government and the EU ratcheted up their talks to settle their differences over the NIP. (According to *The Telegraph*, the voice of the British establishment, US President Joe Biden wanted the matter settled before April, signalling that he was keen to attend the anniversary ceremonies.)[23] Should they fail to settle those differences, the anniversary promises to be a wake rather than a celebration. Even if Stormont is up and running again, however, there is little to toast. Perhaps the single most important lesson of the five years since the twentieth anniversary is that the B/GFA is not working. The public's calls – across the divide – for major reforms to make it more adaptable to the changing realities of the politics on the ground should be acted upon. Even Micheál Martin, in one of his last statements on Northern Ireland as Taoiseach, declared the compulsory power-sharing formulation enshrined in the B/GFA is no longer 'fit for purpose'.[24]

This is achingly obvious.

Interviewees

Bertie Ahern – 26 November 2020

> Leader Fianna Fáil 1994–2008; Taoiseach 1998–2008; an architect of the Belfast/ Good Friday Agreement (B/GFA)

Steve Aiken – 11 December 2020

> Member of the Legislative Assembly (MLA), leader Ulster Unionist Party (UUP) 2019–21; represents the South Antrim constituency

John, Lord Alderdice – 14 March 2020

> Leader Alliance Party 1987–8; negotiator, B/GFA; Speaker of the Northern Ireland Assembly 1998–2004; Senior Research Fellow, Harris Manchester College, University of Oxford, founding Director of the Centre for the Resolution of Intractable Conflict (CRIC)

Martina Anderson – 3 December 2020

> MLA, Sinn Féin, 2007–12, 2020–1; MEP (Member of the European Parliament), 2012–20

Alex Attwood – 13 March 2020

> Social Democratic and Labour Party (SDLP), Minister for Environment in the Northern Ireland Executive 2011–13; represented Belfast West in the Assembly 1998–2017; member of SDLP Good Friday negotiating team

Father Tim Bartlett – 8 July 2021

> Secretary to the Catholic Bishops of Northern Ireland; Catholic Church's spokesman on social affairs in Northern Ireland

Doug Beattie – 14 May 2021

> MLA, Leader of the UUP since 2021; represents the Upper Bann constituency

Paul, Lord Bew – 6 January 2021

> Professor of Irish Politics at Queen's University Belfast since 1991

Francis Black – 24 February 2021

> Independent senator, Seanad Éireann; Chairperson of Ireland's Future since 2016, NGO campaigning for a united Ireland

Niall Blaney – 1 June 2021

> Fianna Fáil, Teachta Dála (TD) for Donegal 2002–11; Seanad Éireann since 2020

John Bradley – 25 March 2021

> Research Professor at the Economic and Social Research Institute (ESRI), Dublin 1981; 2006 international consultant on analysis and modelling of economic development and industrial strategy (EMDS)

Richard Bullick – 15 December 2020

> Special Adviser to Democratic Unionist Party (DUP) first ministers

Máiria Cahill – 19 November 2020

> Former Sinn Féin activist; Northern Irish-born senator, Seanad Éireann, where she represented the Irish Labour Party, 2015–16; a former SDLP councillor, 2018–19; writes weekly column for the *Sunday Independent*

Francis Campbell – 15 March 2021

> British diplomat and academic, policy adviser and private secretary to Prime Minister Tony Blair, Vice Chancellor, University of Notre Dame Australia

Gregory Campbell – 4 March 2021

> DUP MP; represents the East Londonderry parliamentary constituency since 2001

Gerry Carlile – 24 February 2021

> CEO, Ireland's Future – NGO campaigning for a united Ireland

Lesley Carroll – May 2021

> Presbyterian minister; Prisoner Ombudsman, Northern Ireland since 2019; former Deputy Chief Commissioner at the Equality Commission, 2015–19; associate member of the Victims' Forum and a member of the Consultative Group on the Past, 2007–9

Matt Carthy – December 2020

> Sinn Féin TD representing the Cavan/Monaghan constituency since 2020; MEP 2014–20; Sinn Féin Árd Comhairle; Sinn Féin United Ireland Strategy Group

Rose Conway-Walsh – 18 March 2021

> Sinn Féin TD representing the Mayo constituency since 2020; previously a Leader of Sinn Féin, Seanad Éireann, 2016–20

Tim Dalton – 20 May 2021

Secretary General, Dept of Justice 1993–2004; chair, Independent Commission for the Location of Victims' Remains

Mark Daly – 21 April 2021

Fianna Fáil, Cathaoirleach (presiding officer), Seanad Éireann since 2020; former chair of the Committee on the Implementation of the Good Friday Agreement

Nigel, Lord Dodds – 25 March 2021

Deputy leader of the DUP 2008–10; MP for North Belfast 2001–19; leader of the DUP in the British House of Lords

Regina Doherty – 25 March 2021

Fine Gael, member Seanad Éireann and Leader, Fine Gael, in Seanad Éireann; government Leader of Seanad Éireann since 2020

Jeffrey Donaldson – 16 December 2020

MP, leader of the DUP since June 2021; represents Lagan Valley constituency since 1997

Seán Donlon – 28 April 2021

Chair, Press Council of Ireland; former Irish ambassador to the United States; former Secretary General of the Dept of Foreign Affairs; Chancellor, University of Limerick 2002–7; special adviser to Taoiseach John Bruton 1995–7

Chris Donnelly – 27 October 2021

Former Sinn Féin election candidate; political commentator; regular columnist for the *Irish News*

Sammy Douglas – 22 April 2021

MLA for the DUP, represents Belfast East 2011–17; Belfast City Council 2022–

Mark Durkan – 14 December 2020

Leader of the SDLP 2001–10; former MP for Foyle; deputy first minister of the Northern Ireland Executive 2011–12; Minister of Finance 1998–2001; key member of SDLP's Good Friday negotiating team

Colum Eastwood – 26 January 2021

MP, leader of the SDLP since 2015; represents the Foyle constituency since 2019

Sean Farren – 28 February 2020

SDLP, Chairperson SDLP 1980–4; Minister of Higher and Further Education, Training and Employment, 1999–2000; senior member of SDLP's B/GFA negotiating team

Stephen Farry – 28 January 2021

MP, represents North Down since 2019; deputy leader Alliance Party since 2016; Minister for Employment and Learning, 2011–16

Brian Feeney – 10 March 2021

Political columnist for the *Irish News*; former SDLP councillor 1981–93; Lecturer, St Mary's University College Belfast 1979–2016; Head of History 1998–2016

Frank Feighan – 24 March 2021

Fine Gael TD, represents the Sligo-Leitrim constituency since 2020; Minister of State for Public Health, Well Being and National Drugs Strategy since 2020

John FitzGerald – 7 April 2021

Honorary Fellow and Adjunct Professor in the Department of Economics, Trinity College Dublin; formerly Research Professor in the ESRI

David Ford – 12 March 2020

Alliance Party leader 2001–16; MLA for South Antrim 1998–2018, first Northern Ireland Justice Minister 2010–16

John Garry – January 2021

Professor of Political Behaviour at Queen's University Belfast and leads the Democracy Unit, a research centre established in 2019 focusing on the study of democratic theory, institutions and behaviour

Mervyn Gibson – 17 November 2021

Presbyterian Church minister, Grand Secretary to the Orange Lodge of Ireland since 2016

Paul Gillespie – 26 March 2021

Columnist for *The Irish Times*; Adjunct Senior Research Fellow School of Politics and International Relations, University College Dublin (UCD); deputy director of UCD's Institute of British Irish Studies (IBIS)

Harold Good – 23 March 2021

Methodist Church minister, president, Methodist Church in Ireland 2001–2; one of the two independent witnesses who oversaw the decommissioning of paramilitary arms

Will Glendinning – 12 March 2021

Alliance Party, represented West Belfast in Northern Ireland Assembly 1982–6; former chief executive of the Community Relations Council 1997–2002

Paul Gosling – 16 March 2021

Freelance journalist; specializes in the economy, accountancy, co-operatives and government and the public sector

Graham Gudgin – 17 December 2020

Policy Exchange's Chief Economic Adviser; Honorary Research Associate at the Centre for Business Research (CBR) in the Judge Business School at the University of Cambridge

Colin Halliday – 18 February 2021

Former Ulster Defence Association (UDA); runs Lisburn's People's Support Project, helping former prisoners from the UDA and Ulster Freedom Fighters to reintegrate into society

Brandon Hamber – January 2021

Professor, John Hume & Thomas P. O'Neill Chair, International Conflict Research Institute (INCORE) at Ulster University in Northern Ireland

Claire Hanna – 2 December 2020

SDLP MP representing the South Belfast parliamentary constituency since 2019; previously a Belfast City Councillor 2011–15, and MLA 2015–19

Colin Harvey – 13 March 2020

Professor of Human Rights Law in the School of Law, Queen's University Belfast; Fellow, Senator George J. Mitchell Institute for Global Peace, Security and Justice

Katy Hayward – 16 February 2021

Professor of Political Sociology and Fellow of the Senator George J. Mitchell Institute for Global Peace, Security and Justice at Queen's University Belfast; Senior Fellow, UK in a Changing Europe

Chris Hazzard – 1 March 2021

Sinn Féin MP representing South Down since 2017; abstains from Westminster Parliament; member, Sinn Féin Ard Comhairle

Bronagh Hinds – 20 April 2021

Women's rights advocate from Northern Ireland; co-founder Women's Coalition; Deputy Chief Commissioner of the Equality Commission for Northern Ireland (1999–2003); participated in the B/GFA negotiations for the Women's Coalition

Chris Hudson – 12 March 2020

Unitarian minister; negotiator between the loyalist Ulster Volunteer Force (UVF) and the Irish government in the lead-up to the B/GFA

Billy Hutchinson – 9 March 2020

Leader, loyalist Progressive Unionist Party (PUP); MLA for Belfast North 1998–2003; member of Belfast City Council since 2014; ex-prisoner UVF, part of PUP's B/GFA negotiating team

Winston Irvine – 7 December 2021

Former PUP Director of Communications; founding member Loyalist Communities Council (LCC) representing UVF, UDA and Red Hand Commando

Alex Kane – 20 January 2021

Newspaper columnist and political commentator; former Press Officer for the UUP

Tom Kelly – 25 May 2021

> Adviser to the late Seamus Mallon MP 1986–9; SDLP vice chair 1987–9; Executive Director, Social Democratic Group 1989–91, Ireland Policing Board 2001–6; *Irish News* columnist 1994–present

Liam Kennedy – 14 January 2021

> Emeritus Professor of History at Queen's University Belfast; member, Royal Irish Academy

Avila Killmurray – 12 October 2021

> Founding member of the Northern Ireland Women's Coalition; member of its negotiating team for B/GFA talks

Eugen Koh – 17 December 2020; 17 January 2021

> Psychiatrist and psychoanalytic psychotherapist; Senior Fellow, Melbourne School of Population and Global Health, University of Melbourne

John Kyle – 17 February 2021

> UUP Councillor, Belfast City Council, representing East Belfast since 2007; former Interim Leader, loyalist PUP, switched to UUP in 2022

Naomi Long – 4 December 2020

> MLA, represents East Belfast since 2020; Alliance Party leader since 2016; Minister of Justice since 2020

Ben Lowry – 20 January 2021

> Editor, *News Letter*

Chris Maccabe – 12 March 2020

> Former Political Director of the Northern Ireland Office; Honorary Professor of Practice of Conflict Resolution at the Senator George J. Mitchell Institute for Global Peace, Security and Justice, Queen's University Belfast

Pádraig Mac Lochlainn – 16 March 2021

> Sinn Féin TD representing Donegal, and Sinn Féin Party Whip/Chief Whip in the Dáil since 2020.

John Manley – 12 March 2021

> Political correspondent, *The Irish News*

Martin Mansergh – 9 December 2020

> Adviser to Taoisigh Charles Haughey and Bertie Ahern; part of government's negotiating team leading up to the B/GFA and its implementation

Ian Marshall – 28 April 2021

> UUP, former Independent Ulster Unionist Senator Seanad Éireann 2018–20, the first Ulster Unionist elected to the Seanad

Rev. Dr Gary Mason – 8 December 2020

   Methodist minister, Director, 'Rethinking Conflict'

Sam McBride – 11 December 2020

   Northern Ireland editor, *Belfast Telegraph*; former Political Editor, *News Letter*

Philip McGarry – 17 December 2020

   Belfast Health and Social Care Trust consultant psychiatrist and former chair of the Alliance Party

Monica McWilliams

   Member, Independent Reporting Commission (IRC) for disbanding paramilitary organizations; co-founder Women's Coalition, led the Coalition in the B/GFA negotiations; MLA 1998–2003, Chief Commissioner of the Human Rights Commission 2005–11

Jane Morrice – 10 March 2020

   Deputy Speaker Northern Ireland Assembly 1998–2003; a founding member of the Women's Coalition

Duncan Morrow – 13 March 2020

   Professor, University of Ulster, lecturer in politics; former Chief Executive of the Northern Ireland Community Relations Council 2002–12

Michael Moynihan – 21 April 2021

   Fianna Fáil TD representing the Cork North-West constituency since 2020

Niall Murphy – 24 February 2021

   Belfast solicitor; Secretary of Ireland's Future, an NGO campaigning for a united Ireland

Dermot Nesbitt – 10 March 2020

   Election agent for Brian Faulkner 1973–7; junior minister, Office of the First Minister and deputy First Minister 1998–2002; member of the UUP's negotiating team leading to the B/GFA

Mike Nesbitt – 10 December 2020

   MLA, UUP leader 2012–17, representing Strangford constituency since 2011

Paul Nolan – 9 March 2020

   Research Director, Northern Ireland Peace Monitoring Survey

Jim O'Callaghan – 15 March 2021

   Fianna Fáil TD, Dublin Bay constituency, since 2016

Éamon Ó Cuív – 26 March 2021

   Fianna Fáil TD, Galway West constituency, since 1992; Fianna Fáil spokesperson on Regional, Rural, & Island Affairs

Seán Ó hUiginn – 21 May 2021

Head of the Anglo-Irish Division of the Irish Department of Foreign Affairs 1992–7; Second Secretary, Dept of Foreign Affairs 1995–2002; Irish ambassador to the United States 1997–2002

Brendan O'Leary – 3 May 2021

Lauder Professor of Political Science, University of Pennsylvania, and World Leading Researcher; Visiting Professor of Political Science and Mitchell Institute International Fellow at Queen's University Belfast

Matthew O'Toole – 14 May 2021

SDLP MLA representing Belfast South since 2020

Ian Paisley Jr – 16 February 2021

DUP MP representing North Antrim since 2010

Jonathan Powell – 8 December 2020

Downing Street Chief of Staff under Prime Minister Tony Blair; during Blair's time in office, Chief British negotiator on Northern Ireland

Jackie Redpath – 19 March 2021

Shankill community leader in Belfast; awarded an American Ireland Fund Leadership award in 1996, an MBE in 1997 and an Honorary Doctorate from Queen's University Belfast in 2016

Alan Renwick – 9 July 2021

Professor, Deputy Director of the Constitution Unit, University College London (UCL)

Neale Richmond – 19 February 2021

Fine Gael TD representing Dublin Rathdown since 2020; party spokesperson on European Affairs

Trevor Ringland – 17 May 2021

UK Government Special Envoy to the United States on Northern Ireland

Tom Roberts – 9 December 2021

Ex-UVF prisoner; Director of the Ex-Prisoners' Interpretive Centre since 1996

Peter Robinson – 11 March 2020

First Minister of Northern Ireland 2008–16; Leader of the DUP 2008–15

Peter Shirlow – 7 December 2020

Professor, Director, Institute of Irish Studies, University of Liverpool

Philip Smith – 19 March 2021

Ulster Unionist MLA 2016–17, member, Ards and North Down Borough Council since 2019; launched Uniting UK, a pro-union group

Niamh Smyth – 30 April 2021

Fianna Fáil TD representing Cavan-Monaghan-North Meath constituency since 2016.

Graham Spencer – 1 March 2022

Professor of Social and Political Conflict, University of Portsmouth

Sir Quentin Thomas – 29 March 2021

British civil servant who served in the Northern Ireland Office leading a team in talks leading to the B/GFA

Séanna Walsh – 20 January 2021

Sinn Féin, member of Belfast City Council since 2015, and former volunteer in the Irish Republican Army (IRA)

Jim Wells – 10 March 2020

DUP MLA representing South Down constituency 1998–2022; Minister of Health 2014–15

Sammy Wilson – 6 April 2021

DUP MP representing East Antrim constituency since 2015; Chief Whip of DUP House of Commons since 2019

Bibliography

Abernethy, S., 'Majority of Northern voters want minimal disruption to daily life', *The Irish Times*, 8 March 2019, https://www.irishtimes.com/news/politics/majority -of-northern-voters-want-minimal-disruption-to-daily-life-1.3818274 (accessed 14 June 2021).

'About CharterNI', Charter for Northern Ireland [website], 2016, http://www.charterni .org/index.html (accessed 28 June 2022).

'Age structure and sex ratio', Census of population 2016 – Profile 3 an age profile of Ireland [website], Central Statistics Office, 6 July 2017, https://www.cso.ie/en/ releasesandpublications/ep/p-cp3oy/cp3/assr/ (accessed 17 April 2020).

Agreement Between the Government of the United Kingdom of Great Britain and Northern Ireland and the Government of Ireland Establishing the Independent Commission of Information Retrieval, presented to Parliament by the Secretary of State for Foreign and Commonwealth Affairs, 13 September 2016 (Agreement not in force), https://assets.publishing.service.gov.uk/government/uploads /system/uploads/attachment_data/file/554474/Ireland_1_2016_IRC_WEB.pdf (accessed 28 June 2022).

Akenson, D.H., *Education and Enmity: The Control of Schooling in Northern Ireland, 1920–50*, Belfast, Routledge, 1973.

Akenson, D.H., *God's People: Covenant and Land in South Africa, Israel and Ulster*, Ithaca, NY, Cornell University Press, 1992.

Alderdice, Lord J., McBurney, J. and McWilliams, M., *The Fresh Start Panel Report on the Disbandment of Paramilitary Groups in Northern Ireland*. Northern Ireland Executive, 6 July 2016, https://cain.ulster.ac.uk/events/peace/stormont-agreement /2016-06-07_Fresh-Start-Panel_paramilitary-groups.pdf (accessed 28 June 2022).

Alexander, J.C., 'Toward a theory of cultural trauma', in J.C. Alexander et al. (eds), *Cultural Trauma and Collective Identity*, Berkeley, University of California Press, 2004, pp. 1–30.

Angelos, J., 'Will Brexit bring the Troubles back to Northern Ireland?', *New York Times Magazine*, 30 December 2019, https://www.nytimes.com/2019/12/30/magazine /brexit-northern-ireland.html (accessed 12 October 2020).

Archer, B., 'United Ireland would cost up to €30 billion a year and "collapse North's economy"', Belfast, *The Irish News,* 17 September 2019, https://www.irishnews .com/news/northernirelandnews/2019/09/17/news/united-ireland-would-cost -up-to-30-billion-a-year-and-collapse-north-s-economy--1714127/ (accessed 9 December 2021).

ARK, *Northern Ireland Social Attitudes Survey, 1989*, Surveys Online, ARK [website], www.ark.ac.uk/nilt, 16 March 2004, https://www.ark.ac.uk/sol/surveys/gen _social_att/nisa/1989/website/Political_Attitudes/NIRELAND.html (accessed 21 February 2022).

ARK, *Northern Ireland Life and Times Survey, 2019*, 'Political Attitudes Module', ARK [website], www.ark.ac.uk/nilt, 16 June 2020, https://www.ark.ac.uk/nilt/2019/ Political_Attitudes/VIEWGFA2.html (accessed 21 February 2022).

'Arrests follow probes into loyalist paramilitary activity in Belfast and North Antrim', *The Irish News*, 20 August 2021, https://www.irishnews.com/news/northernireland news/2021/08/20/news/arrests-follow-probes-into-loyalist-paramilitary-activity -in-belfast-and-north-antrim-2423232/ (accessed 8 November 2021).

Aughey, A., *Under Siege: Ulster Unionism and the Anglo-Irish Agreement*, London, Hurst, 1989.

Aughey, A., *The Politics of Northern Ireland: Beyond the Belfast Agreement*, Abington, UK, Routledge, 2005.

Bain, M., 'Catholics to be majority of workforce in Northern Ireland for first time in 2020, new figures suggest', *Belfast Telegraph*, 7 February 2019, https:// www.belfasttelegraph.co.uk/news/northern-ireland/catholics-to-be-majority -of-workforce-in-northern-ireland-for-first-time-in-2020-new-figures-suggest -37790936.html (accessed 23 March 2021).

Baker, P., 'A 65% to 17% majority for Northern Ireland remaining in the UK sug-gests little room for doubt', *Slugger O'Toole* [website], 5 February 2013, https:// sluggerotoole.com/2013/02/05/a-65-to-17-majority-for-northern-ireland -remaining-in-the-uk-suggests-little-room-for-doubt/ (accessed 12 October 2020).

Bardon, J., *A History of Ulster,* rev. edn, Newtownards, UK, Blackstaff Press, 2005.

Bardon, J., *The Plantation of Ulster*, Dublin, Gill Books, 2012.

Bardon, S., 'Sinn Féin to campaign against Brexit', *The Irish Times*, 24 December 2015, https://www.irishtimes.com/news/politics/sinn-f%C3%A9in-to-campaign -against-brexit-in-eu-referendum-1.2476720 (accessed 30 September 2020).

Barnes, C., 'Spooks spend two nights hunting for New IRA bomb in North Belfast', *Belfast Telegraph*, 25 October 2020, https://www.belfasttelegraph.co.uk/sunday-life/news/spooks-spend-two-nights-hunting-for-new-ira-bomb-in-north-belfast-39663393.html (accessed 28 March 2021).

Beck, U., *Risk Society: Towards a New Modernity*, London, SAGE Publications, Ltd, July 1992.

Beckett, J.C., *A Short History of Ireland: From Earliest Times to the Present Day*, 6th. ed., London, Hutchinson, 1979.

Beckett, J.C., *The Making of Modern Ireland 1603–1923*, London, Faber and Faber, 2014.

'The Belfast Agreement: An agreement reached at the multi-party talks on Northern Ireland', April 1998, https://assets.publishing.service.gov.uk /government /uploads/system/uploads/attachment_data/file/1034123/The_Belfast_Agreement _An_Agreement_Reached_at_the_Multi-Party_Talks_on_Northern_Ireland.pdf (accessed 23 March 2021).

Betts, J. and Thompson, J., *Mental Health in Northern Ireland: Overview, Strategies, Policies, Care Pathways, CAMHS and Barriers to Accessing Services*, Northern Ireland Assembly Research and Information Service Research Paper, Paper 08/17, 24 January 2017, http://www.niassembly.gov.uk/globalassets/documents /raise/publications/2016-2021/2017/health/0817.pdf (accessed 23 March 2021).

Bew, P., Gibbon, P. and Patterson, H., *Northern Ireland, 1921–2001: Political Forces and Social Classes*, rev. edn, London, Serif, 2002.

Bishop, P. and Mallie, E., *The Provisional IRA*, London, Heinemann, 1987.

Black, L.A., *Suicide: Northern Ireland*, Northern Ireland Assembly Research and Information Service Research Paper, Paper 23/21, 14 April 2021, http://www .niassembly.gov.uk/globalassets/documents/raise/publications/2017-2022/2021 /health/2321.pdf (accessed 25 March 2021).

Blake, L., 'Beyond the binary: What might a multiple-choice EU referendum have looked like?', Democratic Audit [website], 16 July 2018, http://www.democratic audit.com/2016/11/11/beyond-the-binary-what-might-a-multiple-choice-eu -referendum-have-looked-like/ (accessed 13 November 2020).

'Bloody Sunday paratrooper Soldier N dies', London, BBC News, 5 January 2019, https://www.bbc.com/news/uk-northern-ireland-46995647 (accessed 12 February 2021).

Bolton, D., *Conflict, Peace and Mental Health: Addressing the Consequences of Conflict and Trauma in Northern Ireland*, Manchester, UK, Manchester University Press, 2017.

'Border poll survey says 8/10 voters unchanged by Brexit', BBC News, 8 September 2016, https://www.bbc.com/news/uk-northern-ireland-37309706 (accessed 3 August 2021).

'Boris Johnson likens Irish border challenge to congestion charge', BBC News, 27 February 2018, https://www.bbc.com/news/uk-politics-43210156 (accessed 28 March 2021).

Bowcott, O., 'Bill sets five-year limit to prosecute UK armed forces who served abroad', *The Guardian*, 17 March 2020, https://www.theguardian.com/uk-news /2020/mar/18/bill-sets-five-year-limit-to-sue-uk-military-veterans-who-served -abroad (accessed 17 October 2021).

Bowman, J., *De Valera and the Ulster Question: 1917–1973*, Oxford, Oxford University Press, 1990.

Breen, S., 'Just 29% in Northern Ireland would vote for unity, major study reveals', *Belfast Telegraph*, 18 February 2020, https://www.belfasttelegraph.co.uk/news /northern-ireland/just-29-in-northern-ireland-would-vote-for-unity-major -study-reveals-38966196.html (accessed 7 May 2021).

Breen, S., 'Northern Ireland public became more polarised in the run-up to Brexit: Research', *Belfast Telegraph*, 17 June 2020, https://www.belfasttelegraph.co.uk /news/northern-ireland/northern-ireland-public-became-more-polarised-in -the-run-up-to-brexit-research-39291878.html (accessed 7 May 2021).

Breen, S., 'How teaching in Northern Ireland schools divides on "conflict lines"', *Belfast Telegraph*, 15 July 2020, https://www.belfasttelegraph.co.uk/news/education /how-teaching-in-ni-schools-divides-on-conflict-lines-39368683.html (accessed 3 May 2021).

Breen, S., 'Sinn Féin: Nationalists are ignored and excluded in Northern Ireland', *Belfast Telegraph*, 22 March 2021, https://www.belfasttelegraph.co.uk/news /politics/sinn-fein-nationalists-are-ignored-and-excluded-in-northern-ireland -40228119.html (accessed 7 May 2021).

'Brexit: Leo Varadkar warns of Brexit deal "miscalculation"', BBC News, 11 June 2019, https://www.bbc.com/news/world-europe-48602072 (accessed 1 March 2021).

British Council Northern Ireland, *Britain and Ireland: Lives Entwined IV Shifting Borders*, Belfast, British Council, 2014, https://nireland.britishcouncil.org/sites /default/files/britain_and_ireland_-_lives_entwined_iv.pdf (accessed 7 May 2021).

Bruce, S., *God Save Ulster! The Religion and Politics of Paisleyism*, Oxford, Oxford University Press, 1987.

Buckland, P., *The Factory of Grievances: Devolved Government in Northern Ireland 1921–39*, Dublin, Gill & Macmillan, 1979.

Buckland, P., *A History of Northern Ireland*, Dublin, Gill & Macmillan, 1981.

Bunting, B. et al., 'Troubled consequences: A report on the mental health impact of the civil conflict in Northern Ireland', prepared for Commission for Victims and Survivors, Belfast, Bamford Centre for Mental Health and Wellbeing, University of Ulster, in partnership with the Northern Ireland Centre for

Trauma and Transformation and Compass, October 2011, https://www.cvsni
.org/media/1435/troubled-consequences-october-2011.pdf (accessed 23 March
2021).

Burdeau, C., 'Will Northern Ireland's "peace walls" ever come down?', *Courthouse
News Service*, 28 June 2019, https://www.courthousenews.com/will-northern-
irelands-peace-walls-ever-come-down/ (accessed 24 August 2020).

Cadwallader, A., *Lethal Allies: British Collusion in Ireland*, Cork, Mercier, 2013.

Campbell, C., 'Government challenged to take action over scale of paramilitary
activity in Northern Ireland', *The Detail*, 29 April 2016, https://www.thedetail
.tv/articles/hundreds-still-being-victimised-by-paramilitaries-each-year
(accessed 16 June 2020).

Campbell, J., 'NI–ROI economic links to be examined by think tank project', BBC
News, 16 November 2021, https://www.bbc.com/news/uk-northern-ireland
-59310318 (accessed 17 January 2022).

Carswell, S., 'Why are Fine Gael and Fianna Fáil refusing to go into coalition with
Sinn Féin?', *The Irish Times*, 26 January 2020, https://www.irishtimes.com
/news/politics/why-are-fine-gael-and-fianna-f%25C3%25A1il-refusing-to-go
-into-coalition-with-sinn-f%25C3%25A9in-1.4151911 (accessed 28 March 2021).

Cassidy, J., 'Seven jailed over MI5 bugging operation targeting continuity IRA',
Belfast Telegraph, 13 November 2020, https://www.belfasttelegraph.co.uk/news
/courts/seven-jailed-over-mi5-bugging-operation-targeting-continuity-ira
-39743872.html (accessed 23 March 2021).

Chua, A., *Political Tribes: Group Instinct and the Fate of Nations*, New York, Penguin
Books, 2019.

Chua, A. and Rubenfeld, J., *The Triple Package*, New York, Penguin Books, 2015.

Clarke, A., 'The colonisation of Ulster and the rebellion of 1641', in T.W. Moody and
F.X. Martin (eds), *The Course of Irish History*, 4th edn, Boulder, CO, Roberts
Rinehart, 2001.

Clarke, L., 'Survey: Most Northern Ireland Catholics want to remain in UK', *Belfast
Telegraph*, 17 June 2011, https://www.belfasttelegraph.co.uk/news/politics/survey
-most-northern-ireland-catholics-want-to-remain-in-uk-28628245.html (accessed
12 October 2020).

Coakley, J., 'Choosing between unions? Unionist opinion and the challenge of
Brexit', *Irish Political Studies*, vol. 35, no. 3, 2020, pp. 356–77, https://doi.org
/10.1080/07907184.2020.1816375 (accessed 15 January 2021).

Coakley, J. and Todd, J., *Negotiating a Settlement in Northern Ireland, 1969–2019*,
Oxford, Oxford University Press, 2020.

Cochrane, F., *Unionist Politics and the Politics of Unionism,* rev. edn, Cork, Ireland,
Cork University Press, 2001.

Cochrane, F., *Northern Ireland: The Reluctant Peace*, New Haven, CT, Yale University Press, 2013.

Connelly, T., *Brexit and Ireland: The Dangers, the Opportunities, and the Inside Story of the Irish Response*, Dublin, Penguin Ireland, 2017.

Connelly, T., 'Theresa May: How strategic mistakes and the Irish question brought her down', RTÉ News, 25 May 2019, https://www.rte.ie/news/analysis-and -comment/2019/0525/1051593-theresa-may-brexit/ (accessed 5 June 2021).

Connelly, T., 'EU report highlights Brexit effect on north–south cooperation', RTÉ News, 20 June 2019, https://www.rte.ie/news/ireland/2019/0619/1056392-eu -commission-paper-on-north-south-cooperation/ (accessed 23 March 2021).

Conroy, J., 'Kneecapping', updated, Washington, DC, The Alicia Patterson Foundation, 1 April 2011, https://aliciapatterson.org/stories/kneecapping (accessed 13 November 2020).

Corcoran, J., 'United Ireland poll: Two thirds say united Ireland vote risks return to violence', Independent.ie, 2 May 2021, https://www.independent.ie/irish-news/cen -tenaries/centenarypoll/poll-two-thirds-say-united-ireland-vote-risks-return -to-violence-40378476.html (accessed 19 July 2021).

'Cross border poll April 2021', Kantar Public UK Polling Archive [website], Kantar, https://www.kantar.com/expertise/policy-society/kantar-public-uk-polling -archive (accessed 21 February 2022).

Cunningham, K.G., *Inside the Politics of Self-Determination*, Oxford, Oxford University Press, 2014.

D'Alton, I. and Milne, I., *Protestant and Irish: The Minority's Search for Place in Northern Ireland*, Cork, Ireland, Cork University Press, 2019.

Dalby, D., 'Prison officer wounded in Northern Ireland attack dies', *New York Times*, 15 March 2016, https://www.nytimes.com/2016/03/16/world/europe/prison -officer-bombing-northern-ireland.html (accessed 17 October 2021).

Daly, M., Dolan, P. and Brennan, M., 'Northern Ireland returning to violence as a result of a hard border due to Brexit or a rushed border poll: Risk to youth', UNESCO, Dublin, Office of Senator Mark Daly, 18 February 2019, https:// www.senatormarkdaly.ie/uploads/1/3/5/6/135670409/unesco-professors -report-on-return-to-violence.pdf (accessed 18 August 2020).

Daly, M.E. (ed.), *Brokering the Good Friday Agreement: The Untold Story*, Dublin, Royal Irish Academy, 2009.

Daly, M.E., 'Brexit and the Irish border: Historical context', a Royal Irish Academy-British Academy Brexit Briefing, Dublin and London, the Royal Irish Academy and the British Academy, October 2017, https://www.thebritishacademy.ac.uk/ documents/321/brexit-and-irish-border-historical-context.pdf (accessed 23 March 2021).

Darby, J., *Scorpions in a Bottle: Conflicting Cultures in Northern Ireland*, London, Minority Rights Group, 1997.

'David Black murder "meticulously planned"', BBC News, 23 May 2018, https://www.bbc.com/news/uk-northern-ireland-44228059 (accessed 17 October 2021).

Davis, E.E. and Sinnott, R., 'Attitudes in the Republic of Ireland relevant to the Northern Ireland problem: Vol. 1 Descriptive analysis and some comparisons with attitudes in Northern Ireland and Great Britain', [Report], ESRI, 1979, General Research Series, 97', [Report], ESRI, 1979, General Research Series, 97, September 1979, http://hdl.handle.net/2262/84097 (accessed 23 March 2021).

'A decade of opportunity – towards the new republic', Sinn Féin [website], https://www.sinnfein.ie/irish-unity.

Dempster, S., 'Loyalist paramilitary groups in NI "have 12,500 members"', BBC News, *NI Spotlight*, London, 2 December 2020, https://www.bbc.com/news/uk-northern-ireland-55151249 (accessed 6 October 2021).

Dialogue for Peaceful Change, *Navigating Conflict and Change: DPC Handbook Part I*, 2019.

Dillon, M., *Catholic Identity: Balancing Reason, Faith, and Power*, Cambridge, UK, Cambridge University Press, 1999.

'Dissident group Óglaigh na hÉireann calls ceasefire', BBC News, 23 January 2018, https://www.bbc.com/news/uk-northern-ireland-42786530 (accessed 30 September 2020).

Dixon, P., *Northern Ireland: The Politics of War and Peace*, London, Palgrave Macmillan, 2001.

Donaghy, P., 'Northern Ireland life and times survey suggests slight increase in support for Irish unity and cross-community support for abortion reform', *Slugger O'Toole* [website], 16 June 2017, https://sluggerotoole.com/2017/06/16/northern-ireland-life-and-times-survey-suggests-slight-increase-in-support-for-irish-unity-and-cross-community-support-for-abortion-reform/ (accessed 12 October 2020).

Donnelly, C., 'Dublin has been socially distancing from the North long before coronavirus', *The Irish News*, 11 May 2020, https://www.irishnews.com/opinion/columnists/2020/05/11/news/chris-donnelly-dublin-has-been-socially-distancing-from-the-north-long-before-coronavirus-1931829/content.html (accessed 7 November 2020).

Dooley, T., *The Plight of Monaghan Protestants, 1912–1926*, Dublin, Irish Academic Press, 2000.

Dorney, J., 'Casualties of the Irish civil war in Dublin', *The Irish Story* [website], September 2016, https://www.theirishstory.com/2012/06/19/casualties-of-the-irish-civil-war-in-dublin/#.YMYwCflKjD6 (accessed 20 February 2022).

Dorr, N., *Sunningdale: The Search for Peace in Northern Ireland*, Dublin, Royal Irish Academy, 2017.

Downing, J., 'How much longer must this foostering over Sinn Féin and its IRA links go on?', *Independent.ie*, 24 December 2015, https://www.independent.ie /irish-news/politics/how-much-longer-must-this-foostering-over-sinn-fein-and -its-ira-links-go-on--34312459.html (accessed 17 October 2021).

'The Downing Street Declaration', 15 December 1993, https://www.dfa.ie/media/dfa /alldfawebsitemedia/ourrolesandpolicies/northernireland/peace-process --joint-declaration-1993.pdf (accessed 23 March 2021).

Doyle, J., 'UK subvention to North irrelevant to debate on Irish unity', *The Irish Times*, 9 June 2021, https://www.irishtimes.com/opinion/uk-subvention-to-north -irrelevant-to-debate-on-irish-unity-1.4587773 (accessed on 19 July 2021).

Doyle, J., 'Reflecting on the Northern Ireland conflict and peace process: 20 years since the Good Friday Agreement', *Irish Studies in International Affairs*, Royal Irish Academy, vol. 29, pp. 1–16, https://doi.org/10.3318/irisstudinteaffa .2018.0001, 3 August 2021.

'DUP seek victim definition change', BBC News, 5 August 2019, http://news.bbc.co .uk/2/hi/uk_news/northern_ireland/8256468.stm (accessed 13 November 2020).

'DUP–Tory deal secures extra spending in Northern Ireland', BBC News, 26 June 2017, https://www.bbc.com/news/uk-northern-ireland-40402352 (accessed 28 March 2021).

Earley, K., 'Belfast ranks strongly against UK cities for tech jobs and workforce', *Silicon Republic* [website], 8 September 2020, https://www.siliconrepublic.com/ careers/belfast-jobs-employers-workforce-tech-nation-uk-report (accessed 1 December 2021).

Economic Benefits of a United Ireland, Discussion Document, Sinn Féin, November 2020, https://www.sinnfein.ie/files/2020/Economic_Benefits_of_a_United_Ireland .pdf (accessed 23 March 2021).

Edwards, A., *UVF: Behind the Mask*, Newbridge, Ireland, Merrion Press, 2017.

Elliot, S. and Flackes, W.D., 'Systems of government, 1968–1999', in *Conflict in Northern Ireland: An Encyclopaedia*, Newtownards, UK, Blackstaff Press, 1999, https://cain.ulster.ac.uk/issues/politics/elliott99.htm#systems (accessed 23 March 2021).

Elliott, M., *The Catholics of Ulster*, London, Penguin Books, 2001.

Elliott, M., *When God Took Sides*, Oxford, Oxford University Press, 2009.

'EU referendum: Arlene Foster says Brexit vote offers "opportunities"', BBC News, 27 June 2016, https://www.bbc.com/news/uk-northern-ireland-36635182 (accessed 18 February, 2021).

'EU referendum: More UUP councillors backing Brexit', *News Letter*, 21 June 2016, https://www.newsletter.co.uk/news/eu-referendum-more-uup-councillors-backing-brexit-1228480 (accessed 18 February 2021).

Executive, NI, labour force survey religion report 2017 [website], Belfast, 31 January 2019, https://www.executiveoffice-ni.gov.uk/publications/labour-force-survey-religion-report-2017 (accessed 28 June 2022).

'Executive summary – the Ireland/Northern Ireland Protocol: Consensus or conflict?', The Ireland/Northern Ireland Protocol: Consensus or Conflict? [website], University of Liverpool, https://www.liverpool.ac.uk/humanities-and-social-sciences/research/projects/ni-protocol-consensus-or-conflict/, October 2021, https://www.liverpool.ac.uk/media/livacuk/humanitiesampsocialsciences/documents/The,Ireland-Northern,Ireland,Protocol,Consensus,or,Conflict,v3.pdf (accessed February 9, 2022).

Eyerman, R., *Cultural Trauma* (Cambridge Cultural Social Studies), Cambridge, UK, Cambridge University Press, 2001.

Farrell, M., 'Fine Gael and Fianna Fáil: "Civil war" parties?', *The Irish Story* [website], 26 May 2020, https://www.theirishstory.com/2020/05/26/fine-gael-and-fianna-fail-civil-war-parties (accessed 4 September 2021).

Fay, M.T., et al., *The Cost of the Troubles Study: Report on the Northern Ireland Survey: The Experience and Impact of the Troubles*, 2nd edn, Derry/Londonderry, INCORE/University of Ulster and United Nations University, 1999.

Feenan, D., 'Justice in conflict: Paramilitary punishment in Ireland (North)', *International Journal of the Sociology of Law*, vol. 30, 2002, pp. 151–72.

Feeney, B., *Sinn Féin: A Hundred Turbulent Years*, Madison, WI, University of Wisconsin Press, 2003.

Ferguson, N., Burgess, M. and Hollywood, I., 'Who are the victims? Victimhood experiences in postagreement Northern Ireland', *Political Psychology*, vol. 31, no. 6, 2010, Limerick, University of Limerick, and Wellington, Massey University, International Society of Political Psychology (ISSP), 15 November 2010, pp. 881–2, doi/10.1111/j.1467-9221.2010.00791 (accessed 23 March 2021).

Ferriter, D., *Ambiguous Republic: Ireland in the 1970s*, London, Profile Books, 1 January 2012.

Ferriter, D., *The Border: The Legacy of a Century of Anglo-Irish Politics*, London, Profile Books, 2019.

Finn, C., 'Mary Lou McDonald: The idea of Ireland rejoining the Commonwealth needs to be discussed', *TheJournal.ie*, 11 August 2018, https://www.thejournal.ie/ireland-rejoining-the-commonwealth-4174082-Aug2018/ (accessed 3 November 2021).

Finn, C., 'Mary Lou McDonald says Michelle O'Neill does not need to stand aside over attendance at Bobby Storey funeral', *TheJournal.ie*, 2 July 2020, https://www.thejournal.ie/dup-michelle-oneill-bobby-storey-funeral-5139268-Jul2020/ (accessed 3 November 2021).

'First major post-Brexit survey shows no surge in support for Irish unity', *News Letter*, 19 June 2017, https://www.newsletter.co.uk/news/first-major-post-brex-it-survey-shows-no-surge-support-irish-unity-1110344 (7 May 2021).

Fitzmaurice, M., 'Integrated education poll finds 71% believe children should be taught together', *Belfast Live*, 3 August 2021, https://www.belfastlive.co.uk/news/belfast-news/integrated-education-poll-finds-71-21207568 (accessed 3 November 2021).

Foster, J.W. and Smith, W.B. (eds), *The Idea of the Union: Great Britain and Northern Ireland*, Belfast, Belcouver Press, 2021.

Foster, R.F., *Modern Ireland 1600–1972*, London, Penguin Books, 1990.

Foster, R.F., *Luck and the Irish: A Brief History of Change from 1970*, Oxford, Oxford University Press, 2008.

Gallagher, T., 'Identities in Northern Ireland: Nothing but the same old stories?', in M. Crozier and R. Froggatt (eds), *What Made Now in Northern Ireland*, Belfast, Northern Ireland Community Relations Council, 2008, https://www.community-relations.org.uk/sites/crc/files/media-files/What%20made%20now%20in%20Northern%20Ireland.pdf (accessed 23 March 2021).

Gallagher, T., 'New Decade New Approach. What's in it for education?', *Pivotal Blog* [blog], Pivotal Public Policy Forum, 29 January 2020, https://www.pivotalppf.org/cmsfiles/NewsEvents/Pivotal_BLOG_TG-29012020.pdf (accessed 3 May 2021).

Garry, J., 'The EU referendum vote in Northern Ireland: Implications for our understanding of citizens' political views and behaviour', *Northern Ireland Assembly Knowledge Exchange Seminar Series 2016–17*, Northern Ireland Assembly, 2016, https://www.qub.ac.uk/brexit/Brexitfilestore/Filetoupload,728121,en.pdf (accessed 23 March 2021).

Garry, J., McNicholl, K., O'Leary, B. and Pow, J., *Northern Ireland the UK's Exit From the EU: What Do People Think?*, London, UK in a Changing Europe, 2018, https://ukandeu.ac.uk/partner-reports/northern-ireland-and-the-uks-exit-from-the-eu-what-do-people-think/ (accessed 23 March 2021).

General Election Survey, *Northern Ireland General Election Survey 2019*, University of Liverpool, March 2020, https://www.liverpool.ac.uk/humanities-and-social-sciences/research/research-themes/transforming-conflict/ni-election-survey-19/ (accessed 2 February 2022).

Geoghagen, P., 'Legacy of the troubles still haunts Northern Ireland', *Politico EU*, 30 March 2018, https://www.politico.eu/article/northern-ireland-troubles-legacy-good-friday-agreement/ (accessed 8 November 2021).

Gibson, J., 'Overcoming apartheid: Can truth reconcile a divided nation?', *The Annals of the American Academy of Political and Social Science*, vol. 603, no. 1, 1 January 2006, pp. 82–110, https://doi.org/10.1177/0002716205282895.

Gillespie, P., 'Brexit impact on Northern Ireland not as big as we think', *The Irish Times*, 29 February 2020, https://www.irishtimes.com/opinion/brexit-impact-on-northern-ireland-not-as-big-as-we-think-1.4188055 (accessed 6 January 2022).

'Giving workers and families a break: A manifesto for change', Sinn Féin General Election Manifesto [website], https://www.sinnfein.ie/files/2020/Giving_Workers_and_Families_a_Break_-_A_Manifesto_for_Change.pdf (accessed 15 February 2022).

Gladwell, M., *The Tipping Point: How Little Things Can Make a Big Difference*, New York, Back Bay Books, 2002.

Gorvett, J., 'Northern Ireland is a culture war. Brexit is making it worse', *Foreign Policy*, 31 January 2020, https://foreignpolicy.com/2020/01/31/northern-ireland-culture-war-brexit/ (accessed 23 March 2021).

Gosling, P., *Lessons From the Troubles and the Unsettled Peace: Ideas From the Forward Together Podcasts*, Derry/Londonderry, UK, Holywell Trust, 2020.

Gosling, P., *A New Ireland, A New Union: A New Society*, Antrim, UK, W&G Baird, 2020.

Gosling, P., 'A 10 year programme for a new Ireland "makes sense"', *The Detail*, 26 February 2020, https://thedetail.tv/articles/new-ireland (accessed 23 March 2021).

Gosling, P., '"There is something seriously and fundamentally wrong" – Northern Ireland's housing crisis', *Slugger O'Toole* [website], 15 June 2020, http://www.Sluggerotoole.com/2020/06/15/there-is-something-seriously-and-fundamentally-wrong-northern-irelands-housing-crisis/ (accessed 18 November 2020).

Gray, A.M., et al., *Northern Ireland Peace Monitoring Report Number 5*, Community Relations Council, Ulster University, October 2018, https://pure.ulster.ac.uk/ws/portalfiles/portal/71270326/NIPMR_5.pdf (accessed 28 June 2022).

Gray, J., 'Govt publishes troubles pension eligibility guidance', *PensionsAge*, 14 August 2020, https://www.pensionsage.com/pa/govt-publishes-Troubles-pension-eligibility-guidance.php (accessed 3 April 2021).

Green, J. and Yeates, P., 'Written evidence proposing a conditional amnesty', Submitted to House of Commons Select Committee on Northern Ireland (LEG0009), UK Parliament, 28 May 2020, https://committees.parliament.uk/writtenevidence/5708/pdf/ (accessed 13 November 2020).

Gudgin, G., 'Discrimination in housing and employment under the Stormont administration', in Roche, P.J. and Barton, B. (eds), *The Northern Ireland Question: Nationalism, Unionism, and Partition*, Aldershot, UK, Ashgate Publishing, 1999, https://cain.ulster.ac.uk/issues/discrimination/gudgin99.htm (accessed 23 March 2021).

Guelke, A., *Northern Ireland: The International Perspective*, Dublin, Gill & Macmillan, 1988.

Guelke, A., *Politics in Deeply Divided Societies*, Cambridge, UK, Polity Press, 2012.

'Half of UK families £110 worse off a year since general election, while richest 5% are better off by £3,300', New Economics Foundation [press release], 13 December 2021, https://neweconomics.org/2021/12/half-of-uk-families-110-worse-off-a-year-since -general-election-while-richest-5-are-better-off-by-3-300 (accessed 21 February 2022).

Halliday, G., '250 bands apply to parade over twelfth in wake of row', *Belfast Telegraph*, 7 July 2020, https://www.belfasttelegraph.co.uk/news/twelfth/250-bands -apply-to-parade-over-twelfth-in-wake-of-row-39345787.html (accessed 9 December 2021).

Halpin, H., '51% of people in Northern Ireland support Irish unification, new poll finds', *TheJournal.ie*, 11 September 2019, https://www.thejournal.ie/lord-ashcroft -irish-unification-poll-4804372-Sep2019/ (accessed 8 November 2021).

Hamber, B., 'Moment of truth … victims of Northern Ireland's troubled past can't wait forever', *Medium* [blog], 13 December 2020, https://brandonhamber .medium.com/moment-of-truth-victims-of-northern-irelands-troubled-past -can-t-wait-forever-107a061f199c (accessed 9 December 2021).

Hamber, B., 'It's time we stopped kidding ourselves: "New normal" is abnormal', *Belfast Telegraph*, 22 March 2021, https://www.belfasttelegraph.co.uk/life/features /its-time-we-stopped-kidding-ourselves-new-normal-is-abnormal-40222732.html (accessed 9 December 2021).

Hannum, H., *Autonomy, Sovereignty and Self-Determination*, rev. edn, Philadelphia, PA, University of Pennsylvania Press, 1996.

Haverty, D., 'Paramilitaries are surging again in Northern Ireland', *Foreign Policy*, 24 May 2019, https://foreignpolicy.com/2019/05/24/paramilitaries-are-surging -again-in-northern-ireland/ (accessed 6 October 2021).

Hayes, B.C. and McAllister, I., 'Sowing dragon's teeth: Public support for political violence and paramilitarism in Northern Ireland', *Political Studies*, vol. 49, no. 1, 2001, 901–22, https://doi.org/10.1111%2F1467-9248.00346 (accessed 23 March 2021).

Hayward, K., 'Articles by Professor Katy Hayward', UK in a Changing Europe [website], https://ukandeu.ac.uk/author/khayward/.

Hayward, K., *Irish Nationalism and European Integration: The Official Redefinition of the Island of Ireland*, Manchester, UK, Manchester University Press, 2009.

Hayward, K., *Brexit at the Border: Voices of Local Communities in the Central Border Region of Ireland / Northern Ireland,* Belfast, Irish Central Border Network and Queen's University, 15 June 2018.

Hayward, K., 'Life and work across the Irish Border through Brexit', *Annales des Mines*, 2020, pp. 101–5, https://www.annales.org/ri/2020/ri-aout-2020.pdf (accessed 4 September 2021).

Hayward, K., 'Northern Ireland', in Menon, A. (ed.), *Brexit: What Next?* King's College, London, UK in a Changing Europe Initiative, Economic and Social Research Council (ESRC), February 2020, https://ukandeu.ac.uk/wp-content/uploads/2020/02/Brexit-what-next-report.pdf (accessed 23 March 2021).

Hayward, K., and Rosher, B., 'Political attitudes at a time of flux', Research Update 133, *Northern Ireland Life and Times Study, 2019*, ARK [website], www.ark.ac.uk/nilt, June 2020, https://www.ark.ac.uk/ARK/sites/default/files/2020-06/update133.pdf (accessed 28 June 2022).

Hayward, K. and Rosher, B., 'Political attitudes in Northern Ireland in a period of transition', Research Update 142, *Northern Ireland Life and Times Study, 2020*, ARK [website], www.ark.ac.uk/nilt, June 2021, https://www.ark.ac.uk/ARK/sites/default/files/2021-06/update142.pdf (accessed 28 June 2022).

Hedges, J., '"Unionists have nothing to fear" – *An Phoblacht* article welcomed by unionists. Responses to Declan Kearney's "uncomfortable conversations"', *An Phoblacht*, 2 April 2012, https://anphoblacht.com/contents/1390 (accessed 7 July 2021).

Henderson, D. and Little, I. (eds), *Reporting the Troubles*, Newtownards, UK, Blackstaff Press, 2018.

Hennessey, T., *The Northern Ireland Peace Process: Ending the Troubles*, Dublin, Gill & Macmillan, 2000.

Hennessey, T., Braniff, M., McAuley, J., Tonge, J. and Whiting, S., *The Ulster Unionist Party: Country Before Party?* Oxford, Oxford University Press, March 2019.

Herman, J., *Trauma and Recovery: The Aftermath of Abuse – From Domestic Abuse to Political Terror*, New York, Basic Books, 1997.

Hewitt, R., 'Hunger strike by jailed dissident republicans comes to an end', *Belfast Telegraph*, 30 September 2020, https://www.belfasttelegraph.co.uk/news/northern-ireland/hunger-strike-by-jailed-dissident-republicans-comes-to-an-end-39573760.html (accessed 16 January 2021).

'Higher education statistical fact sheet 1 – Higher education age participation index for Northern Ireland, 1994/95 to 2017/18', Department for the Economy, Belfast, https://assets.publishing.service.gov.uk/government/uploads/system/uploads/attachment_data/file/812588/DfE_Higer_Education_Statistical_fact_sheets_1718.pdf, Department for the Economy Higher Education Statistical Fact Sheets [website], https://www.economy-ni.gov.uk/articles/higher-education-statistical-fact-sheets (accessed 9 February 2022).

Historians and the Stormont Agreement – Report on a Workshop Held at Hertford College, 19 October 2016, https://irishhistoriansinbritain.org/?p=321, Historians and the Stormont Agreement [website], https://irishhistoriansinbritain.org/?cat=5 (accessed 28 March 2021).

Hosford, P., 'Third of voters would support Sinn Féin in election, poll finds', *Irish Examiner*, 24 October 2021, https://www.irishexaminer.com/news/politics/arid -40728522.html (accessed 24 January 2022).

Hughes, C., '"The war is over" – Sinn Féin backlash as Mary Lou McDonald says the IRA has gone away', *Extra.ie*, 22 February 2020, https://extra.ie/2020/02/22 /news/politics/sinn-fein-ira-mary-lou (accessed 27 August 2021).

Humphreys, R., *Beyond the Border: The Good Friday Agreement and Irish Unity After Brexit*, Dublin, Irish Academic Press, 2018.

Humphries, C., 'Northern Ireland fears Brexit loss of EU peacemaking and cash', Reuters, 13 September 2017, https://www.reuters.com/article/us-britain-nireland -funding/northern-ireland-fears-brexit-loss-of-eu-peacemaking-and-cash -idUSKCN1BO0WB (accessed 3 April 2021).

'In full: Theresa May's Conservative conference speech 2017', BBC News, 4 October 2017, https://www.bbc.com/news/av/uk-politics-41503214 (accessed 3 April 2021).

Inclusion and Reconciliation in a New Ireland, Sinn Féin, November 2019, https:// www.liverpool.ac.uk/media/livacuk/irish-studies/civicspace/Inclusion,and ,Reconciliation,in,a,New,Ireland.pdf (accessed 28 June 2022).

Independent Reporting Commission [website], https://www.ircommission.org/ publications, *Second Report of the Independent Reporting Commission*, 4 November 2019, https://www.ircommission.org/sites/irc/files/media-files/IRC%20 -%202nd%20Report%202019_0.pdf.

Ingoldsby, S., 'Legacy issues not a priority for people north or south of the border', *The Detail*, 25 February 2020, https://thedetail.tv/articles/legacy-issues-not-a -priority-for-people-north-or-south-of-the-border (accessed 5 June 2021).

Ingoldsby, S., 'While Brexit is a threat to the Good Friday Agreement "it can be managed"', *The Detail*, 28 February 2020, https://thedetail.tv/articles/while -brexit-is-a-threat-to-the-good-friday-agreement-it-can-be-managed (accessed 5 June 2021).

International Foundation for Election Systems (IFES), 'IFES election guide: Country profile: Northern Ireland', *ElectionGuide: Democracy Assistance and Election News*, IFES, Arlington, Virginia, https://www.electionguide.org/countries/id/251/ (accessed 2 February 2022).

'Is the UK heading for break-up?', FT Series, *Financial Times*, 2–6 April 2021, https:// www.ft.com/content/0d2ffa65-08cf-4d98-ad26-fofedadbd6b1 (accessed 19 August 2021).

Ivory, G., 'The meaning of republicanism in contemporary Ireland', in I. Honohan (ed.), *Republicanism in Ireland: Confronting Theory and Practice*, Manchester, UK, Manchester University Press, 1 November 2008, https://www.academia.edu /4435265/The_Meanings_of_Republicanism_in_Contemporary_Ireland (accessed 23 March 2021).

Johnston, R., McCausland, G. and Bonner, K., *The Competitiveness Scorecard for Northern Ireland: A Framework for Measuring Economic, Social, and Environmental Progress*, Coleraine, Ulster University, 2020.

Joyce, J., 'No room for complacency over Sinn Féin in government', *The Irish Times*, 17 January 2022, https://www.irishtimes.com/opinion/no-room-for-complacency -over-sinn-f%C3%A9in-in-government-1.4777807 (accessed 24 February 2022).

Kane, A., 'The past is where we go', *Irish News*, 1 December 2017, https://www .irishnews.com/opinion/columnists/2017/12/01/alex-kane-the-past-is-where -we-go-when-there-is-no-agreement-on-the-present-or-future-1199829/ (accessed 27 February 2021).

Keane, F., 'RIC row threatens to drag us into a dangerous place', *The Irish Times*, 8 January 2020, https://www.irishtimes.com/opinion/fergal-keane-ric-row-threatens -to-drag-us-into-a-dangerous-place-1.4133186 (12 February 2021).

Kearney, D., 'Uncomfortable conversations are key to reconciliation: Increasing understanding and mutual respect by reaching out to unionists', *An Phoblacht*, 2 March 2012, https://anphoblacht.com/contents/28 (accessed 28 June 2022).

Kearney, D., 'Kearney welcomes powerful civic intervention to establish national citizens' assembly', Sinn Féin [website], 4 November 2019, https://www.sinnfein.ie /contents/55274 (accessed 28 June 2022).

Kearney, V., 'Loyalist paramilitaries: "Once you join, it's impossible to get out"', BBC News, 12 February 2019, https://www.bbc.com/news/uk-northern-ireland -politics-47072147 (accessed 19 July 2021).

Kee, R., *Ireland: A History*, London, Abacus, 2003.

Keefe, P.R., *Say Nothing: A True Story of Murder and Memory in Northern Ireland*, New York, Doubleday, 2019.

Keena, C., 'Inside Sinn Féin – where power lies and how decisions are made', *The Irish Times*, 5 March 2020, https://www.irishtimes.com/news/politics/inside -sinn-f%C3%A9in-where-power-lies-and-how-decisions-are-made-1.4193138 (accessed 24 July 2020).

Keena, C., 'Sinn Féin is the richest political party in Ireland', *The Irish Times*, 5 March 2020, https://www.irishtimes.com/news/politics/sinn-f%C3%A9in-is-the-richest -political-party-in-ireland-1.4193124 (accessed 24 July 2020).

Kelleher, L., Smyth, A. and McEldowney, M., 'Cultural attitudes, parental aspirations, and socioeconomic influence on post-primary school selection in Northern

Ireland', *Journal of School Choice*, vol. 10, no. 2, 2016, pp. 200–26, https://doi.org/10.1080/15582159.2016.1153378 (accessed 3 May 2021).

Kelly, G., et al., *The Northern Ireland Peace Monitoring Report: Number Five*, Community Relations Council, Belfast, Ulster University, 10 January 2019, https://ulster-staging.pure.elsevier.com/en/publications/northern-ireland-peace-monitoring-report-number-five (accessed 28 June 2022).

Kelly, T., 'In these long days of lockdown, counting the hours to Irish reunification is hardly a priority … it's all about health, health, and health', *Belfast Telegraph*, 28 April 2020, https://www.belfasttelegraph.co.uk/opinion/comment/in-these-long-days-of-lockdown-counting-the-hours-to-irish-reunification-is-hardly-a-priority-its-all-about-health-health-and-health-39162033.html (accessed 9 December 2021).

Kelly, T., 'Why Micheál Martin's elevation as Taoiseach marks nothing less than the end of the Irish Civil War', *Belfast Telegraph*, 16 June 2020, https://www.belfasttelegraph.co.uk/tablet/comment/why-micheal-martins-elevation-as-taoiseach-marks-nothing-less-than-the-end-of-the-Irish-civil-war-39288439.html (accessed 9 December 2021).

Kennedy, D., *The Widening Gulf: Northern Attitudes to the Independent Irish State, 1919–49*, Newtownards, UK, Blackstaff Press, 1989.

Kennedy, L., *Who Was Responsible for the Troubles? The Northern Ireland Conflict*, Montreal and Kingston, Canada, McGill-Queen's University Press, 2020.

Kennedy-Pipe, C., 'From war to uneasy peace in Northern Ireland', in Cox, M., Guelke, A. and Stephen, F. (eds), *A Farewell to Arms?: Beyond the Good Friday Agreement*, Manchester, UK, Manchester University Press, 2006, pp. 48–9.

Kenny, M., *Goodbye to Catholic Ireland*, Dublin, New Island Books, 2000.

Koenen, K. C., et al., 'Posttraumatic stress disorder in the World Mental Health surveys', *Psychological Medicine*, vol. 47, no. 13, 2017, pp. 2260–74, https://doi.org/10.1017/s0033291717000708 (accessed 23 March 2021).

Kreisberg, L., Northrup, T.A. and Thorson, S.J. (eds), *Intractable Conflicts and Their Transformation*, Syracuse, NY, Syracuse University Press, 1989.

Lally, C., 'Garda commissioner "stands over" IRA–Sinn Féin remarks', *The Irish Times*, 26 February 2020, https://www.irishtimes.com/news/crime-and-law/garda-commissioner-stands-over-ira-sinn-f%C3%A9in-remarks-1.4185888 (accessed 27 August 2021).

Leahy, P., 'Taoiseach warns EU that hard border would threaten return to violence', *The Irish Times*, 18 October 2018, https://www.irishtimes.com/news/politics/taoiseach-warns-eu-that-hard-border-would-threaten-return-to-violence-1.3668341 (accessed 4 October 2021).

Leahy, P., 'Sinn Féin's rise as country's most popular party continues', *The Irish Times*, 6 October 2021, https://www.irishtimes.com/news/politics/sinn-f%C3%A9in-s

-rise-as-country-s-most-popular-party-continues-1.4693036 (accessed 28 June 2022).

Leahy, P., 'Irish Times/Ipsos MRBI opinion poll: Support for Sinn Féin reaches new record', The Irish Times, 10 December 2021, https://www.irishtimes.com/news/politics/irish-times-ipsos-mrbi-opinion-poll-support-for-sinn-f%C3%A9in-reaches-new-record-1.4751548 (accessed 24 February 2022).

Leebody, C., 'Secretary of State Brandon Lewis confirms government seeking statute of limitations on Troubles-related killings', Belfast Telegraph, 14 July 2021, https://www.belfasttelegraph.co.uk/news/northern-ireland/secretary-of-state-brandon-lewis-confirms-government-seeking-statute-of-limitations-on-troubles-related-killings-40652619.html (accessed 1 December 2021).

'Leo Varadkar: United Ireland "further away" after RIC controversy', BBC News, 8 January 2020, https://www.bbc.com/news/world-europe-51035886 (accessed 23 March 2021).

Leroux, M., 'Analysis: The union seems to be more popular in Northern Ireland than unionist parties', News Letter, 14 January 2021, https://www.newsletter.co.uk/news/opinion/analysis-union-seems-be-more-popular-northern-ireland-unionist-parties-3094708 (accessed 19 July 2021).

Loscher, D., 'Irish Times poll: Battles between larger parties increasingly fought along socio-economic lines', The Irish Times, 17 June 2021, https://www.irishtimes.com/news/politics/irish-times-poll-battles-between-larger-parties-increasingly-fought-along-socio-economic-lines-1.4595441 (accessed 8 September 2021).

Lowry, B., 'Loyalist protest meeting in Portadown against Boris Johnson's "Betrayal Act" was packed and angry', News Letter, 25 November 2019, https://www.newsletter.co.uk/news/ben-lowry-loyalist-protest-meeting-in-portadown-against-boris-johnsons-betrayal-act-was-packed-and-angry-1320544 (accessed 7 July 2021).

'LucidTalk poll: Support for a border poll and united Ireland grows', An Sionnach Fionn, 24 February 2020, https://ansionnachfionn.com/2020/02/24/lucidtalk-poll-support-for-a-border-poll-and-united-ireland-grows/ (accessed 23 March 2021).

Lyons, F.S.L., Culture and Anarchy in Ireland 1890–1919 (Ford Lectures 1978), Oxford, Oxford University Press, 1980.

Maillot, A., New Sinn Féin: Irish Republicanism in the Twenty-First Century, London, Routledge, 2004.

'Major and Blair say an EU exit could split the UK', BBC News, 9 June 2016, https://www.bbc.com/news/uk-politics-eu-referendum-36486016 (accessed 27 February 2021).

Mallon, S. with Pollack, A., A Shared Home Place, Dublin, The Lilliput Press, 2019.

Mandelson, P., 'A brief history of Stormont suspensions', Belfast Telegraph, 11 January 2017, https://www.belfasttelegraph.co.uk/news/northern-ireland/a-brief-history-of-stormont-suspensions-35358410.html (accessed 30 September 2020).

Manley, J., 'Boris Johnson says prosecution of British army veterans must end', *The Irish News*, 25 July 2019, https://www.irishnews.com/news/northernirelandnews /2019/07/25/news/boris-johnson-says-prosecution-of-british-army-veterans -must-end-1670146/ (accessed 4 December 2021).

Manley, J., 'Nationalists critical of "amnesty" plans for British troops', *The Irish News*, 16 May 2019, https://www.irishnews.com/news/northernirelandnews/2019/05/16 /news/nationalists-critical-of-amnesty-plans-for-british-troops-1621021/ (accessed 4 December 2021).

Manley, J., 'Protocol matters most to little more than one in 10 unionists – Poll', *The Irish News*, 14 February 2022, https://www.irishnews.com/news/northern irelandnews/2022/02/14/news/protocol-matters-most-to-little-more-than-one -in-10-unionists---poll-2588056/ (accessed 23 February 2022).

Marris, P., *Loss and Change*, London, Routledge & Keagan, 1986.

Martin, M., 'We need to see more reflection in South for any shared future', *Belfast Telegraph*, 22 October 2020, https://www.belfasttelegraph.co.uk/opinion/comment /we-need-to-see-more-reflection-in-south-for-any-shared-future-39653028.html (accessed 18 October 2021).

Mason, R., 'Keir Starmer: Only a federal UK "can repair shattered trust in politics"', *The Guardian*, 26 January 2020, https://www.theguardian.com/politics/2020/jan /26/rebecca-long-bailey-calls-for-greater-powers-for-scotland-and-wales (accessed 15 January 2021).

May, J., 'Read in full: Theresa May's Conservative conference speech on Brexit', *PoliticsHome*, 3 October 2016, https://www.politicshome.com/news/article/read -in-full-theresa-mays-speech-to-the-2018-conservative-party-conference (accessed 5 June 2021).

McAleer, R., 'Northern Ireland is best place to live and start a business – PwC report', *The Irish News*, 17 February 2021, https://www.irishnews.com/business /2021/02/17/news/northern-ireland-is-best-place-to-live-and-start-a-business ---pwc-report-2223636/ (accessed 23 February 2022).

McBride, S., 'RHI inquiry: Arlene Foster admits she didn't even read her own "cash for ash" legislation', *inews.co.uk*, 13 April 2018, https://inews.co.uk/news/northern -ireland/rhi-inquiry-arlene-foster-admits-she-didnt-even-read-her-own-cash-for -ash-legislation-144300 (accessed 23 March 2021).

McBride, S., 'Coronavirus: Sinn Féin's claim pandemic boosts chance of Irish unity "crass"', *News Letter*, 27 April 2020, https://www.newsletter.co.uk/news/politics /coronavirus-sinn-feins-claim-pandemic-boosts-chance-of-irish-unity-crass -2550401 (accessed 4 December 2020).

McBride, S., 'State papers: Terms of border poll discussed by Sinn Féin at private meeting', *Belfast Telegraph*, 3 January 2022, https://www.belfasttelegraph.co.uk

/news/politics/state-papers-terms-of-border-poll-discussed-by-sinn-fein-at
-private-meeting-41204416.html (accessed 23 February 2022).

McClements, F., 'Sinn Féin drops opposition to special criminal court', *The Irish Times*,
30 October 2021, https://www.irishtimes.com/news/politics/sinn-f%C3%A9in-drops
-opposition-to-special-criminal-court-1.4715275 (accessed 8 November 2021).

McDonald, H., 'Sinn Féin calls for vote on Irish reunification if UK backs Brexit', *The
Guardian*, 11 March 2016, https://www.theguardian.com/politics/2016/mar/11
/sinn-fein-irish-reunification-vote-brexit-eu-referendum (accessed 16 January 2021).

McDonald, H., 'Northern Ireland "punishment" attacks rise 60% in four years', *The Guardian*, 12 March 2018, https://www.theguardian.com/uk-news/2018/mar/12/northern
-ireland-punishment-attacks-rise-60-in-four-years (accessed 24 August 2020).

McDonald, H., 'Brexit revives unionist and nationalist divide in Northern Ireland',
The Guardian, 17 June 2020, https://www.theguardian.com/politics/2020/jun
/17/brexit-unionist-nationalist-divide-northern-ireland-survey-identity-political
-allegiances (accessed 24 August 2020).

McDowell, M., 'Sinn Féin's problem with names much more than mere word-
play', *The Irish Times*, 26 February 2020, https://www.irishtimes.com/opinion
/sinn-f%C3%A9in-s-problem-with-names-much-more-than-mere-wordplay
-1.4184786 (accessed 16 January 2021).

McEvoy, J., *The Politics of Northern Ireland*, Edinburgh, UK, Edinburgh University
Press, 2008.

McEvoy, K., et al., *Prosecutions, Imprisonment, and the Stormont House Agreement:
A Critical Analysis Of Proposals On Dealing With The Past In Northern
Ireland*, Belfast, Dealing with the Past in Northern Ireland Research Project,
Queen's University, April 2020, https://www.dealingwiththepastni.com/project
-outputs/project-reports/prosecutions-imprisonment-and-the-stormont-house
-agreement-a-critical-analysis-of-proposals-on-dealing-with-the-past-in-northern
-ireland (accessed 28 March 2021).

McGarry, J. and O'Leary, B., *Explaining Northern Ireland: Broken Images*, Oxford,
Blackwell, 1995.

McGarry, J. and O'Leary, B., *The Politics of Antagonism: Understanding Northern
Ireland*, London, Bloomsbury Publishing, 2018.

McGarry, P.J., 'Paramilitary shootings and assaults', Letter to Editor, *National Center
for Biotechnology Information*, PubMed Central [website], 12 September 2017,
https://www.ncbi.nlm.nih.gov/pmc/articles/PMC5849980/ (accessed 3 May 2021).

McGreevy, R., 'How did plans to remember the RIC and DMP become so con-
troversial?', *The Irish Times*, 7 January 2020, https://www.irishtimes.com/news/
ireland/irish-news/how-did-plans-to-remember-the-ric-and-dmp-become-so
-controversial-1.4133248 (accessed 15 December 2020).

McGreevy, R., 'Why Sinn Féin will not call the state by its name', *The Irish Times*, 24 February 2020, https://pure.qub.ac.uk/en/clippings/why-sinn-f%C3%A9in -will-not-call-the-state-by-its-name (accessed 13 November 2020).

McGuinness, S., 'Four known unknowns of the cost of Irish unity', *The Irish Times*, 26 September 2019, https://www.irishtimes.com/opinion/four-known-unknowns -of-the-cost-of-irish-unity-1.4030297 (accessed 10 January 2021).

McHugh, M., 'Majority in North do not support united Ireland, says Leo Varadkar', *The Irish News*, 27 December 2019, https://www.irishnews.com/news/north- ernirelandnews/2019/12/27/news/majority-in-north-do-not-support-united- ireland-says-leo-varadkar-1800429/ (accessed 1 March 2021).

McKay, S., *Northern Protestants: An Unsettled People*, 2nd edn, Newtownards, UK, Blackstaff Press, 2005.

McKay, S., *Northern Protestants: On Shifting Ground*, Newtownards, UK, Blackstaff Press, 2021.

McKee, L., 'Why suicide rates have skyrocketed for Northern Ireland's "ceasefire babies"', *The Atlantic*, 20 April 2019, https://www.theatlantic.com/health/archive /2016/01/conflict-mental-health-northern-ireland-suicide/424683/ (accessed 12 May 2021).

McKevitt, G., 'On the runs – key questions and inquiry findings', BBC News NI, 24 March 2015, https://www.bbc.com/news/uk-northern-ireland-26359906 (accessed 10 April 2021).

McKittrick, D. and McVea, D., *Making Sense of the Troubles: A History of the Northern Ireland Conflict*, New York, Viking Penguin, 2012.

McKittrick, D. et al., *Lost Lives: The Stories of the Men, Women, and Children Who Died as a Result of the Northern Ireland Troubles*, 2nd edn, Edinburgh, UK, Mainstream Publishing, 1 June 2004.

McNicholl, K., Stevenson, C. and Garry, J., 'How the 'Northern Irish' national iden- tity is understood and used by young people and politicians', *Political Psychology*, vol. 40, no. 3, 2018, 1–19, https://doi.org/10.1111/pops.12523.

McWilliams, D., *Rules for Ireland*, Dublin, Gill Books, 2018.

Meredith, R., 'NI education: No religious mix in "nearly a third of schools"', BBC News, 11 November 2021, https://www.bbc.com/news/uk-northern-ireland -59242226 (accessed 6 January 2022).

Miller, D., *Queen's Rebels: Ulster Loyalism in Historical Perspective*, rev. edn, Dublin, University College Dublin Press, 2007.

Mitchell, D., *Politics and Peace in Northern Ireland: Political Parties and the Imple- mentation of the 1998 Agreement*, Manchester, UK, Manchester University Press, 22 July 2015.

Moloney, E., *A Secret History of the IRA*, 2nd edn, London, Penguin Random House 2007.

Moore, A., 'Funding loyalist communities "will help avert violence during reunification"', *Belfast Telegraph*, 2 January 2020, https://www.belfasttelegraph.co.uk /news/northern-ireland/funding-loyalist-communities-will-help-avert-violence -during-reunification-38829092.html (19 July 2021).

'More than 100 peace wall barriers remain in Northern Ireland', *The Irish Times*, 5 January 2022, https://www.irishtimes.com/news/ireland/irish-news/more-than -100-peace-wall-barriers-remain-in-northern-ireland-1.4769360 (accessed 24 February 2022).

Moriarty, G., 'How the trauma of the Troubles risks being "passed on"', *The Irish Times*, 7 August 2017, https://www.irishtimes.com/news/ireland/irish-news/how -the-trauma-of-the-troubles-risks-being-passed-on-1.3178681 (accessed 16 April 2021).

Moriarty, G., 'Why Soldier F will be charged over Bloody Sunday but other soldiers will not be', *The Irish Times*, 14 March 2019, https://www.irishtimes.com/news /ireland/irish-news/why-soldier-f-will-be-charged-over-bloody-sunday-but-other -soldiers-will-not-be-1.3825921 (accessed 16 April 2021).

Moriarty, G., 'NI bishops express "alarm" at British proposals on the past', *The Irish Times*, 8 April 2020, https://www.irishtimes.com/news/ireland/irish-news /ni-bishops-express-alarm-at-british-proposals-on-the-past-1.4224312 (accessed 16 April 2021).

Moriarty, G., 'Who are the New IRA and what have they done?', *The Irish Times*, 23 April 2019, https://www.irishtimes.com/news/ireland/irish-news/who-are-the -new-ira-and-what-have-they-done-1.3869569 (accessed 16 April 2021).

Moriarty, G. and McClements, F., 'Northern Executive and Assembly to be reinstated after parties reach deal', *The Irish Times*, 11 January 2020, https://www.irishtimes .com/news/politics/northern-executive-and-assembly-to-be-reinstated-after -parties-reach-deal-1.4136263 (accessed 21 December 2020).

Morris, A., 'Loyalists plan "war of attrition"', *The Irish News*, 23 October 2019, https:// www.irishnews.com/news/northernirelandnews/2019/10/23/news/loyalists -plan-war-of-attrition--1745909/ (accessed 16 January 2021).

Morris, A., 'Hyped up talk of unionist betrayal could have dangerous consequences', *The Irish News*, 28 November 2019, https://www.irishnews.com/opinion /columnists/2019/11/28/news/allison-morris-hyped-up-talk-of-unionist-betrayal -could-have-dangerous-consequences-1776681/content.html (accessed 7 July 2021).

Morris, A., 'Loyalist paramilitary groups raking in £250,000 a month member "dues"', *The Irish News*, 3 December 2020, https://www.irishnews.com/news /northernirelandnews/2020/12/03/news/loyalist-paramilitary-groups-raking-in -250-000-a-month-in-members-dues--2149229/ (accessed 16 January 2021).

Morrissey, M. and Smyth, M., *Northern Ireland After the Good Friday Agreement: Victims, Grievance, and Blame*, London, Pluto Press, 2002.

Morrow, D., 'The rocky road from enmity', in C. McGrattan and E. Meehan (eds), *Everyday Life After the Irish Conflict: The Impact of Devolution and Cross-Border Cooperation*, Manchester, UK, Manchester University Press, 2012, pp. 20–9.

Morrow, D., *Sectarianism – A Review*, Belfast, Ulster University, May 2019, https://www.ulster.ac.uk/__data/assets/pdf_file/0016/410227/A-Review-Addressing-Sectarianism-in-Northern-Ireland_FINAL.pdf (accessed 6 January 2022).

Morrow, D. and Byrne, J., *Countering Paramilitary & Organised Criminal Influence on Youth: A Review*, Belfast, The Corrymeela Press, March 2020, https://pure.ulster.ac.uk/ws/files/78933939/Countering_Paramilitary_and_Organised_Criminal_Influence_on_Youth_FULL_REPORT_3_.pdf (accessed 28 June 2022).

Mulholland, M., *The Longest War: Northern Ireland's Troubled History*, New York, Oxford University Press, 2002.

Mullan, K., 'Brandon Lewis still engaging on "statute of limitations" which he describes as a "complicated, sensitive and difficult" area', *Derry Journal*, 22 February 2022, https://www.derryjournal.com/news/crime/brandon-lewis-still-engaging-on-statute-of-limitations-which-he-decribes-as-a-complicated-sensitive-and-difficult-area-3580533 (accessed 28 June 2022).

Murray, A.C., 'Agrarian violence and nationalism in nineteenth-century Ireland: The myth of ribbonism', *Irish Economic & Social History*, vol. 13, 1986, pp. 56–73, http://www.jstor.org/stable/24337381 (accessed 23 March 2021).

Murray, D. and O'Neill, J., *Peace Building in a Political Impasse: Cross-Border Links in Ireland*, Coleraine, UK, University of Ulster, 1991.

Napier, R.J., Gallagher, B.J. and Wilson, D.S., 'An imperfect peace: Trends in paramilitary related violence 20 years after the Northern Ireland ceasefires', *Ulster Medical Journal*, vol. 86, no. 2, 17 May 2017, pp. 99–102, https://www.ncbi.nlm.nih.gov/pmc/articles/PMC5846013/ (accessed 4 September 2021).

National Security Intelligence Work in Northern Ireland, MI5 – The Security Service [website], https://www.mi5.gov.uk/northern-ireland (accessed 21 February 2022).

Nelson, S., *Ulster's Uncertain Defenders: Protestant Political, Paramilitary, and Community Groups, and the Northern Ireland Conflict*, Belfast, Appletree Press, 1984.

'New IRA says border infrastructure would be "legitimate target for attack"', London, Channel 4 News, 16 October 2019, https://www.channel4.com/news/new-ira-says-border-infrastructure-would-be-legitimate-target-for-attack (accessed 5 June 2021).

'New report finds proposed UK government amnesty cannot deliver truth for victims of the Troubles', Committee on the Administration of Justice, 7 September 2021, https://caj.org.uk/2021/09/07/new-report-finds-proposed-uk-government

-amnesty-cannot-deliver-truth-for-victims-of-the-troubles/ (accessed 23 November 2021).

'NI has world's highest rate of post traumatic stress disorder', Ulster University, 5 December 2011, https://www.ulster.ac.uk/news/2011/december/ni-has-worlds -highest-rate-of-post-traumatic-stress-disorder (accessed 23 March 2021).

Nicholas, R.M., Barr, J. and Mollan, R., 'Paramilitary punishment in Northern Ireland: A macabre irony', *Journal of Trauma Injury Infection and Critical Care*, vol. 34, no. 1, 1993, pp. 90–5, https://doi.org/10.1097/00005373-199301000-00017 (accessed 23 March 2021).

'Nigeria: 7 years after Chibok mass abduction, still no solution', *Al Jazeera*, 14 April 2021, https://www.aljazeera.com/news/2021/4/14/nigeria-7-years-after-chibok -mass-abduction-still-no-solution (accessed 19 August 2021).

Nolan, P., 'So, are we going to have a border poll or not?', *Belfast Telegraph*, 17 June 2019, https://www.belfasttelegraph.co.uk/opinion/news-analysis/paul-nolan-so-are-we -going-to-have-a-border-poll-or-not-38223908.html (accessed 23 November 2021).

Nolan, P., 'Border poll to be decided by those with "least commitment to the consti-tutional issue"', *The Detail*, 25 February 2020, https://thedetail.tv/articles/irish -unity-and-disunity (accessed 23 November 2021).

The Non-Medical Use of Prescription Drugs – Policy Direction Issues, Discussion Paper, United Nations Office on Drugs and Crime, Vienna, 2011, https://www .unodc.org/documents/drug-prevention-and-treatment/nonmedical-use -prescription-drugs.pdf (accessed 28 June 2022).

'Northern bank robbery', *Wikipedia*, Wikimedia Foundation, https://en.wikipedia .org/wiki/Northern_Bank_robbery (accessed 16 January 2022).

Northern Ireland, OECD Regional Well-Being [website], Organisation for Economic Co-Operation and Development, https://www.oecdregionalwellbeing.org/UKN .html (accessed February 20, 2022).

Northern Ireland Act 1998, UK General Public Acts – 1998, London, The National Archives, 19 November 1998, https://www.legislation.gov.uk/ukpga/1998/47/contents.

Northern Ireland Affairs Committee, 'New Decade, New Approach', London, UK Parliament, January 2020, https://assets.publishing.service.gov.uk/government /uploads/system/uploads/attachment_data/file/856998/2020-01-08_a_new _decade__a_new_approach.pdf (accessed 23 March 2021).

'Northern Ireland Catholic school population surges to record high', *Belfast Telegraph*, 30 April 2019, https://www.belfasttelegraph.co.uk/news/northern -ireland/northern-ireland-catholic-school-population-surges-to-record-high -38063956.html (accessed 3 November 2021).

Northern Ireland Housing Statistics 2019–20, Northern Ireland Department for Communities [website], https://www.communities-ni.gov.uk/topics/housing -statistics (accessed 28 June 2022), Belfast, 2020, https://www.communities-ni

.gov.uk/publications/northern-ireland-housing-statistics-2019-20 (accessed 28 June 2022). Northern Ireland Life and Times Surveys [website], www.ark.ac.uk/nilt.

Northern Ireland Office, *Addressing the Legacy of Northern Ireland's Past* (CP 498, 2021), https://assets.publishing.service.gov.uk/government/uploads/system /uploads/attachment_data/file/1002140/CP_498_Addressing_the_Legacy_of _Northern_Ireland_s_Past.pdf (accessed 28 June 2022).

Northern Ireland Office, 'Part one, the current system for addressing the past', in Consultation Paper, *Addressing the Legacy of Northern Ireland's Past*, Belfast and London, Northern Ireland Office, 1 May 2018, https://cain.ulster.ac.uk /victims/docs/british_gov/nio/2018-05-11_NIO_Consultation_Paper_Legacy .pdf (accessed 23 March 2021).

Northern Ireland Office, *Addressing the Legacy of Northern Ireland's Past: Analysis of the Consultation Responses*, July 2019, https://assets.publishing-.service .gov.uk/government/uploads/system/uploads/attachment_data/file/814805 /Addressing_the_Legacy_of_the_Past_-_Analysis_of_the_consultation _responses.pdf (accessed 9 December 2021).

'Northern Ireland "one of world's highest rates for anti-depressants"', BBC News, 16 November 2014, https://www.bbc.com/news/uk-northern-ireland-30073669 (accessed 16 April 2021).

Northern Ireland Parades Commission [website], https://www.paradescommission .org/.

Northern Ireland Social Attitudes Survey, 1989, 'Political attitudes module', ARK [website], www.ark.ac.uk/nilt, 16 March 2004, https://www.ark.ac.uk/sol /surveys/gen_social_att/nisa/1989/website/Political_Attitudes/NIRELAND .html (accessed 21 February 2022).

Northern Ireland Statistics and Research Agency, 2011 Census [website], https:// www.nisra.gov.uk/statistics/census/2011-census (accessed 3 February 2022).

Northern Ireland Statistics and Research Agency, *Labour Force Survey Religion Report 2017* [website], Belfast, The Executive Office, January 2019, https:// www.executiveoffice-ni.gov.uk/publications/labour-force-survey-religion -report-2017 (accessed 14 June 2021).

Northern Ireland Statistics and Research Agency, *Northern Ireland Multiple Deprivation Measure 2017* [website], NI Department of Finance, Belfast, November 2017, https://www.nisra.gov.uk/statistics/deprivation/northern-ireland -multiple-deprivation-measure-2017-nimdm2017 (accessed 20 February 2022).

Northern Ireland Statistics and Research Agency, 'Religion in Northern Ireland: 1861–2011', Census 2011 Analysis [website], https://www.cso.ie/en/media/csoie /census/documents/north-south-spreadsheets/Census2011Irelandand NorthernIrelandwebversion1.pdf (accessed 28 June 2022), Belfast, June 2014, https://www.ninis2.nisra.gov.uk/public/census2011analysis/religion/religion Commentary.pdf (accessed 9 February 2022).

Northern Ireland Statistics and Research Agency, *Suicide Statistics: Number of Suicides Registered Each Calendar Year in Northern Ireland* [website], Belfast, 9 October 2021, https://www.nisra.gov.uk/publications/suicide-statistics (accessed 9 February 2022).

Northern Ireland Statistics and Research Agency, *Trends in Domestic Abuse Incidents and Crimes Recorded by the Police in Northern Ireland 2004/05 to 2019/20*, Belfast, Police Service of Northern Ireland *Annual Bulletin*, 20 November 2020, https://www.psni.police.uk/globalassets/inside-the-psni/our-statistics/domestic -abuse-statistics/2019-20/domestic-abuse-incidents-and-crimes-in-northern -ireland-2004-05-to-2019-20.pdf (accessed 28 June 2022).

Ó Beacháin, D., *From Partition to Brexit: The Irish Government and Northern Ireland*, Manchester, UK, Manchester University Press, 2018.

O'Brennan, J., 'Brexit is fuelling tensions in Northern Ireland', Al Jazeera, 14 April 2021, https://www.aljazeera.com/opinions/2021/4/14/brexit-stirring-tension-in -northern-ireland (17 October 2021).

O'Brien, S. (ed.), 'Sinn Féin surges in new poll', *The Sunday Times*, 13 November 2021, https://www.thetimes.co.uk/article/sinn-fein-surges-in-new-poll-5lmblv5px (accessed 9 December 2021).

O'Callaghan, M., '"Old parchment and water": The boundary commission of 1925 and the copper fastening of the Irish border', *Bullán: An Irish Studies Journal*, vol. 5, no. 2, November 2000, pp. 27–55, https://pureadmin.qub.ac.uk/ws/portalfiles /portal/164164784/Parchment.pdf (accessed 23 March 2021).

O'Ceallaigh, D., Gillespie, P. and Gilmore, A. (eds), *Brexit Status Report 2016–2019 and Beyond*, Dublin, Institute of International and European Affairs, 2019, https://www.iiea.com/publications/brexit-status-report-2016-2019-and-beyond (accessed June 16, 2020).

O'Connor, W., 'NI Catholics outnumber Protestants in university', *Independent.ie*, 19 January 2016, https://www.independent.ie/irish-news/education/ni-catholics -outnumber-protestants-in-university-34380510.html (accessed 22 February 2022).

Ó Dochartaigh, N., Hayward, K. and Meehan, E. (eds), *Dynamics of Political Change in Ireland: Making and Breaking a Divided Island*, Abingdon, Oxfordshire, UK, Routledge, 2017.

O'Doherty, M., *Fifty Years On: The Troubles and the Struggle for Change in Northern Ireland*, London, Atlantic Books, 2019.

O'Doherty, M., 'Unionists' priority must be to accept unity debate is real', *Belfast Telegraph*, 27 April 2021, https://www.belfasttelegraph.co.uk/opinion/columnists /malachi-odoherty/unionists-priority-must-be-to-accept-unity-debate-is-real -40359350.html (accessed 23 November 2021).

O'Donovan, P., 'Does Sinn Féin recognise the legitimacy of the Irish State', Fine Gael [website], 25 February 2020, https://www.finegael.ie/does-sinn-fein-recognise -the-legitimacy-of-the-irish-state-odonovan (accessed 22 February 2022).

Office of the Special Representative of the Secretary General for Children and Armed Conflict, *Protect Schools and Hospitals: Guidance Note on Security Council Resolution 1998*, New York, United Nations Secretariat, 2014, https:// childrenandarmedconflict.un.org/publications/AttacksonSchoolsHospitals .pdf (accessed 28 June 2022).

Office for Statistics Regulation, *Systemic Review Programme: Review of Mental Health Statistics in Northern Ireland*, London, September 2021, https://osr .statisticsauthority.gov.uk/wp-content/uploads/2021/09/Review-of-mental -health-statistics-in-Northern-Ireland.pdf (accessed 28 June 2022).

O'Halloran, C., *Partition and the Limits of Irish Nationalism: An Ideology Under Stress*, Dublin, Gill & Macmillan, 1987.

O'Kane, E., 'To cajole or compel? The use of incentives and penalties in Northern Ireland's peace process', *Dynamics of Asymmetric Conflict*, vol. 4, no. 3, 2011, pp. 272–84, https://doi.org/10.1080/17467586.2011.632780 (accessed 23 March 2021).

O'Leary, B., *A Treatise on Northern Ireland, Vol. I: Colonialism*, Oxford, Oxford University Press, 2019.

O'Leary, B., *A Treatise on Northern Ireland, Vol. II: Control*, Oxford, Oxford University Press, 2019.

O'Leary, B., *A Treatise on Northern Ireland, Vol. III: Consociation and Confederation*, Oxford, Oxford University Press, 2019.

O'Leary, B. and McGarry, J., *The Politics of Antagonism: Understanding Northern Ireland*, London, Athlone Press, 1993.

O'Malley, P., *The Uncivil Wars: Ireland Today*, Boston, MA, Houghton Mifflin Co., 1983.

O'Malley, P., *Northern Ireland: Questions of Nuance*, Belfast: Blackstaff Press, 1990.

O'Neill, J., 'Plan to end all NI Troubles prosecutions confirmed', BBC News, 14 July 2021, https://www.bbc.com/news/uk-northern-ireland-57829037 (accessed 13 December 2021).

O'Neill, J., 'Stakeknife: Operation Kenova report into IRA spy due next year', BBC News, 30 September 2021, https://www.bbc.com/news/uk-northern-ireland -58742650 (accessed 8 November 2021).

O'Neill, M., 'British government must respond to UN intervention and withdraw amnesty proposals', Sinn Féin [website], 11 August 2021, https://www.sinnfein .ie/contents/61539 (accessed 3 November 2021).

O'Neill, S. et al., *Towards a Better Future: The Trans-Generational Impact of the Troubles on Mental Health*, Commission for Victims and Survivors, Belfast,

Ulster University, March 2015, 105, https://www.cvsni.org/media/1171/towards -a-better-future-march-2015.pdf (accessed 23 March 2021).

Ó Riain, S., *The Rise and Fall of Ireland's Celtic Tiger: Liberalism, Boom and Bust*, Cambridge, UK, Cambridge University Press, 2014.

O'Rourke, K., *A Short History of Brexit: From Brentry to Backstop*, London, Penguin UK, 2019.

O'Toole, F., 'United Ireland will not be based on "50 percent plus one"', *The Irish Times*, 15 August 2017, https://www.irishtimes.com/opinion/fintan-o-toole -united-ireland-will-not-be-based-on-50-per-cent-plus-one-1.3186234 (accessed 18 February 2021).

O'Toole, F., *Heroic Failure: Brexit and the Politics of Fear*, New York, Apollo, 2018.

O'Toole, F., 'Investigating the Troubles requires a hard-headed exchange: Truth for amnesty', Dublin, *The Irish Times*, 16 June 2020, https://www.irishtimes.com /opinion/fintan-o-toole-investigating-the-troubles-requires-a-hard-headed -exchange-truth-for-amnesty-1.4279721 (accessed 18 February 2021).

O'Toole, F., *We Don't Know Ourselves: A Personal History of Modern Ireland*, New York, Liveright, 2022.

Paramilitary Groups in Northern Ireland, An Assessment Commissioned by the Secretary of State for Northern Ireland, London and Belfast, Secretary of State for Northern Ireland, 19 October 2015, https://cain.ulster.ac.uk/issues/police/ docs/psni_2015-10-19_paramilitary-groups.pdf (accessed 23 March 2021).

Phoenix, E., *Northern Nationalism: Nationalist Politics, Partition, and the Catholic Minority in Northern Ireland 1890–1940*, Belfast, Ulster Historical Foundation, 1994.

Police Service of Northern Ireland, 'Domestic abuse incidents and crimes recorded by the police in Northern Ireland: Update to 31 December 2019', 27 February 2020, https:// www.psni.police.uk/globalassets/inside-the-psni/our-statistics/domestic-abuse -statistics/2019-20/q3/domestic-abuse_-tables-dec-19.ods (accessed 23 March 2021).

Political Studies Association, '20 years of the Good Friday Agreement', 10 April 2018, https://www.psa.ac.uk/psa/news/20-years-good-friday-agreement (accessed 23 March 2021).

'Poll: 65% of voters in Northern Ireland believe Brexit makes Irish unity more likely within ten years', *Belfast Telegraph*, 27 October 2019, https://www.belfasttelegraph .co.uk/news/northern-ireland/poll-65-of-voters-in-northern-ireland-believe -brexit-makes-irish-unity-more-likely-within-ten-years-38635481.html (accessed 12 October 2020).

Pollak, A., 'Sinn Féin are getting ready for government. But are they ready for unity?', *2Irelands2gether* [web blog], 24 May 2021, https://2irelands2gether .com/2020/10/16/sinn-fein-are-getting-ready-for-government-but-are-they -ready-for-unity/ (accessed 18 November 2021).

'Post traumatic stress disorder highest in Northern Ireland', BBC News, 5 December 2011, https://www.bbc.com/news/uk-northern-ireland-16028713 (accessed 16 April 2021).

Powell, J., *Great Hatred, Little Room: Peace in Northern Ireland*, New York, Vintage Books, 2009.

Power, J., 'IRA volunteer Séamus McElwain held in "huge esteem" – Matt Carthy', *The Irish Times*, 26 April 2021, https://www.irishtimes.com/news/politics/ira-volunteer-s%C3%A9amus-mcelwain-held-in-huge-esteem-matt-carthy-1.4548404 (accessed 3 August 2021).

Preston, A., 'Concern as New IRA gets weapons from Hezbollah', *Belfast Telegraph*, 14 September 2020, https://www.belfasttelegraph.co.uk/news/northern-ireland/concern-as-new-ira-gets-weapons-from-hezbollah-39527531.html (accessed 1 March 2021).

Queen's University Belfast, *Queen's on Brexit* [website], https://www.qub.ac.uk/brexit/.

Quinn, A., 'Watch Boris Johnson tell the DUP in 2018 he would never put border in the Irish Sea – today he put a border in the Irish Sea', *News Letter*, 17 October 2019, https://www.newsletter.co.uk/news/politics/watch-boris-johnson-tell-dup-2018-he-would-never-put-border-irish-sea-today-he-put-border-irish-sea-816300 (accessed 7 July 2021).

Quinn, C., 'How to spot the referendum denier', Friends of Sinn Féin USA [website], 9 March 2021, https://www.friendsofsinnfein.com/post/how-to-spot-the-referendum-denier (accessed 27 August 2021).

'Record £15 billion per year for Northern Ireland', Northern Ireland Office, HM Treasury, and The Rt Hon Brandon Lewis CBE MP, 28 October 2021, https://www.gov.uk/government/news/record-15-billion-per-year-for-northern-ireland (accessed 22 January 2022).

Report of the Bloody Sunday Inquiry, Vols I–X, Principal Conclusions and Overall Assessment [website], 14 June 2010, https://www.gov.uk/government/publications/report-of-the-bloody-sunday-inquiry (accessed 28 June 2022).

Retaining and Regaining Talent in Northern Ireland, Pivotal Public Policy Forum NI [website], https://www.pivotalppf.org/, Belfast, 24 March 2021, https://www.pivotalppf.org/cmsfiles/Retaining-and-Regaining-talent-report-V1.pdf (accessed 27 August 2021).

Rieff, D., *Against Remembrance*, Melbourne, AU, Melbourne University Press, 2011.

Rieff, D., *In Praise of Forgetting: Historical Memory and Its Ironies*, New Haven, CT, Yale University Press, 2016.

Robinson, P., 'The DUP cannot allow Sinn Féin demands to be given supremacy', *News Letter*, 18 June 2021, https://www.newsletter.co.uk/news/opinion/columnists/peter-robinson-the-dup-cannot-allow-sinn-fein-demands-to-be-given-supremacy-3277724 (accessed 19 July 2021).

Roche, P.J. and Barton, B. (eds), *The Northern Ireland Question: Perspectives on Nationalism and Unionism*, Royal Tunbridge Wells, UK, Wordzworth Publishing, UK, 2020.

Rose, R., *Governing Without Consensus: An Irish Perspective*, London, Faber & Faber, 1971.

Rouhana, N. and Shalhoub-Kevorkian, N. (eds), *When Politics Are Sacralized: Comparative Perspectives on Religious Claims and Nationalism*, Cambridge, UK, Cambridge University Press, 2021.

Roulston, S. and Cook, S., *Home-School Travel in a Divided Education System: At What Cost?*, Issue Brief, Coleraine, UK, Ulster University, 2021.

Rowan, B., 'Sinn Fein chairman: IRA should say sorry for hurt caused', *Belfast Telegraph*, 3 March 2012, https://www.belfasttelegraph.co.uk/news/northern -ireland/sinn-fein-chairman-ira-should-say-sorry-for-hurt-caused-28722079.html (accessed 7 July 2021).

Rowan, B., *Unfinished Peace: Thoughts on Northern Ireland's Unanswered Past*, Belfast, Colourpoint, 2015.

Ruane, J. and Todd, J., *The Dynamics of Conflict in Northern Ireland: Power, Conflict, and Emancipation*, Cambridge, UK, Cambridge University Press, 1996.

Ruane, J. and Todd, J. (eds), *After the Good Friday Agreement: Analysing Political Change in Northern Ireland*, Dublin, University College Dublin Press, 1999.

Rutherford, A., 'Centenary poll: 44% in Northern Ireland want referendum but would not accept higher taxes to fund reunification', *Belfast Telegraph*, 1 May 2021, https://www.belfasttelegraph.co.uk/news/northern-ireland/the-centenary /centenary-poll-44-in-northern-ireland-want-referendum-but-would-not-accept -higher-taxes-to-fund-reunification-40375678.html (accessed 7 July 2021).

Ryan, P. and McQuinn, C., '"No effort made by Sinn Féin to distance or disown itself from IRA" – Five justice ministers back garda commissioner', *Independent.ie*, 22 February 2020, https://www.independent.ie/irish-news/election-2020/no -effort-made-by-sinn-fein-to-distance-or-disown-itself-from-ira-five-justice- ministers-back-garda-commissioner-38980325.html (accessed 17 October 2021).

Ryder, C. and Kearney, V., *Drumcree: The Orange Order's Last Stand*, London, Methuen, 1 January 2001.

Saville, S.M.O., Hoyt, W.L. and Toohey, J., *Report of the Bloody Sunday Inquiry*, London, Stationery Office, 2010, https://assets.publishing.service.gov.uk /government/uploads/system/uploads/attachment_data/file/279160/0029_x.pdf (accessed 28 June 2022).

Sheahan, F., 'United Ireland: Majority favour a united Ireland, but just 22PC would pay for it', *Independent.ie*, 1 May 2021, https://www.independent.ie/irish-news /centenaries/centenarypoll/majority-favour-a-united-ireland-but-just-22pc-would -pay-for-it-40375875.html (accessed 19 July 2021).

Shirlow, P., *The End of Ulster Loyalism?*, Manchester, UK, Manchester University Press, 2012.

Shirlow, P. and Coulter, C., 'Northern Ireland: 20 years after the cease-fires', *Studies in Conflict and Terrorism*, vol. 37, no. 9, 2014, pp. 713–19, https://doi.org/10.1080 /1057610X.2014.931224 (accessed 23 March 2021).

Should I Stay or Should I Go? Reasons for Leaving Northern Ireland for Study or Work, Pivotal Public Policy Forum NI [website], https://www.pivotalppf.org/, Belfast, 6 December 2021, https://www.pivotalppf.org/cmsfiles//Stay-or-go-final .pdf (accessed 6 January 2022).

Simpson, C., 'Suicide rate for young people in Northern Ireland more than twice that of England', *The Irish News*, 5 March 2020, https://www.irishnews.com /news/northernirelandnews/2020/03/05/news/suicide-rate-for-young-people-in -northern-ireland-more-than-twice-that-of-england-1858622 (accessed 3 May 2021).

Sinn Féin, *Éire Nua: The Social and Economic Programme of Sinn Féin*, Belfast, CAIN and INCORE, 1979, https://cain.ulster.ac.uk/issues/politics/docs/sf/sinnfein79. htm (accessed 9 July 2020).

Smith, P., 'New research shows that for "neithers", the problem with the union is unionists', *News Letter*, 25 January 2021, https://www.newsletter.co.uk/news /politics/philip-smith-new-research-shows-neithers-problem-union-unionists -3111473 (accessed 19 July 2021).

Smith, S., 'NI govt "unlawfully" delayed troubles pension scheme, rules high court', *PensionsAge*, 21 August 2020, https://www.pensionsage.com/pa/NI-govt-unlawfully -delayed-troubles-pension-scheme-rules-high-court.php (accessed 3 April 2021).

Smith, W.B., *The British State and the Northern Ireland Crisis 1969–73: From Violence to Power-Sharing*, Washington, DC, US Institute of Peace, 1 May 2011 (accessed 23 March 2021).

Smyth, C., 'Stormont's petition of concern used 115 times in five years', *The Detail*, 29 September 2016, https://www.thedetail.tv/articles/stormont-s-petition-of-concern -used-115-times-in-five-years (accessed 7 November 2021).

Smyth, L., 'Good Friday Agreement a bluff and hasn't been delivered: Sinn Féin MP Molloy', *Belfast Telegraph*, 19 July 2020, https://www.belfasttelegraph.co.uk /news/northern-ireland/good-friday-agreement-a-bluff-and-hasnt-been -delivered-sinn-fein-mp-molloy-39380124.html (25 March 2021).

Social Investment Fund [website], Belfast, The Executive Office, https://www .executiveoffice-ni.gov.uk/articles/social-investment-fund (accessed 28 June 2022).

'Soldier F: Dropping of Bloody Sunday murder charges adjourned', BBC News, 9 July 2021, https://www.bbc.com/news/uk-northern-ireland-foyle-west-57767339 (accessed 18 October 2021).

Spencer, G., *The State of Loyalism in Northern Ireland*, London, Palgrave Macmillan, 2008.

Spencer, G., *Protestant Identity and Peace in Northern Ireland,* London, Palgrave Macmillan, 2012.

Spencer, G., *The British and Peace in Northern Ireland: The Process and Practice of Reaching Agreement,* Cambridge, Cambridge University Press, 2015.

Spencer, G., *From Armed Struggle to Political Struggle: Republican Tradition and Transformation in Northern Ireland,* New York and London, Bloomsbury Press, 2015.

Spencer, G., *Inside Accounts, Volume I: The Irish Government and Peace in Northern Ireland, from Sunningdale to the Good Friday Agreement,* Manchester, UK, Manchester University Press, 2019.

Spencer, G., *Inside Accounts, Volume II: The Irish Government and Peace in Northern Ireland, From the Good Friday Agreement to the Fall of Power-Sharing,* Manchester, UK, Manchester University Press, 2019.

Spencer, G. and Hudson, C., 'Dialogue needed between unionism and loyalism to create a positive, vibrant and attractive Northern Ireland', *Belfast Telegraph,* 26 July 2020, https://www.belfasttelegraph.co.uk/opinion/comment/dialogue-needed-between-unionism-and-loyalism-to-create-a-positive-vibrant-and-attractive-northern-ireland-39398253.html (accessed 18 December 2020).

Statement on Key Inequalities in Housing and Communities in Northern Ireland, Issue Brief, Equality Commission for Northern Ireland, April 2017, https://www.equalityni.org/ECNI/media/ECNI/Publications/Delivering%20Equality/HousingCommunities-KeyInequalitiesStatement.pdf (accessed 7 May 2021).

Stephan, W.G., Renfro, C.L. and Davis, M.D., 'The role of threat in intergroup relations', in Wager, U., Tropp, L.R., Finchilescu, G. and Tredoux, C. (eds), *Improving Intergroup Relations: Building on the Legacy of Thomas F. Pettigrew,* Oxford, Blackwell, 2008, pp. 55–72, https://doi.org/10.1002/9781444303117.ch5 (accessed December 4, 2020).

Stephan, W.G., Ybarra, O. and Morrison, K.R., 'Intergroup threat theory', in Nelson, T.J. (ed.), *Handbook of Prejudice, Stereotyping, and Discrimination,* New York, Psychology Press, 2009.

Stewart, A.T.Q., *The Narrow Ground: The Roots of Conflict in Ulster,* 2nd edn, London, Faber & Faber, 1989.

'The Stormont House Agreement', 23 December 2014, https://www.gov.uk/government/publications/the-stormont-house-agreement (accessed 12 February 2021).

Sutton, M., *Bear in Mind These Dead: An Index of Deaths from the Conflict in Ireland 1969–1993,* Belfast, Beyond the Pale Publications, 1994.

Symington, M., 'U.K. weighs Northern Ireland amnesty in bid to spare veterans "vexatious prosecutions"', NBCNews.com, 8 November 2021, https://www.nbcnews.com/news/world/uk-weighs-northern-ireland-amnesty-bid-spare-veterans-rcna4806 (accessed 28 June 2022).

Thompson, J., *Addressing the Legacy of Northern Ireland's Past*, Advice Paper, The Commission for Victims and Survivors, January 2019, https://www.cvsni.org /media/1970/jan-2019-addressing-the-legacy-of-northern-ireland-s-past-policy -advice-paper.pdf (accessed 12 October 2020).

Thompson, S., 'Poll: Most Tories would sacrifice union with Northern Ireland for Brexit', Belfast, *The Irish News*, 18 June 2019, https://www.irishnews.com/news /brexit/2019/06/18/news/poll-most-tories-would-sacrifice-union-with-northern -ireland-for-brexit-1644668/ (accessed 23 March 2021).

Todd, J., 'Northern Irish nationalist culture', *Irish Political Studies*, vol. 5, no. 1, 1990, pp. 31–44, https://doi.org/10.1080/07907189008406472 (accessed 3 August 2021).

Todd, J., 'From identity politics to identity change: Exogenous shocks, constitutional moments and the impact of Brexit on the island of Ireland', *Irish Studies in International Affairs*, Royal Irish Academy, vol. 28, 2017, pp. 57–72, https:// www.jstor.org/stable/10.3318/isia.2017.28.15 (accessed 3 August 2021).

Todd, J. 'Unionism, identity and Irish unity: Paradigms, problems and paradoxes', *Irish Studies in International Affairs*, vol. 32, issue 5, 2021, pp. 53–77.

Tomlinson, M.W., 'War, peace and suicide: The case of Northern Ireland', *International Sociology*, vol. 27, no. 4, 16 May 2012, pp. 464–82, https://doi.org/10.1177 /0268580912443579 (accessed 25 March 2021).

Tomlinson, M.W., 'Transition to peace leaves children of the Northern Irish Troubles more vulnerable to suicide', *Politics and Policy* [blog], London School of Economics and Political Science, 30 July 2012, https://blogs.lse.ac.uk /politicsandpolicy/northern-ireland-suicide-tomlinson/ (accessed 23 March 2021).

Tomlinson, M.W., *Dealing With Suicide: How Does Research Help?*, Issue brief, Knowledge Exchange Seminar Series, Belfast, Stormont Assembly, 11 April 2013, http://www.niassembly.gov.uk/globalassets/documents/raise/knowledge _exchange/briefing_papers/tomlinson110413.pdf (accessed 23 March 2021).

Tonge, J., 'After Brexit, what's left for Northern Ireland's unionists?', *Foreign Policy*, 21 December 2019, https://foreignpolicy.com/2019/12/21/northern-ireland-unionism -irish-unity/ (accessed 23 March 2021).

Tonge, J., 'Beyond unionism versus nationalism: The rise of the Alliance Party of Northern Ireland', *The Political Quarterly*, vol. 91, no. 2, April–June 2020, pp. 461–6, https://doi.org/10.1111/1467-923x.12857 (accessed 16 January 2021).

Towards an Agreed and Reconciled Future: Sinn Féin Policy on Reconciliation and Healing, Belfast, Sinn Féin [website], June 2016, https://www.sinnfein.ie/files/2016 /ReconciliationDoc_2016.pdf (accessed 28 June 2022).

Towards a United Ireland — A Sinn Féin Discussion Document, Belfast, Sinn Féin [website], 2016, https://www.sinnfein.ie/files/2016/Towards-a-United-Ireland.pdf (accessed 28 June 2022).

Trimble, D., 'The Belfast Agreement', *Fordham International Law Journal*, vol. 22, no. 4, 1998, pp. 1144–70, https://ir.lawnet.fordham.edu/ilj/vol22/iss4/2/ (accessed 28 June 2022).

Trimble, D., 'Speech by Rt. Hon. David Trimble to the Northern Ireland Forum, 17 April 1998', Northern Ireland Forum, Belfast, 17 April 1998, Ulster University CAIN Archive, https://cain.ulster.ac.uk/events/peace/docs/dt17498.htm (accessed 28 June 2022).

Trimble, D., *To Raise Up a New Northern Ireland: Articles and Speeches by the Rt. Hon. David Trimble MP MLA, 1998–2001*, Belfast, Belfast Press, 2001.

Trimble, D., 'Reflections on the Belfast Agreement', Antony Alcock Memorial Lecture, Belfast, University of Ulster, 24 April 2007, http://www.ricorso.net/rx/az-data/authors/t/Trimble_D/xtra.htm (accessed 28 June 2022).

'Two-thirds of people in the Republic of Ireland support a united Ireland', *Irish Central*, 31 January 2019, https://www.irishcentral.com/news/two-thirds-of-people-in-the-republic-of-ireland-would-vote-for-a-united-ireland (accessed 14 June 2021).

'Ulster Unionist Party supports staying in EU', *Belfast Telegraph*, 5 March 2016, https://www.belfasttelegraph.co.uk/news/northern-ireland/ulster-unionist-party-supports-staying-in-eu-34514128.html (accessed 7 July 2021).

Van der Kolk, B., *The Body Keeps the Score: Brain, Mind, and Body in the Healing of Trauma*, New York, Penguin Books, 2015.

Volkan, V., 'Trauma, identity, and search for a solution in Cyprus', *Insight Turkey*, vol. 10, no. 4, October 2008, pp. 96–110, https://www.jstor.org/stable/26330813 (accessed 3 April 2021).

Volkan, V.D., 'Chosen trauma: Unresolved mourning', in *Bloodlines: From Ethnic Pride to Ethnic Terrorism*, New York, Farrar, Straus & Giroux, 1997, pp. 36–49.

Volkan, V.D., Julius D.A. and Montville, J.V., *The Psychodynamics of International Relationships: Concepts and Theories*, Lanham, MD, Lexington Books, 1990.

Walker, B.M., *A Political History of the Two Irelands: From Partition to Peace*, Basingstroke, UK, Palgrave Macmillan, 2012.

Waller, J., *A Troubled Sleep: Risk and Resilience in Contemporary Northern Ireland*, Oxford, Oxford University Press, 2021.

Whysall, A., 'A Northern Ireland border poll', The Constitution Unit, University College London, March 2019, https://www.ucl.ac.uk/constitution-unit/sites/constitution-unit/files/185_a_northern_ireland_border_poll.pdf (accessed 28 June 2022).

Whyte, J.H., *Church and State in Modern Ireland, 1923–1979*, Dublin, Gill & Macmillan, 1980.

Whyte, J.H., 'How much discrimination was there under the unionist regime, 1921–68?', in Gallagher, T. and O'Connell, J., *Contemporary Irish Studies*, Man-

chester, UK, Manchester University Press, 1983, https://cain.ulster.ac.uk/issues
/discrimination/whyte.htm (accessed 23 March 2021).

Whyte, J.H., *Interpreting Northern Ireland*, Oxford, Clarendon Press, 1991.

Wilson, R., *Northern Ireland Peace Monitoring Report, Number 4*, Belfast, Community
Relations Council, September 2016, https://www.community-relations.org.uk
/sites/crc/files/media-files/NIPMR-Final-2016.pdf (accessed 23 March 2021).

Woodhouse, C., 'Anger as RTE cuts Northern Ireland out of map', *Belfast Telegraph*,
3 September 2017, https://www.belfasttelegraph.co.uk/news/northern-ireland
/anger-as-rte-cuts-northern-ireland-out-of-map-36095292.html (accessed 23
March 2021).

Working Group on Unification Referendums on the Island of Ireland, *Final Report*,
London, The Constitution Unit, School of Public Policy, University College
London, May 2021, https://www.ucl.ac.uk/constitution-unit/sites/constitution
-unit/files/working_group_final_report.pdf (accessed 3 August 2021).

Yeginsu, C., 'In Northern Ireland, Brexit deal is seen as "betrayal"', *New York Times*,
24 October 2019, https://www.nytimes.com/2019/10/24/world/europe/northern
-ireland-brexit.html (accessed 10 April 2021).

'YouGov on the day poll: Remain 52%, Leave 48%', YouGov [website], 23 June 2016,
https://yougov.co.uk/topics/politics/articles-reports/2016/06/23/yougov-day-poll
(accessed 27 August 2021).

Young, D., 'Hutchings challenges admissibility of document naming him as "Soldier
A"', *Irish Examiner*, 11 October 2021, https://www.irishexaminer.com/news/arid
-40718526.html (accessed 13 December 2021).

Notes

INTRODUCTION

1   S. Collins, 'Ahern says Stormont agreement could be possible by end of May',
    The Irish Times, 8 April 2018.

2   P. Leahy, 'Clinton urges compromise to rescue powersharing in North', *The Irish
    Times*, 9 April 2018.

3   Among the attendees: Seamus Costello, leader of the Irish Republican and
    Socialist Party; Andy Tyrie, Ulster Defence Association (UDA) head honcho;
    their charismatic spokesperson Glenn Barr; Thomas Giolla, president of Sinn
    Féin, the political arm of the Official IRA; Martin Smyth, head of the Orange
    Order; and Alban McGuiness (SDLP).

4   Attendees included Peter Robinson; Ruairi Quinn, the Minister of Labour;
    and Michael Noonan, Minister of Justice; Enda Kenny, subsequently
    Taoiseach; Chris Patten, Minister of State for Northern Ireland, subsequently
    the last governor of Hong Kong European Commissioner and currently
    Chancellor of Oxford University; Mary Robinson, subsequently President
    of Ireland; John Hume, leader of the SDLP, subsequently co-winner of the
    Nobel Prize for Peace; Des O'Malley, Fianna Fáil, subsequently leader of
    the Progressive Democrats; Harold McCusker, deputy leader of the Ulster
    Unionist Party (UUP); Seán Donlon, Secretary of the Irish Department of
    Foreign Affairs; and David Goodall, Deputy Secretary to the UK Cabinet. See
    also Department of Taoiseach, Airlie House Conference on Northern Ireland
    [memo], Warrenton, Virginia, United States, 6–9 January, https://cain.ulster
    .ac.uk/nai/1985/nai_TSCH-2015-89-35_1985-01198515.pdf#:~:text=Airlie%20
    House%20Conference%20on%20Northern%20Ireland%2C%20held%20in,
    organised%20by%20the%20Committee%20for%20an%20Irish%20Forum;
    Airlie House Conference on Northern Ireland, 1985. https://openlibrary.org/books
    /OL21434633M; C.D.O. Barrie, Republic of Ireland Department, Airlie House

Conference on Northern Ireland [memo], Warrenton, Virginia, 6–9 January 1985, https://cain.ulster.ac.uk/proni/1985/proni_CENT-3-32A_1985-01-18.pdf.

5   *A Citizens' Inquiry: The Opsahl Report on Northern Ireland*, Andy Pollak (ed.) (Dublin, 1993).

6   Attendees included David Trimble, leader UUP; Jeffrey Donaldson, then UUP; Monica McWilliams, Women's Coalition; David Irvine (PUP); Billy Hutchinson (PUP); Peter Robinson (DUP); Martin McGuinness and Gerry Kelly, Sinn Féin; M. Purdy, 'Nelson Mandela's ties to Northern Ireland', BBC News, 5 December 2013; P. O'Malley, 'The narcissism of small differences: What the IRA learned from the ANC', *Daily Maverick*, 15 October 2020.

7   Under the terms of the EU/UK Withdrawal Act, Northern Ireland remains in the Single Market and customs union. This ensures the free movement of goods between the South and the North but requires checks on goods entering Northern Ireland from Britain to ensure they meet EU customs and regulatory standards. In short, the protocol is tantamount to a border down the Irish Sea. The British government and the Democratic Unionist Party (DUP) demands a replacement with an entirely new arrangement that would do away with checks on goods coming into Northern Ireland from Britain. The EU is not open to renegotiating the Withdrawal Agreement.

8   *Northern Ireland Act 1998*, UK General Public Acts – 1998, London, The National Archives, 19 November 1998, https://www.legislation.gov.uk/ukpga/1998/47/contents.

9   A. Morris, 'Loyalist paramilitaries to target Irish government buildings as 1987 weapons could be used in campaign against NI protocol', *Belfast Telegraph*, 27 March 2022.

10   Article 16 allows one party to the Northern Ireland Protocol (NIP) to unilaterally suspend implementation under a very specific set of circumstances.

11   'Police attacked at Derry republican march on anniversary of Lyra McKee's death', *The Irish Times*, 18 April 2022.

12   A. Morris, 'Loyalism's escalation is a worrying step towards darker days', *Belfast Telegraph*, 28 March 2022.

13   A. Morris, 'Loyalist paramilitaries couldn't back ceasefires now: PUP', *Belfast Telegraph*, 24 March 2022.

14   A. Morris, 'Loyalism's escalation is a worrying step towards darker days', *Belfast Telegraph*, 28 March 2022.

15   IRC Fourth Report (December 2021), https://www.ircommission.org/news-centre/irc-fourth-report; Allison Morris. 'The Northern Ireland-related terrorism threat level in Northern Ireland has been lowered from SEVERE to SUBSTANTIAL for the first time in 12 years', *Belfast Telegraph*, 24 March.

16   'Simon Coveney: "Loyalist paramilitaries behind north Belfast security alert", police say', BBC News, 25 March 2022.

17   Adrian Guelke, *Politics in Deeply Divided Societies* (Cambridge, 2012), p. 9.

18   'Your essential guide to Northern Ireland's elections', *Jnews*, 21 April 2022.

19   Seanin Graham. 'Threat of violence rises as loyalists vent frustrations with protocol', *The Irish Times*, 31 March 2022.

20   Interview with Graham Spencer, 1 March 2022.

21   The party was careful to step away from mention of either a border poll or Irish unity while campaigning for the Assembly. With a series of polls that showed it six to seven points ahead of the DUP and well on its way to becoming the largest party in the Assembly, it didn't want to jeopardize its position by frightening unionist voters into coalescing around the DUP. Hence its emphasis on the cost of living, the economy, mental health issues and others identifying through polling as being of most concerns to voters, issues the Assembly parties could do little about. Its election manifesto was a scant thirteen pages in contrast to the Alliance's, which ran to nearly one hundred pages. Alliance Party Manifesto, https://www.theallianceparty.com/manifesto; Sinn Féin Assembly Election Manifesto, https://vote.sinnFéin.ie/assembly-manifesto-2022.

1. BREXIT

1   G. Osborne, 'Unleashing nationalism has made the future of the UK the central issue', *Evening Standard*, 19 January 2021.

2   M. Hastings, 'How delusions about World War II fed Brexit mania', *Bloomberg*, 3 January 2021.

3   Interview with Gary Mason, 8 December 2020.

4   Interview with Winston Irvine, 7 December 2020.

5   Interview with John, Lord Alderdice, 4 March 2020.

6   F. Cochrane, *Breaking Peace* (Manchester, 2020), p. 8. See also J. Todd, 'From identity politics to identity change: Exogenous shocks, constitutional moments and the impact of Brexit on the island of Ireland', *Irish Studies in International Affairs*, vol. 28 (2017), pp. 57–72; J. Coakley, 'Choosing between unions? Unionist opinion and the challenge of Brexit', *Irish Political Studies*, vol. 35, no. 3, 2020, pp. 356–77; D. O'Ceallaigh, P. Gillespie and A. Gilmore (eds), *Brexit Status Report: 2016–2019 and Beyond*, The Institute of International and European Affairs, 2019. Both the UK in a Changing Europe and the Institute for British-Irish Studies at University College Dublin keep archives on Brexit, including interviews with those directly or peripherally involved in how and why key decisions were made. For the former, go to 'Brexit Witness Archive', UK in a Changing Europe [website], 2022, https://ukandeu.ac.uk/brexit-witness-archive/. For the latter, go to 'Brexit Witness project: Negotiating the Northern Ireland/Ireland dimension of the UK's withdrawal from the EU, 2016–2020', Institute for British-Irish Studies [website], 2015, https://www.ucd.ie/ibis/research/currentresearch/brexitwitnessprojectnegotiatingthenorthernirelandirelanddimensionoftheukswithdrawalfromtheeu2016-2020.

7   T. Shipman and J. Allardyce, 'Union in crisis as polls reveal voters want refer-
    endum on Scottish independence and united Ireland', *The Times*, 23 January 2021.

8   K. McEvoy, A. Bryson and A. Kramer, 'The empire strikes back: Brexit, the Irish
    peace process, and the limitations of law', *Fordham International Law Journal*,
    vol. 43, 2020.

9   F. Campbell, 'Living with partition: A century on', Agape Centre, 29 October 2019.

10 'EU Referendum Results', BBC News, 2020.

11 J. Doyle, 'Reflecting on the Northern Ireland Conflict and Peace Process: 20 years
    since the Good Friday Agreement', *Irish Studies in International Affairs*, 2019.

12 F. O'Toole, *Heroic Failure: Brexit and the Politics of Pain* (London, 2018).

13 Cochrane, p. 177.

14 Cochrane, pp. 177–8.

15 On 8 May 2019, the Irish and UK governments signed a Memorandum of
    Understanding reaffirming the Common Travel Area (CTA) and identifying
    the rights and privileges of Irish and UK citizens within the CTA. It also reaf-
    firmed the commitment to maintain the CTA following Brexit. See 'Common
    travel area between Ireland and the UK', Citizens Information Board, 2022.

16 T. May. 'The Government's negotiating objectives in exiting the EU': PM speech,
    Gov.UK, 17 January 2017.

17 'General election 2017: Why did Theresa May call an election?', BBC News, 9
    June 2017.

18 A. Travis, '"Confidence and supply": What does it mean and how will it work
    for the new government?', *The Guardian*, 11 June 2017.

19 United Kingdom, Parliament, *Confidence and Supply Agreement Between the
    Conservative and Unionist Party and the Democratic Unionist Party*, policy
    paper, Crown, 2020.

20 M. Daly, P. Dolan and M. Brennan, 'Northern Ireland returning to violence
    as a result of a hard border due to Brexit or a rushed border poll: Risks
    for youth', 2019, https://senatormarkdaly.files.wordpress.com/2019/02/unesco
    -professors-report-on-return-to-violence.pdf.

21 P. Maguire, 'Hard border "would be target for violence"', *The Times*, 8 December
    2017; J. Angelos, 'Will Brexit bring the Troubles back to Northern Ireland?', *The
    New York Times*, 8 April 2021.

22 J. Garry et al., 'Northern Ireland and the UK's exit from the EU: What do people
    think?', Economic and Social Research Council, 2018.

23 C. Russell, 'Fear of return to violence if customs checkpoints brought back after
    Brexit', *The Journal*, 4 December 2017.

24 K. McCann, C. Hope and J. Crisp, 'How a phone call from Arlene Foster in the
    middle of lunch ended Theresa May's hopes of an Irish border deal', *The Daily
    Telegraph*, 4 December 2017.

25 Article 49 of the provisional agreement stated that 'in the absence of agreed solu-
    tions, the United Kingdom will maintain full alignment with those rules of the

Internal Market and the Customs Union, which now or in the future, support North South cooperation, the all-island economy, and the protection of the 1998 Agreement'. See also D. Cameron, 'In letter to Donald Tusk, Johnson proposes legal remedy for Irish "backstop"', Yale MacMillan Canter, 20 August 2019.

26 K. Rawlinson, 'Full texts of Boris Johnson's resignation letter and PM's reply', *The Guardian*, 9 July 2018.

27 R. Carroll, M. Savage and T. Helm, 'Britain on verge of historic blunder, warns Johnson at DUP conference', *The Guardian*, 24 November 2018; Steerpike, 'Boris Johnson's speech to DUP conference: "we are on the verge of making a historic mistake"', *The Spectator*, 23 November 2018.

28 United Kingdom, Department for Exiting the European Union, *Northern Ireland: EU Withdrawal Agreement*, bill, Crown, 2019.

29 Commonwealth, *Parliamentary Debates*, House of Commons, 4 September 2019, 664 (Boris Johnson, Prime Minister); C. Gleeson, 'Johnson backed into a corner despite rare Commons win', *The Irish Times*, 26 October 2019.

30 M. Laver, 'Boris the mad general or Boris the Ruthless?', *The Irish Times*, 10 September 2019.

31 H. McGee, 'Leaks, bluster, and secret talks: The inside story of a pivotal week in Brexit', *The Irish Times*, 11 October 2019.

32 'Supplying authorised medicines to Northern Ireland', Gov.UK, 20 December 2020, https://www.gov.uk/guidance/supplying-authorised-medicines-to-northern -ireland.

33 Verónica Huertas Cerdeira (Press officer, Council of the EU), *Brexit: Council adopts decision to conclude the withdrawal agreement* (press release), 30 January 2020, European Council.

34 United Kingdom, 2019, op. cit.

35 A YouGov Poll in July 2019 showed that 59 per cent of Conservative Party members were prepared to see Northern Ireland leave the UK if that was what was needed to secure Brexit (63 per cent were prepared to let Scotland go to achieve the same result). See also M. Smith, 'Most Conservative members would see party destroyed to achieve Brexit', *YouGov* (blog), 18 June 2019; J. Garry et al., 'The future of Northern Ireland: Border anxieties and support for Irish reunification under varieties of UK exit', *Regional Studies*, vol. 55, no. 9, 2021.

36 Interview with David Ford, 12 March 2020.

37 Interview with Sam McBride, 11 December 2020.

38 Interview with Jim O'Callaghan, 15 March 2021.

39 Ibid.

40 M. Lillis, 'The Anglo-Irish Agreement', in M. Daly (ed.), *Brokering the Good Friday Agreement: The Untold Story* (Dublin, 2019).

41 Email correspondence from Seán Ó hUiginn, 3 February 2022.

42 T. Connelly, *Brexit and Ireland: The Dangers, the Opportunities, and the Inside Story of the Irish Response* (Dublin, 2017).

43 Cochrane, p. 82.

44 Ibid.; N. Dooley, 'Frustrating Brexit? Ireland and the UK's conflicting approaches to Brexit negotiations', *Journal of European Public Policy*, 15 March 2022.

45 'Soft' unionists refer to unionists who may be open to Irish reunification under certain circumstances, mostly relating to where they think they would be better off in an all-Ireland state. They are not ideologically and emotionally committed to being British within the United Kingdom.

46 'Northern Ireland General Election Survey', 2019, op. cit.

47 P. Donaghy, 'Northern Ireland Life and Times survey suggests slight increase in support for Irish unity and cross-community support for abortion reform', *Slugger O'Toole*, 16 June 2017. The 2016 Northern Ireland Life and Times (NILT) survey reported that 'support for a united Ireland amongst Alliance voters was 21 per cent in 2016, compared with 12 per cent in 2015 and 8 per cent in 2014'. In addition, 29 per cent of Alliance respondents said the Brexit outcome had made them 'more in favour of Irish unity'. That figure was identical for both Catholic and Protestant Alliance voters.

48 Interview with Naomi Long, 4 December 2020.

49 K. Hayward and B. Rosher, 'Political attitudes in Northern Ireland in a period of transition', *ARK Research Update*, Number 142, June 2021.

50 Ibid.

51 See Chapter 5 for discussion of how different polling methodologies produce different results. S. McBride, 'Northern Ireland has become a more tolerant but more polarised society', *Belfast Telegraph*, 28 May 2022.

52 J. Henley, 'Dutch officials seize ham sandwiches of drivers arriving from UK', *The Guardian*, 11 January 2021.

53 G. Parker et al., 'Inside the Brexit deal: Brexit and its aftermath', *Financial Times*, 22 January 2021.

54 Rt Hon. Boris Johnson, 'Prime Minister's statement on EU negotiations: 24 December 2020', statement from Prime Minister's Office, 10 Downing Street, 24 December 2020.

55 J. Owen et al., *Getting Brexit Done: What Happens Now?*, Institute for Government Insight, January 2020, p. 4.

56 X. Richards, 'Brexit: Westminster forced to compromise on illegal Internal Market Bill', *The National*, 16 September 2020.

57 'Northern Ireland Secretary admits new bill will "break international law"', BBC News, 8 September 2020.

58 J. Douch Guillot (EP Spokesperson and Director General for Communication) and D. Colard (Head of Spokesperson's Unit and Deputy Spokesperson), *Statement of the UK Coordination Group and the leaders of the political groups of the EP* (press release), 11 September 2020, European Parliament.

59 P. Wintour, 'Biden and Pelosi warn UK over risking Good Friday Agreement', *The Guardian*, 16 September 2020.

60   'Fifth ex-PM speaks out against post-Brexit bill', BBC News, 14 September 2020.

61   'Whitehall sources said Jonathan Jones resigned after clashing with the attorney general over the UK's plan to override parts of the Brexit withdrawal agreement' in J. Elgot and O. Bowcott, 'Jonathan Jones' resignation over Brexit lawbreaking met with dismay', *The Guardian*, 8 September 2020. See also 'Senior government lawyer quits over Brexit plans', BBC News, 8 September 2020.

62   D. Staunton, 'Brexit: Johnson says breaking law needed to stop "foreign power" splitting UK', *The Irish Times*, 11 September 2020.

63   P. Leahy and M. O'Halloran, '"It's spin and not the truth": Coveney dismisses UK claims UK may block goods entering Northern Ireland', *The Irish Times*, 13 September 2020.

64   C. McQuinn, 'Simon Coveney accuses Boris Johnson of "spin" as he warns of "damage" to Britain's reputation', *Independent.ie*, 13 September 2020.

65   L. Brooks and S. Morris, 'Plan for post-Brexit UK internal market bill "is an abomination"', *The Guardian*, 9 September 2020.

66   'UK's new Brexit bill is "legal safety net", PM Johnson says', Euronews, 9 September 2020.

67   'Brexit: Boris Johnson says powers will ensure UK cannot be "broken up"', BBC News, 14 September 2020.

68   *Trade and Cooperation Agreement Between the European Union and the European Atomic Energy Community, of the One Part, and the United Kingdom of Great Britain and Northern Ireland, of the Other Part*, opened for signature 30 December 2020, I–23002 (entered into force 1 May 2021).

69   D. Boffey and L. O'Carroll, 'UK and EU agree Brexit trade deal', *The Guardian*, 24 December 2020.

70   M. Matthijs, 'What's in the EU-UK Brexit Deal?', Council on Foreign Relations, 28 December 2020.

71   Ibid.

72   A. Payne, 'Brexit poll finds record majority of British people think leaving the EU was a mistake', *The Insider*, 17 November 2020.

73   A. Sandford, 'Brexit trade deal: Nine claims by Boris Johnson or his ministers that are untrue', Euronews, 6 January 2021.

74   T. Helm, 'Baffling Brexit rules threaten export chaos, Gove is warned', *The Guardian*, 10 January 2021; C. Clohisey, 'Frictionless free trade? Not yet, anyway …', *Accountancy Ireland*, 9 February 2021.

75   Interview with Katy Hayward, 16 February 2021. Hayward is a recognized international expert on Brexit. See also K. Hayward, 'Life and work across the Irish border through Brexit', *Réalités Industrielles*, 2020, pp. 101–5; Queen's University Belfast, 'Insight and Analysis' (website); K. Hayward, *What Do We Know and What Should We Do About the Irish Border?* (Sage Publications Ltd, 2021); 'UK in a changing Europe, articles by Professor Katy Hayward' (website), https://ukandeu.ac.uk/author/khayward/.

76 K. Maclellan and E. Piper, 'Provoking EU, UK sets out new law to fix post-Brexit Northern Ireland trade', Reuters, 17 May 2022.

77 B. Roche and R. McGreevy, '"Main block to protocol deal is British government, not DUP," says Taoiseach', *The Irish Times*, 14 May 2022.

2. THE NORTHERN IRELAND PROTOCOL

1   T. Blair, Foreword to 'Fixing the Northern Ireland Protocol: A way forward', in A. Spisak, T. Blair, 'Institute for Global Change', 1 June 2022. https://institute.global/policy/fixing-northern-ireland-protocol-way-forward.

2   Interview with Ian Marshall, 28 April 2021.

3   R. Shrimsley, 'Democratic unionists are now Irish reunification's secret weapon', *Financial Times*, 20 January 2021.

4   Interview with Katy Hayward, 16 February 2021.

5   Revised Protocol to the Withdrawal Agreement (n.d.), https://assets.publishing.service.gov.uk.

6   L. O'Carroll, 'Brexit: Huge jump in trade between Ireland and Northern Ireland', *The Guardian*, 15 February 2022.

7   F. McClements, 'Unionist leaders jointly declare opposition to Northern Ireland protocol', *The Irish Times*, 28 September 2021.

8   The Anglo-Irish Agreement (1985) between Margaret Thatcher's and Garret FitzGerald's governments acknowledged for the first time that the Irish government had a role to play in Northern Ireland as the guarantor of the rights of the Catholic community. It provided for a physical presence of Irish government officials in Northern Ireland. It was negotiated behind the back of unionists but with the full knowledge of the SDLP. Unionists loathed the Anglo-Irish Agreement (AIA), which they saw as the first step to joint authority. Ultimately, the Belfast/Good Friday Agreement (B/GFA) replaced the AIA.

9   'Ben Lowry: Loyalist protest meeting in Portadown against Boris Johnson's "Betrayal Act" was packed and angry', *News Letter*, 25 November 2019.

10 S. Breen, 'Brexit: Loyalist Bryson warns of "mass resistance" from unionist community', *Belfast Telegraph*, 23 October 2019.

11 J. Tonge et al., 'Same but different? The Democratic Unionist Party and Ulster Unionist Party compared', *Irish Political Studies*, vol. 35, no. 3, 2020.

12 J. Pow, 'The DUP and the protocol', *UK in a Changing Europe*, 10 February 2021; C. Rice, 'Brexit: "My NI business now has the best of both worlds"', BBC News, 4 February 2021.

13 E.J. Ward, 'Boris Johnson says absolutely "no border down the Irish sea"', lbc.co.uk, 15 November 2019; A. Kula, 'Boris Johnson: Only over my dead body will there be a border in the Irish Sea', *News Letter*, 13 August 2020; J. Sargeant, 'Brexit: If the Northern Ireland protocol is not ready by New Year's Eve 2020, the UK could face infringement proceedings at the European Court', *Prospect*,

16 January 2020; J. Sargeant, 'Why this Irish border protocol could see the UK face infringement proceedings', *Prospect*, 16 January 2020.

14 J. Stone, 'EU confirms there will be border checks inside UK under Brexit deal, contradicting Boris Johnson's false claim', *The Independent*, 14 January 2020.

15 P. Daly and M. Baynes, 'Johnson tells Northern Ireland businesses to "bin" customs forms', *Belfast Telegraph*, 8 November 2019.

16 A report by the Treasury said there would be customs declarations and security checks between Northern Ireland and Great Britain. 'Even if a zero-trade deal is reached there will be customs formalities as Northern Ireland will be enforcing EU's customs rules at its ports,' in 'Irish Sea border: What UK/EU withdrawal agreement says on goods movement', *Belfast Telegraph*, 15 January 2020.

17 Ibid.

18 S. Kelly, *Margaret Thatcher, the Conservative Party and the Northern Ireland Conflict, 1975–1990* (Bloomsbury Academic, 2021), p. 152.

19 Ibid., p. 4.

20 H.M. Government CP 502, 'Northern Ireland Protocol: The way forward', July 2021, https://assets.publishing.service.gov.uk/government/uploads/system /uploads/attachment_data/file/1008451/CCS207_CCS0721914902-005_ Northern_Ireland_Protocol_Web_Accessible__1_.pdf.

21 L. O'Carroll, 'Why is UK publishing a "command paper" on Northern Ireland Protocol?', *The Guardian*, 21 July 2021. The command paper called for the removal of any role for EU institutions, continuing with partial implementation of the protocol, an indefinite 'grace period' before the second phase of regulatory align-ment were implemented, abolition of customs paperwork with a 'trust and verify' system where traders from Great Britain selling into Northern Ireland would register their sales in a light-touch system allowing for inspection of their supply chains. *The Guardian* also notes that: 'It sought a dual regulatory system whereby manufactured or phytosanitary goods could be sold in Northern Ireland as long as they meet either UK or EU as determined by either UK or EU regulations.'

22 'Absurdities on the border between Great Britain and Northern Ireland', *The Economist*, 30 January 2021.

23 S. Butler, 'M&S chair attacks "pointless" post-Brexit rules for Northern Ireland', *The Guardian*, 17 May 2022.

24 'Why is the Northern Ireland protocol so contentious?', *The Economist*, 10 March 2021.

25 '"We will examine the Brexit deal from a Northern Ireland perspective", says Arlene Foster', *News Letter*, 24 December 2020; G. Moriarty, 'Northern Executive welcomes Brexit deal despite parties' opposing positions', *The Irish Times*, 24 December 2020.

26 M. McHugh, 'Northern Ireland has "gateway of opportunity" following Brexit', *Belfast Telegraph*, 3 January 2021.

27 Ibid.

28   Ibid.

29   S. McDermott, 'Timeline: How the EU provoked anger in Ireland and the UK with plans for a hard border for vaccines', *TheJournal.ie*, 1 February 2021; J. Sargeant, 'The Article 16 vaccine row is over – but the damage has been done', Institute for Government, 30 January 2021.

30   Sargeant, op. cit.; J. Curtis, *Northern Ireland Protocol: Implementation, Grace Periods, and EU-UK Discussions (2021–2)*, The House of Commons Library, UK Parliament, 11 March 2022.

31   Interview with Ian Paisley, Jr, 16 February 2021.

32   Ibid.

33   Ibid.

34   On the contrary, on 14 March 2022 Northern Ireland's lady chief justice, Dame Siobhan Keegan, along with two other judges in the court, concluded that the protocol had not illegally contravened the Acts of Union 1800, which established Northern Ireland's place in the UK, or elements of the Northern Ireland Act 1998, which followed the peace deal that year. See also L. O'Carroll, 'Northern Ireland Protocol is lawful, court of appeal rules', *The Guardian*, 14 March 2022.

35   Interview with Sammy Wilson, 6 April 2021; In September 2021 after he became party leader, Jeffrey Donaldson withdrew DUP ministers from meetings of the North South Ministerial Council. See also 'DUP to withdraw from North/South political structures, says Donaldson', *Irish Examiner*, 9 September 2021. Despite the fact that the High Court ruled that the boycott was unlawful, the DUP did not attend further meetings that were scheduled for 2021. The issue became moot when Donaldson collapsed the Executive in February 2022. See also A. Erwin, 'DUP boycott of North–South meetings is unlawful, court rules', *Belfast Telegraph*, 11 October 2021.

36   K. Proctor and D. Boffey, '"Fantastic moment": Boris Johnson signs Brexit withdrawal deal', *The Guardian*, 24 January 2020.

37   D. Frost, 'We had to agree to the Northern Ireland Protocol. Now we have to scrap it', *The Daily Telegraph*, 12 May 2022; S. Pogatchnik, 'Ireland: British "bad faith" on protocol sends warning to the world', *Politico*, 13 October 2021; see also Richard Rose in 'Sovereignty cuts both ways, Downing Street has forgotten that', The London School of Economics and Political Science, 14 September 2020.

38   R. Merrick, 'Boris Johnson admits agreeing Northern Ireland Protocol rules but "hoped" EU would not apply them', *The Independent*, 16 May 2022; 'Brexit: London "did not prioritise NI solutions"', BBC News, 14 May 2022.

39   L. O'Carroll, 'Northern Ireland Protocol is lawful, court of appeal rules', *The Guardian*, 14 March 2022.

40   Secretary of State for Northern Ireland by Command of H.M. (1998), 'The Belfast Agreement: An Agreement Reached at the Multi-Party Talks on Northern Ireland', London, The Stationery Office Ltd.

41   P. Robinson, 'Peter Robinson: Unionists might face a choice between keeping Stormont or scrapping the Irish Sea border', *News Letter*, 12 February 2021.

42   'EU offers to scrap most checks on goods heading for N. Ireland', *Financial Times*, 13 October 2021; A. Szucs. 'EU offers solution to Northern Ireland's medicine supply amid post Brexit dispute', Anadolu Agency, 17 December 2021.

43   C. Gallardo, '"No role" for EU court in Northern Ireland disputes, says UK Brexit minister', *Politico*, 25 October 2021.

44   S. Pogatchnik, 'Ireland slams UK protocol demands as insatiable', *Politico*, 11 October 2021.

45   A. Kane, 'The gulf between Coveney and unionists: How it grew and why it's unlikely to change', *Belfast Telegraph*, 9 March 2021.

46   J. Campbell, 'Brexit: EU says UK grace period extension breaches international law', BBC News, 3 March 2021.

47   Kane, op. cit.

48   D. Trimble, 'Tear up the Northern Ireland Protocol to save the Belfast Agreement', *The Irish Times*, 20 February 2021.

49   Ibid.

50   Ibid.

51   Ibid.

52   Ibid.

53   Ibid.

54   Ibid.

55   Ibid.

56   Ibid.

57   Quoted by Sam McBride, 'If even Trimble opposed NI Protocol, how can the EU play the good Friday card,' *Belfast Telegraph*, 30 July 2022.

58   A. Cowburn, 'Brexit: EU "simply can't trust" Boris Johnson's government as a negotiating partner, says Simon Coveney', *The Independent*, 4 March 2021.

59   S. Breen, 'Loyalist terrorists pull their support for Good Friday Agreement over Brexit border in Irish Sea', *Belfast Telegraph*, 3 March 2021. The LCC copied Foster, O'Neill, Martin, Maroš Šefčovič, the EU's new man in charge of the Brexit portfolio and the US consul general.

60   L. Harte, 'Unionist confidence and support for Good Friday Agreement "diminishing rapidly", says DUP's Donaldson', *Belfast Telegraph*, 4 March 2021.

61   'Belfast: Rioting "was worst seen in Northern Ireland in years"', BBC News, 8 April 2021; A. Morris, 'Loyalist youngsters lured to interface violence through fake social media accounts', *Belfast Telegraph*, 9 April 2021; M. Hirst, 'NI riots: What is behind the violence in Northern Ireland?', BBC News, 14 April 2021; 'The ghosts of Northern Ireland's Troubles 'Brexit: EU "simply can't trust" Boris Johnson's government as a negotiating partner, are back. What's going on?', *The New York Times*, 12 April 2021.

62   L. O'Carroll, 'Northern Ireland Police say paramilitaries not behind recent violence', *The Guardian*, 9 April 2021.

63 Interview with Father Tim Bartlett, 8 July 2021.

64 L. O'Carroll, 'Taoiseach says Northern Ireland must not "spiral back to dark place"', *The Guardian*, 10 April 2021; L. O'Carroll, R. Carroll and R. Syal, 'White House expresses concern over Northern Ireland violence', *The Guardian*, 8 April 2021.

65 R. Carroll, 'Ignored, bullied, patronised: Why loyalists in Northern Ireland say no to Brexit "betrayal"', *The Guardian*, 12 June 2021; See more detailed discussions about the riots in Chapters 13 and 15.

66 L. O'Carroll, R. Carroll and R. Syal, op. cit.

67 P. Wintour, 'Biden and Pelosi warn UK over risking Good Friday Agreement', *The Guardian*, 16 September 2020; 'Congressman tells Prime Minister that Good Friday Agreement cannot be undermined', *IrishCentral*, 23 September 2021. 'The declaration states: "We, the undersigned unionist political leaders, affirm our opposition to the Northern Ireland Protocol, its mechanisms and structures and reaffirm our unalterable position that the protocol must be rejected and replaced by arrangements which fully respect Northern Ireland's position as a constituent and integral part of the United Kingdom"', in 'Brexit: Unionist leaders unite in NI Protocol opposition', BBC News, 28 September 2021.

68 'Unionist leaders come together at conference event to denounce NI Protocol', *Belfast Telegraph*, 4 October 2021.

69 S. McBride, 'Shackled to Brexit, Arlene Foster can't admit that it has been disastrous for union – but Irish Sea border is radically reshaping NI', *News Letter*, 24 January 2021.

70 R. Syal, 'MPs pass Brexit trade deal by 521 votes to 73', *The Guardian*, 30 December 2020.

71 S. Breen, 'DUP rejects suggestion party should have agreed to Theresa May's backstop', *Belfast Telegraph*, 21 January 2021.

72 'LT NI quarterly "Tracker" Poll – Spring 2021', LucidTalk, 25 May 2021, https://www.lucidtalk.co.uk/single-post/lt-ni-quarterly-tracker-poll-spring-2021.

73 G. Bowden, 'Lord Frost resigns as Brexit minister', BBC News, 19 December 2021.

74 E. Casalicchio, G. Lanktree and C. Gallardo, 'Everything you need to know about Liz Truss', *Politico*, 15 September 2021.

75 Boris Johnson's future was in doubt after the public learned that staff at 10 Downing Street had attended a party during lockdown when strict social distancing protocols were in place. Johnson had attended some and – until videos surfaced showing his unmistakable presence – subsequently lied about his attendance. 'Boris Johnson: Senior Tories urge PM to quit after party apology', BBC News, 13 January 2022; C. Mason, 'Partygate fines: Are Boris Johnson and Rishi Sunak finished?', 12 April 2022. In April 2022, the Metropolitan Police fined Johnson and Sunak for attending lockdown parties at 10 Downing Street. Then, with Parliament preoccupied with the war in Ukraine, Johnson made a high-profile visit to Kyiv to walk the streets with President Zelensky, distracting

attention from his lies and breaking protocol. The war provided an opportunity for 'global Britain' in the post-EU era to strut its stuff.

76 J. Henley, 'Poll finds Anglo-French antipathy on rise amid post-Brexit bickering', *The Guardian*, 8 December 2021; T. Kingsley, 'Most voters say Brexit has gone badly, new poll finds', *The Independent*, 26 December 2021; A. Menon, 'Covid has been an easy scapegoat for economic disruption, but Brexit is biting', *The Guardian*, 31 January 2022; B. Chapman, 'Brexit: Shoppers face less choice and higher prices as food suppliers ditch UK over new red tape', *The Independent*, 1 February 2022; R. Merrick, 'Fresh delay to Brexit checks on EU imports being considered amid cost-of-living crisis', *The Independent*, 29 March 2022; H. Thomas, 'The UK is still wrestling with the incoherence of Brexit', *Financial Times*, 31 March 2022; C. Blackhurst, 'Haulier shortage encapsulates the trade disaster of Brexit', *The Independent*, 16 April 2022; R. Merrick. 'Brexit has devastated UK exports to smaller countries, study says', *The Independent*, 26 April 2022; P. Aldrick, 'UK sees inflation hitting highest since Falklands War in 1982', *Bloomberg*, 23 March 2022; R. Sullivan, 'Only 18 per cent of Britons think Brexit is going well', *The Independent*, 26 November 2021; J. Stone, 'Brexit trade deals may not deliver any "actual economic" benefits, MPs warn', *The Independent*, 22 March 2022; A. Forrest, 'Brexit will keep wages down and make UK poorer in decade ahead, study finds', *The Independent*, 23 June 2022.

77 M. Lander and S. Castle, 'Boris Johnson survives no-confidence vote over lockdown parties, but is left reeling politically', *The New York Times*, 6 June 2022, https://www.nytimes.com/2022/06/06/world/europe/boris-johnson-vote.html.

78 'Boris Johnson narrowly wins a vote of confidence,' *The Economist*, 6 June 2022, https://www.economist.com/britain/2022/06/06/boris-johnson-narrowly-wins-a-vote-of-confidence; O. Kelleher and N. O'Leary, 'Tory divisions must not dictate UK approach to Protocol, says Coveney', *The Irish Times*, 7 June 2022, https://www.irishtimes.com/politics/2022/06/07/tory-divisions-must-not-dictate-uk-approach-to-protocol-says-coveney/.

79 'Sajid Javid says "enough is enough" and "problem starts at the top" in first Commons statement since quitting', *Yahoo! News*, 6 July 2022, https://uk.news.yahoo.com/sajid-javid-says-enough-enough-112800831.html; A. Isaac, 'Johnson was given 'first-hand account' of allegations against Pincher before promoting him', *Yahoo! Finance*, 4 July 2022, https://finance.yahoo.com/news/johnson-given-first-hand-account-201647795.html.

80 D. Ladden-Hall, '"Breaks" in absurdly chill resignation speech', *The Daily Beast*, 7 July 2022.

81 N. McElhatton and W. Barns-Graham, 'Liz Truss announces green and red channel plan for law changing the Northern Ireland Protocol', *Institute of Export and International Trade*, 17 May 2022.

82 A. Sparrow, 'Liz Truss says decision to ditch parts of the EU Brexit deal is "reasonable and practical"', *The Guardian*, 13 June 2022, https://www.theguardian

.com/politics/live/2022/jun/13/boris-johnson-conservatives-brexit-northern
-ireland-protocol-uk-politics-latest; 'Northern Ireland Protocol Bill', Gov.UK, 28
June 2022, https://www.gov.uk/government/collections/northern-ireland-protocol
-bill. The Bill focuses on four areas. A check-free 'green lane' would be set up for
goods destined for Northern Ireland, while trucks taking goods through the
region across the open border into the Republic of Ireland – and thus the EU
single market – would face 'red channel' checks. The bill ends the role of the
European Court of Justice in enforcing the protocol. The bill would also remove
EU control over state aid and value-added tax in the region. A fourth provision
creates a dual regulatory regime, giving businesses a choice on whether to place
goods on the market in Northern Ireland under either British or EU rules.

83   G. Parker, 'What does Northern Ireland Protocol bill do and why is it contentious?', *The Financial Times*, 13 June 2022.

84   N. O'Leary, '"Historic low point" if British unilateral action on North is
taken – Taoiseach', *The Irish Times*, 8 June 2022, https://www.irishtimes.com/
world/europe/2022/06/08/historic-low-point-if-british-unilateral-action
-on-north-is-taken-taoiseach/.

85   P. Leahy, V. Clarke and S. Burns, 'UK protocol bill "profoundly dispiriting",
says Taoiseach', *The Irish Times*, 14 June 2022, https://www.irishtimes.com
/politics/2022/06/14/uk-protocol-bill-a-fundamental-breach-of-trust-says-martin.

86   D. Hughes, 'EU launches fresh legal action against UK over Brexit protocol',
Evening Standard, 14 June 2022, https://www.standard.co.uk/news/uk/maros
-sefcovic-northern-ireland-uk-governmeneuropean-commission-brexit-b1006272.html.

87   D. Staunton, 'European Commission vice-president Šefčovič warns future
British leader on triggering article 16', *The Irish Times,* 2 September 2022.

88   R. Black, '52 of 90 MLAs sign letter to Johnson rejecting legislation to amend
NI Protocol', *Belfast Telegraph*, 14 June 2022, https://www.belfasttelegraph.co.uk
/news/northern-ireland/52-of-90-mlas-sign-letter-to-johnson-rejecting-legislation
-to-amend-ni-protocol-41748039.html.

89   J. Politi, 'Senior US lawmaker pushes UK to find "solution" to Northern Ireland
stand-off', *The Financial Times*, 22 May 2022, https://www.ft.com/content
/b539a302-f7cd-4f89-ac9e-b6ba4da96ea1.

90   Email with author 18 October 2022.

91   'EU will "respond with all measures at its disposal" if UK brings in law to
change Protocol', *TheJournal.ie*, 17 May 2022.

92   L. O'Carroll, 'EU offers to reduce Northern Ireland border checks to "a couple
of lorries a day"', *The Guardian*, 12 September 2022.

93   R. McCrea, 'Sacrificing Ireland's single market membership to prevent Border
would be dramatic change in policy', *The Irish Times*, 7 January 2022.

3. THE NORTHERN IRELAND STATELET

1   P. Robinson, 'That Northern Ireland has reached its centenary is a reflection of its success', *News Letter*, 15 January 2021.

2   M. O'Doherty, 'Changed normality', *Fortnight@50*, issue 479, September 2020, p. 43.

3   J. Gibney, 'Mr. Churchill goes to Belfast, 8 February 1912', *History Ireland* [website], https://www.historyireland.com/winston-churchill-belfast-8-february-1912/.

4   'By all means necessary', *The Irish Times*, 29 September 2012; J. Connell Jr, 'The 1912 Ulster Covenant', *History Ireland*, issue 5, September/October 2012.

5   Wikipedia [website], 'Larne gun-running', https://en.wikipedia.org/wiki/Larne _gun-running.

6   D. Ó Beacháin, *From Partition to Brexit: The Irish Government and Northern Ireland* (Manchester, UK, 2018), pp. 13–14; M. Farrell, *Northern Ireland: The Orange State* (2nd edition) (London, 1980), pp. 21–63.

7   S. Mallon and A. Pollak, *A Shared Home Place* (Dublin, 2019), p. 157.

8   Ibid., p. 158.

9   Ó Beacháin, p. 14.

10 G. Spencer (ed.), *The British and Peace in Northern Ireland* (Cambridge, UK 2015), p. 57.

11 Wikipedia [website], 'Ireland Act 1949', https://en.wikipedia.org/wiki/Ireland_ Act_1949.

12 P. Roche and B. Barton, 'Introduction', and B. Barton, 'The birth of Northern Ireland in Ireland's revolutionary period', in *The Northern Ireland Question: Perspectives on Nationalism and Unionism*, P. Roche and B. Barton (eds) (Tunbridge Wells, UK, 2020), pp. 1–67.

13 N. Jones, 'The freedom to achieve freedom', *The Critic*, 3 December 2020 [website], https://thecritic.co.uk/the-freedom-to-achieve-freedom.

14 See P. O'Malley, *The Uncivil Wars: Ireland Today* (Boston, MA, 1997), p. 148. Because of lack of attention to its proceedings and neglect and incompetence on the Irish side, the Boundary Commission's findings were shelved. On 25 November 1925, when the London *Morning Star* leaked the commission's pur-ported findings – which would only have resulted in minor changes to existing boundaries, but ended up enlarging the North's territory by adding an area of East Donegal – the South's representative on the three-person commission resigned. Subsequently, the existing borders were agreed by Ireland and the UK as the final borders. See D.H. Akenson, *United States and Ireland* (Cambridge, MA, 1973), pp. 11–12.

15 P.J. Roche and B. Barton (eds), *The Northern Ireland Question: Perspectives on Nationalism and Unionism* (Tunbridge Wells, UK, 2020), p. 201.

16 J. Whyte, 'How much discrimination was there under the Unionist regime, 1921–1968?', in T. Gallagher and J. O'Connell (eds), *Contemporary Irish Studies* (Manchester, UK, 1983), https://cain.ulster.ac.uk/issues/discrimination/whyte .htm#chap1.

17   Spencer, op. cit., p. 57; https://api.parliament.uk/historic-hansard/commons/1973
     /dec/13/northern-ireland-constitution-amendment, Northern Ireland Constitution
     (Amendment) Bill, 1973.

18   The IRA first announced its ceasefire in 1994, broken in February 1996 with the
     London Docklands bombing. For more about the history of the Good Friday
     Agreement, see J. Tonge, 'From Sunningdale to the Good Friday Agreement:
     Creating devolved government in Northern Ireland', *Contemporary British
     History*, vol. 14, issue 3, pp. 39–60.

19   This account is drawn from essays in P.J. Roche and B. Barton (eds), in *The
     Northern Ireland Question: Perspectives on Nationalism and Unionism* (Tunbridge
     Wells, UK, 2020).

20   De Valera's thinking went through several stages. By 1921, he had abandoned
     the 'must be coerced' phase. However, that's the one unionists always recount.
     See J. Bowman, 'De Valera on Ulster, 1919–1920: What he told America', *Irish
     Studies in International Affairs*, vol. 1, no. 1, 1979.

21   Catholic experiences of housing discrimination led to the founding of the
     Northern Ireland Civil Rights Association (NICRA) in Belfast on 9 April 1967,
     which organized the marches associated with the Battle of the Bogside and
     Bloody Sunday in Derry.

22   G. Gudgin, 'Discrimination in housing and employment under the Stormont
     administration' in P. Roche and B. Barton (eds), *The Northern Ireland Question:
     Nationalism, Unionism, and Partition* (London, 1999), pp. 141–88; P. Roche and B.
     Barton, 'A unionist history of Northern Ireland', *The Irish Times*, 19 February 2021.

4. THE BELFAST/GOOD FRIDAY AGREEMENT

1   Interview with Matt Carthy, 2 December 2020.

2   F. Keane, 'Fergal Keane: RIC row threatens to drag us into a dangerous place',
    The Irish Times, 8 January 2020.

3   D. Trimble, 'Multi-party agreement', *Northern Ireland Forum for Political
    Dialogue*, 17 April 1998. https://web.archive.org/web/20010220215835/http://
    www.ni-forum.gov.uk/debates/1998/170498.htm.

4   G. Adams, 'Speech to Sinn Féin Ard Fheis', 18 April 1998, https://cain.ulster.ac
    .uk/events/peace/docs/ga18498.htm.

5   Talks among the major political parties, other than Sinn Féin – purposely left
    out because of its support for the Irish Republican Army (IRA) – led to the
    Sunningdale Agreement, which resulted in a brief period of power-sharing
    (1973); a Northern Ireland Assembly (1981); the Anglo-Irish Agreement (1985),
    the product of talks between the British and Irish governments; multi-party
    talks, again excluding Sinn Féin (1990); informal back channels between the
    British government and the IRA and between the Irish government and repub-
    lican and loyalist paramilitaries (1991); the Peter Brooke initiative, a declaration

that Britain had no selfish or strategic interest in Northern Ireland (1991); the Downing Street Declaration (1993); the Frameworks Documents (1995); and multi-party talks overseen by US Senator George Mitchell (1996), which culminated in the Belfast/Good Friday Agreement (B/GFA) after a concentrated five-day marathon with an imposed deadline. Had there been no agreement by midnight on 10 April 1998, Mitchell would have packed his bags and gone home. See also D. Trimble, Speech by Rt Hon. David Trimble to the Northern Ireland Forum, 17 April 1998, CAIN Web Service; J. Coakley and J. Todd, *Negotiating a Settlement in Northern Ireland, 1969–2019* (Oxford, 2020).

6   D. Trimble, 'The Belfast Agreement', *Fordham International Law Journal*, vol. 22, no. 4 (1998), pp. 1144–70.

7   C. Gleeson, 'The inside story of how the Belfast Agreement was struck', *The Irish Times*, 3 April 2018.

8   E. Mallie, 'Twists and turns of vexed Belfast Agreement Talks revealed', *The Irish Times*, 9 April 2018.

9   G. Spencer, *From Armed Struggle to Political Struggle: Republican Tradition and Transformation in Northern Ireland* (London, 2015), p. 216.

10   Ibid.

11   Ibid., p. 179.

12   Powell, *Great Hatred, Little Room: Making Peace in Northern Ireland* (London, 1999), p. 105.

13   Ibid., p. 109.

14   Ibid., p. 106.

15   'The Agreement: Agreement reached in the multi-party negotiations' (1998), pp. 1–35, https://cain.ulster.ac.uk/events/peace/docs/agreement.htm.

16   Ibid.; Mallon, op. cit., p. 148.

17   ARK, 'The 1998 Referendums', https://www.ark.ac.uk/elections/fref98.htm.

18   F. Cochrane, *Northern Ireland: The Reluctant Peace* (New Haven, CT, 2013), p. 201.

19   Northern Ireland Life and Times Surveys (2020, 2021), Political Attitudes Module, VIEWGFA2 variable.

20   In the 2019 Northern Ireland Life and Times (NILT) survey, 67 per cent of Protestants that said the B/GFA remained the best basis for governing Northern Ireland, with 31 per cent of this total saying it shouldn't be changed and 36 per cent of this total saying it should be amended to work better. In the 2020 NILT survey, 23 per cent of all respondents said the B/GFA remained the best basis for governing Northern Ireland; a further 45 per cent said that although the B/GFA remained the best basis, it was in need of reform. Opposition to the agreement was also up by 5 points, from 10 to 15 points. In the 2021 survey, 65 per cent of respondents expressed support for the Agreement, 25 per cent in full and a further 40 per cent with the caveat it needs revision to make it work better. See Northern Ireland Life and Times Surveys (2020, 2021), Political Attitudes Module, VIEWGFA2 variable.

21   K. Hayward and B. Rosher, 'Political attitudes in Northern Ireland in a period of transition', *ARK Research Update*, Number 142, June 2021.

22   S. McBride, 'State papers: Terms of border poll discussed by Sinn Féin at private meeting', *Belfast Telegraph*, 3 January 2022.

23   Interview with Katy Hayward, 16 February 2021, and email follow-up.

24   Interview with Sam McBride, 11 December 2020.

25   According to the 2021 NILT survey, a decisive majority (65 per cent) believe that the B/GFA remains the best basis for governing Northern Ireland, either as it is or with some reforms. Overall, 76 per cent say they value to some degree Northern Ireland's having devolved powers within the United Kingdom. A University of Liverpool Poll (July 2022) reported that 81.5 per cent of respondents were in favour of 'an independent review of the Assembly and Executive to explore how they could function better'. This was supported overwhelming numbers across the political divide.

26   Interview with Matthew O'Toole, 14 May 2021.

27   E. Flanagan, 'Stormont without NI leadership for third of its lifespan', BBC News, 12 February 2022.

28   J. Doyle, 'Reflections on the Northern Ireland peace process', in *Irish Studies in International Affairs*, special issue, pp. 1–16.

29   Interview with Naomi Long, 4 December 2020.

30   J. McGarry and B. O'Leary, 'The politics of antagonism: Understanding Northern Ireland' in J. Doyle (ed.), 'Reflecting on the Northern Ireland conflict and peace process: 20 years since the Good Friday Agreement', *Irish Studies in International Affairs*, vol. 29, 2018: pp. 1–16. According to Lord Alderdice, he had proposed a weighted majority of 67% and had pressed the Minister, Paul Murphy MP, on it. However, the UUP/SDLP 'were not interested in discussing the proposal because they (especially John Hume) wanted to be the majority parties in their own communities. There was plenty of time to discuss it, but John Hume in particular did not want to consider it because he thought that the UUP/SDLP could get rid of Alliance and divide up the votes between them. What he did not appreciate (as I did) was that Alliance could survive but by creating a dynamic towards "super-Prod vs super-Taig". The DUP would take the UUP's votes and Sinn Féin would mop up the SDLP – which is of course what happened. He could not imagine the SDLP being overtaken by Sinn Féin and indeed kept denying it even after it had happened. The reason this is important is because it shows that rather than John Hume having taken the far-seeing "long view" (as is often maintained) during the Talks, he actually failed to understand the dynamics he was creating. David Trimble told me privately during the Talks that he was not sure that he had done the right thing in accepting Hume's proposal, but once he had accepted it, there was no going back.'' Email to author, 9 January 2023.

31   Interview with David Ford, 12 March 2020.

32 'Labour Force Survey Religion Report 2017: Annual update January 2019', Labour Force Survey Religion Report 2017: Annual Update January 2019, pp. 1–83.

33 Interview with Paul Nolan, 9 March 2020.

34 A. Leach et al., 'Stormont: Where Northern Irish politics splits and where it holds together', *The Guardian*, 22 June 2021.

35 Interview with Doug Beattie, 14 May 2021.

36 The Petition of Concern is a mechanism through which thirty members of the Legislative Assembly (MLAs) can require that an Assembly decision has cross-community support (either 50 per cent of total MLAs and 50 per cent of unionists and nationalist, or 60 per cent of total MLAs and 40 per cent of unionists and nationalists). It was designed to protect minority rights. However, the use of petitions of concern had been rising as both the DUP and Sinn Féin used them simply to veto policy proposals they did not support. These proposals are designed to address the overuse of petitions of concern and restore them to their original purpose. See also Institute for Government, *Northern Ireland: Restoration of the Power-sharing Executive* [website], https://www .instituteforgovernment.org.uk/explainers/northern-ireland-restoration-power -sharing-executive; C. Smyth, 'Stormont's petition of concern used 115 times in five years', *The Detail*, 29 September 2016; A. Leach et al. 'Stormont: Where Northern Irish politics splits and where it holds together', *The Guardian*, 22 June 2021.

37 M. O'Doherty, 'Unionists' priority must be to accept unity debate is real', *Belfast Telegraph*, 27 April 2021; In the 2011 census, 40 per cent identified as British, 25 per cent as Irish, 21 per cent as 'Northern Irish only'; 1 per cent described themselves as both British and Irish only. See 'Census 2011: Key statistics for Northern Ireland', *Northern Ireland Statistics and Research Agency*, December 2012, https://www.nisra.gov.uk/sites/nisra.gov.uk/files/publications/2011-census -results-key-statistics-northern-ireland-report-11-december-2012.pdf. In the NILT (2020) survey, 23 per cent identified as British, not Irish, and 19 per cent as Irish, not British. The same survey reported that 35 per cent of respondents self-identified as unionist, 19 per cent as nationalists and 42 per cent as neither; 'Northern Ireland General Election Survey 2019', NI General Election Survey 2019, NI General Election Survey 2019 (Faculty of Humanities & Social Sciences, University of Liverpool); 'Northern Ireland Life and Times Survey', Northern Ireland Life and Times Survey homepage, ARK, 14 October 2021, https://www.ark.ac.uk/nilt/.

38 The Electoral Office for Northern Ireland, 'Election results 1973–2001', https:// www.eoni.org.uk/Elections/Election-results-and-statistics/Election-results -1973-2001; The Electoral Office for Northern Ireland, 'Election results and statistics 2003 onwards', https://www.eoni.org.uk/Elections/Election-results-and -statistics/Election-results-and-statistics-2003-onwards; CAIN Web Service, 'Assembly Election (NI), Thursday 5 May 2022', https://cain.ulster.ac.uk/issues

/politics/election/2022nia/ra2022.htm. Nationalists calculated as Sinn Féin and SDLP; unionists calculated when relevant as UUP, DUP, PUP and TUV.

39   These numbers may include Alliance, Green, People Before Profit, Green Party, Independents, Labour and Women's Coalition when relevant.

40   Interview with Katy Hayward, 16 February 2021.

41   Flanagan, 2022, op. cit.

42   S. McBride, 'DUP failures leaves unionism at the crossroads, tempted to take the dangerous path of a single party', *Belfast Telegraph*, 8 May 2022. For other commentary on the Assembly 2022 results, see also: 'Sinn Féin has become Northern Ireland's biggest party', *The Economist*, 7 May 2022; 'The Irish Times view on Northern Ireland elections: Silent middle finds its voice', *The Irish Times*, 9 May 2022; S. Breen, 'Michelle O'Neill will be raising glass to DUP leader for his help in historic win', *Belfast Telegraph*, 6 May 2022; R. Carroll and L. O'Carroll, 'Sinn Féin celebrates victory, but DUP warns over Northern Ireland Protocol', *The Guardian*, 7 May 2022; S. Hui and P. Morrison, 'Sinn Féin hails "new era" as it wins Northern Ireland vote', *Associated Press*, 7 May 2022; A. Kane, 'We have changes, yes, but the dynamics remain the same at Stormont after the election', *Belfast Telegraph*, 8 May 2022; F. McClements et al., 'Assembly election: Sinn Féin wins most seats as parties urged to form Executive', *The Irish Times*, 8 May 2022; F. McClements et. al., 'Northern Ireland election: UK calls on DUP to nominate deputy first minister', *The Irish Times*, 8 May 2022; P. Murtagh, 'Unionist heartland reacts: "I feel sick she will be running our country"', *The Irish Times*, 9 May 2022; N. Reimann, 'Sinn Féin becomes biggest party in Northern Ireland Assembly. Milestone may not bring Irish unification nearer', *Forbes*, 7 May 2022.

43   A. Ferguson, 'Sinn Féin calls for united Ireland debate after historic election win', Reuters, 9 May 2022.

44   M. Fletcher, 'Is a united Ireland now inevitable?', *New Statesman*, 27 April 2022; J. Doyle, 'Will the N Ireland election pave the way for a united Ireland?', *Al Jazeera*, 3 May 2022.

45   Northern Ireland Elections, ARK, https://www.ark.ac.uk/elections/; The Electoral Office for Northern Ireland, op. cit.

46   B. Hutton, 'Upper Bann result: UUP leader Beattie defiant as he is re-elected in eighth count', *The Irish Times*, 7 May 2022.

47   An analysis of the assembly results by John Garry, Brendan O'Leary and James Pow in which they add independent parties/individuals to either nationalist, unionist or Alliance blocks according to their pro-unionist, pro-nationalist or 'neither' proclivities produced an Assembly composed of 37 unionist MLAs (25 DUP + 9 UUP + 1 TUV + Alex Easton in North Down and Claire Sudden in Londonderry East), 35 nationalists (27 Sinn Féin + 8 SDLP MLAs) and 18 others (17 Alliance + People Before Profit's Gerry Carroll in West Belfast). In terms of percentages, the Assembly is 41.1 per cent unionist, 38.9 per cent

nationalist and 20 per cent other. On the basis of first-preference votes, the gap between the top two blocs by party candidates was 3,842 in favour of nationalists. However, using the same coding method and adding in the first-preference votes for independents, 'the unionist bloc had a net advantage of 6,416 votes (less than a percentage point). Unionist hegemony is over, the unionist plurality survives by a thread'. See in J. Garry, B. O'Leary and J. Pow, 'Much more than meh: The Northern Ireland Assembly elections', *LSE British Politics and Policy*, 11 May 2022.

48 S. Graham, '"The age of entitlement is over": Alliance surge represents major societal shift', *The Irish Times*, 9 May 2022.

49 A. Kane, 'Rock and hard place of polarizing sectarianism have crashed into each other', *The Irish Times*, 27 August 2022.

50 S. Breen, 'LucidTalk opinion poll: Sinn Féin's Michelle O'Neill nudges closer to top Stormont post as DUP lags behind', *Belfast Telegraph*, 27 March 2022.

51 LucidTalk poll, March 2022.

52 N. Emerson, 'DUP's next mistake is to take patience of the North for granted', *The Irish Times*, 9 May 2022.

53 R. Carroll, 'DUP to block formation of Northern Ireland power-sharing Executive', *The Guardian*, 9 May 2022. As a result of legislation at Westminster (2021), the Assembly has at least twenty-four weeks to nominate an Executive, during which time the Assembly can continue to sit and ministers continue to run their departments. Although MLAs can take their seats and ministers their posts, the absence of the Executive severely undermines the efficacy of Stormont as a legislative body. Without the Executive, there is no North/South Ministerial Council, hence truncated relations between Dublin and Belfast. In a different time, the two governments would step into the breach, find time at the margins of EU meetings to share thoughts, convene the British-Irish Intergovernmental Conference and hammer out an agreement all parties could live with in a New Decades, New Approach (2020).

54 These tests include 'no goods checks between Great Britain and Northern Ireland'. That excludes pre-Brexit checks on livestock and goods, which are moving onwards from Northern Ireland. The other tests are: compatibility with the Act of Union, which says all parts of the UK should be on equal footing when it comes to trade; avoiding any diversion of trade where Northern Ireland customers are forced to switch to non-Great Britain suppliers; no border in the Irish Sea; Northern Ireland citizens to have a role in any new regulations which impact them; no new regulatory barriers between Great Britain and Northern Ireland unless agreed by the Northern Ireland Assembly; honouring the 'letter and spirit' of Northern Ireland's constitutional position as set out in the Good Friday Agreement by requiring upfront consent of any diminution in constitutional status. J. Campbell, 'Brexit: DUP lays out seven steps for NI deal', BBC News, 15 July 2021; 'DUP leader announces seven

tests for HMG plan on NI Protocol', 15 July 2021, https://mydup.com/news
/dup-leader-announces-seven-tests-for-hmg-plans-on-ni-protocol.

55 S. Carswell, 'Most people favour scrapping "Brexit checks" on NI-bound goods',
    The Irish Times, 26 July 2022.

56 S. Breen, 'DUP's support up, but backing for Sinn Féin also on rise as SDLP
    slumps', *Belfast Telegraph*, 20 August 2022; S. Breen, 'DUP's decision not to
    form a Stormont Executive is paying off with the unionist base … like it or not',
    Belfast Telegraph, 21 August 2022.

57 S. Breen, 'DUP's support up, but backing for Sinn Féin also on rise as SDLP
    slumps', *Belfast Telegraph*, 20 August 2022.

58 The Executive Office, Labour Force Survey Religion Report 2017, https://www
    .executiveoffice-ni.gov.uk/news/labour-force-survey-religion-report-2017.

59 J. Manley, 'Ulster Unionists say "no" to DUP/TUV electoral pact plan', *The Irish
    Times*, 16 February 2022.

60 Interview with Doug Beattie, 14 May 2021.

61 Interview with Jeffrey Donaldson, 16 December 2020.

62 The Institute of Irish Studies/University of Liverpool/*Irish News* April 2022 poll
    reported: 'Just over half support re-naming as "joint minister"' and removal
    of the unionist and nationalist designation compared to around a fifth who
    disagree.' Sixty-two per cent support changing the procedure for cross-com-
    munity support, which privileges the views of nationalist and unionist MLAs;
    61.7 per cent believe that '60% of all MLAs … should be enough to demonstrate
    cross-community support in the Assembly'. Nearly 80 per cent agree that if the
    Assembly does not return, MLAs should not be paid; 'There is strong support
    for the Assembly to collectively seek mitigations from the EU', https://www
    .liverpool.ac.uk/media/livacuk/humanitiesampsocialsciences/documents
    /Institute,of,Irish,Studies,Irish,News,Poll,March,2022.pdf.

63 S. McBride, 'Short-termism defines Northern Ireland, but a day of reckoning
    looms', *Belfast Telegraph*, 30 April 2022.

64 E. Carty, 'Peter Robinson: No other republican could have done what Martin
    McGuinness did', *The Irish News*, 21 March 2017.

65 In 2000, the Secretary of State Peter Mandelson introduced the Flags and
    Emblems Act, which sets out a regulation for the flying of flags on government
    buildings. But the legislation neglected to cover the twenty-six district councils,
    which were allowed to set their own policies. 'On 3 December 2012 Belfast City
    Council voted to restrict the flying of the Union flag at the City Hall to eighteen
    designated days each year. The decision sparked a riot on the night the vote was
    taken and was followed by four months of street protests. … On one particular
    night in January there were 84 different seats of protest.' See more in P. Nolan et
    al., 'The flag dispute: Anatomy of a protest', Queen's University Belfast, 2014.

66 'What is the 'cash-for-ash' controversy?', RTÉ documentary, 12 April 2018; S.
    McBride, 'The hidden RHI scandal of how Stormont wasted £90m in green
    energy subsidies', *Belfast Telegraph*, 8 March 2022.

67 S. McBride, *Burned: The Inside Story of the 'Cash-for-Ash' Scandal and Northern Ireland's Secretive New Elite* (Dublin, 2019).

68 Interview with Sam McBride, 11 December 2020.

69 The report revealed that before Sinn Féin ministers made a decision, they conferred with Sinn Féin Headquarters on the Falls Road, and that the special advisers ran roughshod over their ministers. See also R. Carroll, 'Cash-for-ash inquiry delivers damning indictment of Stormont incompetence', *The Guardian*, 13 March 2020; S. McBride, 'The hidden RHI scandal of how Stormont wasted £90m in green energy subsidies', *Belfast Telegraph*, 8 March 2022; D. McGrath, 'Cash for ash: No corruption but much criticism of RHI scheme as report published', *TheJournal.ie*, 20 May 2020.

70 Interview with Alex Atwood, 13 March 2020.

71 R. Wilson, *Northern Ireland Peace Monitoring Report* (Northern Ireland Community Relations Council, 2016), no. 4, p. 5, https://www.community-relations.org.uk/sites/crc/files/media-files/NIPMR-Final-2016.pdf.

72 G. Moriarty and F. McClements, 'DUP and Sinn Féin back Stormont deal', *The Irish Times*, 11 January 2020.

73 Lyra McKee, a 29-year-old journalist from Northern Ireland who wrote for several publications about the consequences of the conflict, an author and LGBT activist, was killed by the New IRA on 18 April 2019 while observing clashes between the dissident republicans and police during rioting in the Creggan estate area of Derry. Her murder caused an outpouring of grief. Her funeral at St Anne's Cathedral was attended by Irish President Michael D. Higgins, Taoiseach Leo Varadkar, Sinn Féin President Mary Lou McDonald, Secretary of State for Northern Ireland Karen Bradley, British Prime Minister Theresa May, First Minister Arlene Foster and deputy First Minister Michelle O'Neill. The priest officiating, Fr Martin Magill, challenged the politicians and received a standing ovation when he asked why it took her death to unite politicians. ('Why in God's name does it take the death of a 29-year-old woman with her whole life in front of her to get to this point?')

74 'New Decade, New Approach', Gov.UK, https://assets.publishing.service.gov.uk/government/uploads/system/uploads/attachment_data/file/856998/2020-01-08_a_new_decade__a_new_approach.pdf.

75 Martin McGuinness (1950–2017) was a senior member of the IRA and Sinn Féin chief negotiator during the multi-party talks leading to the Belfast/Good Friday Agreement (B/GFA). He served as Minister of Education (1999–2002). Following the St Andrews Agreement, he served as deputy First Minister with First Minister Rev. Ian Paisley, the DUP leader, and subsequently with Peter Robinson and Arlene Foster. In January 2017, McGuinness resigned as deputy first minister in protest over the Renewable Heat Incentive scandal. He reportedly suffered from amyloidosis, a condition that attacks the vital organs, and died on 21 March 2017. Among others, President Bill Clinton attended his funeral.

76 'Sam McBride: Stormont has returned with less internal scrutiny and with weaker leaders', *News Letter*, 13 January 2020.

77 D. Bradley, 'Confrontational approach central to getting Stormont back working', *The Irish Times*, 11 January 2020; 'Irish Times view on the Stormont deal: Now to make the institutions work', *The Irish Times*, 10 January 2020.

78 Wikipedia [website], COVID-19 pandemic in Northern Ireland, http://en.wikipedia.org/wiki/COVID-19_pandemic_in_Northern_Ireland.

79 F. McClements, 'Northern Ireland: Pandemic shows parties can "work together" – Foster', *The Irish Times*, 24 May 2020.

80 Interview with Peter Robinson, 11 March 2020.

81 Paul Nolan in a letter to Andy Pollak, quoted in *2Irelands2gether*. https://2irelands2gether.com/2020/05/15/how-covid-19-brought-solidarity-and-kindness-to-northern-ireland.

82 Craigyhill bonfire committee, reddit thread, https://www.reddit.com/r/northernireland/comments/fmfsws/the_craigyhill_bonfire_committee_has_decided_that.

83 G. Halliday, 'Coronavirus pandemic and lockdown bringing out the best in people, Amnesty's survey reveals', *Belfast Telegraph*, 7 May 2020.

84 A. Kane, 'The Executive is on course for a final breakdown', *Belfast Telegraph*, 18 November 2020.

85 M. Bain, 'Executive can't afford repeat of last week, says Foster, but no guarantees on when hospitality will reopen', *Belfast Telegraph*, 18 November 2020.

86 Interview with Philip McGarry, 17 December 2020.

87 J. Breslin, 'Majority say Stormont has hampered NI response to COVID crisis', *Belfast Telegraph*, 1 February 2021.

88 Interview with Sammy Douglas, 22 April 2021.

89 Interview with Brandon Hamber, 8 January 2021.

90 A. Maginness, 'Stormont's marriage of convenience fails another big exam', *Belfast Telegraph*, 13 January 2021.

91 Interview with Paul Nolan, 9 March 2020.

92 NILT 2021, Political Attitudes module, Variable GOVINCR.

93 Black Lives Matter (BLM) is an international human rights movement formed in the United States in 2013, dedicated to fighting racism and anti-Black violence, especially in the form of police brutality. In May 2020, George Floyd, an unarmed Black man, was pronounced dead after Derek Chauvin, a white Minneapolis police officer, knelt on Floyd's neck for more than nine minutes, despite Floyd's repeated protests that he could not breathe. Wide circulation of a bystander's video of Floyd's last minutes triggered massive demonstrations in cities throughout the United States and across the globe, raising questions in many countries about how to deal with the legacy of colonial pasts.

94 L. Harte, 'Unionist anger as republicans named Belfast streets and Queen's University after IRA woman', *Belfast Telegraph*, 24 June 2020.

95 A. Morton, 'Anger as DUP tries to name leisure centre after centenary of Northern Ireland', *Belfast Telegraph*, 20 June 2020.

96 F. McClements, '"My passport's green": Why was Seamus Heaney used in Northern Ireland branding?', *The Irish Times*, 19 December 2020; A. Morton and G. Anderson, 'Council decision not to fly Union flag at half-mast "disrespectful", says DUP man', *Belfast Telegraph*, 12 April 2021.

97 B. Hughes and D. Young, 'No united Ireland for generations to come, UUP leader Doug Beattie insists', *Belfast Live*, 31 March 2022; A. Moore, 'Shared Island Initiative, Day 1 – a Trojan horse for unity or a shared future based on mutual respect?', *Irish Examiner*, 27 December 2020; P. Hosford, 'Unionists' lack of engagement with Shared Island projects disappointing', *Irish Examiner*, 10 December 2021; A. Kula, 'DUP MP warns against Dublin "interference" as Taoiseach talks up his Shared Island Unit', *News Letter*, 22 October 2020.

98 M. Simpson, 'NI 100: How was Northern Ireland's centenary year marked?', BBC News, 30 December 2021.

99 'NI 100: Michael D. Higgins defends decision not to attend centenary event', BBC News, 17 September 2021. The event was organized by the Church Leaders' Group 'as part of their wider programme of collective engagement around the 1921 centenaries, with an emphasis on their common Christian commitment to peace, healing and reconciliation'. The group is made up of the archbishops of the Catholic Church and the Church of Ireland, the Presbyterian Moderator and the presidents of the Methodist Church and the Irish Council of Churches.

100 G. Moriarty, 'Sinn Féin vetoes Stormont stone marking NI centenary', *The Irish Times*, 18 March 2021.

101 'NI 100: Sinn Féin block Belfast City Hall illumination', BBC News, 21 October 2021; LucidTalk Northern Ireland, '"Tracker" Poll-Project: April 2021'. When asked about their feelings on the centenary celebrations, only 40 per cent agreed that indeed there was something to celebrate.

5. REFERENDUM METRICS

1 Interview with Naomi Long, 4 December 2020.
2 Interview with Jonathan Powell, 8 December 2020.
3 Interview with Martin Mansergh, 9 December 2020.
4 Interview with Paul, Lord Bew, 6 January 2021.
5 Interview with Brendan O'Leary, 3 May 2021.
6 Interview with Paul Gosling, 16 March 2021.
7 Interview with Duncan Morrow, 13 March 2020.
8 Secretary of State for Northern Ireland by Command of H.M., *The Belfast Agreement: An Agreement Reached at the Multi-Party Talks on Northern Ireland* (London, 1998), p. 3; see also 'Northern Ireland Act 1998', Legislation.gov.uk (Statute Law Database, 19 November 1998), https://www.legislation.gov.uk/ukpga/1998/47/contents.
9 Interview with Katy Hayward, 16 February 2021; The Shared Island Unit is an initiative of the Irish government that is housed in the department of a Taoiseach.

10 Quoted in Mallon and Pollak, p. 152.

11 P. Hosford, 'Third of voters would support Sinn Féin in election, poll finds', *Irish Examiner*, 24 October 2021.

12 L. Clarke, 'Survey: Most Northern Ireland Catholics want to remain in UK', *Belfast Telegraph*, 17 June 2011.

13 P. O'Malley, *The Uncivil Wars: Ireland Today* (Boston, MA, 1998) pp. 140–1.

14 Professor Peter Shirlow is Director of the Institute of Irish Studies at the University of Liverpool and the author of a number of in-depth studies of loyalism.

15 Interview with Peter Shirlow, 7 December 2020.

16 J. Corcoran, 'United Ireland poll: Two thirds say united Ireland vote risks return to violence', *Independent.ie*, 2 May 2021.

17 Interview with Chris Hudson, 12 March 2020.

18 Interview with Billy Hutchinson, 9 March 2020.

19 Interview with Steve Aiken, 11 December 2020.

20 Interview with Colum Eastwood, 26 January 2021.

21 Ibid.

22 Interview with Naomi Long, 4 December 2020.

23 P. Baker, 'A 65% to 17% majority for Northern Ireland remaining in the UK suggests little room for doubt', *Slugger O'Toole*, 5 February 2013; 'First major post-Brexit survey shows no surge in support for Irish unity', *News Letter*, 17 June 2017; Northern Ireland General Election Survey 2019 (Faculty of Humanities and Social Sciences, University of Liverpool).

24 Interview with Paul Nolan, 9 March 2020.

25 Ibid.

26 Interview with Jane Morrice, 10 March 2020.

27 Interview with Alex Attwood, 13 March 2020.

28 Ibid.

29 Ibid.

30 'Northern Ireland General Election Survey', 2019, op. cit.

31 This interview (March 2019) took place before the DUP in particular demonized Simon Coveney over the Irish government's stand on the Northern Ireland Protocol.

32 Interview with Duncan Morrow, 13 March 2020.

33 Interview with Sam McBride, 11 December 2020.

34 Interview with Stephen Farry, 28 January 2021.

35 Ibid.

36 Interview with Alex Kane, 5 January 2021.

37 CAIN Web Service. 'Results of elections held in Northern Ireland since 1968', 2022.

38 It would restrict voting rights for EU citizens living in England and Northern Ireland who entered the UK after the end of the Implementation Period,

31 December 2020, to those from countries where a bilateral agreement has been agreed between the UK and individual member states. So far this covers Spain, Portugal, Poland and Luxembourg. EU citizens who were living in the UK prior to the end of the Implementation Period will maintain their local voting and candidacy rights in England and Northern Ireland, provided they retain lawful immigration status.

39   A. Whysall, 'A Northern Ireland Border Poll', The Constitution Unit, University College London, 25 June 2019.

40   Corcoran, op. cit.

41   Interview with Peter Robinson, 11 March 2020.

42   'Arrests follow probes into loyalist paramilitary activity in Belfast and north Antrim', The Irish News, 20 August 2021.

43   Interview with Sammy Douglas, 22 April 2021.

44   Interview with Jackie Redpath, 19 March 2021.

45   Interview with Colum Eastwood, 26 January 2021.

46   The Working Group identified five possible configurations for referendums, which they narrowed to three as best meeting the circumstances of both Northern Ireland and the Republic of Ireland.

Under the second, the form of a united Ireland is worked out so far as possible before referendums. The Irish government takes the initiative, 'but with the widest possible consultation throughout the island. If majorities in the referendums, north and south, opted for unification on the proposed model, the two governments would then work together on agreeing the terms of transfer of sovereignty'.

Under the fourth configuration, the referendums on the principle of unification (whether Northern Ireland should remain in the UK or become part of a united Ireland) 'would be held before detailed proposals for a united Ireland had been established'. But in advance, a process for working out detailed proposals for a united Ireland would be set out and known, and the 'default arrangements for a united Ireland would be established' in the event that the 'arrangements for a united Ireland could not be agreed and approved'. Under this configuration, referendums in Northern Ireland and the Republic of Ireland take place on the principle of unification and on the process for working out detailed proposals for a united Ireland. A second referendum follows after the final shape and form of a united Ireland, drafting constitutional amendments and the default arrangements in the event of the united Ireland on offer is rejected. Transfer of sovereignty is relatively slower. One default option would be for Northern Ireland 'to be absorbed into the Republic under the existing Constitution'.

Under the fifth configuration, 'In advance of the [original] referendums, three matters would be agreed [between the governments]: the process for agreeing those detailed future arrangements; the interim arrangements that would apply after transfer of sovereignty, until any replacement arrangements were agreed and approved; and the default arrangements that would apply in the event that detailed future arrangements were not agreed and approved. The interim and default arrangements might well be the same.' The transfer of sovereignty is relatively quick. In the fourth and fifth configurations, once the final model of a united Ireland is agreed on, it would be put to a second referendum, again North and South. But even if they did not pass, default arrangements for incorporating the North into the Republic of Ireland would be known (before the original referendums) and in place. There would be no undoing of the original referendum vote. 'Working Group on Unification Referendums on the Island of Ireland', The Constitution Unit, University College London, 1 November 2021.

47   Ibid., p. xvi.

48   Ibid.

49   Ibid., p. xiii.

50   Ibid.

51   Interview with Brendan O'Leary, 3 May 2021.

52   Interview with Alan Renwick, 9 July 2021.

53   Ibid.

54   Some studies deconstruct the subvention and find that Ireland's share would be a lot less than the £10 billion frequently alluded to. For example, see: J. Doyle. 'UK subvention to North irrelevant to debate on Irish unity', The Irish Times, 9 June 2021.

55   A. Rutherford, 'Centenary poll: 44% in Northern Ireland want referendum but would not accept higher taxes to fund reunification', Belfast Telegraph, 1 May 2021; F. Sheahan, 'Majority favour a united Ireland, but just 22pc would pay for it', Independent.ie, 1 May 2021; Professor John Doyle of Dublin City University suggests that the actual subvention figure would be less than £10 billion and closer to €2.8 billion once pensions, debt repayments, contributions to defence 'out of UK expenditures' and underestimated taxes are excluded.

56   'Record £15 billion per year for Northern Ireland', The Rt Hon. Brandon Lewis CBE MP, Gov.UK, 28 October 2021, https://www.gov.uk/government/news/record-15-billion-per-year-for-northern-ireland.

57   Interview with Paul, Lord Bew, 6 January 2021.

58   J. Stone, 'British public still believe Vote Leave "350 million per week to EU" myth from Brexit referendum', The Independent, 28 February 2018.

59   Ibid.

60   Secretary of State for Northern Ireland by Command of H.M., The Belfast Agreement: An Agreement Reached at the Multi-Party Talks on Northern Ireland (London, 1998), p. 26.

61   Corcoran, op. cit.

62   Interview with Alan Renwick, 9 July 2021.

63   'Cross Border Polls', Kantar Public UK Polling Archive (Kantar, April 2021), https://www.kantar.com/expertise/policy-society/kantar-public-uk-polling-archive.

64 'Northern Ireland General Election Survey', 2019

65 Ibid.

66 Email to author from Brendan O'Leary.

67 Interview with Brendan O'Leary, 3 May 2021.

68 Ibid.

69 'Working Group on Unification Referendums on the Island of Ireland', op. cit., p. xxiii.

70 Ibid.

71 Interview with Brendan O'Leary, 3 May 2021.

72 P. Hosford, 'Unionists' lack of engagement with Shared Island projects "disappointing"', *Irish Examiner*, 10 December 2021.

73 Interview with Francis Campbell, 15 March 2021.

74 Interview with Paul Nolan, 9 March 2020.

75 'Working Group on Unification Referendums on the Island of Ireland', op. cit., p. xix.

76 Ibid.

77 Interview with Naomi Long, 4 December 2020.

78 Ibid.

79 International Foundation for Electoral Systems, Election Guide: country profile: Northern Ireland (part of the United Kingdom), https://www.election guide.org/countries/id/251.

80 Ibid.

81 'Northern Ireland Assembly election turnout for 2022 confirmed', ITV News, 6 May 2022.

82 University of Liverpool, 2019, op. cit., p. 12.

83 Interview with Alan Renwick, 9 July 2021.

84 Northern Ireland Statistics and Research Agency, *Census 2021 Guidance Note on Religious Questions and Religion Outputs*, 22 September 2022, p. 11.

85 Table MS-B19, Census 2021 main statistics religion tables, Census 2021 main statistics for Northern Ireland (phase 1), Northern Ireland Statistics and Research Agency, 22 September 2022, https://www.nisra.gov.uk/publications /census-2021-main-statistics-religion-tables.

86 ARK, Northern Ireland Life and Times Survey, 2020, ARK www.ark.ac.uk/nilt [distributor], June 2021, Background Module, RAGECAT variable.

87 'Northern Ireland Catholic school population surges to record high', *Belfast Telegraph*, 30 April 2019); see also Department of Education, School enrolments – Northern Ireland summary, https://www.education-ni.gov.uk/publications/ school-enrolments-northern-ireland-summary-data.

88 'About 50 per cent more Catholics than Protestants enter higher education', *News Letter*, 20 January 2016, https://www.newsletter.co.uk/news/about-50-per -cent-more-catholics-than-protestants-enter-higher-education-1276383.

89 Department for the Economy, 'Enrolments at NI HEIs by equality categories –
    2016/17 to 2020/21', https://www.economy-ni.gov.uk/articles/higher-education
    -statistical-fact-sheets.

90 Press Release, Census 2021 main statistics for Northern Ireland (phase 1), Northern
    Ireland Statistics and Research Agency, 22 September 2022, https://www.nisra.
    gov.uk/publications/census-2021-main-statistics-for-northern-ireland-phase-1.

91 PfG Analytics, 'Labour Force Survey Religion Report 2017', The Executive Of-
    fice, 31 January 2019, https://www.executiveoffice-ni.gov.uk/publications/labour
    -force-survey-religion-report-2017. Between 1990 and 2017, the proportion of
    the population aged sixteen and over who reported as Protestant decreased
    from 56 per cent to 42 per cent, while the proportion who reported as Catholic
    increased from 38 per cent to 41 per cent. The proportion reported as 'other/non-
    determined' has increased from 6 per cent to 17 per cent over the same period.

92 ARK, Northern Ireland Life and Times Survey, 1998–2014, www.ark.ac.uk/nilt
    [distributor], Political Attitudes module, UNINATID variable.

93 Interview with Katy Hayward, 16 February 2021.

94 In the December 2019 University of Liverpool poll, 51 per cent of Catholics
    voted Sinn Féin, 28 per cent for the SDLP and 13 per cent for the Alliance. No
    Protestants voted Sinn Féin and just 1 per cent SDLP. Among those who said
    they were of 'no religion', 28 per cent voted Alliance, 15 per cent SDLP, 10 per
    cent UUP, 6 per cent Sinn Féin and 6 per cent DUP: 90 per cent of Protestants
    wanted to stay in the UK; 71 per cent of Catholics wanted unification.

95 For example, in the 2001 UK general election, the NILT survey indicates 78 per
    cent of Protestants voted for unionist parties and 82 per cent of Catholics voted
    for nationalist parties. For the 2019 UK general election, the figures were 65
    per cent and 70 per cent respectively; 23 per cent of Protestants and 23 per cent
    of Catholics voted for Alliance and the Green parties. ARK, Northern Ireland
    Life and Times Survey, 2001 (VOTED variable), 2020 (VOTEGE19 variable),
    https://www.ark.ac.uk/nilt/results/polatt.html

96 R. Rose, *Governing Without Consensus: An Irish Perspective* (Boston, MA, 1971).

97 Ibid.

98 'Northern Ireland Social Attitudes Survey: 1989, Surveys Online (ARK, 16 March
    2004), Political Attitudes module, NIRELAND variable.

99 ARK, Northern Ireland Life and Times Survey, 1998, 2007, 2019 and 2020, www.
    ark.ac.uk/nilt, June 1999, Political attitudes module, NIRELAND variable.

100 Discrepancies have been observed between online versus in-person polling
    results. Face-to-face polls include BBC/Ipsos MORI, NILT, University of
    Liverpool 2019, *Irish Times*/Ipsos MRBI and Social Market Research. Online
    polls include Red C, LucidTalk, Lord Ashcroft, BBC Spotlight/LucidTalk,
    Belfast Telegraph/Kantar and University of Liverpool 2021 and 2022. See also P.
    Donaghy, 'The mystery of the shy nationalists – online and face-to-face polling
    on Irish unity', *Slugger O'Toole*, 19 February 2020.

101 R. Lavin, Twitter post, 29 September 2022, https://twitter.com/RachelLavin /status/1575535271335952384?t=LCWTGSzoDipY1T2TujVKLw&s=03.

102 Ibid.

103 S. Abernethy, 'Majority of Northern voters want minimal disruption to daily life', *The Irish Times*, 8 March 2019.

104 Lord Ashcroft, 'My Northern Ireland survey finds the Union on a knife-edge' [full data tables], 11 September 2019, https://lordashcroftpolls.com/2019/09/my -northern-ireland-survey-finds-the-union-on-a-knife-edge/.

105 'Northern Ireland General Election Survey 2019', Faculty of Humanities & Social Sciences, University of Liverpool, 2019, p. 13.

106 'TheDetail: NI and ROI poll projects', LucidTalk, 26 February 2020, https://www .lucidtalk.co.uk/single-post/2020/02/26/thedetail-ni-and-roi-poll-projects.

107 ARK, Northern Ireland Life and Times (NILT) Survey, December 2020, Political attitudes module, REUNIFY variable, https://www.ark.ac.uk/nilt/2020 /Political_Attitudes/REFUNIFY.html.

108 Normally NILT is a face-to-face interview. However, due to COVID restrictions, the 2020 survey was done remotely through online surveys and phone and virtual calls. See technical notes in https://www.ark.ac.uk/nilt/2020/tech20.pdf.

109 'LT NI SUNDAY TIMES January 2021 – NI-wide poll', LucidTalk, 26 January 2021, https://www.lucidtalk.co.uk/single-post/lt-ni-sunday-times-january-2021-state -of-the-uk-union-poll.

110 'LT BBC NI Spotlight poll-project – Northern Ireland (NI) and Republic of Ireland (ROI)', LucidTalk, 23 April 2021, https://www.lucidtalk.co.uk/single -post/lt-bbc-ni-spotlight-poll-project-northern-ireland-ni-and-republic-of -ireland-roi.

111 'Centenary poll: 44% in Northern Ireland want referendum but would not accept higher taxes to fund reunification', *Belfast Telegraph*, 1 May 2021; 'Cross-border poll Northern Ireland', Kantar, April 2021, Polling tables, Table 12, p. 101.

112 'LT NI "Tracker" poll – Summer 2021', LucidTalk, 1 September 2021, Northern Ireland (NI) Tracker Poll Results: August 2021, Poll Questions Results – Main Report, p. 21.

113 'The Ireland/Northern Ireland Protocol: Consensus or conflict?', University of Liverpool, October 2021, p. 7.

114 ARK, Northern Ireland Life and Times (NILT) Survey, December 2021, Political attitudes module, REUNIFY variable, https://www.ark.ac.uk/nilt/2021 /Political_Attitudes/REFUNIFY.html.

115 Lord Ashcroft, 'Northern Ireland: Unification, or the union?', Lord Ashcroft Polls, 13 December 2021.

116 'Opinion Poll April 2022', The Institute of Irish Studies, University of Liverpool/ *The Irish News*, April 2022, p. 7.

117 '4th Attitudinal Survey', The Institute of Irish Studies, University of Liverpool/ *The Irish News*, July 2022, p. 36.

118 C. Woodhouse, 'Support for Northern Ireland to remain part of UK still strong, new poll reveals', *Sunday Life*, 21 August 2022.

119 Wikipedia [website], 'United Ireland', https://en.wikipedia.org/wiki/United_Ireland; see also Professor Jon Tonge's survey described in P. Bradfield, 'Prof. Jon Tonge's survey of all polls [since Brexit] show only 39% support for a united Ireland and over 50% support for the Union', *News Letter*, 5 November 2021.

120 These polling numbers exclude 'Don't Knows' in their calculations for unity or against. Lord Ashcroft, 'My Northern Ireland survey finds the Union on a knife-edge' [full data tables], 11 September 2019, https://lordashcroftpolls.com/2019/09/my-northern-ireland-survey-finds-the-union-on-a-knife-edge.

121 'TheDetail: NI and ROI poll projects', LucidTalk, 26 February 2020, Full Results Data Tables, https://www.lucidtalk.co.uk/single-post/2020/02/26/thedetail-ni-and-roi-poll-projects.

122 ARK, Northern Ireland Life and Times (NILT) Survey, December 2020, Political attitudes module, REUNIFY variable, https://www.ark.ac.uk/nilt/2020/Political_Attitudes/REFUNIFY.html.

123 'LT NI SUNDAY TIMES January 2021 – NI-wide poll', LucidTalk, 26 January 2021, Poll Project Data Tables, https://www.lucidtalk.co.uk/single-post/lt-ni-sunday-times-january-2021-state-of-the-uk-union-poll.

124 'LT BBC NI Spotlight poll-project – Northern Ireland (NI) and Republic of Ireland (ROI)', LucidTalk, 23 April 2021, Northern Ireland (NI) Data – Table Results, https://www.lucidtalk.co.uk/single-post/lt-bbc-ni-spotlight-poll-project-northern-ireland-ni-and-republic-of-ireland-roi.

125 'Cross-border poll (Northern Ireland)', Kantar, April 2021, Polling tables, Table 12, p. 101.

126 'The Ireland/Northern Ireland Protocol: Consensus or conflict?', University of Liverpool, October 2021, p. 7.

127 ARK, Northern Ireland Life and Times (NILT) Survey, December 2021, Political attitudes module, REUNIFY variable, https://www.ark.ac.uk/nilt/2021/Political_Attitudes/REFUNIFY.html.

128 Lord Ashcroft, 'My Northern Ireland survey finds the Union on a knife-edge' [full data tables], 11 September 2019, https://lordashcroftpolls.com/2019/09/my-northern-ireland-survey-finds-the-union-on-a-knife-edge/.

129 C. Woodhouse, 'Support for Northern Ireland to remain part of UK still strong, new poll reveals', *Sunday Life*, 21 August 2022.

130 M. Leroux, 'Should we believe the Opinion Polls on unification', *Fortnight*, no. 480 (Belfast, January 2021), pp. 2–5.

131 Interview with Colum Eastwood, 26 January 2021; For example, the NILT (2010) survey found that DUP support was 18 per cent, well below the 38 per cent the party secured in the 2011 Assembly elections. By contrast, the UUP scored 16 per cent in both the poll and the actual election. On the nationalist side, the SDLP on 17 per cent was comfortably ahead of Sinn Féin's 11 per cent.

In the election the roles were reversed, with Sinn Féin scoring 29 per cent and the SDLP 14 per cent; Clarke, 2012, op. cit.

132 Interview with Brendan O'Leary, 3 May 2021.

133 Referendum intention in 2016: EU referendum voting intention in 2016, 'YouGov on the day poll: Remain 52%, Leave 48%', *YouGov*, 23 June 2016.

134 M. Leroux, 'Analysis: The Union seems to be more popular in Northern Ireland than unionist parties', *News Letter*, 14 January 2021.

135 'The Ireland/Northern Ireland Protocol: Consensus or conflict?', op. cit.; J. Manley. 'Protocol matters most to little more than one in 10 unionists – poll', *The Irish News*, 14 February 2022. Only 2.1 per cent of all respondents in the February 2022 University of Liverpool/*Irish News* opinion poll named constitutional issues as their highest priority. Broken down further, 3.6 per cent of unionists and 2.1 per cent of nationalists chose this as their first priority.

136 Trends calculated from NISA 1989–95, NILT 1998–2020.

137 University of Liverpool, 2019, op. cit., p. 11.

138 Interview with Brendan O'Leary, 3 May 2021.

139 University of Liverpool General Election Survey, December 2019, https://www .liverpool.ac.uk/humanities-and-social-sciences/research/research-themes /transforming-conflict/ni-election-survey-19/.

140 Leroux, op. cit.

141 Ibid.

142 Ibid.

143 K. Hayward and C. McManus, 'Neither/nor: The rejection of unionist and nationalist identities in post-agreement Northern Ireland', *Capital & Class*, vol. 43, no. 1 (2019), pp. 139–55.

144 Northern Ireland General Election Survey, 2019, op. cit.; Northern Ireland Life and Times (NILT) Survey, 2020, op. cit.

145 Some 39.6 per cent of respondents in the 2019 University of Liverpool poll identified as 'neither unionist nor nationalist'. Concomitantly, recent NILT Surveys suggest this dropped from a high of 50 per cent in 2018 to 37 per cent in 2021, reflecting a hardening of identities as the impacts of Brexit, including the protocol, are being experienced differently in the two communities; 'NI survey suggests 50% neither unionist nor nationalist', BBC News, 20 June 2019; NILT Survey, op. cit., 2020, 2021.

146 P. Smith, 'New research shows that for "neithers", the problem with the Union is unionists', *News Letter*, 25 January 2021.

147 J. Tonge, 'Beyond unionism versus nationalism: The rise of the Alliance Party of Northern Ireland', *The Political Quarterly*, vol. 91, no. 2 (2020), pp. 461–6. Says Lord Alderdice, 'Alliance is not neutral. It is not "unionist" in that it does not take a position of being "pro-union no matter what". Since it was formed in 1970, its position has always been that it supported the union with Britain *because* it judged that this was in the best socio-economic interests of the

people of Northern Ireland, *however* it always recognized that could change. There is currently an important debate developing in Northern Ireland about whether Brexit may be altering that balance of socio-economic interests. In saying "debate", I am referring to the community at large, rather than within Alliance, however that question will ultimately become more prominent within Alliance and the party will have to take some kind of view if/when there is a border poll.' Email to author, 9 January 2023.

148 Interview with Katy Hayward, 16 February 2021.

149 Cross-tabulation by Allyson M. Bachta using 2021 NILT survey data.

150 K. Hayward and C. McManus, op. cit., pp. 139–55.

151 Ibid.

152 NILT 2021: ARK. Northern Ireland Life and Times Survey, 2021 [computer file]. ARK www.ark.ac.uk/nilt [distributor], June 2021, Political Attitudes module, UNINATID variable.

153 C. Coulter et al., *Northern Ireland a Generation After Good Friday: Lost Futures and New Horizons in the 'Long Peace'* (Manchester, UK, 2021), p. 193.

154 Northern Ireland General Election Survey, 2019, op. cit.

155 Hayward and McManus, 2019, op. cit.; Northern Ireland Border Poll 2021, op. cit.

156 In 1998, UUP secured 10 per cent of the Neither vote, SDLP 21 per cent and Alliance 16 per cent. By 2013, UUP had lost most of this support and SDLP was shedding support too: UUP at 3 per cent, SDLP at 13 per cent and Alliance 13 per cent, with None (i.e., support no parties listed) or Don't Knows accounting for 51 per cent. By 2021, while the UUP (4 per cent) and SDLP (12 per cent) was relatively unchanged, the None/Don't Knows almost halved (to 27 per cent) and the support to Alliance more than doubled (to 34 per cent). Cross-tabulation of NILT 1998–2021 surveys by Allyson M. Bachta.

157 Hayward and McManus, 2019.

158 Northern Ireland Border Poll 2016, Ipsos, 9 September 2016, https://www.ipsos.com/ipsos-mori/en-uk/northern-ireland-border-poll-2016.

159 Ibid.

160 Interview with Billy Hutchinson, 9 March 2020.

161 H. Arendt, 'Truth and politics', *The New Yorker*, 25 February 1967.

162 Ibid.

163 Quoted in D. Mitchell, *Politics and Peace in Northern Ireland* (Manchester, UK, 2015), p. 19.

164 Ibid., p 19.

165 P. Geoghegan, *Democracy for Sale: Dark Money and Dirty Politics* (London, 2020).

166 Interview with Katy Hayward, 16 February 2021; Hayward is referring to the Working Group Report's coverage of this as an issue of concern.

167 'Cross Border Polls', op. cit.

168 L. Blake, 'Beyond the binary: What might a multiple-choice EU referendum have looked like?', *Democratic Audit*, 11 November 2016.

169 'Is the UK heading for a break-up?', *Financial Times*, 4 April 2021.
170 Corcoran, 2021.
171 Mallon and Pollak, p. 152.

6. THE NORTH

1   S. Breen, 'Sinn Féin: Nationalists are ignored and excluded in Northern Ireland politics', *Belfast Telegraph*, 22 March 2021.
2   Interview with Alex Kane, 5 January 2021.
3   Interview with Ben Lowry, 20 January 2021.
4   M. Fletcher, 'Peace without harmony', in *Imagine: Reflections on Peace*, C. Hale and F. Turners (eds) (Phoenix, AZ, 2020); p. 233–66, 258.
5   C. Mitchell, 'Divided politics, blended lives', *Fortnight*, vol. 479 (2020), pp. 27–9.
6   Interview with Philip McGarry, 17 December 2020.
7   Interview with Lesley Carroll, 19 May 2021.
8   Interview with Máiría Cahill, 19 November 2020.
9   B. Hamber, 'It's time we stopped kidding ourselves: "New normal" is abnormal', *Belfast Telegraph*, 22 March 2021.
10   J. Ruane and J. Todd (2001), 'The politics of transition: Explaining political crises in the implementation of the Belfast Good Friday Agreement', *Political Studies*, vol. 49, p. 938.
11   A.M. McAlinden and C. Dwyer (eds), *Criminal Justice in Transition, the Northern Ireland Context* (Oxford, 2018).
12   'Titanic Belfast crowned as "world's leading tourist attraction"', *The Irish Times*, 2 December 2016.
13   K. Earley, 'Belfast ranks strongly against UK cities for tech jobs and workforce', *Silicon Republic*, 8 September 2020.
14   R. McAleer, 'Northern Ireland is best place to live and start a business – PWC Report', *The Irish News*, 17 February 2021.
15   'Northern Ireland', OECD Regional Well-Being, https://www.oecdregional wellbeing.org/UKN.html.
16   'Northern Ireland General Election Survey 2019', Faculty of Humanities & Social Sciences, University of Liverpool.
17   'Northern Ireland Life and Times Survey', Northern Ireland Life and Times (NILT) Survey homepage (ARK, 14 October 2021).
18   Interview with Colum Eastwood, 26 January 2021; Those identifying as neither Catholic nor Protestant ('no religion'), overwhelmingly – at times doubly – identify as 'neither' unionist or nationalist. With the exception of the 55–64 and 65+ age group, all other age groups report a higher likelihood to claim a 'no political affiliation' identity today than in 1989.
19   'Should I stay or should I go? Reasons for leaving Northern Ireland for study or work', Pivotal Public Policy Forum NI, 6 December 2021, p. 5. The Pivotal

Public Policy Forum NI captured the sentiments of youth who left Northern Ireland to study abroad and have yet to return. The interview excerpts included in this document are anonymous, and all identifiers have been removed. Some responses: 'I'm completely mentally exhausted with the corruption of our government in Northern Ireland, the fact our leaders continue to live in the past and centre policy around religion and sectarianism and continue to withhold human rights. My generation has grown tired of this and need to be in a more forward-thinking, inclusive environment.' 'I don't hear anything about the big issues: jobs, affordable housing and human rights. It's literally flags, language and point-scoring. I got fed up with it and knew I'd have to leave to get away from all that crap.' 'Brexit has really started a lot of trouble where I live in [city in Northern Ireland] and I didn't want to be part of it. I'm sick of protests, flags and all the trouble – I wanted to get out.'

20 C. Lloyd, 'Neighbourhood change, deprivation, and unemployment in Belfast', *The Geographic Journal*, no. 8 (2022), pp. 190–208.

21 Interview with Gary Mason, 8 December 2020.

22 J. Brennan, 'Brexit is fuelling tensions in Northern Ireland', Al Jazeera, 14 April 2021.

23 R. McAleer, 'Catholics outnumber Protestants in public sector workforce for first time', *The Irish News*, 19 May 2022; M. Bain, 'Catholics to be majority of workforce in Northern Ireland for first time in 2020, new figures suggest', *Belfast Telegraph*, 7 February 2019.

24 Interview with Tim Bartlett, 8 July 2021.

25 Ibid.

26 Ibid.

27 S. McGuinness and A. Bergin, 'The political economy of a Northern Ireland border poll', *Cambridge Journal of Economics*, vol. 44, no. 4 (2020), pp. 781–812.

28 Interview with Tim Bartlett, 8 July 2021.

29 J. IJpelaar, T. Power and B. Green, 'Northern Ireland multiple deprivation measures 2017', *Journal of the Statistical and Social Inquiry Society of Ireland*, vol. XLVIII, no. 48 (2,108–19), pp. 163–74.

30 'Half of UK families £110 worse off a year since general election, while richest 5% are better off by £3,300', *New Economics Foundation*, 13 December 2021.

31 D. Morrow, 'Sectarianism in Northern Ireland: A review', Northern Ireland Community Relations Council, 2019, p. 35.

32 Ibid.

33 M. Magill and M. McPeake, 'An anatomy of economic inactivity in Northern Ireland', University of Ulster, 2016, p. 28; R. Johnston, G. McCausland and K. Bonner, 'The competitiveness scorecard for Northern Ireland: A framework for measuring economic, social, and environmental progress', University of Ulster, 2020, pp. 1–195.

34 R. Johnston, G. McCausland and K. Bonner, 'The competitiveness scorecard for Northern Ireland: A framework for measuring economic, social, and environmental progress', University of Ulster, 2020, p. 153.

35 P. Duncan, F. Sheehy and P. Scruton, 'Life in Northern Ireland v the rest of the UK: What does the data say?', *The Guardian*, 2 May 2021; 'Northern Ireland multiple deprivation measures 2017', Northern Ireland Multiple Deprivation Measures 2017, https://www.nisra.gov.uk/sites/nisra.gov.uk/files/publications /NIMDM17-%20with%20ns.pdf.

36 A.M. Gray et al., 'Northern Ireland peace monitoring report', Community Relations Council, October 2018.

37 G. Spencer and C. Hudson, 'Dialogue needed between unionism and loyalism to create a positive, vibrant and attractive Northern Ireland', *Belfast Telegraph*, 26 July 2020.

38 Interview with Naomi Long, 4 December 2020.

39 The New Decade, New Approach document recognized the unsustainability of Northern Ireland's separate school systems. Ulster University's Transforming Education project released a series of twelve reports to public and political stakeholders from April 2019 to March 2021 addressing these issues in contexts such as school governance, testing, teacher education programs and travel costs. See M. Milliken, S. Roulston and S. Cook, 'Transforming education in Northern Ireland', Ulster University (March 2021).

40 R. Meredith, 'NI education: No religious mix in "nearly a third of schools"', BBC News, 11 November 2021; Northern Ireland Assembly, *Integrated Education Bill: Final Stage*, Official Report, 9 March 2022.

41 Morrow, op. cit., p. 26.

42 S. Breen, 'How teaching in Northern Ireland schools divides on "conflict lines"', *Belfast Telegraph*, 15 July 2020.

43 M. Fitzmaurice, 'Integrated education poll finds 71% believe children should be taught together', *Belfast Live*, 3 August 2021.

44 The New Decade, New Approach, the agreement reached in March 2020 that resuscitated the Stormont Assembly and Executive, which were collapsed in 2017 over the Renewable Heat Initiative scandal, provides for a single educational system; T. Gallagher, 'Pivotal blog' (blog), Pivotal Public Policy Forum, 29 January 2020. The Integrated Education Bill (NIA 23/17–22) was introduced to the Assembly on 1 June 2021 and eventually passed with 49 ayes and 38 nays on 9 March 2022. Pointing to the Good Friday Agreement's directive to 'facilitate and encourage integrated education', the bill now places 'a statutory duty on the Department of Education to support integrated education, assess parental preference and to produce a strategy and action plan to aim to meet the demand for integrated education'. In Assembly debates, opponents – the unionist parties – argued that, should the bill pass, it would demonstrate a bias towards only 7 per cent of the student population and ignore the diversity and inclusion initiatives of non-integrated education schools. See Northern Ireland Assembly, *Integrated Education Bill: Final Stage*, Official Report, 9 March 2022.

45 Interview with Brandon Hamber, 8 January 2021.

46   The costs of maintaining Northern Ireland's segregated education system, beside
     the additional environmental costs of the estimated 130,177,516 miles covered by
     post-primary students travelling to schools other than those found in their most
     immediate neighbourhood locations, have been estimated to be between 14.3–
     92.8 million pounds; S. Roulston and S. Cook, 'Home-school travel in a divided
     education system: At what cost?', Ulster University, 2021, pp. 1–8; L. Kelleher,
     A. Smyth and M. McEldowney, 'Cultural attitudes, parental aspirations, and
     socioeconomic influence on post-primary school selection in Northern Ireland',
     Journal of School Choice, vol. 10, no. 2 (February 2016), pp. 200–26.

47   'Statement on key inequalities in housing and communities in Northern Ireland',
     Equality Commission for Northern Ireland, April 2017.

48   C. Burdeau, 'Will Northern Ireland's "peace walls" ever come down?', *Court-
     house News Service*, 28 June 2019; 'More than 100 peace wall barriers remain in
     Northern Ireland', *The Irish Times*, 5 January 2022.

49   Interview with Brandon Hamber, 8 January 2021.

50   P. Gosling, '"There is something seriously and fundamentally wrong" – Northern
     Ireland's housing crisis', *Slugger O'Toole*, 15 June 2020; see also 'Northern Ireland
     Housing Statistics 2019–20', NI Direct Government Services, 2020, pp. 1–13.

51   Gosling, op. cit.

52   A. Madden, 'Concern as Northern Ireland's social housing waiting list could
     take 50 years to clear', *Belfast Telegraph*, 23 August 2022.

53   There is a government-imposed cap on the number of entrants to Northern
     Ireland universities (see also Note 33); 'Retaining and regaining talent in
     Northern Ireland', Pivotal, Public Policy Forum NI, 24 March 2021), p. 2.

54   Pivotal, op. cit., p. 3.

55   Ibid., p. 9.

56   Ibid., p. 3.

57   Interview with Matthew O'Toole, 14 May 2021.

58   Interview with Brandon Hamber, 8 January 2021.

59   D. Morrow, 'The elusiveness of trust', *Peace Review*, 3 January 2001, p. 13–19.

60   Interview with Lesley Carroll, 19 May 2021.

61   E. Koh, Notes on the Opsahl Commission, email to author, May 2020.

62   J. Thompson, 'Addressing the legacy of Northern Ireland's past', The Commission
     for Victims and Survivors, January 2019. www.cvsni.org.

63   B. O'Leary and J. McGarry, *The Politics of Antagonism: Understanding Northern
     Ireland* (London, 1996), pp. 12–13.

64   *Reflections on Peace*, p. 260; 'Troubled consequences: A report on the mental
     health impact of the civil conflict in Northern Ireland', Commission for
     Victims and Survivors (2012); 'NI has world's highest rate of post-traumatic
     stress disorder', Ulster University (5 December 2011); S. O'Neill et al., 'Towards
     a better future: The trans-generational impact of the Troubles on mental health',
     Commission for Victims and Survivors, March 2015.

65 *Troubled Consequences: A Report on the Mental Health Impact of the Civil Conflict in Northern Ireland* (Commission for Victims and Survivors, 2011), p. 6, https://www.cvsni.org/media/1435/troubled-consequences-october-2011.pdf.

66 Ibid.

67 K.C. Koenen et al., 'Posttraumatic stress disorder in the world mental health surveys', *Psychological Medicine*, vol. 47, no. 13 (July 2017), pp. 2,260–74.

68 Interview with Eugen Koh, 28 January 2021; V. Volkan, 'Trauma, identity, and search for a solution in Cyprus', *Insight Turkey*, vol. 10, no. 4 (October 2008), pp. 95–110; V. Volkan, 'Chosen trauma: Unresolved mourning', in *Bloodlines: From Ethnic Pride to Ethnic Terrorism* (New York, 1999), pp. 36–49.

69 Interview with Winston Irvine, 7 December 2020.

70 L. McKee, 'Why suicide rates have skyrocketed for Northern Ireland's "ceasefire babies"', *The Atlantic*, 20 April 2019; M. Tomlinson, 'Dealing with suicide: How does research help?' (Knowledge Exchange Seminar Series, 2013), pp. 1–10.

71 D. McKittrick (ed.) et al., *Lost Lives*, Mainstream, Edinburgh, 1999, p. 1,476.

72 S. O'Neill and R.C. O'Connor, 'Suicide in Northern Ireland: Epidemiology, risk factors, and prevention', *The Lancet*, 29 January 2020, p. 538; A review of suicide statistics examined how 'undetermined' deaths were recorded from 2015 to 2018, deaths caused by the person themselves, but where the intent was unclear. According to the BBC report, 'The corrected rates show that Northern Ireland's suicide rate is lower than Scotland's, but remains higher than those of England, Wales and the Republic of Ireland. Out of the 467 cases reviewed, 84% moved into accidental cause-of-death categories which fall outside the suicide definition, thus resulting in a downward revision of the number of suicide deaths in Northern Ireland between 2015 and 2020. The extent of the downward revision in the number of suicide deaths from previously published figures is almost 30% in each of the years 2015–2017, 23% in 2018 and 17% in 2020'; 'Northern Ireland suicide rate lower than previously reported', BBC News, 26 May 2022, https://www.bbc.com/news/uk-northern-ireland-61589743; 'Review of suicide statistics in Northern Ireland', NISRA, 22 May 2022, https://www.nisra.gov.uk/news/review-suicide-statistics-northern-ireland-0.

73 Tomlinson, quoted in O'Neill and O'Connor, op. cit.

74 'Suicide statistics: Number of suicides registered each calendar year in Northern Ireland', Northern Ireland Statistics and Research Agency, Gov.uk, 19 October 2021.

75 Tomlinson, 2013; O'Neill et al., 2015.

76 He is referring to authorities turning a blind eye towards so called 'punishing shootings'. The IRA still acts as the dispenser of justice in inner-city republican communities. Kneecapping – shooting young offenders in the knee – is a favourite punishment. Sometimes these take place with the acquiescence of the parents; H. McDonald, 'Northern Ireland "punishment" attacks rise 60% in four years', *The Guardian*, 12 March 2018. See Statistics: Police Services of Northern Ireland, https://www.psni.police.uk/inside-psni/Statistics/; 'Terror

within', in L. Kennedy, *Who Was Responsible for the Troubles? The Northern Ireland Conflict* (Montreal, 2020), pp. 97–154; 'They shoot children, don't they?' in L. Kennedy, *Who Was Responsible for the Troubles?*, pp. 155–81.

77 Interview with Philip McGarry, 17 December 2020.

78 M.W. Tomlinson, 'War, peace and suicide: The case of Northern Ireland', *International Sociology* vol. 27, no. 4 (2012), p. 464–82; Tomlinson, 2013; M.W. Tomlinson, 'Transition to peace leaves children of the Northern Irish Troubles more vulnerable to suicide', British Politics and Policy at LSE (LSE, 30 July 2012). https://blogs.lse.ac.uk/politicsandpolicy/northern-ireland-suicide-tomlinson/; O'Neill et al., 2020.

79 The term 'epigenetic' changes refer to particular molecules that stick to particular parts of the DNA. So these are not changes in the gene encoding but they are changes around the DNA. See also S. Jiang et al., 'Epigenetic modifications in stress response genes associated with childhood trauma', *Frontiers in Psychiatry*, vol. 10, November 2019.

80 S. Elliott and W. Flackes, *Conflict in Northern Ireland: An Encyclopedia* (Belfast, 1999), p. 638, 684.

81 Ibid.

82 J. Betts and J. Thompson, 'Mental health in Northern Ireland: Overview, strategies, policies, care pathways, CAMHS and barriers to accessing services', http://www.niassembly.gov.uk/globalassets/documents/raise/publications /2016-2021/2017/health/0817.pdf.

83 L.A. Black, 'Suicide: Northern Ireland', Suicide: Northern Ireland (2021), http:// www.niassembly.gov.uk/globalassets/documents/raise/publications/2017-2022 /2021/health/2321.pdf.

84 'Trends in domestic abuse incidents and crimes recorded by the police in Northern Ireland 2004/05 to 2019/20', (Northern Ireland Statistics and Research Agency, 20 November 2020).

85 'Trends in domestic abuse incidents and crimes recorded by the police in Northern Ireland 2004/05 to 2020/21', PSNI, https://www.psni.police.uk/global assets/inside-the-psni/our-statistics/domestic-abuse-statistics/2020-21/domestic -abuse-incidents-and-crimes-in-northern-ireland-2004-05-to-2020-21.pdf.

86 C. Barnes, 'Northern Ireland is most dangerous place in Europe for women', *Belfast Telegraph*, 28 November 2021; 'Does Northern Ireland have the highest femicide rate in Western Europe?', FactCheckNI, 25 November 2019, https:// factcheckni.org/topics/law/does-northern-ireland-have-the-highest-femicide -rate-in-western-europe/.

87 Interview with Brandon Hamber, 8 January 2021.

88 'The non-medical use of prescription drugs policy direction issues' (United Nations, 2011), https://www.unodc.org/documents/drug-prevention-and -treatment/nonmedical-use-prescription-drugs.pdf.

89 'Systemic review programme: Review of mental health statistics in Northern Ireland' (2021), https://osr.statisticsauthority.gov.uk/wp-content/uploads/2021/09 /Review-of-mental-health-statistics-in-Northern-Ireland.pdf.

90 Interview with Máiría Cahill, 19 November 2020.

91 Interview with Bronagh Hinds, 20 April 2021.

92 Interview with Naomi Long, 4 December 2020.

93 Interview with Gary Mason, 8 December 2020.

94 Interview with Philip McGarry, 17 December 2020.

95 R. Napier, B. Gallagher and D. Wilson, 'An imperfect peace: Trends in paramilitary related violence 20 years after the Northern Ireland ceasefires', *Ulster Medical Journal*, vol. 86, no. 2 (17 May 2017), pp. 99–102; P. McGarry, 'National Center for Biotechnology Information', *National Center for Biotechnology Information* (PubMed Central, 12 September 2017).

96 Interview with Philip McGarry, 17 December 2020.

97 'Paramilitary groups in Northern Ireland', Secretary of State for Northern Ireland, 19 October 2015, p. 1, https://assets.publishing.service.gov.uk/government /uploads/system/uploads/attachment_data/file/469548/Paramilitary_Groups_in _Northern_Ireland_-_20_Oct_2015.pdf.

98 Ibid., p. 2.

99 Ibid.

100 Ibid.

101 Interview with Colin Halliday, 18 February 2021.

102 M. McGlinchey, 'While there's British interference, there's going to be action: Why a hardcore of dissident Irish republicans are not giving up', *The Guardian*, 22 July 2021; See also J.F. Morrison and J. Horgan, 'Reloading the Armalite? Victims and targets of violent dissident Irish republicanism, 2007–2015', *Terrorism and Political Violence*, vol. 28, no. 3, pp. 576–97; M. McGlinchey, 'The unfinished revolution of "dissident" Irish republicans: Divergent views in a fragmented base', *Small Wars & Insurgencies*, vol. 32, nos. 4–5, pp. 714–46, https://www.tandfonline.com/doi/full/10.1080/09592318.2021.1930368.

103 G. Moriarty, 'Behind Maghaberry's walls: The prison left behind by peace', *The Irish Times*, 25 March 2017.

104 R. Hewitt, 'Hunger strike by jailed dissident republicans comes to an end', *Belfast Telegraph*, 30 September 2020.

105 Interviewee wishes to remain anonymous.

106 'David Black murder "meticulously planned"', BBC News, 23 May 2018.

107 D. Dalby, 'Prison officer wounded in Northern Ireland attack dies', *The New York Times*, 15 March 2016.

108 Interviewee wishes to remain anonymous.

109 C. Campbell, 'Government challenged to take action over scale of paramilitary activity in Northern Ireland', *The Detail*, 29 April 2016, https://www.thedetail .tv/articles/hundreds-still-being-victimised-by-paramilitaries-each-year.

110 Ibid.

111 See L. Alderdice, J. McBurney and M. McWilliams, 'The Fresh Start Panel Report on the Disbandment of Paramilitary Groups in Northern Ireland' (Northern Ireland Executive, 6 July 2016) for history of this panel.

112 D. Morrow, 'Sectarianism in Northern Ireland: A review' (2019), p. 31.

113 'Independent Reporting Commission – Second Report', November 2019, https://www.ircommission.org/sites/irc/files/media-files/IRC%20-%202nd%20 Report%202019_0.pdf, p. 5.

114 Ibid.

115 D. Morrow and J. Byrne, 'Countering paramilitary & organised criminal influence on youth: A review' (The Corrymeela Press, March 2020), p. 63.

116 Ibid., p. 63.

117 Ibid., p. 64.

118 Cooperation North originated in 1979 with the goal 'to take action to build mutual respect and understanding [between Ireland and Northern Ireland] through practical co-operation in the economic, social and cultural spheres with no political strings attached'. Charter NI was formed in 2000 and acts as a lobbyist and advocate for East Belfast, North Down and Ards communities. D. Murray and J. O'Neill, *Peace Building in a Political Impasse: Cross-Border Links in Ireland* (Coleraine, UK, 1991); 'About CharterNI' (CharterNI, 2016).

119 Interview with Brian Feeney, 10 March 2021.

120 The Social Investment Fund is an official agency which comes under the Executive Office (the office of the first minister and deputy first minister). It focuses on projects aimed at reducing poverty, increasing employment and improving physical infrastructures; 'Social Investment Fund', The Executive Office, 15 February 2022.

121 C. Simpson, '£100 million "social deprivation" funding "must not repeat mistakes of SIF"', *The Irish News*, 27 June 2018; 'Flawed Social Investment Fund reflects badly on Stormont administration', *The Irish Times*, 9 November 2018.

122 A. Gordon, 'Dee Stitt: Loyalist accuses Arlene Foster of "ruining his street cred"', BBC News, 6 September 2018.

123 For additional academic research on legacy issues in Northern Ireland, see 'Dealing with the past in Northern Ireland', https://www.dealingwiththepastni. com/project-outputs/academic-research?page=2.

124 In July 1995, Bosnian Serb army of Republika Srpska (VRS) massacred approximately 8,000 Bosnian Muslim men and boys in the town of Srebrenica. Despite its UN protection by Dutch UNPROFOR forces, the area was overrun. This incident, in combination with the abuse and forced displacement of 25,000– 30,000 Bosnian Muslim women, children and elderly people, the international community has deemed a genocide.

125 Interview with Gary Mason, 8 December 2020.

126 'Independent Reporting Commission – Third Report', 17 November 2020, https://www.ircommission.org/sites/irc/files/media-files/IRC%20Third%20 Report_0.pdf, p. 8.

127 Interview with Monica McWilliams, 11 March 2020.

128 'Independent Reporting Commission – Fourth Report', 7 December 2021, https://www.ircommission.org/sites/irc/files/media-files/IRC%20Fourth%20 Report%20web%20accessible_1.pdf, pp. 10–11; In 2018, the Independent Reporting Commission made nine recommendations, including: an additional approach to enhance delivery of the Executive Action Plan; establishing an advisory board to the Tackling Paramilitarism Programme Board; taking a whole-of-society approach/shared responsibility; developing neighbourhood policing; focusing on sustainability measures; considering a possible role of local councils in the delivery of Fresh Start; examining the governance of funding arrangements; enhancing the use of asset-recovery powers; and speeding up justice. The additional recommendations made in the second report (2019) focus on strengthening their 2018 recommendations with specific action steps.

129 The programme 'is active across all of Northern Ireland to support people and communities who are vulnerable to paramilitary influence and harm, with commitments being delivered collaboratively by government departments, statutory agencies and partners in the voluntary and community sector. One of the main strategic goals for the Programme is to try to break the cycle of paramilitary activity and organised crime, and to stop another generation getting drawn into this spiral. Through a range of projects and interventions, the Programme is working towards ending recruitment and turning off the tap for these criminal gangs. At the same time, the Programme works with people at risk of paramilitary influence, coercion and violence'. See 'Executive programme for tackling paramilitary and organized crime', Department of Justice, https://www.justice-ni.gov.uk/articles /executive-programme-tackling-paramilitary-activity-and-organised-crime.

130 Interview with Naomi Long, 4 December 2020.

131 Interview with Brandon Hamber, 8 January 2021.

132 Interview with Naomi Long, 4 December 2020.

133 Interview with Paul, Lord Bew, 6 January 2021.

134 K. McEvoy et al., 'Prosecutions, imprisonment, and the Stormont House Agreement: A critical analysis of proposals on dealing with the past in Northern Ireland' (Dealing with the Past in Northern Ireland, 2020), p. 3.

135 Stormont House Agreement, https://assets.publishing.service.gov.uk/government /uploads/system/uploads/attachment_data/file/390672/Stormont_House _Agreement.pdf.

136 B. Rowan, *Unfinished Peace: Thoughts on Northern Ireland's Unanswered Past* (Belfast, 2015), pp. 150–2.

137 Ibid., p. 152.

138 B. Hamber, 'Moment of truth: Victims of Northern Ireland's troubled past can't wait forever for justice', *Belfast Telegraph*, 12 December 2020.

139 Ibid.

140 Interview with Stephen Farry, 28 January 2021.

141 Interview with Gary Mason, 8 December 2020.

142 J. Gray, 'Govt publishes troubles pension eligibility guidance', *Pensions Age Magazine*, 14 August 2020.

143 S. Smith, 'NI govt "unlawfully" delayed troubles pension scheme, rules high court', *Pensions Age Magazine*, 21 August 2020.

144 'Northern Ireland General Election Survey 2019', *NI General Election Survey 2019* (Faculty of Humanities & Social Sciences – University of Liverpool), accessed 2 February 2022.

145 Interview with Harold Good, 23 March 2021.

146 O. Bowcott, 'Bill sets five-year limit to prosecute UK armed forces who served abroad', *The Guardian*, 17 March 2020.

147 '@GRobinsonDUP raises the need for greater protection for Northern Ireland veterans, as he gives support to the Overseas Operations Bill in Parliament', Twitter post, 23 September 2020, https://twitter.com/duponline/status/130881153 4727077888.

148 'Passing of "Overseas Operation bill" shameful – Molloy', Sinn Féin [website], 3 November 2020, https://www.sinnfein.ie/contents/58694.

149 G. Moriarty, 'NI bishops express "alarm" at British proposals on the past', *The Irish Times*, 8 April 2020.

150 Ibid.

151 Ibid.

152 F. McClements, 'Prosecution of Soldier F over Bloody Sunday deaths halted', *Irish Times*, 2 July 2021. See also M. Saville, W. Hoyt and J. Toohey, 'Report of the Bloody Sunday inquiry' (2010), https://www.gov.uk/government/publications /report-of-the-bloody-sunday-inquiry.

153 'Soldier F: Dropping of Bloody Sunday murder charges adjourned', BBC News, 9 July 2021.

154 L. O'Carroll, 'Belfast court quashes decision to stop Bloody Sunday prosecution of Soldier F', *The Guardian*, 23 March 2022.

155 M. McBride, 'Prosecutors drop Troubles cases against ex-soldiers', BBC News, 2 July 2021; 'Joe McCann: Trial of two soldiers collapses', BBC News, 4 May 2021.

156 J. O'Neill, 'Plan to end all NI Troubles prosecutions confirmed', BBC News, 14 July 2021.

157 M. Symington, 'U.K. weighs Northern Ireland amnesty in bid to spare veterans', NBC News, 8 November 2021.

158 D. Young, 'Hutchings challenges admissibility of document naming him as "Soldier A"', *Irish Examiner*, 11 October 2021.

159 For a dedicated academic site dealing with the past, see https://www.dealing withthepastni.com/project-outputs/academic-research.

160 D. Rieff, *In Praise of Forgetting* (New Haven, CT, 2016), p. 106.

161 Ibid.; D. Rieff, 'The cult of memory: When history does more harm than good', *The Guardian*, 2 March 2016.

162 Stevens et al. (2013, p. 76) define continuous stress disorder as 'one possible way of describing the psychological impact of living in conditions in which there is a realistic threat of present and future danger, rather than only experiences of past traumatic events'. See G. Stevens et al., 'Continuous traumatic stress: Conceptual conversations in contexts of global conflict, violence, and trauma', *Peace and Conflict: Journal of Peace Psychology*, vol. 19, no. 2, 2013, pp. 75–84.

163 'Addressing the legacy of Northern Ireland's past', pp. 1–30, https://assets .publishing.service.gov.uk/government/uploads/system/uploads/attachment _data/file/1002140/CP_498_Addressing_the_Legacy_of_Northern_Ireland_s _Past.pdf; M. Symington, 'U.K. weighs Northern Ireland amnesty in bid to spare veterans "vexatious prosecutions"', NBC News, 8 November 2021.

164 C. Leebody, 'Secretary of State Brandon Lewis confirms government seeking statute of limitations on Troubles-related killings', *Belfast Telegraph*, 14 July 2021.

165 K. Mullan, 'Brandon Lewis still engaging in "Statute of Limitations" which he describes as a "complicated, sensitive and difficult" area', *Derry Journal*, 22 February 2022.

166 Ibid.

167 M. O'Neill, 'British government must respond to UN intervention and withdraw amnesty proposals', Sinn Féin [website], 11 August 2021. https://www .sinnfein.ie/contents/61539.

168 L. Clarke, 'Half of all top IRA men "worked for security services"', *Belfast Telegraph*, 21 December 2011.

169 After suspected IRA bomber John Downey produced a letter at trial, his case was dismissed and the letter scheme associated with B/GFA negotiations became public. After an inquiry by the Northern Ireland Affairs committee, it was recommended that the letters have no legal effect. In December 2012, the Northern Ireland Secretary of State said the government would stop processing any outstanding applications associated with the letters; G. McKevitt, 'On the runs – key questions and inquiry findings', BBC News, March 2015.

170 J. Gibson, 'Overcoming apartheid: Can truth reconcile a divided nation?', *The ANNALS of the American Academy of Political and Social Science*, vol. 603, no. 1 (2006), pp. 82–110.

171 McEvoy et al., 2020; 'Prosecutions, imprisonment and the Stormont House Agreement. A critical analysis of proposals on dealing with the past in Northern Ireland', https://caj.org.uk/wp-content/uploads/2020/04/Prosecutions-Imprisonment -the-SHA-LOW-RES.pdf. Under the 1998 B/GFA, those convicted of Troubles would serve a maximum of two years in prison.

172 McEvoy et al., 2020; 'New report finds proposed UK government amnesty cannot deliver truth for victims of the Troubles', Committee on the Administration of Justice, 7 September 2021; 'Agreement between the government of the United Kingdom of Great Britain and Northern Ireland and the government of Ireland

establishing the Independent Commission of Information Retrieval', http://opac.oireachtas.ie/AWData/Library3/FATRdoclaid210116_100026.pdf (2016), pp. 1–12; J. O'Neill, 'Stakeknife: Operation Kenova report into IRA spy due next year', BBC News, 30 September 2021.

173 Kenova, 'About Jon Boutcher', 2022 [website], https://www.kenova.co.uk/about-jon-boutcher.

174 'Tom Lantos Human Rights Commission hearing on Northern Ireland: Accountability at risk', https://chrissmith.house.gov/uploadedfiles/jon_boutcher testimonytlhrchearing_14022022.pdf, p. 2.

175 https://chrissmith.house.gov/uploadedfiles/jon_boutchertestimonytlhrchearing_14022022.pdf. Operation Mizzenmast, Operation Turma and the Barnard Review are all under the umbrella of the Kenova Operation. Operation Kenova can be accessed at http://www.kenova.co.

176 T. Ambrose and L. O'Carroll, 'Evidence police in Belfast colluded with loyalists in the Troubles, report finds', The Guardian, 8 February 2022.

177 Northern Ireland Secretary Brandon Lewis – Statement following Queen's Speech 2022, 10 May 2022, https://www.gov.uk/government/news/northern-ireland-secretary-brandon-lewis-statement-following-queens-speech-2022.

178 'Tweaked Troubles amnesty plan met with opposition', TheJournal.ie, 8 May 2022.

179 Secretary of State Brandon Lewis reintroduced legacy legislation on 17 May 2022. A central element would provide immunity from prosecution for those who co-operated with investigations run by a new information recovery body, the Independent Commission for Reconciliation and Information Recovery (ICRIR). 'Bereaved families can request the ICRIR to conduct investigations, as can the government and others. The body will be headed by a judicial figure appointed by the government and be operational for five years. A panel within the ICRIR will be responsible for deciding if a perpetrator qualifies for immunity. The draft legislation states it must be granted if an individual gives an account judged to be "true to the best of (their) knowledge and belief". Once granted, it cannot be revoked. See in S. Pogatchnik, 'Victims "want no amnesty" for Troubles-era killers, Irish tell UK', Politico, 17 May 2022; J. O'Neill. 'NI Troubles: Legacy bill published by the UK government', BBC News, 17 May 2022.

180 House of Lords, Select Committee on the Constitution, 5th Report of Session 2022–23, Northern Ireland Troubles (Legacy and Reconciliation) Bill, https://committees.parliament.uk/publications/30272/documents/175220/default.

181 R. Black, 'Northern Ireland's Legacy Bill "can be improved", says Heaton-Harris', Belfast Telegraph, 20 September 2022.

182 'Prosecution of "Soldier F" over Bloody Sunday murders resumes', The Irish Times, 28 September 2022.

7. THE SOUTH

1 Interview with Will Glendinning, 12 March 2021.

2 Interview with Mike Nesbitt, 10 December 2020.

3 Interview with Niall Blaney, 1 June 2021.

4 Interview with Billy Hutchinson, 9 March 2020.

5 F. O'Toole, *We Don't Know Ourselves: A Personal History of Modern Ireland* (New York, 2022), p. 541.

6 'Commission to inquire into child abuse', Government of Ireland [website]. http://www.childabusecommission.ie/index.html; See also P. McGarry, 'Catholic Archbishop of Dublin says belief has 'vanished' in Ireland', *The Irish Times*, 16 August 2021; S. Murphy. 'How will Pope Francis' papal visit to Ireland differ from Pope John Paul II's in 1979?', *Extra.ie*, 21 August 2018; Y. Murphy, I. Mangan and H. O'Neill, *Commission of Investigation, Report into the Catholic Archdiocese of Dublin July 2009* (Dublin: Ministry for Justice, Equality, and Law Reform, 2009); Y. Murphy, I. Mangan and H. O'Neill, *Commission of Investigation, Report into the Catholic Diocese of Cloyne December 2010* (Dublin: Ministry for Justice, Equality, and Law Reform, 2010).

7 R. Foster, *Luck and the Irish: A Brief History of Change, 1970–2000* (London, 2007), p. 7.

8 K. Peters, 'Celtic Tiger', Investopedia [website], 13 October 2021, https://www.investopedia.com/terms/c/celtictiger.asp.

9 Foster, op. cit., p. 11.

10 J.B. Burnham 'Why Ireland boomed', *The Independent Review*, vol. 7, no. 4 (Spring 2003), pp. 537–56; P. Bodkin, 'Ireland's sweetheart tax deal for Apple was worth up to €13 billion over a decade', *Fora*, 30 August 2016.

11 J. Burnham, 'Why Ireland boomed', *Independent Review*, vol. 7, no. 4 (Spring 2003), pp. 537–56; R. Ní Mháille, 'Ireland's "Celtic Tiger" economy', *Science, Technology, & Human Values*, vol. 28, no. 1 (Winter 2003), pp. 93–111, https://www.jstor.org/stable/1558024.

12 P. Krugman, 'Leprechaun economics key to understanding US corporate tax proposal', *Irish Times*, 9 April 2021, https://www.irishtimes.com/business/economy/leprechaun-economics-key-to-understanding-us-corporate-tax-proposal-1.4533410; Bodkin, op. cit.

13 E. Burke, 'Ireland is a home for 24 of the world's top biotech and pharma companies', *Silicon Republic*, 29 May 2017.

14 J. Bradley and M. Best, 'Ireland's divided economy: Growth without indigenous innovation', in M. Best, *How Growth Really Happens: The Making of Economic Miracles Through Production, Governance, and Skills* (Princeton, NJ, 2018), p. 178.

15 Interview with Matt Carthy, 2 December 2020.

16 D. Donovan and A. Murphy, *The Fall of the Celtic Tiger: Ireland and the Euro Debt Crisis* (Oxford, 2013), p. 249.

17 Between April 2009 and April 2015, 295,000 foreign citizens left Ireland and 285,000 arrived, for a net –10,000. In the same period, 265,000 Irish citizens left

and 120,000 arrived for a net –145,000. See also A. Barrett and S. McGuinness, *The Irish Labour Market and the Great Recession* (Dublin, 2015); I. Glynn, with T. Kelly and P. Mac Éinrí, *The Re-emergence of Emigration from Ireland: New Trends in an Old Story* (Washington, DC, 2015).

18   S. Collins, 'Irish people second-richest in EU in 2021', *Independent.ie*, 23 March 2022.

19   Kingsley Aitkin, Networking institute, Dublin; email exchange.

20   *Education at a Glance 2019: Ireland*, Organisation for Economic Co-operation and Development (2019), https://www.oecd.org/education/education-at-a-glance/EAG2019_CN_IRL.pdf.

21   'Ratio of children and young people in the total population on 1 January by sex and age', Eurostat, https://ec.europa.eu/eurostat/databrowser/view/YTH _DEMO_020__custom_2165280/bookmark/table?lang=en&bookmarkId =9eddob01-26b5-4038-b148-048279e55e2d.

22   T. Fish, 'The 12 most educated countries in the world', *Newsweek*, 20 June 2021.

23   IDA Ireland, *Education and Skills in Ireland*, https://www.idaireland.com/invest-in-ireland/education-and-skills.

24   IDA Ireland, *Facts About Ireland*, https://www.idaireland.com/newsroom/publications/facts_about_ireland_2018#:~:text=Ireland%20has%20the%20 youngest%20population,educated%20workforces%20in%20the%20world.

25   S. McDermott, 'Ireland has second-highest quality of life in the world, according to the UN', *TheJournal.ie*, 2020; UNDP, *Human Development Report 2020. The Next Frontier: Human development and the Anthropocene* (2020), https://report. hdr.undp.org.

26   D. Carrington, 'Ireland "one of world's best five places" to survive global societal collapse', *The Irish Times*, 29 July 2021.

27   National Competitiveness Council Ireland's Competitiveness Scorecard 2019, July 2019, http://www.competitiveness.ie/publications/2019/ireland-s-competitiveness-scorecard-2019.pdf.

28   Interview with Colum Eastwood, 26 January 2021.

29   Organisation for Economic Co-operation and Development, *Economic Forecast Summary: Ireland* (2021), https://www.oecd.org/economy/ireland-economic -snapshot.

30   C. Kelpie, 'Honohan: We need new accounts to measure economy', *Independent. ie*, 14 July 2016.

31   See Chapter 8: The Two Economies.

32   D. Carolan, 'Inequalities in Ireland: Greater policy coherence needed to tackle stark wealth inequalities which co-exist alongside widespread social discrimination' (2019), https://www.sdgwatcheurope.org/wp-content/uploads/2019/06 /7.3.a-Report-IE.pdf.

33   C. Taylor, 'Anglo collapse taught us one lesson we can't ever forget', *The Irish Times*, 13 November 2021.

34 'Irish corporation tax revenues set to decline from 2023 onwards, says Donohoe', *TheJournal.ie*, 6 January 2022; Taylor, op. cit.

35 Taylor, op. cit.

36 F. O'Toole, 'Ireland would not be viable without 10 big US corporations', *The Irish Times*, 15 January 2021.

37 Ibid.

38 Government of Ireland, Ministry for Climate, Environment, and Communications, *Climate Conversations Summary Report* (2021), https://www.gov.ie/en /consultation/5bd95-climate-conversation-climate-action-plan-2021; 'Climate change: Irish government lays out Climate Action Plan', BBC News, 4 November 2021.

39 'Over 80 per cent of homes in western Ireland are heated with oil, coal or peat fuels that will be hardest hit by carbon tax hikes to discourage their use as the government plans to cut energy emissions by 44–56 per cent', in M. Donnelly, 'Farmers to be hit with extra costs from climate plan', *Farming Independent*, 9 November 2021.

40 L. O'Carroll, 'Ireland would need to cull up to 1.3 million cattle to reach climate targets', *The Guardian*, 3 November 2021; V. Clarke and B. Hutton, 'Emissions targets "not consistent" with Government legislation, says Climate Change Advisory Council', *The Irish Times*, 29 July 2022; P. Leahy and B. O'Sullivan, 'Ireland must take immediate steps to prepare for impact of climate change, Government to be warned', *The Irish Times*, 20 July 2022; 'Irish farmers to be asked to cut emissions by 25%', BBC News, 28 July 2022; 'Ireland targets 25% cut in agriculture emissions but farmers voice anger', *The Guardian*, 29 July 2022.

41 C. Humphries, 'Ireland says halving greenhouse gases will cost 125 billion euros', Reuters, 4 November 2021.

42 S. Carswell and C. McQuinn, 'Farming climate plan imposes "impossible" burden on other sectors, say scientists', *The Irish Times*, 30 July 2022; J. Bray, 'Unprecedented changes needed if climate targets are to be met, cabinet warned', *The Irish Times*, 1 August 2022; G. Howlin, 'Emissions deal reflects significant realignment of political power', *The Irish Times*, 2 August 2022.

43 M.L. McDonald, 'Sinn Féin Ard Fheis 2021', 30 October 2021, https://www.sinn fein.ie/contents/62183.

44 S. Patnaik and K. Kennedy, 'Why the US should establish a carbon price either through reconciliation or other legislation', Brookings, 7 October 2021; A. Dushime, 'Addressing climate change through carbon taxes', World Economic Forum, 16 June 2021.

45 J. Mintz, 'We could grow like a Celtic Tiger too, if we had Irish policies', *Financial Post*, 26 March 2021.

46 'The two-tier nature of the Irish economy', *The Irish Times*, 8 July 2021; R. Shortt, 'ESRI forecasts robust economic recovery', RTÉ, 7 October 2021.

47 E. Burke-Kennedy, 'Unemployment falls to pandemic low of 6.9% as economy rebounds', *The Irish Times*, 1 December 2021.

48 T. Conefrey, R. Hickey and N. McInerney, 'COVID-19 and the public finances in Ireland', Economic Letter, Central Bank of Ireland, vol. 2021, no. 3, pp. 4-5, https://www.centralbank.ie/docs/default-source/publications/economic -letters/vol-2021-no-3-covid-19-and-the-public-finances-in-ireland-(conefrey -hickey-and-mcinerney).pdf#page=4.

49 Ibid.

50 'Annual Report on Public Debt in Ireland 2021 Summary', Gov.ie, 22 February 2022, https://www.gov.ie/en/publication/7373b-annual-report-on-public-debt-in -ireland-2021-summary/.

51 Ibid.

52 Foster, op. cit. p. 188.

53 C. Taylor, 'Fighting inflation is an impossible job in an era of political populism', The Irish Times, 4 June 2022, https://www.irishtimes.com/opinion/2022/06 /04/fighting-inflation-is-an-impossible-job-in-an-era-of-political-populism/; D. McWilliams, 'Ultimately, uncontrolled inflation will be followed by a recession', The Irish Times, 14 May 2022, https://www.irishtimes.com/opinion /david-mcwilliams-ultimately-uncontrolled-inflation-will-be-followed-by-a -recession-1.4876812; 'Irish inflation nears 40-year high of 6.7% in March', Reuters, 7 April 2022.

54 J. Fitzgerald, 'Ireland faces gas rationing as Russia invades Ukraine', The Irish Times, 24 February 2022; C. Keena, 'Ukraine war sees petrol and diesel hit €2 a litre at some service stations', The Irish Times, 6 March 2022; C. Taylor, 'War in Ukraine exacerbates Irish economic problems lurking in the back-ground', The Irish Times, 19 March 2022; C. Phelan, 'Is Ireland headed for recession? Taoiseach Micheál Martin can't make any promises as war rages on', Irish Mirror, 16 March 2022; E. Burke-Kennedy, 'World Bank warns many countries headed for recession', The Irish Times, 7 June 2022, https:// www.irishtimes.com/business/economy/2022/06/07/most-countries-headed -for-recession-world-bank-warns/.

55 E. Burke Kennedy, 'Irish households facing biggest fall in living standards since 2008 financial crisis, ESRI warns', The Irish Times, 23 June 2022.

56 'Electric Ireland announces energy price increases effective from August 1st, 2022', ESB, 2 July 2022, https://www.esb.ie/media-centre-news/press-releases /article/2022/07/01/electric-ireland-announces-energy-price-increases-effective -from-august-1st-2022.

57 Burke-Kennedy, op. cit.; H. O'Connell. 'Cost of living: Bills could rise by €2,000 per year – and over €3,500 when cost of filling car included', Independent.ie, 15 June 2022.

58 'Politics of power set to dominate as winter blackouts loom on horizon', Independent.ie, 31 August 2022.

59 'Electric Ireland to increase gas and electricity again', RTÉ, 1 September 2022.

60   Brian Hutton, 'Cost of living: More than a million people in Ireland struggling to make ends meet', *The Irish Times*, 24 September 2022.

61   Ibid.

62   Carolan, op. cit.

63   Ibid.

64   D. McWilliams, 'The 'Ireland is crap' brigade are way off mark but we need to sort the housing crisis', *The Irish Times*, 22 September 2022.

65   B. Hutton, 'Cost of living: More than a million people in Ireland struggling to make ends meet', *The Irish Times*, 24 September 2022.

66   See B. Roantree et al., 'Poverty, income inequality, and living standards in Ireland' (2021), https://www.esri.ie/system/files/publications/BKMNEXT412_1.pdf; A. Molly, 'Gap between rich and poor was at its narrowest on record but then the pandemic struck', *Independent.ie*, 14 May 2021; Economic and Social Research Institute, *Ireland's young workers 6 times more likely to be on temporary contracts than those over 25* [website], https://www.esri.ie/news/irelands-young-workers -6-times-more-likely-to-be-on-temporary-contracts-than-those-over-25.

67   D. McGrath, 'Brexit not as calamitous for Ireland as feared, politicians told', *Independent.ie*, 9 March 2022.

68   'Ireland and the impacts of Brexit: Strategic implications for Ireland arising from changing EU-UK trading relations', *Copenhagen Economics*, https:// copenhageneconomics.com/publication/ireland-the-impacts-of-brexit. The study's main conclusions are that increased trade costs will lower Irish exports of goods and services by approximately 3–8 per cent in 2030 and Irish GDP by approximately 3–7 per cent in 2030.

69   S. Pogatchnik, 'Brexit slashes Britain's market share in Ireland', *Politico*, 21 December 2021.

70   Ibid.

71   S. Pogatchnik, 'All-Ireland trade booming in post-Brexit economy', *Politico*, 15 February 2022.

72   M. Muvija and W. Schomberg, 'Britain delays full post-Brexit import checks until late 2023', Reuters, 28 April 2022.

73   Pogatchnik, op. cit.

74   Institute for Government, Trade: The UK landbridge [website], https://www .instituteforgovernment.org.uk/explainers/trade-uk-landbridge.

75   G. Aodha, 'Tonnes of new ferry routes have helped to Brexit-proof Irish trade – but choppy waters could yet be ahead', *TheJournal.ie*, 1 March 2021.

76   'The IMDO report shows freight volumes from Dublin port to Liverpool and Holyhead in Anglesey down 19% in the first three-quarters of 2021 compared with 2020 and down by 30% on the two routes from Rosslare in south-east Ireland to the Welsh ports of Pembroke and Fishguard', in L. O'Carroll, 'Goods shipped directly from Ireland to EU up by 50% in six months', *The Guardian*, 30 November 2021.

77　R. Shortt, 'Brexit sees Dublin port UK traffic fall by over 20%', RTÉ News, 27 October 2021.

78　G. Osborne, 'Unleashing nationalism has made the future of the UK the central issue', *Evening Standard*, 19 January 2021.

79　'Election 2020', RTÉ, https://www.rte.ie/news/election-2020/results/#/national.

80　For a comprehensive breakdown of election results, see M. Gallagher, M. Marsh and T. Reidy, *How Ireland Voted 2020: The End of an Era* (London, 2021).

81　'Sinn Féin had around ten times more engagement on Facebook during this year's general election campaign than the State's other political parties, a study has found. The party ran an "anti-elite populist narrative" on social media, where it "vastly outperformed" its political rivals. The study found that Sinn Féin posts on Facebook over the course of the campaign (14 January to 8 February) had 567,020 "interactions" or responses, compared to 49,358 for Fianna Fáil and 55,152 for Fine Gael … Sinn Féin focused on the topic of "change" in its Facebook posts over the course of the election campaign, with more than one in five of its posts referring to the concept. It accounted for two-thirds of all mentions of "change" by all political parties on Facebook during the campaign,' in C. Keena, 'Sinn Féin massively dominant on Facebook during general election', *The Irish Times*, 25 May 2020. See also H. McGee, 'Exit polls by numbers: Who voted what way and where', *The Irish Times*, 8 February 2020.

82　O. Ryan, 'Sinn Féin is the most popular party among all age groups up to 65', *TheJournal.ie*, 9 February 2020.

83　Interview with Bertie Ahern, 26 November 2020. Ahern predictions were close: Sinn Féin won 29 per cent of first preference votes in the May 2022 election. See Chapter 9 and 10 for additional background.

84　S. Collins, 'Detailed election 2020 exit poll results: How voters answered 15 questions', *The Irish Times*, 9 February 2020.

85　Ibid., Sinn Féin, 'Better4housing' [website], https://www.sinnFéin.ie/housing.

86　R. McGreevy, 'Historic coalition agreement ends almost a century of civil war politics', *The Irish Times*, 27 June 2020.

87　See Gallagher, Marsh and Reidy, *How Ireland Voted*.

88　J. Bruton, 'The EU Commission was wrong on Phil Hogan's resignation. The damage may already be done', *Euronews*, 4 September 2020.

89　S. Collins, 'Politicians lose focus obsessing on Zappone saga', *The Irish Times*, 10 September 2021.

90　D. MacNamee, 'Varadkar admits "mistakes were made" in Katherine Zappone appointment', *Nova*, 5 August 2021.

91　T. Doherty, 'Ireland under strictest lockdown in EU, claims Oxford report', *BreakingNews.ie*, 24 February 2021.

92　C. Gleeson, 'Ireland ranked best in the world for dealing with Covid', *The Irish Times*, 27 October 2021.

93 P. Cullen, 'COVID-19: Ireland had one of lowest excess death rates in world, study finds', *The Irish Times*, 10 March 2022; H. Wang, 'Estimating excess mortality due to the COVID-19 pandemic: A systematic analysis of COVID-19-related mortality, 2021–21', *The Lancet*, 10 March 2022.

94 N. O'Leary, 'Ireland in lead with vaccination coverage and lowest death rate in EU', *Irish Times*, 23 November 2021.

95 P. Leahy, 'Public stays with government on COVID measures – for now', *The Irish Times*, 10 December 2021.

96 Red C, 'Sinn Féin dominates current political polling' [website], https://www.redcresearch.ie/sinn-fein-dominates-current-policital-polling/; Red C Business Post, *Opinion Poll Report January 2022* (2022), https://redcresearch.ie/wp-content/uploads/2022/01/Business-Post-RED-C-Opinion-Poll-Report-Jan-2022.pdf.

97 H. McGee, 'Election 2020: Exit poll confirms health, housing, homelessness of most concern to voters', *The Irish Times*, 9 February 2020.

98 Roantree et al., op. cit., p. xii.

99 E. Burke-Kennedy, 'Dublin-centric development "unsustainable", warns ESRI', *The Irish Times*, 24 January 2018.

100 D. Buckley, 'Dublin is ranked fifth in EU for financial services', *Independent.ie*, 30 March 2017.

101 E. Burke-Kennedy, 'Ireland is 13th most expensive place to live, survey shows', *The Irish Times*, 18 January 2021.

102 S. Murray, 'Ireland has the highest prices in the EU – and it's even worse than we think', *Irish Examiner*, 25 June 2022.

103 B. O'Halloran, 'Just 8,000 houses built last year offered for sale on open market, says CIF', *The Irish Times*, 19 February 2020.

104 Central Statistics Office, 'New Dwellings completion', 2022, https://www.cso.ie/en/releasesandpublications/er/ndc/newdwellingcompletionsq12022/; The Housing Agency, 'Welcome to the Housing Agency data hub' [website], 2022, https://www.housingagency.ie/data-hub/welcome-housing-agency-data-hub.

105 S. Starr, 'Why Ireland's housing crisis is intensifying', *Ozy* [blog] (3 April 2020); M. Doyle, 'Property prices rose by almost 8% in 2021', RTÉ, 30 December 2021; D. Houde, 'The 2022 housing crisis of Ireland: Fact or fiction', 2022, https://selectra.ie/moving/tips/housing-crisis-ireland.

106 R.S. Byrne, 'First-time buyers need incomes of almost €80,000 to purchase a home in Ireland, new report reveals', *Buzz*, 24 May 2022.

107 E. Hemani, 'Home rents increase across Ireland at highest rate since 2016', *The Times*, 12 May 2022.

108 O. Kelly, 'Homeless family numbers up 350% since 2014', *The Irish Times*, 13 May 2020.

109 E. Ó Broin, 'Sinn Féin will deliver the largest public housing building programmed in the history of the State', Sinn Féin [website], 20 January 2020, https://www.sinnfein.ie/contents/55773.

110 J. Horgan-Jones, 'Election 2020: Is Sinn Féin's housing policy credible?', *The Irish Times*, 6 February 2020.

111 E. Burke-Kennedy, 'Record tax receipts deliver €5bn surplus for exchequer', *The Irish Times*, 3 August 2022

112 J. Bray, 'Housing for all plan: Taoiseach wants to "end homelessness" by 2030', *The Irish Times*, 2 September 2021.

113 Ibid., para. 4; *Department of Housing, Local Government and Heritage, Housing for All – A New Housing Plan for Ireland* [website], https://www.gov.ie/en /publication/ef5ec-housing-for-all-a-new-housing-plan-for-ireland; E. Burke-Kennedy and C. McQuinn, 'State must double investment to solve housing crisis, ESRI says', *The Irish Times*, June 2021. An investigation by *The Independent* reported that fewer than 1,400 affordable homes would be delivered by the state in Irish cities each year, 2022–6. Over 1,000 will be in Dublin, with just 256 homes built in the other four cities (Cork, Limerick, Galway and Waterford) over the same period; G. Gataveckaite, 'Revealed: How many affordable homes will be built in each county a year', *Independent.ie*, 9 May 2022.

114 E. Burke-Kennedy, 'Electric Ireland prices to rise 23–25% from May', *The Irish Times*, 30 March 2022.

115 D. McWilliams, 'David McWilliams: Housebuyers in Ireland should step away from the market', *The Irish Times*, 4 September 2021.

8. THE TWO ECONOMIES

1 Interview with Will Glendinning, 12 March 2021.

2 Interview with John Bradley, 25 March 2021.

3 Interview with Colum Eastwood, 26 January 2021.

4 Interview with Peter Shirlow, 7 December 2020.

5 Interview with Graham Gudgin, 17 December 2020.

6 Interview with Jim O'Callaghan, 15 March 2021.

7 Interview with Mike Nesbitt, 10 December 2020.

8 Interview with Séanna Walsh, 20 January 2021.

9 Interview with Rose Conway-Walsh, 18 March 2021.

10 'Overview of the UK population: 2020', Office for National Statistics, 25 February 2022, https://www.ons.gov.uk/peoplepopulationandcommunity/populationand migration/populationestimates/articles/overviewoftheukpopulation/latest. The official 2022 census population of the Republic of Ireland was 5.1 million: 'Census of population 2022 – preliminary results', Central Statistics Office, 23 June 2022, https://www.cso.ie/en/csolatestnews/pressreleases/2022pressreleases/press statementcensusofpopulation2022-preliminaryresults/.

11 Interview with Peter Robinson, 11 March 2020.

12 J. Fitzgerald and E.L.W. Morgenroth, 'The Northern Ireland economy: Problems and prospects', *Journal of the Statistical and Social Inquiry Society of Ireland*, vol. XLIX, pp. 64–87, p. 81, April 2020.

13 J. Fitzgerald and E.L.W. Morgenroth, 'The Northern Ireland economy:
    Problems and prospects', Department of Economics, Trinity College, working
    paper no. 01619, July 2019; J. Fitzgerald and E.L.W. Morgenroth, 'The Northern
    Ireland economy: Problems and prospects', pp. 64–87, April 2020; A. Bergin
    and S. McGuinness, 'Who is better off? Measuring cross-border differences
    in living standards, opportunities and quality of life on the island of Ireland',
    Economic and Social Research Institute, Dublin, 2021; J. Fitzgerald, 'Thoughts on
    quality of life, North and South: A response to "Who is better off" by A. Bergin
    and S. McGuinness', *Irish Studies in International Affairs*, vol. 32, no. 2, 2021,
    pp. 161–3; J. Doyle, 'Why the "subvention" does not matter: Northern Ireland
    and the all-Ireland economy', *Irish Studies in International Affairs*, vol. 32, no. 2,
    2021, pp. 314–34; J. Doyle, 'UK subvention to North irrelevant to debate on Irish
    unity', *The Irish Times*, 9 June 2021; A. Bergin and S. McGuinness, 'The political
    economy of a Northern Ireland border poll', *Cambridge Journal of Economics*,
    February 2020; Paul Gosling, *A New Ireland, A New Union, A New Society: A
    Ten-Year Plan?* (Paul Gosling, 2018); G. Gudgin, 'Who is better off, Northerners
    or Southerners?', Queen's Policy Engagement [blog], 16 February 2021, http://
    qpol.qub.ac.uk/who-is-better-off-northerners-or-Southerners.
14 Fitzgerald and Morgenroth, 2019, op. cit.
15 'Interactive Figure 1: Regional economic activity by gross domestic product, UK',
    Office for National Statistics, Ons.gov.uk, https://www.ons.gov.uk/economy
    /grossdomesticproductgdp/bulletins/regionaleconomicactivitybygrossdomestic
    productuk/1998to2020.
16 R. Johnston, G. McCausland and K. Bonner, *The Competitiveness Scorecard for
    Northern Ireland: A Framework for Measuring Economic, Social, and Environ-
    mental Progress* (Coleraine, UK, 2020).
17 D. Jordan, 'Northern Ireland's productivity challenge: Exploring the issues',
    Nevin Economic Research Institute, 13 April 2022, https://www.nerinstitute.net
    /blog/northern-irelands-productivity-challenge-exploring-issues. See also R.
    Zymek and B. Jones, *UK Regional Productivity Differences: An Evidence Review*,
    Industrial Strategy Council, February 2020; see also D. Jordan, 'Northern
    Ireland's productivity challenge: Exploring the issues', *Nevin Economic Research
    Institution*, 13 April 2022, https://www.nerinstitute.net/blog/northern-irelands
    -productivity-challenge-exploring-issues.
18 'Education, skills and training for young people aged 14–19 years old', *Pivotal*,
    https://www.pivotalppf.org/cmsfiles/Pivotal_Report_-Education-skills-and
    -training-for-young-people-aged-14-19-years-old.pdf; 'OECD Skills Strategy
    Northern Ireland (United Kingdom): Assessment and Recommendations',
    OECD Library, https://www.oecd-ilibrary.org/sites/85c17d98-en/index.html?item
    Id=/content/component/85c17d98-en.
19 D. Jordan and J. Turner, 'Northern Ireland's productivity challenge: Exploring the
    issues', *The Productivity Institute*, productivity.ac.uk, https://www.productivity

.ac.uk/wp-content/uploads/2021/11/PIP004-Northern-Irelands-Productivity
-Challenge-FINAL-171121.pdf#page=4; J. Corscadden, 'Cost of living: Northern
Ireland families only have £93 in disposable income per month', *Belfast Live*,
29 July 2022, https://www.belfastlive.co.uk/news/northern-ireland/cost-living
-northern-ireland-families-24594140; 'UK national wellbeing measures: Northern
Ireland data: Personal finance', Northern Ireland Statistics and Research Agency,
https://www.nisra.gov.uk/statistics/uk-national-wellbeing-measures-northern
-ireland-data/personal-finance.

20 J. Fitzgerald, 'Northern Ireland's economy is threatened by more than Brexit',
The Irish Times, 6 September 2019.

21 J. Fitzgerald, 'North needs reform more than unity', *The Irish Times*, 23 October
2020.

22 County Incomes and Regional GDP 2019 – CSO – Central Statistics Office,
Table 9a: GDP Per Person 2011 to 2020, Cso.ie, 16 February 2022. Regional economic activity by gross domestic product, UK – Office for National Statistics,
Table 1: Summary of gross domestic product statistics for selected countries
and regions, 2020, Ons.gov.uk, 30 May 2022. Average rates of exchange for 2020
from The Federal Reserve System, The Fed – Foreign Exchange Rates – G.5A
Annual, Federalreserve.gov, 1 November 2021.

23 S. Collins, 'Irish people second-richest in EU in 2021', *Independent.ie*, 23 March
2022; J. Neugarten, 'Why is Luxembourg considered a tax haven', Investopedia
[website] 25 March 2021.

24 C. Taylor, 'Why Irish households are not, after all, among the best off in
the EU', *The Irish Times*, 23 July 2020. A little data does not presage a trend.
However, the UK's Office of National Statistics found that Northern Ireland's
GDP grew 1.4 per cent in the July–September quarter of 2021, compared with
gains of 0.9 per cent and 0.6 per cent in Scotland and England, respectively.
In Wales, economic activity shrank 0.3 per cent over the same quarter. An
analysis by the National Institute of Economic and Social Research Agency
credited Northern Ireland's continued access to the EU's Single Market as a
key driver. Ireland's Central Statistical Office also has reported record trade
between Northern Ireland and the Republic since January 2021, when the
Northern Ireland Protocol went into effect. S. Pogatchnik, 'Northern Ireland
economy outpacing post-Brexit Britain', *Politico*, 1 June 2022, https://www
.politico.eu/article/northern-ireland-economy-outpace-post-brexit-britain/;
S. Pogatchnik, 'Northern Irish economy outperforming UK thanks to Brexit
protocol: Experts', *Politico*, 11 May 2022, https://www.politico.eu/article
/experts-brexit-protocol-is-boosting-northern-ireland-economy/.

25 P. Honohan, 'Is Ireland really the most prosperous country in Europe?', Central
Bank of Ireland, *Economic Letter*, no. 1, February 2021, 3.

26 Ibid.

27 Ibid., pp. 4, 7. See also J. Fitzgerald, 'Problems interpreting national accounts in a globalised economy – Ireland', Economic and Social Research Institute, *Quarterly Economic Commentary*, 3 June 2015.

28 E. Burke-Kennedy, 'Which has a higher standard of living – Northern Ireland or the Republic?', *The Irish Times*, 18 April 2021.

29 Bergin and McGuinness, 2021, op. cit.; Fitzgerald, 2021, op. cit.; A. Bergin and S. McGuinness, 'A reply', *Irish Studies in International Affairs*, vol. 32, no. 2, 2021, pp. 164–5.

30 Bergin and McGuinness, op. cit.

31 Ibid.; Fitzgerald and Morgenroth, 2019, op. cit.; C. Ó Gráda and K. O'Rourke, 'The Irish economy during the century of partition', *Economic History Review*, 2021, pp. 1–35.

32 A. Bergin and S. McGuinness, 'Modelling productivity levels in Ireland and Northern Ireland', Economic and Social Research Institute, Dublin, November 2022.

33 G. Gudgin, 'The island economies: Comparative living standards', in *The Idea of the Union: Great Britain and Northern Ireland*, John Wilson Foster and William Beattie Smith (eds), pp. 324–43, 38 (Belfast, 2021).

34 P. Devine, 'NI Life and Times Survey – 2010: NIRELND2', Ark.ac.uk, 2011; P. Devine, 'NI Life and Times Survey – 2013: NIRELND2', Ark.ac.uk, 2014; P. Devine, 'NI Life and Times Survey – 2021: NIRELND2', Ark.ac.uk, 2022.

35 Fitzgerald and Morgenroth, 2019, op. cit., p. 73.

36 Ibid., p. 81.

37 'Country and regional public sector finances, UK', Office for National Statistics, Ons.gov.uk, 27 May 2022.

38 J. Fitzgerald, 'Irish unity poses greater risks to Northern Ireland than Brexit does', *The Irish Times*, 13 September 2019.

39 Fitzgerald and Morgenroth, 2020, op. cit., p. 80.

40 'The economic benefits of a united Ireland', Sinn Féin [website], November 2020.

41 Ibid.

42 J. Doyle, 'Why the 'subvention' does not matter: Northern Ireland and the all-Ireland economy', *Irish Studies in International Affairs*, vol. 32, no. 2, 2021, pp. 314–34; J. Doyle, 'UK subvention to North irrelevant to debate on Irish unity', *The Irish Times*, 9 June 2021.

43 Ibid.

44 Fitzgerald and Morgenroth, 2020, op. cit., p. 80.

45 Interview with John Fitzgerald, 7 April 2021.

46 Fitzgerald and Morgenroth, 2019, op. cit. p. 36.

47 Ibid., p. 35.

48 Ibid., p. 36.

49 Interview with John Fitzgerald, 7 April 2021.

50   For a comparison of social welfare systems, North and South, see C. Fitzpatrick and C. O'Sullivan, 'Comparing social security provision North and South of Ireland: Past developments and future challenges', *Irish Studies in International Affairs*, vol. 32, no. 2, 2021, pp. 283–313.

51   J. Fitzgerald, 'North needs reform more than unity', *The Irish Times*, 23 October 2020.

52   Interview with Peter Shirlow, 7 December 2020.

53   Interview with John Fitzgerald, 7 April 2021.

54   Fitzgerald and Morgenroth, 2019, op. cit.; N. Emerson, 'Fading myth of the North's world-beating schools', *The Irish Times*, 30 July 2020.

55   Emerson, 2020, op. cit.

56   D. Jordan, 'What explains Northern Ireland's long-standing problem of low productivity?', *Economics Observatory*, 29 April 2021.

57   Ibid.

58   This standard is defined as obtaining five or more A*–C (English and Math) GCSE passes, which is treated as being the standard for successfully completing secondary school; V.K. Borooah and C. Knox, *The Economics of Schooling in a Divided Society: The Case for Shared Education* (London, 2015), quoted in J. Fitzgerald, 'Investment in education and economic growth on the island of Ireland', *Journal of the Statistical and Social Inquiry Society of Ireland*, vol. XLVIII, 2019, p. 199.

59   Fitzgerald and Morgenroth, 'Northern Ireland economy: Problems and prospects', 2019, p. 75.

60   Ibid.

61   Interview with John Fitzgerald, 7 April 2021.

62   Solidarity Surcharge, https://www.bundesregierung.de/breg-en/solidarity-surcharge-469380; Federal Government of Germany. 'Solidarity surcharge to be discontinued gradually', *Website of the Federal Government*, 21 August 2019.

63   E. Morgenroth, 'A united Ireland would be worse off than the Republic', *The Irish Times*, 15 March 2017.

64   Federal Government Commissioner for the New Federal States, *Annual Report of the Federal Government on the Status of German Unity 2018*, Federal Minister for Economic Affairs and Energy, August 2018.

65   K. Bennhold, 'German elections reveal, and deepen, a new east-west divide', *The New York Times*, 31 August 2019; K. Bennhold, 'Germany has been united for 30 years. Its identity still is not', *The New York Times*, 8 November 2019.

66   J. Gramlich, 'East Germany has narrowed economic gap with West Germany since fall of communism, but still lags', *Pew Research Center*, 6 November 2019.

67   'Economy of East Germany', Wikipedia, 3 May 2022.

68   According to the economist David McWilliams, writing in June 2022, 'The Republic's economy is today roughly six times larger than the North's, generated by a workforce that is only 2½ times bigger. The median income per

head in the Republic is €43,915 versus €33,550 across the Border … 30 per cent higher and the gap is widening.' 'David McWilliams: Truth is the union with Britain has been an economic calamity for Northern Ireland', *The Irish Times*, 18 June 2022. On the other hand, prices that Irish people pay for food, drink, energy, transport, communications and restaurants are 40 per cent above the average for the twenty-seven countries in the EU, second only to Denmark. Charlie Weston, 'Ireland's cost of living soars above EU average as new report reveals just how much prices are rising', *Independent.ie*, 16 June 2022.

69 Gramlich, op. cit.

70 P. Gosling, 'A ten-year programme for a new Ireland "makes sense"', *The Detail*, 26 February 2020.

71 L. Cullen, 'Waiting lists: 53% wait more than a year to see consultant', BBC News, 26 August 2021.

72 K. Hübner and KLC Consulting, *Modelling Irish Unification*, 2015, https://cain.ulster.ac.uk/issues/unification/hubner_2015-08.pdf; other studies that are frequently quoted are P. Gosling, '*The Economic Effects of an All-Ireland Economy*', report (publisher unstated), 2018; G. Gudgin, 'A united Ireland is far from inevitable', *Belfast Telegraph*, 19 December 2018; a critical review of research on the economics of unification appears in J.E. Birnie, 'Economics of nationalism and unionism weighed in the balance and found wanting', in *The Northern Ireland Question: Perspectives on Nationalism and Unionism*, P. Roche and B. Barton (eds) (Ware, UK, 2020).

73 Sinn Féin, op. cit., p. 13.

74 'What do we know – and not know – about the costs of a united Ireland?', *TheJournal.ie*, 26 March.

75 Interview with John Fitzgerald, 7 April 2021.

76 Interview with John Fitzgerald, 7 April 2021; J. Siedschlag and M.T. Koecklin, 'The impact of the UK's EU Exit on the attractiveness of Northern Ireland for FDI and associated job creation effects', Northern Ireland Department of the Economy, https://www.economy-ni.gov.uk/publications/impact-eu-exit-attractiveness-fdi-uk-and-ni-and-associated-job-creation-effects.

77 Interview with John Fitzgerald, 7 April 2021.

78 J. Esmond Birnie, 'The economics of unionism and nationalism' in *The Northern Ireland Question* (London, 1999), pp. 279–314.

79 G. Thumann and M. Daly, *Northern Ireland's Income and Expenditure in a Reunification Scenario*, https://www.senatormarkdaly.ie; Doyle, 2021, op. cit.; Doyle, 9 June 2021, op. cit.

80 E. Burke-Kennedy, 'Northern Ireland's £9.4 bn subvention and the cost of Irish unity', *The Irish Times*, 2 May 2021.

81 Interview with Peter Robinson, 11 March 2020.

82 Interview with Billy Hutchinson, 9 March 2020.

83 S. McGuinness and A. Bergin, 'The Political Economy of a Border Poll', *IZA Institute of Labor Economics, Discussion Paper Series*, no. 12496, July 2019; 'ESRI economist: Any credible assessment of reunification must avoid "static analysis"', https://irishplan.net; S. McGuinness, 'Four known unknowns of the cost of Irish unity', *The Irish Times*, 26 September 2019.

84 For a survey of the challenges facing both health systems, the obstacles to integration – some structural, some cultural – and the barriers to co-operation during COVID, see D. Hennan, 'Cross-border cooperation health in Ireland', *Irish Studies in International Affairs*, vol. 32, no. 2, pp. 117–13.

85 Pat Leahy, '*Irish Times* Poll: Health and housing most important issues for voters', *Irish Times*, 4 February 2020.

86 Ibid.

87 NILT 2019: ARK, Northern Ireland Life and Times Survey, 2020 [computer file]. ARK www.ark.ac.uk/nilt [distributor], June 2020, Political Attitudes module, UIHCARE variable.

88 'Opinion Poll April 2022', The Institute of Irish Studies, University of Liverpool/ *The Irish News*, April 2022.

89 Cullen, 2021, op. cit.

90 Ibid.

91 'Northern Ireland outpatient waiting lists 100 times more than England's?', *FactCheckNI*, 20 September 2019, https://factcheckni.org/topics/health/ northern-ireland-outpatient-waiting-lists-100-times-more-than-englands.

92 P. Gosling, *A New Ireland, A New Union: A New Society* (Antrim, UK, 2020).

93 Interview with Paul Gosling, 16 March 2021.

94 C. Pope, 'More than 900,000 people on hospital waiting lists', *The Irish Times*, 10 September 2021.

95 Bergin and McGuinness, 'Who is better off?', 2021, op. cit.

96 G. Aodha, 'How two different, expensive healthcare systems on this island have managed to (occasionally) work well together', *TheJournal.ie*, 27 March 2021.

97 Bergin and McGuinness, 'Who is better off?', 2021, op. cit.

98 Aodha, op. cit.

99 M. Duffy, 'Explained: What is Sláintecare and what's the controversy about?', BreakingNews.ie, 3 October 2021.

100 P. Cullen, 'One-quarter of State's population on health waiting lists', *The Irish Times*, 6 June 2022, https://www.irishtimes.com/health/2022/06/06/one-quarter -of-states-population-on-health-waiting-lists/.

101 Aodha, op. cit.

102 Ibid.

103 See NILT 2020: ARK. Northern Ireland Life and Times Survey, 2020 [computer file]. ARK www.ark.ac.uk/nilt [distributor], June 2021, Political Attitudes module, NIVALNHS variable.

104 Interview with Will Glendinning, 12 March 2021.

105 This type of psychological fusion is well researched by Oxford University's Centre for the Study of Social Cohesion. See M. Newson, 'United in defeat: Shared suffering and group bonding among football fans', *Managing Sports and Leisure*, 2021; O. Miller, 'Fans of less successful football clubs are more loyal to one another', *University of Kent News Centre*, 19 January 2021.

9. A SHARED ISLAND

1   Interview with Niall Murphy, 24 February 2021.
2   Interview with Niall Blaney, 1 June 2021.
3   Interview with Regina Doherty, 25 March 2021.
4   Interview with Brian Feeney, 10 March 2021.
5   Interview with John Manley, 12 March 2021.
6   Interview with Ian Paisley, Jr, 16 February 2021.
7   Interview with Chris Hazzard, 1 March 2021.
8   Interview with Neale Richmond, 19 February 2021.
9   S. Castle, 'Northern Ireland sees spasm of violence as old tensions resurface', *The New York Times*, 8 April 2021.
10 A. Pollak, 'Border crossings: First-time visitors describe their experience of Ireland North and South', *The Irish Times*, 26 July 2014.
11 F. Sheahan, 'Majority favour a united Ireland, but just 22 pc would pay for it', *Independent.ie*, 1 May 2021; J. Corcoran, 'United Ireland poll: Two thirds say united Ireland vote risks return to violence', *Independent.ie*, 2 May 2021.
12 Sheahan, op. cit.; J. Spain, 'A deep dive into the reality of Ireland's unity poll', *Irish Central*, 6 May 2021.
13 Sheahan, op. cit.
14 'Opinion Poll Report', November 2021. Red C *Business Post*, https://redcresearch .ie/wp-content/uploads/2021/11/Business-Post-RED-C-Opinion-Poll-Report -Nov-2021-.pdf; P. Leahy, 'Large majority of voters favour a united Ireland, poll finds', *The Irish Times*, 11 December 2021.
15 S. Collins, 'Detailed election 2020 exit poll results: How voters answered 15 questions', *The Irish Times*, 9 February 2020.
16 Red C, op. cit., pp. 14–15.
17 Rec C, op. cit., p. 15.
18 Red C, op. cit.; *The Irish Times*/Ipsos MRBI, 11 December 2021.
19 Interview with David Ford, 12 March 2020.
20 Sheahan, op. cit.
21 A. Pollak, 'My single transferable blog: The people of the South are not ready for reunification', 1 November 2021, https://2irelands2gether.com/2021/11/01 /my-single-transferable-blog-the-people-of-the-south-are-not-ready-for -reunification/.

22 It is important to note that not all surveys used the exact same wording in phrases regarding unity. For example, if we consider questions related to unification, there is a difference between how one might respond when asked if they intend to vote a particular way versus whether they want something to occur.

23 When presented with a list of 'workable and acceptable solutions', this number combines the totals of those who answered that unity should happen with one government (41.2 per cent) with those who answered that unity should happen with devolved governments (26.7 per cent).

24 This number combines the totals of those who answered that Northern Ireland should remain in the UK with devolved government (5.1 per cent) with those who answered that Northern Ireland should remain in the UK with Stormont (3.5 per cent).

25 This question is phrased as 'I would be prepared to pay heavier taxes to run a United Ireland'. It doesn't assume that the subject doesn't agree to unite, making this question slightly different than others in the table.

26 'Results of European Values Study, 1999–2000', in T. Fahey, B. Hayes and R. Sinnott, *Conflict and Consensus: A Study of Values and Attitudes in the Republic of Ireland and Northern Ireland* (Leiden, Netherlands, 2006), p. 90. The authors make specific reference to how the questions are worded differently over time and the challenges of comparing trends as a result.

27 32.1 per cent chose an independent Northern Ireland as a constitutional preference.

28 J. Mooney and S. McInerney, 'Smaller majority in republic supports united Ireland', *The Sunday Times*, 17 October 2010.

29 S. McStravick, 'Survey results', *Belfast Live*, 4 November 2015.

30 This number is for those seeking unity in the short to medium term. This number increases to 73 per cent if respondents are told they would pay less taxes with unification. When asked if they would like to see a united Ireland in their lifetime, support increases from 36 per cent to 66 per cent. See also S. McStravick, 'Cross border survey reveals attitudes to a united Ireland, abortion, mixed marriages and more', *Belfast Live*, 5 November 2015.

31 This number combines those preferring direct rule (9 per cent) and devolution (35 per cent) over uniting (36 per cent). The remainder (17 per cent) responded with 'don't know'.

32 These results refer to those whose 'support for a United Ireland [is] influenced by tax'. If asked to pay more taxes, only 31 per cent support a united Ireland. This question is worded differently than it is in other surveys, making comparison between percentages difficult.

33 This number is for when respondents are asked whether they would prefer this in the short to medium term. When asked about their lifetime aspirations, this number decreases to 14 per cent.

34 C. Byrne, 'Sinn Féin's Santa list', RTÉ, 16 December 2016, https://www.rte.ie /news/analysis-and-comment/2016/1216/839321-sinn-feins-santa-list/.

35 Ireland Thinks (@ireland_thinks), 'Increased support for a united Ireland in the latest poll for The Irish Daily Mail', Twitter post, 28 December 2017; https://www.irelandthinks.ie/single-post/2017/12/28/support-for-a-united-ireland-dramatically-increases.

36 When 'don't know's are excluded, the split is 50:50 in spite of higher taxes.

37 Ibid.

38 When 'don't know's are excluded, the split is 60 per cent in support of a united Ireland and 40 per cent against in spite of higher taxes.

39 C. McMorrow, 'Elections 2019: Exit Poll', RTÉ News, 25 May 2019.

40 When those answering as undecided or as non-voters, 77 per cent are in favor of a United Ireland.

41 R. Early, 'Election 2020: We want united Ireland, say four in five voters', 3 February 2020, 'More than 40 per cent of voters said that they wanted to see a united Ireland in the next decade, with a further 19 per cent saying they wanted unity to happen within 20 years. Only 20 per cent of those polled said that they would not like to see a united Ireland. Twelve per cent said they wanted a united Ireland within the next 30 years, with 8 per cent preferring that it happened "more than 30 years from now but within my lifetime".'

42 Among voters who supported Sinn Féin in the 2016 Irish general election, 54 per cent wanted unity within the next 10 years, in contrast to 32 per cent of voters who supported Fine Gael and 39 per cent who supported Fianna Fáil. Half of those who did not vote in 2016 wanted a united Ireland within a decade.

43 S. Collins, 'Detailed election 2020 exit poll results: How voters answered 15 questions', The Irish Times, 9 February 2020.

44 Support varied by age and party affiliation. Among 18- to 24-year-olds, 75 per cent supported a poll within 5 years, compared with 47 per cent among those over 65. In terms of election support, 81 per cent of Sinn Féin voters were in favour of a poll, compared with 52 per cent of Fianna Fáil voters and 44 per cent of Fine Gael voters.

45 Sheahan, op. cit.

46 Of those saying they would like a referendum, 19 per cent responded that they would like to see it happen 'Now' and 50 per cent 'Within five years'.

47 This number is an aggregate of those answering within 20 years (5 per cent) and those answering 'longer than that' (1 per cent).

48 M. Brennan, 'Exclusive Red C poll: A united Ireland, but at what cost?', Business Post, 28 November 2021.

49 Eight per cent said they wouldn't vote; P. Leahy, 'Large majority of voters favour a united Ireland, poll finds', The Irish Times, 11 December 2021.

50 E.E. Davis and R. Sinnott, 'Attitudes in the Republic of Ireland relevant to the Northern Ireland problem: Descriptive analysis and some comparisons with attitudes in Northern Ireland and Great Britain', The Economic and Social Research Institute, September 1979, vol. 1, paper no. 97, pp. 32–3; 52–3; P.

O'Malley, *The Uncivil Wars: Ireland Today* (Boston, MA, 1983), pp. 81–3.

51   O'Malley, op. cit., p. 90.

52   S. Cunningham, 'Just one-in-three in Republic would support united Ireland if taxes rose', *The Irish News*, 19 September 2016.

53   'Programme for government: Our shared future', Gov.ie, June 2020, https://www .gov.ie/en/publication/7e05d-programme-for-government-our-shared-future/.

54   Ibid., p. 104.

55   Ibid.

56   Ibid.

57   Ibid.

58   F. Kelly, P. Leahy, J. Bray, H. McGee and M. O'Halloran, 'Programme for government: What are the main points in the five-year plan?', *The Irish Times*, 14 June 2020.

59   Department of the Taoiseach, 'Building a shared island', Gov.ie, 8 December 2020.

60   A. McMahon, 'Micheál Martin not in favour of "divisive" poll on Northern Ireland border', *Independent.ie*, 7 July 2020.

61   Irish Central Staff, 'Ireland's new Taoiseach says Sinn Féin is "over-focused" on border poll', *Irish Central*, 9 July 2020, https://www.irishcentral.com/news /taoiseach-sinn-fein-over-focused-border-poll; P. Smyth, 'UK has vital Irish Border commitments even in no-deal Brexit, new EU paper says', *The Irish Times*, 20 June 2019.

62   'Arlene Foster and Michelle O'Neill attend North-South Ministerial Council meeting', BBC News, 31 July 2020.

63   A. Kane, 'The mask slips: Micheal Martin picked an odd time to have a pop at unionists', *Belfast Telegraph*, 11 August 2020.

64   P. Ryan, 'Britain may get "turned off" by Northern Ireland, warns Martin', *Independent.ie*, 7 August 2020; G. Halliday, 'Arlene Foster denounces Taoiseach Micheál Martin's "disappointing" comment on NI', *Belfast Telegraph*, 7 August 2020.

65   Ryan, 2020, ibid.

66   Kane, 2020, ibid.

67   Interview with Gary Mason, 8 December 2020.

68   P. Leahy, 'Taoiseach stresses immediate need to forge trust with unionists and Stormont', *The Irish Times*, 11 September 2020.

69   Ibid.

70   Ibid.

71   Ibid.

72   Interview with Mark Durkan, 14 December 2020.

73   Interview with Katy Hayward, 16 February 2021.

74   Interview with Éamon Ó Cuív, 26 March 2021.

75   Leahy, 2020, op. cit.

76 Ibid.

77 Ibid.; P. Leahy, 'Taoiseach stresses immediate need to forge trust with unionists and Stormont', *The Irish Times*, 11 September 2020.

78 A. Moore, 'Shared Island Initiative, Day 1 – a Trojan horse for unity or a shared future based on mutual respect?', *Irish Examiner*, 27 December 2020.

79 P. Smyth, 'EU's "mapping" report stresses need for open Irish border', *The Irish Times*, 20 June 2019. In June 2019, the EU commission published a working paper setting out the results of a mapping exercise conducted jointly with the British, 'mapping' 142 North–South interconnectivity projects and programmes that were deemed to be among the UK's obligations to protect under the terms of the B/GFA. See European Commission, Task Force for the Preparation and Conduct of the Negotiations with the United Kingdom under Article 50 TEU, *Negotiations on Ireland/Northern Ireland, Mapping of North–South Cooperation and Implementation Bodies, Report and Key Findings of the Exercise*, 21 June 2019; See also Smyth, 2019, op. cit.; Rosher and Soares, *Quarterly Survey on the Conditions for North–South and East–West Cooperation: Briefing on the Findings From the 4th Quarterly Survey (October to December 2021)*, Centre for Cross Border Studies, January 2022.

80 Interview with John Bradley, 25 March 2021.

81 D. Hennan, 'Cross-border cooperation health in Ireland', *Irish Studies in International Affairs*, vol. 32, no. 2, pp. 117–36.

82 Interview with Sean Donlon, 28 April 2021.

83 Interview with Stephen Farry, 28 January 2021.

84 Interview with Colum Eastwood, 26 January 2021.

85 Interview with Ian Marshall, 28 April 2021.

86 J. Fitzgerald and E. Morgenroth, 'The Northern Ireland economy: Problems and prospects', pp. 64–87, April 2020.

10. SINN FÉIN

1   Interview with Matt Carthy, 2 December 2020.

2   Interview with Naomi Long, 4 December 2020.

3   Interview with Nigel Dodds, 25 March 2021.

4   Interview with Jeffrey Donaldson, 16 December 2020.

5   Interview with Colum Eastwood, 26 January 2021.

6   Interview with Claire Hanna, 2 December 2020.

7   D. Loscher, 'Battles between larger parties increasingly fought along socio-economic lines', *The Irish Times*, 17 June 2021.

8   J. Dorney, 'Casualties of the Irish civil war in Dublin', www.theirishstory.com, September 2016.

9   M. Farrell, 'Fine Gael and Fianna Fáil: Civil war parties?' www.theirishstory.com, 26 May 2020.

10 Danny Morrison, interview 24 May 1982 in P. O'Malley, *The Uncivil Wars: Ireland Today* (Dublin, 1983), p. 279.

11 '1997 Irish general election', Wikipedia, https://en.wikipedia.org/wiki/1997 _Irish_general_election#Aftermath.

12 '2002 Irish general election', Wikipedia, https://en.wikipedia.org/wiki/2002 _Irish_general_election#Overview.

13 '2011 Irish general election', Wikipedia, https://en.wikipedia.org/wiki/2011 _Irish_general_election#Sinn_F%C3%A9in.

14 '2016 Irish general election', Wikipedia, https://en.wikipedia.org/wiki/2016 _Irish_general_election#Results; '2020 Irish general election', Wikipedia, https:// en.wikipedia.org/wiki/2020_Irish_general_election#Results.

15 Interview with Bertie Ahern, 26 November 2020.

16 F. McClements, 'Sinn Féin drops opposition to special criminal court', *The Irish Times*, 30 October 2021.

17 C. Keena, 'Sinn Féin is the richest political party in Ireland', *The Irish Times*, 5 March 2020.

18 Interview with Alex Attwood, 13 March 2020.

19 'Northern bank robbery', Wikipedia, 16 January 2022.

20 'Paramilitary groups in Northern Ireland', Secretary of State for Northern Ireland, 19 October 2015.

21 C. McCurry, '90% of loyalists say united Ireland vote risks return of violence', *Belfast Telegraph*, 2 May 2021.

22 C. Lally, 'Garda commissioner "stands over" IRA – Sinn Féin remarks', *The Irish Times*, 26 February 2020.

23 C. Hughes, 'Sinn Féin backlash as Mary Lou McDonald says the IRA has gone away', *Extra.ie*, 22 February 2020.

24 P. Ryan and C. McQuinn, '"No effort made by Sinn Féin to distance or disown itself from IRA" – five justice ministers back Garda Commissioner', *Independent.ie*, 22 February 2020.

25 Interview with Naomi Long, 4 December 2020.

26 Northern Ireland Executive, 'Your Executive', https://www.northernireland.gov. uk/topics/your-executive.

27 Interview with Duncan Morrow, 13 March 2020.

28 M. McDowell, 'Sinn Féin's problem with names much more than mere word-play', *The Irish Times*, 26 February 2020; R. McGreevy, 'Why Sinn Féin will not call the State by its name', *The Irish Times*, 24 February 2020; P. O'Donovan, 'Does Sinn Féin recognise the legitimacy of the Irish State?', Fine Gael, 25 February 2020.

29 Interview with Sean Farren, 28 February 2020.

30 Interview with Pádraig Mac Lochlainn, 16 March 2021.

31 J. Downing, 'How much longer must this foostering over Sinn Féin and its IRA links go on?', *Independent.ie*, 24 December 2015.

32 Interview with Rose Conway-Walsh, 18 March 2021.

33 Interview with Pádraig Mac Lochlainn, 16 March 2021.

34 B. Feeney, *Sinn Féin: A Hundred Turbulent Years* (Madison, WI, 2003).

35 Interview with Brian Feeney, 10 March 2021.

36 Ibid.

37 C. Keena, 'Inside Sinn Féin – where power lies and how decisions are made', *The Irish Times*, 5 March 2020.

38 Ibid.

39 Interview with Rose Conway-Walsh, 18 March 2021.

40 Keena, op. cit.; J. Joyce, 'No room for complacency over Sinn Féin in government', *The Irish Times*, 17 January 2022.

41 Ibid.

42 Sinn Féin General Election Manifesto 2020, 'Giving Workers and Families a Break – A Manifesto for Change'.

43 'Economic Benefits of a United Ireland', Sinn Féin, November 2020, https://www.sinnfein.ie/files/2020/Economic_Benefits_of_a_United_Ireland.pdf

44 Ibid.

45 Ibid.

46 Ibid.

47 Inequality Briefing, 'The poorest regions in the UK are the poorest in Northern Europe', https://inequalitybriefing.org/graphics/briefing_43_UK_regions_poorest_North_Europe.pdf.

48 'Economic benefits of a united Ireland', Sinn Féin, op. cit., p. 9.

49 Ibid.

50 Ibid, p. 22.

51 Interview with Matt Carthy, 2 December 2020.

52 Interview with Brian Feeney, 10 March 2021.

53 'For example, the divorce referendum in the South was won by less than 1% of the vote, 50.28% in favour and 49.72% against. If the same criteria were applied to this referendum that has been suggested for a Unity Referendum, divorce would still be illegal', Ciarán Quinn, Sinn Féin representative to the United States and Canada; 'How to spot the referendum denier – by Ciarán Quinn – Sinn Féin Representative to US and Canada', News and Current Affairs, www.eamonnmallie.com, 8 March 2021.

54 Quinn, op. cit.

55 Ibid.

56 *Towards a United Ireland – a Sinn Féin discussion document*, Sinn Féin, 2016, p. 8, https://www.sinnfein.ie/files/2016/Towards-a-United-Ireland.pdf.

57 Ibid., p. 9.

58 Interview with Matt Carthy, 2 December 2020.

59 *Towards a United Ireland*, op. cit., p. 28.

60 Andy Pollak raises the questions he believes are germane to setting out a unification agenda: A. Pollak, 'Sinn Féin are getting ready for government. But are they ready for unity?', 2Irelands2gether.com, 24 May 2021.

61 *Towards a United Ireland*, op. cit., p. 28.

62 Ibid.

63 Interview with Chris Hazzard, 1 March 2021.

64 Ibid.

65 Interview with Séanna Walsh, 21 January 2021.

66 F. Kelly, 'Brexit causing "tectonic plates" of politics to shift, says Varadkar', *The Irish Times*, 13 June 2018.

67 Interview with Chris Hazzard, 1 March 2021.

68 Interview with Séanna Walsh, 21 January 2021.

69 Interview with Chris Hazzard, 1 March 2021.

70 Ibid.

71 Interview with Bertie Ahern, 26 November 2020.

72 After the election, Jeffrey Donaldson vowed that the DUP would not form an Executive until the British government had taken 'decisive action' on the protocol. See more in F. McClements, 'DUP leader rules out return to Executive without "decisive action" on protocol', *The Irish Times*, 10 May 2022; A. Preston, 'Sir Jeffrey Donaldson says DUP is "sending a clear message to EU and UK Government" as he confirms party will not nominate Assembly Speaker', *Belfast Telegraph*, 13 May 2022.

73 M. Brennan, 'Support for Sinn Féin soars to new record level in Red C poll', *Business Post*, 29 May 2022.

74 'Mary Lou McDonald: "I want to lead as Taoiseach if you give us that chance"', *TheJournal.ie*, 30 October 2021.

75 P. Leahy, 'Sinn Féin's rise as country's most popular party continues', *The Irish Times*, 6 October 2021. Important to note here is the potential impact that April 2021's violence may have had on these polls. When 'Don't Knows' are eliminated, the support for Sinn Féin also increases.

76 J. Corcoran, 'Sinn Féin surges to 33pc support but coalition of Fianna Fáil/Fine Gael/Greens still preferred option, poll reveals', *Independent.ie*, 9 January 2022.

77 T. Kingsley, 'Russia makes new threats to nuke Britain with Satan-2 hypersonic missile in just 200 seconds and Finland in 10 seconds', *Independent.ie*, 14 May 2022.

78 M. Fealty, 'Sinn Féin's burns its record on Russia … "the party simply wiped thousands of embarrassing statements from its website"', *Slugger O'Toole*, 16 March 2022; 'The Irish Times view on Sinn Féin's worldview: Disappearing policies', *The Irish Times*, 15 March 2022; S. Collins, 'Sinn Féin's brazen volte-face on Putin should be seen for what it is', *The Irish Times*, 4 March 2022; E. Loughlin, 'Sinn Féin's soft stance on Russia is clearly on the record', *Irish Examiner*, 1 March 2022.

79 Interview with Jim O'Callaghan, 15 March 2021.

80 F. Sheahan, 'United Ireland: Majority favour a united Ireland, but just 22pc would pay for it', *Independent.ie*, 1 May 2021; 'Two thirds of people in the republic of Ireland support a united Ireland', *IrishCentral.com*, 30 July 2016.

81 J. Corcoran, 'United Ireland poll: Two thirds say united Ireland vote risks return to violence', *Independent.ie*, 2 May 2021.

82 Interview with John FitzGerald, 7 April 2021.

83 Interview with Brendan O'Leary, 3 May 2021. In the North, after the May 2022 Assembly elections Sinn Féin held 27 seats in a chamber of 90, and 29 per cent of first-preference votes. It is highly improbable that in a future general election in the republic, any party will secure more than 50 per cent of the TDs. Sinn Féin will either be a minority government in the South, vulnerable to loss in any vote of confidence, or in a coalition as either lead or junior partner. In the North, Sinn Féin will be subject to the co-decision rules of the 1998 Agreement.

84 Ibid.

85 P. Leahy, 'Taoiseach warns EU that hard border would threaten return to violence', *The Irish Times*, 18 October 2018.

86 Andy Pollak in a comment to author.

87 Interview with Matt Carthy, 2 December 2020.

88 Corcoran, 2021, op. cit.

89 D. Kearney, 'Uncomfortable conversations are key to reconciliation: Increasing understanding and mutual respect by reaching out to Unionists', *An Phoblacht*, 2 March 2012.

90 Ibid.; B. Rowan, 'Sinn Féin chairman: IRA should say sorry for hurt caused', *Belfast Telegraph*, 3 March 2012.

91 J. Hedges, '"Unionists have nothing to fear": *An Phoblacht* article welcomed by unionists. Responses to Declan Kearney's "Uncomfortable conversations"', *An Phoblacht*, 2 April 2012.

92 Ibid.

93 'Towards an agreed and reconciled future: Sinn Féin policy on reconciliation and healing', Sinn Féin, June 2016, https://www.sinnfein.ie/files/2016/Reconciliation_Policy_Ard_Fheis_2016.pdf.

94 'Inclusion and reconciliation in a new Ireland', Sinn Féin, November 2019, https://www.liverpool.ac.uk/media/livacuk/irish-studies/civicspace/Inclusion,and,Reconciliation, in,a,New,Ireland.pdf.

95 'Inclusion and reconciliation in a new Ireland', op. cit., p. 2.

96 Ibid.

97 Ibid.; These steps include ones to tackle sectarianism and sectarian segregation, physical walls of division, the erection and flying of flags in the public space and contentious bonfires. There is no mention of education. There are specific proposals on: Commemorations; Dealing with the Legacy of the Past; The Role of Political Institutions, in which the party expresses its intention to incorporate a citizen's anti-sectarian charter into ministers' pledges; Enhancing

Political Leadership and Policy; and Engaging Community and Civic Society. For fuller exposition, see A. Meban, 'Towards an agreed and reconciled future – Sinn Féin latest policy benchmark on promoting reconciliation and tackling sectarianism', *Slugger O'Toole*, 24 November 2019.

98   C. Finn, 'Mary Lou McDonald says Michelle O'Neill does not need to stand aside over attendance at Bobby Storey funeral', *TheJournal.ie*, 2 July 2020.

99   D. Young, 'Michelle O'Neill: "I will never apologise for attending the funeral of my friend"', *Belfast Live*, 3 July 2020.

100 Interview with Paul, Lord Bew, 6 January 2021.

101 G. Halliday, '250 bands apply to parade over Twelfth in wake of row', *Belfast Telegraph*, 7 July 2020.

102 L. Kennedy, *Who Was Responsible for the Troubles? The Northern Ireland Conflict* (Montreal, 2020), p. 64.

103 Op. cit. p 67.

104 D. McKittrick et al., *Lost Lives: The Stories of the Men, Women, and Children Who Died as a Result of the Northern Ireland Troubles* (New York, 2001).

105 Ibid.

106 S. McBride, 'If there was no alternative to IRA violence, then did the IRA – on its terms – succeed?', *Belfast Telegraph*, 23 August 2022.

107 A NILT (1998) survey found that 70 per cent of Catholic respondents said they had no sympathy with republican violence.

108 Ibid., Sam McBride.

109 In 2017, Soldier F was charged with two counts of murder for the deaths of William McKinney and James Wray during the Bloody Sunday massacre by British paratroopers of fourteen civil rights demonstrators in Derry/Londonderry in January 1972. See Chapter 5.

110 'Census of population 2016 – Profile 3: An age profile of Ireland', Central Statistics Office, 17 April 2020, https://www.cso.ie/en/releasesandpublications /ep/p-cp30y/cp3/aad/.

111 Interview with John, Lord Alderdice, 4 March 2020.

112 Interview with Pádraig Mac Lochlainn, 16 March 2021.

113 Ibid.

114 Interview with Chris Hazzard, 1 March 2021.

115 Ibid.

116 Interview with Peter Shirlow, 7 December 2020.

117 C. Keena, 'Sinn Féin is the richest political party in Ireland', *The Irish Times*, 5 March 2020.

118 Interview with Séanna Walsh, 21 January 2021.

119 Interview with Matt Carthy, 2 December 2020.

120 Ibid.

121 Interview with Rose Conway-Walsh, 18 March 2021.

122 Interview with Pádraig Mac Lochlainn, 16 March 2021.

123 Interview with Chris Hazzard, 1 March 2021.

124 Ibid.

125 Interview with Matt Carthy, 2 December 2020.

126 Interview with Séanna Walsh, 20 January 2021.

127 Interview with Matt Carthy, 2 December 2020.

128 Ibid.; The Irish government has commissioned Ireland's ESRI and the UK's NIESR to carry out a macroeconomic study of the island; J. Campbell; 'NI–RoI economic links to be examined by think tank project', BBC News, 16 November 2021.

129 Interview with Chris Hazzard, 1 March 2021.

130 Interview with Matt Carthy, 2 December 2020.

131 S. Breen, 'Opinion poll finds 49% in NI would vote to stay in UK', *Belfast Telegraph*, 20 April 2021.

132 Interview with Chris Hazzard, 1 March 2021.

133 Ibid.

134 Ibid.

135 Ibid.

136 "'He [Gerry] hasn't got his united Ireland, so he's fighting on. He's setting up a united Ireland department within the party, and it has been agreed it will be resourced," said [Des] Mackin.' Quoted in Keena, 'Inside Sinn Féin', op. cit.

137 C. Finn, 'Mary Lou McDonald: The idea of Ireland rejoining the Commonwealth needs to be discussed', *TheJournal.ie*, 11 August 2018.

138 Interview with Chris Hazzard, 1 March 2021.

139 Interview with Matt Carthy, 2 December 2020.

140 M.L. McDonald, 'Full text from Mary Lou McDonald's speech at Sinn Féin Ard Fheis 2021', https://www.sinnfein.ie/contents/62183.

141 J. Joyce, 'No room for complacency over Sinn Féin in government', *The Irish Times*, 17 January 2022.

142 M.L. McDonald, 'Sinn Féin launches commission on the future of Ireland', Sinn Fein [website], 18 July 2022 https://www.sinnfein.ie/contents/64025

143 'The Irish Times view on latest Ipsos MRBI poll: Serious soul-searching needed for Fine Gael', *The Irish Times*, 10 December 2021.

144 L. Smyth, 'Good Friday Agreement a bluff and hasn't been delivered: Sinn Féin MP Molloy', *Belfast Telegraph*, 19 July 2020.

145 J. McCarthy, 'Mary Lou McDonald: Covid-19 more likely to unite us than Brexit', *The Times*, 26 April 2020.

146 Ibid.

147 S. Mallon, 'Tony Blair said to me, "The trouble with you fellows is you have no guns"', *The Irish Times*, 18 May 2019.

148 See Katy Hayward's comments in Chapter 5.

149 'How Martin McGuinness and Ian Paisley forged an unlikely friendship', *Belfast Telegraph*, 21 March 2017.

11. UNIONISM

1   A. Kane, 'Unsettled unionists caught in perfect storm', *The Irish Times*, 22 February 2021.

2   See Chapter 4.

3   Interview with Paul Nolan, 9 March 2020.

4   Interview with Harold Good, 23 March 2021.

5   Interview with Jackie Redpath, 19 March 2021.

6   Interview with Lesley Carroll, 19 May 2021.

7   Interview with John Kyle, 17 February 2021.

8   Interview with Peter Shirlow, 7 December 2020.

9   Taoiseach Garret FitzGerald (1981–2) and (1982–7) attempted to liberalize the constitution and to amend articles prohibiting divorce and Articles 2 and 3 that claimed all of Ireland as the national territory. Liberalization did not envisage prohibiting abortion. FitzGerald hoped to make the country more attractive to Northern Ireland, but fell short on most fronts. However, in subsequent decades the country went through a profound process of liberalization. Divorce and abortion are now permitted. The case for FitzGerald opposing abortion is debatable; see https://www.independent.ie/irish-news/garrets-constitutional-crusade-is-still-puzzling-26806498.html and https://link.springer.com/chapter/10.1057/9781137022066_9.

10 R.L. McCartney, 'The Case for the Unionists' (Belfast, 1981).

11 P. O'Malley, *The Uncivil Wars* (Boston, MA, 1983), pp. 133–8, footnotes 5 and 6.

12 McCartney, 1981 quoted in *The Uncivil Wars*, p. 133.

13 Ibid., p. 134

14 Ibid.

15 Ibid.

16 Ibid.

17 Ibid.

18 Ibid., p. 135.

19 Ibid.

20 Ibid.

21 Ibid.

22 Ibid.

23 Ibid.

24 Ibid.

25 Ibid., pp. 135–6.

26 Ibid, p. 136.

27 Dáil Éireann, parliamentary debates, vol. 56, cols. 2112–6, 29 May 1935, quoted in *The Uncivil Wars*, p. 136.

28 McCartney, 1981, quoted in *The Uncivil Wars*, p. 136.

29 Ibid.

30 Ibid., p. 137.

31 Ibid.

32 Ibid.

33 Ibid., pp. 137–8.

34 Northern Ireland General Election Survey 2019 (Faculty of Humanities and Social Sciences, University of Liverpool).

35 'In 1921 Sir Edward Carson in a speech in the UK parliament opposing the Anglo-Irish Treaty, famously said "What a fool I was! I was only a puppet, and so was Ulster, and so was Ireland, in the political game that was to get the Conservative Party into power,"' quoted in T. Wallace, 'Fools and puppets', *The Flag in the Wind*, 18 February 2021, https://scotsindependent.scot/?p=2956.

36 Interview with Alex Kane, 5 January 2021.

37 Interview with Duncan Morrow, 13 March 2020.

38 F. McClements, 'New light shed on prospect of Catholic majority in North', *The Irish Times*, 14 May 2019.

39 Interview with Steven Aiken, 11 December 2020.

40 Interview with Doug Beattie, 14 May 2021; 'More than two communities: Those who are both, neither, other, and next', in Colin Coulter et al., *Northern Ireland a Generation After Good Friday* (Manchester, UK, 2021), pp. 179–81; J. Garry and K. McNicholl, 'Understanding the "Northern Irish" identity', *Knowledge Exchange Seminar Series 2014–15*. According to Thomas Hennessey et al. in *The Ulster Unionist Party: Country Before Party*, approximately 17 per cent of UUP members identify as Northern Irish, 75 per cent as British, 3 per cent as Ulster, 1 per cent as Irish, 4 per cent as Other. Garry and McNeill, op. cit.; 14 per cent of UUP members identified as Northern Irish (pp. 133–6). See also 'Northern Irish identity and unionism' in Hennessey et al., *The Ulster Unionist Party: Country Before Party* (Oxford, 2019), pp. 135–9.

41 Interview with Doug Beattie, 14 May 2021.

42 Ibid.

43 Interview with John, Lord Alderdice, 4 March 2020.

44 'The unionist parties come together to reject the Northern Ireland Protocol, and call for its replacement with arrangements that respect NI's place in UK', *News Letter*, 28 September 2021. The short statement read: 'We, the undersigned Unionist Political Leaders, affirm our opposition to the Northern Ireland Protocols, its mechanisms and structures and reaffirm our unalterable position that the Protocol must be rejected and replaced by arrangements which fully respect Northern Ireland's position as a constituent and integral part of the United Kingdom.' The signatories were Jeffrey Donaldson (DUP), Doug Beattie (UUP), Billy Hutchinson (PUP) and Jim Allister (TUV).

45 Interview with Jackie Redpath, 19 March 2021.

46 Ibid., clarified in email to author on 30 January 2022.

47 Interview with Richard Bullick, 15 December 2020.

48 Interview with Sammy Douglas, 22 April 2021.

49 Interview with Richard Bullick, 15 December 2020.

50 See A. Aughey, 'Back to the future: The constitutional challenge revisited', in J.W. Foster and W.B. Smith (eds), *The Idea of the Union: Great Britain and Northern Ireland* (Belfast, 2021).

51 Interview with Doug Beattie, 14 May 2021.

52 'Northern Ireland Elections: East Londonderry', *ARK*, 7 May 2022, https://www.ark.ac.uk/elections/ael.htm.

53 T. Connelly, 'Majority believe no united Ireland within next ten years – poll', RTÉ, 21 April 2021.

54 F. Sheahan, 'Majority favour a united Ireland, but just 22pc would pay for it', *Independent.ie*, 1 May 2021.

55 Interview with Gregory Campbell, 4 March 2021.

56 J. Tonge et al., 'Same but different? The Democratic Unionist Party and Ulster Unionist Party compared', *Irish Political Studies* 35, no. 3, 2020, pp. 399–421.

57 Seventy per cent of DUP voters and 58 per cent of UUP voters supported Brexit. See more in Tonge et al., op. cit.

58 Tonge et al., op. cit., p. 419.

59 For an overview of the antipathy of the UUP for the DUP see T. Hennessey et al., *The Ulster Unionist Party: Country Before Party?* (Oxford, 2019), pp. 152–60.

60 At the time of the Westminster elections in 2017, 63 per cent of UUP supporters believed it was right to leave the EU. See Tonge et al., op. cit, p. 406.

61 Interview with Doug Beattie, 14 May 2021.

62 S. McBride, 'Ulster Unionist Party's all things to all people manifesto involves ambition as well as populism', *Belfast Telegraph*, 31 March 2022.

63 H. McDonald, 'Doug Beattie: Anti-NI Protocol rallies are being used to get rid of agreement', *News Letter*, 22 April 2022.

64 'Northern Ireland Assembly Election: 2022 Manifesto', *Ulster Unionist Party*, https://assets.nationbuilder.com/uup/pages/40/attachments/original/1649258439/UUP_Manifesto_2022-_web.pdf, p. 11–12.

65 R. Edwards, 'If it was the democratic will of the people that there has to be a united Ireland then I have to accept that because I'm a democrat', *Belfast Telegraph*, 20 June 2021.

66 S. Beacom, 'Doug Beattie: I want Northern Ireland to have a sporting anthem', *Belfast Telegraph*, 25 April 2022.

67 J. Manley, 'Ulster Unionists say "no" to DUP/TUV electoral pact plan', *The Irish News*, 16 February 2022.

68 Interview with Jeffrey Donaldson, 16 December 2020.

69 University of Liverpool, 'Northern Ireland Survey October 2021, The Ireland/Northern Ireland Protocol: Consensus or Conflict: Executive Summary', https://www.liverpool.ac.uk/media/livacuk/humanitiesampsocialsciences/documents/The,Ireland-Northern,Ireland,Protocol,Consensus,or,Conflict,v3.pdf.

70 Ibid.

71 Ibid.

72 F. Cochrane, *Unionist Politics and the Politics of Unionism Since the Anglo-Irish Agreement* (Cork, Ireland, 2001), p. 35.

73 Ibid.

74 G. Spencer and C. Hudson, 'Unionism has to stop believing it can get to a new place by staying in an old place', *Belfast Telegraph*, 18 February 2022.

75 See W.J.V. Neill, 'Reaching out: Reimagining post centenary unionism', in *The Idea of the Union*, pp. 356–73.

76 C. McGimpsey quoted in G. Spencer, 'The decline of Ulster unionism: The problem of identity, image and change', *Contemporary Politics*, vol. 12, no 1, March 2006, p. 53.

77 M. Elliot, 'Watchmen in Sion: The Protestant idea of liberty', *Field Day*, no. 8 (1985): 6, quoted in G. Spencer, op. cit.

78 Ibid.

79 Ibid.

80 J. Dunlop, *A Precarious Belonging* (Belfast, 1995), quoted in G. Spencer, op. cit.

81 A.T.Q. Stewart, *The Narrow Ground* (London, 1977), quoted in G. Spencer, op. cit.

82 Ibid.

83 S. Bruce, 'Authority and fission: The Protestants' division', *British Journal of Sociology*, vol. 36, no. 4, December 1985, 592–603, quoted in G. Spencer, op. cit.

84 Interview with Dermot Nesbitt, 10 March 2020.

85 Interview with Harold Good, 23 March 2021.

86 Ibid.

87 Interview with Paul Nolan, 9 March 2020.

88 M. Daly, 'Unionists' concerns and fears of a united Ireland', http://www.senator markdaly.ie/unionist-concerns--fears-of-a-united-ireland.html; 'Brexit and the future of Ireland: Uniting Ireland and its people in peace and prosperity', Joint Committee on the Implementation of the Good Friday Agreement, Houses of the Oireachtas, August 2017.

89 Interview with Alex Kane, 5 January 2021.

90 Ibid.

91 D. Morrow, 'Nothing to fear but … ? Unionists and the Northern Ireland peace process', in D. Murray, editor, Protestant Perspectives on the Peace Process in Northern Ireland, University of Limerick, 2000, pp. 11–42.

92 The agreement was negotiated behind the backs of unionists in the belief that had they known about it they would have sabotaged it. The Anglo-Irish Agreement (1985), between the British government with Margaret Thatcher as its prime minister and the Irish government with Taoiseach Garret FitzGerald, acknowledged that the Irish government had rights in Northern Ireland as the guarantor/protector of Catholic rights. Most importantly, it provided a physical presence in Northern Ireland for the Irish government with a secretariat at

Maryfield outside Belfast. Where there were policy differences between the two governments, 'determined efforts' would be made to resolve them.

93 F. McClements, 'DUP boycott driven by NI protocol issues set to continue stalling meetings', *The Irish Times*, 7 January 2022.

94 B. Hutton, 'Peter Robinson's Irish unity remarks "music to the ears" of republicans', *The Irish Times*, 28 July 2018.

95 Interview with Peter Robinson, 11 March 2020.

96 Ibid.

97 'Agreement on the withdrawal of the United Kingdom of Great Britain and Northern Ireland from the European Union and the European Atomic Energy Community', 2019/C 384 I/01, Official Journal of the European Union, 12 November 2019, https://eur-lex.europa.eu/legal-content/EN/TXT/?uri=CELEX :12019W/TXT(02).

98 G. Halliday, '"Suck it up or resist it and bring down Stormont", Peter Robinson tells unionists on NI protocol', *Belfast Telegraph*, 12 February 2021.

99 P. Robinson, 'The Northern Ireland Protocol will spread like cancer through the blood and bones of the Union unless it is removed', *News Letter*, 3 September 2021.

100 Interview with Mervyn Gibson, 17 November 2021.

101 Ibid.

102 P. Robinson, 'Unionists might face a choice between keeping Stormont or scrapping the Irish Sea border', *News Letter*, 12 February 2021; Official Journal of the European Union, op. cit., https://eur-lex.europa.eu/legal-content/EN /TXT/HTML/?uri=CELEX:12019W/TXT(02)&qid=1660990199156&from =EN#d1e714-92-.

103 Ibid.

104 See Note 44 for text of statement.

105 Interview with Dermot Nesbitt, 10 March 2020.

106 'Defending the Good Friday Agreement', https://www.sinnfein.ie/contents/15243.

107 Interview with Dermot Nesbitt, 10 March 2020.

108 Interview with Peter Robinson, 11 March 2020.

109 Interview with Alex Kane, 5 January 2021.

110 Interview with Jim Wells, 10 March 2020.

111 Ibid.

112 Ibid.

113 Interview with Winston Irvine, 7 December 2020.

114 Interview with Richard Bullick, 15 December 2020.

115 Ibid.

116 Ibid.

117 Interview with Doug Beattie, 14 May 2021.

118 Interview with Jeffrey Donaldson, 16 December 2020.

119 Ibid.

120 N. Emerson, 'Leak reveals the DUP knows how much trouble it is in', *The Irish News*, 18 March 2021.

121 'Leaked minutes reveal DUP concerns about future electoral prospects', *The Irish News*, 17 March 2021.

122 S. McBride, 'Leaked internal DUP minutes show fear of looming electoral collapse, and dismay at party's direction', *News Letter*, 16 March 2021.

123 G. Moriarty, 'Brexit: Foster says Northern Ireland Protocol doing "untold damage"', *The Irish Times*, 7 March 2021.

124 Under the Identity and Language (Northern Ireland) Bill introduced in the House of Lords in May 2022 for language and identity, the Irish language would be granted official status in Northern Ireland. This would include allowing the use of Irish in courts and the appointment of Irish and Ulster Scots/Ulster British commissioners. The bill will also create the Office of Identity and Cultural Expression. The commissioners must be appointed by the first and deputy first ministers. However, the legislation also allows for the Secretary of State for Northern Ireland to make the appointments if the first and deputy first minister posts remain vacant. The UK government is also granting Ulster Scots recognition as a national minority under the Framework Convention for the Protection of National Minorities – a status already granted to Irish, Welsh, Scots and Cornish. R. Black and G. Ni Aodha, 'Westminster legislation "a historic advancement for Irish language community"', *Belfast Telegraph*, 25 May 2022.

125 J. Ward, 'Support for DUP falls to 16% after Poots election, poll shows', *The Irish Times*, 22 May 2021.

126 Ibid.

127 Ibid.

128 C. Barnes, 'Latest poll reveals 49% back Northern Ireland remaining in United Kingdom', *Belfast Telegraph Sunday Life*, 29 August 2021.

129 J. Ward, 'Shock poll sees support for DUP drop to 13%, Sinn Féin holds firm at 25%', *breakingnews.ie*.

130 'DUP leader announces seven tests for HMG plans on NI Protocol', DUP [website], 15 July 2021, https://mydup.com/news/dup-leader-announces-seven-tests-for-hmg-plans-on-ni-protocol.

131 '"DUP to withdraw from north/south political structures," says Donaldson', *Irish Examiner*, 9 September 2021.

132 'Northern Ireland Protocol's Article 16 remains "very real option" – Frost', *Irish Examiner*, 17 November 2021.

133 Lisa O'Carroll, 'Why Paul Givan quit – and what it means for Stormont', *The Guardian*, 3 February 2022.

134 Under the terms of the New Decade, New Approach agreement, which the UK Government made retrospective (to cover Given's resignation), if an executive cannot be formed after the Assembly elections, there will be a six-month period with ministers at their posts. If at that point there is still no agreement

on an Executive, the Secretary of State is obliged to call an election within three months. In other words, failure to form an Executive could drag out until February 2023. If there was a failure to form an Executive following a new election, then the whole process could be repeated. See N. Emerson, 'Stormont lurches into new mode of operation', *The Irish Times*, 17 February 2022.

135 Almost two-thirds of respondents [65 per cent] in the University of Liverpool poll believed that the Assembly and Executive should remain in place until May next year, when its mandate ends. See also Northern Ireland General Election Survey October 2021 (Faculty of Humanities and Social Sciences, University of Liverpool).

136 A. Ferguson, 'UK must act unilaterally if N. Ireland Protocol not replaced quickly' – DUP Leader, Reuters, 28 April 2022.

137 M. Canning, 'Unionists more worried about NI Protocol than living costs, reveals LucidTalk poll', *Belfast Telegraph*, 28 March 2022.

138 Ibid.

139 'UUP leader Doug Beattie accuses DUP of "whipping up hysteria" over united Ireland and comments on his poster with a noose around the neck on display at anti-protocol rally in Lurgan', *News Letter*, 10 April 2022; C. Barnes, 'Loyalist dissidents targeted Doug Beattie … Fringe faction Orange Volunteers blamed for sick stunt', *Belfast Telegraph Sunday Life*, 10 April 2022.

140 R. Black, 'Sinn Féin "planning border poll" following Stormont election, claims DUP', *Irish Examiner*, 8 April 2022.

141 University of Liverpool (The Institute of Irish Studies)/*Irish News* opinion poll, April 2022; https://www.liverpool.ac.uk/media/livacuk/humanitiesampsocial-sciences/documents/Institute,of,Irish,Studies,Irish,News,Poll,March,2022.pdf.

142 The Institute of Irish Studies, University of Liverpool/*Irish News* 4th Attitudinal Survey, July 2022, https://www.liverpool.ac.uk/media/livacuk/humanities ampsocialsciences/documents/Institute,of,Irish,Studies,UoL,Irish,News,Poll ,July,2022.pdf.

143 Interview with John Manley, 12 March 2021.

144 L. Ashcroft, 'Northern Ireland: Unification, or the union?', Lord Ashcroft Polls, 13 December 2021.

145 Interview with Bronagh Hinds, 20 April 2021.

146 Interview with Peter Shirlow, 7 December 2020.

147 P. Robinson, 'Unionists are more alienated than I have seen at any time in my 50 years in politics', *News Letter*, 26 March 2021.

148 Ibid.

149 G. Spencer and C. Hudson, 'Unionism has to stop believing it can get to a new place by staying in an old place', *Belfast Telegraph*, 18 February 2022. See also N. Jarman, *Material Conflicts: Parades and Visual Displays in Northern Ireland* (Oxford, 1997), p. 168.

150 Ibid.

151 P. O'Malley, *Northern Ireland: Questions of Nuance* (Belfast, 1990), p. 25.

12. PROTESTANT FEARS

1   Interview with Éamon Ó Cuív, 26 March 2021.

2   Interview with Máiría Cahill, 19 November 2020.

3   Interview with Rev. Harold Good, 23 March 2021.

4   Interview with Colin Halliday, 18 February 2021.

5   Interview with Rev. Gary Mason, 8 December 2020.

6   The Decade of Centenaries refers to inflexion points in Ireland's history in the opening decades of the twentieth century: the 1916 Uprising (1916); first Dáil Éireann (1918); remembrance of Irishmen and women who died fighting on behalf of Britain during the First World War (1914–18), during which more Irish died than in all the uprisings against British rule; the War of Independence (1919–21); the partition of Ireland (1920); the Anglo-Irish Treaty (1921); and the Civil War (1921–2).

7   The RIC was an all-Ireland police force. It was armed. The Dublin Metropolitan Police was an unarmed police force that operated in Dublin. Between them 90,000 policemen served in both forces, the majority of them Irish Catholics. See more in 'How to look for the records of Royal Irish Constabulary', The National Archives, https://www.nationalarchives.gov.uk/help-with-your-research /research-guides/royal-irish-constabulary. 'Flanagan maintained most of these men were ordinary Irishmen doing the job that policemen everywhere do and they had been unfairly treated by Irish history …', in R. McGreevy; 'Commemoration controversy: Who were the RIC, DMP, Black and Tans, and Auxiliaries?' The Irish Times, 10 January 2020.

8   J. Herlihy, The Royal Irish Constabulary: A short history and genealogical guide (Dublin, 2016).

9   'Leo Varadkar: United Ireland "further away" after RIC controversy', BBC News, 8 January 2020; 'Varadkar "stands over" Irish police commemoration', BBC News, 7 January 2020.

10   K. O'Sullivan et al., 'RIC controversy has set back bid for united Ireland, says Varadkar', The Irish Times, 8 January 2020.

11   Ibid.

12   Ibid.

13   Ibid.

14   Ibid.

15   Ibid.

16   P. O'Malley, The Uncivil Wars (Boston, MA, 1983), p. 171.

17   J. Todd, 'Unionism, identity and Irish unity: Paradigms, problems and para-doxes', Irish Studies in International Affairs, vol. 32, no. 2, 2021, pp. 53–77; p. 63; see response by M. Braniff, 'Traditions, lives and new identities in a dynamic political landscape: A response to "Unionism, identity and Irish unity: para-digms, problems and paradoxes"', Irish Studies in International Affairs, vol. 32, no. 2, 2021, pp. 78–81.

18 4.6.1 (A) Submission to Joint Committee on the Implementation of Good Friday Agreement, Brexit and the Future of Ireland: Uniting Ireland and its People in Peace and Prosperity (2017); Dr James Wilson, Committee on the Implementation of the Good Friday Agreement, Seanad Éireann, pp. 282–4.

19 Ibid.

20 The psychiatrist Dr Vamik Volkan highlighted how large groups, consisting of thousands or millions, create their identity by using an external device that enables a common identification by the masses. Such a device often takes the form of what he called 'chosen trauma'. He writes: 'The chosen trauma that created the Northern Protestant identity consisted of the massacres by the Catholics in 1641, the Siege of Derry in 1689 and the triumph of William III over James II at the Battle of the Boyne in 1690.' See V. Volkan, 'Transgenerational transmissions and chosen traumas: An aspect of large-group identity', *Group Analysis*, vol. 34, pp. 79–97, March 2001. For Protestants, another key element of the chosen trauma 'is the Battle of the Diamond in 1795 when the Peep O'Day Boys, a Protestant militia, routed the Catholic defenders, an alliance of Catholic societies aligned with the United Irishmen, inculcating the belief that Protestants needed to address their own defence rather than rely on the forces of the state'. In L.E. Hancock, 'Peace and change', *Narratives of Identity in the Northern Ireland Troubles*, vol. 39, no. 4, October 2014, p. 450.

21 Hancock, op. cit., pp. 443–67.

22 Ibid., p. 459.

23 J. Todd, 'Unionism, identity and Irish unity: Paradigms, problems and paradoxes', *Irish Studies in International Affairs*, vol. 32, no. 2, 2021, pp. 53–77; see response by M. Braniff, 'Traditions, lives and new identities in a dynamic political landscape: A response to "Unionism, identity and Irish unity: Paradigms, problems and paradoxes"', *Irish Studies in International Affairs*, vol. 32, no. 2, 2021, pp. 78–81.

24 'Unionist concerns and fears of a united Ireland: the need to protect the peace process and build a vision for a shared island and a united people', report commissioned by Senator Mark Daly, https://www.senatormarkdaly.ie/uploads/1/3/5/6 /135670409/unionist-report.pdf; Committee on the Implementation of the Good Friday Agreement', Houses of the Oireachtas, 2022, https://www.oireachtas.ie /en/committees/33/committee-on-the-implementation-of-the-good-friday -agreement/.

25 J. Waller, *A Troubled Sleep: Risk and Resilience in Contemporary Northern Ireland* (Oxford, 2021), p. 105, referring to work of psychologists Walter Stephan and Lausanne Renfro on perceived threat; W.G. Stephan, C.L. Renfro and M.D. Davis, 'The role of threat in intergroup relations', in U. Wagner, L.R. Tropp, G. Finchilescu and C. Tredoux (eds), *Improving Intergroup Relations: Building on the Legacy of Thomas F. Pettigrew* (Oxford, [2008]), pp. 55–72.

26 Ibid.

27 Ibid.

28 Ibid.

29 'New Decade, New Approach', https://assets.publishing.service.gov.uk /government/uploads/system/uploads/attachment_data/file/856998/2020-01 -08_a_new_decade__a_new_approach.pdf.

30 'Census 2011: Key statistics for Northern Ireland', Northern Ireland Statistics and Research Agency, December 2012, https://www.nisra.gov.uk/sites/nisra.gov .uk/files/publications/2011-census-results-key-statistics-northern-ireland-report -11-december-2012.pdf, pp. 17–18.

31 'Confirmation bias is the tendency to look for information that supports, rather than rejects, one's preconceptions, typically by interpreting evidence to confirm existing beliefs while rejecting or ignoring any conflicting data', in American Psychological Association (n.d.), *APA Dictionary of Psychology*, https://dictionary .apa.org/confirmation-bias, 10 June 2020; R.S. Nickerson, 'Confirmation bias: A ubiquitous phenomenon in many guises', *Review of General Psychology*, vol. 2, issue 2, 1998.

32 A. Jern, K.K. Chang and C. Kemp, 'Belief polarization in a complex world', quoted in T. Edsall, 'How we think about politics changes what we think about politics', *The New York Times*, 10 August 2022.

33 S. Breen, 'Vast majority of unionists believe NI will still be part of UK in 30 years', *Belfast Telegraph*, 1 February 2021.

34 Ibid.

35 Interview with David Ford, 12 March 2020.

36 Two hundred and ten thousand Irishmen signed up to fight in the First World War, of whom at least 35,000 died. Many did so in the belief that the sooner the war ended the sooner Ireland would achieve home rule for Ireland. Legislation for home rule had already passed Parliament, but implementation was suspended until the war was over; J. Wilson, 'This is why the Irish no longer mark Remembrance Day', *Irish Central*, 11 November 2021; C. DeBarra, 'Opinion: "The poppy argument in Ireland is an ideological battle that's been raging since the 19th century"', *TheJournal.ie*, 7 November 2019; 'Irish PM wears "shamrock poppy" in Parliament', BBC News, 8 November 2017; P. Farrelly, 'Disregarding the poppy will only hinder Irish unity', *Slugger O'Toole*, 17 November 2020.

37 'Preliminary actual and percentage change in population from 1926 to 2022', Table FP002, Central Statistics Office, https://data.cso.ie/table/FP002; 'Average percentage change in the population 1891 to 2016', Table E8053, Central Statistics Office, https://data.cso.ie/table/E8053. 'Protestants' figures are a summation of original figures for "Church of Ireland (incl. Protestants)", "Presbyterians", and "Methodist, Wesleyan".'

38 Additional suggested explanations for the decline in the Protestant population in Ireland from 1911 to 1926 include the impact of Protestants from Ireland killed during the First World War (and subsequent effects on Protestant birth

488

rate) and encouragement to relocate north; see 'Protestant population decline', *The Irish Times*, 22 September 2014.

39   Interview with John Kyle, 17 February 2021.

40   R. Bury, 'Buried lives: The Protestants in Southern Ireland' in P.J. Roche and B. Barton (eds), *The Northern Ireland Question: Perspectives on Nationalism and Unionism* (Belfast, 2020), pp. 315–46.

41   Ibid., p. 319.

42   Ibid., p. 338.

43   J. Banville, introduction to J. G. Farrell, *Troubles* (New York, 2002), p. viii.

44   T. Garvin, *Nationalist Revolutionaries in Ireland, 1885–1928* (Dublin, 1987), p. 99.

45   Bury, op. cit. pp. 331–3.

46   'Ireland's Constitution of 1937 with Amendments through 2012', https://www.constituteproject.org/constitution/Ireland_2012.pdf.

47   'Many of the fears of Northern Irish unionists about what awaits them in a united Ireland, especially in regard to land and the exercise of religion, are unfounded and based on anachronistic and inaccurate interpretations of the past that have lost much in translation as handed down over the past; identity and the danger of it being lost or absorbed have a much stronger base in historical precedent, for that was largely the experience of Southern Protestants after independence.' See M. Coleman, 'The historical basis for unionist fears of a united Ireland', *Queen's Policy Engagement*, 19 July 2019, http://qpol.qub.ac.uk/the-historical-basis-for-unionist-fears-of-a-united-ireland.

48   P. Donaghy, 'Is Northern Ireland dramatically poorer than the Republic?', *Slugger O'Toole*, 26 March 2018.

49   In 2019, Westminster passed legislation to bring the availability of abortion in Northern Ireland in line with the rest of the UK, but Stormont stymied efforts to implement the legislation. In May 2022, Brandon Lewis, the Secretary of State, introduced further legislation in Westminster to override Stormont roadblocks. 'Brandon Lewis to commission abortion services "within weeks" if Stormont does not act', ITV News, 24 May 2022.

50   Interview with Fr Tim Bartlett, 8 July 2021.

51   Interview with Fr Tim Bartlett, 8 July 2021. As a political party, DUP takes an anti-abortion stance. In response to legislation passed in 2019 that placed zero-term limits on abortions in which a foetus was predicted to suffer from severe mental or physical impairment, Paul Given proposed new legislation in early 2021 that would prevent them from being available if the impairment was non-fatal. The bill was barely rejected, with a 45 to 42 vote in the Assembly. See J. McCormack, 'Northern Ireland abortion law changes proposed by the DUP', BBC News, 16 February 2021; J. McCormack, 'Abortion: DUP bill to stop terminations for non-fatal disabilities rejected', BBC News, 14 December 2021; 'DUP will "vigorously oppose" any new abortion laws in North', *The Irish Times*, 19 March 2021.

52 Interview with Matt Carthy, 2 December 2020.

53 Andy Pollak, 'The South is not ready for reunification', John Hewitt Summer School, 26 July 2022.

54 R. McGreevy, 'Irish people should not stereotype the British, says President', *The Irish Times*, 4 December 2020; J. Beresford, 'President Michael D. Higgins warns that Brexit is fuelling anti-English sentiment in Ireland', *The Irish Post*, 5 December 2020; O. Waldron, 'No, Brexit isn't making Irish people hate Brits', *Vice*, 14 February 2019; According to a survey by Good Information Project/ Ireland, '63% of people say their view of Britain has changed since Brexit, and of those, 95% say it has changed for the worse. Overall, that means 59.8% think less of Britain now since the Brexit vote.' See 'More than half of people in Ireland think less of Britain since Brexit', *TheJournal.ie*, 18 December 2021.

55 'NI100: Michael D. Higgins defends decision not to attend centenary event', BBC News, 17 September 2021, https://www.bbc.co.uk/news/uk-northern-ireland -58589593.

56 Interview with Paul, Lord Bew, 6 January 2021.

13. LOYALISM

1   Interview with Naomi Long, 4 December 2020.

2   Interview with Sammy Douglas, 22 April 2021.

3   Interview with Colin Halliday, 18 February 2021.

4   The Resurgam Trust is a unique project aimed at delivering positive change throughout the town of Lisburn by the creation of strong partnerships between statutory and civic associations. It is cross-community based, https://www .resurgamtrust.co.uk.

5   Interview with Peter Shirlow, 7 December 2020.

6   Interview with Rev. Harold Good, 23 March 2021.

7   Interview with Rev. Lesley Carroll, 19 May 2021.

8   Interview with Rev. Gary Mason, 8 December 2020.

9   Interview with Graham Spencer, 1 March 2022.

10 'Q&A: Northern Ireland flag protests', BBC News, 28 November 2014, https:// www.bbc.co.uk/news/uk-northern-ireland-20651163.

11 N. McAdam, 'Orange Order still protesting Drumcree, 20 years on', *The Irish News*, 7 July 2018; 'Protestants and universities: The students hit back', *Belfast Telegraph*, 6 March 2009.

12 E. McCann, 'Why are Catholic schools doing better than Protestant ones?', *The Irish Times*, 3 April 2014.

13 S. Doyle, 'Catholics pupils perform better than Protestants', *The Irish News*, 7 September 2017.

14 W. O'Connor, 'NI Catholics outnumber Protestants in university', *Independent.ie*, 20 January 2016.

15 F. O Connor, *In Search of a State: Catholics in Northern Ireland* (Belfast, 1994); Interview with Fr Tim Bartlett, 8 July 2021.

16 M. Devenport, 'Census figures: NI Protestant population continuing to decline', BBC News, 11 December 2012, https://www.bbc.co.uk/news/uk-northern-ireland -20673534.

17 Interview with Paul Nolan, 9 March 2020.

18 'Unionist concerns and fears of a united Ireland: The need to protect the peace process and build a vision for a shared island and a united people', report commissioned by Senator Mark Daly, https://www.senatormarkdaly.ie/ uploads/1/3/5/6/135670409/unionist-report.pdf.

19 Ibid., p. 45.

20 Ibid.

21 Ibid.

22 P. Marris, *Loss and Change* (Harlow, UK, 1974), p. 97.

23 B. Graham and P. Shirlow, 'The Battle of the Somme in Ulster memory and identity', *Political Geography*, 21 (2002), p. 884.

24 Ibid.

25 Ibid., pp. 886–7.

26 D. Lowry, 'Ulster resistance and loyalist rebellion in the Empire', in K. Jeffery (ed.), *An Irish Empire?: Aspects of Ireland and the British Empire* (Manchester, UK, 2017), p. 191.

27 Graham and Shirlow, op. cit.

28 L. Colley, *Britons: Forging the Nation 1707–1837* (New Haven, CT, 1992).

29 Interview with Graham Spencer, 1 March 2022; email exchange with Graham Spencer, 18 March 2022.

30 Ibid.

31 'Northern Ireland is in a culture war. Brexit is making it worse', *Foreign Policy*, 31 January 2020.

32 Interview with Paul Nolan, 9 March 2020.

33 Interview with Sammy Douglas, 22 April 2021.

34 Interview with John Kyle, 17 February 2021.

35 Interview with Colin Halliday, 18 February 2021.

36 K.A. Shaw, M. Holmes and S. Graham. 'Loyalist engagement survey: Protocol, policing, and politics', *Let's Talk Loyalism*, August 2021.

37 Ibid., p. 9.

38 Ibid.

39 Ibid.

40 Ibid.

41 Interview with Peter Shirlow, 7 December 2020.

42 Interview with Sammy Douglas, 22 April 2021.

14. ACCOMODATING THE BRITISH IDENTITY

1   John Whyte, *Interpreting the Northern Ireland Conflict* (Oxford, 1990), p. 102.

2   Ibid. p. 212.

3   Ibid.

4   Matt Carthy, MEP, Sinn Féin, 'Turn desire for a united Ireland into unstop-pable momentum', 24 February 2022, https://www.mattcarthy.ie/lets-turn-the-desire-for-a-united-ireland-into-an-unstoppable-momentum.

5   Interview with Alex Kane, 5 January 2021.

6   Interview with Ian Marshall, 28 April 2021.

7   Interview with Dr John Kyle, 17 February 2021.

8   Interview with Sammy Douglas, 22 April 2021.

9   Interview with Jackie Redpath, 19 March 2021.

10 Interview with Mervyn Gibson, 17 November 2021; A. Morris, 'Orange Order: Parades issue is not settled', *The Irish News*, 11 September 2021; J. Angelos, 'Will Brexit bring the Troubles back to Northern Ireland?', *The New York Times*, 8 April 2021.

11 Interview with Tim Bartlett, 8 July 2021.

12 J. Todd, 'Two traditions in unionist political culture', *Irish Political Studies*, vol. 2, iss. 1, 1987, pp. 1–26; see also F. Cochrane, *Unionist Politics and the Politics of Unionism Since the Anglo-Irish Agreement* (Cork, 2001), pp. 35–87.

13 Cochrane, op. cit., p. 37; J. Todd, 'The limits of Britishness', *The Irish Review*, 5 (1988).

14 'The Belfast Agreement', Gov.uk, 10 April 1998, p. 2.

15 F. Sheahan, 'Drop the tricolour and create a new flag to respect both sides – poll', *Independent.ie*, 1 May 2021.

16 Michael Brennan, 'Exclusive Red C poll: A united Ireland, but at what cost?', *Business Post*, 28 November 2021.

17 M. Brennan and B. Whyte, 'Poll: Voters say no to new flag and anthem in a united Ireland', *Business Post*, 28 November 2021.

18 P. Leahy, 'Large majority of voters favour a united Ireland, poll finds', *The Irish Times*, 11 December 2021.

19 C. Farrell, 'Quarter of TDs and senators unwilling to change tricolour and national anthem to achieve United Ireland, survey shows', *Irish Sun*, 5 April 2021.

20 J. Quann, 'United Ireland: Is it time for a new national anthem?', *Newstalk*, 10 March 2020.

21 M. Brennan and B. Whyte, 'Poll: Voters say no to new flag and anthem in a united Ireland', *Business Post*, 28 November 2021; P. Leahy, 'Large majority of voters favour a united Ireland, poll finds', *The Irish Times*, 11 December 2021.

22 Interview with Duncan Morrow, 13 March 2020.

23 The Constitution provides that only Irish citizens may be elected president or members of Dáil Éireann. Only Irish citizens may vote in an election for presi-dent or in a referendum. British citizens ordinarily resident in a constituency in

the state are entitled to vote in a Dáil election for that constituency. This is not specifically set out in the Constitution, which merely provides that all citizens and 'such other persons in the state as may be determined by law' are entitled to vote at a Dáil election. At the moment, British citizens resident in the state are determined by law as eligible to vote in Dáil elections under the relevant electoral law. While British citizens resident in Northern Ireland are not entitled to vote in a twenty-six-county general election, under current law (even without a change) they would be eligible in a thirty-two-county state because they would then be resident in a constituency in the state (email exchange with Irish Department of Trade and Foreign Affairs).

24 NILT 2021 variable NINATID: 'Which of this best describes the way you think of yourself: British, Irish, Ulster, Northern Irish, other, don't know?', https://www.ark.ac.uk/nilt/2021/Community_Relations/NINATID.html.

25 Northern Ireland General Election Survey 2021 (Faculty of Humanities and Social Sciences, University of Liverpool); Northern Ireland General Election Survey 2019 (Faculty of Humanities and Social Sciences, University of Liverpool); Northern Ireland General Election Survey 2021 (Faculty of Humanities and Social Sciences, University of Liverpool).

26 R. Rose, *Governing Without Consensus* (London, 1972).

27 R. Rose, op. cit., p. 214.

28 '2011 Census', Table DC2238NI: National Identity (Classification 1) by Religion or Religion Brought Up In, Northern Ireland Statistics and Research Agency, https://www.ninis2.nisra.gov.uk/.

29 'Background to the religion and the "religion brought up in" questions in the census, and their analysis in 2001 and 2011: Guidance note', Table 6, Northern Ireland Statistics and Research Agency, June 2017, p. 9; ARK, Northern Ireland Life and Times Survey, 2021, variable RELIGION, https://www.ark.ac.uk/nilt/2021/Background/, May 2022. (Series data for variable RELIGION available at ARK website.)

30 C. Coulter et al., *Northern Ireland a Generation After Good Friday: Lost Futures and New Horizons in the 'Long Peace'* (Manchester, UK, 2021), pp. 167–81.

31 '2011 Census', Table DC2238NI: National Identity (Classification 1) by Religion or Religion Brought Up In, Northern Ireland Statistics and Research Agency, https://www.ninis2.nisra.gov.uk/.

32 C. Coulter et al., op. cit.

33 Ibid., p. 169.

34 Ibid., p. 171.

35 Ibid., p. 169.

36 It is noted that 'Northern Irish' can be interpreted differently by Protestants, Catholics and those who don't see themselves as either Protestant or Catholic: '[The] Moderate Social Democratic and Labour Party (SDLP) are more inclined than Sinn Féin to discuss the Northern Irish as a people. That is, the Northern Irish are all the people in Northern Ireland, regardless of their self-identity.

The distinction is also found among unionism. The historically more hardline Democratic and Unionist Party (DUP) occasionally refer to all people in the region as 'of Northern Inrush' in efforts to undermine claims of Irishness. The Ulster unionists are relatively more likely to say it as an identity claim and also a matter of personal choice. The centrist Alliance party with its explicitly anti-sectarian message uses it as part of a moderate political project.' K. McNicholl et al., 'How the "Northern Irish" national identity is understood and used by young people and politicians', *Political Psychology*, vol. 40, no. 3, 2019, pp. 487–505, cited in Coulter, 2021, p. 180; see also J. Garry and K. McNichol, *Understanding the 'Northern Irish' Identity*, Knowledge Exchange Seminar Series, 2014–15, http://www.niassembly.gov.uk/globalassets/documents/raise/knowledge_exchange/briefing_papers/series4/northern_ireland_identity_garry_mcnicholl_policy_document.pdf.

37 A. Bachta, Cross tabs using STATA, NILT 2021 variable NINATID: 'Which of this best describes the way you think of yourself: British, Irish Ulster, Northern Irish, other, don't know?'. ARK, Northern Ireland Life and Times Survey, 2021, https://www.ark.ac.uk/ARK/nilt/datasets/, May 2022.

38 Interview with Sammy Douglas, 22 April 2021.

39 C. Humphries and A. Ferguson, 'Northern Ireland loyalists anxious as "stalwart" queen passe', Reuters, 13 September 2022.

40 S. McKay, 'Queen Elizabeth's death is an earthquake for Northern Irish unionists', *The Irish Times*, 8 September 2022.

41 C. Humphries and A. Ferguson, 'Northern Ireland loyalists anxious as "stalwart" queen passes', Reuters, 13 September 2022.

42 Interview with Rev. Harold Good, 23 March 2021.

43 Interview with Graham Spencer, 1 March 2022.

44 *2011 Census: General Report for England and Wales*, Office for National Statistics.

45 M. Bet, 'Queen would remain head of state in an independent Scotland – Ian Blackford', *The Scotsman*, 7 March 2022.

46 G. Arnett, 'Where in Scotland do people feel the most Scottish?', *The Guardian*, 26 September 2013; *2011 Census: Key Statistics for Wales, March 2011*, Ethnic group, Table KS202EW, Office for National Statistics, 11 December 2012, p. 12.

47 M. Easton, 'The English question: What is the nation's identity?', BBC News, 3 June 2018.

48 'Northern Ireland Census 2011 Key Statistics Summary Report: September 2014', Northern Ireland Statistics and Research Agency, September 2014, p. 48.

49 '2011 Census', Table DC2237NI: National Identity (Classification 1) by Religion, Northern Ireland Statistics and Research Agency, https://www.ninis2.nisra.gov.uk; 'People of Northern Ireland', Wikipedia; M. Easton, 'How British is Britain?', BBC News, 30 September 2013.

50 Press Release, Census 2021 main statistics for Northern Ireland (phase 1), Northern Ireland Statistics and Research Agency, 22 September 2022, https://www.nisra.gov.uk/publications/census-2021-main-statistics-for-northern-ireland-phase-1.

51 Ibid.

52 Census 2021 main statistics identity tables, Northern Ireland Statistics and Research Agency, 22 September 2022, https://www.nisra.gov.uk/publications /census-2021-main-statistics-identity-tables; National Identity (Classification 1): KS202NI (administrative geographies), Northern Ireland Neighbourhood Information Service, Northern Ireland Statistics and Research Agency.

53 Ibid.

54 S. McBride, 'If unionists insist on Northern Ireland being British only it can't and won't survive', *Belfast Telegraph*, 23 September 2022.

55 Rose, op. cit., pp. 209–17.

56 Easton, op. cit.

57 D. Hughes, 'Conservatives would cut Northern Ireland loose from UK to deliver Brexit: poll', *Belfast Telegraph*, 19 June 2019.

58 Interview with Winston Irvine, 7 December 2020.

59 Interview with Tom Roberts, 9 December 2020.

60 Interview with John Kyle, 17 February 2021.

61 F. Cochrane, *Unionist Politics*, pp. 35–87.

62 Interview with Paul Nolan, 9 March 2020.

63 *Towards a United Ireland – A Sinn Féin discussion document*, 2016, https://www .sinnfein.ie/files/2016/Towards-a-United-Ireland.pdf, p. 8.

64 Interview with Steve Aiken, 11 December 2020.

65 'Ulster unionists, fearful of being isolated on the island, built a solid house, but it was a cold house for Catholics. And Northern nationalists, although they had a roof over their heads, seemed to us as if they meant to burn the house down. None of us are entirely innocent.' David Trimble, Nobel Prize lecture, 10 December 1998, https://www.nobelprize.org/prizes/peace/1998/trimble/lecture.

66 J. Todd, 'Unionism, identity and Irish unity: Paradigms, problems and para-doxes', *Irish Studies in International Affairs*, vol. 32, iss. 5 (2021), pp. 53–77.

67 Ibid., p. 56.

68 Ibid.

69 Ibid., pp. 76–7.

70 Ibid.

71 T. McTague, 'How Britain falls apart', *The Atlantic*, 5 January 2022.

72 J. Ruane and D. Butler, 'Southern Irish Protestants: An example of de-ethnici-zation?', *Nations and Nationalisms*, vol. 13, no. 4 (2007), pp. 619–35.

73 Ibid., p. 621.

74 'United Kingdom might not exist in a decade, half of UK citizens think: poll', Reuters, 8 November 2019.

75 J. Duffy, 'Support for independence ahead in poll showing majority believe Union will be gone in a decade', *The National*, 22 March 2022.

76 Ibid.

77 Ibid.

78 Ibid.

79 'Should Wales be an independent country?', *Statista*, 18 February 2022.

15. REUNIFICATION

1   R. Humphreys, *Countdown to Unity: Debating Irish Reunification* (Dublin, 2019), p. 153.

2   Interview with Seán Donlon, 28 April 2021.

3   D. Ferriter, 'Lessons from peace process for united Ireland supporters', *The Irish Times*, 26 March 2021.

4   'Unionist concerns and fears of a united Ireland: The need to protect the peace process and build a vision for a shared island and a united people', report commissioned by Senator Mark Daly, https://www.senatormarkdaly.ie /uploads/1/3/5/6/135670409/unionist-report.pdf, p. 13.

5   Interview with Peter Robinson, 11 March 2020.

6   Interview with Alex Attwood, 13 March 2020.

7   Interview with Jim Wells, 10 March 2020. The figures quoted approximate rough calculations based on a UK subvention cost of £9 billion to Northern Ireland (divided by an Ireland population of about 5 million and a UK population of about 67 million). There is debate on how much a net fiscal deficit would be in the event of a united Ireland and transfer of which public expenditure items (national debt, defence spending, pension liabilities). See 'Final Report', Working Group on Unification Referendums on the Island of Ireland, May 2021, p. 110.

8   Interview with Trevor Ringland, 17 May 2021.

9   Interview with Colin Halliday, 18 February 2021.

10 Interview with David Ford, 12 March 2020.

11 Interview with Colin Harvey, 13 March 2020.

12 Mary Lou McDonald, *Claire Byrne Live*, RTÉ News (22 March 2021); S. Pollak, 'Joe Brolly disconnected during RTÉ united Ireland debate after DUP remarks', *The Irish Times*, 23 March 2021.

13 Andy Pollak, 'The South is not ready for reunification', John Hewitt Summer School talk, 26 July 2022

14 J. Corcoran, 'Sinn Féin's push for border poll "alarming", says Varadkar', *Independent.ie*, 2 April 2017.

15 Interview with Bertie Ahern, 26 November 2020.

16 B. Hutton, 'DUP leader: Protocol barriers must be "swept away, not replaced"', *The Irish Times*, 19 July 2021.

17 D. Young, 'SDLP backs call for Republic of Ireland to appoint a "Minister for Reunification"', *Belfast Telegraph*, 27 March 2021; 'New Ireland Commission', Social Democratic and Labour Party, 2022, https://www.sdlp.ie/new _ireland_commission.

NOTES TO PAGES 327-35

18 'Working group on unification referendums on the island of Ireland: final report', Constitution Unit, 26 May 2021, https://constitution-unit.com/2021/05/26/the-working-group-on-unification-referendums-on-the-island-of-ireland-final-report/.

19 J. Manley, 'Protocol matters most to little more than one in 10 unionists – poll', *The Irish News*, 14 February 2022.

20 Interview with Peter Shirlow, 7 December 2020.

21 Interview with Rev. Harold Good, 23 March 2021.

22 Interview with Ian Marshall, 28 April 2021.

23 Interview with Niall Murphy, 24 February 2021.

24 Interview with Niall Blaney, 1 June 2021.

25 Interview with Neale Richmond, 19 February 2021.

26 Interview with Brendan O'Leary, 3 May 2021.

27 Interview with Niall Murphy, 24 February 2021. The government set up NAMA (National Asset Management Agency) in 2009 to take over property loans from the Republic's banks. The value of the properties against which the debts were secured had collapsed, threatening the banks' solvency. See B. O'Halloran, 'Q&A: What is the National Management Asset Agency?', *The Irish Times*, 15 September 2017.

28 D. Loscher, 'Sinn Féin now the leading party of middle class Ireland', *The Irish Times*, 10 December 2021.

29 Ibid.

30 Interview with Matt Carthy, 2 December 2020.

31 M. Gladwell, *The Tipping Point: How Little Things Can Make a Big Difference* (New York, 2000).

32 '2020 Irish General Election', Wikipedia, https://en.wikipedia.org/wiki/2020_Irish_general_election#Results.

33 Gladwell, p. 11.

34 Danny Morrison, Provisional Sinn Féin Ard Fheis, November 1981.

35 Interview with Richard Bullick, 15 December 2020.

36 Interview with Peter Shirlow, 7 December 2020.

37 Interview with Jim O'Callaghan, 15 March 2021.

38 F. Cochrane's book Northern *Ireland Breaking Peace* (Manchester, UK, 2020) was followed with *Northern Ireland: Fragile Peace* (New Haven, CT, 2022).

39 Interview with Graham Spencer, 1 March 2022.

40 Interview with Brendan O'Leary, 3 May 2021

41 'Irish Foreign Affairs Minister Coveney pulled out of Belfast peace event after bomb scare', ITV News, 25 March 2022.

42 R. Edwards and C. O'Neill, 'UVF is "actively planning" to target more Irish politicians', *Belfast Telegraph*, 27 March 2022.

43 Interview with Paul Nolan, 9 March 2020.

44 NILT 2021, variable UNINATID, https://www.ark.ac.uk/nilt/2021/Political_Attitudes/UNINATID.html.

45 See P. Leahy, 'Sinn Féin juggernaut stalls in first post-Covid opinion poll', *The Irish Times*, 13 April 2022.

46 The New Ireland Forum was established by Taoiseach Garret FitzGerald in 1983 to provide for 'consultations on the manner in which lasting peace and stability could be achieved in a new Ireland through the democratic process and to report on possible new structures and processes through which this objective might be achieved. Only nationalists participated in the forum. It outlined three options for a future Ireland: a unitary state, a federal state and a confederal state'; *New Ireland Forum Report*, The Stationery Office, Dublin (1984). https://cain.ulster .ac.uk/issues/politics/nifr.htm. 'In response to the three options, British prime minister Margaret Thatcher famously was quoted as saying "Out, out and out!" In fact, she dismissed the three alternatives one by one at a press conference, each time saying, "that is out", in a response that became known as the "out, out, out" speech: "New Ireland Forum",' Wikipedia, https://en.wikipedia.org /wiki/New_Ireland_Forum; M. Thatcher, 'Press conference following Anglo-Irish Summit ("out … out … out")', 19 November 1984, Margaret Thatcher Foundation, https://www.margaretthatcher.org/document/105790.

47 Interview with Paul Nolan, 9 March 2020.

48 R. Humphreys, *Beyond the Border: The Good Friday Agreement and Irish Unity After Brexit* (Dublin, 2018).

49 'New framework for agreement', *The Framework Documents*, 22 February 1995.

50 *Working Group on Unification Referendum on the Island of Ireland, Final Report*, The Constitution Unit, 202, p. 117.

51 Interview with Bertie Ahern, 26 November 2020.

52 Interview with Jeffrey Donaldson, 16 December 2020.

53 K. Dineen, 'Fianna Fáil leader Micheál Martin says he would not wear a poppy or funny socks if he replaces Leo Varadkar as Taoiseach', *The Irish Sun*, 28 December 2017; 'Where's Fianna Fáil's promised 12-point plan on a United Ireland?', *TheJournal.ie*, 22 July 2019.

54 Interview with Matt Carthy, 2 December 2020.

55 M. Mansergh, 'The political legacy of Seán Lemass', *Études irlandaises*, no. 25–1 (2000).

56 'The West Lothian Question refers to the perceived imbalance between the voting rights in the House of Commons of MPs from Scottish, Welsh and Northern Ireland constituencies and those of MPs from English constituencies following devolution' in 'West Lothian Question', UK Parliament, 2022, https://www.parliament.uk/site-information/glossary/west-lothian-question. After, the UK government devolved powers in a whole range of matters to local administrations in Scotland, Wales and Northern Ireland. MPs from these regions are allowed to vote upon English-specific matters in the Commons, but MPs for English constituencies have no vote on the devolved affairs that are Scotland, Wales or Northern Ireland specific.

57   R. Humphreys, *Beyond the Border: The Good Friday Agreement and Irish Unity After Brexit* (Dublin, 2018).

58   Humphreys, pp. 239–40.

59   E. Birnie and G. Brownlow, 'How is Brexit affecting Northern Ireland's economy?', *Economics Observatory*, 1 February 2021.

60   Interview with Francis Campbell, 15 March 2021.

61   Interview with Peter Robinson, 11 March 2020.

62   John Bruton, participant in *Claire Byrne Live* (RTÉ TV), 'A united Ireland – what would it mean?', 22 March 2021.

63   Interview with Brendan O'Leary, 3 May 2021. A federal state with the Northern institutions constituting one of its parts was among the three models considered by the New Ireland Forum. *Working Group on Unification Referendum on the Island of Ireland, Final Report*, The Constitution Unit, 2021, p. 117, 119; L. O'Carroll, 'How could a vote on the unification of Ireland play out', *The Guardian*, 3 May 2021.

64   J. Garry, B. O'Leary, J. Coakley, J. Pow and L. Whitten, 'Public attitudes to different models of a United Ireland: Evidence from a Citizens' Assembly in Northern Ireland', *Irish Political Studies*, vol. 35, iss. 3, 2020.

65   Ibid., pp. 423–4.

66   Ibid., p. 427.

67   J. Garry, B. O'Leary, P. Gillespie and R. Gjoni, 'Public attitudes to Irish unification', *Irish Studies in International Affairs*, vol. 33, no. 2, 2022, https://muse.jhu.edu/article/854338; J. Garry, P. Gillespie and B. O'Leary, 'What people in the Republic actually think about Irish unification', *The Irish Times*, 23 September 2021. The mini-CA was composed of a cross-section of fifty citizens of the Republic, selected as broadly representative on a range of demographic criteria.

68   J. Garry, P. Gillespie and B. O'Leary, 2021, op. cit.

69   B. O'Leary in email to author, 2 May 2021.

70   J. Garry, P. Gillespie and B. O'Leary, 2021, op. cit.

71   Ibid.

72   The Citizens' Assembly consists of ninety-nine random chosen people, stratified by several criteria including gender, age, location and social class. It is tasked with considering a range of political and socio-economic questions. The Citizens' Assembly established in Ireland in 2016 considered several political questions including the Constitution of Ireland. Questions it has addressed include abortion, fixed-term parliaments, referenda, ageing and climate change. Over eighteen months a report is produced on each topic. The government is required to respond to its recommendations. Citizens' Assembly (Ireland), https://en.wikipedia.org/wiki/Citizens%27_Assembly_(Ireland)#:~:text=The%20Citizens'%20Assembly%20(Irish%3A,including%20the%20Constitution%20of%20Ireland.

73   Interview with Peter Shirlow, 7 December 2020.

74 WGR Final Report, op. cit. p.118.

75 Ibid.

76 Ibid., p. 119.

77 Article 29 of the Irish constitution provides for Ireland re-joining the Commonwealth, which it left in 1949 when Ireland declared itself a republic.

78 WRG Final Report, op. cit.

79 Interview with Jim O'Callaghan, 15 March 2021.

80 J. O'Callaghan, 'The political, economic and legal consequences of irish reunification'. Paper delivered in Sydney Sussex College Cambridge, 23 March 2021, https://jimocallaghan.com/the-political-economic-and-legal-consequences-of-irish-reunification/

81 Ibid.

82 Interview with Jim O'Callaghan, 15 March 2021.

83 Ibid.

84 Devolved Government, British-Irish Intergovernmental Conference (BIIC) CAIN Web Service, https://cain.ulster.ac.uk/issues/politics/conference/.

85 Interview with Neale Richmond, 19 February 2021.

86 N. Richmond, 'Towards a new Ireland'. Paper delivered at Sydney Sussex College Cambridge, 19 April, https://www.finegael.ie/app/uploads/2021/04/Towards-a-new-ireland-Neale-Richmond-2021.pdf.

87 Ibid., p. 18.

88 Interview with Neale Richmond, 18 February 2020.

89 Richmond, op. cit., p. 18.

90 Interview with Neale Richmond, 18 February 2020.

91 T. Hadden, 'Plus ça change … or do we really need to decide now?', Fortnight@50, iss. 479, September 2020, https://fortnightmagazine.org/wp-content/uploads/2021/01/Fortnight@50-2020.pdf, p. 9; 'The Belfast Agreement', Gov.uk, 10 April 1998, p. 2.

92 Interview with Seán Donlon, 28 April 2021.

93 A. Pollak, 'The South is not ready for reunification', John Hewitt Summer School, 26 July 2022.

94 R. Humphreys, 'What do we talk about when we talk about a united Ireland?', Fortnight@50, 2020, pp. 2–4.

95 'Q + A: Here's where the parties stand on a united Ireland and holding a border poll', TheJournal.ie, 6 February 2020.

96 'A united Ireland – what would it mean?', Claire Byrne Live, RTÉ News, 23 March 2021. A poll commissioned for the show found a small majority of people in the South were in favour of a united Ireland. The poll was carried out by Amárach Research, which asked 1,000 adults how they would vote on a United Ireland. Fifty-three per cent said 'Yes to Unification'; 19 per cent said 'No to Unification' and 28 per cent 'Don't Know'; B. Archer, 'Small majority of people in the Republic are in favour of a united Ireland – poll', The Irish News, 23 March 2021.

97   Interview with Bertie Ahern, 26 November 2020.

98   S. McBride, 'Alliance could topple Sinn Féin and DUP as rivals still fail to understand party's growing success', *Belfast Telegraph*, 21 May 2022.

99   Interview with Stephen Farry, 28 January 2021.

100 Interview with Naomi Long, 4 December 2020.

101 C. Woodhouse, 'Support for Northern Ireland to remain part of UK still strong, new poll reveals', *Belfast Telegraph*, 21 August 2022.

102 Interview with Niall Murphy, 24 February 2021.

103 G. Howlin, 'Command and control: How would Sinn Féin navigate government in the Republic?', *The Irish Times*, 24 May 2022.

104 The Institute of Irish Studies, University of Liverpool/*Irish News* Opinion Poll, April 2022, https://www.liverpool.ac.uk/media/livacuk/humanitiesampsocial sciences/documents/Institute,of,Irish,Studies,Irish,News,Poll,March,2022.pdf.

105 J. Wilson, 'McDonald demands border poll after Sinn Féin win', Newstalk Radio, 7 May 2022.

106 Chris Giles, 'UK growth set to be worst in G20 apart from Russia, OECD warns', *The Financial Times*, 8 June 2022.

107 R.J. Partington, 'Brexit is making cost of living crisis worse, new study claims', *The Guardian*, 3 June 2022.

108 R.J. Partington, 'UK living standards "to fall at fastest rate since mid-1950s"', *The Guardian*, 23 March 2022.

109 P. Inman, 'UK inflation will soar to "astronomical" levels over next year, think-tank warn', *The Guardian*, 3 August 2022.

110 B. Walker, 'UK households face worst fall in living standards for 60 years', *New Statesman*, 3 August 2022; B. Chapman, 'UK faces long recession and deepest plunge in living standards on record, Bank of England warns', *The Independent*, 4 August 2022.

111 A. Atkinson and D. Goodman, 'Britain's battered economy is sliding toward a breaking point', *Bloomberg*, 22 June 2022, https://www.bloomberg.com/news /articles/2022-06-27/britain-s-battered-economy-is-sliding-toward-a-breaking -point.

112 R. O'Connor, 'Labour Party leader Keir Starmer will campaign for Northern Ireland to remain part of the United Kingdom if there is a United Ireland referendum', *The Irish Post*, 20 July 2021.

113 K. Andrews, 'Sir Keith Starmer will block independence vote if Labour win election', *The Sunday Times*, 6 July 2022.

114 S. McBride, 'Northern Ireland has become a more tolerant but more polarised society', *Belfast Telegraph*, 18 May 2022, https://www.belfasttelegraph.co.uk /opinion/columnists/Sam-mcbride/northern-ireland-has-become-a-more -tolerant-but-more-polarised-society-41697618.html.

115 'Central Good Relations Fund', The Executive Office, https://www.executiveoffice -ni.gov.uk/articles/central-good-relations-fund.

116 D. Morrow, 'Sectarianism in Northern Ireland – a review', Ulster University, 2017, https://www.ulster.ac.uk.

117 P. Crerar, 'UK aims to end Stormont row before planned Joe Biden visit in 2023', *The Guardian*, 21 September 2022.

118 P. Leahy, 'Border fears return to haunt Irish government', *The Irish Times*, 13 June 2022, https://www.irishtimes.com/politics/2022/06/13/border-fears-return-to-haunt-irish-government/.

EPILOGUE

1   Her proposals were opposed by many Tory MPs who argued that all the benefits went to the better-off, and by Tom Scholar, the Treasury Permanent Secretary, whom she fired. Significantly, she bypassed having the Office for Budget Responsibility vet the proposals for their economic impact, simply announcing they would stimulate economic growth. The budget called for cutting taxes on the financially well off, cutting the stamp duty for property buyers, scrapping bankers' bonus caps and cancelling an increase in corporation tax that had been due to take effect in 2023.

2   D. Milliken, 'Bank of England to buy 65 billion pounds of UK bonds to stem rout', Reuters, 28 September 2022.

3   In the last quarter of 2021 UK GDP was 5.2 per cent smaller, investment 13.7 per cent lower and goods trade 13.6 per cent lower than would have been the case had Britain remained in the EU; J. Springford, 'What can we know about the cost of Brexit so far', 'Centre for European Reform, 9 June 2022, https://www.cer.eu/publications/archive/policy-brief/2022/cost-brexit-so-far.

4   'Brexit: Rejoining EU takes record 14-point lead in latest poll', *The Independent*, 28 October 2022.

5   T. Connelly, 'Truss and the NI Protocol: Reset or ongoing conflict?', RTÉ News, 6 September 2022, https://www.rte.ie/news/2022/0906/1320926-truss-protocol/.

6   L. O'Carroll, 'Tory MP Steve Baker apologises to Ireland and EU for behaviour during Brexit', *The Guardian*, 2 October 2022.

7   D. Young, 'Taoiseach Micheal Martin detects "genuine wish" from UK Prime Minister Liz Truss to resolve Northern Ireland Protocol dispute', *Irish Mirror*, 2 October 2022.

8   'UK and EU edge closer to breakthrough in long -running Brexit saga', *Irish Times*, 8 November 2022.

9   'NI protocol: Issues can be resolved "in a couple of weeks", the EU chief negotiator has said', BBC News, 7 November 2022.

10 S. Morris, 'Rishi Sunak and Ursula von der Leyen agree to "work together" to solve Northern Ireland Protocol row', *Sky News*, 7 November 2022.

11 '"Major breakthrough" on Northern Ireland Protocol issue close', *Belfast Telegraph*, 8 November 2022.

12 L. O'Carroll, 'Sunak hopes to "deepen UK-Irish ties" after Micheál Martin meeting', *The Guardian*, 10 November 2022.

13 After first promising to call new assembly election at one minute past midnight on October 28 (when the six-month time span provided for in legislation for the Assembly to start functioning and for Sinn Féin and the DUP to have formed an Executive was up) and then announcing that he was postponing the election and would not call one for several weeks, perhaps indefinitely, to give EU/UK negotiators room to find a compromise on the protocol, Heaton-Harris managed to earn the opprobrium of all the parties who had been gearing up for an election on 15 December that no one wanted and that would change nothing. However, he did cut MLAs salaries by one-third. S. Ravikumar and A. Ferguson, 'UK delays Northern Ireland election in hope of progress in EU talks', Reuters, 9 November 2022.

14 S. Breen, 'LucidTalk poll: 59% call for Dublin role Northern Ireland if Assembly not restored', *Belfast Telegraph*, 13 November 2022.

15 S. Breen, 'LucidTalk poll: DUP claws back support but Sinn Féin still top party', *Belfast Telegraph*, 4 November 2022.

16 K. Reid, 'UUP leader Doug Beattie says talk of joint authority "not acceptable"', *Belfast Telegraph*, 25 October 2022; J. Breslin, 'Loyalist paramilitaries warn of "dire consequences" if joint authority imposed', *Irish News*, 29 October 2022.

17 J. O'Neill, 'Billy Hutchinson says loyalist community tensions highest since ceasefires', BBC News, 1 November 2022.

18 D. Grennan, 'Ireland is facing biggest decline in living standards since the crash despite budget measures', *DublinLive*, 28 July 2022; E. Burke-Kennedy, 'Ireland is facing biggest decline in living standards since the crash despite budget measures', *Irish Times*, 30 September 2022; L. Burne, 'Irish government "can't rule out" possibility of recession next year', *TheJournal.ie*, 15 November 2022; C. Taylor, 'There is no doubt that the Irish economy is at a turning point', *Irish Times*, 26 November 2022.

19 At the Sinn Féin Ard Fheis in early November 2022, a supremely self-confident Mary Lou McDonald spoke in terms that reinforced her aura of Taoiseach-in-waiting. As regards Irish unification, a priority for a future Sinn Féin government, she acknowledged that while some were 'apprehensive' about the prospect, the time had come to finally settle the question: 'Others say yes to unity, but not now. They're wrong. The time to plan for a peaceful, democratic constitutional change is now.' The Irish government must 'immediately set up a Citizens' Assembly on unity'.

20 P. Leahy, 'North and south methodology: How we took the pulse of Ireland on unity', *Irish Times*, 3 December 2022; P. Leahy, 'Northern Ireland rejects Irish unity by large margin, poll shows', *Irish Times*, 3 December 2022.

21 J. Garry and B. O'Leary, 'Northern Ireland's "persuadables": A pivotal demographic for future referendums', *Irish Times*, 3 December 2022.

22 P. Leahy, 'Large majority of voters favour a united Ireland, poll finds', *Irish Times*, 11 December 2022.

23 'McDonald: "Sinn Féin is ready to lead. Give us that chance"', *TheJournal.ie*, 5 November 2022; B. McDaid, 'Mary Lou McDonald in Irish unity citizens' assembly call as Partition "has failed generations"', *Derry Journal*, 5 November 2022; 'Unity must be immediately addressed', *Irish Echo*, 5 November 2022; For some of the challenges a Citizens' Assembly would face, see K. Sheridan, 'Citizens' assembly on unity would have its work cut out for it', *Irish Times*, 9 November 2022; J. Crisp, D. Penna and T. Diver, 'US sets deadline for EU and UK to agree Northern Ireland Protocol deal', *Telegraph*, 12 November 2022.

24 J. Webber and M. Sandbu, 'Northern Ireland's power-sharing system is "not fit for purpose", says Irish PM', *Financial Times*, 30 October 2022.

Index